The
Book of
Australia

The
Book of
Australia

The Watermark Press

First published in 1990, revised and updated 1997
This edition published in 1997 by
The Watermark Press
PO Box 63, Balmain NSW 2043,
Sydney, Australia

Project Director: Simon Blackall
Managing Editor: Siobhan O'Connor
Head Researcher: Leith Hillard
Production Manager: James Somerled

National Library of Australia
Cataloguing-in-Publication data

The book of Australia : almanac 1997–98

Includes index.
ISBN 0 949284 30 0.

1. Almanacs, Australian. 2. Australia — Encyclopedias.
3. Australia — Miscellanea.

994.003

Produced by The Watermark Press, Sydney
Typeset in 10½/11 pt Berkeley Book
Printed in Australia by Southwood Press

Every effort has been made to ensure that the information given in this book is
correct and that statistics quoted are the latest available at the time of publication.
However, some of the information such as records, positions, office holders and other
information contained herein will certainly change over the course of time. Readers
are therefore advised to make further checks on records, names and statistics as this book
gains in age. The publishers welcome any suggestions and relevant data that will help
to expand and improve the information provided.

Acknowledgement

The publishers would like to acknowledge the considerable assistance received in the course
of compiling this almanac from government departments, arts bodies, unions, environmental
organisations, sporting bodies and many others. In particular, we would like to thank Dr J.
Carson, the Australian Bureau of Statistics, Tourism Victoria and the Bureau of Meteorology.

Cover: Photograph of the Twelve Apostles, Port Campbell National Park,
courtesy of Tourism Victoria

Contents

1 CLIMATE   **1**
Australia's Weather. Weather Phenomena. Records. Aboriginal Seasons in the Northern Territory. Climatic Data for Capital Cities. Climate & the Greenhouse Effect. Meteorology.

2 GEOGRAPHY   **35**
Australia's Area. The Coastline. Australian Territories. The States & Territories. Landform Structures. Altitude. Mountains & Plateaus. Plains. Caves. Soils. Desert. Wilderness. Rivers. Lakes. Water Resources. Irrigation.

3 FLORA & FAUNA   **77**
Australia's Flora. Poisonous Plants. Introduced Plants. Australia's Floral Emblems. Australia's Fauna. Native Animals. Introduced Species. Birds. Reptiles. Amphibians. Fishes. Molluscs. Coelenterates. Crustaceans. Arthropods. Dangerous Animals. State Faunal Emblems. Endangered Vertebrate Fauna.

4 ENVIRONMENT   **137**
Some Issues. The Greenhouse Effect. Biodiversity. International Treaties & Conventions. Major Organisations. National Parks & Conservation Reserves. Wilderness Areas. World Heritage Listings.

5 POPULATION   **163**
Australia's Changing Population. Demographics. Births. Deaths. Marriages. Families & Households. Immigration. Religion. Labour. Welfare.

6 HISTORY   **193**
Prehistory. Discovery & Exploration. European Colonisation. Convict Settlement. Exploration. The Gold Rush. The Post Gold Rush Boom. Squatters. The Depression 1890–1893. Federation. World War I. The Great Depression. World War II. The Post-War Years. The Menzies Era. The Vietnam War. The Whitlam Era. The Fraser Years. The Eighties — A Timeline. Mabo & the *Native Title Act 1993*. An Australian Republic? The Nineties — A Timeline. The Wik Decision.

7 GOVERNMENT   **235**
Australia's Government. Federal Parliament. Governors-General. State Parliament. Elections. Political Parties. Local Government.

8 LAW   **267**
Australia's Legal System. The High Court. The Federal Court. Family Law. State & Territory Courts. Police. National Crime Authority. Independent Commission Against Corruption. Industrial Relations Commission. The Ombudsman. Human Rights & Equal Opportunity Commission. Aboriginal & Torres Strait Islander Commission. Administrative Appeals Tribunals. Freedom of Information. Legal Aid. Royal Commissions. Law Reform Commission. National Crime Authority. Consumer Affairs. Australian Competition & Consumer Commission. Australian Security Intelligence Organisation. Crime & Justice.

9 THE ECONOMY   **297**
Overview. Government Finance. National Accounts. Banking. Foreign Trade. Prices. Employment, Social Security & Welfare. Australian Stock Exchange. Australian Securities Commission. Primary Industries. Forestry. Fishing. Mining. Energy. Housing. Tourism. Manufacturing. Retail.

10 TRANSPORT & COMMUNICATIONS   **333**
Telecommunications. Postal Services. Transport. Road Transport. Rail Transport. Water Transport. Aviation.

11 DEFENCE   **355**
Australia's Defence Policy. Defence Structure. Personnel. Expenditure. Training & Education. Australian Defence Force Command. The Royal Australian Navy. The Australian Army. The Royal Australian Air Force. Acquisition & Logistics. The Forces Executive. Budget & Management. Strategy & Intelligence. Science & Technology. Defence Force Awards. Australian Security Intelligence Organisation.

12 HEALTH   **393**
Commonwealth Department of Health & Community Services. Health Insurance. The Hospital System. The Medical Profession. Aboriginal & Torres Strait Islander Health. Government Health Bodies. Nutrition. Health Organisations. Drugs in Australia. Communicable Diseases. Occupational Health. Mental Health. Care for the Elderly. Disabled People. Childcare.

13 EDUCATION, EMPLOYMENT & TRAINING   **421**
The Commonwealth's Role. Department of Employment, Education, Training & Youth Affairs. The Education System. Schooling. Higher Education. Aboriginal Education. Student Assistance. Overseas Students. Educational Administration. Training. Employment. Income Support. Employment Support Services.

14 THE MEDIA   **447**
Changes in the Australian Media. Regulation of the Commercial Media. A Decade of Media Ownership. Program Standards — Australian Content & Quotas. Government Broadcasting. Television. Radio. Print. Print Media Ownership. Regulatory Bodies. Unions. News Agencies. Industry Awards.

15 THE ARTS   **487**
Overview. Major Organisations. Arts Festivals. Dance. Film. Fine Arts. Theatre. Music. Libraries. Literary Awards. Publishing.

16 SPORT   **527**
Disabled Sport. The Olympic Games. The Commonwealth Games. Athletics. Australian Rules. Rugby League. Rugby Union. Soccer. Boxing. Cricket. Golf. Horse Racing. Motor Racing. Motorcycling. Speedway Racing. Sailing. Surfing. Triathlon. Swimming. Tennis. Netball. Hockey.

INDEX   **591**

1
Climate

Australia's Weather

Australia has a relatively harsh and variable continental climate. It boasts a wide range of climatic zones, from the tropical regions in the north, the arid expanses of the interior, the temperate regions in the south, to the subtropical maritime climate along the coast. Temperatures can range from above 50°C to well below zero, although extremely cold temperatures, as recorded in other continents, do not occur in Australia because of the lack of mountain ranges and the expansive surrounding oceans. It is also a relatively dry continent, with 80% of the area having a median rainfall of less than 600 mm per year and 50% less than 300 mm.

SEASONAL WEATHER

SUMMER

Summer (December–February) is fine and warm in southern Australia due to the passage of high pressure systems. Northern Australia, however, experiences hot, rainy summers because of moist, warm monsoonal air travelling from north to south. Tropical cyclones are a regular summer feature around northern and north-eastern Australia, with about three cyclones hitting the north and north-west coast per season.

WINTER

Winter (June–August) in southern Australia brings cool, moist westerly winds, with cold snaps occurring in the south-east when cold air from the Southern Ocean travels northwards, covering areas of up to 2000 km. In northern Australia, winter is mild with dry south-east trade winds, due to high pressure systems passing from west to east across the continent, often remaining stationary over the interior for several days and extending for up to 4000 km.

In latitudes less than 20°S, the reference is not so much to summer and winter, but to the wet and the dry.

RAINFALL

ANNUAL

It is no wonder Australia is widely known as 'The Dry Continent', with 80% of the country having a median rainfall of less than 600 mm per year and 50% less than 300 mm. The lowest rainfall median, in the Lake Eyre region of South Australia, is only about 100 mm. Another low rainfall area is the Giles-Warburton Range region in Western Australia, which has a median rainfall of about 150 mm.

A vast region, extending from the west coast near Shark Bay, across the interior of Western Australia and South Australia to south-west Queensland and north-west New South Wales, has an annual median rainfall of less than 200 mm, although occasionally 400 mm of rain may fall here within a few days.

Regions with rainfall medians above 600 mm per year include the east coast of Queensland, western Tasmania (3565 mm) and the Snowy Mountains area in New South Wales (320 mm).

SEASONAL

In the tropical region of Australia (from Broome in north-west Australia across to Rockhampton in northern Queensland), summer brings heavy periodic rain, while winter is generally dry.

The subtropical areas from Brisbane to Sydney and as far west as Bourke (New South Wales) and Longreach (Queensland), receive heavy periodic summer rains, with some significant rain in winter.

Some temperate regions, including the south-east of Australia, from Bourke down to Melbourne, and Sale on the coast, receive mainly reliable rain in summer and winter. Other temperate regions, such as the south-west coast, the Victorian coast and inland areas only get irregular light rain in summer.

Arid subtropical regions (from Port Hedland in the north-west across to Mt Isa and Bourke) are very dry in summer with variable rain while winter is dry with mainly irregular light rain. Temperate arid regions, which include the interior from North West Cape to Cobar in western New South Wales, have very dry summers with very little rain, and dry winters with variable rain.

RAINFALL VARIABILITY

Arid regions in Australia experience the highest variation in rainfall while temperate regions generally experience low to moderate rainfall variations.

In the tropics, random cyclones cause extreme variations in rainfall from year to year. Variability of rainfall in eastern Australia is strongly linked to the Southern Oscillation. This is gauged by the Southern Oscillation Index (SOI), which measures the difference in sea level between Tahiti, in the central Pacific, and Darwin, in northern Australia. High SOI levels mean above average rainfall over eastern Australia; low SOI levels mean below average rainfall.

RAINFALL FREQUENCY

Most of the continent receives less than 50 rain days per year. Tasmania is the wettest Australian state with over 150 rain days per year, rising to a maximum of over 200 rain days in western Tasmania. At the other extreme, the area extending from the north-west coast through to the interior of the continent has less than 25 rain days a year and is Australia's driest region.

RAINFALL INTENSITY

Rainfall intensity is measured over a period of 24 hours (9 a.m. to 9 a.m.). Most of the very high 24-hour falls (above 700 mm) occur on the Queensland coast, where a tropical cyclone moving close to mountainous terrain provides ideal conditions for torrential rain.

RECORD RAINFALL

Bellenden Ker at the top end of Queensland has experienced a 24-hour total rainfall of 960 mm, recorded between 3 p.m. and 3 p.m. in January 1979. However, it is not shown below because it did not fall within the official time frame. Also in Queensland is Crohamhurst, which recorded the highest daily rainfall of 907 mm, within the proper time frame of 9 a.m. to 9 a.m., in February 1893.

The wettest years on record in Australia include 1979 at Bellenden Ker in the top end of Queensland, when 11 251 mm of rain fell, and 1950 at Tallowood Point in New South Wales, when 4540 mm of rain was recorded.

HIGHEST DAILY RAINFALL

State	Town	Rainfall (mm)	Date
New South Wales	Dorrigo	809	21 February 1954
Victoria	Tanybryn	375	22 March 1983
Queensland	Beerwah (Crohamhurst)	907	3 February 1893
South Australia	Motpena	273	14 March 1989
Western Australia	Whim Creek	747	3 April 1898
Tasmania	Cullenwood	352	22 March 1974
Northern Territory	Roper Valley	545	15 April 1963

THUNDERSTORMS AND HAIL

Thunderstorms are common in northern Australia, especially during the summer wet season. About 74 thunderstorms hit Darwin each year. They are also quite frequent in the eastern highlands where there are about 40-60 a year. (Thunderstorms are measured by thunder days, where thunder occurs more than once.) This is due to the upsurge of moist air streams. In summer, hail measuring 10 mm in diameter can fall on the eastern highlands, causing considerable damage to crops.

In the southern regions, thunderstorms occur less than ten times a year, although when they do, in the winter and spring months, they are occasionally accompanied by hail capable of piercing light galvanised iron and causing widespread damage.

SNOW

There are no permanent snowfields in Australia. Some snow may persist through summer around Mount Kosciuszko (2228 m) in the far south of New South Wales, but the Australian Alps are usually only covered with snow for varying periods from late autumn through to early spring. Mountains in Tasmania are frequently covered with snow above 1000 m in these seasons, and snow sometimes falls lower than 1000 m.

Snowfalls at levels below 500 m do occasionally occur in southern Australia, but these are usually light and only short-lived. The Blue Mountains west of Sydney, and west from there to Bathurst and Orange, and the New South Wales Southern Highlands are places where this occurs.

FROST

Frost may strike when the temperature reaches 2°C or less. In Australia, the incidence of frost varies from none in northern Australia to more than 200 days per year in the south-eastern uplands area south of the Hunter Valley in New South Wales. The length of a frost period for the year is taken as the number of days between the first and last recording of an air temperature of 2°C or less.

The area in Australia most subject to frost is the eastern uplands running from north-eastern Victoria to the Darling Downs in southern Queensland, where it can cause serious crop losses. Frosts usually occur there for three to five months of the year. Central Tasmania has similar conditions for three to six months of the year. In Australia's southern regions, frost occurs for about 100 days inland, dropping gradually to less than 50 days near the coast. In Tasmania, the frost period exceeds 300 days a year on the uplands, decreasing to less than 20 on the coast.

Heavy frosts, which occur in temperatures at freezing level or below, can occur as many as 100 times a year in the highlands. This figure gradually decreases to 20 times on the coast. The southern half of Western Australia, all of South Australia and, perhaps surprisingly, the Alice Springs district of the Northern Territory experience heavy frosts.

CLOUD AND FOG

CLOUD

The amount of cloud cover over a certain area generally follows the rainfall pattern. Thus in the dry Australian interior there is little cloud, while towards the coast and over the eastern highlands, cloud cover increases. In southern Australia, winter is generally more cloudy than summer. In the north, skies are cloudier in the summer wet season, but mainly cloudless in the winter dry season.

FOG

For fog to occur, climatic elements such as temperature, wind, humidity and cloud cover must all be favourable. It usually occurs in valleys and hollows, and may vary significantly over distances as short as 1 km. Fog can persist during the day, but only rarely lasts until the afternoon over the Australian interior. It tends to occur more in the south of Australia than the north, although parts of the eastern coastal areas are relatively fog prone, even in the tropics.

FOG AVERAGES   Australia's capital, Canberra, has the highest amount of fog per year, averaging 47 days, 29 of these occurring between May and August. Brisbane averages 20 days of fog per year, while Darwin usually has only two days of fog per year during July and August.

TEMPERATURE

ANNUAL AVERAGES

Average annual temperatures in Australia range from 28°C along the Kimberley Coast in the extreme north of Western Australia down to 4°C in the alpine areas of south-eastern Australia.

AVERAGE MONTHLY MAXIMUMS

In January, at the height of summer, average monthly maximum temperatures can exceed 40°C in north-west areas, while the interior of Australia can experience temperatures in excess of 35°C. In July, during winter, maximum monthly temperatures range from 30°C near the north coast, down to 5°C in the alpine areas of the south-east.

AVERAGE MONTHLY MINIMUMS

The lowest average temperatures experienced in Australia in January range from 27°C on the north-west coast, to 5°C in the alpine areas of the south-east. In July, average minimums can fall below 5°C in areas south of the tropics and away from the coast, with alpine areas recording the lowest temperatures; the July average can be as low as –5°C.

AVERAGE DAILY MAXIMUMS

In January, average daily summer temperatures vary from a top of 36°C in Port Hedland on the West Australian coast, through to a top of 15°C in eastern Tasmania. Temperatures have exceeded 45°C at nearly all inland areas over 150 km from the coast, and at many places on the southern and north-western coasts.

Extreme temperatures over 50°C occur more in western New South Wales than in other areas due to hot winds blowing across from the north-west interior of the continent.

In July, average daily maximum temperatures remain high in the Top End from Darwin to Thursday Island, but reach a low of 9°C in the Australian Alps.

AVERAGE DAILY MINIMUMS

During summer in Australia, the average minimum temperature ranges from as low as 5°C in the Australian Alps to a minimum of 24°C from Darwin to Thursday Island. In July, the average daily temperatures vary from 0°C on the southern coast to 21°C from Darwin across to Thursday Island. Temperatures have fallen below –5°C at most inland places within a few kilometres of southern coasts. In the tropics, extreme minimums below 0°C have been recorded as far north as Herberton, Queensland, where the temperature has plummeted to –5°C.

HEATWAVES

A heatwave in Australia is usually classified as successive days where the temperature is higher than 40°C. They are relatively common in summer over parts of Australia, although most coastal areas rarely experience more than three successive days of such conditions, with the exception of the north-west coast of Western Australia. As heatwaves move inland away from the coast, they become longer, extending to ten and sometimes 20 consecutive days of high temperatures.

During three days in January 1939, the south-eastern coast of Australia experienced a severe heatwave: Adelaide had a record temperature of 47.6°C; Melbourne a record of 45.6°C; and Sydney a record of 45.3°C.

HUMIDITY

Australia is a dry continent in terms of the humidity or water vapour content in the air. Moisture contents measured from the air by the Bureau of Meteorology are referred to as the relative humidity pattern.

Over the interior of the continent there is a marked dryness during most of the year, while the coast, except in the north-west, stays comparatively moist. In northern Australia, the highest humidity occurs during the summer wet season, and the lowest in the winter dry season. In most of southern Australia, the highest humidity values are experienced in the winter rainy season (June–August) and the lowest in summer.

RELATIVE AVERAGE HUMIDITY

SUMMER   Recorded at 9 a.m. in January, humidity averages are lowest in the interior of the country at around 20%, rising to 80% in the northern region between Darwin and Cairns. At 3 p.m., relative humidity averages are lowest in the north-west interior with a minimum of 20%, while along the south-eastern coast around Victoria it reaches 80%.

WINTER   In July at 9 a.m., the relative average humidity is 20% in the north-west region of Western Australia, with Broome experiencing a minimum of 20%. At the other end of the scale, in Perth and Victoria, relative average humidity reaches 90% maximum. At 3 p.m., north-west Queensland and north-eastern Western Australia experience the lowest humidity values, with minimums of 20% in Normanton and Halls Creek. Maximums of 70–80% are experienced in northern Tasmania and in south-east Victoria around Portland.

SUNSHINE AND GLOBAL RADIATION

There is little difference between global radiation and sunshine, however, sunshine is more dependent on variations in cloud coverage than global radiation, which includes diffuse radiation from the sky as well as direct radiation from the sun. There is, therefore, usually a high correlation between daily global radiation and daily hours of sunshine. Around Port Hedland on the north-west coast, the average daily global radiation is high (640 milliwatt hours), as is the average daily sunshine, which is approximately 10 hours.

GLOBAL RADIATION

In January, the average daily amount of global radiation is highest around the north-west coast of Australia and in the inland areas on the eastern and western sides of the continent. The maximum for this period is 900 milliwatt hours around Meekatharra and Wiluna. Birdsville and Alice Springs record 800 and 750 milliwatt hours respectively. The top end of the mainland and southern Tasmania experience the lowest averages at 550–650 milliwatt hours. In July, southern Tasmania once again records the lowest averages, with only 150–200 milliwatt hours, while the north-west coast and the inland areas on the eastern and western sides of the mainland still experience the top averages for this time of year, with between 700 and 850 milliwatt hours (particularly around Birdsville in Queensland).

SUNSHINE

Most of the continent receives more than 3000 hours of sunshine a year, or nearly 70% of the possible total. Central Australia and the mid-west coast of Western Australia receive sunshine slightly in excess of 3500 hours, while at the other end of the scale totals of less than 1750 hours occur on the west coast and highlands area of Tasmania. In southern Australia, the duration of sunshine is greatest around the month of December when the sun is at its highest elevation, and lowest in June when the sun is low. In tropical northern Australia, sunshine is generally greatest about August–October prior to the wet season, and weakest about January–March during the wet season.

DAILY AVERAGES In January, Birdsville in the centre of Australia has, on average, 10 hours of sunshine per day, as does the south-west coast of Australia. The top end of Australia, from Broome in Western Australia to Townsville in northern Queensland, has the lowest averages, ranging from 6–7 hours.

In July, Tasmania and the south coast of Victoria have the lowest amount of sunshine, with averages of 3–5 hours, while central Australia and the south-west inland areas of Western Australia experience between 10 and 11 hours of sunshine.

EVAPORATION

Evaporation data is used mainly for water conservation, irrigation and plant growth studies. Records noting the rate and amount of evaporation did not begin until 1967. Evaporation is determined by measuring the amount of water evaporated from a free water surface exposed in a pan to the elements. Such evaporation depends on a mixture of temperature, humidity and wind values.

AVERAGE ANNUAL EVAPORATION

Central Australia experiences the most evaporation with annual averages ranging from 4200 mm in the north of Western Australia (the highest in Australia) to 3200 mm around Mt Isa in Queensland. In Tasmania and parts of the Victorian coast, averages of 1200 mm (Australia's minimum) occur.

In the tropics, the onset of summer brings increasing cloudiness and higher humidity causing less evaporation. The highest amount of evaporation occurs around November.

South of the tropics, average monthly evaporation follows the seasonal changes in global radiation: the highest levels of evaporation occur in December and January and the lowest in June and July.

WIND

Australia's two most common wind streams are easterlies in the north and westerlies in the south, due to mid-latitude high pressure systems. Wind variations are greatest around the coast, where land formation and sea breezes are important. In Australia, high wind speeds and wind gusts are linked to tropical cyclones: gusts reaching 200 km/h have been recorded on several occasions in northern Australia, accompanying cyclones.

WIND DIRECTION AND SPEED AVERAGES

Recorded in January at 9 a.m., southerly winds are strongest over the south of the continent, often blowing at over 30 km/h, while winds from the east blow at 11–30 km/h. In the north of the continent, westerly winds blow consistently at up to 30 km/h. Some northerly gusts reach speeds greater than 30 km/h, although they are usually gentler; about 1–11 km/h.

By 3 p.m. in January, wind is coming in much more strongly from the south-east, measuring from 11 km/h to over 30 km/h. In the north, winds from the north and west are also blowing much more strongly and are more consistently over 30 km/h.

In July at 9 a.m., the south of Australia experiences strong westerly winds at speeds over 30 km/h, with some gusty winds coming from the north. Winds in the north of Australia are blowing steadily and with increasing speed, reaching a maximum of over 30 km/h, from the south-east.

By 3 p.m. in July, the westerly winds in the south of the country are blowing steadily at speeds over 30 km/h, while in the north the southerly wind remains consistent at 11 km/h to 30 km/h. The easterly wind has picked up and is blowing steadily at over 30 km/h across some parts of northern Queensland.

DROUGHTS

A drought occurs when there is not enough water to meet a specific demand. Australia has been stricken by a number of major droughts, with some lasting up to a decade, destroying crops and killing thousands of livestock.

Since the 1860s, there have been 13 major droughts in Australia, those of 1895–1903 and 1982–1983 being among the most devastating in terms of extent and their effect on primary production. In 1902, it is estimated that the Australian sheep population of 100 million was reduced by half. The latest drought, which spanned from 1992–1996, caused widespread devastation, loss of crops and livestock throughout eastern Australia. It was largely attributed to a climatic cycle called 'El Nino'.

The other major droughts were in 1864–1868, 1880–1886, 1888, 1911–1916, 1918–1920, 1940–1941, 1944–1945, 1946–1947, 1957–1958 and 1965–1968.

FLOODS

Widespread flooding rainfall may occur anywhere in Australia, however it tends to happen more in the north and in the eastern coastal areas. Floods are at their most destructive and damaging in the more densely populated coastal river valleys of New South Wales, all of which experience relatively frequent flooding, and along the eastern uplands near the east coast of Queensland and New South Wales. Flood rains may also occur at irregular intervals in the Murray–Murrumbidgee system of New South Wales and Victoria, the coastal streams of southern Victoria and the north coast streams of Tasmania.

FLOOD WARNING SYSTEMS

The Bureau of Meteorology has developed a radio-linked flood warning system, which effectively acts as a flood forecaster. The system consists of field stations which transmit rainfall and river level information by radio links to a receiving station, which automatically alerts the user when pre-determined alarm conditions are reached.

CLIMATIC DISCOMFORT

The climatic elements which give physical discomfort are primarily air temperature, vapour pressure and the wind. This discomfort is termed climatic discomfort by meteorologists.

In Australia, a great deal of climatic discomfort is experienced due to humidity, temperature and other factors. Defining criteria for discomfort is difficult, however, because personal reactions to the weather differ greatly according to health, age, clothing, occupation and acclimatisation factors. One of the most common ways of measuring climatic discomfort is the relative strain index (RSI), devised in 1963 by Lee and Henschel. Discomfort occurs when the RSI exceeds 0.3 at 3 p.m., with high discomfort occurring at 0.4 and above.

AMOUNT OF CLIMATIC DISCOMFORT

The highest amount of climatic discomfort occurs in the Kimberley region in the north of Western Australia, due mainly to heat. This discomfort gradually decreases to low levels of discomfort on the south-west coast. Queensland coastal areas have low levels of discomfort because of onshore winds and the cooling effect of the nearby eastern uplands. In the tropics near Cairns, for example, the higher altitude helps to lower the amount of climatic discomfort. The State with the least discomfort is Tasmania, which has about one day per year. (The amount of climatic discomfort is measured by the number of days the RSI exceeds 0.3 at 3 p.m.)

Weather Phenomena

BUSHFIRES

VICTORIA AND SOUTH AUSTRALIA   Widespread bushfires occurred on Ash Wednesday, 16 February 1983, as a direct result of record low rainfall between April 1982 and February 1983. They covered virtually all of Victoria and much of the settled areas of South Australia. A total of 46 lives were lost in Victoria, along with the destruction of 1700 homes. In South Australia, 26 people lost their lives.

TASMANIA   The most severe bushfires in Tasmanian history occurred on 7 February 1967, following the driest summer this century and the third driest on record. There were 62 deaths and 1400 houses, and major buildings were gutted, resulting in property damage estimated at tens of millions of dollars.

NEW SOUTH WALES   In a three-week period from 1993–1994, more than 800 fires were fuelled by high winds, temperatures as high as 40°C and vegetation that was extremely dry after a long period of drought. More than 800 000 ha were destroyed in the fires, which extended along the coastal and adjacent inland regions, some of which were lit by arsonists.

CYCLONES

Tropical cyclones follow erratic paths and their frequency varies, with an average of six affecting the tropical coast each year.

QUEENSLAND   On 24 December 1971, Cyclone Althea struck Townsville with gusts of up to 196 km/h (the highest recorded on the Queensland mainland), and caused damage estimated at around $50 million. Severe flooding occurred afterwards in which three people died.

In January 1970, Cyclone Ada hit a number of Whitsunday Islands and the central Queensland coast near Proserpine, causing an estimated $12 million damage and killing 13 people.

On 6 March 1956, Cyclone Agnes struck Townsville and Cairns, killing four people in accompanying floods. Damage was estimated at almost $16 million.

WESTERN AUSTRALIA   On 13 March 1979, cyclone Hazel killed 15 crew members of a Taiwanese fishing boat as it headed into shore. About $15 million in damages and losses occurred.

On 7–8 December 1975, Cyclone Joan hit Port Hedland with the insurance loss estimated at $20 million. The highest wind gust recorded was 212 km/h, and the cyclone caused extensive flooding throughout the North Kimberley, De Grey, Fortescue and East Gascoyne divisions of Western Australia.

Cyclone Bobby struck the north-west coast of Australia in February 1995, claiming seven lives.

NORTHERN TERRITORY   On Christmas morning in 1974, Cyclone Tracey struck Darwin with wind speeds of up to 300 km/h. Fifty people were killed, 16 were reported missing and more than 30000 were evacuated. It was Australia's worst cyclone in terms of lives lost, and remains the most well-known natural disaster in Australia.

DUST STORMS

VICTORIA In Melbourne on 8 February 1983, a huge dust storm engulfed the city. This was a side effect of the 1982–1983 drought, with enormous quantities of topsoil from Victorian farmlands covering the city.

ELECTRICAL STORMS

WESTERN AUSTRALIA During a severe electrical storm on 17 September 1974 in Willeton, a Perth suburb, two people speaking on the telephone were knocked unconscious when lightning struck lines they were using. On 13 November in the same year, also in Willeton, lightning once again struck another person using the phone during an electrical storm. He received burns to the throat and tongue.

FLOOD

NEW SOUTH WALES On 23 April 1990, floodwaters engulfed the entire town of Nyngan, north-west of Dubbo. About 2200 people were airlifted to higher ground 8 km out of town. This is the only time an entire town has been evacuated by air, in Australia. The floods occurred when the Bogan River broke its banks due to extra water it was carrying from swollen tributaries. Within two hours the floodwaters had increased from floor to ceiling height, reaching 5.2 m; 1.01 m above the previous record from the 1976 floods. Other nearby towns such as Cobar and Bourke were cut off for up to two weeks because of the road damage.

VICTORIA Record flooding hit Victoria in May 1974, inundating areas of Melbourne along the Maribyrnong River. Flood levels were the highest on record along the Broken, Kiewa, Mitta Mitta and Maribyrnong Rivers and at Wangaratta on the Ovens River. In Shepparton on the Goulburn River, flood levels were the highest since 1916.

HAIL

QUEENSLAND On 1 January 1969, a severe local storm at Buaraba Creek, in the Lowood district of Queensland, left cattle embedded in ice from hail drifts up to 3.7 m deep. More than 200 cattle were killed and there was widespread crop damage.

WESTERN AUSTRALIA On 13 April 1918, about 5 km south of Bullfinch, a severe storm occurred with enormous hail. One piece which broke through a tent measured 15 cm by 7.5 cm. (The largest ever hailstone, 19 cm in diameter and weighing 750 g, fell in the USA.)

On 13–14 October 1980, geographically unusual hail accompanied thunderstorms at Turkey Creek (Western Australia) and Katherine (Northern Territory). It was the first time since 1958 that hail had occurred as far north as Katherine.

LIGHTNING

TASMANIA   On 24 May 1975, 50 people were hit by lightning when it struck a sports ground at Latrobe. One person needed to be hospitalised.

THUNDERSTORMS AND GALES

VICTORIA   In February 1972, a thunderstorm lasting only an hour and a half, but producing record rainfall, flooded the centre of Melbourne. It received about 100 000 tonnes of water.

On 15 November 1982, severe local storms passed over northern and north-eastern suburbs of Melbourne, with a gust of wind at 139 km/h recorded at Melbourne airport.

QUEENSLAND   On 18 January 1985, a thunderstorm hit Brisbane with wind speeds reaching 183 km/h at Brisbane airport. The winds were accompanied by severe hail. About 80 000 premises lost electricity and 20 000 buildings were damaged with Brisbane insurance companies paying out $177 million.

Five years before, on 16 December 1980, thunderstorms and tornado squalls caused about $10 million damage in Brisbane, when 5000 houses were damaged and aeroplanes were overturned at the airport.

TORNADOS

NEW SOUTH WALES   On 1 January 1970, a tornado swept through the Bulahdelah State Forest (70 km north/north-east of Newcastle) completely destroying more than a million trees. Probably the most intense tornado ever documented in Australia, it would have caused a major disaster had it passed over a populated area.

VICTORIA   A tornado at Sandon on 13 November 1976, with wind speeds of up to 165 km/h, caused an estimated $2–3 million damage. An elderly couple were killed when they were blown out of their car which the tornado lifted 12 m into the air and carried 100 m.

On 4 October 1979, a tornado struck the north-west town of Red Cliffs. Wind at speeds of between 120–140 km/h and hailstones the size of golfballs rained down on the town in mid-afternoon. The tornado caused an estimated $20 million damage to houses, fruit and wheat crops.

QUEENSLAND On 4 November 1973, Australia's most devastating tornado in terms of property damage (1390 buildings damaged), hit Brisbane. Winds were estimated at 217–253 km/h.

WESTERN AUSTRALIA On 3 September 1983, a tornado moved into Scarborough from the Indian Ocean and caused damage in excess of $1 million. Explosive effects from the strong differential pressure of the tornado caused a delicatessen to explode, blowing out plate glass windows and scattering the shop's contents onto the street.

RECORD COLD SPELLS

TASMANIA From 23–25 June 1972, record low temperatures were experienced in Tasmania, causing widespread ice damage to vehicles and water pipes. In Launceston on the 24th, the temperature reached –7.8°C (the previous record low was –5.6°C); in Hobart on 25 June it was –2.8°C (previous record low –2.4°C), and at Bothwell on the 24 June, the temperature plunged to –12.8°C.

On 30 June 1981 at Shannon, Tarraleah and Butlers Gorge, the lowest ever temperature for the State was recorded at –13.0°C.

NORTHERN TERRITORY In July 1976, there were below average temperatures in the Alice Springs district, with an unusual reading of –7.5°C recorded in Alice Springs itself.

SNOWFALLS

NEW SOUTH WALES On 5 July 1900, exceptional snowfalls were recorded over the central districts of the State. Snow was 2.4 m deep in places. Lightly constructed buildings collapsed under the weight of about 70 cm of snow in Bathurst and Blayney. Between Locksley and Rydal, snow fell to a depth of 122 cm. Forbes in the central west of the state received some 25 cm in what was proclaimed to be its first recorded snowstorm.

VICTORIA AND SOUTH AUSTRALIA Between 21 June 1981 and 30 June 1981, snow fell in South Australia as far north as Wilpena and Blinman; on the Mt Lofty ranges; in the Barossa Valley, and in all districts in Victoria except the Mallee and Southern Gippsland. In some places, it was the first snow for at least a quarter of a century. The South Australian snowfalls ranged in depth from 2–10 cm.

TASMANIA On 4–5 August 1976, extensive snowfalls were recorded throughout Tasmania with an average depth of 50–75 mm. Many inland areas recorded low temperatures and, with the snowline reaching the 150-m level, there were severe stock losses and major roads were cut off. Several Hobart suburbs were so snowbound that people were able to ski to work.

During July 1974, heavy snowfalls measuring up to 400 m deep fell, cutting off several highways. About 40 skiers were stranded on Mount Field by the heavy drifts.

Records

RAINFALL

- The highest rainfall measured for one hour in Australia is 136 mm at Wongawilly, New South Wales on 18 February 1984.
- The highest rainfall in one day occurred in Beerwah (Crohamhurst) in Queensland with 907 mm of rain falling on 3 February 1893.
- The wettest town in Australia is Tully, on the east coast of northern Queensland between Cairns and Cardwell, with a median of 4084 mm of rain per year.
- The rainiest State is Tasmania, with over 150 days of rain per year and more than 240 days of rain per year in western Tasmania.
- The Australian town with the greatest variance in rainfall is Whim Creek in Western Australia. Although it received 747 mm in a single day in 1950, only 4 mm of rain fell in the whole of 1924.

TEMPERATURE

- The hottest place in Australia is around Marble Bar in Western Australia (150 km south-east of Port Hedland), where the summer average is 41°C and daily top temperatures may exceed 40°C for several days at a time.
- The world's longest heatwave occurred at Marble Bar, the only place in the world where temperatures of more than 37.8°C have been recorded on as many as 161 consecutive days between 30 October 1923 and 7 April 1924.
- The most uncomfortable place in terms of heat in Australia is also Marble Bar, when the 0.3 RSI reached 179 days and the 0.4 RSI reached 86 days between 1957 and 1974.
- The hottest temperature ever recorded in Australia was 53.1°C at Cloncurry in Queensland on 16 January 1889.
- July is the coldest month of the year for all Australian States.
- The coldest temperature ever recorded in Australia was −23°C at Charlotte Pass in New South Wales on 28 June 1994.
- the coldest temperature ever recorded along the tropical coastline was −0.8°C in Mackay, Queensland.

FROST

- The highest average frost recorded in Australia is at Kiandra in New South Wales (at 1400 m), where there is an average of 228.3 frosty nights per year (i.e. where the temperature drops below 2.2°C) and an average 176.7 nights of heavy frosts per year (where the temperature is freezing or below).
- In May 1976, frosts occurred on 26 mornings in the Australian Capital Territory, double the May average for the Territory.

HUMIDITY

- The most humid place in Australia is Thursday Island, which has an average relative humidity of 80% at 9 a.m. and 71% at 3 p.m.

SUNSHINE

- The greatest amount of sunny days in January in Australia occur in parts of central South Australia and southern Western Australia, where it averages 11 hours of bright sunshine per day.
- The sunniest winter days in Australia occur in July in the top end of Western Australia and Northern Territory, which average 10 hours of bright sunshine per day.

WIND

- The windiest city in Australia is Perth with an average wind speed of 15.6 km/h.
- The least windy city in Australia is Canberra with an average wind speed of 5.4 km/h.
- The highest recorded gust of wind in Australia was 259 km/h at Mardie in Western Australia on 19 February 1975.
- The highest gust of wind recorded in a capital city in Australia was 217 km/h in Darwin.

FLOOD

- One of the worst floods in Australia occurred in Nyngan, New Soutth Wales, on 23 April 1990. The whole town of 2200 people was evacuated by air when flood waters rose from floor to ceiling height in two hours.

HISTORY OF AUSTRALIAN WEATHER

- The first weather map in Australia was published in 1877.
- The pioneer of the practice of naming cyclones was Clement Wragge, an Australian meteorologist with the Queensland Government Meteorology Department from 1887–1903.
- Staffing of Macquarie Island meteorological station as a base for Mawson's Antarctic expedition began in 1913.
- In 1921, a meteorological station was set up on remote Willis Island in the Coral Sea Islands Territory. The only inhabitants of the territory are the three staff of the station.
- The first weather forecast broadcast over radio aired in 1924.
- In 1948, radar was used for the first time to measure wind.
- Australia joined the World Meteorological Organisation (WMO) in 1950 and has played a leading role in their activities since that time.
- The first meteorological observations came from Mawson Station in the Antarctic in 1954.
- The first television weather report was broadcast in 1956.
- In 1962, the first automatic weather station was set up.
- In 1962, the first weather satellite pictures were received from the TIROS satellite.
- In 1978, regular transmissions began from the Japanese geostationary satellite.

Aboriginal Seasons in the Northern Territory

The Aboriginal peoples living in and around Kakadu National Park recognise an annual cycle of at least six seasons, as opposed to the western system of four main seasons.

GUNUMELENG   This is the time just before the wet season starts in the top end of Australia. It is a season of hot weather which becomes more and more humid, with thunderstorms building up in the afternoon and bringing scattered rain. Around this time, people move camp from the flood plain to shelter from the intense storms that come in the wet season.

GUDJEWG   Otherwise known as the wet season, it is a time of violent thunderstorms, heavy rain and extensive flooding. The heat and humidity brings on the greening of the outback and plant and animal life blossom.

BANGERRENG This season is also called the 'knock 'em down' season, as violent storms flatten the 2-metre high spear grass. It is also the time when most plants are flowering or fruiting, and animals are caring for their young.

YEGGE Drying winds signal it is time to begin burning the bush to clear the country and encourage new growth. These early season fires are to protect against more destructive fires in the hotter months. Yegge also brings early morning mists that hang low over the plains and the waterholes, which become covered in waterlilies.

WURRGENG This is when the Kakadu region experiences its coldest weather, with low humidity and day temperatures of 30°C and nights as low as 17°C. Creeks and flood plains dry up and burning continues, dampened by the dew at night.

GURRUNG During this season there is some wind and it is very hot. The countryside seems lifeless, put to sleep by the heat of the day. Thunderheads begin to build again with the advent of Gunumeleng.

Climatic Data
for Capital Cities

SYDNEY

Latitude 33° 52' S, Longitude 151° 12' E. Height above mean sea level (MSL): 42 m.

SYDNEY TEMPERATURE

Month	Mean max. (°C)	Mean min. (°C)	Mean (°C)
January	25.8	18.4	22.1
February	25.5	18.5	22.0
March	24.6	17.4	21.0
April	22.2	14.6	18.4
May	19.7	11.3	15.5
June	16.7	9.2	12.9
July	15.9	7.9	11.9
August	17.5	8.9	13.2
September	19.7	10.9	15.3
October	21.9	13.4	17.7
November	23.5	15.5	19.5
December	25.0	17.3	21.1
Averages	21.5	13.6	17. 4

TEMPERATURE EXTREMES
The highest temperature recorded in Sydney was 45.3°C on 14 January 1939, and the lowest was 2.1°C (air) on 22 June 1932 and −4.4°C (ground) on 4 July 1983.

SYDNEY RAINFALL

Month	Mean monthly (mm)	Mean rain days	Highest intensity (mm)
January	102	13	180
February	113	13	226
March	135	14	281
April	124	13	191
May	121	13	212
June	131	12	131

SYDNEY RAINFALL (CONTD)

Month	Mean monthly (mm)	Mean rain days	Highest intensity (mm)
July	101	11	198
August	80	11	328
September	69	11	145
October	78	12	162
November	63	12	235
December	65	12	126
Total	1214	148	—

RAINFALL EXTREMES

In Sydney, the greatest monthly rainfall occurred in June 1950 of 643 mm. The greatest amount of rain in one day, 281 mm, fell on 28 March 1942. The driest month was August 1885, when it only rained on one day.

MELBOURNE

Latitude 37° 49' S, Longitude 144° 58' E. Height above mean sea level: 35 m.

MELBOURNE TEMPERATURE

Month	Mean max. (°C)	Mean min. (°C)	Mean (°C)
January	25.8	14.0	19.9
February	26.7	14.3	20.0
March	23.8	13.0	18.4
April	20.1	10.6	15.3
May	16.5	8.5	12.5
June	13.9	6.7	10.3
July	13.3	5.7	9.5
August	14.8	6.5	10.7
September	17.1	7.7	12.4
October	19.5	9.3	14.4
November	21.8	10.9	16.4
December	24.1	12.7	18.4
Averages	19.7	10.0	14.9

TEMPERATURE EXTREMES

The highest temperature ever recorded in Melbourne was 45.6°C on 13 January 1939, and the lowest was –2.8°C (air) on 21 July 1869 and –6.7°C (ground) on 30 June 1929.

MELBOURNE RAINFALL

Month	Mean monthly (mm)	Mean rain days	Highest intensity (mm)
January	47	8	176
February	48	7	238
March	53	9	191
April	58	11	195
May	58	14	142
June	49	14	115
July	48	15	178
August	51	15	111
September	59	14	201
October	69	14	193
November	59	12	206
December	58	10	182
Total	665	143	—

RAINFALL EXTREMES

The wettest month ever in Melbourne occurred in February 1972 when it rained a total of 238 mm, while the heaviest rainfall occurred on 29 January 1963 when a total of 108 mm fell on the city. In April 1923, however, there was no rain at all, making that the driest month ever in the city.

BRISBANE

Latitude 27° 28' S, Longitude 153° 2' E. Height above mean sea level: 41 m.

BRISBANE TEMPERATURE

Month	Mean max. (°C)	Mean min. (°C)	Mean (°C)
January	29.4	20.8	25.0
February	29.0	20.6	24.8
March	28.0	19.4	23.7
April	26.1	16.7	21.3
May	23.2	13.4	18.3
June	20.8	10.9	15.9
July	20.4	9.6	15.0
August	21.8	10.3	16.1
September	24.0	12.9	18.5
October	26.1	15.9	20.9

BRISBANE TEMPERATURE (CONTD)

Month	Mean max. (°C)	Mean min. (°C)	Mean (°C)
November	27.8	18.2	22.9
December	29.1	19.9	24.5
Averages	25.5	15.7	20.6

TEMPERATURE EXTREMES

The highest temperature ever recorded in Brisbane was 43.2°C on 26 January 1940. The lowest temperature ever recorded was 2.3°C (air) in December 1894 and February 1896 and –4.5°C (ground) on 11 July 1890.

BRISBANE RAINFALL

Month	Mean monthly (mm)	Mean rain days	Highest intensity (mm)
January	164	13	872
February	161	14	1026
March	143	15	865
April	87	11	388
May	73	10	410
June	68	8	647
July	57	7	330
August	46	7	373
September	47	8	138
October	76	9	456
November	99	10	413
December	130	12	441
Total	1151	123	—

RAINFALL EXTREMES

In Brisbane, the highest ever rainfall in one month, 1026 mm, occurred in February 1983. The wettest day ever recorded in Brisbane was on 20 January 1887, when 465 mm of rain fell in one day. Brisbane has also recorded several dry months with no rain.

ADELAIDE

Latitude 34° 56' S, Longitude 138° 35' E. Height above mean sea level: 43 m.

ADELAIDE TEMPERATURE

Month	Mean max. (°C)	Mean min. (°C)	Mean (°C)
January	29.5	16.4	23.0
February	29.3	16.6	23.0
March	26.8	15.1	21.0
April	22.7	12.6	17.7
May	18.7	10.3	14.5
June	15.8	8.3	12.1
July	15.0	7.3	11.1
August	16.4	7.8	12.1
September	18.9	9.0	13.9
October	22.0	10.9	16.5
November	25.1	12.9	19.1
December	27.7	15.0	21.3
Averages	22.3	11.9	17.1

TEMPERATURE EXTREMES

The highest temperature ever recorded for Adelaide was 47.6°C on 12 January 1939, with the coldest temperatures ever recorded being −0.4°C (air) on 24 July 1908 and −6.1°C (ground) on 24 June 1944.

ADELAIDE RAINFALL

Month	Mean monthly (mm)	Mean rain days	Highest intensity (mm)
January	20	4	84
February	21	4	155
March	24	5	117
April	44	9	154
May	68	13	197
June	72	15	218
July	66	16	160
August	61	15	157
September	51	13	148
October	44	11	133
November	31	8	113
December	26	6	101
Total	528	119	—

RAINFALL EXTREMES

In Adelaide, the most rain in one month, 218 mm, occurred in June 1916. The wettest day ever recorded was 7 February 1925, when 141 mm of rain fell.

PERTH

Latitude 31° 57' S, Longitude 115° 51' E. Height above mean sea level: 19.5 m.

PERTH TEMPERATURE

Month	Mean max. (°C)	Mean min. (°C)	Mean (°C)
January	29.6	17.7	23.5
February	29.9	17.9	23.7
March	27.8	16.6	22.2
April	24.5	14.1	19.2
May	20.7	11.6	16.1
June	18.2	9.9	14.1
July	17.3	9.0	13.2
August	17.9	9.1	13.5
September	19.4	10.1	14.8
October	21.2	11.5	16.3
November	24.6	14.0	19.2
December	27.3	16.2	21.7
Averages	**23.2**	**13.1**	**18.2**

TEMPERATURE EXTREMES

The hottest temperature ever recorded in Perth was 44.7°C on 12 January 1978. The lowest temperature (air) was 1.2°C recorded on 7 July 1916, while the lowest temperature (ground) was –3.9°C on 31 May 1964.

PERTH RAINFALL

Month	Mean monthly (mm)	Mean rain days	Highest intensity (mm)
January	8	3	55
February	12	3	166
March	20	4	145
April	45	8	149
May	124	14	308
June	183	17	476
July	174	18	425
August	137	17	318
September	80	14	199
October	55	11	200
November	21	6	71
December	14	4	81
Total	**873**	**119**	—

RAINFALL EXTREMES

Perth's wettest ever month occurred in June 1946, when 476 mm of rain fell, but there have been various months when no rain has fallen. The most rain ever to fall in one day in Perth was 99 mm on 10 June 1920.

HOBART

Latitude 42° 53' S, Longitude 147° 20' E. Height above mean sea level: 54 m.

HOBART TEMPERATURE

Month	Mean max.	Mean min.	Mean
	(°C)	(°C)	(°C)
January	21.5	11.7	16.5
February	21.6	11.9	16.7
March	20.0	10.7	15.2
April	17.1	8.8	12.9
May	14.9	6.8	10.5
June	11.8	5.1	8.5
July	11.5	4.4	7.9
August	12.9	5.1	9.1
September	14.9	6.3	10.6
October	16.9	7.6	12.2
November	18.5	9.1	13.8
December	20.2	10.6	15.4
Averages	**16.8**	**8.2**	**12.4**

TEMPERATURE EXTREMES

On 4 January 1976, the hottest day every recorded in Hobart, the temperature reached 40.8°C. The city's lowest temperature (air) was −2.8°C on 11 July 1981 and 25 June 1972, while the lowest ground temperature, −7.7°C, was recorded on 24 June 1963.

HOBART RAINFALL

Month	Mean monthly (mm)	Mean rain days	Highest intensity (mm)
January	48	11	150
February	40	10	171
March	47	11	255
April	53	12	248

HOBART RAINFALL (CONTD)

Month	Mean monthly (mm)	Mean rain days	Highest intensity (mm)
May	49	14	214
June	57	14	238
July	53	15	157
August	52	15	161
September	53	15	201
October	63	16	193
November	56	14	188
December	57	13	206
Total	628	160	—

RAINFALL EXTREMES

Hobart's wettest month was March 1946, when rainfall measured 255 mm. On 15 September 1957, Hobart experienced its wettest ever day with rainfall measuring 156 mm.

DARWIN

Latitude 12° 25' S, Longitude 130° 52' E. Height above mean sea level: 31 m.

DARWIN TEMPERATURE

Month	Mean max (°C)	Mean min	Mean
January	31.7	24.7	28.2
February	31.4	24.6	28.0
March	31.8	24.4	28.1
April	32.6	23.9	28.3
May	31.9	21.9	26.9
June	30.4	19.8	25.1
July	30.3	19.2	24.8
August	31.2	20.6	25.9
September	32.4	23.0	27.7
October	33.0	24.9	29.0
November	33.1	25.2	29.2
December	32.5	25.2	28.9
Averages	31.9	23.1	27.5

TEMPERATURE EXTREMES

The hottest day ever recorded in Darwin occurred on 17 November 1982, when the temperature hit 40.5°C. The lowest ever air temperature of 10.4°C, was recorded on 29 July 1942.

DARWIN RAINFALL

Month	Mean monthly (mm)	Mean rain days	Highest intensity (mm)
January	409	21	906
February	355	20	815
March	316	19	1104
April	99	9	357
May	17	2	299
June	2	—	41
July	1	—	10
August	6	1	84
September	18	2	130
October	72	6	339
November	142	12	371
December	224	16	665
Total	**1661**	**108**	—

RAINFALL EXTREMES

Darwin's wettest ever month was March 1977, when 1014 mm of rain fell on the city. The most rain ever to fall in one day, 296 mm, was recorded on 7 January 1987. During June and July in Darwin, it is usual for no rain to fall.

CANBERRA

Latitude 35° 19' S, Longitude 149° 11' E. Height above mean sea level: 577 m.

CANBERRA TEMPERATURE

Month	Mean max (°C)	Mean min	Mean
January	27.7	12.9	20.3
February	26.9	12.9	19.9
March	24.4	10.7	17.5
April	19.6	6.5	13.1
May	15.1	2.9	9.0
June	12.0	0.8	6.4
July	11.1	-0.3	5.4
August	12.8	0.8	6.8
September	15.9	2.9	9.4
October	19.1	5.9	12.5
November	22.5	8.4	15.5
December	26.0	11.1	18.5
Averages	**19.4**	**6.3**	**12.9**

TEMPERATURE EXTREMES

On 1 February 1968, Canberra recorded its hottest ever day, with the temperature at 42.2°C. The city's lowest temperature (air) was –10.0°C on 11 July 1971 while the lowest temperature (ground) was –15.1°C on the same day.

CANBERRA RAINFALL

Month	Mean monthly (mm)	Mean rain days	Highest intensity (mm)
January	60	8	185
February	57	7	148
March	54	7	312
April	50	8	164
May	48	9	150
June	37	9	126
July	39	10	104
August	49	12	156
September	52	11	151
October	69	11	161
November	62.	9	135
December	49	8	215
Total	626		109

RAINFALL EXTREMES

The wettest month ever recorded in Canberra was March 1950, when 312 mm of rain fell. The heaviest rainfall in one day was recorded on 21 October 1959, when 105 mm of rain fell on the city.

Climate and the Greenhouse Effect

There is no conclusive evidence that any warming trend is due to the greenhouse effect. Scientists concede, however, that there is evidence that amounts of greenhouse gases are rising rapidly and that this must lead to significant global warming in the next few decades. In fact, eight of this century's hottest years have occurred in the 1980s, with 1987 and 1988 the hottest years recorded as yet for at least a century.

Tidal records also show that the average global sea level has risen by about 10 cm in the past 100 years. However, these increases could just be normal climatic variations as we head into an uncertain climatic future with only about 100 years of weather recording with which to compare. It also cannot be assumed that all changes brought about by the greenhouse effect will be bad. Some climatic change could be good, such as less aridity in subtropical deserts.

Meteorology

THE BUREAU OF METEOROLOGY

Official weather observations did not begin until 1859 in Sydney, although Australia's early explorers compiled weather reports for their journeys. The first weather forecasts were published in the press on 1 January 1908. Country areas were sent the forecasts by morse code, while metropolitan areas set up a system of flags on tall buildings to indicate the weather. Early weather reports consisted of one daily forecast for the States, metropolitan areas and oceans.

Although the Bureau managed to set up an observation station on Macquarie Island during Mawson's Antarctic expedition in 1913, and on remote Willis Island in the Coral Sea in 1921, collecting data and forecasting the weather did not really begin until the post-war boom. The Bureau expanded greatly during this period, resulting in regular meteorological observations at Mawson Station in Antarctica, the first automatic weather station, and regular transmissions from the Japanese geostationary satellite.

MODERN SERVICES

Today, the Bureau issues more than one million forecasts and warnings each year, provides more than one million aviation briefing and documentation services, and handles about half a million inquiries on weather information and forecasts. Some 3000 forecasts and warnings are put out each day to the general public through the media. About 12 million calls are made each year by the public to recorded weather information services.

FORECASTING FOR SPECIAL USER GROUPS

Forecasts and other sorts of weather information are also provided on a daily basis to the aviation industry, defence services, shipping, primary producers, offshore oil rigs and a range of other commercial interests.

WEATHER WARNINGS

One of the most important functions of the Bureau is to issue warnings about dangerous weather conditions including cyclones, floods, gales, thunderstorms, cold snaps and fire. It operates specially staffed centres in time of flood and bushfire, and has a network of Tropical Cyclone Warning Centres in Brisbane, Darwin and Perth, where information from ships, aircraft, offshore automatic weather stations and radar-equipped observing stations is collected so that no cyclone goes undetected.

COLLECTING WEATHER INFORMATION
The Bureau has more than 60 stations covering Australia, including the Antarctic and islands in the Pacific and Indian Oceans, which collect information from various sources such as:
- radar or radio-tracked balloons that measure wind, temperature and humidity at various levels in the stratosphere;
- polar orbiting satellites which provide data on temperature, moisture content, wind values at various levels above the earth's surface and cloud imagery;
- more than 400 part-time observers who provide surface weather reports several times a day;
- more than 6000 volunteers who provide monthly rainfall totals;
- a fleet of more than 80 selected ships that radio valuable weather data when they are travelling in Australian waters;
- the Japanese Geostationary Meteorological Satellite which provides three-hourly pictures day and night;
- American and Russian satellites which provide more detailed but less frequent pictures as they pass over; and
- satellites which receive and transmit weather data from remote automatic weather stations, drifting ocean buoys and wide-bodied jet aircraft fitted with instruments to record and transmit weather data.

METEOROLOGICAL RESEARCH

Most of the Bureau's research has been in forecasting, with centres such as the International Antarctic Meteorological Research Centre in Melbourne set up in 1965, and the Commonwealth Meteorology Research Centre set up in conjunction with the CSIRO in 1969. In 1985, the Bureau of Meteorology Research Centre was set up; another joint CSIRO and Bureau centre. These centres aim to make advances in meteorological science in the Southern Hemisphere and Australian region, improve accuracy and precision of weather warnings, make more detailed forecasts for aviation and refine long-range forecasting.

AUSTRALIA'S INTERNATIONAL ROLE

Since becoming one of the first members of the World Meteorological Organisation (WMO) in 1950, Australia has played a leading role in activities such as World Weather Watch and the World Meteorological

Centre in Melbourne, Washington and Moscow. Many Bureau officers are also members of WMO bodies who are developing meteorology for aviation, shipping and agriculture. The Bureau also runs training courses for overseas students as well as offering general and technical support to other countries.

COMMONWEALTH SCIENTIFIC AND INDUSTRIAL RESEARCH ORGANISATION (CSIRO)

Most commonly known as the CSIRO, this government-funded body performs a wide range of scientific and industrial research. The Division of Atmospheric Research is the only section that deals with climatic research and weather monitoring. Established in the late 1940s, this division carries out a wide range of research: monitoring changes in the earth's climate by computer, looking at land and sea surfaces, studying radiation and the greenhouse effect, and gathering air samples from Australia's research base on Macquarie Island.

2
Geography

Australia's Area

The total land area of Australia, including Tasmania, is 7 682 300 km², which makes it the world's smallest continent and the sixth largest country in terms of size. The area of Australia is 32 times the size of the British Isles, approximately double the size of Europe, excluding Russia, and equal to the United States without Alaska. The area claimed by Australia in the Antarctic region is 6 044 063 km².

THE TEN LARGEST COUNTRIES IN THE WORLD BY AREA

Country	Approx. Area (km²)
Russia	17 075 000
Canada	9 976 150
China	9 596 690
USA	9 372 610
Brazil	8 511 965
Australia	7 682 300
India	3 166 830
Argentina	2 766 890
Khazakhstan	2 717 000
Sudan	2 505 810

AREA OF AUSTRALIA BY STATE OR TERRITORY

The area of the states was calculated in 1973 by the Division of Mapping of the Department of National Resources. The length of Australia's coastline also was determined at this time.

State or Territory	Approx. Area (km²)	% of Total Area
New South Wales	801 600	10.43
Victoria	227 600	2.96
Queensland	1 727 200	22.48
South Australia	984 000	12.81
Western Australia	2 525 500	32.87
Tasmania	67 800	0.88
Northern Territory	1 346 200	17.52
Australian Capital Territory	2 400	0.03
Australia	**7 682 300**	**100.00**

THE EXTREMITIES OF AUSTRALIA

THE NORTH

The northernmost point of the Australian mainland is the tip of Cape York, Queensland, at latitude 10°41'S. Australia's most northerly town is Thursday Island; the town shares the island's name.

Thursday Island was originally named Friday, with Thursday being given to a neighbouring island. The two names were transposed prior to the printing of the charts. It is situated north of Cape York Peninsula, Queensland, at 10°41'S, and is separated from the mainland by Endeavour Strait.

THE SOUTH

The southernmost point of Australia is South Cape, Tasmania, at latitude 43°39'S. The southernmost point of the Australian mainland is Wilson's Promontory, Victoria, which is 225 km south-east of Melbourne.

THE WEST

The westernmost point of Australia is West Point on Dirk Hartog Island, off the coast of Western Australia. Steep Point on the Western Australian coast is the westernmost point of the Australian mainland, north of Geraldton, at longitude 113°9'E.

THE EAST

Cape Byron on the north coast of New South Wales is the Australian mainland's easternmost point at 153°39'E.

CROSS-DISTANCES

The distance between the northernmost and southernmost points of mainland Australia, Cape York to South Cape, is approximately 3680 km.

The distance between the easternmost and westernmost points of mainland Australia, Steep Point to Cape Byron, is approximately 4000 km.

The Coastline

The length of mainland Australia's coastline is estimated at 33 535 km. The length of the total coastline, including Tasmania, is 36 735 km. There are four principal types of coastline in Australia: rock coasts, mainland beach coasts, barrier beach coasts and tidal plains.

Rock coasts, which are basically cliffs of varying heights, occur mainly in the south and north-west of Australia.

Mainland beach coasts, while they may include rocky areas, are largely open beaches. These are commonly the broad expanses of sand which form part of the stereotypical images of Australia's sun and sand lifestyle.

Barrier beach coasts occur where beaches have formed some distance from the original shore, near rocky promontories. This results in lagoons or estuaries forming between the barrier beach and the old shoreline.

Tidal plain coasts are most often characterised by salt marshes or mangrove swamps. In tropical areas, they can also be marked by fringing coral. Tidal plains are common between Port Hedland, Western Australia, and the Northwest Cape, but do occur elsewhere. Unfortunately, because of the 'unattractive' nature of mangroves and the lack of recognition of their vital role in the ecosystem, many of these ecologically important areas have been lost to development in the more populous areas of Australia.

COASTLINE LENGTH

State or Territory	Length (km)	% of Total Length
New South Wales	1 900	5.17
Victoria	1 800	4.90
Queensland	7 400	20.14
South Australia	3 700	10.07
Western Australia	12 500	34.03
Tasmania	3 200	8.71
Northern Territory	6 200	16.88
Australian Capital Territory (incl. Jervis Bay)	35	0.10
Australia	**36 735**	**100.0**

COASTLINE LENGTH BY STATE OR TERRITORY

The coastline distance of the states was determined in 1973 by the Division of Mapping of the Department of National Resources. Taken from maps of 1:250 000 scale, it was determined by plotting points 500 m apart and then adding the straight-line distance between them. The high-water mark was used and therefore mangrove and coral reefs were excluded.

THE WATERS SURROUNDING AUSTRALIA

As an island, Australia is bounded by seas and oceans on all sides. They are: the Indian Ocean to the west; the Timor, Arafura and Coral Seas to the north; the South Pacific Ocean to the east; the Southern Ocean to the south; and the Tasman Sea to the south-east.

Bass Strait separates Tasmania from the mainland and varies in width from 130 km to 250 km. The main islands in Bass Strait are King, Flinders and Cape Barren. The closest country to Australia is Papua New Guinea, which lies across the Torres Strait at a distance of only about 140 km from the tip of Cape York Peninsula.

AUSTRALIAN FISHING ZONE

The Australian Fishing Zone (AFZ) established in 1979 encompasses the area extending 200 km from the territorial sea baseline of Australia (excluding the territorial waters of other countries) and covers a total of 8 900 000 km². All species of whale are a protected species in the AFZ.

Under the Law of the Sea Convention, Australia has an obligation to allow licensed foreign fishing vessels access to areas which are surplus to domestic requirements.

THE CONTINENTAL SHELF

In proportion to its size, Australia has the largest continental shelf of any continent. The continental shelf is the area around the continent submerged under relatively shallow sea. The shelf extends to Papua New Guinea in the north and around Tasmania in the south. It varies in width from the coast from 30 km to more than 240 km.

FEATURES OF OUR COASTLINE

THE GREAT BARRIER REEF

Situated off the north-east coast of Australia and stretching for 2000 km along the Queensland coast, the Great Barrier Reef is the largest coral structure in the world. It is not a single reef, but rather consists of nearly 3000 individual coral reefs — the most complex living coral reef system in the world.

The reef varies in age from 2 million to 18 million years old, and runs from Bramble Cay (latitude 9°8'S) off Papua New Guinea to Lady Elliot Island (latitude 24°8'S) 155 km south-east of Gladstone. It covers an area of more than 200 000 km².

The Great Barrier Reef Marine Park was established in 1975 to protect this region. It covers 98.5% of the reef area taking in a total of 355 883 km², making it the largest marine park in the world. The Great Barrier Reef has also been placed on the World Heritage List in recognition of its natural importance. It is one of ten areas in Australia recognised by UNESCO as being of world heritage importance. (*See* Environment.)

There are two types of islands in the reef; high or continental islands, such as Hayman and Brampton Islands, and low coral cays, such as Green Island off Cairns. *Continental islands* are, as their name suggests, made up of the same rocks as the mainland and are really partly submerged, mainland hills. There are more than 2000 of these within the Great Barrier Reef Marine Park. Of these, at least 750 have fringing reefs attached to them.

Cays are composed entirely of debris produced by the reef through storms and bioerosion. This debris builds up and forms cays which can stabilise and support vegetation. There are more than 300 cays in the Great Barrier Reef; about 90 of these have vegetation. The highest are Heron and Green Islands, which, along with Lady Elliot Island, have tourist resorts.

FRASER OR GREAT SANDY ISLAND

Australia is also home to the largest sand island in the world - Fraser Island off the south-east coast of Queensland. Approximately 120 km long and between 25 and 50 km wide, the island covers more than 160 km². Sandhills rise to almost 240 m in places and there are numerous freshwater perched lakes, some of which are more than 60 m deep. Lake Boemingen is the largest, covering an area of 2 km². The island is also noted for its dense rainforest, with fine stands of turpentine trees.

Originally known as Great Sandy Island, its current name of Fraser Island is in honour of Eliza Fraser, who was shipwrecked near the island in 1836 and spent three weeks stranded there before being rescued.

SHARK BAY

Shark Bay, in north-western Western Australia, is an area of great natural beauty. It is also home to stromatolites, ancient rock formations built over hundreds of years by blue-green algae, one of the earliest forms of plant life. Stromatolites formed up to 3500 millions years ago, and some of the oldest stromatolites at Shark Bay are known to have formed over a period of 1000 years or more.

THE GREAT AUSTRALIAN BIGHT

The widest indentation in the Australian coastline is the Great Australian Bight, which extends from West Point in South Australia to Cape Parsley in Western Australia. It covers a distance of 1100 km and has steep cliffs along much of the coastline which are often more than 70 m high and reaching 120 m in places. These cliffs form the southern border of the Nullarbor Plain, one of the largest flat bedrock surfaces in the world.

A feature of the Nullabor Plain is its blowholes. Actually vents from a large system of underground caves, there are thought to be around 10 000 blowholes on the plain. As the caves heat and cool throughout the day, air rushes in and out of the holes. At times, the noise is almost deafening.

TWELVE APOSTLES

Found along the coastline of Victoria near Port Campbell, these rock stacks are part of the Port Campbell National Park. They rise in dramatic formation from the sea, up to 100 m above sea level. In 1990, a natural rock bridge from the ocean cliffs to one of the rock stacks, known as London Bridge, collapsed into the sea. A sightseer was trapped on the surviving rock stack at the time of the collapse, and had to be rescued by helicopter.

CAPE YORK PENINSULA

Cape York Peninsula is 700 km long and, at its northernmost tip, is separated by only 140 km water from Papua New Guinea. The vegetation ranges from coastal tropical rainforest to scrubland, open forest and dry plains. It is home to Australia's largest butterfly, the Cape York birdwing (*Ornithoptera priamus*), which is a stunning, almost lime green colour, with black markings. The tip of Cape York is the most northerly point of Australia. The Great Dividing Range runs almost its entire length.

THE GULF OF CARPENTARIA

The largest gulf on the northern coast, the Gulf of Carpentaria reaches a width of almost 700 km between Limmen Bight on the western coast and the mouth of the Coleman River on the coast of Cape York. It is bordered by Arnhem Land to the west and the Gulf Country (land less than 100 m above sea level) to the south.

THE BEACHES

The Australian coast has thousands of kilometres of sandy beaches, divisible into two basic types: *mainland beach coasts* and *barrier beach coasts*.

Mainland beach coasts are extensive stretches of sand, occurring along the coast of western Victoria and along the coast of the Southern Ocean.

Barrier beach coasts are formed when sand accumulates against offshore headlands to form lagoons and estuaries between the beach and the old shore line. These are commonest on the east coast where extensive barrier beach coasts are broken at times by sheer rock cliffs.

Coastal beaches result from the balance between: the effects of the standard wave action along the coastline; erosional storm waves; and longshore currents bringing sand to the area.

EIGHTY MILE BEACH

Situated 300 km E/NE of Port Hedland in Western Australia, this arc of barren sand dune coast and salty marshland faces the Indian Ocean. It is a western extension of the Great Sandy Desert.

NINETY MILE BEACH

Bordering Bass Strait on the Victorian mainland, this beach stretches from Yatram to beyond Lakes Entrance. Ninety Mile Beach is an uninterrupted stretch of sand ridge and dune beach more than 140 km long, created from a build-up of sea-transported sand.

Australian Territories

MAINLAND TERRITORIES

JERVIS BAY TERRITORY

Handed over by New South Wales in 1915 to provide the Australian Capital Territory with sea access, Jervis Bay Territory is a separate Territory. It encompasses an area of 7360 hectares, including 800 hectares of territorial waters in Jervis Bay.

In 1971, 4118 ha, about two-thirds of the territory, was declared the Jervis Bay Nature Reserve; in 1985, Bowen Island, another 51 ha, was declared part of this reserved area. The remaining one-third consists of Royal Australian Navy land, private leases, Aboriginal land and unoccupied Commonwealth land. There is a permanent population of about 170 at Wreck Bay village and about 90 in Jervis Bay village. There are an additional 450 people based at HMAS *Creswell*, a naval college, and at other naval installations.

The other mainland territories are the Australian Capital Territory and the Northern Territory. Both are covered in greater detail later.

EXTERNAL TERRITORIES

NORFOLK ISLAND

The Territory of Norfolk Island includes Norfolk, Philip and Nepean Islands, located in the south-west Pacific Ocean at longitude 167°59'E and latitude 29°02'S, 1676 km north-east of Sydney.

Norfolk Island is approximately 8 km long and 5 km wide with an area of about 35 km². Its coastline is 32 km long. Discovered in 1774 by Captain Cook, it was used for much of its early settlement as a penal station for the most hardened convicts. In 1856, 194 descendants of the mutineers from the *Bounty* were brought there from Pitcairn Island. Today, about half of the population is made up of descendants from these original settlers.

Norfolk Island became a Territory of Australia in 1913. Since 1979, the island has had its own Legislative Assembly consisting of nine elected members. An Administrator, appointed and financed by Australia, represents the Australian government. Residents of Norfolk Island are unable to vote in Australian elections or to claim Social Security benefits. Norfolk Island receives no economic support from Australia and relies on tourism as its main source of revenue.

HEARD AND McDONALD ISLANDS

Transferred to Australian control from the UK in 1947, this group of islands lies near the Antarctic. Heard Island is 43 km long and 20 km wide, and is the largest of the group, with an area of 860 km². It is of volcanic origin and its highest point, Big Ben (2745 m), is an active volcano. The island was sighted in 1833, but not named until 1855.

Briefly used by sealers and expeditioners, a scientific base was set up on Heard Island in 1946, but this was closed in 1955 when Mawson Station, Antarctica, was opened. Since that time various visits to and studies of Heard Island have been made; it is seen as the last unspoilt habitat of the Antarctic region. Australia maintains a summer research station on Heard Island, but it is basically uninhabited except for seabirds and seals.

The McDonald Islands are a group of three small, rocky islands 43 km west of Heard, situated in the southern Indian Ocean between longitude 72° and 74°30'E and latitude 52°30' and 53°30'S, 4100 km southwest of Fremantle. The first landing on the McDonald Islands was in 1971.

AUSTRALIAN ANTARCTIC TERRITORY
Transferred to Australia from British claims in 1933, the Australian Antarctic Territory encompasses all land south of 60°S latitude and between 45°E and 160°E longitude, except for the French Terre Adelie. The Australian Antarctic Territory covers an area of 6 119 818 km².

Australia has had a permanent presence in Antarctica since 1954 when the first permanent Australian research station was set up at Mawson. Two other mainland stations have been established since then, named Casey and Davis. Australia also maintains bases used for summer research programs at: Dovers in the Prince Charles Mountains, south of Mawson; Law in the Larsemann Hills; Edgeworth David in the Bunger Hills; and Commonwealth Bay. The Antarctic science program is primarily concerned with weather and climate studies, marine science, environmental science, geoscience and sciences specific to polar regions.

COCOS (KEELING) ISLANDS
The Cocos (Keeling) Islands are a group of 27 coral islands, in the form of two atolls, which were discovered in 1609 by Captain William Keeling of the East India Company. In 1836, Charles Darwin visited the islands on the HMS *Beagle* and it is believed he based his theories on coral reef formation on observations made there.

Located in the East Indian Ocean 2768 km north-west of Perth and 3700 km west of Darwin, the total area of the islands is 14 km². The largest of the group is West Island, which is about 10 km long and 0.5 km wide.

Responsibility for the islands had been held by a number of different governments over the years until they became part of Australia in 1978. In 1955, they became an Australian territory by agreement between the British and Australian governments.

Alexander Hare arrived in the Cocos Islands in 1826 and the Scottish sea captain John Clunies-Ross settled there in 1827. Hare later left the islands, but Clunies-Ross stayed on. It was not until 1857 that the Cocos Islands were annexed by Britain. In 1886, Queen Victoria gave all land above the high-water mark to the Clunies-Ross family, under the proviso that the Crown had the right to use land for public purposes. In 1973, the Cocos (Keeling) Council was set up to advise the Administrator who is appointed by the Australian Governor-General.

The Australian government purchased the Clunies-Ross family's interests in 1978, apart from their home and land, and the Cocos Islands became part of Australia. In 1984, the residents of the islands voted by referendum to integrate with Australia.

Home Island and West Island are the only two islands which are inhabited, mostly by descendants of the Malay labourers imported to farm copra.

CHRISTMAS ISLAND

Christmas Island was discovered in 1615 and named on Christmas Day in 1643. It is located in the East Indian Ocean between 10°25'S and 105°40'E. Although it has no indigenous population, Christmas Island is inhabited by people of predominantly Chinese/Malay origin. It has been mined on and off for its large phosphate deposits since Britain claimed the island in 1888, although this industry is now coming to an end. Efforts are now being made to develop the tourism and fishing industries to provide an alternative source of income for the islands. In 1958, Christmas Island became an Australian territory and almost all residents are now Australian citizens or permanent residents.

The island is situated 2623 km north north-west of Perth. It is the rugged summit of an undersea mountain, with an area of 135 km² and a central plateau which at some points reaches heights of 360 m above sea level. The coastline is surrounded, except for a few spots, by sea cliffs between 20 and 60 m high. Rainforest covers most of the island.

CORAL SEA ISLANDS TERRITORY

The Coral Sea Islands Territory covers a sea area of 780 000 km² east of the Great Barrier Reef, between the Reef and longitude 156°06'E and latitudes 12° and 24°S. Some of the islands are extremely small sand and coral islands. While some have grass or scrub cover, none has permanent fresh water. The area experiences tropical cyclones and a number of meteorological stations are based on reefs. The only inhabited island is Willis Island, where the weather station has a staff of three.

The territory was formed under the *Coral Sea Islands Act 1969*. Local wildlife includes migratory birds and the world's largest and most endangered species of sea turtle, the luth or leathery turtle. As a result of the need to protect the flora and fauna, the Lihou Reef and Coringa-Herald National Nature Reserves were formed in 1982. The Australia–Japan and Australia–China Endangered and Migratory Birds Agreements protect numerous species here.

ASHMORE AND CARTIER ISLANDS

Cartier Island and Ashmore Reef, which comprises Middle, East and West Islands are situated in the Timor Sea, on the outer edge of the continental shelf, between 790 and 850 km west of Darwin and 100 km south of the Indonesian island of Roti. The islands are small and low, and are uninhabited. They are composed of coral and sand, with a cover of grass.

The islands came under Australian Commonwealth authority in 1931 and, in 1933, were annexed to the Northern Territory. In 1978, when the Northern Territory became self governing, the islands again became the responsibility of the Commonwealth.

The area is a nature reserve to protect the abundant birdlife, turtles and bêche-de-mer. Australia–China and Australia–Japan agreements protect endangered migratory birds. An Australian presence at Ashmore Reef protects wildlife and enforces landing regulations during the fishing season.

The States and Territories

BOUNDARIES

The following boundaries were settled by 1901, apart from the Australian Capital Territory, which was only established in 1911, and Jervis Bay Territory, which was established in 1915. In 1926, the Northern Territory was divided into Central and North Australia, but the two were reunited in 1933.

NEW SOUTH WALES

New South Wales is bounded along its east coast by the South Pacific Ocean and on the southern border with Victoria by the Murray River (which is within New South Wales's boundaries) from its source in the Great Dividing Range and then directly from there to the coast at Cape Howe. The western boundary, which it shares with South Australia, is the 141st meridian of longitude. The northern boundary, between New South Wales and Queensland, follows the 29th parallel of latitude until it meets the Macintyre and Dumaresq Rivers, where it follows them and then runs along the crest of the McPherson Range to Point Danger on the east coast of Australia.

VICTORIA

When the border between Victoria and South Australia was first surveyed, inadequate equipment and a number of problems meant that the line was accidentally placed at 140°58'E longitude rather than at the 141st meridian longitude as decided. Despite litigation and appeal to the Privy Council, this mistake has never been corrected and the border stands about 3.6 km to the west of where it was meant to go. The New South Wales/South Australia border does lie along the 141st meridian and this anomaly creates a dogleg at the intersection of the three States.

The northern boundary of Tasmania is decreed to be the line of 39°12'S latitude, approximately 7 km south of Wilsons Promontory, and this is generally recognised as Victoria's southern border.

QUEENSLAND
Queensland is bordered on its eastern side by the Pacific Ocean and on the northwest coast by the Gulf of Carpentaria. The western border with the Northern Territory is the 138°E meridian of longitude, turning at Poeppels Corner, which marks the northern junction of Queensland, South Australia and the Northern Territory, and then running along the 26th parallel to Haddon Corner. At Haddon Corner, the border turns south again and runs down the 141st meridian of longitude.

SOUTH AUSTRALIA
The northern border of South Australia lies along the 26°S latitude and its western border with Western Australia runs straight down the 129th meridian of longitude. It is bordered on the south by the Great Australian Bight.

WESTERN AUSTRALIA
Western Australia borders the Northern Territory and South Australia along the 129° meridian of longitude. Its only other border is its seaboard, which borders the Timor Sea in the far north-west, the Indian Ocean in the west and the Great Australian Bight in the south.

TASMANIA
The state of Tasmania is an island surrounded by sea. The northern seaward boundary of Van Diemen's Land (as it was) was set in 1825 as the line of 39°12' latitude. Tasmania is bounded on the north by Bass Strait, the east by the Tasman Sea and to the west and south west by the Southern Ocean.

NORTHERN TERRITORY
The northern border of the Northern Territory is its coastline, which is bounded from east to west by the Timor Sea, the Arafura Sea and the Gulf of Carpentaria.

AUSTRALIAN CAPITAL TERRITORY
Of all the states and territories, only the Australian Capital Territory is completely landlocked, although its control over the Jervis Bay Territory does, in theory, allow it sea access. The western border of the Australian Capital Territory lies along the Bimberi-Franklin Brindabella Ranges in the south of New South Wales.

POEPPEL'S CORNER

The point where Queensland, South Australia and the Northern Territory meet is known as Poeppel's Corner. Located in the Simpson Desert, it is named for Augustus John Poeppel, who marked the spot in 1883 with a coolabah tree stump and then went back and corrected it the next year.

TIME ZONES

Australia is divided into three time zones. The 'hours ahead' figure is based on Universal Time (UT), formerly Greenwich Mean Time (GMT):

Zone	Hours ahead	Meridian of longitude	Areas within zone
Eastern Standard Time	10	150°E	Queensland New South Wales Australian Capital Territory Victoria Tasmania
Central Standard Time	9.5	142° 30'E	South Australia Northern Territory Broken Hill/Western New South Wales
Western Australian Standard Time	8	120°E	Western Australia

All these time zones were set in the 1890s. Central Standard Time was originally set at 135° meridian of longitude, but changed in 1898 to its present position. The Northern Territory also changed, as it was under South Australia's administration at this time.

DAYLIGHT SAVING

Summer time in some states varies from the standard times because of daylight saving, by which clocks are brought forward by one hour during the summer months. Daylight saving was first introduced during World War I and then revived in World War II, and again in the 1970s. Not all states participate and those that do often start and/or finish on different dates, creating several different time zones during the year.

Landform Structures

There are three major landform structures that make up Australia. They are the Western Shield, the Central Basin and the Eastern Uplands, which are described below.

THE WESTERN SHIELD
The oldest landform on the Australian continent, the Western Shield, contains rocks which are at least 1500 million years old; some may be twice as old. Forming nearly two-thirds of Australia's area, the Western Shield is an ancient plateau, or series of plateaus, which averages between 300 and 600 m in height.

The Western Shield covers the whole of Western Australia, most of the Northern Territory, northern South Australia and small areas of New South Wales and Queensland.

THE CENTRAL BASIN OR INTERIOR LOWLANDS
This region runs north–south across Australia from the Gulf of Carpentaria to the Great Australian Bight. It consists of low-lying lands which around 50 million years ago were sea and lake beds. This area now covers about 20 separate artesian basins, including the Great Artesian Basin. The area has an average altitude of less than 150 m above sea level. Land use is largely agriculture and grazing, with irrigation improving fertility.

THE EASTERN UPLANDS
Formed when the floor of the Tasman Sea was forced against the eastern edge of Australia, the Eastern Uplands are a broad belt of ranges and ridges running from Cape York to Tasmania, the majority of which is also known as the Great Dividing Range.

NATURAL LANDFORM FEATURES BY STATE OR TERRITORY

NEW SOUTH WALES
There are four distinct regions in New South Wales, which run roughly north-south from the coastline. The first is the coastal district, an area of valleys and plains which border the Pacific Ocean on the eastern side and runs up to the highland belt, or tablelands, along the western side.

The tablelands are part of the Great Dividing Range, which runs the length of Eastern Australia. In New South Wales, this region varies from 50 km to 160 km in width. The western slopes of the tablelands form the next region. They gradually descend into the fourth and largest region, the western plains district which covers almost two-thirds of the State.

VICTORIA

The Great Dividing Range forms a highland belt which curves to run east–west across the centre of Victoria. North of Melbourne, a low wide pass known as Kilmore Gap allows access over the Great Dividing Range to the northern districts. To the east of this pass, the highlands contain large plateau-like areas known as the high plains, where the Victorian snowfields are situated. To the west, the highlands are lower and more gently sloped. The Grampians, a series of sandstone ridges, are situated here.

The highlands form a division between: the northern regions of the Wimmera Mallee and the North Plains; and the southern regions which are the coastal plains and hill lands.

Plains in the south-west cover the area from the Grampians down to Warrnambool and Colac, an area of 2300 km². Volcanic in origin, they consist of vast basalt flows with some volcanic cones rising above the plain such as Mount Elephant.

The uplands in the south include the Mornington Peninsula and the Otway Ranges. There are also some rugged highlands to the south-west of the Gippsland area.

QUEENSLAND

Queensland consists of five main landform regions. The coastal plains region which lies along the eastern seaboard consists of valleys and plains, and varies quite considerably in width, stretching to 200 km in places.

The eastern highlands, which comprise the northern part of the Great Dividing Range, stretch from Cape York Peninsula all the way down to the border with New South Wales, in places reaching right down to the coastline. They form the watershed for rivers running to either side.

Covering almost two-thirds of the State are the western plains, which include the Channel Country in the southwest and the Simpson Desert. After heavy rains, the Cooper and Diamantina creeks flood into the plains area of the Channel Country, giving it its name. The northwestern uplands are similar to areas of the eastern highlands; this area includes Mount Isa and the Barkly Tableland, which extends into the Northern Territory.

The offshore area of Queensland, which includes the Great Barrier Reef as well as other reefs and offshore islands, makes up a unique region and the largest living coral formation in the world.

SOUTH AUSTRALIA

The central region of South Australia is known as 'the shatter belt' as it has been fractured by faults relatively recently, in geographical terms. This encompasses the highland belt which consists of the Mt Lofty Ranges and the Flinders Ranges, the Yorke and Eyre Peninsulas, and the Spencer and St Vincent Gulfs. Kangaroo Island, the largest island off the South Australian coast, is an extension of these highlands and was once joined to the mainland.

The western half of the state is made up of a low plateau edged on the southern side by the Nullarbor Plain, which reaches to the coast of the Great Australian Bight. The centre of this area is dominated by the Great Victoria Desert. In the north-west, several ranges rise above the plains, the main one being the Musgrave Ranges.

The Murray River runs through South Australia from the New South Wales border to Lake Alexandrina, from which it flows into the sea, a distance of 640 km. Mallee lands surround the river valley and to the south lie the Coorong and Ninety Mile Beach.

In the far south-east are Mount Gambier and other dormant volcanoes. This area is the site of the most recent volcanic activity in Australia.

The Lake Eyre Basin in the central north district is a vast shallow depression which fills only rarely after very heavy rain.

WESTERN AUSTRALIA

The Great Plateau is the dominant geographical feature of Western Australia; it covers more than 90% of the State's area with a general height of 300-450 m above sea level. Above this plateau rise occasional ranges, but generally its surface consists of gently undulating land. This area is the Western Pre-Cambrian Shield, which covers two-thirds of Australia. The inland reaches of this area contain vast areas of arid land such as the Gibson and Great Sandy Desert. In some places, this plateau reaches right to the coast producing shoreline cliffs and numerous offshore islands. The Kimberley region between King Sound and Joseph Napoleon Gulf is a good example of this.

Coastal plains, sometimes only 20 km in width, are spaced along the western seaboard.

TASMANIA

The most mountainous state, Tasmania is dominated by a series of plateau blocks which are a continuation of the Great Dividing Range. These are most often bounded by steep escarpments called tiers. Glacial activity in the last ice age has left steep sided valleys and basins where lakes have formed.

The only relief from the rugged terrain is in the central eastern lowlands around the valleys of the Huon, Derwent and Tamar-Esk rivers, and the small area of lowland in the north. It is in these places that towns and cities have been established.

NORTHERN TERRITORY

The low flat northern coastline of the Northern Territory is intersected by numerous rivers and bordered with many islands. The coastline consists of sandy beaches, mud flats and mangrove swamp.

The central basins region of the Northern Territory is semi-arid country of low elevation, broken by ridges and ranges. It rises slowly in the south to the area known as the 'Centre', where the landscape consists of a number of ranges with large basins between them and with giant rock formations, like Uluru (Ayers Rock), rising suddenly from the surrounding countryside.

AUSTRALIAN CAPITAL TERRITORY

Positioned in the southern tablelands of New South Wales, the Australian Capital Territory contains a number of north–south aligned ridges and valleys.

Canberra itself is set in a valley surrounded by mountains. A number of rivers, tributaries of the Murrumbidgee which flows south-north through the Territory, runs through the Australian Capital Territory.

Canberra itself is set at an average altitude of 600 m and the highest peak in the Australian Capital Territory is Bimberi Peak at 1914 m.

VOLCANIC ACTIVITY

Australia is the only continent without current volcanic activity; the last eruption here happened more than 1400 years ago.

A billion years ago in the west, there were many active volcanoes: beds of volcanic rock can be found there that are 1000 m thick. Much more recent is the activity in the east, where the remains of volcanic rocks form such striking formations as the Glasshouse Mountains in Queensland and the Warrumbungles in New South Wales. Mount Warning, near Cape Byron on northeastern New South Wales is actually the eroded crater of the giant Tweed Volcano, which extends north into Queensland. This inactive volcano last exploded about 23 millions years ago.

The most recent eruption by a volcano in Australia occured at Mount Gambier, which last erupted more than 1400 years ago; the Blue Lake is a former volcanic crater.

Altitude

The average altitude of Australia is 300 m above sea level; approximately 87% of the total land mass is lower than 500 m; and 99.5% is lower than 1000 m. Australia is the lowest and flattest of the continents, while the Antarctic is the highest, with an average elevation of 2200 metres. The Australian continent is so flat because it lies near the centre of one of the earth's tectonic plates, which means that geologically it has not been subject to much movement for about 200 million years. Although some mountains do exist, many others have been worn down by erosion during this quiet period. New Zealand, on the other hand, lies on the edge of a tectonic plate. This has resulted in much geological activity such as earthquakes and volcanic eruptions, and mountains being formed and rapidly eroded.

THE HIGHEST POINT IN AUSTRALIA

Mount Kosciuszko, in the Australian Alps, in New South Wales, is the highest point on the continent at 2228 m. It was named by the Polish explorer Paul de Strzelecki, who, on 12 March 1840, was probably the first European to climb the mountain. The highest point on Australian territory, however, is Mawson Peak on Big Ben, which is found on Heard Island. Mount Hotham in Victoria is the highest village in Australia at a height of 1747 m.

THE LOWEST POINT IN AUSTRALIA

Lake Eyre, situated northwest of Adelaide, is, at 15 m below sea level, Australia's lowest point. Covering an area of 9300 km², this huge salt pan, which is dry most of the time, is also the largest lake in Australia.

HIGHEST POINT BY STATE OR TERRITORY

The most mountainous state of Australia is Tasmania. However, the highest point in Australia, Mount Kosciuszko, is in New South Wales.

State	Mountain	Height (m)
New South Wales	Mt Kosciuszko	2228
Victoria	Mt Bogong	1986
Queensland	Mt Bartle Frere	1611
South Australia	Mt Woodroffe	1439
Western Australia	Mt Meharry	1244
Tasmania	Mt Ossa	1617
Northern Territory	Mt Zeil	1509
Australian Capital Territory	Bimberi Peak	1912

Mountains and Plateaus

AUSTRALIAN MOUNTAINS HIGHER THAN 1500 M

Mountain	Metres	State
Mt Kosciuszko	2228	New South Wales
Mt Townsend	2214	New South Wales
Mt Jagungal	2061	New South Wales
Mt Bogong	1988	Victoria
Mt Feathertop	1922	Victoria
Bimberi Peak	1912	Australian Capital Territory
Mt Loch	1862	Victoria
Mt Cope	1837	Victoria
Mt Cobberas	1836	Victoria
The Pilot	1831	New South Wales
Mt Buller	1804	Victoria
Mt Howitt	1742	Victoria
The Horn	1723	Victoria
Mt Buffalo	1721	Victoria
Chandlers Peak	1684	New South Wales
Mt Tamboritha	1646	Victoria
Mt Bartle Frere	1622	Queensland
Tinderry Peak	1619	New South Wales
Mt Ossa	1617	Tasmania
Round Mt	1615	New South Wales
Mt Murray	1609	Victoria
Point Lookout	1600	New South Wales
Brumlow Top (Barrington Tops)	1586	New South Wales
Legges Tor	1573	Tasmania
Mt Baw Baw	1566	Victoria
Cradle Mountain	1545	Tasmania
Mt Zeil	1531	Northern Territory
Ben Lomond	1527	Tasmania
Mt Saint Bernard	1524	Victoria
Mt Bajimba	1524	New South Wales
Mt Kaputar	1524	New South Wales
Mt Torbreck	1522	Victoria
Ben Lomond	1520	New South Wales
Mt Rumbee	1503	New South Wales

THE GREAT DIVIDING RANGE

Also known as the Eastern Highlands or the Great Divide, this extensive area of highland extends from the Cape York Peninsula in far northern Queensland, through eastern Queensland to the Grampians in western Victoria. It varies in width from 160 km to more than 300 km. While it lies very close to the eastern coast in some places, it is up to 250 km inland in others. In some areas, it is named as individual ranges, in others as mountains, plateaus and tablelands. The highest point in the Great Dividing Range is also Australia's highest point, Mount Kosciuszko.

THE AUSTRALIAN ALPS

This highest section of the Great Divide runs south from Kiandra in New South Wales to the Gippsland region in north-eastern Victoria, where it is known as the Victorian Alps. Kosciuszko National Park covers most of the high-altitude area, which is snow-covered during the winter months. Thredbo and Perisher, the major New South Wales ski fields, are both situated within the park. Victoria's Mount Hotham and Mount Buffalo ski fields are part of the Australian Alps. The Australian Alps are a major watershed and the source of the Murray and the Murrumbidgee Rivers, two of Australia's great river systems.

THE WARRUMBUNGLE RANGE

This range in central western New South Wales is an eroded shield volcano, formed by volcanic activity about 13 million years ago. It consists of a cluster of volcanic plugs, the tallest of which is Mount Exmouth (1228 m). It occupies a circular area approximately 64 km in diameter and stretching for 130 km. Like Queensland's Glasshouse Mountains, the Warrumbungles form part of a volcanic series which stretches from central and northern New South Wales to south-eastern Queensland. The Warrumbungle National Park covers 914 ha.

BLUE MOUNTAINS

Running between Coxs River and Mount Wilson in New South Wales, this region is a sandstone plateau, dissected into forested valleys and gorges by sheer cliffs. The maximum altitude in the mountains is 1100 m. The name is thought to have come about from the blue haze given off by eucalypts, which gives the mountains their characteristic 'blue' appearance when seen from a distance. This phenomenon is common to most heavily forested areas in the mountains and ranges in every state.

ATHERTON TABLELAND

Atherton Tableland is a fertile plateau on the Great Dividing Range, with an average altitude of 762 m and an area of approximately 32 000 km². It is located west to south/south-west of Cairns in northern Queensland. The area has rich volcanic soil, and features lush rainforest, caves, gorges, lakes and waterfalls. There are also two crater lakes, Eacham and Barrine, which are further evidence of the plateau's former volcanic activity. Much of the Atherton Tableland is now used for agriculture such as dairy farming and tobacco and tea plantations.

NOTABLE RANGES OUTSIDE THE GREAT DIVIDING RANGE

BARKLY TABLELAND
Barkly Tableland is an area of 130 000 km², extending from the north-east of the Northern Territory into Queensland. It is a plateau of grassy hills and tropical pastures, and has an annual rainfall of 250–500 mm, making this an ideal cattle-raising area.

FLINDERS RANGES
The most extensive highland region in South Australia, the Flinders Ranges extend more than 400 km in a north–south alignment. They form a northern extension of the Mount Lofty Ranges. The Flinders Ranges are characterised by sheer scarps, deep valleys and steep gorges. Arkaroola, in a remote part of the area, is unusual in that it has hot springs, a sign of volcanic activity rarely seen on the continent.

THE KIMBERLEY PLATEAU
Situated in the far north of Western Australia, this vast plateau is dissected by river gorges bordered by steep fault ranges such as the Durack Range to the east and the King Leopold Range to the southwest.

The Bungle Bungle Range in the east Kimberley region is a spectacular sandstone massif, which is one of the best examples of sandstone ruiniform relief (an erosional landform) in the world. Its weathered spires and domes are very distinctive, with some resembling giant beehives and others sharp and pointed. The vegetation around the ranges is mainly spinifex and mulga.

MACDONNELL RANGES
The largest area of highlands in Northern Territory are the Macdonnell Ranges, which are 380 km long. The highest point within the ranges is Mount Zeil at 1510 m, and it is situated 145 km west/north-west of Alice Springs. The ranges are folded mountains cut with steep gaps formed by streams such as the Standley Chasm. Australia's deepest gorge, its walls are up to 80 m high and only 4 m apart.

MONOLITHS

MOUNT AUGUSTUS

Rising to a height of 1105 m above sea level and measuring 8 km by 3 km, the little-known Mount Augustus is located 320 km east of Carnarvon in Western Australia. An upfaulted monoclinal gritty conglomerate, or monadnock, it is twice the size of Uluru (Ayers Rock) in the Northern Territory and rises 377 m above the surrounding terrain.

ULURU AND THE OLGAS

Uluru (Ayers Rock) rises above an open plain, to 863 m above sea level. It is 426 km south-west of Alice Springs. The base circumference is approximately 9 km and the rock measures 2.5 km long by 1.5 km wide. It covers an area of 468 hectares. Uluru, a monadnock or resistant rock standing above surrounding country, is composed of sand, gravel and boulders deposited in the Pre-Cambrian age more than 600 million years ago, and compacted by seas which covered the region. It stands 348 m above the surrounding plain and is connected to the bedrock underneath.

The tallest of the Olgas is Mount Olga, also a monadnock, which rises to an altitude of 1069 m. This group of rounded red sandstone mountains is distinctive for its shape which is thought to be caused by aeolian erosion; sand being blown constantly against their surfaces.

Plains

DARLING DOWNS

The Darling Downs are a fertile plain of 90 060 km^2 to the west of Brisbane, at an altitude ranging between 350 m and 600 m above sea level.

CANNING BASIN

An arid region in the north-west of Western Australia, this basin spreads to the south from Derby to the mouth of the De Grey River and across to the Kimberley region. It is generally below 200 m above sea level, and does not exceed a height of 400 m. The Great Sandy Desert forms part of the basin.

NULLARBOR PLAIN

The Nullarbor Plain is a limestone plateau bordered on the southern side by the Great Australian Bight and on the northern side by the Great Victoria Desert. Straddling the states of South Australia and Western Australia, it runs for a distance of 725 km east–west and extends north for 400 km. The Nullarbor Plain is the largest flat bedrock surface in the world. Its maximum altitude is 200 m and it covers an estimated area of 270 000 km^2.

Characterised by steep coastal cliffs that reach 120 m in height, the porous limestone of which the plain consists means that the low rainfall seeps through the rock to form subterranean caves and lakes. Its name comes from the Latin *nullus arbor* meaning 'no tree'.

The longest sea cliffs in Australia can be found along the Nullarbor Plain, stretching from the Eyre Telegraph Station to Israelite Bay in Western Australia. They are about 250 km in length.

Caves

There are different kinds of caves in Australia: rock shelters or open caves; coastal caves; lava caves; and limestone and dolomite caves.

Most caves are found in limestone, the result of acidic water action which dissolves the stone over hundreds of years. Caves in Australia have formed in rock aged between 1000 million years and a few thousand years old.

PRINCIPAL CAVES BY STATE OR TERRITORY

NEW SOUTH WALES   With 300 caves, the Jenolan Caves are the most extensive system in New South Wales. These extensive limestone caves were discovered in 1838 by James Whalan, while he was hunting the bushranger McKeown. The caves, a popular tourist attraction since the Edwardian era, are a complex series of caverns and passages, and underground rivers. The limestone has been formed into stalactites and stalagmites in many places, and underground pools of azure blue, such as the Pool of Cerberus, lie eerily in the smoothly eroded white rock.

The Yarrangobilly Caves in the Kosciuszko National Park south-west of Canberra are the deepest caves on the mainland.

VICTORIA   There is little limestone in Victoria and therefore few caves. The most notable are at Buchan near the border with New South Wales, where there are about 300 known caves. The Dukes-Fairy-Royal-Federal system is the largest in Victoria and runs for 3000 m.

QUEENSLAND   The deepest cave in Queensland is Goolie Cave (120 m) at Morinish, where caves formed when soil was washed out from between granite boulders. The Chillagoe-Mugana-Rockwood-Redcap system in the Chillagoe-Mungana National Park inland from Cairns has approximately 350 limestone caves.

SOUTH AUSTRALIA   South Australia has dune-limestone caves running parallel to the coast near the Victorian border and ending in the Naracoorte

Range 87 km inland. A vast amount of fossil bone, the remains of Australia's early animals, was found in the 3000 m long Victoria Fossil Cave. South Australia is also home to the second longest cave in Australia and the longest on the mainland: Corra-Lynne Cave.

The Nullarbor Plain also has a vast system of caves or 'blowholes' running underneath its surface. At Koonalda Cave, some of the oldest Aboriginal art to be found anywhere in Australia can be seen. The petro-glyphs, or rock art, are thought to be more than 20 000 years old. Aboriginal peoples were quarrying stone at this site around 25 000 years ago.

WESTERN AUSTRALIA   There are some 300 caves beneath the surface of the Nullarbor Plain in the south of Western Australia, part of the same system found in South Australia. In the Madura district lies the Mullamullang cave system, one of the longest cave systems in Australia. Also below the Nullarbor Plain is the Abrakurrie Cave which includes the largest single chamber in this area.

Yallingup Cave is the most northerly of several limestone caves found on the west coast south of Bunbury and north of the Margaret River.

TASMANIA   The 20 deepest caves in Australia are all in Tasmania, and also five of the longest. As many caves have yet to be completely explored, there could well be deeper and longer caves to be found there. The deepest cave, Anne-A-Kananda, is found near Mount Anne to the west of Hobart. It was discovered in 1982 and is 373 m in depth. Mole Creek, Kubla Khan and Croesus are among the most beautifully decorated caves in Australia. The Junee Florentine area is thought to be the thickest area of limestone in Australia and has more than 422 caves. The Ice Tube-Growling Swallet cave in this area is 11 000 m long and 345 m deep.

Exit Cave at Ida Bay is Australia's longest recorded cave. Situated south of Hobart, it is 17 km long. In July 1990, three members of a school party died in the Ida Bay district when rains flooded Mystery Creek Cave.

NORTHERN TERRITORY   The Aboriginal peoples have painted in many of the numerous rock shelter caves which exist in the Northern Territory. A lot of the caves around the base of Uluru have great importance to Aboriginal mythology and many have significant paintings.

Cutta Cutta Cave south of Katherine is the longest in the Northern Territory and runs for 2000 m. Also near Katherine is the Turkish Bath Cave, so named because the temperature in the cave is often 35°C or higher.

THE LONGEST CAVES IN AUSTRALIA

Name	State	Length (m)
Exit Cave System	Tasmania	17 000
Corra-Lynn Cave	South Australia	13 300
Mullamullang Cave	Western Australia	12 100
Old Homestead Cave	Western Australia	12 000
Growling Swallet	Tasmania	11 000
The Queenslander	Queensland	10 000
Easter Cave	Western Australia	7 655
Jenolan Show Caves	New South Wales	7 200
Mimbi Caves	Western Australia	7 000
Five Corners Cave	South Australia	6 500
Cocklebiddy Cave	Western Australia	6 200
Colong Caves	New South Wales	6 000
Herberts Pot	Tasmania	5 730
Johannsen's Cave	Queensland	5 550
Kalkadoon Cave	Queensland	5 400
Kubla Khan	Tasmania	3 657
West Eagles Nest	New South Wales	3 600
Mammoth Cave	New South Wales	3 510
Serendipity	Tasmania	3 500
Royal Arch Cave	Queensland	3 050

The longest known cave in the Southern Hemisphere is Mamo Kananda in
Papua New Guinea, which is 55 km long.

THE DEEPEST CAVES IN AUSTRALIA

Name	State	Depth (m)
Anne-A-Kananda	Tasmania	373
Ice Tube (Growling Swallet)	Tasmania	354
Khazad-Dum	Tasmania	323
Serendipity	Tasmania	282
Cauldron Pot	Tasmania	263
Owl Pot	Tasmania	244
Tassy Pot	Tasmania	238
Arrakis	Tasmania	235
Mini-Martin (Exit System)	Tasmania	220
Milk Run	Tasmania	208
Sesame 2 (Sesame Cave)	Tasmania	207
Flick Mints Hole	Tasmania	204
Mystery Creek Cave	Tasmania	203
Porcupine Pot	Tasmania	202

Name	State	Depth (m)
The Chairman	Tasmania	197
Cyclops Pot	Tasmania	192
Big Tree Pot	Tasmania	189
Deep Thought	Tasmania	187
Peanut Brittle Pot	Tasmania	186
Udensala	Tasmania	181

There are only 24 caves in the world deeper than 1000 m and the deepest of these is Reseau Jean Bernard Cave in France, which is 1535 m. The deepest cave in the Southern Hemisphere is Nettlebed Cave in New Zealand, which is 687 m deep.

Soils

Soil profile is the arrangement of the soil into layers or horizons, made distinct by variety of colour, texture and structure. The three main horizons are topsoil, subsoil and substratum. Further divisions are made of horizons, into zones. The substratum grades down to the bedrock, which is the unaltered parent material, the upper levels being the result of external influences such as climate, organisms, topography and time.

Soil texture is related to the size of soil particles and thus determines the soils' water-holding capacity, which in turn is important for estimating plant growth.

Sandy soils are coarse and porous with consequently high water retention. Loams have roughly equal quantities of sand, clay and silt which give good water retention and good drainage capacity. Clays are made up of 40% or more clay and hardly any sand. Water has trouble moving freely through clay.

Type	Texture	Sub-types	% of Aust. soil
Sands	uniform coarse	calcareous bleached sands brownish-earthy sands	30
Duplex Soils	subsoil finer than topsoil	red duplex (i.e. desert loams, red podzols or red-brown earths) yellow duplex (i.e. yellow podzols)	20

Type	Texture	Sub-types	% of Aust. soil
Massive Earths	gradational	red and yellow earths	17
Loams	uniform medium	calcareous, non-calcareous	13
Cracking Clays	uniform fine	black, grey, brown and red-brown earths	11
Calcareous Earths	gradational		6
Structured Earths	gradational	porous sub-soil or non-porous (smooth) Subsoil (krasnozems or red loams, red podzols, prairie soils or chocolate soils)	3
Non-Cracking Clays	uniform fine		less than 1%
Organic Soils	organic for top 30 cm	peats	less than 1%

LAND DEGRADATION

Land degradation is one of the most serious problems facing the Australian environment. Australians soils are complex and have been formed over millions of years, hence the lack of mountains on the continent, where existing mountains have been worn away through time.

Since European settlement, however, humans have managed to cause considerable damage to the intricate and variable soil system of Australia. Many soils are naturally salt-affected or have a high salt content in their groundwater. These soils have formed over a great length of time and are easily degraded by land use such as agriculture and irrigation. Overzealous or unwise use of the soil and its resources has caused several forms of land degradation in Australia.

DRY LAND SALINITY

Wholesale clearing of land for pasture or other uses has caused an increase in groundwater salinity. In some areas, such as around the Murray River, clearing the land has destroyed the delicate balance between soil and vegetation. Native trees and plants that previously kept the salinity in check by taking up rainwater are no longer there and consequently the groundwater salinity rises. As the groundwater rises to the surface, salt is left behind, making the land unusable and devoid of vegetation.

IRRIGATION SALINITY AND WATERLOGGING

Although eastern Australia has a vast system of artesian groundwater, a resource renewed by rainfall, indiscriminate use for irrigation has caused serious land degradation in some areas. Poorly maintained or leaking irrigation channels, poor drainage and overwatering have increased groundwater levels. This leads to waterlogging and increased salinity. Many bores spout water continually and unnecessarily, and may be broken or surplus to requirements. This has led to land degradation in the Murray–Darling Basin and near Emerald in Queensland, as well as other areas.

An education program is now under way not only to increase people's awareness of this problem, but also to implement practical solutions for overcoming it.

WATER EROSION

When vegetation is removed from sloping soil, the soil becomes vulnerable to erosion by rainwater or waterways. The topsoil is lost, causing further erosion, and waterways can silt up because of the extra soil being carried along their courses. Another side effect is the increased run-off of nutrients, particularly fertilisers, into the waterways. In the right conditions, such as drought or in a slow-flowing river, this can lead to outbreaks of the deadly blue-green algae and other algal forms. This has been a particular problem recently in the Murray–Darling river system of New South Wales and the Hawkesbury River west of Sydney.

WIND EROSION

When areas with low annual or intermittent rainfall lose their vegetation cover, the soil is carried away by the wind. This can be the result of drought or overgrazing of land. Light-textured soils are particularly susceptible to this and the devastating effects of wind erosion can be seen in western New South Wales and the mallee scrub of western Victoria, and also on the sand plains of South Australia and Western Australia.

Wind erosion can also have devastating effects in coastal areas, where sand dunes are placed under great stress by overdevelopment and alteration to the natural environment, such as the clearing of mangroves. The sand dune system is a fragile one, and extensive development of the coastline and clearing of land for housing or tourism puts this system at great risk. Many areas are suffering the effects of this; along Queensland's Gold Coast, much of the beach has been washed away by king tides because of the strip development which stretches all along the coast.

Sand mining is another threat to sand dune systems, although in recent years greater awareness has led to the scaling down or, in some cases, banning of this venture. Companies are now encouraged and sometimes compelled to regenerate the land after they have finished mining. In the case of Fraser Island off the coast of Queensland, sand mining was halted completely after protests by environmentalists who were concerned any mining at all would destroy the fragile ecosystem of Australia's largest sand island.

SOIL STRUCTURE DEGRADATION

Agriculture can exact a heavy toll from the soil. Overcultivation, over-grazing and compression of the soil by heavy machinery reduce the amount of air in the soil, a vital part of its structure. This can lead to anaerobic soil, i.e. soil without air, rendering it useless for crops and pasture. Water run-off increases and therefore so does water erosion, increasing the degradation and destroying productivity.

LOSS OR DEGRADATION OF VEGETATION

As land has been cleared for settlement and agriculture across Australia, much of the native vegetation has been lost. This can lead to decreased soil stability or unproductive land, as the delicate balance between the soil and its vegetation is destroyed. Overgrazing does not allow the vegetation to regenerate and, in forested areas, tree dieback is often the result. When combined with the problems of erosion, run-off and soil salinity, the land becomes useless for agriculture.

Desert

Australia is claimed to be the driest continent (outside the polar regions) because of its low precipitation and run-off, and its extensive arid zone. The average rainfall is 420 mm and Australia has one of the highest rates of evaporation in the world.

Desert is defined as an arid area characterised by little or no rainfall where vegetation is scanty or absent. More than 20% of Australia's surface is desert and there are areas of semi-desert bordering it. Australia's arid and semi-arid zones cover about 66% of the continent.

EXTENT OF PHYSIOGRAPHIC DESERT TYPES IN AUSTRALIA

Type	Area (km^2)	% of Arid Zone
Shield	697 000	14
Upland and piedmont	818 000	16
Stony	894 000	18
Riverine and clay plains	650 000	13
Sand	1 916 000	38
Lakes	50 000	1
Total	5 025 000	100

PRINCIPAL AUSTRALIAN DESERTS

GIBSON DESERT

Crossed from east to west for the first time in 1874 by Ernest Giles, the Gibson Desert is named after one of his party who died on the journey. It is a vast expanse of arid country made up of sand dunes and gibber plains, areas covered in rocks and pebbles worn smooth by abrasive wind-blown sand. The Gibson Desert is located in the middle of Western Australia.

GREAT SANDY DESERT

A vast area in Western Australia between the Kimberley Plateau and the Gibson Desert, it consists mainly of sand hills and stony desert areas. The Great Sandy Desert was first crossed east-west in 1873 by P. E. Warburton. The Great Sandy Desert covers the inland part of the Pilbara region, which stretches for 440 000 km² east–west from the Indian Ocean to the Northern Territory border and north–south from the Tropic of Capricorn to the Kimberley region.

GREAT VICTORIA DESERT

The Great Victoria Desert lies south of the Warburton Range and above the Nullarbor Plain, partly in Western Australia and partly in South Australia. This area is made up of vast stretches of parallel sand dunes.

SIMPSON DESERT

The first recorded European to enter the Simpson Desert was Charles Sturt in 1845. It was first crossed in 1939 by C. T. Madigan, who had made the first aerial survey of the region in 1929. He named it after the South Australian Branch president of the Australian Geographical Society at that time.

The Simpson Desert covers an area of 780 000 km² around the border area of the Northern Territory, Queensland and South Australia.

Wilderness

Defined as entirely natural country unadulterated by the effects of modern technology, the values of wilderness areas are numerous. Some of the most important scientific reasons for protecting them are for the genetic resources they can and do hold, and as a pure and unaffected environment to observe and monitor environmental and climatic trends.

In Tasmania, 18% of the landscape falls into the wilderness category, with the south-west wilderness area being by far the largest. The Western Tasmania Wilderness National Parks are on the World Heritage List.

PROTECTION

Within the national parks system there is a provision for wilderness areas to be set apart from the usual and recreational functions of a park. This is generally considered to be the most efficient way of protecting wilderness areas.

MAJOR WILDERNESS AREAS

QUEENSLAND   Cape York Peninsula

SOUTH AUSTRALIA   Lake Eyre

WESTERN AUSTRALIA   Prince Regent River and Kimberleys, Great Sandy Desert, Gibson Desert, Great Victoria Desert

TASMANIA   South-west Tasmania

NORTHERN TERRITORY   Arnhem Land, Tanami Desert, Simpson Desert

Rivers

TYPES OF RIVER

There are two major classes of rivers in Australia, rivers of coastal margins with moderate rates of fall and rivers of central plains with slight fall. The majority of Australian coastal rivers originate in the Great Dividing Range, which is also the major watershed in Australia.

Many Australian rivers only flow in the wet season.

THE LONGEST RIVER SYSTEM

The Murray–Darling is the longest river system in Australia. The Murray is approximately 2530 km long, while the Darling River is 1900 km, making the whole system about 3500 km.

The Murray River starts in the Snowy Mountains and flows into the sea through Lake Alexandrina just south of Adelaide in South Australia. It drains an area of 1 062 530 km² (about one-seventh of Australia's total area), including part of Queensland, most of New South Wales and a large part of Victoria. This system is the only continuously flowing river system of any length inland and supplies 50% of South Australia's water.

Major tributaries of the Murray are the Lachlan, Murrumbidgee and Goulburn Rivers. The Murray River was discovered by Europeans in 1824 by Hume and Hovell.

RIVERS OF THE GREAT DIVIDING RANGE

NEW SOUTH WALES

The Hawkesbury River runs for 480 km. Throughout its length, it goes under a number of names, starting in the Cullarin Range as the Wollondilly and becoming the Warragamba at its junction with the Cox's River. Upon meeting the Nepean River, it assumes that name before becoming the Hawkesbury when it is joined by the Grose River. The Hawkesbury River empties into the sea at Broken Bay just north of Sydney.

Another coastal river of New South Wales, indeed its largest, is the Hunter River, which drains an area of 28 000 km^2. It runs through the Hunter Valley area west of Newcastle, a winegrowing and thoroughbred horse breeding area. The Hunter River empties into the Pacific Ocean at the city of Newcastle.

Other important rivers in New South Wales include the Richmond, Tweed, Clarence and Shoalhaven Rivers, which are coastal rivers, and the Barwon–Darling, Castlereagh, Macquarie, Bogan and Murrumbidgee–Lachlan Rivers, which flow inland.

VICTORIA

The Snowy River rises close to Mount Kosciusko in New South Wales and flows for 435 km. With its major tributary, the Eucumbene River, the Snowy River is extremely important in the major hydro-electric power project in Australia, the Snowy Mountains Scheme. South-flowing waters of these rivers are harnessed through two tunnel systems and from there diverted inland to the Murray and Murrumbidgee rivers. Other Victorian rivers include the Mitta Mitta, Ovens, Goulburn and Campaspe rivers.

QUEENSLAND

Major rivers in Queensland which rise in the Great Dividing Range are the Barron, Tully, Herbert, Burdekin, Mackenzie–Dawson, Brisbane, Fitzroy, Logan rivers — all coastal — and the Mitchell, Gilbert, Barcoo, Bulloo and Condamine-Balonne rivers, which flow inland.

The Burdekin River rises in the Seaview Range and runs from there 720 km to the ocean near Ayr, south of Townsville. It has a catchment area of 130 000 km^2 and 14 tributaries. The Burdekin and the Fitzroy rivers are the two largest in north-east Australia.

MAJOR RIVERS OUTSIDE OF THE
GREAT DIVIDING RANGE

QUEENSLAND

The Flinders River flows in an arc for around 840 km to an estuary at the south-east corner of the Gulf of Carpentaria. Other rivers include the Gregory, Leichhardt and Cloncurry rivers. The Leichhardt River is named after a German explorer, Friedrich Leichhardt.

WESTERN AUSTRALIA

The Gascoyne is Western Australia's longest river. It runs for a length of 820 km, meeting the sea at Carnarvon. Other major rivers in Western Australia are the Murchison, Ashburton, Fortescue, De Grey, Fitzroy, Drysdale and Ord rivers.

The Ord River rises in the Albert Edward Range near the Western Australia border with the Northern Territory and flows through the Kimberley region to the Cambridge Gulf near Wyndham. In 1960, the first stage of the Ord River Irrigation Scheme was started and the region now supports a range of agricultural crops. The scheme was originated so cotton could be grown in the area, but the prohibitive costs involved meant that Ord River cotton was more expensive than cotton produced elsewhere in the world. Several other crops have been tried since, but without the spectacular success predicted when the scheme was announced. The Ord has the largest flow of any of Australia's rivers.

TASMANIA

The longest river in Tasmania is the Derwent River, which runs for a length of 193 km. Tasmanian rivers have short rapid courses due to the configuration of the country, which is more mountainous than found elsewhere in Australia.

NORTHERN TERRITORY

Rising in the Macdonnell Ranges where it cuts deep gorges in the ridges, the Todd River flows through Alice Springs — but only in wet years. The rest of the time the river bed is dry, but water does flow underneath its sandy surface. The famous Henley-on-Todd Regatta, which is held annually, features bottomless boats with crews running along the dry river bed to cross the finishing line.

Lakes

TEMPORARY OR SALT LAKES
The largest lakes in Australia are drainage dumps from internal rivers. These lakes often become beds of salt and dry mud in dry seasons. Lake Eyre is the largest of these and covers an area of 9323 km^2. It is rarely full, but is a spectacular sight when in flood.

Most often found in arid and semi-arid inland areas such as the Great Victoria, Gibson and Great Sandy Deserts, salt lakes are usually linked to inland rivers which only occasionally carry water and so fill up only infrequently, often many years apart.

GLACIAL LAKES
Particularly found in central and south-western Tasmania, these lakes were shaped by glaciers during the Great Ice Age and are dammed by the moraine material, which was held in the glacier, when it melted. Lake St Clair in Tasmania, Australia's deepest lake at more than 200 m, is an example of this type. In 1982, the Lake St Clair/Cradle Mountain National Park was placed on the World Heritage List.

VOLCANIC CRATER LAKES
Australia's most famous crater lake must be Blue Lake in Mount Gambier, South Australia, which has four crater lakes. Blue Lake is the largest with a crater circumference of 4.8 km, and is so named because from November to February each year the lake appears intensely blue.

Crater lakes are most common in Victoria and Queensland. Eacham and Barrine Lakes in north-eastern Queensland are both situated in rainforest national parks in the Atherton Tableland. Land subsidence due to volcanic activity resulted in the formation of Lake Corangamite in south-west Victoria.

FAULT ANGLE LAKES
Lake George near Canberra is a fault angle lake. It has a steep scarp on the western side caused when the floor of the lake subsided due to faulting. It is 24 km long and 10 km wide.

COASTAL LAKES
The majority of coastal lakes occurs in the east and south resulting from the build-up of sand and shingle, and changes in the sea level.

The largest coastal lake in Australia is Lake Macquarie in New South Wales. Situated near Newcastle, it covers an area of 110 km^2. Just to the north of here is the Myall Lakes region, a coastal system of waterways and lakes popular with holidaymakers seeking solitude and peace.

Lake Illawarra in New South Wales periodically becomes a lagoon when its entrance from the sea becomes blocked up with sand.

In Victoria, the Gippsland Lakes region is a complicated system of lakes and waterways. The Gippsland Lakes, which lie behind Ninety Mile Beach, are the longest chain of lagoons in Australia. The largest of these lagoons is Lake Wellington, which is fed by the Avon and Latrobe Rivers. In 1889, an inlet was made into the lake where Lakes Entrance now stands. Most of the area is only accessible by boat.

Artificial Lakes

Some of the largest lakes in this category are Eucumbene, Jindabyne, Tantangara and Talbingo which are part of the Snowy Mountains Scheme in New South Wales. Lake Argyle was formed when the Ord River, in Western Australia, was dammed for an irrigation scheme.

The Largest Lakes in Australia

The largest lakes in Australia are all salt lakes. They are, in descending order: Lake Eyre at 9323 km^2; Lake Torrens at 5776 km^2; and Lake Gairdner at 4776 km^2.

Great Lake in Tasmania is the largest natural freshwater lake in Australia. It extends about 25 km from north to south, and varies in width from 5–8 km. Lake Argyle is the largest permanent lake in Australia, formed artificially when the Ord River was dammed in 1971 as part of a major irrigation project. Lake Argyle's capacity is 5672 million litres.

Australia's Deepest Lake

Lake St Clair in Tasmania is the deepest lake in Australia, at 200 m deep. It is also the source of the Derwent, which is Tasmania's longest river. There are more than 4000 lakes in north-west Tasmania.

Water Resources

Surface and ground water resources are limited in Australia because the country has: a limited number of high mountain barriers; a high proportion of arid or semi-arid land (two-thirds); unreliable rainfall; and high temperatures and high levels of evaporation.

The important thing, therefore, is to use water resources efficiently and ensure groundwater supplies are carefully managed so that land degradation does not occur.

This has resulted in an extensive construction program to control water resources through the use of dams, reservoirs, large tanks and other forms of storage.

Measure	Symbol	Amount
kilolitres	KL	1×10^3 litres
megalitres	ML	1×10^6 litres
gigalitres	GL	1×10^9 litres
teralitres	TL	1×10^{12} litres

USE OF WATER RESOURCES

Drainage Division	Mean Annual Run-off	Divertible Resource	Developed Resource	Use
Bulloo-Bancannia	1.1	–	0.0	0.00
Gulf of Carpentaria	92.5	13.2	0.1	0.12
Indian Ocean	4.0	0.3	–	0.00
Lake Eyre	6.3	0.2	–	0.01
Murray-Darling	24.3	12.4	10.0	8.05
N-E Coast	83.9	22.9	3.5	0.97
S-E Coast	41.9	15.1	4.3	2.03
S-W Coast	6.7	2.9	0.4	0.38
SA Gulf	0.9	0.7	0.1	0.23
TAS	52.9	10.9	1.0	0.17
Timor Sea	80.7	22.0	2.0	0.10
Western Plateau	1.6	0.1	0.0	0.00
Australia	**398.00**	**100.00**	**21.5**	**12.06**

GROUND WATER

Especially in the inland of Australia, there are vast areas of land which are underlaid by artesian basins. Artesian water is water stored in porous rock encased between layers of impermeable rock (aquifer). If it is under sufficient pressure, the water will be brought to the surface when the aquifer is penetrated by a bore. If this pressure is inadequate to raise it all the way and pumps must be used to bring it up it is called sub-artesian.

The largest of these basins in Australia (and one of the world's largest) is the Great Artesian Basin. It covers an area of 1 700 000 km^2 below the surface of New South Wales, Queensland, South Australia and the Northern Territory.

Ground water is a renewable resource, as the aquifers are topped up with water from rainfall, and is used for mining or rural purposes. However, in many cases the artesian basins are being placed under great strain by indiscriminate use of artesian bores for irrigation or poor maintenance and inadequate drainage leading to water wastage. Moves are now under way to increase awareness of the need to use artesian bores carefully and also to cap or repair and modify bores where their use is unnecessary or inefficient.

MAJOR ARTESIAN BASINS OF AUSTRALIA

Basin	Area (km²)	State
Great Artesian Basin	1 700 000	New South Wales, Queensland, South Australia, Northern Territory
Canning Basin	474 000	Western Australia
Georgina-Daly Basin	450 000	Queensland, Northern Territory
Murray Basin	300 000	New South Wales, Victoria, South Australia
Eucla Basin	180 000	South Australia, Western Australia

MAJOR DAMS AND RESERVOIRS IN AUSTRALIA

Name	Year Completed	Gross Capacity (GL)	Height of wall (m)
New South Wales			
Eucumbene	1958	4 798	116
Hume	1936, 1961	3 038	51
Warragamba	1960	2 057	137
Menindee Lakes	1960	1 794	18
Burrendong	1967	1 678	76
Blowering	1968	1 628	112
Copeton	1976	1 364	113
Wyangala	1936, 1971	1 220	85
Burrinjuck	1927, 1956	1 026	79
Victoria			
Dartmouth	1979	4 000	180
Eildon	1927, 1955	3 390	79
Thomson	1984	1 175	164
Queensland			
Burdekin	1986	1 860	55
Fairbairn	1972	1 440	49
Wivenhoe	1985	1 150	59

Name	Year Completed	Gross Capacity (GL)	Height of wall (m)
Western Australia			
Lake Argyle (Ord)	1971	5 797	99
Tasmania			
Lakes Gordon and			
Pedder i.e.	1974		
Gordon,		11 316	140
Scotts Peak,			43
Serpentine,		2 960	38
Edgar			17
Miena	1967	3 356	28
Lake St Clair	1938	2 000 (est.)	3

Irrigation

TYPES OF IRRIGATION

The dominant form of irrigation in Australia is flood irrigation. Alternatives are spray, furrow and trickle (or drip) irrigation.

Flood irrigation is used especially in the cultivation of rice (which has been grown in the Murrumbidgee Irrigation Area of New South Wales since 1924), pasture, wheat and millet.

Spray irrigation uses water pumped direct from rivers, to irrigate uneven ground or sandy soils. It is commonly used for citrus fruit, vegetables and pasture. Overhead sprinkling of salinated water can cause defoliation so below tree sprinklers have to be used.

Furrow irrigation is used for vegetables and row crops.

NATIONAL AND INTERSTATE PROJECTS

NEW SOUTH WALES, VICTORIA AND SOUTH AUSTRALIA   About two-thirds of Australia's irrigated land is in south-east Australia, along the Murray River and its tributaries, whose flow is controlled for irrigational use. There is a storage capacity of 27 gigalitres (GL) in the Murray–Darling Basin, 12 GL of which is along the Murray River.

There are 24 storages in the Murray-Darling Basin, four of which are shared with Victoria and South Australia, and one with Queensland. It is currently estimated that 40% of the Murray River's resource is being utilised. The Murray–Darling Basin Commission manages the project.

NEW SOUTH WALES AND QUEENSLAND   The resources of border rivers, particularly the Dumaresq River, are shared according to the New South Wales–Queensland Border Rivers Agreement, under which the Glenlyon Dam on Pike Creek in Queensland has been constructed.

The Snowy Mountains Hydro-Electric Scheme was commissioned in 1949 and largely completed by 1974. This is a dual-purpose scheme generating hydro-electricity and irrigation resources. Water from the Snowy River and its tributary, the Eucumbene, is diverted by tunnels into the Murray and Murrumbidgee rivers. Other rivers employed are the Tumut, Tooma and Geehi. Irrigation resources of 2300 GL (average) per annum in the Murray and Murrumbidgee rivers, result from the scheme.

(The electricity output averages more than 5000 GW per annum.)

STATE PROJECTS

NEW SOUTH WALES   In New South Wales, irrigation is the largest consumer of water; it uses an average 75% of total water resources. There are two types of irrigation in New South Wales: license holders who pump from rivers, using approximately 1 500 000 ML annually; and irrigation areas and districts on the Murray, Murrumbidgee and Lachlan rivers. These areas cover 6300 properties over an area of 1 400 000 ha, one-third of which is usually irrigated using 1 400 000 ML per year. Bore water is also utilised in these districts.

Increasing salinisation in the Murray–Darling Basin is a serious problem, reducing productivity and increasing production costs. There is also a severe environmental cost as vegetation and ecosystems are destroyed in salt-affected areas.

VICTORIA   The main irrigation systems in Victoria are: the Goulburn–Campaspe–Loddon System; the Murray Valley Irrigation Area and Torrumbarry Irrigation System; the Southern Systems in the Macalister district; the Werribee and Bacchus Marsh System; and the Wimmera–Mallee Domestic and Stock Supply System.

QUEENSLAND   The eight main irrigation areas in Queensland and their resources are: the Dawson Valley using the Dawson River; the Burdekin River, south of Townsville; Mareeba-Dimbulah using the Tinaroo Falls Dam; St George using the Beardmore Dam; Emerald using the Fairbairn Dam; Bundaberg using the Fred Haigh Dam and the Kolan and Burnett Rivers; Eton in the hinterland of Mackay, using the Kinchant Dam; and Lower Mary River using the Borumba Dam.

SOUTH AUSTRALIA   Irrigation in South Australia began in 1887 in the Renmark district. Recently, water diversions amounting to more than 381 090 ML are being made in the Murray River in South Australia for various irrigation schemes. There are also considerable areas irrigated from underground sources.

WESTERN AUSTRALIA   There are seven irrigation systems in Western Australia: the Waroona, Harvey, Collie River and Preston Valley Irrigation Districts between Donnybrook and Waroona; the Carnarvon Groundwater Supply Scheme; the Ord Irrigation Project and the Camballin Irrigation Area.

The first attempt at large-scale tropical irrigation was the Ord Project in remote northern Western Australia. The project currently irrigates 14 000 ha of clay and sandy soils, with an ultimate capacity of 72 000 ha.

TASMANIA   The three major irrigation schemes in Tasmania are: the Cressy Longford Irrigation Scheme; the South East Irrigation Scheme Stage 1; and the Winnaleah Irrigation Scheme. The majority of land irrigated is by private pumping or water storage schemes.

NORTHERN TERRITORY   Irrigation operates in the following areas: near Darwin; Adelaide River; Daly River; Katherine; Ti Tree; and Alice Springs. The use of irrigation is developing, but is still not extensive within the Northern Territory. Most of the territory uses bore water from the Great Artesian Basin.

USE OF IRRIGATION IN GL

Drainage Division	Pasture	Crops	Horticulture	Total
Gulf of Carpentaria	17	45	13	74
Indian Ocean	0.1	2	7	9
Lake Eyre	-	3	-	4
Murray–Darling	4 120	2 440	1 090	7 650
North East Coast	71	803	92	966
South Australian Gulf	28	2	45	76
South East Coast	711	137	176	1 020
South West Coast	168	24	75	267
Tasmania	46	47	4	97
Timor Sea	20	46	5	70
Australia	**5 180**	**3 550**	**1 510**	**10 200**

WATER RESOURCES USED FOR IRRIGATION (1990)

Water Source	Percentage of total
State irrigation schemes	51.4
Rivers, lakes	28.1
Farm dams	6.4
Artesian water	13.6
Town or country reticulation systems	0.4

3
Flora & Fauna

Australia's Flora

The geological history of Australia has had a large impact on the type of flora and fauna that is found in the continent today. It is now generally believed that Australia has been separated from other continents for the past 60 million years, except for periods during the ice ages when water levels were so low that there were land connections with Papua New Guinea. This is why many of the tropical plants in the north of the continent originate from Asia.

This isolation, combined with geological changes, means that Australia still has many unique species, for example, 75% of the 6000 land plants in the southwestern corner of Western Australia are not found anywhere else. At the same time, many orders which appear elsewhere in the world are missing here.

VEGETATIVE REGIONS

Climate also plays a significant part in the survival of flora and fauna. Australia is the driest continent in the world. Two-thirds of the country is classified as arid or semi-arid; coupled with this, over almost the entire continent, evaporation is greater than rainfall. Parts of Australia can be extremely dry for months or sometimes years, while others can be extremely wet. In order to survive, plants and animals have had to evolve to cope with these conditions so that, generally speaking, their success has produced an astonishing and unusual richness in spite of the harshness of the climate and terrain. It has been estimated that there are more than 15 000 species of flowering plants in Australia, which can be divided between the following six vegetative regions, as specified by the CSIRO:

- *Tall, closed, tropical forest and rainforest:* characterised by lush, maximum growth, large forest trees, epiphytes, ferns, climbers and shade-loving plants.
- *Tall, open, dry forest:* consisting predominantly of eucalypts, grasses, ground orchids and hardy shrubs.
- *Tall, open or closed shrubland, and low open or closed shrubland:* with flowering shrubs, undershrubs, perennials and grasses.
- *Grassland (savannah):* the predominant cover is shrubs, low trees, colourful plants and creepers, ground orchids, and epiphytic orchids in the moister areas.
- *Hummock grassland:* encompassing all the dry deserts, in which are found colourful flowering prostrate plants, low shrubs, succulents and colourful flowering annuals after heavy rainfall.
- *Alpine grassland and woodland:* trees, flowering shrubs, herbaceous plants, ferns and shade-loving plants.

NATIVE TREES

Trees are perennials, that is, they live for a number of years. They have a permanent, self-supporting, woody main stem and grow more than 5 m in height, with branches growing some distance from the ground. The toughness and resistance to drought of Australian trees enables them to thrive in the most arid regions of the country. Australia has approximately 41 million hectares of native forest, covering about 5.4% of the continent. This constitutes an estimated 57% of pre-European trees. Three-quarters of the rainforests found in Australia at the time of European settlement has now disappeared — through clearing and development. About 85% of the remaining rainforest in Australia is in conservation reserves.

EUCALYPTS

Approximately 68% of Australia's forest trees and a large portion of the woodlands are eucalypts and 18% are tropical eucalypts. They are found throughout the continent and Tasmania. There are about 450 distinct species of eucalypt in Australia, as well as many other related species. They are often called gum trees, a name which derives from the gum-like substance which some eucalypts exude from wounds to the bark. Their scientific name *Eucalyptus* means 'well covered' and refers to their flower-bud, which has a cap.

The smallest species of eucalypts are the mallees, the majority of which grow in Western Australia. These trees grow to a height of about 1 metre. The tallest eucalypts grow in the coastal forest regions, some of them to a height of more than 90 m, making them the tallest flowering plants in the world. Australia's tallest tree is the mountain ash (*Eucalyptus regnans*). The tallest living example of this grows in Tasmania, to a height of more than 98 m. In the 1880s, however, a mountain ash was measured at 132.6 m after felling. Even allowing for the inaccuracy of historical records, this would make it a very large tree indeed. It would also make it taller than the tallest living tree in the world, a redwood in America measuring 112.1 m. Ironically, although bushfires can appear to devastate Australian forests, the mountain ash relies on this phenomena for its survival as a species. Only the intense heat of a bushfire can release the seed of the mountain ash from its pod, so what, for some other species, may mean a serious setback, for the mountain ash means regeneration.

Different kinds of bark have produced a number of common names such as gums (smooth bark shed annually in ribbons or plates); boxes (rough bark around the trunk with smooth-barked upper limbs); stringybarks (thick, fibrous brown- and grey-coloured bark); peppermint (less fibrous than stringybarks, but often having aromatic leaves); ironbarks (hard, furrowed, dark bark); bloodwoods (mostly tropical species with loose, flaky bark); and ashes (rough, fibrous bark around the base and smooth bark higher up). The river red gum (*Eucalyptus camaldulensis*) is the most widespread of the eucalypts. One of the most distinctive is the scribbly gum (*Eucalyptus haemastoma*), which has 'scribbles' on its bark caused by the larvae of a moth which burrows beneath its surface.

The Tasmanian blue gum (*Eucalyptus globulus*) is the species of gum most often found planted overseas. The introduction of eucalypts in other countries is seen by some as a blessing and others as a curse. Eucalypts are often introduced as they are relatively quick growing and can survive in arid areas where other trees find it difficult to establish. In some countries, such as Brazil, eucalypt plantations have been used to provide a ready source of timber for use as fuel in industry.

In the south-west of Western Australia, a few karri (*Eucalyptus diversicolor*) forests have survived European settlement. These tall, majestic trees can grow more than 60 m in height. One, the Gloucester Tree, near Pemberton, was used a lookout from which to spot bushfires before the introduction of spotter planes.

Other species include: the snow gum (*Eucalyptus pauciflore* subsp. *nipohphila*), found in the subalpine areas of southern New South Wales and northern Victoria; the red ironbark (*Eucalyptus sideroxylon*), with its very black bark; the narrow-leaved ironbark (*Eucalyptus crebra*), which is found from the tip of Cape York Peninsula in Queensland to New South Wales; the flooded gum (*Eucalyptus grandis*); the spotted gum (*Eucalyptus maculata*), which has a pitted surface on its trunk and patches of colour on the bark; the manna gum (*Eucalyptus viminalis*), which grows up to 50 m and is the preferred habitat of koalas — its sugary sap also attracts sugar gliders; the red bloodwood (*Eucalyptus gummifera*), which exudes a blood-red sap; the lemon-scented gum (*Eucalyptus citriodora*), whose leaves smell strongly of lemon when crushed; and the tallowwood (*Eucalyptus microcorys*), which produces a very fine hardwood timber suitable for floors.

Perhaps one of the most famous individual gum trees in Australia is the Dig Tree. The Dig Tree, a coolibah (*Eucalyptus microtheca*), is found on the banks of Cooper Creek in western Queensland. It once bore the message 'Dig 3 ft. N.W. Apr. 21 1861'. It was here that William Brahe left a message and buried supplies for the doomed explorers Robert O'Hara Burke and William Wills. Although Burke and Wills, and fellow explorer John King, found Brahe's message, they set off for Mount Hopeless in South Australia rather than remaining near the tree, thinking that Brahe and his men were far away in Menindee, New South Wales. Brahe returned to the site, found no sign of the men and gave up hope. The three struggled back to the tree later, however, but Burke and Wills died within a few days; only King survived.

ANGOPHORA

Often mistaken for eucalypt or gum trees, and indeed commonly known apple gums, the *Angophora* genus is widespread, particularly in New South

Wales and Victoria. The branches of the tree, species of which grow up to 30 m, are usually extremely gnarled. Hollows in the trunks and limbs are popular with birds and marsupials as nesting places. Species include: the rough-barked apple (*Angophora floribunda*), found in coastal forests in Queensland, New South Wales and Victoria; the dwarf apple (*Angophora hispida*), a smaller species found in sandstone soils in dry forests in New South Wales; and the smooth-barked apple (*Angophora costata*), widespread in coastal regions, particularly around Sydney in New South Wales.

ACACIAS

The *Acacia* species are more commonly called wattles. There are about 1000 species of acacia in Australia, making it the largest genus in Australian flora. Widely distributed throughout Australia, the acacias are well known for their beautiful golden flowers, which appear in spring. They also stabilise Australia's fragile soils and provide food and shelter for native birds and animals.

The golden wattle (*Acacia pycnantha*) is Australia's floral emblem. Other acacias include: the Cootamundra wattle (*Acacia baileyana*) which is cultivated widely both here in Australia and overseas; the blackwood wattle (*Acacia melanoxylon*) often used for furniture and cabinet work; the kangaroo thorn (*Acacia paradoxa*); the sweet wattle (*Acacia suaveolens*), a widespread heathland shrub; the coast myall (*Acacia glaucescens*), widely distributed in New South Wales; the myrtle wattle (*Acacia myrtifolia*), commonly found growing in the sandstone areas of eastern Australia; and the small, shrubby mulga (*Acacia aneura*), which grows in Australia's arid and semi-arid areas, and is used for ornamental woodwork.

BANKSIAS

There are about 70 species of evergreen trees and shrubs from the genus *Banksia* in Australia. The genus was named after English botanist Sir Joseph Banks, who travelled to Australia with Captain Cook on his exploratory journey aboard the Endeavour between 1768 and 1771. The majority of banksias grow in the south-western part of Western Australia, but they also occur in all mainland areas and Tasmania. The clustered flowers provide food for birds such as the honeyeater and also small marsupials.

The most popular species include the heath banksia (*Banksia ericifolia*), a reddish-flowered banksia common in coastal sandstone areas; the silver banksia (*Banksia marginata*), which is found in habitats as varied as coastal heath, subalpine forest and dry, inland plains; the large-leafed swamp banksia (*Banksia robur*), found in swampy areas along the Queensland and New South Wales coasts; the salt-tolerant coast banksia (*Banksia integrifolia*), common in coastal heathland and behind sand dunes (in some areas, it grows right on the beach); the marsh banksia (*Banksi paludosa*), found in marshy areas in coastal heaths and woodlands, and which has a narrower spike than other species; and the saw or 'old man' banksia (*Banksia serrata*), found in coastal areas all along the east coast of Australia and Tasmania.

BLACK BEAN TREE

The black bean tree or Moreton Bay chestnut (*Castanospermum australe*) is endemic to the rainforests of Queensland and New South Wales. An evergreen tree, it grows to about 40 m in height. The black bean tree attracts flocks of nectar-eating birds when it flowers in the late spring and early summer. Although its fruit is extremely poisonous, black bean timber is seen as superior for cabinet making.

BOTTLEBRUSHES

The bottlebrushes (*Callistemon* spp.) are part of the family of Myrtaceae, which also includes tea trees and melaleucas (paperbarks). These trees and shrubs are commonly known as bottlebrushes because of the shape of their large red cylindrical flower spikes. The crimson bottlebrush (*Callistemon citrinus*) is perhaps the most well known species, as it is commonly found in gardens and parks. Its natural habitat is the coastal plains and also the foothills of the Blue Mountains west of Sydney. Other bottlebrushes species include: the wallum bottlebrush (*Callistemon pachyphyllus*), found in swampy coastals heaths in northern New South Wales and southern Queensland; *Callistemon subulatus*, which grows along the banks of streams and rivers in Victoria and New South Wales; and the weeping bottlebrush (*Callistemon viminalis*), a widespread species found along stream and river banks in Queensland and northern New South Wales.

CASUARINAS OR SHE-OAKS

The casuarina or she-oak trees (*Casuarina* and *Allocasuarina* spp.) derive their name from the fact that their foliage looks like the feather of the cassowary. Species include: the she-oak (*Allocasuarina distyla*), found in heathland and dry forest in Queensland and New South Wales; the river she-oak (*Casuarina cunninghamia*), found along river banks; and *Allocasuarina monilifera*, a small shrub found in Tasmania and Victoria.

PAPERBARKS

The paperbarks or *Melaleuca* spp. are so named because of their distinctive papery bark, and are related to the bottlebrush. Indeed, the flowers of the paperbarks often resemble those of the bottlebrush. The species vary in height, from low shrubs up to 5 m to trees growing up to 20 m. Species include: the broad-leaved paperbark (*Melaleuca qinquenervia*), usually found in swampy coastal areas in Queensland, New South Wales and the Northern Territory; the prickly-leaved paperbark (*Melaleuca styphelioides*), found in various habitats; the swamp paperbark (*Melaleuca ericifolia*), a tall shrub found along river banks and swamps in New South Wales, Victoria and Tasmania — this bark was used by Aboriginal peoples to make canoes and water baskets; and snow-in-summer (*Melaleuca linariifolia*), a bushy shrub found along the coast in Queensland and New South Wales.

LILLY PILLY

The lilly pilly (*Acmena smithii*) is found in temperate rainforest and damp forest areas, particularly around Sydney. It has fleshy fruits and dark green, glossy leaves.

MACADAMIA

The macadamia tree (*Macadamia integrifolia*) is native to Australia and not Hawaii, as is commonly thought in some overseas countries. It occurs naturally in the rainforests of southern Queensland and northern New South Wales, but commercial production of macadamia nuts is now underway in several areas of north-eastern Australia.

Once again, the nutritious nut has long been recognised by the Aboriginal peoples as a good source of protein, fat and carbohydrate. This crop is simple to harvest as the ripe nuts simply fall to the ground and their protective casing splits when they are ready. The nut's shell, however, is extremely hard and requires some force to open. Possibly the only bird or animal in the wild able to do this is the black cockatoo, which has an extremely strong, sharp beak. Humans need to resort to stones or special nut crackers designed to open macadamias.

MORETON BAY FIG

There are several *Ficus* species in Australia, the most well known of which is probably the Moreton Bay (*Ficus macrophylla*), which grows up to 25 m. A strangler fig, in the wild, it forms huge buttress roots around its host plant, eventually strangling and killing the host plant and leaving hollows in its base.

The Moreton Bay fig is found naturally in Queensland, and the mid-south coast and north coast of New South Wales. Many parks and gardens around Sydney and Brisbane have plantings of this majestic tree.

TEA TREES

Tea trees are members of the Myrtaceae family, along with melaleucas (paperbarks) and bottlebrushes. Although many species are shrubs, there are some tree species. The Aboriginal peoples have long understood the antiseptic and healing properties of the oil of one particular species of this tree, the medicinal tea tree (*Melaleuca alternifolia*). Tea tree plantations now produce this oil and it can be found in antiseptic cream, oils, medicinal shampoos and insect repellents. Other species include: the coast tea tree (*Leptospermum laevigatum*), common on sand dunes in coastal areas; the peach tea trea (*Leptospermum squarrosum*), found in Queensland and New South Wales in damp areas along coastal streams and adjacent areas; the woolly tea tree (*Leptospermum lanigerum*), found along streams and river banks in New South Wales, Victoria, Tasmania and South Australia; the slender tea tree (*Leptospermum brevipes*), found in Queensland, New South Wales and Victoria; and the prickly tea tree (*Leptospermum juniperum*), found in Queensland, New South Wales, Victoria and South Australia.

QUANDONG

This native tree is sometimes called the native peach. The fruit of the quandong (*Santalum acuminatum*) has long been eaten by the Aboriginal peoples and it was a popular fruit during early European settlement. Its bright red fruit was used in conserves, tarts and pies. Both the flesh of the quandong and the kernel inside the fruit's shell can be eaten, although the flesh can be rather tart if it is not ripe.

Found in arid and semi-arid areas across much of southern Australia, it reaches up to 6 m in height. The quandong is related the the sandalwood (*Sandalum spicatum*), a native of Western Australia's arid regions which is now harvested under strict controls and exported to Asia for its aromatic oil.

NATIVE SHRUBS

Shrubs are woody perennial plants less than 8 m tall, often with stems growing from or near to the ground. Australia possesses a great many different groups of native wildflower shrubs which may have the same common name as trees, but are much shorter in height. For example, there are eucalypt shrubs, so named because they are small and bushy and therefore more suited to this classification than to trees.

In the same way, many species of *Acacia* and *Banksia*, as well as most of the *Grevillea*, *Hakea*, *Dryandra*, *Eremophila* (emu bush), *Callistemon* (bottle-brushes) and *Kunzea* are called shrubs. Plants in the genus *Hakea* include shrubs with bright pink, red, purple or white bottlebrush or round 'pincushion' shaped flowers. Those in the genus *Dryandra* are found only in south-western Australia and have stiff, wirelike flowers and prickly foliage. The genus *Grevillea* has long racemes of flowers ranging from the fiery scarlet to the creamy in colour.

There are more than 90 species of *Boronia* shrubs, which are found only in Australia and more than half of them originate in Western Australia. Many of the plants have scented leaves which are used in the manufacture of perfume.

Perhaps the best-known of Australia's plants is the waratah, from the genus *Telopea*. There are three species in New South Wales and one in Tasmania. The main characteristic of the waratah is its brilliant scarlet flowers on an erect stem.

MONOCOTYLEDONS

Monocotyledons are plants which produce seeds and have only one primary leaf, which appears after the seed coat has been shed by the germinated seed. Examples of these are the grasses (including agricultural cereals), bulb plants (such as lilies and orchids) and palms. The leaves have parallel venation, there is no true bark, the roots may be fibrous and there is no major central tap root.

Wildflowers in this category include the families Orchidaceae, Amaryllidaceae, Palmae, Liliaceae, Agavaceae, Haemodoraceae and Iridaceae. The kangaroo paw (*Anigozanthos* spp.) belongs to the family Haemodoraceae and is so called because its flowers resemble the paw of a kangaroo. These flowers can vary from yellow and green to orange and red, and even black. Kangaroo paws are indigenous to the south-west of Western Australia, but are now widely cultivated as garden plants.

The Christmas bell (*Blandfordia cunninghamii* and *Blandfordia nobilis*) grows in swampy country in coastal eastern Australia and flowers just before Christmas. It is named after Englishman George Spencer-Churchill (1766–1840), the then Marquis of Blandford, who was a keen horticulturalist. The colour of its bells varies from yellow to deep orange.

The carnivorous pitcher plant *Nepenthis mirabilis* is found in Cape York, Queensland. Its leaves have been modified to trap small insects which provide food for the plant. Other carnivorous plants are found in Australia, mostly in the south-western region of Western Australia, possibly because of the low nutrient content of some of the soils found there.

LILIES

There are numerous species of lily in Australia. The the bulbine lily (*Bulbine bulbosa*), a yellow-flowered lily, is found in open forest, grassland and rocky outcrops at higher elevations in Queensland, New South Wales, Victoria, Tasmania and South Australia. The Aboriginal peoples used its bulb-like tuber as a source of food, roasting and eating it. Other lily species include: the yellow garland lily (*Calostemma luteum*), found in Queensland, New South Wales and Victoria, which likes damp areas and floodplains; the nodding blue lily (*Stypandra glauca*), which has dainty blue flowers and grows in sandy or stony soils in Queensland, New South Wales, Victoria and South Australia; and the common fringe lily (*Thysanotus tuberosus*), a widespread purple-flowered lily which has three fringed petals.

ORCHIDS

Orchids are perennial herbs (plants with stems that are not woody and which die down after flowering). They grow terrestrially or on another plant (epiphytically), and their chief distinguishing features are that the style, stigma and anthers are joined together into a column, at the tip of which the anthers are clustered together. The pollen is contained in structures called pollina.

Most orchids belong to the terrestrial group and die back every year, although some are evergreens, with thick fleshy roots. Some of these terrestrial orchids are saprophytic, that is, they live on dead or decaying plant matter such as moulding leaves and wood. The epiphytes cling to trunks or branches of trees or to rocks. Their roots absorb nutrients from decayed vegetable matter and need a warm, humid environment for growth. For this reason, therefore, they tend to be restricted to coastal regions.

The donkey orchid (*Diuris longifolia*) flowers in the spring and occurs in much of Australia, except for Queensland and the Northern Territory. It is particularly dominant after a bushfire and the shape of its yellow flowers roughly suggests a donkey's head.

The dotted sun orchid (*Thelymitra ixiodes*) is one of the most common sun orchids found in Australia. Unless the sun is shining, the blue or violet flowers of the dotted sun orchid do not fully open. It is a terrestrial orchid and grows in all states.

There are two known species of underground orchid in Australia. The Western Australian underground orchid (*Rhizanthella gardneri*) has cream to pink flowers, and is found near Corrigin in Western Australia. The eastern Australian underground orchid (*Rhizanthella slateri*) has been found in the Lamington Plateau in Queensland, and at Bulahdelah and the Blue Mountains in New South Wales.

Other orchid species include: the king orchid (*Dendrobium speciosum*), which has sprays of white, cream of yellow flowers and is common along the east coast of Australia; the white-flowered tongue orchid (*Dendrobium linguiforme*), found on trees and rocks in Queensland and New South Wales; the beech orchid (*Dendrobium falcorostrum*), an uncommon but exquisite species which grows on the Antarctic beech tree in areas of Queensland and New South Wales; the pink rock orchid (*Dendrobium kingianum*), which grows in crevices and on rocks and cliff faces in parts of Queensland and New South Wales; and the hyacinth orchid (*Dipodium punctatum*), a leafless orchid found in Queensland, New South Wales, Victoria, Tasmania, South Australia and the Northern Territory. This latter species is a saprophyte, which mean that it cannot be moved from its native environment because of its symbiotic relationship with a particular soil fungus found in the dead or decaying organic matter in which it grows.

PALMS AND CYCADS

Native palms and cycads are to be found in both Australia's tropical and temperate zones. The cabbage or cabbage tree palm (*Livistona australis*) has fan-shaped leaves and grows up to 20 m. It is found in rainforest and sheltered forest. The young tips of the palm were used as a food by the Aboriginal peoples and early European settlers. Settlers also used the fronds to weave hats and baskets. Other palm species include: the bangalow or piccabeen palm (*Archontophoenix cunninghamia*), a majestic palm which grows up to 20 m and is found naturally in coastal rainforest; *Carpentaria accuminata*, the lone species of the *Carpentaria* genus, which grows up to 20 m in height and has feathery, graceful leaves; the umbrella palm (*Hedyscepe canterburyana*), a slim palm which grows up to 10 m in height and has prominent rings on its trunk; the curly or sentry palm (*Howea belmoreana*), which grows about 8 m in height and has stiff, arching, dull green fronds; the kentia or thatch palm (*Howea forsteriana*), which has a slender trunk and long, feathery, dark green leaves and grows up to 10 m; the Atherton palm (*Laccospadix australasica*), a single-trunked palm with glossy leaves that grows up to 6 m in height; the fan palm (*Licuala ramsayi*), easily identifiable because of its fan-like fronds; the walking-stick palm (*Linospadix monostachya*), a smaller palm which grows up to 4 m in height and has feather leaves with sharp tips; the black palm (*Normanbya normanbyi*), a slender, grey-trunked palm which grows up to 15 m in height; the solitaire palm (*Ptychosperma elegans*), a single-trunked palm with dark green leaves which grows up to 10 m in height; the Macarthur palm (*Ptychosperma macarthurii*), a clumping palm with slender stems which grows up to 8 m and has long clusters of pendulous bright red fruits; and the Norfolk palm (*Rhopalostylis baueri*), a single-trunked feathery palm found on Norfolk Island.

Cycads often look like palms. These are tropical and subtropical species that have an unbranched stem with palm-like leaves. They are not monocotyledons, but belong to the class Cycadidae. Cycad species include: *Lepidozamia peroffskyana*, a palm-like tree which grows up to 6 m in height and has a cone somewhat like a pineapple in the centre of its crown; and the burrawang (*Macrozamia communis*), whose trunk is very short or grows underground, and whose pineapple-like cones contain poisonous seeds. The Aboriginal peoples use the seeds of the burrawang as food, but have perfected a technique of ridding them of toxins. Eaten unprepared, they are highly poisonous.

GRASS TREES

The grass tree (*Xanthorrhoea* sp.) and Austral grass tree (*Xanthorrhoea australis*) are extremely ancient plant forms. They grow in open forest, heath and cleared areas throughout Australia (including Tasmania), and have a thick central spike which bears small, scented flowers in spring and early summer. Grass trees flower particularly well after bushfires, which is one of the reasons for the longevity of some individual specimens — in some cases, many hundreds of years. The single trunk can reach up to 2 m in height, and a 'skirt' of thin, grass-like leaves up to 1 m in length surrounds the trunk at its crown like a fringe, hence the name. It is from this crown that the flower spike grows.

DICOTYLEDONS

The seeds of these plants have two cotyledons or seed leaves. They also have true bark, often a tap root and their flowers are usually in multiples of four or five. Some of the most common genera in this group, in Australia, are *Helichrysum* (the everlasting spp.), *Helipterum* (the sunrays), *Waitzia*, *Podolepis*, *Celmisia*, *Senecio* (the groundsels), *Olearia* (the daisy bushes) and *Craspedia* (the billy-buttons). Also, aquatic plants belonging to the family Nymphaeaceae, many herbaceous plants in the family Papilionaceae and plants in the very large Umbelliferae family are included.

Sturt's desert pea (*Clianthus formosus*) occurs in dry areas of all states except for Tasmania and appears after heavy rains. It has distinctive scarlet and black flowers.

The giant waterlily (*Nymphoides gigantea*) grows in the wetter parts of northern Australia from New South Wales to northern parts of Western Australia. The giant waterlily's pink or blue flowers can be seen throughout the summer. The fringed waterlily or large marshwort (*Nymphoides geminata*) is found in swamps, ponds and streams, and on muddy river banks. Its has heart-shaped leaves and fringed yellows flowers that appear in spring and summer. The fringed waterlily can be found in all states of mainland Australia, with the exception of Western Australia, and the Northern Territory.

The yellow daisy-like flower of the golden everlasting (*Helychrysum bracteatum*) appears from August to December throughout central Australia. The white everlasting (*Helichrysum baxteri*) has white flowers with a yellow centre, and is found in sandy coastal heathlands and further in from the coast in New South Wales, Victoria and South Australia.

The snow daisy (*Celmisia asteliifolia*), also known as the silver daisy, can be found in the alpine areas of New South Wales, Victoria and Tasmania. It flowers in summer in a massed display that looks quite spectacular. The snow daisy bush (*Olearia lirata*) grows in cool forests in mountains and subalpine regions. The white, daisy-like flowers form in clusters and flower in early summer. This particular species is found in New South Wales, Victoria and Tasmania.

The bridal daisy bush (*Olearia microphylla*) is a small shrub found in forest areas in Queensland and New South Wales. It has delicate, white, daisy-like flowers that bloom in showy masses all over the bush in late winter and spring.

The flannel flower (*Actinotus helianthi*) and lesser flannel flower (*Actinotus minor*) are both found in heathland and open forest, particularly around the Sydney region in New South Wales. The flannel flower has greyish, velvety foliage, hence the name flannel, and it grows in a low, spreading bush. The daisy-like flowers are also velvety, and are white in colour and sometimes have green tips.

FUNGI

Fungi cannot photosynthesize and have to take their food from dead or living organic matter. They can be divided into four classes: Myxomycetes (slime moulds); Phycomycetes (filamentous fungi); Ascomycetes (yeasts with many cellular forms); and Basidiomycetes (large fungi of which there are about 2000 species in Australia, including edible mushrooms, toadstools, agarics and bracket fungi).

Species include: the boletus mushroom (*Boletus* spp.), a large, spongy mushroom which grows in soil and often turns blue when cut; *Amanita xanthocephala*, a distinctive mushroom with an orange-red cap which grows to 5 cm in diameter and is found in dry sclerophyll eucalypt forest; the shaggy ink cap (*Coprinus comatus*), an elongated white mushroom found in open areas, which has a cap that turns black from the bottom; the flame fungus (*Clavulinopsis miniata*), an orange fungus which grows in the compost soil of wet forest; the jelly fungus (*Tremella fuciformis*), which grows on dead timber in moist gullies; the beefsteak fungus (*Fistulina hepatica*), which grows on living trees or stumps, and is a reddish colour with slimy texture; and the bird's nest fungus (*Cyathus* sp.), a greyish brown fungus found in rich soil and rotting timber.

As with all fungi, many Australian species are toxic or their toxicity is unknown. Picking and eating mushrooms without proper identification can be extremely hazardous.

LICHENS

Lichens are primitive plants which consist of a fungus and an alga living in close association. Tree-dwelling forms are common in Australia. Species include: the crustose *Graphis* spp. and *Lecidea* spp. which grow on trees; and the fruticose or branching lichens such as the feathery *Usnea inermis*, the strap-like *Ramalina celastri* and the grey *Parmotrema perlatum*. The latter three species grow on shaded logs.

MOSSES

Mosses, or Bryophytes, are widespread in rainy or humid places, and less common in arid areas. They usually form large colonies on moist soil, rocks or wood, and have important soil-binding qualities. The moss flora of Australia is rich and diverse.

Species include: thallose liverworts such as *Lunularia cruciate*, which likes damp earth; leafy liverworts such as the *Lepidozia* sp. which is common on rotting timber in wet forest; trailing or hanging mosses such as the *Papillaria* sp., which is commonly epiphytic and grows on wood, although it can be found on rocks, and is found in moist forest; and

Campylopus bicolor, commonly found on sandstone in open forest and sometimes growing in extremely widespread clumps.

CLUB MOSSES, HORSETAILS AND FERNS

Three of the four genera of club mosses (primitive spore-bearing plants) grow in Australia. Native horsetails do not exist here. There are about 380 species of fern in Australia and most grow in the northern subtropical area of Queensland, although some grow in all other states.

Species include: the common maidenhair (*Adiantum aethiopicum*), a widespread species common in cultivation, which grows in moist, rocky sites in the wild; the fishbone water fern (*Blechnum nudum*), which grows in groups along watercourses; the bird's nest fern (*Asplenium australasicum*), which has large, wide fronds which grow from a central base leaving a large hollow in the middle rather like a bird's nest; the hen-and-chicken fern or mother spleenwort (*Asplenium bulberiferum*), which has arching, dark green fronds from which bulbils grow, hence the name; the bushy club moss (*Lycopodium deuterodensum*) a fern ally dominant in the Devonian-Carboniferous period and still widespread today; the soft tree fern (*Dicksonia antarctica*), a tree-like fern which grows up to 6 m; the rough tree fern (*Cyathea australis*), which grows up to 12 m tall and prefers shady gullies or sunny slopes; and the staghorn fern (*Platycerium superbum*), a large, epiphytic fern with huge fronds that resemble stag's horns.

Poisonous Plants

The most poisonous plants are usually flowering plants. Sometimes all their tissues are toxic and sometimes only a particular part of the plant (such as the leaves) which can cause harm. In Australia, some of these dangerous plants are native and some are introduced. Some of the plants have proved poisonous to introduced livestock. For example, major stock poisonings have been caused by the York Road poison plant, Cooktown ironwood, lantana and laburnum. Some cause irritation and blistering on contact, such as the tar tree, the giant stinging tree, ivy, rhus, Bathurst burr, couch grass and geranium. Following is a list of some poisonous plants grouped according to the part which is poisonous.

WHOLE PLANT   Agapanthus, angel's trumpet, apple of Sodom, arum lily, begonia, bracken fern, buttercup, Carolina jessamine, Christmas rose, columbine, cunjevoi, daffodil, daphne, dumbcane, foxglove, fruit salad plant, gold rain tree, ivy, laburnum, belladonna lily, lobelia, oleander, petty spurge, poinsettia, poppy (corn, Iceland and opium), snow-on-the-mountain, taro, thorn apple, toadstools (certain species), yew.

STEMS Yellow oleander (and seeds).

LEAVES Anemone, azalea, box, cherry laurel (and berries), croton, deadly nightshade (and green berries), delphinium (and seeds), fennel (only in large quantities), flax, hydrangea, iris, larkspur, old man's beard, potatoes (and green potatoes), privet (and berries), rhododendron (and flowers), rhubarb, sorrel (in large quantities), tomato, winter sweet (and berries).

SEEDS Bean-prayer, bird of paradise (and pods), castor oil plant, delphinium (and leaves), yellow oleander (and stems), rosary pea, wisteria (and pods).

PODS Bird of paradise, wisteria (and seeds).

FLOWERS Rhododendron.

BERRIES Buckthorn, cherry laurel (and leaves), cotoneaster, deadly nightshade (green berries), duranta, elder (uncooked berries), holly, lantana, privet (and leaves), Virginia creeper, white cedar, winter sweet (and leaves).

UNRIPE NUTS Almond.

FRUITS Ornamental chilli, pepper tree.

KERNELS Apricot, peach, plum.

ROOTS Elder (and uncooked berries).

Introduced Plants

Hundreds of exotic species have been introduced into Australia, some with devastating effects on the environment and agriculture. Of course, some species are introduced by migratory birds, but other disastrous introductions can be laid at the feet of the European settlers. As awareness and practical solutions to the problems that some exotic species become more prevalent, many 'bad' foreign plants are now being exterminated or brought under control.

The blackberry, now classified as a noxious plant, was probably introduced by Philip Oakden, a settler in Launceston, Tasmania. Although he planted only a few cuttings brought from England, the blackberry was spread through planting by other Europeans and also by fruit-eating birds. It was also quickly spread on the south-eastern Australian mainland in areas where the climate suited its growth, and became a problem in pasture and also on land cultivated for crops. A rust fungus is now being used as a biological control.

There are several introduced plants which are classed as weeds, as they do not have any value to the land and, in fact, inhibit agriculture or the growing of commercial crops. Four weeds of this nature are annual ryegrass (*Lolium rigidum*), a Mediterranean species introduced for pasture, but which seriously inhibits wheat and other cereal crops in southern Australia; skeleton weed (*Chandrilla juncea*), also from the Mediterranean and also affecting wheat and cereal crops; wireweed (*Polygonum aviculare*), which infests pasture and cereal crops; and wild oats (*Avena* spp.), which not only affects cereal crops, but also tea, cotton and grapes.

Agriculture is not the only thing which can be adversely affected by the introduction of certain exotic species, the natural environment can also be deleteriously altered. The bitou bush (*Chrysanthemoides monilifera*) was introduced from South Africa for ornamental cultivation, but it was later used to stabilise sand dunes in coastal areas, particularly along Australia's eastern temperate coast. It has now overtaken native vegetation in many places, killing off naturally occurring species and negatively altering the coastal plant ecosystem.

The giant sensitive plant (*Mimosa pigra*) has become a pest in northern Australia, particularly in the Kakadu National Park in the Northern Territory. It has spread rapidly over floodplains in the Northern Territory, choking out native species.

Lantana (*Lantana camara*) is an extremely vigorous noxious plant which is widespread in New South Wales and Queensland. It thrives particularly well in rainforest areas where there is high rainfall. Initially intended for use as an ornamental hedge, it has also spread rapidly through grazing country in areas with fertile soil, which can be a problem because of some species toxicity to cattle.

Many people view Paterson's curse or salvation Jane (*Echium plantagineum*) as an attractive addition to the Australian environment. In summer, its purple blooms cover grazing pasture like a blanket. Although in some states it has been declared a noxious weed, in others it is viewed with more tolerance. In some areas, Paterson's curse is even used as a stock feed at certain times of the year when pasture is scarce.

The water hyacinth is an introduced floating water plant which is regarded as a weed in many other tropical areas, as well as in Australia. It is now widespread throughout the Australian mainland, but is not found in Tasmania. It chokes up natural waterways, freshwater lagoons and lakes, destroying the delicate balance of the natural ecosystems.

Australia's Floral Emblems

State or Territory	Floral Emblem
New South Wales	Waratah *(Telopea speciosissima)*
Victoria	Common heath *(Epacris impressa)*
Queensland	Cooktown orchid *(Dendrobium bigibbum)*
South Australia	Sturt's desert pea *(Clianthus formosus)*
Western Australia	Kangaroo paw *(Anigosanthos manglesii)*
Tasmania	Tasmanian blue gum *(Eucalyptus globulus)*
Northern Territory	Sturt's desert rose *(Gossypium sturtianum)*
Australia	Golden wattle *(Acacia pycnantha)*

Australia's Fauna

*T*he enormous geological changes to the Australian land mass combined with the country's long isolation have created a highly unusual collection of fauna. These animals, birds, insects and spiders have had to learn to adapt to the often very dry conditions in Australia. The long lack of external contact means that Australia still has two particular species of mammal, the monotremes, which are so ancient in origin that they are virtually living fossils. At the same time, many species found elsewhere in the world are missing here: there are no great apes in the Australian forests, hoofed animals are a recent introduction and there are no members of the order Insectivora.

Australia has about 282 species of mammals, of which almost half are marsupials and the rest are either placental mammals or monotremes. Most are unique to Australia.

Native Animals

MONOTREMES

Monotremes have been called living fossils by some because they share some of the characteristics of birds, reptiles, fishes, marsupials and placental mammals. On the one hand, they lay eggs; on the other, like mammals, they are warm-blooded, furred vertebrates which breathe air and have young which feed on the mother's milk.

PLATYPUS   The platypus (*Ornithorhynchus anatinus*) has webbed feet, a duck-like bill, a broad tail like a beaver's, and is covered in thick dark brown fur. It lays eggs and suckles its young, and can be found in the freshwater areas of eastern mainland Australia from Cape York Peninsula in Queensland to the southwest of Victoria, and also in Tasmania. The platypus lives in a burrow just above water level and is an extremely shy mammal. It can occasionally be seen in streams and shallow, flowing rivers at dusk. Adult males have a spur on each hind ankle, which is connected to a poison gland. The venom is strong enough to kill small animals.

ECHIDNA   The echidna (*Tachyglossus aculeatus*) is also erroneously known as the spiny anteater, a name which comes from its diet of termites and ants. It lives in a variety of habitats, including rainforest, scrubland, arid regions and generally rocky areas. The echidna's body is covered in brown hair and it has sharp quills on its back, which can reach 6 cm in length. If the echidna feels it is under attack, it will roll up into a ball so that only its quills are exposed, thus protecting it from predators. To compensate for poor eyesight, the echidna has an acute sense of smell to locate food, which it licks up with a long, sticky tongue.

MARSUPIALS

Many marsupials do not possess a placenta and instead have a pouch in which their tiny young develop.

BANDICOOT

There are seven species of bandicoot in Australia, ranging in size from that of a large rat to that of a rabbit. Probably the best known is the long-nosed bandicoot (*Perameles nasuta*), which is found in most of eastern Australia, and the short-nosed or brown bandicoot of the genus *Isoodon*, which can be found throughout Australia. Some species of bandicoot, such as the western barred bandicoot (*Perameles bougainville*), are now endangered. The western barred bandicoot is now thought to survive only on Bernier Island and the nearby Dorre Island off the coast of Western Australia near Shark Bay. At one time, this species was commonly found over a vast proportion of southern Australia.

KANGAROO

There are around 48 different species of kangaroo in Australia, ranging in size from the man-sized red kangaroo (*Megaleia rufa*) to the smaller wallabies, wallaroos, potoroos, bettongs and rat-sized kangaroos, the latter being less than 300 mm long. Some of these species are now considered extinct, although it is possible that they may still exist. Habitats vary from the dryland to the rainforest. Most kangaroos are herbivorous and, with the exception of Queensland's tree-climbing kangaroos (Bennett's tree-climbing kangaroo and Lumholtz's tree-climbing kangaroo), are ground dwellers. Large kangaroos can briefly reach speeds exceeding 45 km/h and leap 11 m or more in a single hop.

The species thought to be extinct include: the desert rat-kangaroo (*Caloprymnus campestris*), considered extinct since 1935; the broad-faced potoroo (*Potorous platyops*), considered extinct since 1875; the central hare-wallaby (*Lagorchestes asomatus*), considered extinct since 1932; and the Eastern hare-wallaby (*Lagorchestes leporides*), considered extinct since 1890.

Several species are also severely endangered, including: the banded hare-wallaby (*Lagostrophus fasciatus*), now found only on two islands off the coast of Western Australia near Shark Bay; the burrowing bettong (*Bettongia lesueur*), a burrowing marsupial once widespread throughout mainland Australia, but now restricted to four islands off the coast of Western Australia; the brush-tailed bettong (*Bettongia pencillata*), which now survives only in three small pockets — in the south-west of Western

Australia, and in two places in eastern Queensland; the Proserpine rock-wallaby (*Petrogale persephone*), which inhabits rocky outcrops in two small pockets of northeast Queensland; and the rufous hare-wallaby (*Lagorchestes hirsutus*), a once widespread species now found only in small populations in the Northern Territory, the Tanami Desert and two islands, Bernier and Dorre Islands, off the coast of Western Australia.

THYLACINE   The largest of Australia's marsupial carnivores existing in recent times, the thylacine or Tasmanian tiger (*Thylacinus cynocephalus*) first declined in numbers with the arrival of the dingo on the Australian mainland at least 4000 years ago. Its survival in Tasmania before European settlement was due to the fact that the dingo was not introduced there. Unfortunately, the thylacine, with its distinctive striped coat and dog-like appearance, had been hunted to extinction by Europeans by 1914.

Believed to be extinct, the last zoo specimen died in 1933. It is thought possible, however, that this species may still be alive in the Tasmanian wilderness and there have been reported, but unverified, thylacine sightings in recent times.

KOALA   There is only one species of koala (*Phascolarctos cinereus*), a herbivorous nocturnal marsupial, and its natural habitats are the forests and woodlands of eastern coastal areas from southern Queensland to South Australia, including Kangaroo Island. It lives almost exclusively in trees and, until the late 1920s, was in danger of extinction. Since then it has become a protected species. However, disease and environmental changes have a continuing impact on its numbers. The koala prefers to eat the leaves of the red, manna and grey gums, and many of these eucalypts have been felled to make way for development or agricultural land.

MARSUPIAL MOLE   Like the koala, there is only one species of marsupial mole (*Notoryctes typhlops*) and it is considered one of the most unusual of the marsupials. Covered in fine fur, it has strong claws, a nose covered by a horny shield and eyes that are rudimentary, making it almost blind. It inhabits sandy areas in south, central and western Australia, and spends much of its time tunnelling through the earth in search of invertebrates for food. It is a fairly common species, but rarely seen because of its habits.

NUMBAT   The only member of its species, the numbat (*Myrmecobius fasciatus*) has a long bushy tail, a pointed snout and conspicuous white stripes across its back. An endangered species, the numbat is now found only in certain parts of south-western Western Australia where its range is restricted because of its diet of termites. Also known as the banded anteater, it was once widespread over much of southern Australia, extending into Victoria and New South Wales.

BILBY   The bilby (*Macrotis lagotis*) is a long-eared rat-like mammal which is now seriously endangered, in part due to the introduction of the rabbit to Australia. Once widespread over western and inland Australia, it is now found only in the north of Western Australia, the centre of the Northern Territory and the far south-west of Queensland.

POSSUM   The name 'possum' was used by Captain Cook's men in 1770 because they thought the creature looked like the North American opossum. In fact, Australian possums, nocturnal marsupials, belong to several different families. The most widely distributed species is the common brushtail possum (*Trichosurus vulpecula*), often seen in suburban gardens. The brushtail builds nests in trees, roofs and holes in the ground. The ringtail possum (*Pseudocheirus peregrinus*) has a prehensile tail, with which it clings to branches. The ringtail inhabits dense coastal scrub in eastern mainland Australia — New South Wales, Victoria, northern Queensland — and south-western Australia and Tasmania. It lives in hollow limbs or spherical nests in shrubs or plants such as the tree fern. The sugar glider (*Pteraurus breviceps*) can glide up to 50 m through the air. It feeds on the nectar and pollen of eucalypts and banksias, as well as insects and the gum of acacias and eucalyptus sap. The greater glider, has a flying membrane which stretches from elbow to ankle. The eastern pygmy possum (*Cercartetus nanus*) is a native of eastern Australia. It feeds mainly on banksia nectar and is common in regions where these plants are found.

WOMBAT   There are four species of wombat in Australia, of which the most widely distributed is the common wombat (*Vombatus ursinus*) which can be found in forested regions of the south-east, from Queensland to Tasmania. The southern hairy-nosed wombat (*Lasiorhinus latifrons*) has adapted to living in arid conditions and occurs in the drier areas of South Australia and Western Australia. It is able to conserve moisture in its body and during summer feeds only at night. The northern hairy-nosed wombat (*Lasiorhius krefftii*) is an extremely endangered species thought to be found in a small pocket of north-east Queensland.

PLACENTAL MAMMALS

The young of placental mammals are able to develop considerably inside the mother before birth, and to suckle her milk afterwards. Placental mammals are the most numerous and highly evolved of the vertebrates.

BAT   There are about 58 species of bat in Australia, of which ten are species of the larger fruit bat or flying fox. These eat mostly fruit and blossoms, and include the grey-headed flying fox (*Pteropus poliocephalus*), which is found in Queensland and New South Wales, and the little red fruit bat found in Queensland, New South Wales and Western Australia. There is a large colony of up to 20 000 grey-headed flying foxes in the Sydney suburb of Gordon. During the day, they can be seen hanging upside down on dead tree branches, with their wings wrapped around their bodies. At night, they fly south across Sydney to areas such as the Royal Botanic Gardens and The Domain in the city centre, and Moore Park just south of the city centre. Certain other bats in Australia are insectivorous, including the little brown bat and the ghost, or false vampire bat.

DINGO   Similar to the domestic dog, the Australian dingo (*Canis familiaris dingo*), or warrigul, is thought to be descended from the wolf and varies from a yellow colour in dry areas to a reddish gold in mountainous country. It generally occurs in inland South Australia and New South Wales, the eastern highlands of New South Wales and Victoria, and also in Queensland, the Northern Territory and Western Australia. Thought to have come to Australia about 4000 years ago, the dingo usually hunts by night, alone or in pairs, for birds, reptiles, insects and carrion. It also preys on mammals such as sheep and calves, and for this reason is classified as a harmful pest in some areas.

DUGONG   Believed to be the source of the mermaid myth, the dugong is a large marine mammal, which is also called the sea-cow because it grazes on sea-grasses and suckles its young at its teats. Resembling a fish in shape, the male has short ivory tusks. The female has a pair of mammary glands under her forelimbs and gives birth to only one calf at a time. Dugongs move in herds of up to several hundred and it is believed that one of the largest surviving populations in the world now lives in the waters of the Great Barrier Reef, although this is now under threat because of tourist development. In general, they occur in northern coastal waters from Broome in Western Australia to Moreton Bay in Queensland.

WHALE   There are two main suborders of whale: the Mysticeti or baleen whales; and the Odontoceti or toothed whales. The former eats by drawing large quantities of sea water into its mouth and then straining it out again to trap the small crustacea inside.

The species of baleen whale found around Australia include the southern right whale and the humpback whale. The humpback whale migrates annually to Antarctica for summer and returns to warmer Australian waters in the winter to calve. Toothed whales, in contrast, actively hunt down fish and squid and swallow them whole. The sperm whale, killer whale and pilot whale are representatives of this group. Whale numbers were seriously depleted by the whaling industry during the 19th and early 20th centuries, but the international ban on whaling has seen numbers increase or stabilise to some extent.

Introduced Species

FERAL MAMMALS

Species not native to Australia, but introduced since European settlement for farming, utility, pets and sport include: dogs, cats, sheep, buffalo, goats, cattle, pigs, rabbits, foxes, camels, horses and donkeys. Animals such as rats and mice were introduced mistakenly in ship cargoes. Certain other animals, such as ostriches and alpacas, have recently been introduced into Australia to be professionally farmed for their hides and fleece.

In some cases, these exotic animals have had disastrous effects on the fragile Australian environment. Possibly the most damaging of these animals is the rabbit. Rabbits have multiplied to such an extent — because of their extremely rapid breeding cycle — that they endanger native animals because of the competition for range and food. They have also had a devastating effect on the soil, particularly in semi-arid areas or where there is irregular rainfall, as they eat all the groundcover, leaving the soil exposed to erosion.

Hard-hooved animals also have a negative impact on the Australian soil and hence the vegetation, and feral populations of animals such as goats, pigs and buffalo are now culled in an effort to reduce their numbers to more manageable levels or, indeed, to get rid of them entirely. Deer are another type of introduced hard-hooved animal that causes problems in national park areas. Efforts are being made to have deer culled or destroyed, but are being met by the 'Bambi' factor, i.e. resistance from people who do not want to see this species killed for sentimental reasons. Foxes, introduced in ignorance by hunt-loving English settlers in the early 19th century, also have a harmful impact on the environment and native fauna.

Birds

Birds are warm-blooded vertebrates, distinguishable from other animals by their feathers. There are about 8600 species of birds in the world, and nearly 800 of these are in Australia or Australian waters. Of these 800, about 400 are endemic and the rest migratory.

EMUS AND CASSOWARIES

Australia is the only country where there are two families of large flightless birds, both still living.

The emu (*Dromaius novaehollandiae*), is the second largest bird in the world, after the ostrich, and is the only member of the family Dromaiidae. It cannot fly, but can run in bursts of up to 50 km/h. It can reach about 190 cm in height and is unique to Australia, found throughout the continent except the north-east and in densely populated areas. It feeds on grasses, fruits, berries and insects. Emu chicks have striped plumage, which they eventually shed for their adult coat of shaggy grey-brown feathers.

Confined to the rainforests of northeast Queensland, the southern cassowary (*Casuarius casuarius*) has a horny helmet on top of its head and a long, knife-like claw which can do considerable damage to its victim. It has been known to kill humans when provoked. Its head is bare and its throat blue, with scarlet touches at the nape. It has a large body, like the emu, which is covered in purplish black, drooping feathers.

GREBES

There are three species of the grebe in Australia: the great-crested grebe (*Podiceps cristatus*), the hoary-headed grebe (*Poliocephalus poliocephalus*) and the little or Australasian grebe (*Tachybaptus novaehollandiae*). Diving water-birds, their feet are placed well back along the body and each toe is joined by a lobe of skin rather than by webbing. Since their tail is very short, they use their feet for steering both in the water and the air. Though not very swift swimmers, they are excellent divers and are mostly carnivorous, feeding on small water animals. They are found in fresh, brackish and coastal salt waters, and their nests are usually floating rafts of waterweed anchored to waterside vegetation.

PENGUINS

The penguin is an oceanic flightless seabird, with a protective layer of blubber which insulates it from the extreme cold of its natural environment in the Antarctic and sub-Antarctic regions. It usually comes ashore only to breed, when it can be seen in large colonies, although the little penguin can often be found resting on shore. Of the 11 species of penguin, only one breeds and resides on mainland Australia, the little or fairy penguin (*Eudyptula minor novaehollandiae*), but at least nine other species have been recorded in Australian waters.

The little penguin occurs along the southern coast from Fremantle in Western Australia round to northern New South Wales and measures only about 33 cm long. Penguins can swim extremely quickly due to the fact that their wings are completely stiff — speeds of 40 km/h have been recorded — and they can jump almost 2 m high from the sea onto pack ice in the Antarctic and sub-Antarctic regions.

The king penguin (*Aptenodytes patagonica*) is probably the most well known species. This large penguin grows up to 90 cm tall and has a long straight beak with orange markings, and it also has orange markings on its neck. An upright species, it is white on its stomach and a steel-blue, almost black, on its back. The king penguin has been spotted in waters south and west of Tasmania.

The adelie penguin (*Pygoscelis antartica*) is smaller than the king penguin at up to 74 cm, and lacks any orange markings. Its upper parts are black, including its throat, with white underparts and pink feet. It has been spotted occasionally in waters off the far south-east of Tasmania.

The magellanic penguin (*Spheniscus magellanicus*) grows up to 70 cm, and its marking are black and white like the adelie penguin, but with a distinctive horseshoe band of white around its breast, and black and white markings on its breast. It has been seen in the waters of Bass Strait, between Victoria and Tasmania.

ALBATROSSES

There are nine species of this extremely large seabird found in the oceans and seas around southern Australia. They have large heads and beaks, large bodies and characteristically long, slender wings. Albatrosses are able to glide very quickly and very low over the sea, with very little wing movement. Like many seabirds, they come ashore only to breed.

Species include: the wandering albatross (*Diomedea exulans*), which can have a wing span of up to 3.5 m and has been seen along the coast of Australia from Perth in Western Australia to the mid-north coast of Queensland; the royal albatross (*Diomedea epomophora*), the largest of the species seen in Australia at up to 140 cm, but whose wing span is not as great as the wandering albatross; and the sooty albatross (*Phoebetria fusca*), a slim, graceful species with chocolate brown plumage.

TUBE-NOSED SEABIRDS — FULMARS, PETRELS, PRIONS AND SHEARWATERS

The oceanic seabirds in this grouping vary in size from very large to small, but they all have external nostrils at the end of tubes. They range in size from the giant petrels to the smaller prions and include fulmars, gadfly petrels, petrels, prions and shearwaters. Some 40 species are found along the Australian coast, but only one is endemic: the short-tailed shearwater or Tasmanian mutton-bird (*Puffinus tenuirostris*), which has been commercially exploited since the early 19th century when sealers killed it for food and feathers. This industry is now controlled, with a short open season between March and April.

Species of this grouping include: the southern giant-petrel (*Macronectes giganteus*), with a wing span of up to 2 m; the northern giant-petrel (*Macronectes halli*), which is similar to the southern giant-petrel; the providence petrel (*Pterodroma lessonii*), an endangered species which breeds on Lord Howe Island; Gould's petrel (*Pterodroma inexpectata*), another endangered secies which breeds on rock islands off the coast of New South Wales and New Caledonia; the blue petrel (*Halobaena caerulea*), which the often found in the company of prions and follows ships; the Antarctic prion or dove (*Pachyptila desolata*); and the Manx shearwater (*Puffinus puffinus*), which breeds on offshore islands in the Northern Hemisphere.

Amazingly, there has been a recorded sighting in Australia of a particular specimen of this latter bird, the Manx shearwater, which had originally been banded in the UK.

STORM-PETRELS AND DIVING-PETRELS

The storm-petrels are small, dark seabirds, again with tubular nostrils on the ridge of their beaks. They feed from a swimming position or by making shallow dives under the water. The diving-petrels are small to medium in size, and are similar to their Northern Hemisphere relatives. Unlike the storm-petrels, they feed exclusively by diving and chasing their food — zooplankton, crustaceans and small fish — underwater.

Species include: Wilson's storm-petrel (*Oceanites oceanicus*), which is found all along the coast of mainland Australia and Tasmania, although it breeds in the Antarctic Circle; the grey-backed storm-petrel (*Oceanites nereis*), which has prominent tubular nostils and breeds in the South Indian and South Atlantic oceans; and the common diving-petrel (*Pelecanoides urinator*), a plump bird which breeds on islands off the coast of Victoria and Tasmania.

CORMORANTS, PELICANS AND ALLIES

The six families of this order comprise tropicbirds, frigatebirds, gannets and boobies, cormorants, darters and pelicans. Their common features are that all four toes are joined by webbing and that they have sealed nostrils which enable the birds to dive for food. The beaks of birds in this order are always longer than their heads.

The Australian pelican (*Pelecanus conspicillatus*) is typical of this type of bird, with its large, pouched beak. However, unlike other pelicans found elsewhere in the world, it does not dive for food. The Australian pelican is found all over the mainland of Australia, with the exception of the desert areas of Western Australia and in Tasmania.

The boobies are quite distinctive looking birds — not endemic to Australia — which mainly inhabit coastal tropical areas and offshore islands, and commonly nest in trees. The red-footed booby (*Sula sula*) is particularly unusual, and either has an all white body and wings with black markings, or a completely brown body and wings. It has bright red feet and blue and red markings on the beak, and a blue ring around the eye.

HERONS, IBISES, STORKS AND ALLIES

These birds are all long-legged and most of them wade in marshes, tidal estuaries and along river margins in search of food. Herons are well-represented in Australia and the most common is probably the white-faced heron (*Ardea novaehollandiae*), distributed throughout the continent and Tasmania, and also, mistakenly, called the blue crane.

Ibises can be distinguished by their long, downcurved bills. There are three species of ibises in Australia: the glossy ibis (*Plegadis falcinellus*); the white ibis (*Threskiornis molucca*); and the straw-necked ibis (*Threskiornis spinicollis*). Spoonbills have a characteristic wide spoon-shaped tip to their bills. There are two species of spoonbills in Australia: the royal spoonbill (*Platalea regia*) and the yellow-billed spoonbill (*Platalea flavipes*).

The jabiru or black-necked stork (*Ephippiorhynchus asiaticus*) is Australia's only stork species and occurs along the northern and eastern coasts of the mainland in wetland areas.

SWANS, GEESE AND DUCKS

Of the 148 species of waterfowl in the family Anatidae, there are only 23 found in Australia — two species have been introduced, ten are endemic and the rest are migratory. The small number is due largely to the dryness of the continent and the lack of favourable habitats for them.

Native to Australia, the black swan (*Cygnus atratus*) occurs mostly south of the Tropic of Capricorn. Unlike the introduced white mute swans, black swans breed in colonies.

The magpie goose (*Anseranas semipalmata*) is now largely restricted to northern parts of Australia. The Cape Barren goose (*Cereopsis novaehollandiae*) occurs mostly in the south, on offshore islands and along southern coastal areas of Victoria, South Australia, Tasmania and Western Australia. The latter is fully protected as a rare species. Other species include the green pygmy-goose (*Nettapus pulchellus*) and the white or cotton pygmy-goose (*Nettapus coromandelianus*).

The most common and numerous of the ducks in Australia are the grey teal duck (*Anas gracilis*) and the Pacific black duck (*Anas superciliosa*). Others include the freckled duck (*Stictonetta naevosa*), the pink-eared duck (*Malacorhyncus mebranaceus*), the maned or wood duck (*Chenonetta jubata*) and the musk duck (*Biziura lobata*).

DIURNAL BIRDS OF PREY

Active during the day, these birds of prey are found throughout the world, except in the Antarctic, and all have sharply hooked, down-curved beaks and strong taloned feet. They belong to the orders Accipitriformes and

Falconiformes. Of the five families, only three are present in Australia: the Accipitridae which includes eagles, kites, goshawks and harriers; the Falconidae which includes six species of falcon; and the osprey (*Pandion haliaetus*) which is in a family by itself.

EAGLES   There are three species of eagle in Australia: the wedge-tailed eagle (*Aquila audax*), the little eagle (*Hieraaetus morphnoides*) and the white-bellied sea-eagle (*Haliaeetus leucogaster*). The former is Australia's largest bird of prey and can be found in a variety of habitats, mostly in open areas, all over the Australian mainland and Tasmania. It has a wing span of up to 2.5 m.

OSPREY   The osprey (*Pandion haliaetus*) is often called the 'fish eagle'. A coastal bird of prey, it feeds exclusively on fish. After diving for its prey, it often carries it in its claws like a torpedo.

FALCONS   These swift-flying birds usually swoop on their prey, often small mammals, after soaring at great heights. Species include: the black falcon (*Falco subniger*); the peregrine falcon (*Falco peregrinus*); the Australian hobby or little falcon (*Falco longipennis*); and the Australian kestrel or nankeen (*Falco cenchroides*).

FOWL-LIKE BIRDS

There are six families in this group, but only four are represented in Australia: mound-builders of the family Megapodiidae; pheasants, fowls, and true quails, of the family Phasianidae; button-quails of the family Turnicidae; and the plains-wanderer, a single-species genius unique to Australia of the family Pedionomidae. All are characterised by having three toes in front and a shorter toe behind. The common pheasant and the peafowl have both been introduced.

MOUND-BUILDERS   There are three species of mound-building birds in Australia: the orange-footed scrub fowl (*Megapodius reinwardt*), the mallee fowl (*Leipoa ocellata*) and the Australian brush-turkey (*Alectura lathami*). The last two are endemic. This family is the only group of vertebrates, other than amphibians and reptiles, that do not use their body heat to incubate their eggs or young. Instead, they use the heat of rotting vegetation, burying the eggs in mounds of soil and vegetation. The Australian brush-turkey is found in rainforest, woodland and scrub, mostly in coastal areas, from the mid-north coast of New South Wales to the tip of the Cape York Peninsula in Queensland.

PLAINS-WANDERER   The plains-wanderer (*Pedionomus torquatus*) is unique to Australia and in danger of extinction. A small, fast-running bird, it is rather like a quail, but with a more upright stance and the longer legs of a wading bird. This species is quite rare, and is found in grassland, open paddocks, cereal crops and stubble in the inland areas of southern Queensland, inland New South Wales, western Victoria and eastern South Australia. Recent sightings have mainly been restricted to a small area of South Australia, Victoria and western New South Wales.

CRANES, RAILS AND ALLIES

There are about 30 species from this group in Australia which include cranes, rails, crakes, coots, bustards, jacanas and various hens, including the purple swamphen (*Porphyrio porphyrio*) and the dusky moorhen (*Gallinula tenibrosa*). They are generally ground-dwelling birds with powerful pointed bills and large feet. Many of the species rarely fly and some are flightless.

The brolga crane (*Grus rubicundus*) is endemic to Australia and one of the world's largest cranes, growing up to 140 cm. It is found in northern and eastern parts of the continent, and gives an impressive dancing display. The other species of crane here is the sarus crane (*Grus antigone*), which was first sighted in northern Queensland in 1966. Similar to the brolga crane, it has pink legs and red markings on its head and neck. The Australian bustard (*Ardeotis australis*) can be found in most parts of Australia, but is the only bustard species here.

PLOVERS, WADERS, GULLS AND TERNS

Waders in Australia range from the tiny stints to the medium-sized curlews, and live mostly along the seashores, swamps, river margins and lakes. Many of these spend the summer in Australia and migrate to the Northern Hemisphere during the winter. There are more than 20 species of gull and tern in Australia, some of which are migratory. Most live in colonies, especially when breeding. These include the common silver gull (*Larus novaehollandiae*), the Pacific gull (*Larus pacificus*), the crested tern (*Sterna bergii*) and the sooty tern (*Sterna fuscata*).

PIGEONS AND DOVES

There are about 25 species of the family Columbidae in Australia. The larger, plumper species are generally called pigeons and the smaller ones, doves. In contrast to other birds, pigeons drink by continuously sucking instead of tipping their heads back to swallow.

The forest species are usually brilliant in colour, with the open or plains species being more drab. The male of the superb fruit-dove (*Ptilinopus superbus*) is found in the tropical and subtropical forests of Australia's eastern coast. It has rich green feathers on its upper body, with a pale green face and purple breast, with scarlet purple markings on its head and neck.

PARROTS AND COCKATOOS

There are about 60 species of parrot, cockatoo and related birds in Australia belonging to the order Psittaciformes. Of these, 48 live only in Australia and they occur in every habitat from rainforest to desert. The characteristics of this group include short hooked bills and strong claws, with two toes pointing forwards and two backwards. They can be divided into three subfamilies: cockatoos, lorikeets and typical parrots. Cockatoos are the largest of the Australian parrots and most have a conspicuous crest and very strong bill. They feed both on the ground and on trees. Species include: the sulphur-crested cockatoo (*Cacatua galerita*) and the galah (*Cacatua roseicapilla*), both of which are often kept as pets. Other species include: the red-tailed black cockatoo (*Calypyorhynchus lathami*); the gang gang cockatoo (*Callocephalon fimbriatum*), found in the forests and woodland of south-eastern New South Wales and eastern Victoria; and the long-billed corella (*Cacatua tenuirostris*).

There are seven species of lorikeet in Australia, five of them endemic. Largely arboreal, they can gather in large flocks and feed on nectar, pollen and fruit using brushlike tongues. Perhaps the most recognised of these are the rainbow lorikeet (*Trichoglossus haematodus*) and the red-collared lorikeet (*Trichoglossus rubritorquis*).

Most of the world's parrots belong to this same subfamily, the Psittacinae. In Australia, these include the fig-parrots, fruit-eating and long-tailed parrots and the broad-tailed parrots. Perhaps the most brilliantly coloured are the eastern rosella (*Platycerus eximius*); the crimson rosella (*Platycercus elegans*); the scarlet-chested parrot (*Neophema splendida*), a grass parrot; the superb parrot (*Polytelis swainsonii*); and the male Australian king parrot (*Alisterus scapularis*). Possibly the most well known Australian parrot is the budgerigar (*Melopsittacus undulatus*), a small, slim parrot with a distinctive musical chirruping. Its natural habitat is the dry interior of Australia. However, since 1840, when John Gould took four aviary-bred birds back to England, the budgerigar has been bred and domesticated as a cagebird throughout the world.

CUCKOOS AND COUCALS

There are 14 species of cuckoo in Australia, of which 13 are parasitic (i.e. the females lay their eggs in the nest of an unwitting host). One, the pheasant coucal (*Centropus phasianinus*), builds its own nest and rears its own brood. Most Australian species breed in Australia during the summer and then migrate further north, sometimes as far as northern Asia, during the winter.

One of the most notorious species of cuckoo is the common koel (*Eudynamys cyanocephala*), which often nests in urban areas and has an unmistakable, loud call of either 'ko-eel' or 'quodel, quodel, quodel'. This carrying call can drive people mad in spring and early summer.

HAWK OWLS AND BARN OWLS

Owls are characterised by their vision and hearing, hooked beaks and strong claws, as well as almost silent flight. There are two major families of owl, Tytonidae (barn owls) and Strigidae (hawk owls). Four species of the former occur in Australia and four of the latter. The smallest, most familiar and most widespread is the southern boobook (*Ninox boobook*), so named because of its distinctive call. Other species include the barn owl (*Tyto alba*) and the quite rare sooty owl (*Tyto tenbricosa*).

FROGMOUTHS AND NIGHTJARS

Frogmouths and nightjars are characterised by large mouths, small legs and weak feet. Frogmouths generally feed on the ground at night on insects, centipedes, snails and sometimes mice. By day, they can be superbly camouflaged because of their colouring and capacity for extreme stillness. Species include the tawny frogmouth (*Podargus strigoides*); the Papuan frogmouth (*Podargus papuensis*) and the spotted nightjar (*Eurostopodus argus*).

SWIFTS

The white-rumped swiftlet (*Aerodramus spodiopygius*) is the only resident breeding swift in Australia, but the white-throated needletail (*Hirundapus caudacutus*) and fork-tailed swift (*Apus pacificus*) are two regular visitors. Swifts spend most of their lives on the wing and are characterised by an ability to fly extremely fast: speeds of 150 km/h have been estimated. They cannot perch and have to hold on to vertical surfaces when grounded.

KINGFISHERS, ROLLERS AND ALLIES

The birds of this order, Coraciiformes, are generally brightly coloured and their front three toes are partly joined. All nest in hollows, for example in trees, walls, or stream or river banks. Of the 90 species of kingfisher in the world, 11 occur in Australia and are characterised by their large heads, short legs, wings and tail, thick necks and long beaks.

The laughing kookaburra (*Dacelo novaeguinae*), with its unmistakable laugh-like call, and the red-backed kingfisher (*Todiramphus pyrrhopygius*) are endemic to Australia. The rainbow bee-eater (*Merops ornatus*) and the dollarbird (*Eurystomus orientalis*) are also part of this grouping.

The laughing kookaburra is one of Australia's best-known birds and also the largest in the kingfisher family. Its name is Aboriginal in origin, but it is also often referred to as the laughing jackass or bushman's clock — probably because it calls most usually at dawn and dusk. Found generally in woodland and open forest from Cape York Peninsula to Victoria and South Australia, it has been introduced into Tasmania and Western Australia. It has also adapted well to suburban life. Its diet includes insects, snakes, lizards, rodents and small birds. The blue-winged kookaburra (*Dacelo leachii*) is very similar in appearance to the laughing kookaburra, but the male of this species has mostly azure blue wings and azure tail feathers.

The dollarbird (*Eurystomus orientalis*) is the only kind of roller in Australia; it is so named because of the off-white patches on its wings. Distributed throughout northern and eastern Australia, it migrates to Malaysia for the winter. The rainbow bee-eater (*Merops ornatus*) has several alternative common names including: rainbow bird, golden swallow, gold-miner and gold-digger. It is brilliantly coloured and occurs in all kinds of open country, but migrates north for the winter.

PERCHING BIRDS

Sixty per cent of all the birds in the world come into this order, the Passeriformes. They are all small or medium in size and have three of their toes in front, with one behind. This back toe can lock round a branch so that the bird will not fall off its perch. There are at least 50 different families in this order. Some of the groups are described below.

BIRDS OF PARADISE   Australia has four of the 41 species of birds of paradise, although they are more common to Papua New Guinea. They occur in the rainforests of the north-eastern region of Australia and are renowned for their spectacular plumage and courtship display. One species is called the trumpet manucode (*Manucodia keraudrenii*) and the other three are riflebirds, perhaps because their plumage colour resembles the uniform of British Army rifle regiments. These are the paradise riflebird (*Ptiloris paradiseus*); Victoria's riflebird (*Ptiloris victoriae*) and the magnificent rifle-bird (*Ptiloris magnificus*).

BOWERBIRDS AND CATBIRDS   This family, Ptilonorhynchidae, is confined to Australia and Papua New Guinea. Of the 18 species, ten occur in Australia. They usually inhabit rainforest and open forest areas in central and northern Australia and are famous for the structures which the males build to attract a female to a particular place where courtship and mating can take place.

The satin bowerbird (*Ptilorhynchis violaceaus*) is probably the best known, and the male has been known to collect all kinds of oddments for its bower, including bright plastic clothes pegs and ring pulls from aluminium soft drink cans.

HONEYEATERS   Honeyeaters range in size from the 11 cm scarlet honey-eater (*Myzomela sanguinolenta*) to the 48 cm yellow wattlebird (*Anthochaera paradoxa*) of Tasmania, but they all have a slim body, long tail, slightly downcurved beak and a brush tongue for gathering nectar from flowers. Miners are medium-sized honeyeaters, so called because of the golden colour of their feet and beaks. With nearly 70 species found here, honeyeaters make up the largest bird family in Australia and occupy every type of habitat.

LYREBIRDS   The superb lyrebird (*Menura novaehollandiae*) is found from south-east Queensland to southern Victoria, while Albert's lyrebird (*Menura alberti*) is found in the dense rainforest of the McPherson Range on the Queensland/New South Wales border. The males of both species are famous for their beautiful plumage and courtship display.

SCRUB-BIRDS   The noisy scrub-bird (*Atrichornis clamosus*) and the rufous scrub-bird (*Atrichornis rufescens*) make up the family Atrichornithidae. They are noted for their powerful voices, and sturdy legs and feet, and for having no wishbone. Both live in dense undergrowth; the rufous scrub-bird in the rainforest of north-eastern New South Wales and southern Queensland, and the noisy scrub-bird in the Two Peoples Bay and Mt Many Peaks areas of Western Australia. The latter was thought to be extinct after 1889, but was rediscovered in 1961.

AUSTRALIAN WARBLERS

This group of small insect-eating birds unique to Australia includes the fairy-wrens, which have tiny bodies and long cocked tails. The male plumage is much brighter than the female, particulary during breeding. Species include: the superb fairy-wren (*Malurus cyaneus*); the splendid fairy-wren (*Malurus splendens*), the male of which has brilliant blue plumage of varying hues all over its body, head and wings; the variegated fairy-wren (*Malurus lamberti*); the white-winged fairy-wren (*Malurus leucopterus*), mainly a brilliant blue except for white patches on its wings; and the southern emu-wren (*Stipiturus malachurus*), an uncommon species found in swamps, wetlands, scrub, subalpine grassland and the button-grass plains of Tasmania.

GRASS-FINCHES AND ALLIES

The native species of these tiny to small seed-eating birds are, particularly in the male, colourful and/or distinctively patterned. They usually occur in fast-flying flocks and build intricate domed grass nests. Species include: the

Gouldian finch (*Erythrura gouldiae*), a colourful finch once common across the north of Australia, but now endangered; the crimson finch (*Neochmia phaeton*), also from the north of Australia and usually found in long grasses near water; the beautiful firetail (*Stagonopleura bella*), found in south-eastern Australia, which favours tea tree and casuarina thickets; the red-eared firetail (*Stagonopleura oculata*), which is restrictd to the far south of Western Australia; and the blue-faced finch (*Erythrura trichroa*), an extremely rare species found on the edge of rainforest and in mangroves in a small pocket in the far north-east of Queensland.

BUTCHERBIRDS AND CURRAWONGS

These medium to large birds have dinstinctively patterned grey, black and white plumage. Possible the most well known are the Australian magpie (*Gymnorhina tibicen* and *Gymnorhina hypoleuca*), large black and white birds which are sometimes mistaken for the pied currawong (*Strepera graculina*), and vice versa. The magpies have far more dominant white markings (particularly on the neck and wings), however, and are slightly smaller than the pied currawong. The pied currawong is mostly black with a yellow eye and a white patch underneath its wing and in its tail. The grey butcherbird (*Cracticus torquatus*), black-backed butcherbird (*Cracticus mentalis*) and pied butcherbird (*Cracticus nigrogularis*) are smaller than both the magpie and the currawongs, and white is far more dominant in their black and white markings.

RAVENS AND CROWS

These glossy, black birds have a distinctive harsh 'cawing' call. Species include the Australian raven (*Corvus coronoides*), which grows up to 56 cm; the little raven (*Corvus mellori*), whose call is 'car, car, car'; the Torresian crow (*Corvus orru*), which is widespread across the north and northern inland of Australia; and the little crow (*Corvus benetti*), widespread across the inland and west of mainland Australia.

Reptiles

Reptiles are cold-blooded vertebrates whose bodies are covered with scales. They breathe air and, in general, their young hatch from eggs, except in the case of some snakes and lizards which are born alive. There are approximately 750 known species of reptiles in Australia. The following are examples of the most interesting or well known.

TURTLES

Turtles and tortoises have a protective horny carapace attached to their backbone and ribs and a small head. When very active, they must come to the surface to breathe. There are six species of marine turtle in Australia, found along the north coast of the continent. There are no terrestrial species of tortoise here and, in Australia, the freshwater varieties of turtle are commonly known as tortoises.

BROAD-SHELLED RIVER TURTLE   The largest Australian freshwater species (*Chelodina expansa*), it can grow to 50 cm.

LUTH OR LEATHERY TURTLE   The largest marine species, the luth turtle (*Dermochelys coriacea*) can weigh up to 750 kg and reach almost 3 m in length. It occurs along the western and eastern coasts of the mainland, but is seriously endangered.

SNAKES

Snakes are cold-blooded limbless creatures with neither eyelids nor ear-openings. They bite their prey with fangs, inside which are poison glands, and then swallow it whole. There are more than 110 species of land snake in Australia and 32 sea snakes. However, only a few of them are dangerous to humans.

CHILDREN'S PYTHON   There are ten species of python in Australia and they are generally nocturnal and slow-moving in habit. The children's python (*Liasis childreni*) was named after a British scientist, Dr Children of the British Museum. It is found throughout Australia, except for Victoria and Tasmania.

COMMON DEATH ADDER   One of the most poisonous snakes in Australia, the common death adder (*Acanthophis antarcticus*) is short in length (up to 1 m), of varied coloration and found virtually throughout the continent, except in Victoria and Tasmania. It is a secretive snake, and often lies half-buried in soil or plant litter.

EASTERN BROWN SNAKE   One of Australia's most dangerous snakes, the eastern brown snake (*Pseudonaja textilis*) is widespread across eastern Australia and grows up to 1.5 m. This snake is not normally aggressive, but will attack unprovoked if nesting.

EASTERN TIGER SNAKE   As this species of snake is more common in towns and cities in the south-eastern mainland of Australia, there are more recorded bites from this snake. Although not as poisonous as the taipan, the eastern tiger snake (*Notechis scutatus*) can kill humans if the bite is left untreated. It inhabits forest, pasture and floodplain areas, and grows up to 1.2 m in length.

FIERCE SNAKE   The fierce snake (*Oxyuranus microlepidotus*) could probably be considered Australia's most venomous snake, but there has been only one recorded human victim. It is not only extremely poisonous, but, like the taipan, it is also extremely aggressive; most snakes will retreat when disturbed. It is found in the arid regions of eastern central Australia and grows up to 2.5 m.

RED-BELLIED BLACK SNAKE   A glossy, thin black snake with a distinctive red ribbon marking on its belly, the red-bellied black snake (*Pseudechis porphyriacus*) is found on the eastern mainland, particularly near water. It grows up to 1.5 m in length and is venomous to humans.

TAIPAN   The taipan (*Oxyuranus scutellatus*) is Australia's most venomous snake. Its bite was invariably fatal before the development of an antivenin. This snake contains more venom than any reptile in Australia; enough to kill 200 sheep. Found across northern Australia from northern New South Wales to northern Western Australia, it grows up to 2.5 m long.

YELLOW-BELLIED SEA SNAKE   There are about 32 species of sea snake around the Australian coastline, of which the yellow-bellied sea snake (*Pelamis platurus*) is the most widely distributed.

LIZARDS AND GOANNAS

There are five families of lizard in Australia: geckoes, legless lizards, skinks, dragons and goannas, these make up the 450 or so known species in Australia. There are about 4000 known lizard species in the world. Whereas snakes possess a lower jaw held together by elastic ligaments (allowing enormous stretching), lizards have a fixed lower jaw, limiting the size of its prey.

DRAGONS   There are 50 or so species of dragon lizards in Australia. All are rough-scaled, have short, blunt tongues and generally eat termites, larger insects and small mammals. The frilled lizard (*Chlamydisaurus kingii*) inhabits the warmer, northern regions of the country and, when in danger, raises a red and yellow coloured frill of skin attached to the bones in its throat — and also opens wide its mouth, which is bright orange or pink.

GECKOES   There are about 65 species of gecko in Australia and these are generally nocturnal, have broad tails used as food stores and lay two hard-shelled white eggs. The largest known species in Australia is the leaf-tailed gecko (*Phyllurus cornufum*), which grows to 25 cm in length.

GOANNAS   Of the 30 known species of goanna in the world, there are about 20 in Australia. Also known as monitor lizards, they are covered in small scales, have a long forked tongue and vary in size from 18 cm (short-tailed goanna) to 2.4 m (perentie — *Varanus giganteus*). The fastest are probably the sand and black goannas, which can reach speeds of 40 km/h.

LEGLESS LIZARDS   One of the differences between a snake and a legless lizard is that the lizard has a blunt tongue, whereas the snake has a long forked one. Also, the legless lizard, like the gecko, can discard its tail as a means of defence and a snake never can. The largest of the legless lizards, of which there are some 30 species in Australia, is the common scaly-foot lizard (*Pygopus lepidopodus*). It can reach 75 cm in length.

SKINKS   The skink family is the largest of the five major groups of lizard in Australia, with about 250 known species in the country. All possess the following characteristics: plates, rather than scales, on their heads; very short legs; a broad, blunt tongue and deeply buried eardrums. They are usually between 30 mm and 60 mm in length. Living in arid or semi-arid areas, the blue-tongue lizard (*Tiliqua multifasciata*) shows its cobalt blue tongue when alarmed.

CROCODILES

Apart from venomous snakes and spiders, probably the most feared living creature in Australia is the crocodile. There are two species of crocodile in Australia, found in the north and north-east, but there are no alligators. The crocodile's front feet show traces of webbing, but its back feet are strongly webbed and used when swimming slowly. When swimming fast, the crocodile folds its feet away and uses the large flat tail as a paddle. Normally fairly sluggish, crocodiles can move with surprising speed when capturing prey, particularly in the water.

SALTWATER OR ESTUARINE CROCODILES   Found in coastal rivers, mangroves and swamps, the saltwater or estuarine crocodile (*Crocodylus porosus*) usually grows to between 5 m and 7 m in length. It is grey, brown or blackish in colour on the top, with darker mottling, and off-white beneath. Generally nocturnal, it feeds on fish, crustaceans, reptiles, birds and mammals, and has killed and injured human beings. This is the species responsible for the so-called 'death roll', where it takes its prey into the water and rolls it until drowned, and then stores it on an underwater ledge until eating.

FRESHWATER CROCODILES   Usually found in freshwater lagoons near the coast and in the hinterland, the freshwater crocodile (*Crocodylus johnstoni*) can reach about 3 m in length. In colour, it is olive-green or grey above with mottled sides and off-white beneath. It is considered to be harmless to humans and has a thinner snout than the saltwater or estuarine crocodile.

Amphibians

The only native amphibians in Australia are frogs, of which there are nearly 200 species, representing five families. There are undoubtedly more species, as yet undiscovered. The only toad is an imported species called the cane toad (*Bufo marinus*), brought in to control beetles in sugar cane plantations in Queensland. One of Australia's most attractive native species is the corroboree frog (*Pseudophryne corroboree*), which lives above the timber line in the Australian Alps. It has striking yellow and black stripes and markings.

There is concern among scientists that many frogs are rapidly becoming endangered species, which are particularly susceptible to changes in environment resulting from land clearing and development. There are further concerns about the damage caused by the cane toad, which has now spread from the far north of Queensland down to Lismore in northern New South Wales.

Fishes

From the more than 300 000 species of fish known worldwide, about 3000 have been recorded in Australian waters. The seas around the continent are rich in marine life, but ichthyologist John S. Lake has listed only 231 species of freshwater fish. This imbalance is mostly because Australia is such a dry continent. Of these 231, only 130 live all their lives in fresh water, yet some of the marine fish also spend part of their life cycle in fresh water.

CARTILAGINOUS FISHES

The skeleton of the cartilaginous fish is composed of cartilage or gristle, and instead of scales, some have smooth skins while most are covered in a rough skin with millions of protruding toothlike parts embedded in it. In sandy and silt-ridden parts of the sea, they can make use of a spiracle, or opening on top of the head, through which water is brought in and passed over the gills. Also, instead of a gill cover they have between five and seven slits through which water escapes once oxygen has been removed by the gills. This grouping includes sharks and rays.

SHARKS

Sharks can range in size from the 0.5-m cat sharks to the 18-m whale shark (*Rhincodon typus*). The larger ones have voracious appetites and occasionally aggressive behaviour, but on the whole they are timid when confronted by man. Some of them — especially the great white or white pointer, blue pointer, tiger, bull and perhaps hammerhead sharks — have been involved in attacks on humans, particularly along the eastern and southern coastlines of Australia. The first recorded encounter was in 1791 and, since then, there have been more than 200 fatalities and 300 people injured from shark attacks in Australian waters. However, when considered against other threats to human life, this figure is relatively small.

BLUE POINTER SHARK   The blue pointer shark (*Isurus glaucus*), also called the mako or mackerel shark, is distinguished by the deep blue colour of its back. It has a reputation for aggressive behaviour and is able to leap up to 6 m clear of the water.

BULL SHARK   The bull shark (*Carcharuns leucas*) is found in waters around Australia and there are recorded attacks on humans, making it, along with the great white and tiger sharks, among the most dangerous to people.

GREAT WHITE SHARK   The great white shark (*Carcharodon carcharias*) was common in Australia, although it is also found in most tropical and temperate seas of the world. Unfortunately, its numbers are now vulnerable because of overzealous hunting for sport and the trade in sharkfins. It can have as many as 200 teeth set in rows and has become well known, if a trifle hysterically, for attacks on humans.

GREY NURSE SHARK   Although harmless, the grey nurse (*Carcharias taurus*) is an endangered species due to many years of hunting by anglers and spearfishers. It has been a protected species since 1984.

HAMMERHEAD SHARK   The hammerhead (*Sphyrna lewini*) can grow up to 5 m and has been recorded in all states of Australia. It has a widened head and feeds on large fish. It is thought to be dangerous to man.

PORT JACKSON SHARK   The Port Jackson shark is from a primitive family of shark (*Heterodontus portusjacksoni*), of which Australia has two species. It is named for the place it was first seen by European settlers, Port Jackson in Sydney. It ranges around the southern coastline from Western Australia to Queensland. The Port Jackson shark eats molluscs, crustaceans and other small marine creatures.

TIGER SHARK The tiger shark (*Galeocerdo cuvier*) is named after the distinctive tiger stripe markings on the bodies of the young sharks. Their natural habitats are the cooler waters of offshore reefs. It has been known to attack humans.

WHALE SHARK Together with the basking shark (*Cetorhinus maximus*), the whale shark (*Rhincodon typus*) is the largest fish of the sea. It can reach a length of about 18 m. Most sharks have their mouths under their heads, but that of the whale shark is placed at the front, like that of the bony fishes. Ningaloo Reef off Western Australia is home to a significant colony of whale sharks.

RAYS

Most rays have wide pectoral fins and a long tail on which can be one or more serrated spines capable of causing extreme pain. They generally have blunt teeth for eating molluscs and are widespread in Australian waters.

LONG-TAILED RAY This particular ray (*Himantura uarnak*) is commonly found in many estuaries, sheltered bays and offshore waters in Queensland, the Northern Territory, Western Australia and New South Wales. It can reach 1.75 m across the fins and has a venomous spine on its tail.

MANTA RAY Manta rays are large, graceful, harmless creatures that often swim together in small groups. They can measure over 5 m across and, unlike most other rays, eat plankton which they sieve out of the water with whale-like gill rakers. They occur in the offshore waters of Queensland, the Northern Territory, Western Australia and New South Wales.

BONY FISHES

There are about 2700 species of bony fishes in Australia. All of them have a bone skeleton and their gills are covered by an operculum, which acts as a shield. Most are covered by scales, though some, such as eels, are not. Their body shapes vary enormously between species and their size can range from a few millimetres to up to 3 m. The majority of edible fish caught in Australia are bony fishes.

NORTHERN SPOTTED BARRAMUNDI   Also known as saratoga and gulf barramundi (*Scleropages jardini*), this fish is found in certain rivers in the Northern Territory and north Queensland. It can grow to nearly 1 m in length and weigh nearly 20 kg. Unusually, the female incubates the eggs she has laid in her mouth.

QUEENSLAND LUNGFISH   This fish belongs to the Ceratodontidae family, and there is only one species in Australia. Unlike other fishes, which take in oxygen from the water that passes over their gills, the Queensland lungfish (*Neoceratodus forsteri*) also has a pair of nostrils on its underside which enables it to come to the surface and gulp air directly. Originally found only in the Burnett and Mary rivers in south-eastern Queensland, it has now been introduced in other rivers as far south as the Tweed in New South Wales.

AUSTRALIAN SALMON   Actually a marine perch, the Australian salmon (*Arripis trutta*) was given the name by the early settlers because it resembled the salmon and was fine sport for anglers. It occurs around the southern coastline from southern Queensland to Geraldton in Western Australia, and is an important food fish since a mature salmon can weigh about 6 kg and shoals can contain as much as 12 000 tonnes of fish.

MURRAY COD   The most important freshwater food fish in Australia, the Murray cod (*Maccullochella peeli*) is also Australia's largest and can weigh up to 60 kg. It is found throughout the Murray–Darling river system and has been introduced into the Dawson and Mary rivers in Queensland, and the Clarence and Richmond rivers, the Burrinjuck and Burrendong Dams, and Lake Eucumbene in New South Wales.

CATFISH
There are two catfish families in Australia, the Ariidae (fork-tailed) and the Plotosidae (eel-tailed). The former occur round the northern coastline and the latter swim throughout the Murray–Darling system of rivers. Both kinds have sharp dorsal spines, a scaleless skin and the characteristic whiskers round the mouth, called barbels.

EELS
Eels are found in both salt and freshwater and there are more than 60 species in Australia. The long-tailed moray eel (*Thyrsoidea macrura*) can grow to 3.5 m long and is the largest reef eel in the world. The salt-water Australian conger eel (*Leptocephalus wilsoni*) usually lives in rock crevices. If surprised, like some of the other eels, it may bite. The serpent eel (*Ophisurus serpens*) is one of the group of snake eels, which are often as brightly coloured as land snakes.

JAWLESS FISHES

Hagfish and lamprey are distinguished from eels because they have no lower jaw, but instead use a ring of horny material which they attach to their prey. Lampreys are freshwater species and hagfish occur off the coast of southern and eastern Australia.

SEA SQUIRTS, ACORN-WORMS AND LANCELETS

As opposed to the vertebrates, these creatures possess a notochord, a stiffened structure, rather than a backbone, which is made of cartilage or bone. Sea squirts are perhaps the most well known and one species is the 'cunjevoi', which is used as bait.

ECHINODERMS

The name for this group is derived from the Greek *echinos*, meaning hedgehog, since so many are covered with spines. All live in the sea, are built radially and so have no definite head or tail. Their body wall is stiffened by calcareous plates and they also have tube feet which operate on hydraulic principles. Without well-defined eyes, they rely on sense organs to detect smell, light, taste, touch and the pull of gravity.

SEA STARS

Sea stars have five or more arms joined together into a star shape as well as hundreds of tube feet ending in suckers which help it grip firmly. The biscuit star and the sunstar are examples of this class, but the crown of thorns is probably the most well known and controversial. This latter species, which is an aggressive feeder, is spreading throughout the Great Barrier Reef in large numbers, and some experts feel it is destroying the delicate ecosystem of the living coral.

CROWN OF THORNS   One of the largest sea stars, the crown of thorns (*Acanthaster planci*) can reach 45 cm across its arms, which may number between seven and seventeen. Its spines are poisonous and it eats hard corals by enveloping them with its stomach and then absorbing the material using digestive enzymes, leaving the skeleton behind. A crown of thorns can eat an area about the size of its central disc every day.

Controversy began in 1962 when there was a population explosion of the sea stars on the Great Barrier Reef. Opinion is divided about whether they are likely to destroy the reef or whether the rise in their numbers is a natural phenomenon which will encourage species diversity by consuming the fast-growing corals.

SEA URCHINS

Many sea urchins have spines — some are wide and blunt like those of the slate pencil urchins; others are long and sharp, as in those of the needle urchins. Sea urchins have long tube feet and also pedicellariae, which are small jawed structures which prevent tiny creatures from settling between their spines.

FEATHER STARS

Feather stars have a central disc, made up of the mouth and stomach, to which is attached a number of thin arms with side branches which resemble feathers.

SEA CUCUMBERS

Also known as holothurian, trepang or bêche-de-mer, the sea cucumber is a long cylinder with a mouth at one end and an anus at the other. Some sea cucumber species eat by taking in sand and mud from the ocean floor, digesting the food material contained within and others by using tentacles to bring food to the mouth.

BRITTLE STARS

Also called snake stars, brittle stars are different to sea stars in that they have a more definite central disc and less obvious tube feet. They move by bending their arms but, if picked up, may drop a piece or the whole arm in the same way that geckoes can lose their tails.

Molluscs

There are about 10 000 known species of mollusc in Australia, most of which occur in the sea, some in freshwater and a few on land. Soft-bodied creatures, they form a shell around themselves for protection. In spite of a large number of body shapes, all molluscs have a skin fold, called the mantle, which secretes the shell.

Many molluscs have a strongly developed foot under their body, and some have a feeding rasp called a radula.

CHITONS

An ancient form of life, chitons live in the sea and feed off algae during the night. Their bodies are covered by eight pieces of shell held together by an encircling leathery band. Chitons are often called coat-of-mail shells.

GASTROPODS

Also called univalves, not all gastropods have shells, but when they do it is a single spiral one. Many species also have an operculum or shield for closing the shell when the animal withdraws into it.

CONE SHELLS

Of the genus *Conus*, the radula of the cone shell has been reduced to only a few individual teeth, which are stored in a sac. Each tooth is hollow and filled with poison and one is shot into the intended victim — species of snails or fishes. The venom kills quickly and can also be highly dangerous to humans.

LAND SNAILS

There are some 400 species of land snails in Australia and they are found throughout the mainland. Some eat plants while others are carnivorous, eating other snails and small creatures. Under very dry conditions, many secrete a heavy mucous to seal their operculum shut to retain moisture.

BIVALVES

In bivalves, two almost equal shells protect the soft animal inside and these shells are held together by an elastic ligament, like a hinge. There is also a strong muscle which allows the bivalve to close quickly when in danger. Bivalves are filter feeders.

OYSTERS

Australia has about ten species of oyster, but the ones with commercial value as food are the Sydney rock oyster (*Saccostrea commercialis*) and the Tasmanian oyster .

Pearls are secretions of mother-of-pearl built up round foreign bodies in their tissues. However, although clams, mussels, cockles and other bivalves will produce pearls, the best in Australia are obtained from two inedible species, the gold-lip oyster (*Pinctada maxima*) and the black-lip oyster (*Pinctada margaritifera*).

SCALLOPS

Scallops come from the genus *Pecten* and have one flat shell. The other, which lies on the sea floor, is convex. Most bivalves have lost their eyes, however, scallops have a line of rudimentary eyes which rim their mantle and sense shadow and changes in light. Scallops can move quite quickly by snapping their valves, or shells together, thus forcibly ejecting a controlled stream of water.

CEPHALOPODS

The foot of the cephalopod has been considerably modified so that some of it has become arms and some a siphon, with which jets of water are injected and ejected, partly to enable it to sense certain chemicals, and therefore food, in the water and partly to help it to swim faster. Some have kept the shell, in others it has disappeared altogether. Unlike most molluscs, the eyes of the cephalopods are as complex and well-developed as most mammals.

OCTOPUSES

All octopuses have eight arms and there are several species in Australian waters. All can inject venom into their prey and many can also eject a cloud of ink behind them which helps them hide and escape from predators. They are able to change colour more quickly and efficiently than almost any other creature in the animal kingdom. Most no longer have a shell.

The blue-ringed octopuses (*Hapalochlaena maculosus* and *Hapalochlaena lunulata*) can deliver a fatal bite to humans if handled and no antivenin has yet been developed. They live in rock pools around most of the temperate and warm temperate coastline, and measure about 10 cm across the extended tentacles. Their skin is a pinkish-brown, with irregular blue markings.

CUTTLEFISH

Cuttlefish have ten arms, two of which are longer than the others and have suckers on the ends to hold prey. They live in the open sea and often feed in large numbers at night.

Coelenterates

The word *coelenterata* comes from the Greek meaning 'hollow intestine'. These animals have an internal cavity surrounded by a body wall two cells deep, with a jelly-like substance in between. The inner layer digests food brought in through the mouth. The outer layer forms a protective skin with specialized cells containing stings, a coiled thread bathed in poison. These stinging cells can be present in large numbers and are used to capture prey or defend the animal against attack, and can be sufficiently strong to be extremely painful, even lethal, for humans.

HYDROZOA

An amazingly diverse group of animals belong to the class Hydrozoa, ranging from coral-like animals to the bluebottle or Portuguese man-of-war. The hydrozoan corals are only related very remotely to true coral.

PORTUGUESE MAN-OF-WAR   The best known of the Hydrozoans, the Portuguese man-of-war or bluebottle (*Physalia* sp.) has been thus named because it looks like a tiny blue galleon on the water. Its feeding tentacles, however, hang below the surface and prey on small animal life using powerful stinging cells. If onshore winds are blowing, particularly on to the east coast, they can become a painful, but not fatal, hazard for bathers.

JELLYFISH

Some jellyfish are freshwater species, although most live in estuaries or the sea. They can vary in size from a few centimetres across the bell to 2 m in diameter. The tentacles may be as much as 30 m long.

BOX JELLYFISH   There are two species of box jelly fish, but only one, the sea wasp (*Chironex fleckeri*), is found in Australian waters. It is one of the most dangerous of the stinging animals and is, in fact, deadly. Its quick-acting venom affects the heart and breathing, and rapidly break downs red blood cells. Its four-sided bell is usually not much more than 15 cm across, but at each corner hangs a 3-m long cluster of tentacles which are loaded with batteries of stinging cells. It is found generally in northern waters, from Broome in Western Australia to Gladstone in Queensland, particularly in summer when the strong south-easterly wind dies down.

ANTHOZOA

This is the general term for the class of marine animals which include sea anemones and corals. It means 'flower animal' and can be applied to either single coral polyps or large colonies, most of which have the typical coelenterate structure of a tissue bag surrounded at its open end by stinging tentacles.

SEA ANEMONES

Unlike jellyfish, the sea anemones are fixed by a basal disc to the sea reef or mud and their 'body' is a cylinder crowned by a mouth disc with stinging tentacles. Most sea anemones are brightly coloured and can be as beautiful as the corals. The largest species in Australia is *Stoichatus kenti*, a sea anemone found on the Great Barrier Reef and measuring up to 1 m across.

CORALS

Corals can be divided into two groups. The first are soft corals from the order Alcyonacea which have eight feathery tentacles and tiny, hard crystalline structures called sclerites in their tissues, these are more common on inshore reefs. The other are hard, or stony, corals from the order Scleractinia which have a white skeleton of limestone with six tentacles or more, in multiples of six. Some corals, such as the mushroom corals, live singly, but most are colonial with individual polyps gradually growing outwards and dividing into two. The type of life form is largely dependent on its position on the reef; availability of light and wave energy are the most important controls. Most corals also depend on the existence of minute plants, zooxanthellae, which live in the cells of the polyp tissues and which while consuming the polyp waste products, supply the coral with as much as 98% of its food requirements. Their presence greatly helps the rate at which the polyps can grow.

Crustaceans

Crustaceans have appendages on the head and often a horny carapace which covers the thorax. Several thousand species of crustacea are found in Australia and they are divided between eight subclasses. Perhaps the most familiar are in the subclass Malacostraca, which includes crabs, crayfish, prawns, shrimp and krill.

MALACOSTRACA

HERMIT CRABS
Hermit crabs use the empty shells of other molluscs to protect their soft abdomens.

LOBSTERS AND CRAYFISH
These are characterised by a long abdomen and a large tail fan. In addition to lobsters, the Balmain bug and Moreton Bay bug are also edible. Freshwater crayfish are sometimes called yabbies, and are now being commercially farmed as food.

TRUE CRABS
There are about 700 species of crab in Australia in both marine and freshwater environments. Included in this group are the aemaphore, ghost, soldier, box, blue swimmer and sponge crabs.

Arthropods

Arthropod means 'jointed foot', which is the main characteristic of the huge number of animals contained in this phylum. They dominate the sea, freshwater and land — there are more than 65 000 insect species so far classified in Australia and these outnumber all the other plants and animals. Unlike the vertebrates, they have no internal skeleton, but instead have a jointed outside covering called an exoskeleton which has to be moulted to allow for growth.

ARACHNIDS

Spiders, scorpions, mites and ticks are all included in this class, and all have two parts to their body: the cephalothorax (head and thorax) and the abdomen. They have no antennae and no wings, and almost all are carnivores.

SPIDERS

Classified in the subphylum Chelicerata, there are about 1700 species in Australia, most of which are endemic. They have eight legs and a number of simple eyes (usually eight but some have six), as well as a pair of fangs on the front of the head which are connected to a poison gland. All spiders are able to spin silk from spinnerets on their abdomen. Some use this for creating webs to catch their prey, some to line their burrows and others for throwing nets.

BIRD-EATING SPIDERS   There is one species of this group in Australia, *Selenotypus plumipes*, which is found in the Northern Territory and Queensland. It is Australia's largest species of spider and has been known to capture and eat small birds. Frogs are also an important part of its diet. They normally grow up to 150 mm in leg span width, although there is a recording of a specimen measuring 240 mm found in the Northern Territory.

FUNNEL-WEB SPIDERS   This group of spiders has two pairs of lungs and parallel down-pointing fangs which mean they have to rear up on their hind legs to strike. They usually live on the ground in burrows or silk-lined tubes under rocks and logs. Funnel-webs occur only in Australia and there are at least nine species belonging to the genus *Atrax*, of which the best known is the Sydney funnel-web (*Atrax robustus*), which is found from Newcastle in New South Wales along the wet coastal forests through to south-eastern Victoria. Its rapid-acting venom can be fatal to humans, but an effective antivenin was developed in 1981. Although its venom is not as poisonous as that of the redback spider if compared by volume, the funnel-web's larger size and correspondingly larger dose of venom mean it is regarded as more deadly.

NET THROWERS   These spiders are from the genus *Dinopis* and are found in the wet forest regions of Australia. They generally hunt at night by spinning a web which they hold between the two front pairs of legs. When the prey comes into range they spread the net wide and drop it over the victim.

REDBACK SPIDERS   The redback spider (*Latrodectus mactrans*) is found throughout Australia and is also distributed throughout the world: in New Zealand it is called the 'katipo' and, in America, the 'black widow'. The female measures about 10 mm along its abdomen and it is she, rather than the male, who bites. This can be extremely painful for humans and was lethal before an antivenin was discovered in 1956. The web of the redback is very strong and, although the usual prey are insects, sometimes large beetles, lizards and even house mice are killed. It is also an extremely common species and could be found in most gardens and parks throughout Australia. It prefers cool, damp places — hence, the redback on the toilet seat of the popular song.

SYDNEY TRAPDOOR SPIDER   Generally found in the gardens and bushland around Sydney and in the moist forests of eastern Australia, the trapdoor (*Dyarcyops fuscipes*) burrows into the earth and constructs a funnel of silk, the end of which is brought a few centimetres above the ground and sealed with a door of silk. It is often mistaken for the funnel-web, but is brown in colour as opposed to the shiny, almost plastic appearance of the Sydney funnel-web spider.

TICKS AND MITES

Ticks and mites are different from other arachnids in that their thorax and abdomen are fused and the mouth parts have been changed into a puncturing device. The mature animal has eight legs.

There are less than 2000 species of mite in Australia. Most are parasitic and live off liquid food from plants and other animals such as poultry, birds, grass and insect larvae. Some affect man and can cause severe itching.

Ticks are blood-feeding parasites; there are about 73 species in Australia. They live on wild and domestic animals, reptiles, birds and humans. They can transmit a number of diseases and some can cause paralysis. Those causing most problems are the scrub or paralysis tick (*Ixodes holocyclus*) and the cattle tick (*Boophilus microplus*).

SCORPIONS

There are about 30 species of scorpion in Australia and they belong to the Scorpionidea class. Their characteristic thin, segmented tail carries a poison gland at the tip and an injecting spine. They are nocturnal and eat insects, spiders, centipedes and other small animals, but if disturbed by man they can inflict a painful sting.

CENTIPEDES

The centipede has a long, segmented, flattened body and belongs to the Chilopida class. Each segment carries a pair of legs and, in the case of the leading section, these have been modified into poison jaws. The common species in Australia usually have about 50 pairs of legs. They are carnivorous and attack insects, small lizards and mice. Their bite is unlikely to produce more than a painful swelling in humans.

MILLIPEDES

Millipedes can be distinguished from the centipedes by their cylindrical rather than flat body and by the fact that each segment carries two pairs of legs. Also, the mouth parts lack poison glands and they feed on vegetable matter.

INSECTS

Insects are invertebrates with one pair of antennae and three pairs of jointed legs. The most successful class of animals, more than 700 000 species of insect have so far been classified in the world and there are at least three times this number waiting to be identified. So far, about 140 000 species have been classified in Australia. Insects live in huge numbers throughout the globe, in the air, on land and in fresh water, the only habitat they have not colonised successfully is the ocean.

Different insects use different ways of moving from egg to mature adult. Some hatch as a replica of the parent and others vary in shape and form as they go through different stages of development.

The following are a selection of the most interesting:

SILVERFISH
The silverfish comes from a primitive group of insects and has a segmented body covered in silvery scales. The domestic variety are pests. Others live in forest litter and under the bark of trees.

MAYFLIES
Mayflies come from the order Ephemeroptera and their life cycle makes them unique in the insect world. Once the nymph emerges from the egg in fresh water, it feeds and moults a number of times before rising to the surface of the water. Here, it throws off its skin and becomes a winged 'subimago' which, in a few minutes or hours, depending on the species,

moults again and becomes the fully mature adult. Mayflies are an important part of the diet of many freshwater fish and anglers often make replicas of them to act as lures for trout and other sporting fish.

DRAGONFLIES AND DAMSELFLIES
Belonging to the order Odonata, these are not true flies because they have two pairs of wings. Dragonflies rest with their wings held horizontally out from the body. There are 170 species in Australia. Damselflies are more delicate and hold their wings folded together, they are strong fliers and can reach speeds of 80 km/h. There are 100 species here.

Both dragonflies and damselflies prey on other insects on the wing, for this reason they have large eyes which cover most of the head.

COCKROACHES
There are about 450 species of cockroach in Australia, of the order Blattodea. They are generally nocturnal creatures, mostly inhabiting areas of natural vegetation, but about six introduced species have become domestic pests. The largest Australian species (*Macropanesthia rhinoceros*), from northern Queensland, can grow to 80 mm in length and weigh 30 g.

PRAYING MANTISES
Praying mantises are remarkable for the way in which they wait for prey with their long forelegs held folded, as if in prayer. Their total stillness is only broken when the victim comes in range and a rapid strike is made. There are more than 100 species widely distributed throughout Australia, but the most common is the green praying mantis (*Orthodera ministralis*).

EARWIGS
From the order Dermaptera, the earwig is a nocturnal creature, rarely seen during the day. Their most characteristic feature are the large forceps-shaped appendages on the tail. Most species are vegetarian, although some are omnivorous.

GRASSHOPPERS AND CRICKETS
The characteristics of this group, called Orthoptera are chewing mouthparts, large hind legs which enable them to jump powerfully and the ability to make a variety of sounds, especially at night, by rubbing one part of the body against another.

Long-horned grasshoppers are mainly vegetarian, most of them live in bushes and trees where they are well camouflaged. Males rub their forewings together to produce sound. Short-horned grasshoppers are ground dwellers, feeding on grasses and other plants. They are usually active during the day and make sound by rubbing their hind legs against a section of their forewings.

When food is plentiful, grasshoppers can cause great devastation by forming dense swarms, the Australian plague locust (*Chortoicetes terminifera*) can be a problem over much of the eastern half of Australia.

Crickets are usually brown or black in colour and generally nocturnal. They can be distinguished from grasshoppers by their long 'tails' and their front wings which lie flat on the back.

STICK INSECTS

These are large, long-legged, thin-bodied insects which are grey-green, grey-brown in colour and resemble twigs or leaves. From the order Phasmatodea, they feed on plant material and are generally solitary though swarms can occur. The longest Australian stick insect can be found on the east coast and is the *Acrophylla titan*, the female of which can grow to about 30 cm. The heaviest species of stick insect is the spiny leaf insect (*Extatosoma tiaratum*), which can weigh up to 30 g.

TERMITES

Although often called white ants, termites and ants are not closely related. There are more than 2000 species of termite in tropical, subtropical and temperate environments and about 250 species in Australia, mostly in northern Queensland, the Northern Territory and northern Western Australia. Using a complex social structure, they live in colonies, generally in mounds which may reach as high as 7 m and contain material weighing several tonnes. They feed on cellulose, often from wood, which, although it can be useful in breaking down forest debris, can also be highly destructive in human environments.

BUGS

In Australia, the word 'bug' describes insects of the Hemiptera order, which have the common characteristic of a sucking beak enabling them to pierce and draw up the juices from plant tissue. This group includes cicadas, aphids, plant hoppers, scale insects, psyllids, water boatmen, water scorpion, back-swimmers, water-striders, shield bugs and assassin bugs.

CICADAS   Well known for their shrill call, which is produced with a pair of membranes called tymbals situated on each side of the base of the abdomen, cicadas are often seen as a symbol of the Australian summer. Muscles vibrate these tymbals up to 500 times a second and the sound is then amplified through a resonating chamber behind. There are about 200 species in eastern Australia and they vary between 2 cm and 5 cm in length.

LACEWINGS

Lacewings belong to the Neuroptera order and they have two pairs of wings of almost equal length which have a beautiful network of fine veins. They also have long antennae, which helps to distinguish them from dragonflies; many fly rather weakly.

SCORPION-FLIES
The name of the scorpion-fly comes from species in the Northern Hemisphere, where the males have the tip of their abdomen curled over like a scorpion. They have long bodies, antennae, wings and long legs, the last of which are used for seizing prey. Some have an elaborate courtship where the male takes the body of its prey to the female.

FLIES
True flies belong to the Diptera order and have only one pair of wings, the second having been reduced to a pair of knobs called halteres. Their mouthparts are designed for sucking liquid. Diptera can be divided into two sub-orders: Nematocera, which have long antennae and whose adults are usually small, thin and delicate, living in damp or aquatic conditions. These include mosquitoes, midges and craneflies.

The second sub-order is the Brachycera, where the adults are usually larger and more strongly built, such as the housefly (*Musca dornestica*). This is an enormous order of insects; there are more than 6250 species in Australia, and they can have a significant effect on the health of humans and also that of domestic stock.

The sheep blowfly (*Lucila cuprirul*) causes many problems with sheep. The larvae, which hatch from the eggs laid by the fly, feed on the animal. The wound then attracts other species, which extend the infestation.

FLEAS
From the order Siphonaptera, fleas have a flattened narrow body with large hind legs used to jump onto a host, either mammals or birds. Their mouthparts-have been adapted to suck blood as food. Fleas carried bubonic plague from rats to man and also acted as carriers of myxomatosis from sick to healthy rabbits.

MOTHS AND BUTTERFLIES
Moths and butterflies belong to the order Lepidoptera and form the second largest insect order, after beetles. There are more than 11 000 species in Australia made up of six families of butterflies and more than 70 families of moths. Most feed on liquids such as nectar and have a long proboscis for this purpose which coils up under the head when not in use. The wings and body of the adults are covered in small scales which are really modified hairs. It is these scales which give the creatures their often brilliant colours. Butterflies generally fold their wings vertically above their body while moths hold them out horizontally. Butterflies tend to be active during the day, while moths are usually nocturnal, and butterflies are generally more

delicate and brightly coloured than moths. Their antennae are generally 'clubbed' at the ends, while those of moths are feathery. All butterflies and moths go through a life cycle of four stages: egg, larva (caterpillar), pupa (chrysalis) and adult.

The Hercules moth (*Coscinocera hercules*) is Australia's largest moth, with a wing span of 24 cm. It belongs to the Saturnidae family and is found in northern Queensland. One of the swallowtail butterflies of the family Papilionidae, the Ulysses butterfly (*Papilio ulysses*) is a large, iridescent blue and velvet black species found in the rainforests of far north Queensland. The Cape York birdwing (*Ornithoptera priamus*) is Australia's largest butterfly. It has distinctive lime green and black markings, and has a wing span of up to 140 mm.

ANTS, BEES AND WASPS
Ants, bees and wasps belong to the order Hymenoptera and tend to have a characteristic 'wasp waist' between the first and following segments of the abdomen. The forewings are usually larger than the hind wings, some do not possess wings at all. On the whole they possess a strong social behaviour.

ANTS   Australia has about 1500 species of ant, representing about 10% of the world total. Their social structure includes three castes: females (both winged and wingless); males (winged); and workers (wingless and neuter). The average size of an ant colony in Australia is about 2000 ants. The most primitive living ant (*Nothomyrmecia macrops*) occurs in Australia. It is a pale brown, nocturnal creature about 10 mm long and is thought to resemble a species which lived about 80 million years ago.

Most pest species, such as the Argentine ant, the black house ant and the hospital ant, have been introduced.

BEES   There are about 3000 species of bees in Australia. They feed their young on nectar and pollen and are generally solitary in behaviour, the female makes a burrow in soil, wood or plant stem in which to rear her young. Some, however, are social and create nests with a queen and many workers. Usually, they have hairy legs for gathering pollen and a long tongue for gathering nectar.

Members of the genus *Trigona* are small, stingless, social bees and are found in the northern half of Australia. Their honey is much prized by Aboriginal peoples as food. The introduced honey bee (*Apis mellifera*) is now widespread throughout southern Australia.

WASPS   Australia has about 6000 species of wasp, some of which, like bees, are social creatures, others are not. Once a burrow or nest has been built, a wasp hunts for prey (usually spiders, flies, grasshoppers or beetles) stings and then stores them as food for their larvae. Two of the best known nest-builders are the paper wasp, which uses wood and bark to make its nest, and the mason wasp, which uses mud to create 'cells' in the nest.

BEETLES

This order of insects, the Coleoptera, makes up one-third of all the known species of animals: 40% of all insects are beetles. In Australia alone, there are some 20 000 species, living mostly on the ground — although some live in fresh water.

The front pair of wings of most beetles are hard and act as covers for the more delicate hind wings. They also protect the softer parts of the body from dry air in arid areas. All beetles have chewing mouthparts and the majority feed at night.

PERIPATUS

Peripatus look like a kind of worm, but have some of the characteristics of the jointed-legged arthropods and some of the segmented worms. There are at least five species in Australia.

SEGMENTED WORMS

Called annelids, these worms have marked sections which can be seen both inside and outside and well-developed nervous and circulatory systems. They are found on land, in fresh water and in the sea. Leeches belong to this group.

MOSS ANIMALS

Most of these tiny creatures live in the sea inside a protective shell. The moss animals can form large colonies and some species cause fouling on ships' hulls.

ROUND WORMS

Some of these cylindrical, unsegmented worms are free-living, others are parasites who live on crops, domestic animals and man. There are enormous numbers present in soil.

RIBBON WORMS

These are flat, unsegmented worms which are carnivorous and have a long proboscis which can be extruded over victims.

FLATWORMS

Included in this phylum are the tapeworms, flukes and planarians. Some of the flatworms are free-living, while some are parasitic and can cause serious health problems in both humans and stock.

SPONGES

The body wall of a sponge is made up of two layers, in this wall are small holes called pores. The pores help to circulate water which supplies the animal with food and oxygen. Some sponges are freshwater but most are marine.

PROTOZOANS

These animals consist of only one cell. They are found in all habitats, those which cause disease are popularly called microbes.

Dangerous Animals

Australia is well stocked with dangerous creatures; it has more venomous species of snakes than any other continent and its spiders are among the most poisonous in the world. Usually these animals only become aggressive towards humans if they are attacked or disturbed in some way. The following, however, are some of the animals that should be treated with extreme care:

BOX JELLYFISH OR SEA WASP   Found in tropical waters from Broome, Western Australia, to Gladstone, Queensland.

BUSH TICKS   Found in the rainforests of eastern Australia.

CONE SHELLS   Found in the northern waters from Brisbane, Queensland, to Geraldton, Western Australia.

CROCODILES   Estuarine or saltwater, found in coastal rivers and swamps of northern and north-eastern Australia.

FISH   Porcupine fish, puffer fish (widespread), stonefish (northern waters from Brisbane, Queensland, to Geraldton, Western Australia), stingray (widespread).

OCTOPUSES Blue-ringed or blue-banded (widespread).

PLATYPUSES Eastern Australia from Cape York to south-west Victoria.

SHARKS Great white, blue pointer, tiger, bull, possibly hammerhead — generally found in the eastern and southern waters of Australia.

SNAKES Broad-headed (east coast of Australia), taipan (northern Australia), death adder (widespread except southern Victoria, south-western South Australia and Tasmania), tiger (southern Australia and Tasmania), brown (different areas according to species), king brown or mulga (widespread), copperhead (south-eastern Australia and Tasmania), red-bellied black (eastern Australia), sea snake (mostly around Ashmore Reef in the Timor Sea).

SPIDERS Sydney funnel-web (160 km in and around Sydney, New South Wales), redback (widespread).

State Faunal Emblems

State or Territory	Faunal Emblem
New South Wales	Platypus (*Ornithorhynchus anatinus*)
	Kookaburra (*Dacelo novaeguineae*)
Victoria	Leadbetter's possum
	(*Gymnobelideus leadbeateri*)
	Helmeted honeyeater
	(*Lichenostomus melanops cassidix*)
Queensland	Koala (*Phascolarctos cinereus*)
	Brolga (*Grus rubicunda*)
South Australia	Hairy-nosed wombat
	(*Lasiorhinus latifrons*)
Western Australia	Numbat (*Myrmecobius fasciatus*)
	Black swan (*Cygnus atratus*)
Tasmania	No official emblems
	Unofficial:
	Thylacine (*Thylacinus cynocephalus*)
	or Tasmanian devil (*Sarcophilus harrisii*)
Northern Territory	Red kangaroo (*Macropus rufus*)
	Wedge-tailed eagle (*Aquila audax*)
Australian Capital Territory	Gang-gang cockatoo
	(*Callocephalon fimbriatum*)

Endangered Vertebrate Fauna

The following list of endangered vertebrate fauna was last amended in 1995. There are more than 100 000 endangered invertebrates, many of which have not yet been classified, and have not been included in the following list. Many of these have not been sighted for up to 100 years and are probably extinct.

MAMMALS Burrowing bettong (boodie), brush-tailed bettong (woylie), northern bettong, desert rat-kangaroo, central hare-wallaby, rufous hare-wallaby, eastern hare-wallaby, banded hare-wallaby, toolache wallaby, bridled nailtail wallaby, crescent nailtail wallaby, Proserpine rock wallaby, broad-faced potoroo, long-footed potoroo, Leadbeater's possum, northern hairy-nosed wombat, pig-footed bandicoot, western barred bandicoot, desert bandicoot, greater bilby (dalgyte), lesser bilby, thylacine (Tasmanian tiger), numbat, Julia Creek dunnart, long-tailed dunnart, sandhill dunnart.

RODENTS White-footed rabbit-rat, lesser stick-nest rat, greater stick-nest rat, short-tailed hopping mouse, northern hopping-mouse, dusky hopping-mouse, long-tailed hopping-mouse, big-eared hopping-mouse, Darling Downs hopping-mouse, Alice Springs mouse, Shark Bay mouse, false water-rat, central rock-rat.

WHALES Blue whale, humpback whale, southern right whale.

BIRDS Gould's petrel, providence petrel, Abbott's booby, Christmas Island frigatebird, red goshawk, plains-wanderer, Lord Howe Island woodhen, Cocos buff-banded rail, lesser noddy, little tern, Norfolk Island parrot, Coxen's fig parrot, night parrot, orange-bellied parrot, ground parrot, Alexandra's parrot, golden-shouldered parrot, hooded parrot, paradise parrot, Norfolk Island boobook owl, Christmas Island hawk-owl, plumed frogmouth, noisy scrub-bird, purple-crowned fairy-wren, Carpentarian grass-wren, thick-billed grass-wren, western bristlebird, eastern bristlebird, rufous bristlebird, Lord Howe Island currawong, western whipbird, 40-spotted pardalote, Norfolk Island silvereye, helmeted honeyeater, black-eared miner, Gouldian finch, northern scrub robin, Norfolk Island thrush.

AMPHIBIANS Round frog, Mt Baw Baw frog, platypus (gastric-brooding) frog, gastric-brooding frog, elegant microhylid, rock-dwelling microhylid, long-nosed tree frog.

REPTILES   Luth or leathery turtle, western swamp tortoise, lined burrowing skink, Lancelin Island striped skink, pedra branca skink, bronze-backed legless lizard, worm snake, black-striped snake, broad-headed snake.

CARTILAGINOUS FISHES   Grey nurse and great white sharks.

FISHES   Swan galaxias, Clarence galaxias, Lake Eacham rainbow fish, eastern freshwater cod, trout cod.

Source: Australian National Parks and Wildlife Service

4

Environment

*T*he environment and its protection play an essential role in day-to-day life in Australia. Australia is at the forefront of international innovation in environmentally based government projects and policies and is renowned for its conservation of both flora and fauna. Despite this, Australia still faces the same environmental problems as other countries that support industry, development and technology.

Environmental issues became a major concern in the 1970s and 1980s when individuals, lobby groups and organisations became increasingly aware of pollution to Australia's water, air and the gradual degradation of land. Widespread outrage and concern over the destruction of rainforest and wilderness areas led to the declaration of several World Heritage listings. The Great Barrier Reef became a protected area following demands for its preservation by the public. By 1982, more than 1100 national conservation groups had more than 600 000 members, exceeding the membership of all political parties combined.

Current contentious issues include woodchipping and deforestation; erosion and salinisation of land and the resultant soil deficiency or infertility; marine pollution and preservation of indigenous land and sacred sites at the expense of mining contracts.

Some Issues

ECOLOGICALLY SUSTAINABLE DEVELOPMENT

In 1989, a meeting of Australian conservation groups, unions and industry worked with the government to generate a discussion paper on ecologically sustainable development (ESD). They defined it as 'using, conserving and enhancing the community's resources so that ecological processes, on which life depends, are maintained, and the total quality of life, now and in the future, can be increased'.

The national ESD plan aims to guide the development of natural resources according to four general rules:

- Economic considerations must be balanced against environmental considerations when formulating policies and undertaking development.
- Environmental resources must be adequately valued, ensuring that resources will be available for future generations.
- Decisions made about the management of resources must be conservative when dealing with issues of risk and irreversibility.
- The worldwide scale of resource management issues must be taken into consideration.

NATIONAL LANDCARE PROGRAM

In the 1980s, soil conservation was recognised as a major issue; it was at this time that the National Landcare Program (NLP) was implemented. With the sustainable management of all resources as its ultimate aim, the NLP is open to contributions from the farming and industrial sectors, governments and the conservation movement, the community and land and water managers.

There are three areas to the program:
• community-based policies and programs dealing with natural resources;
• Federal, State and Territory governments' joint arrangements on natural resources management issues; and
• research and development undertaken by the government on issues of national concern.

Some of the major issues tackled by the NLP include catchment management, salinity, water and land resource management, vegetation protection and regeneration and the conservation of biological diversity. The One Billion Trees and Save the Bush schemes have resulted in the planting or regeneration of about 550 million trees.

The NLP originally set a target of 22 000 Landcare groups to be established by the end of the 1990s. This target was reached in 1994, and more than 325 000 people are now involved in Landcare: an estimated 28% of pastoral farmers and 19% of dairy farmers are active members.

In conjunction with the Surfrider Foundation and Dune, the NLP also released the results of a major study of Australian beaches in 1996. It found that they were under serious threat from development, stormwater pipes and litter. In addition, about three billion litres of sewage effluent are discharged near the beaches each day, with about 22% of the ocean outfalls discharging only slightly treated effluent.

About 1612 beaches were included in the survey which signalled the dangers of coastal development without limits. As the coast from Adelaide around to Cairns is in the process of becoming a string of suburbs, the study also highlighted beaches where sand dunes had completely disappeared under marinas, golf courses, resorts and other constructions. Between 1974 and 1989, for example, 33% of the bushland along the southeast Queensland coast was lost.

RECYCLING

Recycling is one of the most significant ways to reduce the negative effects of bulk wastage disposal. In Australia, recycling is the responsibility of the individual, but there are incentives offered by government and industry to do so. The main articles recycled are glass, paper, aluminium, plastics, food scraps and clothing. Individual municipal councils have kerbside collection schemes and neighbourhood drop-off facilities which encourage active recycling practices. According to the 1992 Federal government's National Waste Management and Recycling Strategy, the following targets for recycling were set for 1996 (most were attained by 1994):

Type of product	Amount recycled
Paper packaging	71%
Newsprint	40%
Glass	45%
Aluminium cans	65%
Steel cans	25%
Plastic containers	25%
Paperboard liquid containers	20%

In 1994, of the 2.7 billion aluminium cans sold, 1.73 billion or 65% were collected or returned for recycling, an increase of 54% since 1973, when aluminium recycling was introduced into Australia.

Of the 3 million tonnes of paper consumed in Australia in 1994, 1.2 million tonnes was collected for recycling. Sydney households reduced their weekly solid waste from 21.6 kg in 1993 to 18.6 kg in 1995. With recent changes to the paper manufacturing industry, the percentage of recycled material has increased dramatically. Other recycling percentages for 1994 include: PET plastic bottles, 29%; glass products, 45%.

ECOTOURISM

Ecotourism is the largest tourism growth industry in Australia, with visitors flocking to Australia's national parks and other reserves to see the unique flora and fauna and enjoy the relatively unspoilt landscape. Many of these areas are fragile, however, and cannot sustain the developments that inevitably come with large tourist numbers without losing the very qualities that visitors come to experience. Few of the businesses contribute to the maintenance of the natural environments they utilise. The industry's challenge is to find a balance between encouraging tourists and protecting the environment.

To this end, an Ecotourism Code of Environmental Conduct has been formulated. This code recognises that planning and effective management of developments, regular monitoring of environmental indicators and the imposition of necessary constraints on visitors are all factors that must be be addressed at all times.

CLEAN UP AUSTRALIA DAY

In 1989, the first Clean Up Australia Day exercise took place in the form of Clean up Sydney Harbour. Now an annual event, the concept was put forward by Ian Kiernan, 1994's Australian of the Year. The idea has expanded to become a nationwide day set aside for volunteers to clean up the land, sea and rivers of human-made pollution: about 500 000 people cleaned up over 8000 sites in 1994. The scheme's popularity has since spread to over 80 countries worldwide, with approximately 30 million people taking part in Clean up the World Day in 1993.

The Greenhouse Effect

The greenhouse effect is not a new phenomenon, but a permanent feature of our planet that is being boosted by gases produced by human activities. Named by a Swedish chemist who coined the term 'greenhouse effect' in 1896, it describes the warming of the earth caused by 'greenhouse gases' such as carbon dioxide and methane. These gases form a 'thermal blanket' around the earth, allowing some sunlight to reach the planet's surface, but preventing some of the infra-red or heat radiation given off by the earth from escaping into space.

Although greenhouse gases make up a very small part of the total volume of the atmosphere, they can have a significant effect on it.

CONTRIBUTING FACTORS TO THE GREENHOUSE EFFECT

Over the past century, there has been a steady rise in carbon dioxide in the atmosphere due to fossil fuel burning (including carbon dioxide emissions from cars) and increased human population and activity. The surface warming of the Earth due to carbon dioxide, would lead to more evaporation of water and more water vapour, the dominant greenhouse gas. With an ability to absorb heat energy, increases in water vapour would produce a greater greenhouse warming effect, as would methane, emitted largely as a result of the boom in world population, as well as animal digestion, coal mines and natural gas fields, swamps and other areas with decaying or dead matter.

Australia's relatively high dependence on fossil fuels (compared with other developed nations), the lack of nuclear power and the limited opportunities for hydro-electricity generation all restrict the available options to reduce ozone depleting emissions. The energy sector is the largest contributor to greenhouse gas emissions, with motor vehicles contributing 18%; almost double that of industry.

As a co-signatory of international ozone protection treaties such as Vienna Convention for the Protection of the Ozone Layer (1989), Montreal Protocol on Substances that Deplete the Ozone Layer (1990) and the Framework Convention on Climatic Change (1992), Australia is committed to the reduction in levels of ozone depleting gases and has pledged to reduce its gas emissions in line with international recommendations by the turn of the century. The National Greenhouse Gas Inventory (1994), however, indicated that carbon dioxide emissions are on the increase, and that Australia will not meet the target of a cut in emissions to 20% below the 1988 levels by 2005, if the government does not enforce a more stringent policy.

In 1995, the Australian government placed a blanket ban on the manufacture and importation of equipment which produced harmful chlorofluorocarbon (CFC) gases.

Biodiversity

The loss of biological diversity is one of the nation's most urgent environmental problems. Since European settlement, Australia has lost an estimated 75% of its rainforests, and about 40% of its total forest area. Almost 70% of native vegetation has been removed or modified for agriculture, urban development and forestry since 1788. The rate of land clearance has rapidly accelerated, with as much clearing done during the past 50 years as in the 150 years before that. It continues at a rate of more than 600 000 hectares each year, with most destruction taking place in New South Wales and Queensland.

The pastoral industry covers about 70% of the continent, with grazing is believed to be partly responsible for the extinction of 34 plant species. In the past 50 years, 463 exotic plant species have been introduced as pasture. While only 5% of exotic species have proved viable as fodder, 13% have become problem weeds. Plant species not native to Australia now account for about 15% of our total flora and are spreading at an alarming rate.

There is currently no national legislation addressing biodiversity. The 1995 national Strategy for the Conservation of Australia's Biological Diversity, however, is a positive step.

FAUNA EXTINCTION RATES

In 1996, the World Conservation Union (IUCN) released its Red List of endangered animals throughout the world. It named 58 Australian mammals, 45 birds, 37 reptiles, 25 amphibians, 27 fishes and 281 invertebrates which are either critically endangered, endangered or vulnerable. For those groups for which there is sufficient information to assess the current state, the trends are disturbing. Some 5% of Australia's higher plants, 9% of birds, 23% of marsupials, 7% of reptiles, 16% of amphibians and 9% of freshwater fish are extinct, endangered or vulnerable.

Australia's record of mammal species extinctions is the worst for any country: 50% of the world's mammal extinctions over the past 200 years have been Australian species. In the past two centuries, the country has lost ten of 144 species of original marsupial fauna and eight of the 53 species of native rodents. There are only about 65 northern hairy-nosed wombats (*Lasiorhinus kreftii*) left in the world, while only a few hundred western barred bandicoots (*Parameles bougainville*) remain, along with just 200 orange-bellied parrots (*Neophema chrysogaster*), which breed in Tasmania, and about 100 western swamp turtles (*Pseudemydura umbrina*), which are found in two small swamps near Perth, Western Australia.

Feral pests or introduced animals have rapidly multiplied in the wild and pose an enormous threat to native plants and animals. About 18 exotic mammals have become feral: wild dogs, feral cats, pigs, foxes, goats and rabbits are just some of these. Estimates of feral cat numbers range between 3.8 and 18.4 million, with a single average-sized cat needing to consume about 2188 birds or animals each year to survive. Feral pests also threaten native animal populations by competing for scarce resources.

Some marine species such as whales and seals, which were hunted in Australian waters until recently, now show signs of recovery. Dugong numbers, however, have dropped by half in the past eight years, while the southern bluefin tuna and great white shark both face extinction. The latter was given protected species status in Tasmania in 1996 and has been nominated for listing under the national *Endangered Species Protection Act*. Certainly humans are proving to be far more lethal to the great white than it is to us. Myths of shark attack abound, but the truth is that of the 127 000 people who die in Australia each year, just one is the victim of shark attack. The great white is not even to blame for every attack. An Australian is more likely to die from a lightning strike or a bee sting, yet the hunting of the great white shark for sport and shark fins continues.

International Treaties & Conventions

Australia plays a contributing role in the development of and adherence to international treaties and conventions relating to the environment. Australia is a party to the following treaties and conventions:
• Antarctic Treaty (signed by Australia in 1961)

- Convention for the Protection of the World Cultural and Natural Heritage (1975)
- Convention on the Nature in the South Pacific (1990)
- International Convention for the Regulation of Whaling (1948)
- UN Convention on the Law of the Sea (1982)
- Convention on Early Notification of a Nuclear Accident (1987)
- Treaty Banning Nuclear Weapons Testings in the Atmosphere, in Outer Space and Under Water (1963)
- International Convention for the Prevention of Pollution from Ships (1988)
- International Convention on the Prevention of Marine Pollution by Dumping of Wastes and Other Matter (London Dumping Convention) (1985)
- Basel Convention on the Transborder Movement of Hazardous Waste (1992)
- Convention on Wetlands of International Importance (1975)
- Convention on Trade of Endangered Species or Wild Fauna and Flora (1976)
- International Plant Protection Convention (1952)
- Vienna Convention for the Protection of the Ozone Layer (1989)
- Montreal Protocol on Substances that Deplete the Ozone Layer (1990)
- Convention on Biological Diversity (1993)
- UN Framework Convention on Climatic Change (1994)
- Basel Convention to Ban International Trade in Toxic Waste (1994)
- Non-proliferation of Nuclear Weapons Treaty.

Major Organisations

AUSTRALIAN NATURE CONSERVATION AGENCY

Formerly the Australian National Parks and Wildlife Service, the Australian Nature Conservation Agency (ANCA) is the Federal government's main nature conservation authority. Working cooperatively with State and Territory governments, the ANCA utilises the Endangered Species and Feral Pests Programs along with the National Reserves System, and assists and advises community groups. Under the authority of four Acts of Parliament, the ANCA manages marine wildlife, and regulates the import and export of wildlife. As the Australian administrator of a number of international agreements, the agency also regulates whaling, the conservation of wetlands, protection of migratory species and nature conservation in the South Pacific.

The ANCA manages about 18 conservation areas, some jointly with their traditional owners. These areas and reserves include marine parks in the Coral Sea and Indian Ocean, along with Kakadu, Uluru-Kata Tjuta, Jervis Bay and Christmas and Norfolk Islands national parks.

The ANCA also supports scientific research and the documentation of native flora and fauna through the Australian Biological Resources Study, monitoring wildlife and plant populations, and formulating strategies for their long-term management.

COMMONWEALTH ENVIRONMENT PROTECTION AGENCY

The Commonwealth Environment Protection Agency (CEPA) is an agency of the Commonwealth Department of Environment, Sport and Territories. Interacting with other government agencies, it aims to ensure a uniform approach to the protection of Australia's environment.

CEPA is concerned with issues such as air pollution, waste minimisation, water quality and the related issue of waste dumping at sea, and the safe management of hazardous waste, contaminated sites, biotechnology and agricultural and industrial chemicals. It is also involved in coordinating national ozone protection projects, assisting in the development of an Australian environment technologies industry, and running programs for industry which show the financial and environmental benefits of product and production redesign. CEPA also conducts Environmental Impact Assessments and administers the National Pollutant Inventory which compiles details of pollutants within the Australian environment.

GREENING AUSTRALIA

Greening Australia is a national, community-based organisation working to save and restore native vegetation and repair and protect land and water resources. Greening Australia implements the Commonwealth government's 1989 One Billion Trees (OBT) Program. Under the program, Greening Australia raises community awareness, provides practical advice and helps groups with information and resources for local projects.

In 1993–1994, the OBT contract was for $4.3 million and Greening Australia raised another $9.7 million through sponsorship, by providing consultancy services, from membership fees, merchandising, linking employment programs to vegetation and environmental repair work, and from other State and Commonwealth programs. For every $1 of the $14 million received, Greening Australia generated $5 more from contributions in time, materials and financial support made by individuals and communities to facilitate vegetation works worth more than $70 million.

The One Billion Trees Program has stimulated a massive growth in revegetation, the number of groups supported by Greening Australia, the area of land and waterways being protected, and public awareness of the need to address and reverse Australia's vegetation loss.

AUSTRALIAN CONSERVATION FOUNDATION

The Australian Conservation Foundation (ACF) is an independent, non-profit membership-based organisation which works to achieve positive solutions to environmental problems. The ACF's work program includes environmental campaigning, research and policy development, green investment, paper recycling and promotion of public awareness. The ACF has 70 full-time staff and is supported by a team of volunteers and a membership in excess of 22 000 people.

Major ACF achievements include:
- assisting in the establishment of the Great Barrier Reef as a marine park and World Heritage area;
- campaigning for the establishment of Kakadu as a national park and World Heritage area;
- in association with the Wilderness Society, the successful campaign which stopped the damming of the Franklin River, Tasmania (1983);
- the establishment of World Heritage areas in the tropics and Tasmania;
- an alliance with The National Farmer's Federation which won $320 million in federal funds for a ten-year land management program (1989);
- an instrumental role in persuading the Australian Government to adopt the target of reducing greenhouse gas emissions by 20% by the year 2005.

GREENPEACE

Founded in 1971, Greenpeace is now the world's largest environmental organisation with nearly five million supporters and offices in 30 countries. In Australia, Greenpeace has over 90 000 supporters. Though well known for its non-violent direct actions, such as manoeuvring inflatable boats between whales and whaling ships, most of Greenpeace's battles are won behind the scenes, with much time and effort spent lobbying governments and corporations and gathering scientific evidence.

Greenpeace's achievements include actions which encouraged the halting of French nuclear testing in the Pacific; and advocacy against large-scale driftnetting, which threatens dolphins and other marine creatures, leading towards the practice being declared illegal by the UN. Nets once 50 km long are now just 4–5 km long. Other victories include the 1991 decision to impose a 50-year ban on mining in Antarctica; successfully working with local groups to protect Jervis Bay (New South Wales) from development; exposing an oil company's illegal ocean discharges and forcing technology changes at its refinery in Sydney; the establishment of the Southern Ocean Whale Sanctuary (currently under threat from Japanese 'scientific' whaling) and the prevention of offshore oil drilling at Ningaloo Reef (Western Australia), where the whale shark is found.

Greenpeace's goals for the future include the protection of biodiversity with its campaign against rainforest destruction; protecting the marine environment from driftnetting, overfishing and commercial whaling; protecting the atmosphere by campaigning for a reduction in the burning of fossil fuels; stopping toxic pollution by encouraging the production of goods and services without the use or inclusion of toxic substances, including chlorine; halting international trade in toxic waste, and stopping the nuclear threat with campaigns targeting the nuclear industry, nuclear disarmament, uranium mining, reprocessing and waste disposal.

WILDERNESS SOCIETY

Established in 1976, the Wilderness Society has played a key role in the preservation of millions of hectares of Australian wilderness. The Society received international acclaim for its 1983 protest against the damming of Tasmania's Franklin River. Successful campaigns for the protection of threatened areas have been carried out in relation to Kakadu in the Northern Territory, South Australia's Kangaroo Island and Shark Bay in Western Australia. The passing of wilderness legislation in New South Wales, Victoria and South Australia was, in part, a response to advocacy from the Wilderness Society.

The current national campaigns focus on native forests, under threat from the woodchip export industry; Cape York in Queensland, a biologically diverse area; outback and Commonwealth wilderness areas; community education, and liaising and coordinating campaigns with overseas conservation groups.

National Parks & Nature Conservation Reserves

There are a total of 461 national parks in Australia. The area covered is 22 311 609 hectares or about 2.9% of the land surface of Australia. In addition to this, 41 240 760 hectares are reserved as marine and estuarine protected areas (MEPAs).

The first official national park was established in 1879 - the Royal National Park near Sydney. The greatest development of national parks has occurred since the 1950s. In 1967, the National Parks and Wildlife Service was established by the New South Wales government, and other States soon followed. In 1975, the Commonwealth government set up the Australian National Parks and Wildlife Service (ANPWS), now replaced by the Australian Nature Conservation Agency (ANCA).

National park status can only be revoked by a resolution in both Houses of Parliament.

AUSTRALIA'S MAJOR NATIONAL AND CONSERVATION PARKS

The following shows the area of different parks in each State along with their principal features. This is followed by a listing of national parks of 10 000 hectares or more in that State. Marine and estuarine protected area (MEPA) figures include elements of reserves which are primarily land (terrestrial).

NEW SOUTH WALES

Designation	Area (ha)	Number
National parks	3 322 321	92
Nature reserves	586 917	207
State recreation areas	86 330	12
Aboriginal areas	11 505	5
Historic sites	2 616	13
Marine and estuarine protected areas	100 803	8

Name	Area (ha)	Principal Features
Banyabba	12 560	Undisturbed catchment
Barrington Tops	39 121	Subalpine woodland, temperate rainforest
Blue Mountains	247 021	Sandstone gorges, eucalypt forest
Border Ranges	31 508	Rim of volcanic caldera, rainforest
Brisbane Water	11 372	Coastal inlets, sandstone flora
Budawang	16 106	Budawang Range
Bundjalung	17 679	Coastal heaths and lagoons
Deua	81 821	Forested ranges, wild river, limestone caves
Dharug	14 834	Sandstone scenery, Aboriginal rock engravings
Gibraltar Range	17 273	Granite ranges, heaths, swamps
Goulburn River	69 875	River and sandstone

Name	Area (ha)	Principal Features
Guy Fawkes River	35 630	Meandering river
Kajuligah	13 660	Belah open woodland
Kanangra Boyd	68 276	Gorges, caves, wilderness, Boyd Plateau
Kinchega	44 180	Darling River, lakes, water fowl
Kosciuszko	647 837	Alpine and subalpine flora, glaciated landscape
Ku-ring-gai Chase	14 837	Sandstone plateau, flat rock engravings
Macquarie Marshes	18 031	Wetlands, river red gum
Mallee Cliffs	57 969	Mallee flora and fauna
Marramarra	11 759	Hawkesbury River, mangroves
Mootwingee	68 912	Semi-arid woodland, mulga, Aboriginal sites
Morton	162 674	Sandstone gorges, Shoalhaven
Mount Kaputar	36 817	Extinct volcano
Mungo	27 847	Evidence of over 40 000 years of human occupation
Myall Lakes	31 562	Coastal lakes and dunes, heaths
Nadgee	17 116	Coastal heath, eucalypt forest
Nattai	47 504	Sandstone plateau, wilderness, rare plant species
New England	29 985	Escarpment, subtropical rainforest
Nocoleche	74 000	Wetlands, channels of Paroo, Cuttaburra Rivers
Nombinnie	70 000	Mallee flora and fauna
Nymboida	18 998	Wild river, wilderness
Oxley Wild Rivers	90 414	Wild rivers, deep gorges, waterfalls, rainforest
Pilliga	75 910	Forested plains
Round Hill	13 629	Mallee flora and fauna
Royal	15 069	Sandstone, heaths, rainforest
Solitary Islands	85 000	Seabird sanctuary
Sturt	310 634	Gibber desert, cliffs
Tinderry	12 796	Granite peaks
Wadbilliga	77 009	Brogo wilderness
Warrumbungle	21 715	Volcanic landscape, rock pinnacles
Washpool	27 715	Rainforest, waterfalls, wilderness
Willandra	19 386	Flood plains, water courses
Winburndale	10 047	Forest remnant
Wollemi	488 060	Sandstone plateau, volcanic outcrops, wilderness

Name	Area (ha)	Principal Features
Yathong	107 241	Mallee flora and fauna
Yengo	139 861	Sandstone, McDonald River catchment
Yuraygir	20 032	Coastal heath

VICTORIA

Designation	Area (ha)	Number
National parks	2 525 191	33
Wilderness parks	202 050	3
Wilderness zones	640 000	19
Flora and fauna reserves	214	1
Marine and estuarine protected areas	46 660	6

Name	Area (ha)	Principal Features
Alpine	642 080	High plains, alpine and subalpine flora
Angahook-Lorne	21 000	Dry and wet eucalypt forests
Avon	39 650	Catchment of the Avon
Baw Baw	13 300	Alpine heaths, mountain ash, rare fauna
Big Desert	142 300	Sand dunes, mallee
Black Range	11 700	Heaths and wild flowers
Bronzewing	12 415	Mallee flora and fauna
Bunyip	13 900	Mountain ash forests
Burrowa-Pine Mt	18 400	Granite landforms
Coopracambra	38 800	Gorge of Genoa River, granite outcrops
Corner Inlet	18 000	Intertidal flats, fish spawning, migratory birds
Croaningolong	87 500	Coastal heaths, wilderness, dunes, lagoons
Dergholm	10 400	Open woodland, swamps
Eildon	24 000	Lake Eildon
Errinundra	25 600	Plateau, wet eucalypt forest, rainforest

Name	Area (ha)	Principal Features
Gippsland Lakes	17 500	Sand spit
Grampians	167 000	Sandstone ranges, Aboriginal rock art
Hattah-Kulkyne	48 000	Mallee flora and fauna, waterbirds
Holey Plains	10 576	Sand and limestone, diverse vegetation
Kinglake	11 430	Timbered ridges and gullies, lyre birds
Lederberg	14 100	Gorges
Little Desert	132 000	Mallee flora and fauna
Mount Buffalo	31 000	Granite plateau with cliffs, subalpine flora, fauna
Mount Lawson	13 150	Granite plateaus, open forests
Murray-Sunset	633 000	Mallee, woodlands, pink lakes
Nooramunga	15 000	Inlet islands, habitat for migratory birds
Otway	12 750	Wet mountain eucalypt forests
Snowy River	98 700	Deep gorge, wild river
Wabba	20 100	Forests of North East High Country
Wilsons Promontory	49 000	Granite coastal and mountain scenery
Wyperfeld	356 800	Mallee flora and fauna
Yarra Ranges	76 000	Mountain ash forest, Leadbeater's possum

QUEENSLAND

Designation	Area (ha)	Number
National Parks	6 217 434	210
Marine and estuarine protected areas	4982 907	59

Name	Area (ha)	Principal Features
Archer Bend	166 000	Sandy plains, gallery forest along rivers
Bartle Frere	79 500	Rainforests
Blackdown Tableland	32 000	Forested plateau, cliffs and gorges

Name	Area (ha)	Principal Features
Bladensburg	33 700	Mitchell grass plains
Bowling Green Bay	55 000	Largely wetland, includes granite Mount Elliot
Bulleringa	54 400	Geologically diverse area
Bunya Mountains	11 700	Araucarian vine forest
Camooweal Caves	13 800	Swampy gum, silver leaf box, coolibah
Cape Melville	36 000	Granite range and coastal plain
Cape Tribulation	16 965	Tropical rainforest, wild coastline
Carnarvon	251 000	Sandstone plateaus and gorges
Chesterton Range	16 100	Ironbark, lancewood, poplar box, cypress pine
Conway	24 200	Rainforests, islands
Coolloola	54 700	Sand mass, lakes, rainforest, heath
Currawinya	151 300	Mulga, poplar box, dunefields, lakes
Daintree	59 028	Vine forest, mountain scenery
Diamantina	470 000	Contains 26 ecosystem types in the Channel Country
Dipperu	11 100	Lagoons
Dryander	13 000	Granite Gloucester Island
Eungella	51 400	High plateau, vine and eucalypt forest
Expedition	104 000	Sandstone plateau and gorges, Robinson Gorge
Girraween	11 399	Granite landscapes, open forest
Great Barrier Reef	34 380 000	Coral reef ecosystem
Great Basalt Wall	30 500	Edge of lava flow, waterfalls
Great Sandy	83 700	Fraser Island, sand mass, rainforest, heath
Hell Hole Gorge	12 700	Waterholes and gorges of Powell Creek
Hinchinbrook Island	39 900	Mountains, mixed forest, mangroves
Homevale	32 650	Tropical, subtropical and dry rainforest
Idalia	144 000	Tablelands
Iron Range	34 600	Rainforest, tropical fauna
Jardine River	237 000	Tropical wilderness, wetlands, heaths
Kinkuna	13 300	Wetlands
Lake Bindegolly	11 930	Dunefields, shrublands, sandplains
Lakefield	537 000	Savannah woodland, swamps

Name	Area (ha)	Principal Features
Lamington	20 500	Plateau, subtropical rainforest
Lawn Hill	262 000	Ridges of North Western Highlands
Lochern	24 293	Channel Country land system
Lumholtz	124 000	Tropical rainforest, rare plants, waterfalls
Main Range	11 500	Rainforest, includes Mount Cordeaux
Malaleuca	11 890	Brigalow Belt park, softwood scrub
Mariala	27 300	Soft mulga
Mitchell, Alice Rivers	37 100	Open woodland, gallery forest
Moorrinya	32 607	Desert Uplands park
Moreton Island	16 800	Sand mass, lakes, dunes
Mount Barney	11 900	Solitary mountain
Mount Spec	10 600	Tropical woodland and rainforest
Palmgrove	25 600	Softwood and brigalow scrub
Rokeby	291 000	Peninsula
Simpson Desert	1 012 000	Sand ridge desert, desert fauna
Staaten River	470 000	Open woodland, gallery forests
Sundown	11 200	Severn River Gorge, forested ridges
Taunton	11 626	Brigalow scrub
Thruston	25 652	Open woodlands, river red gum
Undara Volcanic	54 700	Crater and lava tubes
Welford	124 000	Mulga Lands park, Barcoo River floodplains
White Mountains	108 000	Quartz sandplains with granite peaks
Whitsunday Island	10 900	Volcanic rocks, low vine forest, hoop pines

SOUTH AUSTRALIA

Designation	Area (ha)	Number
National parks	4 224 925	17
Wilderness areas	43 730	1
Marine and estuarine protected areas	15 849	14

Name	Area (ha)	Principal Features
Bascombe Well	32 000	Limestone plain, heath
Billiat	59 148	Sand hills, mallee wildlife
Cape Gantheaume	24 316	Coastal wilderness
Coffin Bay	30 380	Coastal sand dunes
Coorong	46 745	Coastal sandspit
Danggali	253 660	Plains country, spinifex scrub
Elliot Price	64 570	Lake Eyre peninsula
Flinders Chase	73 841	Wild coastline, woodland
Flinders Ranges	94 908	Eroded rock formations
Gammon Ranges	128 228	Rugged mountain wilderness
Hambidge	37 992	Sand ridges, mallee flora and fauna
Hincks	66 285	Dunes, mallee flora and fauna
Kulliparu	45 114	Open scrub, endangered wildlife
Lake Eyre	1 356 000	Salt lake, water fowl
Lake Gairdner	553 408	Salt lake
Lake Gilles	45 100	Sand ridges, mallee
Lake Torrens	570 000	Salt lake
Lincoln	29 060	Coastal scenery, mallee
Messent	12 246	Lake, sedge flats, water fowl
Mount Rescue	28 385	Sand hills and plains
Munyaroo	12 385	Coastal landscape, mallee woodland
Murray River	13 287	River red gum forest
Ngarkat	207 960	Sand ridges, mallee heath
Nullarbor	593 000	Coastal cliffs, limestone caves, salt bush
Pinkawillinie	127 164	Mallee scrub
Pureba	144 470	Sand ridge desert, granite outcrops
Scorpion Springs	30 366	Sand ridges, heath
Simpson Desert	692 680	Sand ridge desert, small desert marsupials
Tallaringa	1 249 900	Sand ridge desert
Victoria Desert	2 132 600	Great Victoria Desert of mulga and mallee
Witjira	776 900	Mound springs
Yumbarra	327 589	Sand ridges, mallee and spinifex

WESTERN AUSTRALIA

Designation	Area (ha)	Number
National parks	2 951 980	85
Nature reserves	12 837 331	1 148
Marine and estuarine protected areas	1 145 940	7

Name	Area (ha)	Principal Features
Badgingarra	13 121	North sand plain
Barlee Range	104 544	Spinifex covered ranges
Barrow Island	23 483	Native mammals now rare on mainland
Boorabbin	26 000	Sandplain shrub land
Cape Arid	279 382	Coastal scenery
Cape Le Grand	31 578	Rugged coastline, Mount Le Grand
Cape Range	50 581	Limestone, Slothole and other canyons
Chinocup	19 825	Habitat for small mammals and waterbirds
Collier Range	235 162	Spinifex and soft grass
De La Poer Range	74 935	
D'Entrecasteaux	114 567	Coastal heaths and lakes
Dragon Rocks	32 219	Rare flora and fauna
Drysdale River	448 264	Savannah grassland
Dundas	780 883	Claypans, lakes, woodland
Dunn Rock	27 349	
Fitzgerald River	329 039	Coastal ranges and inlets
Francois Peron	52 529	Peninsula in Shark Bay, dolphins at Monkey Mia
Frank Hann	61 420	Wild flowers
Gibson Desert	1 859 289	Spinifex plains and mulga, lakes
Goongarrie	60 397	Mulga
Great Victoria Desert	2 495 777	Sandridges, mulga, spinifex
Hamelin Pool	132 000	Stromatolites
Jibadji	208 866	Woodland, heath and scrub
Kalbarri	186 050	Murchison River Gorge
Karijini	606 597	Hamersley Range, gorges, spinifex, mulga
Karroun Hill	309 678	Rare birds
Kennedy Range	141 660	Cliffs, mulga scrub plains
Lake Campion	10 752	

Name	Area (ha)	Principal Features
Lake Magenta	107 615	Saltpans and freshwater lakes
Lake Muir	11 301	Lakes and swamps, black swans
Lake Shaster	10 505	
Leeuwin-Naturaliste	19 007	Limestone caves, spectacular coastal scenery
Lesueur	26 977	Diversity of plants
Millstream-Chichester	190 736	Semi-arid range, Aboriginal rock engravings
Moore River	17 543	Wild flowers
Mount Frankland	30 830	Karri forest
Mount Manning	153 293	Mulga, rare flora
Mungaroona Range	105 842	High tablelands, ravines
Namburg	18 319	Exposed limestone pinnacles, coastal scenery
Neale Junction	723 073	Sand ridges
Ningaloo	225 003 (State) 194 257 (C'wealth)	Coral reef ecosystem
Nuytsland	625 344	Long unbroken high cliffs, wild scenery
Ord River	78 842	Mangroves, crocodile habitat
Parry's Lagoon	36 111	Wetlands, waterbirds
Peak Charles	39 959	Granite, mallee
Pinjarega	18 221	
Plumridge Lakes	308 990	Sand dunes, blue bush
Point Coulomb	28 676	Dry savannah plain
Prince Regent River	634 952	Prince Regent River Gorge, rainforest
Purnululu (Bungle Bungle)	208 823	Unique sandstone plateau
Queen Victoria Spring	272 598	Desert flora and fauna
Rudall River	1 569 459	Salt lakes, catchment of Rudall River
Shark Bay	748 735	Rare fauna, Dugong habitat
Shannon	52 598	Karri forest, river basin of the Shannon
Stirling Range	115 661	Rocky range, great diversity of plant species
Walpole Nornalup	15 861	Karri and tingle forest, estuary scenery
Walyahmoning	20 925	Sand plains, granite outcrops
Wanagarran	11 069	Coastal heaths

Name	Area (ha)	Principal Features
Wandana	54 821	Victoria plateau
Wanjarri	53 248	Great diversity of birdlife, mulga
Watheroo	44 474	Spring wild flowers
Yalgorup	12 888	Coastal heaths and lakes
Yeal	10 336	
Yellowdine	32 798	Granite outcrops, salt lakes
Yeo Lake	321 946	
Zuytdorp	363 822	

TASMANIA

Designation	Area (ha)	Number
National parks	1 366 809	14
Nature reserves	41 124	51
State recreation areas	5 725	9
Aboriginal sites	712	2
Historic sites	15 757	15
Marine and estuarine protected areas	6 722	5

Name	Area (ha)	Principal Features
Ben Lomond	16 527	Snowfield, plateau and cliffs
Central Plateau	89 200	High plateau, glacier landscape with lakes
Cradle Mountain/ Lake St Clair	161 108	Mountain glaciers, lakes, rainforest
Douglas Apsley	18 080	Sclerophyll forest
Franklin/Gordon/ Wild Rivers	440961	Wilderness river gorges, limestone caves
Freycinet	11 930	Granite peaks and rock slabs, coastal wilderness
Macquarie Island	12 785	Sub-Antarctic island, seabirds
Maria Island	11 550	Rare birds, forest
Mount Field	16 265	Glacier, sub-alpine environment
Mount William	13 899	Coastal heath
Walls of Jerusalem	51 800	Part of Central Plateau, lakes, pine forest

NORTHERN TERRITORY

Designation	Area (ha)	Number
National parks	1 597 054	9
National parks — Aboriginal	180 356	1
Historical reserves	9 692	15
Marine and estuarine protected areas	229 279	3

Name	Area (ha)	Principal Features
Cape Hotham	12 900	Swamp and monsoon rainforest vegetation
Cobourg	229 000	Marine reserve
Connells Lagoon	25 890	Black soil plains
Elsey	13 840	Roper River, rainforest, thermal pool
Finke Gorge	45 843	Palm Valley
Gregory	978 100	Tropical merging into semi-arid area
Gurig	220 700	Mangrove swamps, diversity of fauna
Kakadu	1 980 400	Escarpment plains, Aboriginal art, lagoons
Katherine Gorge	80 350	Tropical woodland
Keep River	56 889	Aboriginal relics, lagoons, ranges
Litchfield	146 118	Escarpment, waterfalls, termite mounds
Nitmiluk	100 002	River gorges, tropical woodland
Uluru-Kata Tjuta	132 566	Monoliths, flora and fauna
Watarrka	71 720	Deep gorge, eroded sandstone
West MacDonnell	205 756	Rocky ranges

AUSTRALIAN CAPITAL TERRITORY

Designation	Area (ha)	Number
National parks	105 845	1
Nature reserves	7 891	6

Name	Area (ha)	Principal Features
Namadgi	105 900	Granite peaks, sub-alpine flora

AUSTRALIA — COMMONWEALTH

Designation	Area (ha)	Number
National parks	2 055 949	5
Nature reserves	2 029 575	5
Marine and estuarine protected areas	34 712 600	2

Name	Area (ha)	Principal Features
Territory of Heard Island and McDonald	1 138 260	Active volcano, ice cap and glaciers
Ashmore Reef	58 412	Coral reefs, seabird colonies, turtle nesting
Coringa Herald	885 724	Coral reefs, seabird and turtle habitat
Elizabeth Middleton Reefs	188 000	Coral atolls, black cod
Lihou Reef	843 691	Coral reefs, sandy cays, seabirds, turtles
Mermaid Reef	53 984	Shelf atolls in Rowley Shoals

(Australian Nature Conservation Agency (ANCA) IUCN 1996 digital data set of Marine and Terrestrial Protected Areas. ANCA has received the data on Marine and Terrestrial Protected Areas from a wide range of State and Territory agencies responsible for the management of Protected Areas. Data has been provided on the basis that it will not be sold by ANCA or a third party. Any attempt by an agency to on-sell the data will place ANCA in breach of licence agreements with a number of custodian agencies. Where an agency wishes to use this data supplied by ANCA for commercial gain they are required to contact ANCA directly to seek approval.)

Wilderness Areas

Defined as entirely natural country unadulterated by the effects of modern technology, the values of wilderness areas are numerous. Some of the most important scientific reasons for protecting them are for the genetic resources they can and do hold, and as a pure and unaffected environment to observe and monitor environmental and climatic trends.

Approximately 18% of Tasmania falls into the wilderness category, with the southwest wilderness area being by far the largest. The Western Tasmania Wilderness National Parks are on the World Heritage List.

PROTECTION

Within the national parks system, there is a provision for wilderness areas to be set apart from the usual and recreational functions of a park. This is generally considered to be the most efficient way of protecting wilderness areas.

Approximately half of the nation's forests have been cleared, with forests now only covering about 5% of Australia. Only 13% of these areas are currently protected.

MAJOR WILDERNESS AREAS

Some of the most significant areas are the Cape York Peninsula in Queensland; Lake Eyre in South Australia; Prince Regent River and the Kimberley region, the Great Sandy Desert, Great Victoria Desert and Gibson Desert, all in Western Australia; the forests and wild rivers of Southwest Tasmania, and Arnhem Land and the Tanami and Simpson Deserts in the Northern Territory.

World Heritage Listings

The World Heritage Committee was set up in 1975 by UNESCO to protect the world's irreplaceable heritage of cultural and natural places. There are approximately 340 places on the World Heritage List including such places and natural wonders as the Great Wall of China, the Pyramids at Giza in Egypt and the Grand Canyon National Park in the USA.

Ten Australian properties have been assessed by the World Heritage Committee as having 'outstanding universal value'. These are:

• Great Barrier Reef, Queensland (34 870 000 ha)
• Lord Howe Island Group (145 000 ha)
• Willandra Lakes Region of western New South Wales (600 000 ha)

- Kakadu National Park, Northern Territory (1 980 000 ha)
- Tasmania Wilderness, Tasmania (1 383 640 ha)
- Uluru-Kata Kjuta National Park, Northern Territory (132 566 ha)
- Central Eastern Rainforests — Stage 1, New South Wales (203 564 ha)
- Wet Tropics of Queensland (920 000 ha)
- Shark Bay, Western Australia (2 320 000 ha)
- Fraser Island, Queensland (181 000 ha).

5
Population

Australia's Changing Population

*A*ustralia has changed dramatically since the First Fleet arrived in Sydney Cove on 26 January 1788, with 1487 Europeans on board. At that time, the Aboriginal population was roughly estimated at anywhere between 200 000 and 750 000 people. As of 30 June 1995, there were approximately 18 173 600 people settled throughout Australia, with Aboriginal peoples making up only 1.7% of the total population.

Once a country settled by young, mainly Anglo-Saxon men and women, Australia is now a multicultural society, with many recent migrants coming from the Asia–Pacific region. It is also a country with an ageing population and a declining birth rate, due to women choosing to marry later and also have less children later in their lives. This chapter looks at these trends in Australia's population as the country heads towards the turn of the century.

Demographics

THE CENSUS

Official statistics on Australia's population are recorded every five years through the Census, a survey sent out to every Australian household. Known as the Census of Population and Housing, it is organised by the Australian Bureau of Statistics (ABS). It attempts to take a count of all people in the country and collects information about their age, sex, family, housing, profession and income.

The first nationwide census was taken at federation in 1901. It revealed a population of 3 773 801 people, but Aboriginal Australians were excluded, as they were until 1967. Of the population at this time, 77.1% were born in Australia and 22.7% were born overseas, with 0.2% unstated. By far the largest group from overseas was the United Kingdom and Eire which accounted for 18% of the overseas born.

The last Census occurred in 1996 with the statistics due out in 1998. Although as accurate as possible, the Census is not entirely representative of the Australian population as it ignores those people moving around the country and/or those who are not at home at the time of survey.

DISTRIBUTION

Most of Australia's population is concentrated around two coastal regions. The larger area extends from Queensland south-east through to South Australia, and contains about 75% of the nation's population. The smaller area is in the south-west of Western Australia. The two areas are separated by 2000–3000 km² of sparsely populated countryside that make up three-quarters of the total size of mainland Australia. This area includes the whole of the Northern Territory and parts of all five mainland States.

The external Australian territories with permanent populations are Norfolk Island: 2367; Christmas Island: 1275; and Cocos (Keeling) Islands: 647.

New South Wales was the most populous State in 1995, followed by Victoria and Queensland, as the following table shows.

ESTIMATED POPULATION BY STATES AND TERRITORIES 1995

State	Population
NSW	6 116 200
VIC	4 503 400
QLD	3 276 700
SA	1 473 800
WA	1 731 800
TAS	473 200
NT	174 100
ACT	304 200
Total	18 056 100

URBAN AND RURAL POPULATION DISTRIBUTION AT SELECTED DATES

Census Year	Total Urban Population (%)	Total Rural Population (%)
1947	68.7	31.1
1966	82.9	16.9
1971	85.6	14.3
1976	86.0	13.9
1981	85.7	14.2
1986	85.4	14.5
1991	85.3	14.6

* Urban and rural proportions do not add up to 100% as the proportion of migratory population is not included.

URBAN AND RURAL

Australia's population seems quite evenly spread across the continent, the official population density figure being two persons per km². However, the Australian population is becoming increasingly urbanised with economic conditions forcing many of the rural population into the cities.

In 1995, approximately 85% of the population lived in State and Territory capitals or in other major cities with more than 100 000 people. Capital cities have also been the consistent choice for settlement by the majority of overseas migrants, who in 1995 made up approximately 23% of the total population.

ESTIMATED RESIDENT POPULATION OF CAPITAL CITIES 1995

Capital City	Resident Population	Proportion of State/ Territory population (%)
Sydney	3 772 700	62.0
Melbourne	3 218 100	71.5
Brisbane	1 489 100	45.7
Adelaide	1 081 000	73.3
Perth	1 262 600	72.9
Hobart	194 700	41.0
Darwin	79 100	45.6
Canberra	331 800	99.9

ABORIGINAL AND TORRES STRAIT ISLANDER POPULATION

In 1994, the indigenous population was 303 261, approximately 1.7% of the total Australian population. This was an increase of 33.2% from 1986 and of 6.9% since 1991. There are an estimated 1385 indigenous communities in Australia, with 81% of these in remote areas. New South Wales is the State with the largest indigenous population, with 80 440 indigenous people living there.

Proportion of Indigenous Population Living in Each State

The percentage of indigenous people living in each state is as follows:

New South Wales	26.5%
Victoria	6.3%
Queensland	26.3%
South Australia	6.1%
Western Australia	15.6%
Tasmania	3.3%
Northern Territory	15.2%
Australian Capital Territory	0.7%

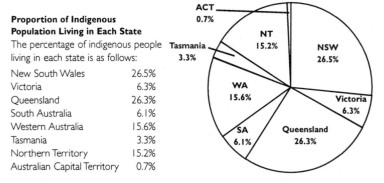

Approximately 27% of the country's indigenous population live in capital cities, while 26.9% of the Northern Territory's population is Aboriginal and/or Torres Strait Islander.

POPULATION DENSITY

Situated in the most densely populated region in the world, Australia is dramatically out of step with its neighbours. In Asia, the average population density is 85 people per square kilometre while in Australia it is just two. Canberra has one of the lowest population densities of any city in the world: 331 800 people, or eight per hectare, live in a city that stretches 40 km from north to south. This is about a tenth of the population density of a European city.

GROWTH

Australia's population has increased by more than 4 000 000 over the past 20 years. The estimated resident population in 1996 was 18.2 million, a slight increase over the previous year. Despite the fact that overseas migration has been a significant factor in population growth figures for over two decades, this figure represents the lowest level of immigration since 1975–1976. The size of migrant intakes into Australia at a given time can set the pattern for direction in total population growth.

POPULATION GROWTH BY STATE
YEAR ENDING 1995

State	Growth (%)
New South Wales	1.3
Victoria	0.8
Queensland	2.6
South Australia	0.3
Western Australia	1.9
Tasmania	0.1
Northern Territory	2.7
Australian Capital Territory	1.1
Australia	**1.3**

AGE AND SEX COMPOSITION

AGE

Australia's population is ageing. The median age has been rising consistently since the beginning of the 1970s, due to a declining birthrate and a lower mortality rate at most ages. At 30 June 1993, the median age was 33.0 years.

In 1982, 9.9% of the population was aged 65 and over. This figure had risen to 11.7% in 1993, while those aged 0–14 years had declined from 37.7% to 32.6% in the same period. These two groups, the over 65s and under 15s, currently make up 33.3% of the population; this figure is known as the dependency ratio.

The expected increase in this ratio at the over 65 end of the scale is reflected in the projected growth of the population over 75 years of age. During the period 1986–1991 there were 52 000 people, rising to about 400 000 people in 1991–2001. It is estimated that by 2020, the country's population will have stabilised at 23 million, with the over 65s making up about 20% of this figure.

Percentage Breakdown of Total Age Groups in 1995

- 65+ years 11.9%
- 0–14 years 21.4%
- 45–64 years 20.7%
- 15–44 years 46%

SEX

The ratio of men to women in Australia is calculated by the number of males per 100 females. This ratio varies according to age. At birth there are about 105 men to women, but higher male mortality evens out this ratio until the numbers of men to women are about equal at around 60 years of age. With increasing age, women start to outnumber men.

Since the 1950s, as the intake of overseas migrants has become less male dominated, the overall sex ratio has declined. In 1995, there were about 99.4 males to every 100 females in Australia.

Births

Registering births has been compulsory throughout Australia since 1856, but it is only since the 1950s that these vital statistics have been published.

BIRTH RATE

In 1995, there were 256 240 births, one of the highest figures since the baby boom days of the early 1970s. The highest ever number of births in Australia was in 1971, when a record of 276 400 was set. An increasing birth rate is also explained by a reduction in infant mortality due to improving health care and advances in science and medicine. In 1994, the birth rate was 14.5 per 1000 population, with 258 051 babies born that year.

FERTILITY

Australia's fertility rates have been low since the 1980s, although they still remain higher than in western Europe, North America and in Japan.

In 1994–1995, the total fertility rate was 1.85 births per woman. This figure represents the sum of age specific birth rates and gives a projected figure representing the number of children born to a woman in her child-bearing life. This is based on the age specific rates for the different ages (shown below). This figure has dropped from 2.86 in 1970.

The crude birth rate in 1995 was 14.1 per 1000 population and this contrasts with the 1970 figure of 20.6 per 1000 population. Despite this decline in the fertility rate, the number of births has continued to increase, due to the higher numbers of women at a reproductive age.

ANNUAL BIRTH RATES PER 1000 WOMEN BY AGE

Year	15–19 years*	20–24 years	25–29 years	30–34 years	35–39 years	40–44 years	45–49 years[Δ]
1982	27.5	104.0	144.9	80.6	25.6	4.6	0.3
1984	23.6	96.0	143.0	83.0	25.6	4.4	0.3
1986	21.8	90.0	141.9	88.7	27.2	4.3	0.2
1988	20.2	81.8	137.2	93.4	30.5	4.6	0.2
1990	22.1	79.4	137.9	101.7	34.7	5.5	0.2
1992	21.9	74.9	132.6	104.6	38.4	6.1	0.3

* Includes births to mothers under 15.
[Δ] Includes births to mothers over 49

AGE

As the table above clearly shows, women are choosing to have children at a later age. While the fertility rates are dropping overall and births to women aged 15–19 years, 20–24 years and 25–29 years have dropped, births to women aged 30–44 years have risen noticeably especially in the last few years. In 1987, the births to women aged 30–34 years overtook those to women in the 20–24 years age group.

This change also reflects the rising median age for marriage. In 1971, the median age for women's first marriage was 21.1 years while in 1994 it was 25.1 years. However, more children are being born outside marriage. The figure for ex-nuptial births was 9.3% in 1971, rising to 25.6% in 1994.

CHANGES TO FAMILY STRUCTURE

As the number of women in the workforce increases, women are choosing to have children later in their lives and closer together. In 1971, 46.5% of married women had a child within the first two years of marriage, but by 1994 this figure had fallen to 30.7%.

The number of women having three or more children is decreasing. In 1971, 22.5% of women had three or more children while in 1994 this figure had dropped to 7.1%.

Deaths

Australia boasts some of the lowest mortality levels and highest life expectancy rates in the world. The compulsory registration of death began at the same time as those of birth in 1856. Statistics have only been published on a regular basis since the 1950s.

DEATH RATE

The number of deaths in Australia has been falling consistently for 25 years, although the late 1980s showed a slight increase. In 1995, the number of deaths was 125 348, a 0.2% decrease in the crude death rate from the previous year (the number of deaths occurring per 1000 population): from 7.1 to 6.9.

MORTALITY LEVELS

Mortality levels are measured by the crude death rate and are influenced by changes in the age of the population over periods of time. Mortality rates have declined since the early 1970s, and are continuing to do so, due in part to advances in medicine and science.

The adjusted death rate, taking into account the age structure of the population, fell from 12.0 per thousand in 1971 to 8.4 per thousand in 1992 for males, and from 7.3 to 5.1 per thousand for females during the same period.

AGE AND SEX FACTORS

Death rates are lower for women than for men in Australia — a trend consistent with most of the world. In 1994, the female death rate was about one-third of males in the 15–24 years age group, while in many other age groups, the female death rate was about half that of the male. This has led to an increase in the number of females, especially in older groups of the population.

INFANT MORTALITY RATE

The infant mortality rate per 1000 live births in 1995 was 5.7. The infant death rate in the Northern Territory is more than double this figure, however, as the Aboriginal and Torres Strait Islanders who comprise 26.9% of the Territory's population suffer from a higher infant death rate.

Infant deaths occur mostly within the 28 days after birth, and are usually caused by conditions that existed before or during birth. Some of these conditions can also cause stillbirths (foetal deaths).

Hypozia, birth asphyxia and other respiratory conditions account for 36.2% of total infant deaths; conditions originating in the prenatal period account for 27.6%, while 25% of infant deaths are caused by maternal conditions such as complications of the placenta, placental cord and membranes.

With funds coming from the proceeds of the national Red Nose Day, research into Sudden Infant Death Syndrome (SIDS) has found that a majority of deaths are caused by the child being placed to sleep on its stomach and overheating while sleeping. There is also a possible link to smoking in the household. The number of SIDS deaths has declined since these findings were made public in the early 1990s.

COMPARATIVE INFANT MORTALITY RATES (1994)

Country	Deaths per 1000
Japan	4
Australia	6
United Kingdom	6
New Zealand	7
United States	8
Thailand	26
China	31
South Africa	52
Afghanistan	164

LIFE EXPECTANCY

People are generally living longer in Australia today. A rise in life expectancy, due to medical advances and improvements in health care and public awareness of health issues, has offset the death rate to some extent over the last two decades.

Between 1982 and 1992, the life expectancy for males has increased from 71.3 to 74.1 years, while the age for women has correspondingly risen from 78.2 to 80.4 years. A contributing factor to this increase in life expectancy has also been the decline in infant mortality, dropping in the period 1970–1972 to 1995 from 17.2 per thousand to 5.7 per thousand.

COMPARATIVE LIFE EXPECTANCY RATES

Country	Median life expectancy
Japan	80
Australia	77
United States	77
New Zealand	76
United Kingdom	76
China	71
Thailand	69
South Africa	63
Indonesia	63
Afghanistan	44

CAUSES OF DEATH

The three main causes of death in Australia are diseases of the circulatory system (44.4%), neoplasms (26.2%) and respiratory diseases (8.1%). In 1992, they made up a total of 78.7% of registered deaths for both men and women. For the age group ranging from 1–44 years, the leading causes of death are violence, accidents and poisoning, especially in the 15–24 years age group, where these causes of death accounted for more than 75% of the total number of deaths.

CAUSES OF DEATH PER 100 000 (1994)

Cause of Death	Death rate
Circulatory system diseases	308
Respiratory system diseases	56
Digestive system diseases	22
Neoplasms	192
Diseases of nervous system and sense organs	17
Infectious and parasitic diseases	6
Endocrine, nutritional, metabolic diseases and immunity disorders	23
Congenital anomalies	4
All other diseases	40
Ill-defined conditions	3
Accidents, poisonings, violence	40
Total	**710**

AGE AND SEX-RELATED CAUSES

When the deaths of males and females from particular age groups are examined, differences become apparent when comparing the main causes of death. For example, from 25–44 years, men are three times more likely to die from heart disease, accidents, poisoning and violence than women in that age group.

CANCER   Cancer, or malignant neoplasms as it is officially referred to in death statistics, is a major cause of death in the 45–64 age group, accounting for approximately 40% of deaths. Digestive and peritoneum cancer make up about 30% of these deaths in men and women, while respiratory and intrathoracic cancer accounts for 21% of deaths in men and 13% of women. In 1993, 19% of women died from breast cancer in this age group. The cancer death rate per 100 000 population in 1993 was 166 deaths.

HEART DISEASE   Heart disease is the biggest killer of people aged 65 years and over. In 1993, it accounted for 33% of all deaths in Australia. However, this figure is not spread evenly across the two sexes. Men are at greater risk of dying from heart disease than women, with heart disease being the number one killer for men over 40 years of age. For women, heart disease does not become the major cause of death until after 70 years of age. The death rate per 100 000 population from heart disease in 1993 was 168 deaths.

Marriages

Registration of marriage has been compulsory across the nation since 1856. The total number of registrations for each year can be traced back to the 1860s and more detailed information is available from 1910 onwards.

NUMBERS OF MARRIAGES

Despite the growth in overall population, the number of marriages in Australia has continued to fall since it reached a record of 117 600 marriages in 1971. The crude marriage rate (marriages per 1000 population) for 1970–1975 was 8.3.

Since then the rate has dropped steadily. In 1995, 109 325 marriages were recorded giving a crude marriage rate of 6.0. The falling rate of marriages in Australia is due in part to the legal and social acceptance of de facto relationships.

FAMILY LAW ACT 1975

The introduction of the *Family Law Act 1975*, which gave easy and faster access to divorce, noticeably affected the number of marriages. Before this

Act was passed, about 80–85% of marriages were first marriages for both partners, but after 1976 this figure dropped dramatically and in 1992 was 63.7% of all marriages.

Marital Status

The marital status of Australians in 1993 revealed that 4 171 100 persons over 15 years had never married; 7 994 600 were married; 861 200 were widowed; and 803 300 were divorced.

Trends show that the median age at marriage is getting higher for both men and women, having increased from 23.3 years in 1971 to 27.2 years in 1994 for men and from 21 years to 25.1 years for women.

Divorce

The promulgation of the *Family Law Act* in 1975, which came into effect in January 1976, facilitated the dissolution of marriage by providing a single ground for divorce — namely irretrievable breakdown of marriage, established by one year's separation. Its reduction of the separation period from five years to one year and the removal of the need to prove guilt or fault resulted in the number of divorces rising from an annual average of 17 350 between 1971 and 1975 to 47 502 between 1991 and 1995.

The total number of divorces in 1995 was 49 636. The overall incidence of divorce was 2.7 per 1000 people; this crude divorce rate has remained steady for three years.

While children were involved in 61.6% of divorces in 1982, that number had decreased to approximately 52% in 1992.

Duration of Marriages

The median duration of marriage decreased from 12.5 years in 1971 to 10.9 years in 1994. The highest divorce rate for males occurred in the 25–29 age group with 21.0 per thousand married men completing proceedings. The most common age group for women was the under 25, with 22.3 per thousand married women divorcing.

Families and Households

Families

In the 1991 census, one- and two-person households made up about 53% of all Australian households. The average number of persons per household fell from 3.3 in 1971 to 2.8 in 1986 and 2.6 in 1994. This decline is due partly to the shrinking size of the average family and changing social attitudes. It also reflects Australia's ageing population, with more people over 65 living by themselves after their partners have died or dependants have left home.

FAMILY TYPE AND COMPOSITION, AUSTRALIA 1992

Family Type	Number
Without dependent children	
Couple	1 619 980
Couple & adult family member	434 880
Related adults	255 190
With dependent children	
Couple & 1 dependent child	497 520
Couple & 2 or more dependent children	1 218 960
Couple & 1 dependent child & adult family member	193 490
Couple & 2 or more dependent children & adult family member	121 410
Single parent & 1 dependent child	185 780
Single parent & 2 or more dependent children	170 040
Single parent & 1 dependent child & adult family member	51 260
Single parent & 2 or more dependent children & adult family member	26 640
TOTAL FAMILIES	4 775 150

SOLE PARENTS

The number of sole parents in Australia reached 324 171 at the 1991 Census. Of this figure, 46 334 were men and 277 837 were women. Both divorced men and women were the most common type of sole parent, with 99 300 women making up the majority of this figure. The number of unmarried mothers was also relatively high at 60 033 women.

HOUSEHOLD INCOME

Household income refers to the sum of the gross weekly income of all household members. The average weekly household income across the workforce was $723.26 in 1994. The lowest average weekly household income was $134.00, while the highest average weekly household income was $1302.

The cities of Canberra and Darwin had households with the highest average weekly incomes: $1037 and $864 respectively. The capital cities with the lowest incomes in this survey category were Hobart ($687) and Perth ($708).

Household Expenditure

Household expenditure surveys measure spending patterns of private households. These patterns vary according to income and other factors such as household size, composition, location and principal source of income. This data is then used to review the Consumer Price Index, loosely referred to as the cost of living index.

In 1984, weekly household expenditure averaged $361.84, while in 1994 it was recorded at an average of $602. In 1994, almost half of this was spent on food, transport and housing: on average, $111 on food and non-alcoholic beverages, $94 on transport and $85 on housing. Australians also spent about $80 per week on recreation, $33.70 on clothing and footwear, $27.15 on medical care and health expenses, and $39.60 on household furnishings and equipment. At the very top of the expenditure list, however, was the cost of income tax: $137 weekly.

State Levels of Income Tax

Those living in the Australian Capital Territory paid the highest average weekly income tax at $243.70 a week, while Tasmania recorded the lowest average with $103.40 a week paid. Residents of the Northern Territory ($168.22), New South Wales ($149.40) and Victoria ($130.50) paid the next highest average, followed by residents of Queensland ($128.30), Western Australia ($125.60) and South Australia ($123.90).

The Cost of Living in Various States

New South Wales and Victoria were the States with the highest levels of average weekly expenditure: $623.80 and $601.80 respectively. A survey taking in only capital cities, however, showed that Canberra and Darwin registered the highest costs of living with weekly household expenditure reaching $749.40 and $685.50 respectively. The city of Canberra registered the highest costs in almost every category of expenditure, while Tasmania was the cheapest State to live in in terms of weekly household expenditure, averaging $535.30 a week.

FOOD AND NON-ALCOHOLIC BEVERAGES The capital city Darwin recorded the highest average weekly expenditure at $127.10, while Canberra came in second at $126.80. Once again the States spending the most were New South Wales ($118.20) and Victoria ($111.10), while Tasmania ($102.10) and South Australia ($99.10) spent the least.

TRANSPORT, HOUSING AND HEALTH   The city of Canberra comes at the top of the capital city expenditure list for transport: $127.70, while Darwin households spend, on average, more each week for housing: $116.20. The States spending the most in these categories were Queensland ($95.40) for transport, closely followed by New South Wales ($94.10) and Victoria ($93.60). The State at the bottom of the list for transport costs was South Australia ($83.90).

On a State and Territory basis, housing costs were greatest in New South Wales ($95.40) and Victoria ($83.10), while in Tasmania costs mounted to only ($62.90) on average.

Households in New South Wales spent the most on health expenses and medical care: $28.60 on average. South Australia followed close behind with spending of $28.40, while Tasmanians spent the least at $24.40 per person. The capital city spending the most in this category was Canberra: $28.40 on average.

Immigration

Immigration began with the arrival of the First Fleet at Port Jackson in 1788 carrying 1487 people. By 1839, the colony's population had reached 77 000 people, although it consisted mainly of military personnel and convicts, with only 18 free settlers.

In the 1850s, gold was discovered and there was an influx of migrants to Australia. Amongst the new arrivals were a significant number of Chinese which sparked off racial conflict and anti-Chinese riots. This led to the White Australia Policy (the *Immigration Restriction Act*) in 1901, which prevented non-European people settling in Australia. This policy continued until 1945, after the government had become worried during World War II about Australia's ability to defend itself, given the size of the population (7 300 000). Policy then changed to allow immigration equalling the annual natural increase of 1%, but many restrictions remained in place until well after World War II.

Since then, migrants have included World War II refugees from various European countries, large intakes of Vietnamese refugees and other Asian people, and an increase in the number of New Zealanders coming to live in Australia. About 11.5% of Australia's total migrant arrivals originate from New Zealand.

Under the trans-Tasman Travel Arrangement, New Zealanders do not require a visa or entry permit and this agreement extends to children born to Australian citizens overseas, those who have become Australian citizens overseas, and residents of the territory of Norfolk Island.

BIRTHPLACE OF MAJOR SETTLER ARRIVALS

Country	1993	1994	1995
United Kingdom	9 480	8 960	10 690
New Zealand	6 690	7 770	10 500
Vietnam	5 650	5 430	5 100
Hong Kong	5 520	3 330	4 140
Total arrivals	76 330	69 770	87 430

AGE AND SEX OF PERMANENT ARRIVALS

AGE

Permanent arrivals in Australia have tended for some time to be fairly young, with a lot of young families arriving in the country.

Between 1971 and 1985, over 3.6% of immigrants were aged above 65 years, but in 1995 this figure dropped to 2.5%. The median age of these settlers however has been rising; in 1971 the average age was 23.1 years rising to 27.8 years in 1994.

SEX

Traditionally, male settlers have dominated Australia's immigration programs, but in 1988 the male-to-female ratio was at an historic low of 99.9 males per 100 females. Currently, males predominate in the 0–14 years and 35–54 years age groups.

ASIAN IMMIGRATION

The trend towards Asian immigration began with the first groups of Vietnamese refugees in the late 1970s and has been increasing ever since. Most migrants come from Vietnam, Hong Kong, Malaysia and the Philippines, making up collectively, over 25% of total overseas arrivals in 1992. (Migrants from New Zealand, on the other hand, account for approximately 8% of current annual immigration.)

Since 1978–1979, family immigration has become more significant. The arrival of family members now accounts for over 40% of all migrants settling in Australia.

REFUGEES

Since 1945, Australia has accepted more than 495 000 refugees, including 170 000 World War II refugees from Europe. Although Australia takes refugees from about 40 countries, Indo-Chinese people account for just over a quarter (29%) of total refugee arrivals. In 1995, however, the greatest number of refugees (5100 from a total of 13 632) came from the Former

Yugoslav Republic; 2245 refugees were from Iraq and 1032 were from the former USSR and Baltic States.

Australia also has international legal responsibilities through its membership of the Executive Committee of the United Nations High Commission for Refugees (UNHCR). The final decision to accept refugees, however, rests with the Australian government.

A MULTICULTURAL SOCIETY

In 1994, well over 20% of Australians were born in another country. More than half this number came to Australia from non-English speaking countries in Europe, the Middle East, Asia and South America. With their Australia-born children, these people constitute about 40% of the total population.

At 1994, the ethnic mix of Australia was roughly Anglo-Celtic 74%, Asian 5% and others 21%. By the year 2001, predictions put the ethnic mix at: Australian-born residents 64%; English-speaking countries 14%; and Non-English speaking countries 22%. By the year 2040, the projected ethnic mix is estimated at: Anglo-Celtic 53.5%; Asian 26.0% and others 20.5% of the population.

The number of migrants to Australia increased by 25% in 1994–1995. The biggest increases were among South Africans and Iraqis. Professionals as a percentage of total migrants increased by 36%.

POPULATION BY BIRTHPLACE, 1991

Country	Number
Argentina	10 660
Australia	12 725 160
Austria	22 150
Cambodia	17 630
Canada	24 130
Chile	24 150
China	78 870
Cyprus	22 150
Czechoslovakia (as then known)	17 780
Egypt	33 200
Fiji	30 540
France	15 920
Germany	114 910
Greece	136 330
Hong Kong	58 980
Hungary	27 200

Country	Number
India	61 610
Indonesia	33 270
Ireland	52 440
Italy	254 780
Japan	25 990
Korea (North and South)	21 000
Laos	9 660
Latvia	9 280
Lebanon	69 000
Malaysia	72 610
Malta	53 810
Mauritius	16 890
Netherlands	95 870
New Zealand	276 060
Papua New Guinea	23 740
Philippines	73 660
Poland	68 960
Portugal	18 010
Singapore	24 560
South Africa	49 420
Spain	14 780
Sri Lanka	37 280
Turkey	27 840
Ukraine	9 040
United Kingdom	1 118 680
United States	50 540
Uruguay	9 690
Former USSR	25 890
Vietnam	122 350
Yugoslavia (as then known)	161 060
Other	234 300

PERMANENT DEPARTURES

People leaving Australia permanently have a significant restraining effect on population growth. Between 1990 and 1995, a total of 171 370 people left the country (an average of 28 562 per year). The ratio of permanent departures to arrivals is about 13%. This is due, in part, to two policies: family reunion and the refugee resettlement program, which mean family members and refugees are less likely than other settlers to return to their own country.

INTERNAL MIGRATION

Statistics on internal migration, i.e. migration from one part of Australia to another, have only been available since the 1971 Census. Since this time, the flow of persons interstate has dramatically increased.

In the period 1971–1976, 569 500 people moved interstate, while from 1981–1986, 716 555 people had moved. This figure continues to increase with New South Wales and Victoria recording the greatest losses, losing out to destinations such as Queensland, the Australian Capital Territory and Western Australia.

INTERSTATE MIGRATION

Year	NSW	Vic.	Qld	SA	WA	Tas.	NT	ACT
1982	-19 580	-14 430	35 450	-4 880	3 560	-2 020	2 070	-170
1987	-9 520	-13 100	19 720	-3 980	6 580	1 510	-120	1 940
1990	-35 980	-7 830	38 100	-250	3 010	2 790	-1 170	1 330
1994	-13 540	-31 900	49 070	-3 470	3 660	-2 160	-1 510	-150

AUSTRALIAN CITIZENSHIP

Until 1948, when the *Australian Citizenship Act* was passed, all people who were naturalised became British subjects. After the Act was passed, they automatically became Australian citizens.

Australian citizenship is obtained:

• at birth in Australia, provided one parent is an Australian citizen or legal resident;
• at birth overseas, if one parent is Australian; or
• by a citizenship grant to a person residing in Australia.

New settlers may become Australian citizens if they have lived in Australia for two years, are of good character, have an adequate grasp of English and intend to live permanently in Australia.

Australian citizens made up 87.7% of the population at the 1991 Census, with 12.2% of these being born overseas.

Religion

Since the 1933 Census, it has been clearly stated that answering the question on religion is not obligatory, although details on religious affiliation have been collected in all censuses. By 1991, 25% of the population answered the question on religion with 'no religion' or declined to answer. About 12.7% of the population described themselves as atheists.

The data shows that the Australian population is approximately 74% Christian with 27% associating themselves with the Catholic Church and 24% with the Anglican Church. There are approximately 4.6 million Catholics in Australia; the largest of all religious groups.

The remaining 23% of the Christian population is dispersed between several other groups, with only three denominations consisting of more than 2% of the population: the Uniting Church (8%), Presbyterian (4%), and Orthodox (3%).

The proportion of non-Christian religions in Australia has increased from 0.8 in 1971 to 3% in 1991. At the 1991 Census, Muslims comprised 0.9% of the total national population, while there were 139 800 Buddhists and 74 100 Jews.

RELIGIOUS BELIEFS OF TOTAL POPULATION AT SELECTED CENSUS DATES BY %

Year	Church of England	Catholic	Other Christian	Total Christian	Non-Christian	Not stated or no religion
1971	31.0	27.0	28.2	86.2	0.8	13.1
1976	27.7	25.7	25.2	78.6	0.9	20.5
1981	26.1	26.0	24.3	76.4	1.4	22.3
1986	23.9	26.1	23.0	73.0	2.0	25.0
1991	23.9	27.3	22.8	74.0	2.6	23.4

Labour

The Australian labour force is defined broadly as those persons aged 15 years and over, employed or unemployed during a particular week. The size and composition of the labour force is influenced by age, for example increases or decreases in the population aged 15 years and over, as well as sex and marital status.

The total labour force in Australia in June 1996 was approximately 9.1 million. Of this figure, 8.4 million were employed: 4.8 million males and 3.6 million females. The unemployment rate in June 1996 was 8.2% (766 700 people).

EMPLOYMENT

A person is considered to be employed if she or he is doing any work at all, regardless of the number of hours worked.

In Australia the average working week for a person working full-time is 35 hours or more, while part-time workers work less than 35 hours a week.

In June 1996, there were 4 201 300 full-time male workers and 550 400 part-time. Women accounted for more part-time work, with 1 560 200 employed on a part-time basis. 2 042 200 women worked full-time. About 1 555 800 part-timers had no wish to work more hours.

A large percentage of the Australian workforce, 4 156 900 (women and men), were employed in the private sector in 1994, while 1 588 300 found work in the public service.

EMPLOYED PERSONS BY INDUSTRY AND AVERAGE WEEKLY HOURS WORKED, 1994

Industry	No. of people ('000)	Average hours worked Male	Female
Agriculture, forestry, fishing	409	49	30
Mining	89	44	34
Manufacturing	1 082	41	33
Food, beverages, tobacco	163	40	32
Metal products manufacturing	180	40	31
Other manufacturing	78	42	30
Electricity, gas, water supply	92	36	33
Construction	560	41	21
Wholesale trade	504	43	32
Retail trade	1 124	39	26
Accommodation, cafés restaurants	347	39	28
Transport, storage	366	43	32
Communications	128	37	32
Finance, insurance	317	40	31
Property, business services	674	42	30
Govt. administration, defence	368	37	31
Education	552	39	32
Health, community services	672	39	28
Cultural, recreational services	168	37	28
Personal, other services	301	36	29

OVERTIME

The average weekly overtime hours per employee in all industries was 2.0 hours for the year ending June 1994.

The average weekly hours worked by full-time workers in one week in 1995 was 40.8 hours and by part-time workers 15.4 hours.

UNEMPLOYMENT *see* Welfare

WAGES

The concept of a basic wage was first developed after the economic depression of the 1890s by the trade union movement. Since then several methods have been used to set the basic wages, although it was not until 1967 that the Australian Conciliation and Arbitration Commission introduced a minimum wage which varied according to job requirements, industry and sex. The Australian Industrial Relations Commission has now replaced the ACAC.

AVERAGE WEEKLY TOTAL EARNINGS
ALL EMPLOYEES, FEBRUARY 1996

State	Males	Females	Total Average
New South Wales	700	467	594
Victoria	676	441	570
Queensland	596	411	507
South Australia	631	402	527
Western Australia	692	415	561
Tasmania	618	392	510
Northern Territory	677	469	576
Australian Capital Territory	760	526	640
Australia	**668**	**439**	**563**

NON-WAGE BENEFITS

Most employees receive some form of non-wage benefits, although this is now under threat with the introduction of new industrial relations policies of the Howard coalition government. Superannuation is the most common non-wage benefit, followed by leave benefits such as annual leave and sick leave, which are given to two-thirds of the workforce.

However, it is employees at the highest income levels that are the most likely to receive other employment benefits such as telephone, transport, goods and services, housing, health costs, shares, study leave, entertainment, union fees and, in some cases, children's education expenses.

WOMEN IN THE WORKFORCE

A major feature of post-war Australian society has been the increasing number of women entering the workforce. In 1947, women represented 22.4% of the labour force; this figure had increased to 41% at the end of 1989. In 1996, women's participation in the workforce stood at 53.6%. The participation rate for men, in contrast, was 73.4%.

MIGRANT WOMEN

The participation rate for women born outside Australia in other than English speaking countries was 48.6% at the end of June 1996. This figure is lower than that of Australian-born women at 57.2%.

TYPE OF EMPLOYMENT

In 1994, approximately 80% of female wage and salary earners were employed in four main industries: 511 400 in community services, 731 800 in wholesale and retail trades, 464 500 in finance, property and business services and 330 900 in manufacturing.

TRADE UNIONS

In the past few years there have been a number of union amalgamations with smaller unions swallowed up by larger ones. In 1993, there were almost 90 unions with fewer than 1000 members; the following year there were about seventy-five. Unions with more than 50 000 members now have a greater percentage of total union membership: from 65% in 1992 to 77% in 1994. While about 50% of workers belonged to unions in 1982, that figure had declined to 35% in 1994.

MEMBERSHIP OF TRADES UNIONS (1994)

Size of Union Membership	Number Separate Unions	Total Membership
Under 1000	76	21 000
1000–4999	33	76 000
5000–19 999	20	200 200
20 000–49 999	11	360 500
50 000 and over	17	2 231 800
Total	157	2 890 200

INDUSTRIAL DISPUTES

In 1995, 635 industrial disputes began, leading to the loss of about 547 600 working days. A total of 344 300 employees were involved in these disputes. This shows a marked decrease from 1989, when 1402 disputes commenced with the loss of 1 202 400 working days lost. In 1994, the lowest number of industrial disputes for 54 years was recorded: just 558. In that year the coal industry suffered the greatest loss of working days: 5960 per 1000 employees.

WORKING DAYS LOST
PER 1000 EMPLOYEES (1994)

State	No. of days
New South Wales	95
Victoria	55
Queensland	112
South Australia	32
Western Australia	40
Tasmania	30

Welfare

Australia has a long tradition of social security, i.e. payment for the aged, disabled, widowed persons, sole parents, the orphaned, the unemployed and the sick, as well as assistance to families and other groups. Most are subject to income and assets tests and a decision handed down in the 1990 Budget has extended the tax file system to cover virtually all income-tested payments.

VARIOUS SOCIAL SECURITY PAYMENTS
(JUNE 1995)

Payment type	Amount paid out ($)
Families with children	
Basic Family Payment	2 017 000 000
Additional Family Payment	3 535 000 000
Sole Parent Pension	2 552 000 000
Double Orphan Pension	2 000 000
Home Childcare Allowance	618 000 000
Unemployed	
Job Search Allowance	3 389 000 000
Newstart Allowance	3 672 000 000
Mature Age Allowance	357 000 000
People with disabilities/the sick	
Disability Support Pension	4 525 000 000
Rehabilitation Allowance	1 000 000
Sickness Allowance	413 000 000
Mobility Allowance	31 000 000
Child Disability Allowance	185 000 000

Payment type	Amount paid out ($)
Retired	
Age Pension	11 884 000 000
Special circumstances	
Special Benefit	224 000 000
Bereavement Allowance	1 000 000
Widow Pension	481 000 000
Widow Allowance	32 000 000

UNEMPLOYMENT

A person is considered unemployed if they meet three criteria: they are not employed, are available for work and taking active steps to find work. Applicants must also prove their unemployment is not due to industrial action and register with the CES.

The unemployment rate is expressed as a percentage of the total labour force. In August 1996, unemployment was 8.5%, with 575 200 Australians looking for full-time work and 155 400 seeking part-time employment.

In June 1995, there were approximately 246 000 long-term unemployed Australians: about 33% of all unemployed people and 2.7% of the total labour force. A long-term unemployed person is defined as someone who has been seeking work for longer than one year. This figure was highest during the recession of 1990–1991.

UNEMPLOYMENT BENEFITS

Otherwise known as 'the dole', this benefit is available to those unemployed over 18 years and under the pension age. It is subject to an income test, and also an assets test for those over 25 years.

There have been two types of income support in this category: Job Search Allowance for those who have been unemployed for less than one year, and Newstart Allowance for the long-term unemployed.

In the year ending June 1995, approximately 393 830 people received the former, while 379 830 received the latter payment. The total number of about 773 660 people comprised 225 470 women and 548 190 men.

From September 1995 onwards, these two payments were amalgamated into one; Newstart Allowance. In addition to this, there is the Youth Training Allowance for those under 18 years of age. Aiming to ensure that young people do not become long-term unemployed, this initiative offers access to training and insists on close and regular contact with the CES and its officers.

PAYMENTS FOR PEOPLE
WITH DISABILITIES AND THE SICK

SICKNESS ALLOWANCE

This benefit is available to people aged at least 16 years, but under the pension age, who are temporarily unable to work due to illness or injury. All people applying for the sickness allowance must undergo an income and assets test. Except in special cases, the payment is usually limited to 12 months.

At the end of June 1995, approximately 46 050 people had been assisted in this category.

DISABILITY SUPPORT PENSION

This payment is made to those over 16 years of age who are physically or intellectually impaired or who suffer from a psychiatric disorder and are therefore unable to work at least 30 hours each week. The benefit is not taxable, but all recipients must be Australian citizens and undergo an income and assets test.

Approximately 324 670 men and 139 760 women received this payment in the year ending June 1995.

MOBILITY ALLOWANCE This allowance is for people over 16 who have a disability that prevents them using public transport without a reasonable amount of assistance. It is not means tested and specifically applies to those who have paid employment for at least eight hours each week, or need to get to vocational training.

In the year ending June 1995, about 22 300 people were receiving support in this category.

CHILD DISABILITY ALLOWANCE

This payment is made to a parent or guardian of a dependent child to 24 years of age, who suffers either physical, intellectual or psychiatric disability. The payment is not subject to a means test, but the child must live at home and require substantial care.

There were about 87 120 children in this category whose parent/s or guardian received this allowance at the end of June 1995.

PENSIONS

AGE PENSION

This pension was first introduced on 1 July 1909, making it the earliest form of social security in Australia. Men and women who have reached the ages of 65 and 60 respectively receive an age pension providing they are Australian citizens. The qualifying age for women is to be gradually raised to 65 years by the year 2013. This payment is generally subject to an income and assets test.

At the end of June 1995, the government had paid the pension to about 1 578 700 people, 1 034 130 of them women.

CARER PENSION
This payment is made to a person who provides long term and constant care to someone who is aged or has a severe disability. The person may take part in training or paid work outside the house for up to 10 hours a week. The rate of payment is the same as for the Age Pension and is subject to the same means test.

PAYMENTS FOR FAMILIES WITH CHILDREN
BASIC FAMILY PAYMENT   People with children under 16 years or dependent students aged 16 to 18 years who do not receive any other benefit, are eligible to apply for this allowance, subject to a means test. (All payments to students of 16 years and over are dealt with by the AUSTUDY scheme.) Multiple births usually attract an additional payment that is received by the mother until the children are six years of age. There can be no payment if family assets come to more than $584 500.

ADDITIONAL FAMILY PAYMENT   In the year ending June 1995, there were some 836 590 families receiving the additional family payment.

DOUBLE ORPHAN PENSION   This is available to guardians of children under 16 and dependent full-time students aged 16 to 24 years whose parents are both dead, or one parent is dead and the other cannot care for the child. Guardians of refugee children whose parents are outside Australia are also eligible.

In the year ending June 1995, this payment was made in relation to 1700 children.

SOLE PARENT PENSION
This was introduced on 1 March 1989, replacing part of the former widow's pension and the supporting parent's benefit. It is paid out to people bringing up children under 16 years or a child within the Child Disability Allowance. The child can be a natural or adopted child, and must have been in the person's legal custody, control or care for more than 12 months. The following people are eligible for this pension: a separated, divorced, widowed or unmarried person (de facto relationships qualify); a person who has been imprisoned for at least 14 days, or a person who is unable to live with their partner because of that person's illness.

In the year ending June 1995, about 324 940 people had received the sole parent benefit.

SPECIAL CIRCUMSTANCES

SPECIAL BENEFIT   This payment applies to people who do not qualify for any social security, and who because of age, physical or mental disability or domestic situation cannot earn a sufficient income for themselves and their dependants. Special Benefit is a discretionary payment for people in financial hardship and cannot exceed the relevant rate of Newstart or Youth Training Allowance. Special Benefit may be reduced when other assistance is received.

In the year ending June 1995, 20 440 people were granted this benefit.

WIDOW PENSION

This pension is being gradually phased out, but in the year ending June 1995, there were about 54 940 recipients.

BEREAVEMENT ALLOWANCE   Introduced in 1990, this allowance means widowed persons can receive payment during a period of adjustment when funeral arrangements are being made, financial matters are being settled and, perhaps, work is being sought. The allowance is granted to a person who was either married or in a de facto relationship with the deceased. The allowance is paid for up to 14 weeks after the partner's death.

There were just 47 recipients of this benefit in the year ending June 1995.

OTHER FORMS OF ASSISTANCE

There are a number of other schemes administered by Social Security that aim to protect those experiencing a number of categories of hardship: Drought Relief Payment, Farm Household Support Scheme and Disaster Relief Payment are some of the examples.

FRINGE BENEFITS

The Commonwealth government also provides those eligible with a range of benefits: the Pensioner Concession Card, Health Benefits Card, Health Care Card, Commonwealth Seniors Health Card, Pharmaceutical Allowance, Childcare Assistance, Rent Assistance, Telephone Allowance and Remote Area Allowance are just some of the additional benefits available.

6
History

Prehistory

*A*ccording to modern scholarship, Australia was once joined to Africa, South America, Antarctica, India and some parts of the earth now covered by the ocean, in a supercontinent called Gondwanaland.

PREHISTORIC TIMELINE

Era	Period		Absolute Years
Pre Cambrian			
Palaeozoic	Cambrian		600 million
(Primary)	Ordovician		500 million
	Silurian		440 million
	Devonian		400 million
	Carboniferous		345 million
	Permian		270 million
Mesozoic	Triassic		225 million
(Secondary)	Jurassic		185 million
	Cretaceous		135 million
Tertiary	Eocene		60 million
	Oligocene		40 million
	Miocene		25 million
	Pliocene		8 million
Cainozoic	Pleistocene	Paleolithic	2 million
	Holocene	Mesolithic	10 thousand
		Neolithic	
		Bronze Age	
		Iron Age	

PRE-CAMBRIAN ERA

The Pre-Cambrian Era describes the period which began about 600 million years ago. The only life forms that existed were seaweeds and soft-bodied invertebrates. Some of the few fossils found from this time are jellyfish discovered in South Australia. Rocks of this age exist throughout Australia, except in Victoria.

PALAEOZOIC ERA

During the Cambrian Period much of the surface of Australia was covered by seas which were quite deep over New South Wales, Victoria and

Tasmania. The age of marine invertebrates began at this time. Life was then still limited to the sea, but this period left an abundance of fossils. Trilobites, an ancient and extinct creature whose bodies were a flattened oval shape, are some of the earliest known fossils.

The Ordovician period had the greatest number of trilobites. Graptolites, an early order of coelenterates, also existed and molluscs began to spread. Major mountain formation and volcanic activity began.

It was during the Silurian period that the first land plants began to appear. Air breathing animals also made their first appearance as well as primitive fishes and brachiopods. This is known as the Age of the Fishes.

The Devonian period saw more volcanic activity. The first amphibians began to appear. Plant life gradually became more complex and corals abounded. Seas still covered the eastern part of Australia but the centre and western areas were above sea level.

The Carboniferous period saw the rise of amphibians. Insects were abundant and the earth was covered in tall land plants. An Ice Age began which lasted into the Permian period, when many shallow seas were formed over the continent by melting ice.

In the Permian period, trilobites died out and insects and amphibians spread. Cycads, a palmlike order of plants, formed and much of Australia's coal deposits were laid down.

MESOZOIC ERA

In the Triassic period, about 225 million years ago, Gondwanaland is thought to have first started to break away from the major landmass which combined all present day continents. Then, 45 million years ago, the ancient continent Sahul, which consisted of the Australian mainland, Tasmania and Papua New Guinea, separated from the supercontinent of Gondwanaland. From this time flora and fauna were isolated from the rest of the world.

The Triassic period also saw the dawn of the Mesozoic period, the Age of Reptiles, when the first dinosaurs and primitive mammals appeared. Australian dinosaurs included the *Rhaetosaurus* and the *Austrasaurus*, plant-eating dinosaurs which grew to a length of about 15 metres. The plesiosaur *Kronosaurus queenslandicus* and the *Ichythyosaurus australis* were both swimming reptiles.

Dinosaurs reached their peak in the Jurassic Period. Primitive birds also began to appear at this time.

Flowering plants such as the banksia started to appear in the Cretaceous period. Dinosaurs died out and seas again covered much of Australia between the Great Dividing Range and the western plateau.

TERTIARY ERA

During the Eocene period, mammals, especially marsupials, evolved. In Australia, the *Diprotodon* began to appear. Grasses spread. Shallow seas remained over the Carnarvon area of Western Australia.

The Oligocene period, which began about 40 million years ago, saw volcanic activity in the south and east of Australia.

In the Miocene period, the land bridge with Papua New Guinea was cut and mammals became the dominant life form. Rainforests date from this period and flourished along Australia's east coast. Along the south coast volcanic activity was widespread.

The Pliocene period marks the emergence of primitive people. The eastern highlands and western plateau of Australia were uplifted. Marsupials and birds continued to develop.

CAINOZOIC ERA

The Cainozoic era, which began with the Pleistocene period about two million years ago, saw the development of humans. For much of this early time the earth was subject to glacial phases which, in Australia, were particularly extensive in Tasmania and south-eastern Australia.

THE ARRIVAL OF HUMANS

A remarkable find made in 1996 at Jinmium in the Northern Territory, just over the Western Australian border, is causing anthropologists and prehistorians to discard long-held theories about Aboriginal occupation of Australia. The sculpted boulders and thousands of circular engravings found there have been dated at up to 75 000 years old, more than twice the age of French rock paintings at Chauvet previously thought to have been the world's oldest rock art. Excavations carried out at the site unearthed artefacts and ochre estimated at between 116 000 and 176 000 years old, thereby dramatically pushing back the date of Aboriginal occupation of the continent. This also goes back before the date that, based on fossil and genetic evidence, modern humans — *Homo sapiens* — are thought to have emerged from Africa. Australia, therefore, may have been originally occupied by a now extinct human species that lived in South-East Asia. This is an idea that excites much anthropological controversy.

It had previously been thought that between 40 000 and 60 000 years ago, during the last Great Ice Age, *Homo sapiens* first crossed from South-East Asia to the Australian mainland, which at the time was joined to Papua New Guinea and Tasmania in the supercontinent Sahul. It is almost certain that colonisation was not made at one single time. There is conjecture that at least two distinct morphological types of human arrived in Australia.

This journey, possible due to low sea levels, still involved some relatively short sea journeys across deep channels which at their narrowest would never be less than 60 km wide. It is this permanent sea barrier that has kept Australia's flora and fauna so isolated and unique.

LAKE MUNGO

Previously the most firmly dated human remains were found near Lake Mungo in western New South Wales, showing that humans existed in that area 38 000 years ago. Lake Mungo is now dried up, but it used to be a large freshwater lake full of fish and bird life. The lake is in the Willandra Lakes Region, which is now protected by a World Heritage listing for both its cultural and natural significance.

Another important find in this district was the cremated remains of a young woman dating back 25 000 years; the first recorded cremation in the world. This skeleton also has a very thin skull, which contrasts with the remains found at Kow Swamp in northern Victoria, where the skulls found were much thicker. The Kow Swamp remains were uncovered in approximately 1970 and date back at least 10 000 years. This is further evidence leading some experts to the conclusion that there were two different races of inhabitants in Australia. These earliest inhabitants were hunter–gatherers who lived by gathering edible seafood and plants and hunting wild animals. The stone tools they used have been identified as belonging to the 'core tool and scraper tradition'.

The animals which would have existed at the time of first habitation include the *Thylacoleo*, a marsupial lion with large shearing teeth, and the *Diprotodon*, a grazing wombat-like animal, the largest species of which was the biggest marsupial ever known. There were also giant kangaroos which were one-third larger than the largest present-day species of kangaroo.

Discovery & Exploration

The first recorded visitors to Australia in modern times were the Dutch. It is believed, however, that the Chinese and the Portuguese, both of whom made journeys to the islands north of Australia, may have accidentally or intentionally visited before the Dutch. Certainly, there is evidence that the Portuguese may even have charted part of the east coast, but kept the discovery secret.

In December 1605, the Portuguese explorer Pedro Fernandez de Quiros left Callao in Peru and journeyed south. De Quiros made it as far as the New Hebrides, naming the islands Australia del Espiritu Santo. Although de Quiros turned back after this, the other ship in the party led by Luis Vaz de Torres sailed through the Torres Strait. His records, however, make no mention of sighting land to the south.

THE DUTCH

The first recorded landing by Europeans on Australian soil was made by a Dutch party in the boat Duyfken led by Willem Jansz, which landed on the west coast of Cape York Peninsula in March 1606.

The Dutch East India company had been operating since 1602, following the Portuguese trade route round the Cape of Good Hope and north from there around the African coast, across to Ceylon and down to Java. In 1611, a Dutch captain pioneered a new, faster route using the westerlies that run along the roaring forties. The new route from Holland to Java was to sail east from the Cape of Good Hope using the westerlies to cross to the vicinity of the west coast of Australia, before turning north to Java.

By 1616, all Dutch ships were using this route. Many miscalculated and were blown off course, sailing near to the west coast or even the south coast of Australia. The first to do so was the *Eendracht* skippered by Dirk Hartog, which landed on an island now known as Dirk Hartog Island near Shark Bay in Western Australia on 25 October 1616. The party left an inscribed pewter plate recording this visit.

Between 1616 and 1640 many Dutch ships touched on parts of the west coast which later became known as New Holland.

ABEL TASMAN

In 1642, the Dutch East India Company decided to send an expedition to search for the great south land. The Governor-General of the Dutch East Indies, Anthony Van Diemen, commissioned Abel Tasman.

Tasman made two journeys. On the first in 1642–1643 he discovered and named Van Diemen's Land, now known as Tasmania, and the west coast of the islands of New Zealand.

On the second journey in 1644, Tasman charted the northern Australian coastline from Cape York Peninsula in Queensland to North West Cape on the coast of Western Australia.

WILLEM DE VLAMINGH

In 1696, a Dutch sailor called Willem de Vlamingh charted much of the western Australian coastline. During his visit, de Vlamingh found the pewter plate left by Dirk Hartog and also named the Swan River that flows through the present-day city of Perth.

The Dutch lost interest after these expeditions, finding their hopes of wealth through trade in the south dashed, and abandoned the land without further exploration.

THE ENGLISH

The first English ship to reach Australia was an East India company ship *Ityal*, which was wrecked near the west coast in 1622.

In 1688, a party led by the vagabond William Dampier in the pirate ship *Cygnet* landed at Shark Bay on the west coast of Australia and found, as the Dutch did before him, little to recommend the land. After Dampier's return journey in 1699 aboard the *Roebuck*, he published books on the botany and inhabitants encountered during this voyage.

CAPTAIN COOK

Lieutenant James Cook left England in the *Endeavour* in August 1768. His first purpose was to journey to Tahiti in the South Pacific to study the transit of the planet Venus across the face of the sun on 3 June 1769. By observing this transit, the distance of the sun from the earth could be calculated.

Cook was also instructed to chart New Zealand and take possession of it for the English, and to search for the great south land, about the existence of which he was sceptical. After charting and claiming New Zealand, he decided to return home via Van Diemen's Land and turned towards the undiscovered east coast of New Holland. The prevailing winds carried him north of his intended route and, at daylight on 19 April 1770, land was sighted by and named after Cook's first lieutenant. Point Hicks in Victoria has since been renamed Cape Everard.

For the next nine days, the boat travelled north along the coast searching for safe anchorage. They eventually found Botany Bay and landed on 28 April 1770 near the site of modern-day Sydney. The party spent a week exploring this area and the two botanists on board, Daniel Solander and Joseph Banks, gathered specimens. The Endeavour then resumed its journey northwards along the coast.

On 11 June, the boat struck a reef near Trinity Bay and stopped for a month to repair damage. On 22 August, Cook landed on and named Possession Island north of Cape York, also claiming as New South Wales the east coast north of latitude 38°S in the name of King George III. From here Cook sailed north through Torres Strait and home.

Cook found the eastern coast of Australia far more hospitable than the western coast and observed the native people with sympathy, not the contempt expressed by previous explorers.

In 1771, Cook commanded *Adventure* and *Resolution* in a renewed search for the great south land and, in 1773, they became the first boats to enter the Antarctic Circle and see the ice barrier. On his third voyage of 1777–1779, Cook was killed by Hawaiian islanders.

European Colonisation

Cook's discovery of Botany Bay sealed Australia's fate as the new British penal colony with Joseph Banks suggesting it as an ideal site. Britain's prisons were overflowing and the achievement of American independence in 1776 prevented further transportation there. The decision was formally announced in 1787 by King George III. Other than the death sentence, transportation to Botany Bay was the most severe punishment with terms ranging from a minimum exile of seven years to 14 years or life, with hard labour involved at all levels. A prisoner could be transported for a crime as minor as stealing a handkerchief or a loaf of bread.

THE FIRST FLEET

Arthur Phillip, a captain in the Royal Navy, was chosen to lead the first convict expedition to the new colony. In May 1787, the First Fleet, made up of 11 store and transport ships, set sail from England bound for Botany Bay. There were approximately 1475 people on board, with an estimated 211 marines, 548 male and 188 female convicts. The cargo also included two bulls, five cows, four stallions, three mares, 19 goats, 74 pigs, 29 sheep, five rabbits, 18 turkeys, 29 geese, 35 ducks and 209 fowls.

Phillip's flagship, the *Supply*, reached Botany Bay on 18 January 1788 before the rest of the fleet, but Phillip decided it was unsuitable for permanent settlement. The bay was shallow and unprotected, the soil was poor and the surroundings swampy. The fleet sailed north into Port Jackson, described by Phillip as 'the finest harbour in the world', and landed at Sydney Cove on 26 January 1788. They had been at sea for eight months. The British flag was hoisted the same day; the day that is now celebrated as Australia Day each year. The colony was formally proclaimed on 7 February 1788.

THE ORIGINAL INHABITANTS

At the time of white settlement it is believed that there were more than 600 Aboriginal clans in Australia, ranging in size from about 100 to 2000 people. The total population at that time is very roughly estimated at somewhere between 200 000 and 750 000. Each clan had its own territory which was linked to its ancestors through features of the land (sacred sites).

This population had been reduced by more than two-thirds by the 1930s. They were decimated by introduced diseases such as smallpox, measles, influenza and venereal disease, against which they had few biological defences. The appropriation of land and resources and deliberate killing by the settlers were also responsible for the heavy loss of life, with the suffering greatest amongst the clans living in areas where early settlements were established.

The forcible takeover of land, the rape of Aboriginal women and enslaving of children were major causes of early conflict. Hunting spears were no match for the military's firepower, and those who survived were faced with starvation and the impoverishment and loss of their traditions as they were cut off from the sites of greatest cultural, spiritual and ceremonial significance.

RESISTANCE

Black resistance to the white invasion took many forms and was a feature of life on the fringes of European settlement from the first months at Sydney Cove to the early 20th century.

As the settlers slowly pushed inland, Aboriginal people engaged in forms of economic warfare, burning buildings and crops and murdering large numbers of sheep and cattle. Settlers were also killed in retaliation for the stealing of land and destruction of sacred sites. The whites responded with dramatic force, and by the early 1800s it was common practice for a Governor to order a party to drive Aboriginal people from any area where violence had occurred. This later became known as 'dispersing the blacks', a practice particularly popular with squatters and often involving mass murder.

An estimated 2000 Europeans and 20 000 Aborigines died violently in these frontier conflicts.

THE TASMANIAN ABORIGINAL PEOPLE

Aboriginal clans in Tasmania were almost wiped out by white invaders within 75 years of the first white settlement in 1803. Most of the estimated 4000 to 5000 Aboriginal people were killed in the first 20 years. In 1829, the survivors were rounded up and removed to an island in Bass Strait. The dispossession decimated the population and by 1858 only 15 people remained alive. 'Queen' Truganini, who died in 1876, is generally thought to have been the last full-blooded Tasmanian Aboriginal elder, but it is possible that some groups survived on isolated Bass Strait islands.

BENNELONG

The Aboriginal men Bennelong and Colbee were captured at the order of Governor Phillip, who was eager to learn their language and customs and gain further knowledge of the land and its resources. Bennelong quickly became proficient in English, dined at Government House and began living in a brick hut built for him by the Governor on the site where the Sydney Opera House now stands. The site is named Bennelong Point in his honour.

When Phillip returned to England in 1792 he took Bennelong and Yemmerrawanyea with him. The latter Aboriginal man did not manage to survive the English cold and died there at 18 years of age. Bennelong amused the English, who plied him with alcohol and then laughed at his drunken antics. By the time he returned to Australia in 1795 his health was broken and he discovered that he was wanted by neither black nor white. His own people disowned him because he had left the tribe and he was barely accepted in white society. He died in 1813.

Convict Settlement

For the first two years, the threat of starvation hung over the young penal colony, as neither convicts nor marines had much knowledge of farming. The settlement had to rely on supply ships from England for food and other provisions. Unskilled convicts were put to work straight away clearing land and building roads, while blacksmiths, carpenters, bricklayers and stonemasons worked on churches, courthouses and other public buildings. The convicts were housed in barracks, where they received scant food and clothing.

Punishment for those thought slack in their work or who were caught trying to escape ranged from the treadmill and the road party (where convicts worked side by side in leg irons) to flogging or, at worst, hanging.

Transportation to other penal settlements such as Norfolk Island was a severe punishment. Situated off the east coast of New South Wales, the island was settled shortly after 1788 as a secondary penal settlement. Convicts who had committed a second offence after arriving in the colony were sent here, as were the less obedient convicts. It quickly developed a notorious reputation as a brutal island prison and a place of banishment for the worst convicts.

Macquarie Harbour, on the remote west coast of Tasmania, was founded as a penal settlement in 1822, while Port Arthur on the south-east coast was established in 1930. It became the largest penal settlement in the colony, incarcerating a total of 30 000 convicts over its 47-year history. It was thought to be impossible to escape from, as the only access was over an isthmus, guarded constantly by soldiers with dogs. In 1996, it was the scene of the world's worst documented peace time shooting, with 32 people killed.

FARMING

The reliance on supply ships from England, which were often late, made Phillip realise that the settlement in Sydney Cove had to become self-supporting. He searched for suitable farming land and found the fertile river valleys of the Parramatta and Hawkesbury Rivers. Farms were established at both sites, with Aborigines mounting fierce attacks on the settlers, especially along the Hawkesbury River. In 1789, when his sentence expired, the convict farmer James Ruse was given 0.6 ha of land at Parramatta on which to start a farm, along with grain, tools, two sows and six hens. He and his wife, also an emancipated convict, harvested a substantial wheat crop and were rewarded with the colony's first land grant: 12 ha of land named 'Experiment Farm' by Governor Phillip.

EMANCIPATION

Phillip devised a system of emancipation to act as an incentive for ex-convicts to pioneer the country. There were three levels. Through hard work or good conduct, convicts could earn a ticket of leave allowing them to work for themselves within a nominated area providing they made regular contact with authorities. The second and most common was a conditional pardon; convicts were granted their liberty as long as they did not leave the colony. An absolute pardon allowed an ex-convict total freedom as well as a small land grant.

THE RUM CORPS

When Phillip returned to England in 1792, his departure signalled the end of civil administration. No new Governor was appointed and the NSW Corps ran the colony, headed by a senior army officer, Major Francis Grose. At this time, incoming ships were selling their much needed supplies to the struggling settlement at inflated prices and making a huge profit. When a young lieutenant, John Macarthur (*see* Economy, wool industry), was forced to buy a cargo of rum with his supplies, the officers decided to turn it to their advantage and set up a monopoly on rum provisions. As a result, rum became the de facto currency of the colony and the officers became known as the Rum Corps.

Grose also started the practice of granting land to officers, who, in turn, enticed convicts to work after government hours by paying them in rum. Slowly, the officers absorbed the riches of the new colony and became an elite and arrogant group.

THE RUM REBELLION

Grose was later replaced by Governor King, under whom the Rum Corps became even more powerful. William Bligh then replaced King as Governor. An English naval officer, he had commanded the Bounty on a voyage to Tahiti when his crew, led by Fletcher Christian, staged the famous mutiny in response to his unpredictable rages. It was with the same temperament that Bligh tried to govern New South Wales.

He threatened to arrest and try for treason key figures in the Rum Corps and, in January 1808, his officers rebelled and deposed him in what is commonly known as the Rum Rebellion. He was held prisoner for a year before returning to England. Those responsible for the rebellion were court-martialled.

THE MACQUARIE ERA

The power of the rum monopoly was finally broken with the appointment of Governor Lachlan Macquarie in 1810, who introduced old Spanish dollars as the new colonial currency. A former Lieutenant Colonel in the British army, Macquarie headed the colony until 1822, improving roads and commissioning buildings which transformed the settlement.

Greenway, an ex-convict who was given 14 years transportation for forgery, was Macquarie's chief architect. Greenway was pardoned by Macquarie after he designed the Hyde Park Barracks. He is also remembered for St Matthew's Church at Windsor, the lighthouse at South Head (at the entrance to Sydney Harbour), the stables at Government House (now the New South Wales Conservatorium of Music), St James Church in King Street, and the 'Rum Hospital', so called because Macquarie gave the contractors 200 000 litres of rum as payment. Today, the hospital's former north wing forms the central part of New South Wales Parliament House.

Exploration

It took the European settlers only 75 years to explore effectively the entire continent of Australia, a remarkable achievement given the harsh climate and lack of water in some parts of the country. Although short expeditions were mounted under Governor Phillip, the first major expedition was not until 1813.

THE BLUE MOUNTAINS

The Blue Mountains are so called because of the blue haze covering them, thought to be caused by sunlight shining through vapour released by eucalypts. They proved a barrier to exploration for 25 years. The European method of crossing mountains was by following valleys through the range, but valleys in the Blue Mountains end in cliffs about 300 m high.

Blaxland, Wentworth and Lawson finally crossed the range in 1813 by keeping to the ridges, and reached the area now known as Lithgow. They returned to Sydney to report on the new grasslands found and the following year the surveyor George Evans was sent to lay foundations for a road to Bathurst. A gang of convicts under William Cox built this road to Bathurst in six months. When completed it allowed settlers to move to rich grazing lands in the west.

The New South Wales Surveyor General, John Oxley, was sent out by Macquarie to discover more about the new land to the west. With his assistant George Evans and botanist Allan Cunningham, he found a number of rivers including the Macquarie, Castlereagh and Hastings Rivers before striking a fertile coastal valley which he called Port Macquarie. Oxley was to make many more trips after this. Travelling now by sea, his most famous discovery occurred in 1823 when he was the first European to see the Brisbane River.

HUME AND HOVELL

Hamilton Hume, born in Parramatta in 1797, and William Hovell, an immigrant, opened up large areas of southern Australia in 1824. Instructed to walk to Spencer Gulf in South Australia, they made it as far as Corio Bay in Port Phillip along roughly the same route followed today by the Hume Highway. On their way, they became the first Europeans to discover one of Australia's most important rivers, which they named after Hume. It was later renamed the Murray River.

JOHN EDWARD EYRE

Eyre arrived in Sydney in 1833 and began working in the bush, becoming one of the first 'overlanders' in Australia, taking stock from Liverpool to the Monaro district. Later he spent years trying to find a way of moving stock from South Australia to Western Australia, discovering during his travels both Lake Torrens and Lake Eyre.

In 1841, Eyre set out from Fowler's Bay, but his party was attacked by Aborigines, leaving just Eyre and an Aborigine called Wylie to travel on to King George Sound. The land they found along the way was desert, with no feed or water for stock.

CHARLES STURT

Charles Sturt was born in India and arrived in Australia as Secretary to Governor Darling in 1827. With Darling's support, he set off in 1828 to follow the course of the Macquarie River, hoping to find an inland sea in central Australia into which all rivers ran. Instead, he found and named the Darling River. Sturt made another small trip, but became ill and returned to England to recover. When he returned to Australia in 1843, he had secured finance for an exploratory expedition through the entire interior. His party set off from Adelaide in 1844, crossing the Stony Desert and reaching the Simpson Desert. Here they turned back, discovering Cooper Creek on their return to Adelaide.

SIR THOMAS MITCHELL

Thomas Mitchell was born in Scotland, arriving in Sydney with his family in 1827. When the NSW Surveyor-General John Oxley died the following year, Mitchell took up this post.

He was responsible at first for improving roads to Bathurst, Goulburn and Liverpool. After Governor Darling returned to England, however, Mitchell persuaded the acting Governor, Patrick Lindsay, to support him in an exploratory expedition.

He set out in 1836, travelling from the Murray River along the Victorian coast to Portland. The land he found was fertile and scenic and he called it 'Australia Felix'.

JOHN MACDOUGALL STUART

Stuart was born in Scotland and came to Australia in 1839 at the age of 23. He joined a number of expeditions to open up land around South Australia, travelling around the Great Australian Bight and the Davenport Range.

Stuart is remembered most, however, for his exploratory trip of 1860. Attempting to find a transcontinental route from South Australia to the Northern Territory, he became the first European to reach the geographical centre of Australia, just west of Alice Springs, on 23 April. In 1861, on another expedition, Stuart left Adelaide and crossed through the centre of the continent before reaching the northern tip of Australia in 1862. This last trip left Stuart almost totally blind and he died two months after returning to England in 1864.

BURKE AND WILLS

Of all the inland explorers, Robert Burke and William Wills remain the best known. They were commissioned by the Royal Society of Victoria to find a transcontinental route to the north. In August 1860, the party set off with 23 horses and 15 men, recognising that they were racing to beat John MacDougall Stuart.

When they arrived at Menindee, Burke decided to form an advance party with Wills, William Brahe and John King. They reached Cooper Creek two months later, but Burke decided to push on to the Gulf of Carpentaria, leaving Brahe and some assistants to wait for the others. Although they came within sight of the sea, they were stopped by swamps and storms, and turned back to Cooper Creek. When they arrived, however, it was deserted. Brahe had left that morning for the Darling. They decided to travel to Mt Hopeless, a police outpost 240 km away. By dreadful misfortune, while they were away the remainder of the expedition returned to Cooper Creek and from there to Melbourne after finding no message from Burke.

Burke and Wills died wandering around the base camp. John King, however, was rescued by local Aboriginal tribespeople and kept alive until he was found by a search party.

The Gold Rush

The discovery of gold marked a turning point in Australian history, helping to transform it from a penal colony in to a young but prosperous country.

DISCOVERY OF GOLD

Gold was first discovered near Bathurst, New South Wales, by Edward Hargraves on 12 February 1851. Gold fever immediately struck Sydney, with wild stories circulating about gold nuggets being picked up off the ground. The lure of easy money quickly drained Sydney's workforce as they headed off for the diggings.

By August, the fever had spread to Melbourne when Thomas Hiscock discovered the alluvial goldfields at Ballarat in Victoria. Melbourne and Geelong were virtually deserted by people leaving for the goldfields, although the rough and primitive conditions there drove many back to the cities within a year.

The news of these gold finds had reached the rest of the world by the end of 1851. People from England, Scotland, Ireland, America and China soon poured into Australia to try their luck.

THE END OF TRANSPORTATION

Beginning with the First Fleet in 1788, about 165 000 convicts were transported to Australia. The last 10 000 went to Western Australia between 1850 and 1868. The British realised that gold would bring Australia wealth and that convict labour was therefore no longer necessary.

The last convicts transported to Tasmania arrived in 1853. To celebrate the end of transportation, the legislative council of Van Diemen's Land changed the colony's name to Tasmania to honour its European discoverer, Abel Tasman.

THE EUREKA STOCKADE

Soon after the gold diggers arrived in Ballarat and Bendigo, the Victorian legislative council took steps to police the goldfields. All diggings were placed under the control of a chief commissioner who enforced licence regulations. Diggers could not search, dig or remove gold without paying the £1 10s for a licence. Inspections of licences were held regularly and a fine was incurred for failure to pay a licence fee.

By 1854 most of the surface gold had been found and the value of gold had fallen. Diggers were finding the licence fee difficult to pay and the often brutal licence hunts by the police intensified a general feeling of discontent. They began demanding political reforms such as universal adult suffrage, ballot votes, annual parliamentary elections and the abolition of property interests to become a member of parliament. The Ballarat Reform League was set up, led by Peter Lalor, and began to lobby for reform.

THE UPRISING

Violence broke out in November 1854, when the owner of the Eureka Hotel in Ballarat, charged with murdering a digger, was let off. The pub was burned to the ground and more than 20 000 diggers joined together, burning their licences in a huge bonfire and building a stockade.

On 3 December 1854, with only 150 diggers remaining (the rest having become discouraged) almost 300 police and soldiers arrived and ordered the diggers to surrender. When they refused the troops charged. Within 15 minutes the fight was all over. About 25 diggers were killed, 30 were wounded and the rest taken prisoner.

The result of this bloody uprising was the replacement of the licence fee with a miner's right (payment of £1 a year). Goldfields were included in electoral boundaries and those with miner's rights were allowed to vote.

ANTI-CHINESE RIOTS

In 1855–1856, Chinese immigrants arrived at the goldfields in large numbers. By 1857, there were 23 623 Chinese in Victoria, and 24 062 by 1861 (only six of whom were women). At the time there were 203 966 Europeans at the Victorian goldfields: 130 535 men and 73 431 women. Diggers began to develop a territorial fear of the Chinese whose culture was completely alien. Laws were passed in Victoria and New South Wales to restrict Chinese entry, but the Chinese landed in South Australia instead and walked across to the goldfields.

In 1857, there was a riot against the Chinese on the Buckland River in Victoria, but the worst racist violence occurred in New South Wales. On 30 June 1861, anti-Chinese hatred came to a head at Lambing Flat, near Young in New South Wales. About a thousand men put up a 'No Chinese' banner and then rode out to the Chinese quarters, armed with bludgeons and whips. The Chinese people were grabbed by their hair by men on horseback and left to be beaten up by those on foot. Police eventually arrived at the end of the day and arrested the rioters, but they were later released and went unpunished.

GOLD IN WESTERN AUSTRALIA

Gold was first discovered in the Kimberley region in 1886. Four years later, gold was found in Kalgoorlie, where millions of dollars worth of gold is still mined each year.

The discovery of gold in Western Australia changed Australia's poorest and most underdeveloped state into the richest and most progressive, almost overnight. Western Australia became known as the 'Golden West', and people flocked there during the 1890–1893 Depression to try their luck on the goldfields.

BUSHRANGERS

Bushrangers existed in the colony's early days, but after the gold rush they enjoyed quite extensive popular support and when arrested and taken for trial to the cities, large crowds would cheer as they rode by.

Ben Hall, Frank Gardiner and 'Mad Dog' Morgan were all notorious. The most famous and celebrated bushranger, however, was Ned Kelly. Kelly wore an iron mask and his notorious gang eluded the police for two years. Kelly was finally arrested at Glenrowan, Victoria, in 1880, and was hanged in Melbourne at the age of twenty-six.

The Post Gold Rush Boom

LAND TRANSPORT

At the time of the gold rush, walking, travelling by horseback or using two-wheeled bullock drays were almost the only ways of moving around Australia. By 1853, a coach service was established by four Americans between Melbourne and the Victorian goldfields, known as Cobb & Co. The network soon covered the eastern colonies and constantly extended inland, carrying mail and passengers for about 75 years with only four fatal accidents in that time.

The first railway in Australia began operating in 1854 in Victoria, from Melbourne to Port Melbourne, carrying goods over 4 km of track. It was funded by the colonial government. By 1880, railways had crossed the

Great Dividing Range and, by 1888, the four main railway systems of Queensland, South Australia, Victoria and New South Wales had joined up at the respective borders (*see* Transport).

RIVER TRAVEL AND SHIPPING

In 1853, the first locally built paddle-steamer sailed down the Murray River, heralding a new era of travel in Australia. Soon hundreds of paddle-steamers were towing wool and wheat up and down the Murray, Murrumbidgee and Darling Rivers. It proved a cheaper way to move cargo, and towns along these rivers prospered through increased trade.

Ships also improved during this period. The First Fleet took eight months to reach Australia and news from Europe could take even longer to reach the colony. By 1816, the average voyage from England to Australia took five months. In the 1840s, shipbuilding was revolutionised by the advent of clippers, an American design which streamlined sailing ships and reduced the average trip from London to Sydney to about 14 weeks. The opening of the Suez Canal in 1869 and the development of steamships eventually cut the time down to about 50 days.

COMMUNICATIONS

OVERLAND TELEGRAPH LINE

This was Australia's first link with the rest of the world. In 1870, the Postmaster General of South Australia, Charles Todd, began to supervise the building of the overland telegraph line to Port Darwin, relying largely on maps drawn by the explorer Stuart ten years earlier. Construction took two years, in which time they pushed through about 3250 km of bush and desert. The two ends of the line eventually met north of Alice Springs on 22 August 1872, and the Australian connection was then linked with a cable between Java and Darwin.

KANAKA TRADE

While gold was being mined in New South Wales and Victoria, Queensland had struck gold of a different kind. The climate was perfect for growing sugar cane and sugar became one of the most important colonial exports.

In 1863, a successful Queensland businessman, Robert Towns (after whom Townsville was named), began importing cheap labour from the Pacific to work on sugar plantations, creating a slave trade that existed until 1904. Kanakas were contracted to work on sugar plantations for a three-year term, in return for wages and keep. This rarely happened in practice, however, and in 1884 when thousands of Kanakas were put to work, at least one out of every seven died because of the appalling conditions they were forced to endure.

In the early years of federation, in line with its White Australia policy, the Federal government passed the *1901 Pacific Islander Labourers Act*, stopping the use of Kanaka labour and repatriating these workers within five years.

Squatters

Investment in land during the mid-1800s bought respectability as well as political power. Running sheep was the most lucrative business and the most popular way of doing this was to lease crown land by paying an annual lease or licence fee. Those who did this became known as squatters.

The squatters were responsible for pioneering the inland country after NSW became increasingly populated in the mid-1800s. They would travel with bullock drays packed with necessities and, when suitable land was found, build a hut and set out to stake a claim on running the land. They faced many problems such as bushfire, drought and lack of labour but their biggest problems were Aboriginal attacks and sabotage.

RELATIONS WITH ABORIGINAL PEOPLE

The squatters' expansion over most of the eastern part of the country meant dispossession and death for local Aboriginal tribes. Squatters would often organise parties of men to go out and hunt Aboriginal people, exterminating them like pests. Others used more subtle measures such as poisoning flour given to Aboriginal people or poisoning their waterholes.

By the end of the 19th century, Aboriginal people had been pushed into special reserves or missions run mostly by the church to protect their declining numbers and to keep them off land seized by the white invaders. Half-caste and Aboriginal children were forcibly removed from their parents and sent to the cities to earn their living as domestic servants. Some ran away from these attempts to 'civilise' them, while others grew up never knowing their parents or cultural background.

MYALL CREEK MASSACRE

In 1838, a party of white men near Myall Creek, New South Wales, captured some Aboriginal men, tied them together, shot them and then burned their bodies. When a white man reported the murders the men were arrested and brought to trial. White society was in an uproar, but it was not over the horrific nature of the crime. Rather, it was considered an outrage that killing Aboriginal people could be considered a crime. At the first trial, the men were found not guilty and four of them were released. When a retrial was called, the seven remaining men were hanged.

Massacres and retaliation between Aboriginal peoples and whites became more frequent as a result.

LAND REFORM

The squatters' domination of land ownership began to decline during the 1850s when city dwellers began to demand access and selection of land. They believed the squatters were wasting the land and impeding agricultural progress with their huge sheep runs. The squatters predicted that free selection would be disastrous due to the settlers' lack of experience in the bush and their inability to cope with the harsh climate.

Despite these dire predictions, New South Wales, Victoria, Queensland and South Australia all passed legislation allowing any person to buy land for a set price per acre. For most of the new settlers, the squatters' gloomy warnings unhappily came true. Most lived in slum conditions, and many lost their properties when the banks foreclosed. It was only with the advent of agricultural machinery after the turn of the century that they began to improve their standard of living.

The Depression 1890–1893

In July and August 1890, a financial crash occurred in Argentina which had worldwide implications. It also had a very damaging effect on Australia's economy, inflated by years of expansion by government and the private sector, and financed largely through loans from London. When these London financial institutions crashed after Argentina, funds were withdrawn from Australia. As a result, one bank failed in 1892, and 13 banks in Victoria, New South Wales and Queensland closed soon after.

Country areas were also hard hit. Their produce was now fetching less than 50% of its previous price, while interest rates at banks continued to rise. Land values plummeted.

THE GREAT MARITIME STRIKE

When the Depression hit, the trade union movement was well and truly established. The rights of shearers, wharf-labourers and other manual workers were protected by the unions and the debate about a minimum wage was beginning to warm up.

In contrast, the great maritime strike began with the officers, not the manual workers. The officers walked out, encouraged by the success of the trade union movement, to form their own union. Employers refused to accept the officers' desire for a union and began advertising for non-union or 'scab' labour. Within a month tens of thousands of waterside workers, miners, pastoral workers and others were on strike in sympathy.

Although the strike was defeated, bush workers took it up again. In 1894, the government responded by siding with the employers, arresting union leaders and throwing them in prison. These strikes fuelled the move towards uniting the States. (*See* Government for a timeline to Federation.)

Federation

THE CEREMONY

The Commonwealth of Australia was officially proclaimed on 1 January 1901 by Australia's first Governor-General, Lord Hopetoun. The day before the ceremony Hopetoun commissioned Edmund Barton, a strong federationist, as Australia's first Prime Minister.

The Federation Ceremony was held at Centennial Park in Sydney in a temporary pavilion made for the occasion. A procession of floats and statesmen set off from the Domain, winding its way past grandstands which lined the route, to Centennial Park where a crowd of about 100 000 waited. Lord Hopetoun entered the pavilion to loud applause and after the attendant choir sang and prayers were recited, Hopetoun took the oath of office. He then read messages from the Queen and the British government and the Federal anthem was sung.

Just 21 days later, on the 22 January 1901, Queen Victoria died.

THE FIRST FEDERAL ELECTION

Edmund Barton served as interim Prime Minister until the first federal election was held on 29 and 30 March 1901. After the election he became Australia's first elected Prime Minister, leading a group of mainly liberal protectionists. Two other party groupings existed at this time: the Free Traders, a loosely organised party led by George Reid, the former NSW premier; and the Labor Party which became Australia's first federal political party in 1902. The Labor Party gave their support to Barton, giving him a working majority in the House.

The first Parliament was opened on 9 May 1901 by the Duke of York. It was housed in the Exhibition Building in Melbourne until 1927, when the seat of government moved to Canberra.

On 31 March 1901, when the first Commonwealth census was taken, Australia's population stood at 3 773 801 people.

THE AUSTRALIAN FLAG

Upon Federation, Australia had no national flag and competitions were run in two Melbourne papers in search of a design. In 1901, the government joined the quest by offering additional prizemoney.

The competition was won by five identical designs chosen from 32 823 entries. The flag was hoisted for the first time on 3 September 1901. Originally the star below the Union Jack was six-pointed, but was soon changed to a seven-pointed star.

THE WHITE AUSTRALIA POLICY

In 1901, the Immigration Restriction Bill was introduced into the House by Alfred Deakin who later served as Prime Minister. Watson, the first federal Labor leader, agreed about the necessity of a white Australia to maintain the standard of living of the working class.

The *Immigration Restriction Act* was passed, imposing a 50-word dictation test on potential immigrants in any European language chosen by the immigration official. Residents of less than five years could also be subjected to the test and deported if they failed. In 1905, the Act was amended so that a prescribed language rather than specifically a European language was tested, and in the same year the law was relaxed to allow Indian and Japanese students, tourists and businesspeople to stay a maximum of five years. In 1912, this new ruling was extended to Chinese people.

The Commonwealth Government discriminated against Aboriginal Australians as well, and they were not given the right to vote when the *Commonwealth Franchise Act* was passed in 1902. In fact, it was not until 1962 that all Aboriginal people became entitled to vote at federal elections and referendums.

When the aged pension was introduced, it excluded Aboriginal Australians, Asians not born in Australia, natives of Africa and the islands of the Pacific. The Australian Workers Union at this time excluded Asians, Aboriginal Australians and half-castes in their constitution.

CONCILIATION AND ARBITRATION

An Act of Federal Parliament in 1903 established the Commonwealth Court of Conciliation and Arbitration. Part of its role was to be the supreme arbitrator in situations which extended beyond state boundaries.

In 1907, Henry Bourne Higgins, the court's second President, found that the wages being paid by the Sunshine Harvester Company were not fair and reasonable. He proceeded to define and implement a minimum wage, a concept which, though altered and amended, has remained a basic precept of Australian life. (*See* Law.)

EARLY FEDERAL POLITICS

The three-party system which existed in the early years of Federal Parliament meant that no party could achieve an outright majority. Until 1909, the Protectionist Party had held government with the support of the Labor Party. Alfred Deakin, who replaced Barton when he resigned to join the High Court bench in 1903, had served three terms as Prime Minister.

In 1909, the two liberal parties, the Protectionists and the Free Traders, amalgamated under the title of the Liberal or Fusion Party. As a result, an election was called in 1910 and the Labor Party, under the leadership of Andrew Fisher, obtained an outright majority.

In power for three years, this government created the Commonwealth Bank. Canberra was chosen as the site for Australia's capital and a competition for the design of the city was held and won by American architect Walter Burley Griffin. (*See* Government.)

In 1911, a previously decided system of compulsory military training was introduced for all males between the ages of twelve and twenty-six. (*See* Defence.) In 1913, a Liberal government won the election with a majority of one and a minority in the Senate. This led, in 1914, to a double dissolution, the first in Australia's history.

During the ensuing election campaign World War I broke out.

World War I

World War I began on 4 August 1914 when Britain declared war on Germany. The day before this the Australians had offered an expeditionary force of 20 000 men to be under the control of the British government, and the ships of the Royal Australian Navy (RAN) to be under the control of the British Admiralty. This offer was accepted on 6 August and four battalions each from New South Wales and Victoria were promised, as well as another four between the other States.

In his election campaign, Andrew Fisher, leader of the Labor Party, promised that 'Australians would stand beside our own to help and defend her to our last man and shilling'. On 5 September, the Labor Party was returned to government.

AUSTRALIA AT WAR

The first major engagement of the RAN was with the German light cruiser *Emden* on 9 November 1914 in the Indian Ocean near the Australian Territory of the Cocos Islands. In a confrontation with the Australian light cruiser *Sydney*, the *Emden* was sunk.

Enlistment in the Australian Imperial Force (AIF) began on 8 August 1914 and on 1 November the first group, consisting of 20 000 men, including New Zealanders, left for England. During the voyage the destination was changed due to lack of accommodation in England, and they landed at Alexandria on 3 December.

The Australian and New Zealand Army Corps (ANZACs) were quartered in training camps in Egypt by the beginning of 1915. When the Gallipoli campaign was devised, the ANZACs played a major role due to their proximity to the region.

Gallipoli

The plan behind the Gallipoli campaign was to take control of the Dardanelles, a passage leading through to the Black Sea, opening it to Allied shipping. On 25 April, today commemorated in Australia as ANZAC Day, thousands of Australian troops stormed the beach at Gallipoli. The attack was badly planned and undermanned. Many Australian soldiers were killed and wounded as they stormed ashore at Anzac Cove.

About 8000 Australians were killed and 20 000 were wounded during the campaign. Those who survived stayed for eight months until they were allowed to withdraw.

Overall, there were about 34 000 killed and about 80 000 Allied soldiers wounded.

The Western Front

After the Gallipoli campaign, most of the ANZACs went to the Western Front to the trenches near Armentieres. The 1st, 2nd and 4th Divisions took part in the First Battle of the Somme, which had started on 1 July 1916 soon after they arrived. By the end of this battle, the Australians had suffered 23 000 casualties.

The Australian troops also sustained many casualties in 1917 in the battles of Bullecourt in April and May, at Messines in June and in the Ypres and Passchendaele offensives.

Conscription

In Australia another battle was being waged over conscription. Billy Hughes, who had been Attorney General under Andrew Fisher, became Prime Minister in 1915 after Fisher resigned to take up the post of Australian High Commissioner in London. After touring England and the Western Front in 1916, Hughes returned convinced that conscription was the only way to raise the numbers needed. When Hughes announced his decision to hold a referendum on conscription, he was expelled from the

Labor Party by the Sydney Political Labour League. The conscription referendum was held on 28 October 1916 and the answer was no. The vote was 1 100 033 to 1 087 557.

Soon after, Hughes walked out of a parliamentary meeting asking those who supported him to follow; 23 of the 65 people present did. They formed a minority government with the Liberals' support and soon after the parties joined to form the Nationalist Party. At the next election, held in May 1917, the Nationalists were returned to power and Hughes called another referendum over conscription. Held on 20 December 1917, the vote was even more decisively against conscription. The vote was 1 015 159 for and 1 181 747 against.

THE ARMISTICE

At 11 a.m. on 11 November 1918, the firing ceased. In all, 331 781 Australians had gone to war. Of the 416 809 who joined the services during the war, all were volunteers. Of these, 59 342 were killed and 152 171 wounded. No other country in the Empire suffered as high a loss in proportion to its population as Australia.

The Great Depression

The Great Depression of 1929–1933 began on 24 October 1929 with the crash of the American stockmarket. This financial crisis spread worldwide.

Australia was hit harder than most countries because the economy relied on overseas loans and the sale of primary products, such as wool and wheat. Between 1928 and 1930, national income fell from £640 million to £560 million. When the value of wool fell by nearly half in 1929, the country was plunged into crisis. Farms were lost, shops and businesses closed and debts increased. The basic wage was reduced. Unemployment rose to a record 30%. Many unemployed breadwinners left the cities to find work in the country while shanty towns and soup kitchens mushroomed in the cities.

THE NIEMEYER PLAN

In August 1930, Sir Otto Niemeyer from the Bank of England visited Australia as an economic adviser. Addressing a Premiers' conference called by Labor Prime Minister James Scullin, his advice reflected the conventional economic thinking of the time.

He recommended the adoption of deflationary policies, believing Australia had to reduce its high standard of living created by heavy borrowing and the protection of local industry. He recommended retrenchment and wage cuts. Under his influence, the State and Territory Premiers tried to balance their budgets and decrease their reliance on borrowed funds.

RECOVERY

Although the economy began to recover from the Great Depression during the 1930s, the effects were felt for a long time. The Labor government of the day, led by Joseph Lyons, concentrated on bringing down unemployment and establishing financial security.

During this time, Australian society was becoming increasingly urbanised, due mainly to the lack of transport and opportunity in the outback and also the growth of secondary industry. Although unemployment was still quite widespread, Australian industry was showing promising potential when World War II broke out.

World War II

World War II started on 3 September 1939. Prime Minister Robert Menzies announced that Britain had declared war on Germany after Hitler invaded Poland, and that Australia was also at war. His announcement was greeted quietly by the Australian public, unlike the patriotic scenes that accompanied Australia's involvement in World War I. Compulsory military training was introduced, amateur radio operations were banned and enemy foreigners were rounded up.

World War II was different from World War I in that there was a threat on two fronts: Asia and Europe. The Menzies government was preoccupied by a possible future expansion by the Japanese into the South Pacific, but was also determined not to let Britain down in the fight against the Nazis and Italian Fascists.

The war was fought between the Allies (including Britain and her dominions, France, Russia and the United States) and the Axis powers (Germany, Italy and Japan).

THE WAR IN EUROPE

At the end of 1939, the first Australian contingent left for Palestine for training before heading to Europe to fight the Italians and Germans. When Germany invaded Greece in 1941, Australian and New Zealand forces, known as the ANZAC Corps, were sent to help the Greek army. Despite the combined effort, Crete fell to the Germans. In June 1941, the Australians joined the Allies in Syria and Lebanon to prevent the Germans advancing to the Persian Gulf. The Germans and Italians were also fought against in the Middle East and North Africa and, in 1941, Tobruk and Benghazi were captured by the Allies. When troops were diverted to the war against the Japanese in the Pacific, however, Tobruk fell. In 1942, the Allies staged an offensive at El Alamein against the Germans and Italians, retaking Tobruk and Tripoli.

THE JAPANESE

While the war was being fought in Europe, the Japanese were slowly advancing south. During this time, Australian Prime Minister Arthur Fadden was defeated by John Curtin, who led the Labor Party to victory in the 1941 election.

He was not long in office before the Japanese attacked the American base at Pearl Harbour on 7 December 1941. The invasion of Australia now seemed a real threat and the country prepared itself for a war on Australian soil. One by one, Japan took Hong Kong, Borneo, the Philippines, Singapore, northern New Guinea and many of the Solomon Islands. Darwin was bombed and the civilian population evacuated, ships were sunk off the New South Wales coast and Japanese midget submarines penetrated Sydney Harbour.

It was at this time that Curtin, after receiving little support from Churchill in Britain, turned to the Americans for help.

THE AMERICANS

General Douglas Macarthur arrived in Melbourne, Victoria, on 17 March 1942, and was made Supreme Commander of the Allied forces in the South-West Pacific.

The Japanese suffered their first real defeat when a combined American-Australian force drove them back from Port Moresby, New Guinea, and away from the eastern coast of Queensland in May 1942; this was the Battle of the Coral Sea. In March 1943, several Japanese ships were sunk in the Battle of the Bismarck Sea and the long battle to push the Japanese back from the Pacific began.

HIROSHIMA AND NAGASAKI

On 6 August 1945, an American plane dropped an atomic bomb on Hiroshima; on 9 August 1945, a second atomic bomb was dropped on Nagasaki. The Japanese surrendered. On 15 August 1945, the new Australian Prime Minister, Ben Chifley, who had replaced Curtin after his death, announced to the Australian public that the war with Japan was over.

By the end of the war in 1945, 993 000 Australians had enlisted in the three defence forces: 28 753 were killed and there were 95 746 casualties. Of the 22 376 Australians held as prisoners of war of the Japanese, 8031 died while captive.

The Post-War Years

After the war, demobilisation of men and women and their rehabilitation into civil life proceeded quickly and smoothly. Apart from a housing shortage, the post-war years were a time of great optimism in Australia. There was a baby boom, plenty of jobs, and the overall population rose from 7 500 000 to 11 million due to the arrival of almost 2 million migrants between 1945 and 1966. Welfare was improved and extended after a 1946 referendum gave the Federal government increased social security powers. The standard of living rose as the economy grew stronger, and the demand for primary products, especially wool, increased.

The Snowy Mountains Scheme was devised (*see* Geography, irrigation) to divert the waters of the Snowy River to the dry western plains in NSW. Legislation to nationalise all civil airlines was introduced. In 1945, a *Banking Act* was introduced to regulate banking and protect the Australian dollar and public credit. The 40-hour working week was established across the country.

The Chifley government fell from favour in 1949, however. Strikes were held on the waterfront and in the shipping industry, and coal miners went out on strike over hours, wages and leave claims. When Chifley sent in the army to break a seven-week- old coal strike, complaints about the government became louder. The last straw was the proposal to nationalise the banks. As a result, the 1949 election was lost to the Liberals.

The Menzies Era

After the defeat of Menzies and the United Australia Party in 1941, the coalition split and the Liberal Party was formed in 1944 with Menzies as the leader. The Liberals quickly found support in the electorate, due in part to their strong stance against communism, and, at the 1949 election, they took office. Menzies remained in power from 19 December 1949 to 20 January 1966, the longest and most unbroken rule by an Australian Prime Minister.

At the time he was elected, communism was sweeping across Eastern Europe: Poland, Czechoslovakia, Hungary, East Germany, Bulgaria,

Romania, and Yugoslavia all had communist governments by 1948. Communist parties in Italy and France were becoming more popular and, on 1 October, the Cultural Revolution led by Mao Tse- tung proclaimed the People's Republic of China.

COMMUNIST PARTY DISSOLUTION BILL

On 27 April 1950, Menzies introduced the Communist Party Dissolution Bill to the House of Representatives. The Bill claimed that the Communist Party of Australia was planning the overthrow of the government and was therefore an illegal party.

The Bill was declared invalid by the High Court in March 1951. A referendum was held on 22 September 1951 to give the Australian people a chance to vote on whether the Communist Party should be banned: 2 317 927 voted for the ban and 2 370 009 voted against.

THE KOREAN WAR

A year after the Menzies government was elected, Communist North Korea invaded South Korea on 25 June 1950. US President Truman denounced the North Koreans and pledged American support to the Korean government. Australia, in turn, pledged support to the Americans and went to war. When the armistice was signed in July 1953, some 281 Australians had been killed or were missing in Korea.

INTERNATIONAL TREATIES

On 12 July 1951, the United States, Australia and New Zealand initiated a security treaty called the ANZUS treaty.

In Manila in October 1954, France, the United States, Australia, New Zealand, the United Kingdom, Pakistan, Thailand and the Philippines signed a treaty to establish the South-East Asia Treaty Organisation (SEATO) to protect against the perceived common enemy of communism.

THE PETROV AFFAIR

On 3 April 1954, Vladimir Petrov, a third secretary in the Soviet Embassy in Canberra, asked for political asylum. Menzies made an announcement to Parliament that Petrov had left the Soviet embassy with Soviet spy documents which he presented to ASIO. A Royal Commission was set up to enquire into the affair.

Press speculation pointed to a connection with Labor Party leader Dr Evatt and the 'spy network'. The Commission was held just before the 1954 election, discrediting the Labor Party and returning the Liberals to power. Evatt resigned as leader of the Labour Party and was replaced by Arthur Calwell (*see* Government, political parties).

The Vietnam War

The Vietnam War began in 1954, after France and China agreed to divide Vietnam between North and South. The North was under the Communist government of Ho Chi Minh and General Vo Nguyen Giap, and the South under the dictatorship of Ngo Dinh Diem. Fighting broke out between the communist North, supported by the Viet Cong in the South, and the non-communist South Vietnam regime, supported by the United States. By December 1961, President John F. Kennedy, had pledged American support to the South Vietnamese government to defeat the communist attack from the North.

AUSTRALIAN INVOLVEMENT

The Vietnam War broke out just as Menzies had been returned to power in the 1954 election. He was quick to respond. By 1955 he had sent troops to Malaya, and the following year he announced that they could be used against the communists. In 1964, he introduced selective conscription for military service; those selected could be sent overseas for military service for two years. Then, in April 1965, he announced that Australia was sending over a battalion of soldiers to assist America's intervention in the war.

Labor leader, Arthur Calwell, firmly opposed the decision to send Australian troops to Vietnam, believing it was a civil matter.

MENZIES' RETIREMENT

On 20 January 1966, Menzies retired after more than 16 years as Prime Minister. In one of his last speeches to Parliament, he described himself as 'British to my boot straps'. Australia's longest serving Prime Minister was a royalist and, at a Canberra dinner for Queen Elizabeth II in 1963, he said, 'I did but see her passing by, And yet I love her till I die.' He was later knighted by the Queen.

ANTI-VIETNAM PROTESTS

Deputy Leader Harold Holt replaced Menzies as leader and increased Australian forces in Vietnam from 1500 to 4500 in March 1966. President Johnson visited Australia later that year and Holt promised that Australia would go 'all the way with LBJ'. While many Australians supported Johnson, he was also greeted by hostile and vocal anti-war demonstrators.

By 1967, uneasiness over Vietnam was growing. Some disapproved of America's imperial intervention in a small country like Vietnam, while others were worried that Australia would be on the losing side. The majority were alarmed by the use of napalm, phosphorous, and fragmentation bombs. In 1970, over 70 000 people marched in Melbourne in the largest anti-Vietnam War protest.

JOHN GORTON

Gorton eventually replaced Holt as Prime Minister on 10 January 1968, after Holt drowned at Portsea, Victoria in December 1967. His body was never found.

At his first press conference on 17 January 1968, Gorton announced that Australia would not send any more troops to Vietnam. When the Viet Cong launched their Tet offensive that month, however, an Australian presence was maintained in Vietnam. It was gradually decreased in 1970, and in 1972 Gough Whitlam, in one of his first decisions in office, announced that all Australian troops would be withdrawn from Vietnam.

A total of 49 211 Australians served in Vietnam: 501 were killed and 2069 were wounded.

The Whitlam Era

On 2 December 1972, a Labor government headed by Gough Whitlam, came to power. Labor's slogan for the election, 'It's time', captured the feeling of the population, who wanted a change after 23 years of Liberal government. Whitlam had a grand vision for Australia. He wanted to bring about genuine equality for all Australians through reforms in education and health care. He immediately announced the government's intention to abolish university fees, increase spending on primary and secondary education, decrease subsidies to private schools, grant land rights to Aboriginal Australians and relax divorce laws.

The speed with which his government implemented these reforms worried some conservatives, who voiced their criticisms loudly in the media. Thus the Whitlam government was attacked early in its term for being idealistic and hopeless administrators.

Whitlam was ruling without a majority in the Senate and, by April 1974, a number of bills passed by the House of Representatives, including a bill outlining the national health insurance scheme (Medibank), had been rejected by the Senate.

DOUBLE DISSOLUTION

In response to this attack from the Senate, Whitlam asked the Governor-General Sir Paul Hasluck for a double dissolution (*see* Government) on 10 April 1974. When Whitlam went to the polls on 19 May that year, inflation was rising and critics were calling Labor's support programs in education, health and Aboriginal Affairs, extravagant.

Despite this, Labor was returned to power, but still with a minority in the Senate. Leadership of the Liberal Party changed after the election with Billy Snedden replaced by Malcolm Fraser, an ambitious man who set about discrediting the Whitlam government.

THE LOANS AFFAIR

This 'scandal' was to be the turning point in the fortunes of the Whitlam government. The Minister for Minerals and Energy, Rex Connor, announced a plan to buy back some of Australia's mineral wealth that had been sold to America and Japan, by raising a loan from the Arab world. This was not the traditional means of obtaining loans and the government had first to receive the approval of the Loans Council.

The council agreed and in late 1974, Tirath Khemlani was authorised to act as an intermediary in the Arab world. In December, the Executive Council organised a temporary loan for Connor from the United States of $4000 million. On 6 March 1975, deputy leader Dr Cairns was authorised to borrow $US500 million overseas. He also signed a letter to a Melbourne financier authorising him to raise money overseas.

When news of this reached the Opposition, Cairns was forced to admit to the letter's existence and a campaign against the Labor Party was mounted in the press by the Opposition. In October 1975, the Khemlani Affair came out into the open.

THE DISMISSAL

The Opposition, believing the Whitlam government to be on the verge of collapse, decided to block the Supply Bill. This would have forced an election in the House of Representatives. Whitlam decided to wait it out and lasted for several weeks with no compromise in sight.

On 11 November 1975, Governor-General Sir John Kerr used his constitutional power to dismiss the Whitlam government. Malcolm Fraser, leader of the Opposition, was appointed caretaker Prime Minister until an election could be organised. On the steps of Parliament House, Whitlam said to the crowd, 'Well may we say, "God Save the Queen", because nothing will save the Governor-General.' He also called Fraser 'Kerr's cur'. Fraser's coalition government was duly elected in the polls that followed.

The Fraser Years

Fraser's government was overwhelmingly returned in the 1975 election. He declared that 'life wasn't meant to easy', encapsulating the direction in which the new government would turn the country. Huge cuts were made in every kind of government spending except defence, and funding of ASIO was increased dramatically. Medibank was abolished, but despite these measures the economy did not pick up.

When the Whitlam government was dismissed, inflation was at 15% and the unemployment rate was over 4% (the worst since the Great Depression). Under the Fraser government unemployment rose from 4.4% (November 1975) to 5.5% (1977), interest rates increased to 14.5% and inflation remained in double figures.

Despite this, Fraser was returned on 10 December 1977, and Whitlam resigned as Leader of the Labor Party to be replaced by Bill Hayden. Fraser also won the 1980 election convincingly, but by then criticism was becoming louder over the sale of Australia's natural resources to foreign investors at bargain prices. By 1981, $6 billion worth of foreign capital was invested in Australia, an increase of some $5 billion over the previous year.

On 3 February 1983, Fraser asked the Governor-General Sir Zelman Cowen for a double dissolution. At the same time, Bill Hayden resigned as Opposition Leader and Robert Hawke, a former ACTU President, became the new Labor leader. On 5 March 1983, the Hawke Labor Government was elected and Malcolm Fraser resigned as leader of the Liberal Party, conceding defeat.

The Hawke/Keating Labor Government

In 1983, Labor under the leadership of Bob Hawke won the election with a 25-seat majority. Together Hawke and Paul Keating, then Treasurer and later to become Prime Minister, oversaw a 13-year period of dramatic political and social reform, with Labor winning a record five terms. In the first year alone, the government floated the Australian dollar, abolished controls on foreign exchange and deregulated the banks.

One of the greatest achievements of the early years was the Prices and Incomes Accord, enabling the government to keep a check on inflation and wages. The cooperative relationship between government and trade unions secured a period of greater industrial harmony with the number of strikes reaching an all-time low.

The establishment of Medicare in 1984 set a new social policy standard, while the development of a more significant role for Australia on the world stage brought about changes in long-held views of the nation's identity. Tariff barriers came down and Australia, accustomed to the cushioning provided by protectionism, was forced to compete in the rough-and-tumble world marketplace.

Increasingly, the Hawke and Keating governments recognised that for the nation to forge a place for itself internationally, it must fully acknowledge its geographical position and engage with its neighbours in the Asia-Pacific region. Hawke's idea for an Asia-Pacific Economic Cooperation (APEC) was enthusiastically embraced and rapidly advanced by Keating when he became Prime Minister in 1991.

The two initiatives which earned Keating both the most accolades and the most enemies were his often-voiced comments on the necessity for an Australian Republic, and his Native Title legislation in response to the High Court's Mabo decision.

It is arguable that the rapid changes implemented by the Keating government and the radical shift in thinking it encouraged, came to alienate the majority of Australians. The loss of faith in the government and the direction in which it was taking the country was amply demonstrated in the 1996 election. John Howard and the Liberal National coalition won a landslide victory, enabling them to form a government after 13 years on the opposition benches.

The Eighties — A Timeline

<u>1983</u>

- Australia won the America's Cup, a yacht racing series at Newport, Rhode Island, USA, ending 112 years of American domination of the race. (*See* Sport, sailing.)
- Some of the worst recorded bushfires ('Ash Wednesday') occurred in Victoria and South Australia after record low rainfall the previous year. (*see* Climate, weather phenomena.)
- A Royal Commission into British nuclear tests in South Australia was established.
- The bungling of a training exercise at the Sheraton Hotel in Melbourne by the Australian Secret Intelligence Service (ASIS) made headlines and was investigated by Justice Hope. Training officers had not informed the hotel or ASIS of the exercise and ASIS had to pay out over $650 000 to the Sheraton.

1984

- 'Advance Australia Fair' was officially made Australia's national anthem by referendum.
- The $100 note and the one dollar coin made their first appearance.
- The Hawke Government was re-elected for a second term.
- The national health insurance scheme Medicare was introduced. (*See* Health.)
- The Nuclear Disarmament Party (NDP) was formed, signalling the emergence of a new force in politics, i.e. non-aligned political parties and independent candidates.
- The first of three articles based on conversations tapped by NSW police were published in the Age newspaper and became known as the Age Tapes. The tapes were investigated by the Costigan Royal Commission. One of the Commission's main findings resulted in the conviction of former High Court Judge Lionel Murphy charged with attempting to pervert the course of justice.
- Seven people were killed and about 30 people were injured when two motorbike gangs, the Bandidos and the Commancheros, held a shoot-out in the Viking Tavern car park in the western suburb of Milperra, Sydney. This incident became known as the Milperra massacre.

1985

- Uranium exports to France were banned.
- Deregulation of the banking industry occurred after the government invited applications to set up foreign banks in Australia.

1986

- Australia was constitutionally severed from the United Kingdom.
- Halley's Comet appeared in the night sky.
- The Pope visited Australia.
- An Australian communications satellite was launched, known as AUSSAT.
- The United States refused to recognise security obligations to New Zealand under the 1952 ANZUS Treaty after the New Zealand government banned nuclear warships from New Zealand waters. However, Australia continued its bilateral defence relationship with New Zealand and with the United States.
- Prime Minister Hawke launched the promotional 'Buy Australian' campaign, in an attempt to encourage Australians to reduce spending on imports.

1987

- A Royal Commission into Deaths in Custody of Aboriginals and Torres Strait Islanders began in October, after a string of incidents where Aboriginal people were found hanged in police cells.
- Lindy Chamberlain was cleared of the charge of murdering her baby daughter Azaria at Ayers Rock in 1981 by a Darwin court. Lindy Chamberlain maintained that a dingo had taken her baby and the resulting court case became one of the most sensational cases of the 1980s.
- Tennis player Pat Cash became the first Australian since John Newcombe in 1971 to win the men's singles at Wimbledon.

1988

- Australia's Bicentennial Year. Australia celebrated 200 years of European settlement with mixed feelings. Demonstrations by Aboriginal groups and supporters occurred, but the celebrations went on. A re-enactment of the First Fleet's entry into Sydney Harbour was staged.
- The new Parliament House in Canberra was officially opened by the Queen.
- Darling Harbour in Sydney was officially opened by the Queen.
- The two dollar coin was introduced.
- World Expo '88 was held in Brisbane.

1989

- Two major bus accidents occurred on the Pacific Highway, at Kempsey and Grafton, New South Wales, killing a total of 55 people.
- An earthquake hit Newcastle in New South Wales, killing 13 people and injuring about 130 more.
- The pilot's dispute, originally over a wage rise, disrupted air travel for three months. During this period, international airlines were called in to help ease the disruption to domestic flights.
- Tony Fitzgerald, handed down the findings of the Fitzgerald Inquiry. The Inquiry was set up in response to media revelations about crime and corruption in Queensland. Public hearings began in July 1987.
- A Labor government, led by Wayne Goss, won the November Queensland elections, ending 32 years of rule by the National Party. Sir Joh Bjelke Peterson was Premier for 17 of those years.

The Nineties — A Timeline

1990

- Australian opera singer Dame Joan Sutherland, who first launched her career in 1969 and often sang as a guest artist for the Australian Opera, announced her retirement in September.
- A financial crisis occurred in Victoria when a run on the Pyramid Building Society froze depositors' money. Tricontinental, a merchant bank purchased by the Victorian State Bank, collapsed, leaving many people without their life savings. Tricontinental had granted a number of bad loans after other major banks had rejected them.
- The Hawke government was narrowly returned to power for a record fourth term for a Labor Prime Minister.
- Deregulation of the two airline policy for the domestic market was announced and several new airlines were formed, the largest being Compass Airlines.
- The government announced that 49% of Australian Airlines and 49% of Qantas would be sold to private investors.

1991

- Paul Keating becomes Prime Minister after challenging Bob Hawke for the leadership of the Labor Party.
- The Wool Corporation is forced to abandon the reserve price scheme after 17 years.
- The final report from the Royal Commission into Aboriginal Deaths in Custody recommends sweeping reforms.
- The Coalition Opposition proposes a goods and services tax plan.
- Uranium mining is banned at Coronation Hill, Kakadu.
- The Royal Commission into WA Inc. reveals widespread corruption.
- Nine people are killed in a massacre by a lone gunman at Strathfield Shopping Centre, Sydney.

1992

- Lindy and Michael Chamberlain receive a $1.3 million compensation payout.
- The Anglican Synod allows the ordination of women.
- The Australian Armed Forces accept homosexual recruits.
- The landmark High Court Mabo decision is reached.
- The opening of the Sydney Harbour Tunnel.
- 1c and 2c coins are phased out of circulation.

1993

- The introduction of the *Native Title Act*.
- The highest unemployment rate ever is recorded, with newspapers reporting that, 'Australia hits the wall'.
- The Labor Party wins a record fifth successive term, with Keating dubbing it a victory for the 'true believers'.
- The Unknown Soldier is interred in the War Memorial, Canberra.
- Sydney, New South Wales, wins its bid to hold the Olympic Games in the year 2000.

1994

- Bushfires devastate areas around Sydney and the NSW central coast, causing the loss of four lives and extensive loss of property.
- Laws discriminating against homosexuality in the State of Tasmania are challenged by the Federal government and by the United Nations.
- The release of the Federal government report on Australia as a Republic.
- Alexander Downer is elected Leader of the Opposition.
- One person dies in the bombing of the National Crime Authority offices in Adelaide.

1995

- The Attorney-General's attempt to extradite failed business entrepreneur and former Quintex boss, Christopher Skase, from Majorca, Spain, is rejected by the Spanish court system and Skase leaves debts of hundreds of million dollars in Australia.
- The worst drought of the 20th century begins to subside.

1996

- In New South Wales, a Royal Commission is launched to investigate police corruption within the New South Wales Police Force. Justice Wood is appointed Royal Commissioner.
- John Howard's Liberal/National Party coalition wins the federal election.
- Following the Labor Party's defeat at the Federal election, former prime minister Paul Keating resigns from parliament after 27 years in politics.
- In Victoria, premier Jeff Kennett and his Liberal government retain power in the state elections.
- The world's worst documented mass shooting during peace time occurs at Port Arthur, Tasmania, with 32 people shot dead.
- Robert Beallar becomes Australia's first Aboriginal judge when he is appointed to the bench of the New South Wales District Court.

- In the wake of strong calls for tigher regulations on gun ownership following the Port Arthur massacre in Tasmania, Prime Minister John Howard attends a rally of pro-gun protesters in Sale, Victoria, wearing an anti-shrapnel jacket.
- An Aboriginal rock art site is uncovered in the tropical forests of the Kimberley region in Western Australia. The site, east of Kununnura, contains petroglyphs dating back 75 000 years, pushing back the date of the earliest known rock art in Australia by 50 000 years. Evidence is also found that Australia has been occupied by humans for up to 176 000 years, far longer than previously thought.

Mabo and the Native Title Act 1993

In May 1982, Eddie Mabo and several other Meriam people of the Murray Islands in Torres Strait began proceedings against the state of Queensland in the High Court. They argued that Murray Island (Mer) had been continuously occupied by the Meriam people since time immemorial, and sought a recognition of their rights to their traditional land at common law. Although the islands had been annexed by the sovereign in the form of the colony of Queensland in 1879, they argued that this did not validly extinguish their rights.

In 1992, the High Court upheld their claim by a six to one majority. The court ruled that the continent was not *terra nullius* — land belonging to no one — at the time of European settlement, and that native title survived settlement. The judgment recognised that Aboriginal people had lived in Australia for thousands of years and enjoyed rights to their land according to their own laws and customs. The Meriam people were 'entitled as against the whole world to possession, occupation, use and enjoyment of (most of) the lands of the Murray Islands'.

The Commonwealth government responded to the historic High Court decision by passing the *Native Title Act 1993*. Native title is defined as the rights and interests possessed under traditional laws and customs of Aboriginal and Torres Strait Islander peoples. The Act aims to validate and clarify all titles throughout Australia, mining, pastoral and native, ensuring equality before the law. While recognising the cultural and property rights of indigenous people, it also recognises that land developers need access to land and certainty of title, and governments need to manage land resources. The Act works in five ways:

- recognising and protecting native title;
- providing for the validation of any past land grants that may otherwise have been invalid because of native title;

- providing a system with which to deal with native title lands in the future and places conditions on such dealings;
- establishing a method to ascertain the existence of native title, and determining compensation for any acts affecting it; and
- creating a land acquisition fund for dispossessed Aboriginal and Torres Strait Islander peoples who would not be able to claim native title.

An Australian Republic?

Since Federation in 1901, the issue of republicanism versus the retention of the monarchy has been hotly debated. In 1993, Prime Minister Paul Keating established the Republic Advisory Committee to examine the minimum constitutional changes required to form a Federal Republic of Australia. Consideration was not to be given to changes which would 'otherwise change our structure of government, including the relationship between the Commonwealth and the States'. It was required to address the following:
- the removal of all references to the monarch in the Constitution;
- the need for and creation of an Australian head of state;
- how the head of state might be selected and removed;
- reconciling the present powers of the Governor-General and the future powers of a head of state; and
- the implications for the states and territories.

The Report of the Republic Advisory Committee was published the same year, detailing a range of options and generating a series of further questions. The Committee found that there were practical and workable solutions, legal and otherwise, that address all the points examined:
- Section 128 of the Constitution permits amendments to be made following a vote of the Australian people.
- The Constitution would need to be amended in only three substantive ways.
- A republic could be established without fundamentally changing the constitutional principles on which the Australian system of government is based.
- An Australian head of state appointed and removable by a two-thirds parliamentary majority could be regarded as more independent than the present Governor-General.
- The conventions presently limiting the powers of the Governor-General could also be applied to a new head of state, ensuring that he or she would not have too much power.
- The rights and autonomy of the States would not be impinged upon by a move to a republic. It is even feasible that a State could retain the monarch as its head of state (if the monarch agrees to it).

- The establishment of an Australian republic is primarily a symbolic change with arguments turning more on questions of national identity than questions of substantive changes to our system of government.

The Wik Decision

On 23 December 1996, the High Court delivered its judgment in the Wik People vs Queensland case. The High Court determined that the granting of certain pastoral leases in Queensland does not give the lessees the right to exclusive possession and therefore did not extinguish native title. More precisely, the High Court determined that:

Native title can only be extinguished by a written law or an act of the Government which shows a clear and plain intention to extinguish native title;

Statute creating pastoral leases in Queensland did not show an intention to extinguish native title;

Pastoral leases were created in Australia to meet the special needs of the emerging Australian pastoral industry in circumstances unknown in England;

Pastoral leases did not give exclusive possession to the pastoralists (meaning not having to share the land with others);

The granting of a pastoral lease does not necessarily extinguish all native title rights;

Native title rights could continue at the same time that the land was subject to a pastoral lease;

Where there is conflict in the exercise of those rights, native title rights were subordinate to those of the pastoral lease holder.

To determine what native title rights they have, the Wik People must present evidence to the Federal Court. This court also has the power to determine which of those rights can coexist with pastoral leases. Only native title rights that are not inconsistent with the rights of a pastoralist can coexist, and where there is any inconsistency with the latter's rights these rights override native title. Furthermore, the *Native Title Act 1993* that followed on from the High Court's Mabo ruling validated any grants of pastoral leases which might have been invalid because of native title. Native title does not, in itself, confer ownership on native title holders.

The Liberal/National Party federal government was, at April 1997, considering both extinguising native title on pastoral leases and amending the *Racial Discrimination Act* in relation to the owning and use of property.

7

Government

Australia's Government

*A*ustralia is administered by a three-tiered system of government. At the top of this system is the national or federal government; below that are the state and territory governments followed, on a community level, by a system of local government.

Australia has a federal system of government, that is, the power to make laws is shared between the federal and state parliaments. The federal parliament makes laws which affect the whole country, but only on those subjects which the Australian constitution specifically allocates to it. While some of these are exclusive to the federal parliament, most are also retained by the states, and where this leads to contradiction federal law prevails over state law.

Federal Parliament

THE AUSTRALIAN CONSTITUTION

The Australian Constitution is a document which was drawn up detailing the composition of the Australian federal parliament, its role and powers and its relationship with the existing state governments.

The constitution came into effect upon federation in 1901. The document is divided into eight chapters. Chapter one covers 'The Parliament', which consists of the Queen through her representative the Governor-General, the Senate and the House of Representatives. This first chapter is divided into five parts: general; the Senate; the House of Representatives; both houses of parliament; and the powers of parliament.

Chapter two outlines the 'Executive Government'; chapter three 'The Judicature' (establishing the High Court of Australia); chapter four covers 'Finance and Trade'; chapter five addresses 'The States'; chapter six allows for new states as they may occur; chapter seven, called 'Miscellaneous', covers the positioning of the federal capital and the appointment of deputies to the Governor-General. Chapter eight lays down the ways in which the constitution may be changed.

REFERENDA

The only way to alter the constitution is through a referendum of the people of Australia. The Bill must first pass through both houses of parliament; or through one house twice, in not less than three months.

The referendum is then put to all voters in each state and territory, and changes must be approved by a majority of voters (in Australia) and a majority of voters in a majority of states. The difficulties in gaining such a strong and wide-ranging majority can be seen by the fact that, between federation and 1995, only eight of a contested 42 proposals have been successful.

TOWARDS FEDERATION: A TIMELINE

24 OCTOBER 1889

Henry Parkes, speaking in Tenterfield, gives a widely publicised speech calling for a conference of Australasian governments to consider the federation of the colonies.

FEBRUARY 1890

A meeting is held in Melbourne to discuss federation with delegates from the six Australian colonies and from New Zealand. Henry Parkes moves a resolution calling for 'the union of the colonies, under one legislative and executive government on principles just to the several colonies'. This is passed unanimously, as is the resolution to meet again to consider an 'adequate scheme for a federal Constitution'.

MARCH-APRIL 1891

The first National Australasian Convention is held in Sydney with seven representatives from each colony and three from New Zealand. Henry Parkes acts as president. Three drafting committees are set up to work on the constitutional, financial and judicial aspects of federation. A draft Constitution Bill is produced. On 9 April 1891, the Constitution Bill is adopted, with minor amendments by the National Australasian Convention.

31 JULY 1893

A conference of federation leagues is held at Corowa, where it is resolved that each of the colonial parliaments should pass Acts to provide for the popular election of delegates to a federating constitutional convention, whose work should then be voted on by public referenda. New South Wales, Victoria, South Australia and Tasmania do; however, Queensland and Western Australia do not.

MARCH–APRIL 1897

A second National Australasian Convention is held, this time in Adelaide. All colonies are represented by ten elected delegates except for Western Australia, whose delegates are chosen by parliament, and Queensland which does not participate. As at the first convention, drafting committees are set up for constitution, finance and the judiciary. On 12 April, after the committees had reported, Edmund Barton presents a draft Bill. On 22 April, the convention is adjourned and delegates return to their state parliaments to consider the draft Bill.

2–24 September 1897
The National Australasian Convention resumes, sitting to consider the 286 amendments proposed in state parliament debate.

20 January–17 March 1898
National Australasian Convention resumes, this time sitting in Melbourne, and finally adopts a Federation Bill, which is sent to be put to referenda.

3 June 1898
The first referenda on federation are held in New South Wales, Victoria, South Australia, Tasmania and fail to get the minimum number of votes required by the Enabling Act which, by amendment, had been raised to 80 000 votes. Voting figures are shown below.

First Referenda Results on Australian Federation

State	For	Against
New South Wales	71 595	66 228
Victoria	100 520	22 099
South Australia	35 800	17 320
Tasmania	11 797	2 716

29 January 1899
A Premiers' Conference is held in Melbourne to discuss opposition to the draft Bill, and to suitably amend it.

April–July 1899
Second referenda are held in New South Wales, Victoria, South Australia and Tasmania to increased majorities in favour of federation.

Second Referenda Results on Australian Federation

State	For	Against
New South Wales	107 420	82 741
Victoria	152 653	9 805
South Australia	65 990	17 053
Tasmania	13 437	791

September 1899
Queensland, having passed an Enabling Act, holds a referendum which produces a narrow majority in favour of federation.

QUEENSLAND REFERENDUM ON AUSTRALIAN FEDERATION

State	For	Against
Queensland	38 488	30 966

MARCH 1900
An Australian delegation arrives in London to negotiate Enactment of the draft Federation Bill.

9 JULY 1900
Queen Victoria gives her assent to the Federating Act.

31 JULY 1900
Western Australia votes yes in a referendum for federation.

WESTERN AUSTRALIAN REFERENDUM ON AUSTRALIAN FEDERATION

State	For	Against
Western Australia	44 800	19 691

17 SEPTEMBER 1900
The Queen proclaims that, on 1 January 1901, an Australian Commonwealth will come into existence combining all six of the Australian colonies, which would become the six states of the federation.

THE FIRST PARLIAMENT

The first federal parliament of Australia was convened on 29 April 1901 by the Governor-General, His Excellency The Earl of Hopetoun. It was housed in the Exhibition Building in Melbourne.

The parliament was officially opened on 9 May 1901 by the Duke of Cornwall and York (later King George V). The Senate consisted of 36 senators and the House of Representatives of 75 members. The first Speaker was Sir Frederick Holder.

THE FEDERAL CAPITAL
In 1899, the New South Wales government set up a Royal Commission to find a site for the federal capital. Over the next few years, a number of sites were chosen but rejected and it was not until 1908 that the federal parliament voted the Canberra/Yass district Australia's future federal capital. In 1909, the New South Wales parliament surrendered the land.

On 1 January 1911, 2359 km^2 in the Canberra district were declared the Federal Capital Territory (renamed the Australian Capital Territory in 1938). An international competition was proposed for the design of the federal capital and it was finally won by an American architect called Walter Burley Griffin, who had worked as chief assistant to Frank Lloyd Wright.

PARLIAMENT HOUSE

The design for the provisional Parliament House was the subject of an Australia-wide competition in 1923. The winning entry was by Sydney architect G. Sydney Jones.

On 9 May 1927, the Duke of York (later King George VI) opened Parliament House and the seat of government moved from Melbourne to Canberra. This provisional Parliament House was designed to have a life of 50 years. It allowed room for only 75 members and 36 senators so that, by the mid-1970s when that number had doubled, a new building was needed.

In 1978, federal parliament approved the construction of a new and permanent Parliament House on Capital Hill. The design was selected from 329 entries received from 28 countries in an open competition. The winning design was from the American architectural firm of Mitchell/ Giurgola & Thorp, and was chosen unanimously by the jury. The main architect for the project was Romaldo Giurgola.

On 8 May 1988, the new Parliament House was opened.

STRUCTURE AND COMPOSITION

The federal parliament of Australia is bicameral, that is to say, it is made up of two houses; the Lower House is known as the House of Representatives and the Upper House is the Senate.

The constitution states that the number of members of the House of Representatives 'shall be, as nearly as practicable, twice the number of the senators'. This is known as the nexus provision.

Originally there were 75 members of the House of Representatives (MHRs) and 36 senators.

Originally, only the states were represented in the federal parliament and it was not until 1922 that the Northern Territory gained a member of the House of Representatives (MHR), who was not given full voting rights in the Lower House until 1968. The Australian Capital Territory gained an MHR in 1948 and acquired full voting rights in 1966. In 1974, the Australian Capital Territory was allowed a second MHR and, at present, it is allowed three MHRs.

Both territories were given two senators each in 1975; however, unlike state senators, who are re-elected every six years, the Northern Territory and Australian Capital Territory senators face re-election at every House of Representatives general election.

CURRENT NUMBERS IN THE UPPER AND LOWER HOUSES BY STATE OR TERRITORY

State	Senate	House of Representatives
New South Wales	12	50
Victoria	12	37
Queensland	12	26
South Australia	12	12
Western Australia	12	14
Tasmania	12	5
Northern Territory	2	1
Australian Capital Territory	2	3
Total	76	148

STANDING ORDERS

The permanent rules and orders which regulate the operations of both houses of parliament are called standing orders. There are separate sets of standing orders for each house.

LEGISLATION

The legislative power of the Commonwealth is vested in the Commonwealth parliament. The constitution states that the parliament shall have the 'power to make laws for the peace, order, and good government of the Commonwealth'.

There must be concurrence from all parts of the parliament: the two Houses and the Queen (through her representative, the Governor-General), for legislation to pass. To amend the constitution itself, however, a Bill must also be put to referendum in each state and territory, and changes must be approved not only by a majority of voters, but a majority of voters in a majority of states.

HOUSE OF REPRESENTATIVES

The Lower House of the Federal Parliament is called the House of Representatives. It is the people's House in the Federal Parliament and is composed of members chosen directly by the people.

The principal role of the House of Representatives is as legislator, that is the making of laws. When a proposed law is introduced to Parliament it is known as a 'Bill'. When a Bill is passed through both houses and is signed by the Governor-General, it becomes an Act of Parliament. By the terms of the constitution, the Senate may not initiate appropriation or taxation bills, nor amend them.

The government is centred in the House of Representatives. After an election, the Governor-General commissions the party with the majority in the Lower House to form a government. The Prime Minister must be a member of the House of Representatives (MHR) and most of the Ministers are chosen from here.

MEMBERSHIP

The number of members of the House of Representatives allocated to each state is proportional to the number of people in the state, unlike the Senate, and each member represents a reasonably equal number of people.

The number of members of the House of Representatives (MHRs) chosen from each state is proportionate to the number of people in that state. However, the constitution sets down that no state shall have less than five members and Tasmania has always had this minimum number even though the size of its population may not have justified it.

The number of MHRs was 75 at the opening of Parliament in 1901. In 1934, this was reduced to 74 members and then, in 1949, it was increased, in line with the nexus provision, to 123 MHRs.

The official term for MHRs is three years from the first meeting of the house, although in practice it may be less than this if the government decides to call an early election.

OFFICE HOLDERS

THE SPEAKER   The Speaker is the chief officer of the House of Representatives and is an MHR elected to the position. His role is both to preside over the Lower House without bias while it is sitting and also to act as the representative of the house. Often known as the Presiding Officer, all speeches in debate must be addressed to the Speaker or his or her representative in the Chair. The Speaker calls for members to speak, alternating between the government and the opposition. The Speaker of the House, in the case of a tied decision, has the right to a casting vote.

CHAIRMAN OF COMMITTEES   When the Speaker is absent, the Chairman of Committees acts in his/her place as Deputy Speaker and is in turn relieved by Deputy Chairmen of Committees. The Chairman of Committees presides over the House when it considers bills in detail as a committee 'of a whole'.

THE LEADER OF THE HOUSE   This position is held by a government Minister appointed by the Prime Minister. The Leader of the House fixes the order that items of government business are dealt with and makes sure that the passage of this business is never disrupted or delayed. He or she also determines the time allocated for debates in negotiation with his or her counterpart in the opposition, known as the Manager of Opposition

Business. The Leader of the House consults with and works closely with the government whips.

CONSTITUTION OF THE HOUSE OF REPRESENTATIVES BY PARTY 1949–1996

Year	No. of Seats	ALP	LP	CP	NAT	NCP	CLP	IND
1949	121	47	55	19				
1951	121	52	52	17				
1954	121	57	47	17				
1955	122	47	57	18				
1958	122	45	58	19				
1961	122	60	45	17				
1963	122	50	52	20				
1966	124	41	61	21				
1969	125	59	46	20				
1972	125	67	38	20				
1974	127	66	40	21				
1975	127	36	68	9	13	–	1	–
1977	124	38	67	–	10	8	–	–
1980	125	51	54	–	10	9	–	–
1983	125	75	33	–	17	–	–	–
1984	148	82	45	–	21	–	–	–
1987	148	86	43	–	19	–	–	–
1990	148	78	55	–	14	–	–	1
1996	148	49	75	–	18	–	1	5

ALP — Australian Labor Party
LP — Liberal Party
CP — Country Party
NAT — National Party of Australia

NCP — National Country Party
CLP — NT Country Liberal Party
IND — Independent

SENATE

The Upper House of the federal parliament is called the Senate.

Since the membership from all the states is equal, the larger, more populous states, who have more members in the Lower House, are prevented from dominating the Parliament. A similar system operates in the United States Senate, where every state is represented by two Senators, regardless of the states' population. The smaller states of Australia insisted on equal representation if they were to join the federation in 1901.

The Senate has almost equal legislative powers to those of the House of Representatives, except that a provision in the constitution states that laws for imposing taxation or for appropriation may not originate in the Senate nor may they be amended by it. (However, the Senate may in effect request that the Lower House amend a Bill or block the passing of a Bill.) This provision is designed to keep this power with the government, which is centred in the House of Representatives.

Whereas the government holds a majority in the House of Representatives and Bills proposed by the government are usually passed through the Lower House, the government rarely has a majority in the Senate. Indeed, the balance of power may be held in the Senate by a minority party or independent senators. Therefore, the Senate remains an independent arbiter and may not necessarily vote to pass a Bill or may choose to amend it. The Senate is an important house of review.

MEMBERSHIP

There are equal numbers of senators elected from each of the states. Originally this number was 36, that is six per state. This has been increased twice: in 1948, it was raised to 60 Senators, ten from each state, and in 1983 to 72 members; 12 from each state. Both the federal territories — the Northern Territory and the Australian Capital Territory — have, since 1975, been allowed two Senators each. Each state votes for the senate as a single electorate, that is, all voters within a state use the same ballot paper and vote for the same candidates.

The term of office for Senators is six years except for the four Senators from the federal territories, who are only elected for three years. The Senate is divided in half so that every three years, half of the positions will be subject to election. The term of service of a senator begins on the first day of July following the election.

Senators serve a fixed term of six years unless it is shortened by a double dissolution. Casual vacancies in the Senate were previously a problem, as it was difficult to assemble a whole state for the election of one candidate. The constitution was amended in 1977 to allow these vacancies to be filled by the party or group that the retiring senator comes from, maintaining the political balance in the Upper House. Also, the new senator now runs for the term of the original Senator.

In the case of a double dissolution, half of the senators are elected as short-term senators and the others are elected as long-term senators to retain the staggered terms.

OFFICE HOLDERS

THE PRESIDENT   The President of the Senate is the principal office holder in the Upper House. The President presides over the Senate, deciding the order that the Senators speak in and maintaining order in the Upper House. The President is also the representative of the Senate. Elected by a secret ballot, the President, who must be a senator, usually holds the office for a three-year term.

Unlike the Speaker of the House of Representatives, the President of the Senate is not entitled to a casting vote and tied decisions in the Upper House are taken as negative.

DEPUTY PRESIDENT AND CHAIRMAN OF COMMITTEES   When the President is absent, the Deputy President and Chairman of Committees acts in his/her place and is in turn relieved by Temporary Chairmen of Committees. As the Chairman of Committees, he/she presides over the Upper House when it considers Bills in detail as a committee 'of a whole'.

COMMITTEE CHAIRMEN   The chairmen of Senate committees are elected by the members of their committee and are responsible for that committee.

DOUBLE DISSOLUTION

Where conflicts arise between the House of Representatives and the Senate, the constitution allows for the deadlock to be resolved by a double dissolution of both houses of parliament and re-election of all members. It is the Prime Minister's prerogative to ask the Governor-General for a double dissolution. This situation is recognised by the constitution when the House of Representatives has twice passed a proposed law and the Senate has twice refused it. There must be a three-month period between the Senate's first failure to pass the Bill and its reintroduction in the Lower House.

If, after a new election, the House of Representatives again passes the law and it is again blocked by the Senate, a joint sitting is held where both the Upper and Lower Houses vote as one. There have been six double dissolutions since federation: in 1914, 1951, 1974, 1975, 1983 and 1987. Only once has a joint sitting been held to vote on proposed laws which were the subject of a double dissolution, this happened in 1974. Three times, after a double dissolution, the government has been re-elected (1951, 1974, 1987), and three times the opposition has been successful (1914, 1975, 1983).

PARLIAMENTARY COMMITTEES

A number of parliamentary committees exist to examine various issues of interest in detail. These allow committee members to work in particular areas of interest and to specialise in these areas.

The first House of Representatives committee was set up on 6 June 1901 to look into Commonwealth coinage. The first Senate committee of inquiry examined steamship communication between the mainland and Tasmania, it was set up on 26 July 1901.

Until fairly recently, the majority of committees were like these first two: select, ad hoc committees set up to investigate a specific topic and then disbanded. However, a few important standing (that is permanent) committees were set up in this time. The 1960s saw the development of many Senate select committees and in 1969 the Senate Standing Orders Committee started to study the value of a system of committees.

In 1970, the Senate introduced seven legislative and general purpose, and five estimates standing committees. The numbers of committees were later increased to eight and six respectively. This period also saw the establishment of standing committees in the House of Representatives and in 1978 select committees were set up to examine specific Bills that passed through the Lower House. Thirteen Bills were considered in this way until 1980, when this process was discontinued. Estimates committees were also set up in the House of Representatives in the late 1970s to examine the main appropriation Bill. These were not re-established after 1981.

A committee considers a wide range of evidence in its inquiries and then prepares a report which is presented to the House, or, in the case of joint committees, to both Houses.

SENATE COMMITTEES
There are a number of different standing committees existing in the Senate.

Internal or domestic committees concentrate on the administration and procedures of the houses of parliament. Some of these committees often meet with a similar committee in the House of Representatives.

The legislative and general purpose committees of the Senate conduct inquiries into matters which concern the Senate and which it would like more detailed information on. There are also committees of legislative scrutiny.

The estimates committees of the Senate examine the estimates of expenditure by government departments contained in the main appropriation Bills of the May Budget and the additional appropriation bills in November. In addition to these, there are various and changing select committees; and joint committees which contain members of both Houses.

HOUSE OF REPRESENTATIVES COMMITTEES
The standing committees of the House of Representatives include internal, or domestic, committees and investigative, or scrutiny, committees.

Domestic committees concern themselves with the administration and procedures of the Houses. Some of these often meet with a similar committee in the Senate. Scrutiny committees in specific areas exist to consider these topics on an ongoing basis.

In addition to these, there are various and changing select committees; and joint committees which contain members of both Houses.

JOINT COMMITTEES
Joint committees consist of members of both Houses. It is felt by some that this system avoids duplication of inquiry.

There are three types of joint committee: joint statutory committees, joint committees and joint select committees. Joint statutory committees are set up by acts of Parliament.

AUSTRALIAN PRIME MINISTERS

Term	Prime Minister
1 Jan 1901–24 Sept 1903	Sir Edmund Barton
24 Sept 1903–27 April 1904	Alfred Deakin
27 April 1904–17 Aug 1904	John Christian Watson
18 Aug 1904–5 July 1905	George Houstoun Reid
5 July 1905–13 Nov 1908	Alfred Deakin
13 Nov 1908–2 June 1909	Andrew Fisher
2 June 1909–29 April 1910	Alfred Deakin
29 April 1910–24 June 1913	Andrew Fisher
24 June 1913–17 Sept 1914	Sir Joseph Cook
17 Sept 1914–27 Oct 1915	Andrew Fisher
27 Oct 1915–14 Nov 1916	William Morris Hughes
14 Nov 1916–17 Feb 1917	William Morris Hughes
17 Feb 1917–8 Jan 1918	William Morris Hughes
10 Jan 1918–9 Feb 1923	William Morris Hughes
9 Feb 1923–22 Oct 1929	Stanley Melbourne Bruce
22 Oct 1929–6 Jan 1932	James Henry Scullin
6 Jan 1932–7 Nov 1938	Joseph Aloysius Lyons
7 Nov 1938–7 April 1939	Joseph Aloysius Lyons
7 April 1939–26 April 1939	Sir Earle Christmas Grafton Page
26 April 1939–14 March 1940	Robert Gordon Menzies
14 March 1941–28 Oct 1940	Robert Gordon Menzies
28 Oct 1940–29 Aug 1941	Robert Gordon Menzies
29 Aug 1941–7 Oct 1941	Arthur William Fadden
7 Oct 1941–21 Sept 1943	John Curtin
21 Sept 1943–6 July 1945	John Curtin
6 July 1945–13 July 1945	Francis Michael Forde
13 July 1945–1 Nov 1946	Joseph Benedict Chifley
1 Nov 1946–19 Dec 1949	Joseph Benedict Chifley
19 Dec 1949–11 May 1951	Robert Gordon Menzies
11 May 1951–11 Jan 1956	Robert Gordon Menzies
11 Jan 1956–10 Dec 1958	Robert Gordon Menzies
10 Dec 1958–18 Dec 1963	Robert Gordon Menzies
18 Dec 1963–20 Jan 1966	Robert Gordon Menzies
20 Jan 1966–14 Dec 1966	Harold Edward Holt
14 Dec 1966–19 Dec 1967	Harold Edward Holt
19 Dec 1967–10 Jan 1968	John McEwen
10 Jan 1968–28 Feb 1968	John Grey Gorton

Term	Prime Minister
28 Feb 1968–12 Nov 1969	John Grey Gorton
12 Nov 1969–10 March 1971	John Grey Gorton
10 March 1971–5 Dec 1972	William McMahon
5 Dec 1972–19 Dec 1972	Edward Gough Whitlam
19 Dec 1972–11 Nov 1975	Edward Gough Whitlam
11 Nov 1975–22 Dec 1975	John Malcolm Fraser
22 Dec 1975–20 Dec 1977	John Malcolm Fraser
20 Dec 1977–3 Nov 1980	John Malcolm Fraser
3 Nov 1980–11 March 1983	John Malcolm Fraser
11 March 1983–1 Dec 1984	Robert James Lee Hawke
1 Dec 1984–24 July 1987	Robert James Lee Hawke
24 July 1984–April 1990	Robert James Lee Hawke
4 April 1990–20 Dec 1991	Robert James Lee Hawke
20 Dec 1991–24 March 1993	Paul John Keating
24 March 1993–11 March 1996	Paul John Keating
11 March 1996–	John Winston Howard

FEDERAL MINISTRY AND CABINET
(AS AT NOVEMBER 1996)

Name	Portfolio(s)
John Howard	**Prime Minister**
John Herron	Aboriginal and Torres Strait Islander Affairs
Tim Fischer	**Trade** (Deputy Prime Minister)
Alexander Downer	**Foreign Affairs**
Peter Costello	**Treasurer**
Rod Kemp	Assistant Treasurer
John Anderson	**Primary Industries and Energy**
Warwick Parer	Resources and Energy
Sen. Robert Hill	**Environment** (Leader of the Government in the Senate)
Warwick Smith	Sport, Territories and Local Government
Sen. Richard Alston	**Communications and the Arts** (Deputy Leader of the Government in the Senate)
Peter Reith	**Industrial Relations** (Leader of the House)
Sen. Jocelyn Newman	**Social Security**
John Moore	**Industry, Science and Tourism** (Vice-President of the Executive Council)
Peter McGauran	Science and Technology (Deputy Leader of the House)
Geoff Prosser	Small Business and Consumer Affairs
Ian McLachlan	**Defence**

Name	Portfolio(s)
Bronwyn Bishop	Defence Industry, Science and Personnel
Bruce Scott	Veterans' Affairs
John Sharp	**Transport and Regional Development**
Dr Michael Wooldridge	**Health and Family Services**
Judi Moylan	Family Services
John Fahey	**Finance**
David Jull	Administrative Services
Sen. Amanda Vanstone	**Employment, Education, Training and Youth Affairs**
David Kemp	Schools, Vocational Education and Training
Philip Ruddock	Immigration and Multicultural Affairs
Daryl Williams	Attorney-General and Justice

Note: Each grouping represents a portfolio. Cabinet ministers are shown in **bold** type. All ministers are members of the House of Representatives unless otherwise indicated.

LABOR PARTY SHADOW MINISTRY
(AS AT MARCH 1996)

Name	Shadow Ministry(ies)
Kim Beazley	**Leader of the Opposition**
Gareth Evans	Deputy Leader of the Opposition
	Treasurer
Sen. John Faulkner	Leader of the Opposition in the Senate
	Social Security
Sen. Nick Sherry	Deputy Leader of the Opposition in the Senate
	Finance and Superannuation
Simon Crean	Industry and Regional Development
	Manager of Opposition Business
Bob McMullan	Industrial Relations
	Assistant to the Leader of the Opposition on Public Service Matters
Michael Lee	Health
Dr Carmen Lawrence	Environment
	The Arts
	Assistant to the Leader of the Opposition on the Status of Women
Sen. Bob Collins	Primary Industries, Northern Australia and Territories

Name	Shadow Ministry(ies)
Laurie Brereton	Foreign Affairs
Peter Baldwin	Education and Youth Affairs
Sen. Peter Cook	Commerce and Small Business
Sen. Nick Bolkus	Attorney-General and Justice
Martin Ferguson	Employment and Training
Arch Bevis	Defence
Duncan Kerr	Immigration
	Assistant to the Leader of the Opposition on Multicultural Affairs
Sen. Chris Schacht	Communications
Stephen Martin	Veteran's Affairs
	Sport and Tourism
Lindsay Tanner	Transport
Neil O'Keefe	Resources and Energy
Jenny Macklin	Aged, Family and Community Services
Stephen Smith	Trade
Mark Latham	Competition Policy and Assistant to the Shadow Treasurer
	Local Government
Daryl Melham	Aboriginal Affairs
	Assistant to the Shadow Foreign Minister on Arms Control
Martyn Evans	Science and Information Technology
Laurie Ferguson	Administrative Services
Sen. Belinda Neal	Consumer Affairs
	Assistant to the Shadow Minister for Health

Note: Ministers are members of the House of Representatives unless otherwise indicated.

Governors-General

The Governor-General of Australia is the Queen's representative in the Federal Parliament. Although the position was held until 1931 exclusively by Englishmen, since 1965 it has been held by those born in Australia and it is presumed that this trend will continue.

Also shown within the following list are administrators who served until a new Governor-General could be appointed.

GOVERNORS-GENERAL AND
ADMINISTRATORS SINCE FEDERATION

Term	Name
1 Jan 1901–9 Jan 1903	John Adrian Louis Hope Earl of Hopetoun Governor General and Commander-in-Chief of the Commonwealth of Australia
17 July 1902–9 Jan 1903	Hallam Tennyson Lord Tennyson Officer administering the Government of the Commonwealth of Australia
9 Jan 1903–21 Jan 1904	Hallam Tennyson Lord Tennyson
21 Jan 1904–9 Sept 1908	Henry Stafford Northcote Lord Northcote
9 Sept 1908–31 July 1911	William Humble Ward Lord Dudley
31 July 1911–18 May 1914	Thomas Denman Lord Denman
18 May 1914–6 Oct 1920	Sir Ronald Craufurd Munro-Ferguson
6 Oct 1920–8 Oct 1925	Henry William Forster Lord Forster
8 Oct 1925–2 Oct 1930	John Lawrence Baird Lord Stonehaven
3 Oct 1930–22 Jan 1931	Arthur Herbert Tennyson Somers Cocks Officer administering the Government of the Commonwealth of Australia
22 Jan 1931–22 Jan 1936	Sir Isaac Alfred Isaacs
23 Jan 1936–30 Jan 1945	Brigadier-General Alexander Gore Arkwright Hore-Ruthven Lord Gowrie
3 Sept 1944–30 Jan 1945	Major-General Sir Winston Dugan Officer administering the Government of the Commonwealth of Australia
30 Jan 1945–11 May 1947	Henry Duke of Gloucester, HRH
9 Jan 1947–11 May 1947	Major-General Sir Winston Dugan Officer administering the Government of the Commonwealth of Australia
11 May 1947–8 May 1953	Sir William John McKell
8 May 1953–2 Feb 1960	Field Marshal Sir William Joseph Slim
2 Feb 1960–3 Feb 1961	William Shepherd Morrison Viscount Dunrossil

Term	Name
4 Feb 1961–3 Aug 1961	General Sir Reginald Alexander Dallas Brooks Officer administering the Government of the Commonwealth of Australia
3 Aug 1961–22 Sept 1965	William Phillip Sidney De L'Isle 1st Viscount De L'Isle
7 May 1965–22 Sept 1965	Colonel Sir Henry Abel Smith Officer administering the Government of the Commonwealth of Australia
22 Sept 1965–30 April 1969	Richard Gardiner Casey Lord Casey
30 April 1969–11 July 1974	Sir Paul Meernaa Caedwalla Hasluck
11 July 1974–8 Dec 1977	Sir John Robert Kerr
8 Dec 1977–20 July 1982	Sir Zelman Cowan
20 July 1982–16 Feb 1989	Sir Ninian Martin Stephen
16 Feb 1989–15 Feb 1996	William George Hayden
15 Feb 1996–	Sir William Deane

State Parliament

From 1788 until 1823, a period of 35 years, the Governor of New South Wales held virtually absolute power in the colony.

The first Governor was Captain Arthur Phillip, known as the Captain-General and Governor-in-Chief over the Territory called New South Wales and its Dependencies. Phillip served from 26 January 1788 until 10 December 1792. In 1823, the British Parliament passed an Act to establish a Legislative Council in New South Wales with a minimum of five and a maximum of seven members, to advise the Governor. These members would be nominated by him. On 1 December that year, five members were appointed and the Legislative Council met for the first time on 25 August 1824.

Tasmania was the next to have a nominated Legislative Council, in 1825 when the colony was founded, followed by Western Australia in 1832 and South Australia in 1842.

REPRESENTATIVE GOVERNMENT

In 1842, an Act was passed through the British Parliament allowing the first representative government in Australia. The Legislative Council of New South Wales was increased to 36 members, 24 of whom were to be elected in public elections. The first election was held in 1843.

In 1850, the *Australian Colonies Government Act* was passed, making Victoria a separate colony and granting representative government (consisting of two-thirds elected to one-third nominated members) to all the colonies (Victoria, South Australia and Tasmania), but not to Western Australia. These Legislative Council elections were held in 1851. Western Australia was allowed representative government in 1870.

RESPONSIBLE GOVERNMENT

The same *Australian Colonies Government Act* authorised the colonies of New South Wales, Victoria, South Australia and Tasmania to prepare draft constitutions. These constitutions were prepared in 1853 and, between 1855 and 1856, the constitution Acts for New South Wales, Victoria and Tasmania were passed and each colony set up a bicameral parliament with a premier and cabinet. South Australia was granted responsible government in 1857 and Queensland in 1859 when it separated from New South Wales. Western Australia was finally granted responsible government in 1890.

SYSTEMS OF STATE PARLIAMENT

All state parliaments are bicameral, except in Queensland where the Upper House was abolished in 1922. All the other states have an Upper House known as the Legislative Council. In New South Wales, Victoria and Western Australia, the Lower House is known as the Legislative Assembly; in South Australia and Tasmania it is known as the House of Assembly.

The Northern Territory became self governing in 1978. It has a Lower House only, which is known as the Legislative Assembly. The leader of the government is known as the Chief Minister. As of 1989, the Northern Territory had self-government in the form of a Legislative Assembly consisting of 17 members.

Following the *Australian Capital Territory (Self Government) Act 1988*, the first election for the Australian Capital Territory Legislative Assembly was held on 4 March 1989. Seventeen members were elected in a single multi-member electorate. The government is run by a Chief Minister currently supported by three other ministers.

Each of the states has its own constitution. These were originally modelled on the British House of Commons.

MEMBERSHIP OF STATE AND TERRITORY PARLIAMENTS

House	NSW	Vic.	Qld	SA	WA	Tas.	NT	ACT
Upper House	45	44	–	22	34	19	–	–
Lower House	109	88	89	47	57	35	25	17

PREMIERS AND OPPOSITION LEADERS
OF THE STATES AND TERRITORIES

State	Premier/Chief Minister	Opposition Leader
New South Wales	Robert Carr Australian Labor Party	Peter Collins Liberal Party of Australia
Victoria	Jeffrey Kennett Liberal Party of Australia	John Brumby Australian Labor Party
Queensland	Rob Borbridge National Party of Australia	Peter Beattie Australian Labor Party
South Australia	John Olsen Liberal Party of Australia	Michael Rann Australian Labor Party
Western Australia	Richard Court Liberal Party of Australia	Geoff Gallop Australian Labor Party
Tasmania	Tony Rundle Liberal Party of Australia	Michael Field Australian Labor Party
Northern Territory	Shane Stone Country Liberal Party	Maggie Hickey Australian Labor Party
Australian Capital Territory	Kate Carnell Liberal Party of Australia	Andrew Whitecross Australian Labor Party

Elections

SUFFRAGE

Suffrage is the right of a person to vote in an election. Australia now has universal adult suffrage. In the first election in New South Wales in 1843, suffrage was restricted by minimum property values. South Australia was the first place in the world to introduce universal male suffrage (1856) and the first in the British Commonwealth to introduce adult female suffrage (1894).

The different states of Australia have developed differently in regard to suffrage enfranchisement and the different dates are given below. In 1973, the age to qualify for voting was reduced from 21 to 18 years of age.

Suffrage Enfranchisement

Franchise	NSW	Vic.	Qld	SA	WA	Tas.
Men over 21	1858	1857	1872	1856	1893	1896
women over 21	1904	1910	1907	1894	1898	1905

In 1902, all adults were given the right to vote at federal elections. However, Aboriginal peoples and Torres Strait Islanders were only given limited rights to vote in federal elections in 1949. It was not until 1962 that all Aboriginal peoples and Torres Strait Islanders became entitled to vote at federal elections and at referendums, although they were included in adult male suffrage in South Australia when it was introduced in 1856. In 1984, enrolment and voting became compulsory for Aboriginal peoples and Torres Strait Islanders.

Eligibility to Vote

The following conditions apply for eligibility to vote in Australian elections:
- You must be 18 years old to vote, although 17-year-olds can enrol as provisional voters, i.e. they will be put on the roll immediately they turn 18 years of age.
- You must be an Australian citizen, you must have lived at your present address for at least one month and you must be of sound mind.
- People convicted of treason and not pardoned are ineligible to vote, as are those who are serving prison sentences of five years or longer.

British subjects were once eligible to vote in federal and state elections, but this ceased on 25 January 1984 (1 August 1983 in Queensland). However, those British subjects that were enrolled at this time have been allowed to retain their voting rights.

There are a number of special provisions for voters who for some reason cannot meet the normal provisions for enrolment, such as people with no fixed address, people working in Antarctica and others who may not be able to attend a polling booth on election day for one reason or another.

The Electoral Process

Elections in Australia are always held on Saturdays between the hours of 8 a.m. and 6 p.m. Each electorate is managed by a Returning Officer who organises temporary staff who run the polling booths, but whose job also involves the declaration of the poll and the return of the Writ.

THE WRIT Elections begin with the issue of the Writ by the Governor or Governor-General, on advice from the government. The Writ authorises the election and specifies: the date and time that the electoral roll must close; the day that nominations close; the day for the election; and the day by which the Writ must be returned (which is 60 days after issue in the case of State elections and 100 days in Federal elections). The Writ is distributed to the Returning Officers in each electorate. When the Writ is returned it must have on it the name of the elected candidate, endorsed by the Returning Officer.

ELECTORAL SYSTEMS

Originally, Australia used the first-past-the-post plurality system of election inherited from Britain. Queensland introduced the preferential system in 1892 and it was soon adopted for all other single member constituencies. The preferential system is used still in single-member electorates and also for the alternately elected two-member constituencies of the Tasmania and Victoria Upper Houses.

Since 1949, the Australian Senate has used a modified Hare-Clark system of proportional representation. This system is also used in the Tasmanian Lower House, in the New South Wales and South Australian Upper Houses, which are voted for as single electorates, and in the Western Australian Upper House, which since 1987 has used multi-member electorates.

The New South Wales parliament uses an optional preferential system of voting which allows a voter to fill in no preferences or only as many as they wish. This is used with both the Hare-Clark proportional system in the Upper House and also with the preferential system in the Lower House.

PREFERENTIAL OR ALTERNATIVE VOTE

In preferential voting, voters must fill each square of their ballot papers from 1 onwards (in all boxes) according to preference. To be elected, a candidate must gain an absolute majority of votes, that is half of the votes plus one. When there are three or more candidates, it is possible that no candidate will get an absolute majority. In this case, the candidate with the least amount of votes is declared defeated and their votes are redistributed according to second preferences. This process continues until a member is elected. If a voter's second preference is for a defeated candidate then the ballot paper is declared exhausted. Exhausted ballots are subtracted from the total vote to form a subtotal which is used to redetermine the number of votes needed for a majority.

PROPORTIONAL REPRESENTATION

In proportional representation, the ballot paper is divided into two halves. Voters have the option of either: assigning preferences from 1 onwards for individual candidates, filling in every square; or by making a ticket vote, that is voting for one party's candidates by marking a 1 in the party or group squares at the top of the ballot paper. In a ticket vote, preferences are given automatically; they have already been chosen by the party and are shown on their how-to-vote material.

Candidates must receive a certain amount of the vote known as a 'quota'. This is determined by the following equation:

$$\text{quota} = \frac{\text{total number of 1st preference votes}}{\text{number to be elected} + 1} + 1$$

Once a candidate has achieved the quota, and has been elected, any extra votes are called surplus votes and are redistributed. Rather than assigning preferences from the surplus votes only, however, all candidate's votes are redistributed according to the second preference indicated, but at a reduced, transfer value according to the following equation:

$$\text{transfer value} = \frac{\text{number of elected candidates surplus votes}}{\text{number of candidates 1st preference votes}}$$
(excluding exhausted ballots)

If all available seats are not filled using this method then the candidate with the least votes is eliminated and their votes redistributed according to second preference. This process continues until all positions are filled.

OPTIONAL PREFERENTIAL
The New South Wales parliament uses an optional preferential system of voting which allows a voter to fill in preferences or not fill in preferences at all, or only fill in as many as they wish. This is used with both the Hare-Clark proportional system in the Upper House and also with the preferential system in the Lower House.

THE AUSTRALIAN CAPITAL TERRITORY ELECTION
The d'Hondt voting system is named after Professor Victor d'Hondt of the University of Ghent who helped devise it more than 100 years ago. It is used in several democratic Western European countries.

In the first election of the Australian Capital Territory Legislative Assembly, the d'Hondt system was modified and combined with parts of the Senate system of proportional representation and various methods of preferential voting to produce a unique system of voting.

Counting in the election took two months. This delay led to some controversy and enquiries have since been carried out into the system and into likely alternatives. At the time of publication, it looked as though a referendum would be held where voters were asked to choose their preferred voting system.

Political Parties

Government in Australia has been dominated for a long time by three main parties, the Australian Labor Party, the Liberal Party of Australia and the National Party. Since their formation in 1977, the Australian Democrats have kept a significant presence in the Senate, often, with independent senators, controlling the balance of power.

The 1980s saw the rise of many independent political parties. One of the first to form was the Nuclear Disarmament Party (NDP) in 1984, with rock singer Peter Garrett of the band Midnight Oil contesting a seat in the Senate at the 1984 election. He was unsuccessful and, in 1985, a split forced the NDP from the public eye.

Increasing public awareness of environmental issues saw the growth of numerous 'green' parties during the 1980s. The only 'green' party to win at the ballot box however, has been the Tasmanian Greens led by Dr Bob Brown, who now holds the balance of power in the Tasmanian Assembly: 5 Green members, 13 Labor members and 17 Liberal members.

AUSTRALIAN LABOR PARTY

The Australian Labor Party (ALP) is the oldest political party in Australia. In 1891, the first state Labor Parties were formed. The first Labor government was elected in Queensland in 1899 for a period of just seven days.

At Federation in 1901, a federal party was formed with J. C. Watson as the first leader. At the first Commonwealth elections in 1901, 16 Labor members were elected to the House of Representatives and eight to the Senate. These successful candidates met before the first sitting of Parliament on the 8 May 1901 and agreed to form a federal party. The first federal Labor government took office in May 1904, with Watson as Prime Minister. It was a minority government and only lasted three months. In 1907, Andrew Fisher succeeded Watson as Labor leader. The second Labor government was elected in November 1908, but it was also a minority government and lasted only until June 1909.

In April 1910, the Labor Party won a majority in both Houses, and Fisher's Labor government remained in power until May 1913. Although they lost the election in May 1913, they won after a double dissolution in September that year and Fisher was Prime Minister when Australia entered World War I.

In October 1915, when Fisher resigned to become Australian High Commissioner in London, William (Billy) Hughes, prominent in Labor politics for a long time, became Prime Minister.

During 1916 and 1917, there were bitter struggles over conscription. Hughes believed strongly in conscription and decided to take the issue to referendum, but he was expelled from the Labor Party before it was held.

The campaign was a bitter one, especially for the anti-conscriptionists; however, when the vote was held on 28 October 1916, the answer was no to conscription. Hughes walked out of a parliamentary meeting and asked those who supported him to follow; 23 of the 65 did. Hughes and his followers, in coalition with the Liberals, formed the new federal Nationalist Party which took government at the next election on 5 May 1917.

The remaining members of the ALP struggled in a weakened party, originally led by Frank Tudor, then by Matthew Charlton and finally by James Scullin, who became Prime Minister when the Labor Party won the election in October 1929. The Scullin government did not hold a majority in the Senate and lost support in the House of Representatives in 1931, failing to win at the subsequent election. An ex-Minister of the Scullin government, Joseph Lyons, who left with other dissidents in opposition to government economic policy joined the Opposition to form the United Australia Party and Lyons became Prime Minister.

During the 1930s, open warfare broke out between the different factions within the Labor Party and many splinter parties were formed. John Curtin took over as leader in 1935 and under his leadership the federal Labor Party was gradually rebuilt until, in 1941, Curtin became war-time Prime Minister. In 1945, Curtin died in office and was replaced by Joseph Chifley, whose government served until December 1949. Chifley died in 1951 and was replaced by Dr H. Evatt.

In 1954, the Labor Party narrowly lost the federal election. At this time, the Petrov Royal Commission was being held and the Labor Party was attempting to purge itself of groups originally set up to combat the Communist influence in the union movement; that is both the Industrial Groups and 'The Movement', a secret organisation led by B. A. Santamaria. Those who left or were expelled organised themselves into the new Democratic Labor Party.

Under Evatt, the Labor Party lost three federal elections and he resigned as leader in 1960. He was replaced by Arthur Calwell and in 1961 the Labor Party almost won the federal election.

In 1966, Gough Whitlam took over the leadership of the ALP. Labor again narrowly lost in the 1969 election, but then won in 1972. Whitlam proceeded to initiate wide-ranging reform, but was frustrated in many areas by the Opposition majority in the Senate, which led to a double dissolution in May 1974. The Whitlam government was re-elected in the subsequent election, but failed again to gain a majority in the Senate.

During 1975, the Whitlam government was involved in a number of controversial incidents and, in October of that year, the Senate blocked supply until the government agreed to an election. When Whitlam refused, the Governor-General of the time, Sir John Kerr, dismissed the Labor government and appointed the Opposition as caretaker government.

The Labor Party was defeated at the next election and again in 1977. Bill Hayden took over the leadership of the Labor Party in 1977 and in 1980 they came within 13 seats of winning.

At the next election in 1983, the Labor Party came to office under the leadership of former ACTU boss Bob Hawke, who held government for a total of four terms until December 1991, when Paul Keating challenged the leadership and became leader of the Labor Party and Prime Minister. Keating remained as Prime Minister until March 1996, when the ALP was defeated at the federal election by John Howard's Liberal/National Party coalition.

LIBERAL PARTY OF AUSTRALIA

The Liberal Party of Australia was formed in 1944. Robert Menzies, who was disturbed at the disunity of the various anti-Labor organisations, organised conferences in Canberra in October and in Albury in December, to try and form a united federal party. The result was the unification of 18 separate organisations who stood for 'liberal, progressive policy and are opposed to socialism with its bureaucratic administration and restriction of personal freedom'. In reality, it was a unification of conservative ideals.

The conference in Canberra voted to form the Liberal Party of Australia. At the Albury meeting, the Liberal Party of Australia was formally inaugurated and the members adopted a federal constitution.

At the first federal election they contested, the Liberal Party won 17 seats. In 1949, Menzie's Liberal Party gained office, in coalition with the Country Party. Menzies remained Prime Minister until his retirement in 1966; a total of five terms which, with his previous three terms in the early 1940s, adds up to a total of 18 years (16 of these consecutively), making him Australia's longest serving Prime Minister.

Upon his retirement, Menzies was replaced by Harold Holt, who in December 1967 disappeared while swimming in the sea off Portsea in Victoria. John McEwen, the Country Party Deputy Prime Minister, took over as acting Prime Minister for a short period until John Gorton was elected the new leader of the Liberal Party and became Prime Minister in January 1968.

Gorton served as Prime Minister until March 1971 when he was challenged for the leadership by William McMahon (later Sir William) who took over leadership. McMahon resigned in December 1972 after the Labor election victory. Billy Snedden led the Liberal Party during this period of Opposition and was replaced in early 1975 by Malcolm Fraser, who went on to lead the party until 1983, becoming caretaker Prime Minister when Sir John Kerr sacked the Labor government in 1975, and then winning the subsequent federal election.

The Liberal Party under Fraser went on to win the next election and the next two in 1977 and 1980, serving until 1983 when the Hawke Labor government came to power. Fraser resigned in March 1983 after losing the election to the Labor Party.

The Liberal Party was then in opposition from 1983 to 1996, and the leadership changed or was challenged a number of times. John Howard regained leadership of the party from Alexander Downer in 1995, and led the Liberal/National Party to victory in the 1996 federal election.

NATIONAL PARTY

Formed officially in 1920 as the Australian Country Party, the National Party has its roots in the farmers' associations which formed as a result of the 1890s Depression. At this time, these associations supported particular candidates who promoted their causes.

In 1916, a meeting was held in Melbourne, attended by members of these farmers associations from New South Wales, Victoria, Queensland and Western Australia. It was decided to establish a federal constitution and platform to guard the interests of farmers; the inaugural meeting of the Australian Farmers' Federal Organisation was held on 17 April 1917.

In the December 1919 election, 15 of the organisation's endorsed candidates were elected. On 22 January 1920, a meeting of country members was held, where it was decided to form the Australian Country Party, led temporarily by W. J. McWilliams. On 19 March 1920, McWilliams announced to the House of Representatives that the Country Party was an independent body committed to securing 'closer attention to the requirements of the primary producers of Australia than they have hitherto received'.

In the next election in December 1922, the party campaigned in its own right and returned 14 members in the Lower House. In 1923, they formed a coalition with the government under Hughes' successor Stanley Bruce, as a minority partner.

They have remained in coalition on a federal level with the Liberal Party since its inception in 1944, except for the period 1972–1974 when in Opposition. At the 1975, 1977 and 1996 elections, the Liberal Party won enough seats to gain power independently, however, the coalition remained intact. In 1987, when Sir Joh Bjelke Petersen announced a bid for federal politics, relations between the Liberal and National parties were compromised and although Bjelke Petersen pulled out, the coalition was terminated for a period, until August 1987.

In 1939, Sir Earle Page served as Prime Minister for a short period following the death of Lyons. Other National Party leaders to have served as Prime Ministers are Arthur Fadden who served from August to October in 1941 after Menzies resigned, and John McEwen who filled in for less than a month when Harold Holt disappeared.

The federal party changed its name in 1975 to the National Country Party of Australia and then in October 1982 to the National Party. The party is currently led by Tim Fischer, and is part of the coalition government formed with the Liberal Party at the 1996 federal election.

AUSTRALIAN DEMOCRATS

The Australian Democrats party was formed in 1977 by Don Chipp, who resigned that year from the Liberal Party, which he had represented in the House of Representatives since 1960, serving as a minister in two governments.

Chipp was passed over for a place in the Fraser ministry and became disillusioned with the way that Malcolm Fraser was leading the government. He resigned from the Liberal Party and retained his seat in the House of Representatives as an independent member.

At this time, Chipp was apparently approached by supporters of a number of small parties with the idea of forming a new party. He held a number of meetings around Australia, the first in April 1977 at Perth Town Hall, where it was voted unanimously to form a new party. After further well-attended meetings around the country, a national constitution was drawn up and the Australian Democrats were launched.

During the next six months, the party set up branches throughout Australia and prepared draft policies on areas of federal government responsibility. Later that year, the Democrats won their first seat when Robin Millhouse was elected to the South Australia parliament. Janine Haines entered the federal parliament in November 1977 when she was chosen by the South Australia Parliament to succeed resigning senator R. Hall. Her term finished at the end of June 1978.

In the 1977 federal election, both Don Chipp and Colin Mason were elected to the Senate, beginning their terms as Janine Haines finished hers. In 1980, the Australian Democrats won three more Senate seats, giving them five senators in the parliament from July 1981 and enabling them to hold the balance of power in the Senate. In 1984, the Democrats had seven senators. Don Chipp retired from Parliament in 1986 and Janine Haines was elected leader of the party. In the 1990 federal election, Janine Haines resigned her Senate position and stood for a House of Representatives seat. She was defeated at the polls and resigned as leader.

The Australian Democrats representation in the Senate currently stands at seven senators. The present leader of the party is Cheryl Kernot.

Local Government

Local government is the final level of government in Australia's three-tiered system. It consists of councils governing at a community level. There are 840 councils in Australia, however, this number includes Aboriginal community governments in the Northern Territory and Queensland which are a recent innovation and do not function in the same way as the traditional councils, of which there are 835.

Almost the whole area of Australia comes within the jurisdiction of a local government area. The exceptions to this are the Australian Capital Territory, and sparsely populated parts of New South Wales, South Australia and the Northern Territory.

COUNCIL RESPONSIBILITIES

The role and power of councils varies considerably between states, as each state has enacted differing legislation with regard to local government. Thus, within each state the diversity of the different councils reflects the different needs and composition of the local community they serve.

Local government bodies in each state are required to perform, or allowed certain powers. Their authority is limited to these specific areas. State governments retain the right to dismiss a council and replace it with a commissioner or administrator. The responsibilities of local government bodies are basically maintenance and improvement of the local environment, regulation of development and community based activity. Specific work undertaken includes: maintenance and construction of roads, pavements, guttering and parks; rubbish collection; street cleaning and lighting.

Gardens, sports grounds and camping facilities often fall within the jurisdiction of local government. Many councils run public libraries, swimming pools, child care services and fire fighting services. They often provide services for the community such as meals on wheels, counselling, hostels, immunisation and health care. The council also controls planning and development within its jurisdiction.

The amount of services provided by a council is often linked to the amount of revenue collected.

REVENUE

Councils raise revenue through rates levied on land and property owners. This is the main source of revenue and is levied in two ways; either site value or rental value (calculated on a yearly basis). These two systems are known by a number of different names, but basically refer to an improved and unimproved value. Values are assessed by a council or government valuer who inspects properties periodically.

Federal and state government, charitable, religious and educational premises are often exempt from rates. Other revenue is collected through state government grants (usually given for specific projects), charges for public works and services, rent of council properties, profits from commercial activities, licence fees and fines. The states have various naming systems to describe a council. These are outlined below. In most states, these distinctions are based on permanent population figures.

STATE DETAILS

NEW SOUTH WALES

New South Wales local government is divided into city, municipal and shire councils. The four largest cities; Sydney, Parramatta, Newcastle and Wollongong, are run by lord mayors; cities and municipalities are run by mayors; and shires by shire presidents. The members of the city and municipal councils are known as aldermen or alderwomen. Members of shire councils are known as councillors.

Council members are elected for a term of four years and voting in council elections is compulsory. The voting system used is proportional representation in wards with three or more seats and preferential in the others.

VICTORIA

Many Victorian councils, especially in the Melbourne metropolitan area, have recently amalgamated despite resistance. The local government divisions in Victoria are cities, towns, boroughs and shires.

Melbourne has a lord mayor, while the other cities, towns and boroughs are run by mayors. Shires are run by shire presidents. Members of all councils are known as councillors.

Council members are elected for a three-year term and voting in council elections is compulsory. The voting system used is preferential.

QUEENSLAND

Brisbane is the only capital city that is run by a single council. This council controls the entire metropolitan area, known as Greater Brisbane, which covers an area of 1000 km². (This compares with Sydney and Melbourne which have about 50 councils each.)

The local government divisions in Queensland are known as cities, towns and shires. Brisbane is run by a lord mayor, other cities and towns by mayors; and shires by shire chairmen.

Council members are elected for a three-year term and voting is compulsory for all residents of Queensland. In Brisbane, the preferential system is used, while everywhere else, electors have as many votes as there are positions.

SOUTH AUSTRALIA

In South Australia, the divisions are cities, corporate towns and district council areas. Adelaide has a lord mayor and the cities and towns are run by mayors. Council district areas are run by shire presidents.

In South Australia, council members are known as councillors, but the positions of alderpeople are held by councillors with experience elected for a whole area rather than within a ward. Council members are elected for two-year terms; half of the members retiring each year at an annual election.

Voting in council elections is voluntary and everyone, including those who are not Australian citizens, is eligible to vote.

WESTERN AUSTRALIA

Western Australia is divided into cities, towns and shires. Perth has a lord mayor and the other cities and towns are run by mayors. Shires are run by shire presidents.

Council members serve a three-year term and elections are held annually for a third of the members.

Voting is voluntary, but restricted to Australian citizens or British subjects who own or occupy property. Plural voting exists; certain people who pay rates over a certain limit are allowed two votes.

TASMANIA

Tasmania has four city councils: Hobart, Launceston, Glenorchy and Devonport. Hobart has a lord mayor and the other three cities mayors. The rest of the state is divided into districts known as municipalities and run by wardens.

Council members serve a three-year term, with a third of the members going to election each year. Voting is voluntary and, while it is restricted to Australian citizens and British subjects who own or occupy property, alien owners are allowed to get a qualified elector to vote on their behalf.

NORTHERN TERRITORY

Darwin has the only city council in the Northern Territory. It is run by a lord mayor. There are at present five town councils, one shire and one corporation. As well as this, there are 48 community governments. Council elections are held every four years on the last Saturday in May.

Community governments differ from traditional councils in a number of ways. To adopt community government, a petition with at least ten signatures must be sent to the Northern Territory Minister for Local Government requesting that they consider the proposal. The minister and his department then help the community devise a tailored system of government within the outlines of the scheme.

In this way, no two community governments will be exactly the same. There are five common policies behind the Northern Territory system of local government: community choice; community accountability; community management; community development and self-sufficiency.

Council members are elected by secret ballot in a first-past-the-post system. Terms run for one year and there must be eight weeks notice given for elections. The government is run by a president who is elected by the council members.

Community governments in general serve more functions than a traditional council, becoming more involved with local industry and management.

8
Law

Australia's Legal System

*T*he Australian legal system is based on the British system of law, but with certain refinements which take into account the Federation of Australian States. Even though there are a few small differences between the different States, in general it could be said that basic laws are the same throughout Australia. The Australian constitution created the High Court as the Supreme Federal Court of Australia. Later, other Federal Courts were created to cope with matters such as bankruptcy, industrial disputes and Family Law. State Courts usually deal with all criminal matters.

The High Court

The High Court of Australia is the highest court in the Australian judicial system. Its role is to interpret and uphold the Australian Constitution and serve as the supreme tribunal and arbiter in cases of constitutional dispute between the Commonwealth and the states. Its role as the ultimate court of appeal for cases from the States' Supreme Courts, combined with its unchallengeable jurisdiction on constitutional matters, places it at the top of the Australian judicial system.

HISTORY

Established under Section 71 of the Constitution, the High Court held its first sitting on 6 October 1903 in the Banco Court of the Supreme Court building in Melbourne. The Court was initially composed of three Justices. By 1912, this number had increased to seven, although the Great Depression forced numbers down to six. The present level of seven Justices was not restored until 1946.

Courtrooms and Registry offices specifically for the High Court's use did not exist before 1923 in Sydney and five years later in Melbourne. Until that time, the Court had used the State Supreme Court facilities in each of those cities. The High Court finally found a permanent home in May 1980, when the new High Court building on Lake Burley Griffin, Canberra, was opened by Queen Elizabeth II.

APPOINTMENTS TO THE COURT

Appointments of Justices to the High Court are made by the Governor-General on the advice of the Federal Attorney-General, who in turn consults the Attorneys-General of the States.

There have been ten Chief Justices and 35 Justices since the High Court was established in 1903. Until 1977, Justices of the High Court were appointed for life, but a referendum held in that year decided that future appointees would retire at the age of seventy.

PRESENT JUSTICES OF THE HIGH COURT

Chief Justice Gerard Brennan
Justice Daryl Michael Dawson
Justice John Leslie Toohey
Justice Mary Genevieve Gaudron
Justice Michael Hudson McHugh
Justice Michael Donald Kirby
Justice William Montague Charles Gummow

The Federal Court

The Federal Court of Australia, established under the *Federal Court of Australia Act 1976*, interprets legislation relating to Commonwealth matters or those which exceed State and Territory borders. It has registries and conducts hearings in all parts of the country, with most hearings open to the public. The average number of judgments made available for publication is in excess of 1000 per year.

There are approximately 40 judges of the Federal Court in Australia. They are appointed by the Governor-General under the *Federal Court of Australia Act 1976*.

JURISDICTION

The Federal Court is made up of two main divisions: the Industrial Division which handles cases relating to the *Industrial Relations Act 1988*, and the General Division which exercises jurisdiction under many other Commonwealth Acts. The most notable of these are the *Aboriginal and Torres Strait Islander Commission Act*, *Administrative Appeals Tribunal Act*, *Australian Securities Commission Act*, *Bankruptcy Act*, *Foreign Acquisitions and Takeovers Act*, *Native Title Act* and the *Trade Practices Act*.

The Federal Court hears almost all civil matters arising under Federal law and some summary criminal matters. The majority of cases the court deals with are:
• bankruptcy of individuals;
• liquidation or winding up of corporations;
• restrictive (anti-competitive) trade practices;

- consumer protection from misleading or unconscionable conduct by corporations;
- judicial review of administrative decisions made under Commonwealth enactments;
- income and sales tax appeals from the Administrative Appeals Tribunal and objections to decisions made by the Commissioner of Taxation;
- intellectual property (along with the Supreme Courts of States and Territories);
- native title claims for land as well as for compensation;
- anti-discrimination under Commonwealth legislation on the basis of sex or race.

Family Law

In 1975, Australian couples were given access to quicker and less complicated divorces when the *Family Law Act* was passed. The Act was established by the Family Court of Australia and addressed the questions of child custody, maintenance and issues of property.

The most significant change introduced by the Act is that matrimonial conduct and questions of fault are no longer taken into account when divorce applications are lodged. Only one reason, irredeemable breakdown of marriage, is necessary to obtain a divorce. To meet this ground for divorce, married couples must have been separated for more than twelve months with no foreseeable prospect for their reunion.

The provisions of the Act, in reference to maintenance, custody and welfare, have recently been broadened to include all offspring of a couple, including those outside marriage. These changes operate in all States and Territories, except Western Australia, where ex-nuptial children are subject to State laws.

THE FAMILY COURT

The Act also created the Family Court which provides a number of facilities to couples. One of the most important is the counselling service, available to couples involved in cases at the court as well as those not involved in proceedings who need to discuss marriage problems, custody and access issues and property settlements.

POWERS

The Family Court will not usually grant a divorce decree if adequate arrangements have not been made for the care of children involved. The *Family Law Act* states that both parents are guardians and, unless an opposing court order is presented, parents have joint custody of a child or children until the age of eighteen. The Family Court also considers applications for sole custody.

The Family Court has jurisdiction over disputes concerning family assets. It has the authority to transfer possession of property and also assesses how much each partner has contributed, financially and non-financially, to the marriage.

APPOINTMENTS

Those appointed to the Family Court are considered carefully, not only for professional qualifications and experience, but also for personal qualities of compassion and understanding. Trained counsellors and legally qualified registrars and deputy registrars are employed by the Family Court.

OTHER BODIES

The Court is assisted in its work by two statutory bodies also established under the *Family Law Act*. These are the Family Law Council, which provides advisory support to the court; and the Australian Institute of Family Studies, a national research and information dissemination organisation.

The Child Support Agency was established in 1988 to collect and enforce maintenance payments under the Child Support Scheme. The agency is now responsible for assessment of the amount of child support to be paid, taking into account the incomes of both parents and the number of dependent children involved.

State and Territory Courts

State and Territory courts have initial jurisdiction in all matters under State and Territory laws as well as original jurisdiction in cases involving Federal law, unless they have been specifically passed to the Federal courts. Most criminal cases, regardless of whether they fall under commonwealth, state, or territory law, are heard in the state and territory courts.

APPEALS

The process of appeals begins in the lower courts and can continue through to the High Court if the person is not satisfied by a decision. After passing through the lower courts, appeals are taken to the State County and District Courts and then to the state and territory Supreme Courts. The next course of action is by way of application to appeal to the High Court.

Police

Every Australian State and the Northern Territory has its own police service, each responsible for maintaining the laws within their own jurisdictions. In the Australian Capital Territory, community policing is undertaken by the Australian Federal Police (AFP). The AFP's services are contracted by the Australian Capital Territory government. The AFP also provides community policing services for Australia's external territories of Christmas Island, the Cocos (Keeling) Islands, Norfolk Island and the Commonwealth territory of Jervis Bay in New South Wales. The AFP is the principal law enforcement agency through which the Commonwealth pursues its law enforcement interests.

AUSTRALIAN FEDERAL POLICE

The Australian Federal Police (AFP) is unique in Australian law enforcement in that its functions relate both to community policing and to investigations of offences against Commonwealth law which involve law enforcement in Australia and overseas.

With its head office located in Canberra, the AFP has regional offices in every Australian state and territory, including a community policing structure which serves the Australian Capital Territory under an arrangement with the Australian Capital Territory government. The AFP has liaison posts in 15 cities in 13 countries, and a representative attached to Interpol in Lyon, France. The AFP also provides members for the United Nations peacekeeping operations in Cyprus and has assisted in establishing law and order in Cambodia, Mozambique and Haiti.

The AFP was established in 1979 as a result of the recommendations made by Sir Robert Mark in his review of the organisation of police resources in the Commonwealth. The AFP incorporated the Commonwealth and the Australian Capital Territory police forces and later the functions of the Federal Narcotics Bureau of the Australian Customs Service (ACS). The first challenge for the AFP was to forge a new organisational entity from the three separate structures it replaced.

Later developments included the transfer in 1984 of the function of protective service guarding to a new organisation, the Australian Protective Service (APS); the creation and subsequent transfer to ACS of a new unit, the Coastal Protection Unit; and more recently the forging of a strategic alliance with the National Crime Authority (NCA).

FUTURE DIRECTIONS

The AFP is currently going through a process of change. Changes are being characterised by a demonstrated commitment to fostering a professional ethos and by employing a flexible team-based approach, empowering individuals and emphasising the importance of working with other law enforcement agencies at the international, national and community levels.

The transition from a basically hierarchical rule-bound organisation to one which fosters initiative, learning and empowerment has seen a move away from a traditional police rank structure. Outside the community policing function of the Australian Capital Territory, AFP officers below the rank of assistant commissioner are now all classed as federal agents.

The AFP has approximately 2800 personnel, made up of 1500 federal agents, 650 community police members and 650 staff members.

RESPONSIBILITIES

The AFP investigates crimes against the Commonwealth, including counterfeiting and money laundering, drug trafficking, fraud, illegal immigration and organised crime.

DRUGS   Drug traffickers used a variety of means to bring narcotics into Australia. Some attempted to bring drugs through customs barriers at airports either in or on their persons or in their luggage, while others shipped drugs in the mail or concealed in items of freight. Others have attempted to bring narcotics into Australia on cargo ships, fishing boats and pleasure craft.

The AFP, in cooperation with other Commonwealth, State and Territory and overseas law enforcement agencies, is continually working to stop illicit drugs from finding their way onto the streets of Australia.

FRAUD   The difficulties experienced with some major fraud investigations arise from the fact that some criminal organisations have bigger budgets than the agencies investigating them. These organisations tend to have large financial resources to afford them the best legal, accounting and other professional services to defend themselves and their assets.

White-collar criminal activity involves breaches of State and Commonwealth criminal and regulatory legislation. The pursuit of evidence often will be helped by access to the intelligence and information holdings of agencies such as the AFP, State police services, the Australian Transaction Reports and Analysis Centre (AUSTRAC) and the Australian Securities Commission (ASC). Considerable emphasis is placed on the cooperative aspect of investigations.

ORGANISED CRIME   Organised crime was defined by the Commonwealth Law Enforcement Review (CLER) as a systematic and continuing conspiracy to commit serious offences. Organised crime involves fraud, extortion, drug trafficking and money laundering.

Technological, political and economic factors that have enhanced the growth of legitimate businesses have also aided the growth of organised crime which has taken advantage of technological change, the globalisation of the world's economy, and the larger movement of people, cash and goods around the world. Criminal networks are not inhibited by rules, protocols or political borders.

Australian-based criminal groups continue to cause the most damage to the Australian community and operate in most major cities. They are generally unstructured, loose-knit organisations in which the members cooperate for particular criminal ventures. Membership of these groups is not necessarily linked to ethnicity, and intelligence shows that their criminal activities tend to be in 'traditional' fields such as armed robberies, illegal gambling, warehouse robberies and counterfeiting. Being long established in the Australian community, these traditional criminal groups are more visible than the ethnic-based groups.

EMERGING TRENDS

Computer-related crime has become a challenge to the investigative capacity of the AFP in the 1990s. Investigations into computer related crime have highlighted areas of potential fraud and unauthorised collection of data as well as the transmission of terrorist and racist material and child pornography on the Internet.

National Crime Authority

The National Crime Authority (NCA) has been given special powers under Commonwealth, State and Territory legislation to counter organised crime in Australia and reduce its impact on the community. It is not a police service, but an organisation comprised of multidisciplinary teams of police, lawyers, financial and intelligence analysts and support staff. Cooperation and coordination with Australia's law enforcement agencies is an integral part of the NCA's work.

Independent Commission Against Corruption

The Independent Commission Against Corruption (ICAC) was established in March 1989 by the *Independent Commission against Corruption Act 1988*. The ICAC's role is to expose and minimise corruption in the 400 000-strong New South Wales public sector; its catalyst was a realisation by the then state government of high public concern about corruption in that sector.

The ICAC operates separately from government and is accountable to the people of New South Wales through the Parliament, specifically the Parliamentary Committee on the ICAC. All New South Wales public sector departments, statutory authorities, local governments and public officials, including politicians and the judiciary, are subject to ICAC's charter.

The ICAC's main responsibilities, as determined by the Act, are initiating investigation, corruption prevention and education. The private sector is outside the Commission's powers, except where it interacts with the public sector in areas such as contracting and tendering. Most work arises from reports by public sector agencies and information from members of the public. The Commission has discretion as to which matters it will pursue but has special obligations in regard to complaints from members of the public and matters referred by the Parliament. It can form taskforces with other government agencies.

FUNCTIONS

INVESTIGATIONS   Exposing and deterring corrupt conduct by investigating and reporting on allegations of corruption. Complaints of corrupt conduct, which may be made anonymously, can be notified by phone, letter or in person. The ICAC, however, does not operate on the basis of hearsay or rumour, nor does it operate as a complaint resolution body.

CORRUPTION PREVENTION   Minimising or preventing corruption opportunities by working with the public sector to improve procedures and operating systems. Corruption prevention complements investigations by following the exposure of corrupt conduct with improvements to operating systems, thereby eliminating or reducing the chance of such behaviour recurring.

EDUCATION   Attitudinal change is used proactively by the ICAC. Strategies and products to lift awareness of the risks, costs and preventive actions relating to corruption have been designed for the community and public officials. Challenging interactive curriculum materials have also been produced to teach ethical attitudes in schools and universities.

THE COMMISSIONER

Ian Temby, QC, was the first ICAC Commissioner. When his five-year non-renewable contract expired, he was succeeded by Barry O'Keefe, AM, QC, in November 1994. Mr O'Keefe, a former Chief Judge of the New South Wales Supreme Court Commercial Division, has also been appointed to a non-renewable five-year term under the *Independent Commission Against Corruption Act 1988*.

The commission's statutory functions and powers are exercised by the commissioner, who also acts as chief executive. The *Independent Commission Against Corruption Act* allows the New South Wales Governor to appoint assistant commissioners to conduct hearings or perform statutory functions during periods of leave taken by the commissioner.

Budget and Staffing

The ICAC has its own budget provided directly by the NSW Parliament. Recurrent expenditure is approximately $14 million annually. Total staff is approximately 140 people.

Special Powers

The ICAC's wide-ranging powers include the following:
- the commission has the right to require a public authority or public official to provide a statement of information, and any person can be asked to produce specific documents or things;
- the right of ICAC officers, authorised by the commissioner, to enter specific premises occupied by a public authority or public official, and inspect any document or thing in the premises and copy any document;
- an authorised justice or the commissioner may issue a search warrant if satisfied that reasonable grounds exist for doing so;
- commission officers can apply to a New South Wales Supreme Court judge for a warrant to use a device under the *Listening Devices Act 1984* or apply to a Federal Court judge for a warrant to record phone calls under the *Telecommunications (Interceptions) Act 1979*;
- the power to arrest a witness who fails to comply with a summons to give evidence;
- the power to arrange protection for witnesses.

Prosecutions and Disciplinary Actions

The Commission has the power to make findings of corrupt conduct against individuals. However, where evidence of a criminal or disciplinary offence is found during an investigation, the ICAC refers the former to the NSW Director of Public Prosecutions and the latter to the chief executive officer, or equivalent, of the relevant public sector agency.

Industrial Relations Commission

Replacing the Australian Conciliation and Arbitration Commission, the Australian Industrial Relations Commission (IRC) is a Federal body established under the *Industrial Relations Act 1988* (the Act) to arbitrate in industrial matters which extend beyond State and Territorial boundaries. The Act has been amended by approximately 20 other Acts of Parliament, most substantially by the *Industrial Relations Reform Act 1993* and, most recently, by the Coalition Government's Workplace Relations Bill 1996.

The principal object of the IRC is to provide a structure for the prevention and settlement of industrial disputes, as far as possible by conciliation, and where necessary by arbitration. It aims to settle industrial disputes quickly and fairly, with as little disruption as possible to the Australian community and economy. Its general functions are:

- to provide and maintain safety net award provisions through an award system, and also to provide minimum entitlements consistent with certain treaty obligations;
- to ensure that the award system provides for secure, relevant and consistent wages and conditions of employment so that it is an effective safety net underpinning direct bargaining;
- to facilitate and approve enterprise bargains;
- to conciliate unlawful termination claims and, where agreed by the parties, to deal with the claim by consent arbitration.

The Workplace Relations Bill 1996 has substantially enhanced the role of the IRC. It has gained award jurisdiction for superannuation and outworkers, while also setting some conditions for part-time workers. The commission regained the power to handle equal pay for equal work cases and, in exceptional circumstances, can arbitrate on some non-award matters in the public interest.

STRUCTURE

The Industrial Relations Commission consists of a president, two vice presidents and such numbers of senior deputy presidents, deputy presidents and commissioners as are appointed by the Governor-General.

Generally matters are dealt with by a single member, but there are some issues, such as demarcation disputes, which can only be determined by a presidential member. Matters which involve the formulation or alteration of terms of award agreements can only be heard by a full bench of the Industrial Relations Commission.

DECISIONS

After a matter is concluded, either by conciliation or arbitration, the Industrial Relations Commission member may issue a decision or, where required, an order. A decision is a statement of findings and reason for the determination which is subsequently reflected in the Commission's order. The order is a legally binding instrument having the force of Federal law.

In addition to the IRC, there are three bodies that provide for the regulation of industrial relations at the Federal level:
* the Australian Industrial Registry;
* the Industrial Relations Court of Australia; and
* the Awards Management Branch.

AUSTRALIAN INDUSTRIAL REGISTRY

The functions of the Australian Industrial Registry are to provide administrative support to the Industrial Relations Commission. Notifications of disputes and other applications are lodged with the Registry. The registry maintains the files and records of the commission, including the rules of organisations. The registry also undertakes a number of functions in relation to the regulation of organisations registered under the Act.

INDUSTRIAL RELATIONS COURT OF AUSTRALIA

This specialist industrial court takes over all industrial relations matters from the Federal Court and deals with matters sent to it by the High Court. It is a judicial tribunal which interprets and enforces the statutory rights and duties laid down by the Act and the awards made pursuant to the Act. Its jurisdiction extends to such matters as claims for unlawful termination of employment, review of unfair contracts, prosecutions for offences against the Act and awards, as well as disputed elections within organisations and infringements of the rules of organisations.

AWARDS MANAGEMENT BRANCH

As part of the Department of Industrial Relations, the Awards Management Branch is responsible for providing advice on award entitlements and obligations, and for ensuring compliance with awards of the Industrial Relations Commission and observance of requirements under the Act. An inspector may institute proceedings for non-observance of awards and/or breaches of the Act.

The Ombudsman

The role of an ombudsman is to protect the rights and interests of the Australian public. The ombudsman is an independent statutory officer, ultimately responsible to Parliament, who investigates complaints about government departments, authorities, local councils and members of the police force. In Australia, ombudsmen operate on a national and regional level. There is a Commonwealth Ombudsman, whose jurisdiction also covers the Australian Capital Territory, as well as seven ombudsmen who oversee the states and territories. The names of those holding the positions in 1996 are shown below.

Jurisdiction	Ombudsman
Commonwealth	Ms Philippa Smith
New South Wales	Ms Irene Moss
Victoria	Dr Barry Perry
Queensland	Mr Fred N. Albietz
South Australia	Mr Eugene Biganovsky
Western Australia	Mr Robert Eadie
Tasmania	Mr Ron Green
Northern Territory	Mr Peter Boyce

THE COMMONWEALTH OMBUDSMAN

Established under the *Ombudsman Act 1976*, the Commonwealth Ombudsman is independent of Commonwealth departments and authorities and must remain impartial when dealing with complaints. The ombudsman has the power to investigate all administrative actions of Commonwealth departments and authorities. He or she can demand to see files and other records and enter Commonwealth premises, as well being able to order the presence of public servants and demand their testimony.

The ombudsman is assisted by one deputy ombudsman and investigative officers.

THE COMPLAINT PROCESS

Although not a hard-and-fast rule, the ombudsman generally only investigates a complaint after the person has taken the matter to the relevant department or body, but remains unsatisfied. All investigations by the ombudsman into the complaint are confidential.

The next step is when the ombudsman asks the department to explain its decision. Once she or he has gathered all available information and made a decision, the complainant is notified. The ombudsman has no powers to enforce a decision. If he or she decides the complaint is justified, a report can be made to the relevant department. If the department fails to accept the Ombudsman's recommendations, then the Ombudsman may report to the Prime Minister and to Parliament.

LIMITS OF POWER

The ombudsman cannot investigate the actions of a minister or a judge. Ministers are answerable to Parliament in the case of alleged impropriety and a judge's decision can be appealed against. Disputes regarding employment conditions between the government and its employees are also outside the terms of reference of the ombudsman's powers, and are looked into by the Industrial Relations Commission.

COMPLAINTS ABOUT POLICE

Complaints about the police can be made either to the police department or to the ombudsman, although the police department must notify the ombudsman of any complaints received. These complaints may be investigated by an internal police investigation body or by the ombudsman. Staff may be present at a police interview, and once the police have completed their report, it must be turned over to the ombudsman, who then decides whether or not they agree with the outcome. If not, they can go to the police commissioner. If this does not resolve the situation, the matter is then referred to the Attorney General.

Human Rights and Equal Opportunity Commission

Promoting the understanding and practice of human rights principles is the main aim of the Human Rights and Equal Opportunity Commission (HREOC), formerly the Human Rights Commission. Established in December 1986 by the Federal government, the HREOC runs a program of public enquiries and community education, as well as investigating complaints from the public. The commission covers three main areas: human rights, racism and sexism.

The HREOC has responsibility for five Acts of Parliament: the *Human Rights and Equal Opportunity Commission Act 1986*, the *Sex Discrimination Act 1984*, the *Racial Discrimination Act 1975*, the *Privacy Act 1988* and the *Disability Discrimination Act 1992*.

HUMAN RIGHTS AND EQUAL OPPORTUNITY COMMISSION ACT 1986
This Act sets down in law the rights of every individual to a decent standard of living, including appropriate access to education and medical facilities, and equal opportunity before the law, as well as the freedom to express their religious and political views, in accordance with the principles established by the other anti-discrimination Acts.

The Act is responsible for Australia's compliance with the following international human rights instruments:
- The International Covenant on Civil and Political Rights;
- Declaration of the Rights of the Child;
- Declaration on the Rights of Disabled Persons;
- Declaration on the Rights of Mentally Retarded Persons; and
- Convention Concerning Discrimination in Respect of Employment and Occupation.

SEX DISCRIMINATION ACT 1984   This Act gives effect to the Convention on the Elimination of All Forms of Discrimination Against Women and promotes recognition of the principle of equality between men and women. It also aims to eliminate sexual harassment.

The Act specifies that discrimination occurs when a person is treated less favourably than another in the same or similar circumstances because of sex, marital status, pregnancy or family responsibilities.

RACIAL DISCRIMINATION ACT 1975   This Act enacts Australia's compliance with the International Convention on the Elimination of All Forms of Racial Discrimination. Its major purpose is to promote the equality before the law of all persons regardless of their race, colour or national or ethnic origin, and to make discrimination against such people unlawful in public life.

PRIVACY ACT 1988   This Act ensures the protection of personal information held by Federal government departments and agencies; restricts the use of consumer credit information to credit related purposes, and ensures that tax file numbers are collected and used only for expressly authorised government purposes. It establishes rules about the collection of personal information, storage and security, access by individuals to their personal records, and limits on the use and disclosure of personal information. The terms of the Act do not extend to state or local government bodies or to private organisations except in regard to tax file numbers.

DISABILITY DISCRIMINATION ACT 1992   This Act gives effect to Australia's obligations under the International Covenants on Civil and Political Rights and Economic, Social and Cultural Rights, and the International Labour Organisations Convention. The major objects of the

Act are to make discrimination against people on the grounds of any actual or perceived disability unlawful in public life, and to eliminate harassment and victimisation of such people.

STRUCTURE

The HREOC is made up of a President, a Human Rights Commissioner, a Race Discrimination Commissioner, a Sex Discrimination Commissioner, a Privacy Commissioner, a Disability Discrimination Commissioner and an Aboriginal and Torres Strait Islander Social Justice Commissioner.

The latter appointment was made in 1993 to highlight existing breaches of the human rights of Aboriginal and Torres Strait Islander people. This Commissioner works with the Aboriginal and Torres Strait Islander Commissioner, the Council of Aboriginal Reconciliation, and organisations established by Aboriginal and Torres Strait Islander communities, as well as with indigenous organisations in other countries and international organisations.

The position of Human Rights Commissioner is allowed for under the provisions of the Act while the other four positions exist in recognition of Australia's commitment to its international obligations. All members of the commission are appointed by the Governor-General on the recommendations of the government.

Commissioners are responsible for dealing with complaints and examining proposed legislation in their respective spheres. They can exercise statutory powers of inquiry, conciliation and settlement in relation to complaints under the terms of the Human Rights and Equal Opportunity Commission Act and the Acts relevant to their positions.

It remains the government's prerogative to determine how to enact the recommendations as the position of commissioner carries no legal power.

Aboriginal and Torres Strait Islander Commission

The Aboriginal and Torres Strait Islander Commission (ATSIC), established under the *Aboriginal and Torres Strait Islander Commission Act 1989*, is the chief representative indigenous organisation in Australia. It is the main Commonwealth agency for administering and advancing Aboriginal and Torres Strait Islander programs, and also advises various authorities on indigenous issues, contributes an indigenous point of view in national debates and negotiations, and ensures that indigenous people have access to the full range of mainstream services. ATSIC also made a crucial contribution to the establishment of the *Native Title Act 1993* and the Indigenous Land Fund.

REPRESENTATION

Through 35 elected regional councils, Aboriginal and Torres Strait Islander people are able to set priorities and take decisions on many social and economic programs set up to combat indigenous disadvantage. Regional councillors assist in drawing up regional plans, make funding decisions on ATSIC programs in their region, and lobby other agencies in the region to meet their responsibilities.

They also elect a commissioner to sit on the ATSIC Board with one commissioner elected from the Torres Strait and another two appointed by the Minister for Aboriginal and Torres Strait Islander Affairs. The board makes national funding and policy decisions.

PROGRAMS

In 1996–1997, ATSIC administered a program budget of approximately $830 million. Most of the funding goes to indigenous organisations, enabling them to provide community services such as housing, legal aid, broadcasting, employment, economic development and the promotion and maintenance of culture and identity.

COMMUNITY DEVELOPMENT EMPLOYMENT PROJECTS

ATSIC's largest program accounts for almost one third of the program budget. Often described as a work for the dole scheme, the Community Development Employment Projects (CDEP) participants give up their entitlement to unemployment benefits while ATSIC funds the community to pay wages and buy equipment and materials necessary.

The work undertaken improves living conditions and helps develop businesses. With over 28 000 participants in 276 communities, CDEP is the main source of employment in indigenous Australia.

COMMUNITY HOUSING AND INFRASTRUCTURE PROGRAM

The Community Housing and Infrastructure Program (CHIP) is ATSIC's second largest area of expenditure, although the primary responsibility for essential services lies with State and Territory governments.

It is estimated that there is a $4 billion backlog of capital needs in this area. Since 1990, ATSIC has identified the area of housing as one of the most urgent problems facing indigenous people and has subsequently provided funds to indigenous housing organisations owning about 30% of all housing rented to indigenous people.

HEALTH INFRASTRUCTURE PRIORITY PROJECTS

The Health Infrastructure Priority Projects (HIPP) targets large-scale projects in areas of high need, providing the infrastructure necessary for good health in indigenous communities.

THE BUSINESS FUNDING SCHEME AND THE
COMMUNITY ECONOMIC INITIATIVES SCHEME

The Business Funding Scheme and the Community Economic Initiatives Scheme provide individuals and communities with loans and grant funding to create, buy or expand small businesses. The Housing Loans Scheme assists families to buy their own home subject to a means test.

ATSIC supports a network of representative bodies under the *Native Title Act 1993* to advance claims under that Act, and plays a major role in native title policy. In the cultural area, ATSIC supports more than 50 arts and crafts projects, mostly in remote Australia, as well as indigenous broadcasting services that include seven licensed broadcasters and 11 regional media groups. It is also involved in more than 90 language maintenance projects across Australia.

Administrative Appeals Tribunal

The Administrative Appeals Tribunal is an independent body, established under the *Administrative Appeals Tribunal Act 1975*. The Tribunal may review certain decisions of Commonwealth Ministers, officials and authorities where jurisdiction has been conferred by the legislation under which the decision was made; at present it may review decisions under 290 Commonwealth enactments. The tribunal may affirm or vary a decision and remit the matter to the decision-maker with directions or recommendations. It may also encourage parties to reach agreement through processes such as mediation.

The tribunal has district registries in each State and Territory.

MEMBERSHIP

As of 30 June 1996, the Administrative Appeals Tribunal had 102 members, including the president (who must be a Family Court judge). There were 26 presidential members, 21 senior members, and 55 part-time members. Eleven of the tribunal's members were Federal Court judges and four were Family Court judges.

HEARINGS

The Administrative Appeals Tribunal adapts its procedures to meet the circumstances of each case. It may use conferences, mediation and formal hearings, depending on the issues and needs of the parties.

Freedom of Information

The *Freedom of Information Act 1982* was passed to give the public greater access to government departmental information as well as making ministers' documents more readily available. It ensures that 'rules and practices affecting members of the public in their dealings' with government authorities are available.

Persons seeking information under freedom of information (FOI) do not have to reveal their reasons for the request. It is up to the departmental officer to make sure any request complies with the terms of the Act. Certain classes of documents and material remain unavailable to the public despite FOI laws.

EXEMPTIONS

There are certain documents which are exempt from the terms of the Act. These are Cabinet and Executive Council documents; documents concerning enforcement of law and protection of public safety; Other major exemptions are documents concerning national security, defence, international relations, relations with the States, and documents exempt by reason of secrecy provisions or affecting personal privacy.

Agencies exempt under the Act include intelligence agencies and all those commercial organisations in competition with the private sector.

REVIEWS

Many requests for FOI documents, if not refused, result in the release of pages of blacked-out material. The Act does, however, allow for applications to be made to the Commonwealth Ombudsman or the Administrative Appeals Tribunal for review of official decisions refusing access. The tribunal is invested with the power to refer the question of whether disclosure is against the public interest to a Document Review Tribunal, established in pursuance of the Act.

Legal Aid

There are a number of legal aid and legal assistance schemes in Australia which help people who cannot afford a lawyer or proper legal defence.

LEGAL AID COMMISSIONS

Each State and Territory has a statutory Legal Aid Commission, jointly funded by the Commonwealth and the State, providing legal assistance in both Federal and State matters. The Legal Aid Commissions are the principal providers of legal aid. They provide legal advice, minor legal assistance and legal representation in a range of matters including family, criminal, civil and administrative law matters.

To qualify for legal aid, a person must generally pass a means test which looks at income and assets. In non-criminal matters, they generally also have to satisfy a merit test.

ABORIGINAL LEGAL SERVICES

There are a number of Aboriginal Legal Services operating throughout Australia. They are funded through the Aborignal and Torres Strait Islander Commission (ATSIC). Although they are independent of each other, they provide similar services, including legal advice and representation to people of Aboriginal and Torres Strait Islander descent and their spouses.

COMMUNITY LEGAL CENTRES

Community Legal Centres (CLCs) provide legal advice and assistance and some legal representation. Some CLCs are specialist services. Some are generalist services, but may only provide assistance to residents of the local area. Most CLCs are funded by government grants administered by the state Legal Aid Commissions. Some are funded by charities, universities and private law firms. CLCs are staffed by employed solicitors and volunteer lawyers and law students.

COMMONWEALTH SCHEMES

The Commonwealth Attorney-General's Department administers schemes providing legal aid in a limited number of specifically Commonwealth areas. Assistance is only available through these schemes after an application for aid has been rejected by a state Legal Aid Commission.

CHAMBER MAGISTRATE

Chamber Magistrates and Clerks of local courts provide free legal advice and assistance to people conducting their own matters in the local court.

OTHER LEGAL ASSISTANCE SERVICES

A wide range of other government and non-government organisations provide legal information, advice and assistance. These include the Law Societies in each State, the Family Court and State government departments responsible for housing, consumer affairs and motor vehicle and work-related accidents. People who contact the Legal Aid Commission in their State, but do not qualify for legal aid, can be referred to another agency which may be able to help.

Royal Commissions

Commonwealth governments establish Royal Commissions to investigate matters of particular public concern. A Royal Commission is usually called in response to a public perception, as registered by the government of the day, that an issue has assumed such extraordinary dimensions that it is no longer able to be dealt with by standard public investigative procedure. The Governor-General, on the government's advice, then commissions a person or persons to inquire into and report on specified subjects.

POWERS

The *Royal Commissions Act 1902* grants a Royal Commission the power to order the attendance of witnesses and obtain their testimony and to demand the production of whatever material they consider of relevance. It is an offence, under the Act, to fail to comply with a commissioner's directive. In addition, the Act protects commissioners and witnesses, within reason, against legal liability.

RESULTS

Once an investigation has been completed, the Royal Commissioner presents the finished report to the Governor-General for consideration by the government. Royal Commission reports are usually tabled in Parliament.

SOME ROYAL COMMISSIONS CONDUCTED SINCE 1980

- Royal Commission on the Use and Effects of Chemical Agents on Australian Personnel in Vietnam
- Royal Commission into British Nuclear Testing in Australia
- Royal Commission into Alleged Telephone Interceptions
- Royal Commission into the Chamberlain Convictions
- Royal Commission into Grain Storage, Handling and Transport

- Royal Commission into the Australian Secret Intelligence Service
- Royal Commission into Relations Between the Civil Aviation Authority and Seaview Air
- Royal Commission into Aboriginal and Torres Strait Islander Deaths in Custody

Law Reform Commission

The Australian Law Reform Commission is an independent statutory authority which operates under the *Australian Law Reform Commission Act 1996* (Commonwealth). The commission is responsible to Parliament through the Attorney-General. The function of the commission is to give policy advice to the government on reform of the law, in pursuance of references to the commission made by the Attorney-General.

POWERS

The Law Reform Commission's powers encompass the laws of the Commonwealth and Territories. New enabling legislation allows the commission to consider proposals for uniformity or complementary laws between the States, Territories and the Commonwealth. State laws are subject to examination by law reform agencies in each State. The commission meets regularly with members of other commissions, and with representatives of the Attorney-General's department, for the purpose of coordinating an integrated national agenda for law reform.

FUNCTIONS

The Law Reform Commission's functions include reviewing Commonwealth laws for the purpose of systematically developing and reforming the law by bringing it into line with current conditions, removing defects and simplifying the law, adopting more effective methods for administering the law, and dispensing justice and improving access to justice.

In performing these functions, the commission is to ensure that its recommendations do not trespass on personal rights and liberties, and that they give regard to Australia's international obligations and to considerations of access to justice.

COMMISSION MEMBERS

The Law Reform Commission is made up of a president, deputy president and at least four other members, each of whom is appointed by the

Governor-General either as a full-time or part-time member for a maximum duration of seven years.

National Crime Authority

The National Crime Authority's (NCA's) mission is to counter organised crime and reduce its impact on the Australian community, working in partnership with other law enforcement agencies. The NCA was established under the *National Crime Authority Act 1984* following a series of Royal Commissions, the majority of which investigated drug trafficking, and revealed the existence of complex and entrenched webs of organised crime. No existing law enforcement agency had the necessary powers, or national scope, to tackle the problem effectively.

The NCA is Australia's first national crime-fighting agency with a specific brief to investigate organised crime. Underpinning legislation exists in every State and Territory; it is the States and Territories, in conjunction with the Commonwealth, that are responsible for setting and placing in order of priority the NCA's work.

ROLE

The NCA works in cooperation and coordination with other law enforcement agencies to investigate and collect intelligence on numerous aspects of organised crime, including drug dealing, money laundering, extortion, fraud, currency and company violations, and violence.

The NCA is not a police service, but an investigative agency which utilises multidisciplinary teams of police, financial investigators, lawyers, intelligence analysts and support staff. It gathers admissible evidence relating to offences, which is then passed to the appropriate prosecuting authorities.

In addition to its investigative and intelligence roles, the NCA is involved in making recommendations to relevant ministers on law and administrative reform.

POWERS

The NCA conducts two types of investigations: general and special. Special investigations make up the majority of the NCA's work, and result from matters referred to it by the Commonwealth and/or State and Territory governments and approved by the Inter-Governmental Committee on the NCA. Special investigations enable the NCA to use powers not available to police services. These coercive powers include the ability to compel people to produce documents and give evidence under oath at in-camera hearings. General investigations are not conducted under a reference from government and do not involve the use of coercive powers.

When the NCA was established, civil rights had to be balanced against the need for the NCA's coercive powers. As a result, the NCA is the most accountable law enforcement agency in Australia, and checks and balances exist to ensure the authority is also efficient and effective.

Consumer Affairs

The Federal Bureau of Consumer Affairs is responsible for consumer protection as determined under the *Trade Practices Act 1974*. This Act deals with unfair practices and provides legal protection against sellers, manufacturers and importers. It also aims to ensure product safety with its power to recall or ban goods deemed unsafe.

RESPONSIBILITIES

The Federal Bureau of Consumer Affairs has both an administrative and educative role. It teaches consumers about their rights, encouraging their representation on government and private sector decision making bodies. It also initiates the resolution of disputes between the consumer and business or industry, providing information on consumer law and ensuring that product safety and product information provisions are enforced at all times. It also advises the Federal Minister for Consumer Affairs and various government agencies on consumer policy.

Australian Competition and Consumer Commission

Established in November 1995 by a merger of the Trade Practices Commission and the Prices Surveillance Authority, the Australian Competition and Consumer Commission (ACCC) is responsible for enforcing the *Trade Practices Act 1974* and the *Prices Surveillance Act 1983*. It prohibits misleading and deceptive conduct and representations, and outlaws a range of unfair trading practices.

From July 1997, the ACCC will also be responsible for eliminating anti-competitive conduct in the telecommunications industry, particularly important now that this field is opening up in Australia.

Australian Security Intelligence Organisation

The Australian Security Intelligence Organisation (ASIO), established in 1949, is an advisory body with no powers to enforce security measures. It offers advice and intelligence to the government and appropriate agencies on issues relating to the security of Australian people, property and interests, and how any risks might be managed and harm avoided or reduced. Governments use this intelligence to make decisions about any action required to maintain national security.

The *Australian Security Intelligence Organisation Act 1979* identifies the primary activities threatening national security: sabotage, espionage, politically motivated crime and violence, foreign interference and attacks on the defence system. ASIO functions, as detailed by the Act, include both the overt and covert gathering and analysing of intelligence, with extraordinary powers sometimes granted to use intrusive investigative methods such as telephone interception. The organisation also contributes to Australia's counter-terrorism response capability. *See* chapter 11. 'Defence'.

Crime and Justice

There is no single justice system in Australia. Although the country became a Federation in 1901, the States have maintained their own administrative powers, with each State and Territory responsible for the management of criminal justice within its own boundaries. This means that there are eight police forces, eight judicial systems, and seven prison systems (since the Australian Capital Territory has no gaols) in Australia.

CRIME

WHITE COLLAR CRIME
The term 'white collar crime' is used to cover non-violent crimes committed by professionals, in particular embezzlement and company fraud. However, its meaning has been broadened in recent years to include tax evasion, insider trading, social security fraud, Medicare fraud (which involves doctors billing the national health scheme for services never performed), price-fixing and consumer fraud.

Governments throughout Australia have established investigative bodies, such as the National Companies and Securities Commission (MCSC), to deal exclusively with these problems.

ORGANISED CRIME

Organised crime is premeditated activity, involving two or more persons, for the purpose of the illegal procurement of goods and services. It includes orchestrated activities in gambling, SP bookmaking, prostitution and illicit dealings involving drugs. It is often characterised by the laundering of illegal money through a legitimate business or by computer manipulation. Organised crime often flourishes because public officials are bribed to give protection and support to crime rings.

Governments in Australia have established bodies such as the National Crime Authority (NCA) and the Independent Commission Against Corruption (ICAC) in NSW to combat organised criminal activity.

ENVIRONMENTAL CRIME

Public concern over environmental pollution, particularly that caused by large corporations, has prompted governments in Australia to extend criminal law to cover the pollution of rivers and estuaries, illegal dumping of chemical waste and improper work practices which result in pollution and damage to the environment.

VIOLENT CRIME

Violent crimes, also known as crimes against the person, are crimes which may cause injury or death to a person. They include murder, manslaughter, assault, rape and sexual assault, kidnapping and abduction. Armed hold-ups, robbery and extortion are also classified as violent crimes because they involve threat or use of force against a person.

Robberies make up one-third of all serious violent crimes, with more than 30% involving the use of weapons.

PROPERTY CRIME

Property crime refers to arson, burglary, larceny, car theft, forgery, fraud, and vandalism. The difference is that these crimes do not involve the use of threat or force.

Larceny is the most common, representing four out of ten property crimes. About half the larcenies reported involved shoplifting.

A quarter of all residential burglaries occurred without forced entry. In 90% of residential burglaries the offender entered the dwelling through a door or window. About 50% of these burglaries occur during the daytime when most homes are empty.

About 1.3% of motor cars registered became the targets of theft. More than 80% of motor cars stolen are recovered, although many are damaged.

DRUG OFFENCES

Drug offences relate to the cultivation, manufacture, importation, trafficking, sale, possession, and use of narcotic and dangerous drugs.

Sex Offences

Sex offences are indecent assaults on men or women, and indecent behaviour and sexual assaults on children. Several State parliaments have made legislative changes to broaden the definition of rape to include acts of sexual violence not previously regarded as rape. A husband can now be charged with the rape of his wife. Prosecution in these cases is still quite difficult due to the complexities involved in proving rape in marriage.

Rapes account for almost 10% of serious violent crimes. Most rapes involve lone offenders and lone victims.

Homicide

Homicide is not a very common crime in Australia. There was a total of 288 homicides in Australia in 1994, with firearms involved in 16.3% of these crimes. The majority of these killers proved to be relatives, friends, or acquaintances of the victims, and about a quarter of homicides occur between spouses or partners.

Serial killers and Multiple Murders

7 people killed — Hoddle St, Melbourne, Victoria
8 people killed — Queen St, Melbourne, Victoria
7 people killed — Terrigal, New South Wales
6 people killed — Strathfield, New South Wales
32 people killed — Port Arthur, Tasmania

In 1996, Ivan Milat was convicted of the murders of seven backpackers, mostly travellers from overseas, who disappeared over a period of 3 years from 1989–1992. Their remains were buried in the Belanglo State Forest near Bowral in New South Wales.

In response to the Port Arthur massacre in 1996, the world's worst documented peacetime shooting, the federal and state governments agreed to the following changes to the national gun laws:

- all governments agree that the possession of firearms is not a right, but a conditional privilege.
- new classifications introduced determine genuine reasons for owning, possessing or using a firearm.
- in addition to the 'genuine reason' test, some categories of firearms may be subjected to a 'genuine need' test of their own.
- apart from exemptions for military, police and occupational categories of shooters who are licensed for a particular purpose (such as the extermination of feral animals), all self loading centre fire and rim fire rifles and pump action shotguns are banned.
- the tightening of all gun licensing requirements.
- an Australia-wide firearms registration system now holds details of all licence holders and their firearms.

- all licence holders are required to complete an accredited course in safety training.
- licences can be refused or cancelled and firearms seized.
- the amendment of Customs Regulations to prohibit the importation of banned firearms and their ammunition.

WHERE CRIMES OCCUR

Crime trends in Australia appear to be related to its demography, wealth and the high level of urbanisation. During 1994, the majority of violent crimes occured in residential areas (57.6% of murders; 55.7% of attempted murders; 62.0% of sexual assaults). The risk of burglary in cities with a population of more than one million is almost three times that of towns and rural areas, while the risk of assaults and robberies is two times greater.

TRENDS

Examination of information collected over a period between 1974 and 1993 reveals a steady increase in the level of most crimes. There also appears to be a significant increase in the proportion of crimes reported to the police. There are a number of reasons for this: the police adoption of policies that encourage the reporting of crimes, especially in the areas of sexual assaults and domestic violence; the mass ownership of motor vehicles; increasing numbers of women in the workforce with more houses left unattended during the day; a subsequent proportional increase in the number of insurance policy holders, with the insurance companies demanding that policy holders report all crimes to police before claims can be validated. (*Note:* Police annual report figures shown in this survey differ from Australian Bureau of Statistics crime data.)

- While the rates of non-lethal violence have increased by more than 400%, the homicide rate has remained steady.
- Police figures suggest a 219% increase in robberies; a 423% increase in serious assaults, and a 155% increase in acts of sexual violence.
- The most common crime reported to police in 1994 was unlawful entry with intent, with 63.3% of the premises involved being residential.
- There has been an increase in police numbers per 100 000 people from 178 in 1974 to 244 in 1992.
- In 1993, about 489 200 Australians were victims of crime.

The tables overleaf detail the types of crimes reported to police in recent years, the number in which firearms were a factor and the number of prisoners by offence committed in 1993.

CRIMES REPORTED TO POLICE
PER 1000 PERSONS/HOUSEHOLDS

Crime	1974–75	1982–83	1991–92
Break, enter and steal	4.42	9.76	11.19
Motor vehicle theft	3.61	6.22	8.01
Robbery	0.21	0.43	30.67
Sexual assault	0.05	0.11	0.28
Other serious assault	0.22	0.51	1.15
Fraud	2.22	3.72	7.14
Drug offence	0.71	2.72	5.03
Homicide	0.02	0.02	0.02

OFFENCES IN WHICH FIREARMS
WERE USED, 1994

Crime	Percentage
Murder, manslaughter	16.3
Attempted murder	23.7
Armed robbery	35.9
Kidnapping/abduction	3.8
Sexual assault	0.1

NUMBER OF PRISONERS BY
OFFENCE, 1993

Type of Crime	No. of Prisoners
Homicide	1 492
Assault	1 736
Sex offences	1 893
Robbery	2 009
Break and enter	2 231
Dealing/trafficking drugs	1 298
Possession/use of drugs	187
Fraud and misappropriation	691
Driving offences	663
Total	12 200

Of these prisoners, 601 are serving life sentences, 69 are incarcerated at the Governor's pleasure and 8718 are serving a sentence between a minimum and maximum set term.

9
The
Economy

Overview

In the 1990s, the Australian economy has shown steady growth, although unemployment remains high at close to 9%. Compared with many European nations, the level of unemployment in Australia is modest, but for a country that has enjoyed relatively full employment for almost 60 years, it is unacceptably high. Most economic predictions are that the rate of employment will not improve in the forseeable future given that the federal government has scheduled a phase down in tariffs on imported goods to between 0% and 5% by the year 2000. Manufacturing efficiency requires fewer people to produce more, and with the increased competition from imports, most industries have no option but to improve their production levels.

The recession of the 1990s also marked the start of major reforms to the whole Australian economy with many public enterprises such as the national airline Qantas, the Commonwealth Bank and postal and telegraphic services being either privatised or turned into corporations.

In line with these reforms, productivity in the mid-1990s increased markedly while the inflation rate remained relatively low. The difficult task for the Australian government will be to maintain growth while containing inflationary pressures.

The prolonged drought in the early 1990s in much of New South Wales and Queensland had a catastrophic effect on rural incomes. Wool and beef prices remain low, although grain prices rose dramatically for a period in early 1996. The mining sector, which is the main earner of foreign currency for the nation, continues to expand but a stronger Australian dollar has reduced profitability.

The Australian economy has often been likened to a roller coaster, zooming endlessly up and down from boom to recession depending on the world requirements for commodities. Successive governments have tried to control these wild swings by encouraging local industry through subsidies and protective tariffs, hoping thereby to reduce Australia's dependency on sales of primary produce (wool, wheat, meat, mining). Protected industries, however, like monopolies, are rarely efficient. More recently, Australian economic policies have followed the laissez-faire aspects of the United States and the European Common Market.

Unfettered by restrictions, the Australian financial market took on a global aspect in the 1980s and the financial sector of the economy boomed. People and businesses borrowed more money to buy and do more things than ever before. In the process the nation's gross foreign debt, that is to say the total amount owed to other countries, more than tripled and then doubled again so that by late 1996 it was in excess of $235 billion. When the amount owed by other countries to Australia is deducted from this figure, the net indebtedness is $191.2 billion. Public sector debt accounts for $97 127 million of this. The ratio of net foreign debt to GDP for the year ending September 1996 was 38.8%. This in turn caused the International Monetary Fund to issue a warning that Australia's indebtedness had exceeded what it considerered to be a safe limit. For a brief period in the late 1980s, the federal government recorded a surplus of income over expenditure, but by 1996 this had slipped to a deficit in the vicinity of $8 billion. The newly elected government then instigated policies that would severely curtail expenditure with the intention of bringing the national accounts back into surplus within one or two years.

Government Finance

Income tax provides approximately 60% of government revenue. It is compulsory to pay taxes on any activity which gives an economic advantage and profit whether as a company, landowner, importer or wage earner. Taxes are paid regularly at set times and this goes towards the general source from which the government finances its expenditure. After income tax, the main source of government income is by way of sales and excise taxes on alcohol, tobacco, petrol and most manufactured products. The percentages of sales tax vary according to product, with tobacco and alcohol attracting the highest taxes.

There is no general tax, such as a goods and services tax (GST), or a value added tax (VAT), as is levied in most countries that are members of the OECD. The introduction of a goods and services tax to supersede the somewhat labrynthine sales tax system has been proposed by both the

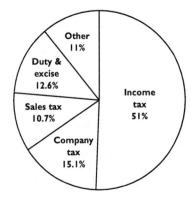

Government Revenue (August 1996)

Revenue (A$)	
Income tax	65.9 billion
Company tax	19.7 billion
Sales tax	13.9 billion
Duty and excise	16.4 billion
Other	14.3 billion
Total	**130.2 billion**

Government Expenditure
(August 1996)

Expenditure (A$)

Welfare	51.4 billion
Econ. services	7.8 billion
General services	7.2 billion
Payments to states	16.8 billion
Defence	10 billion
Health	19.4 billion
Education	11.1 billion
Other	6 billion
Total	**129.7 billion**

SURPLUS: $474 million

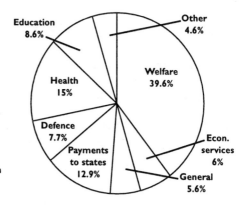

major parties in recent years. Political manoeuvrings, however, have engendered a suspicion of the goods and services tax in the minds of the electorate and set back its introduction for some time.

COMMONWEALTH OR FEDERAL

The federal government is responsible for public finance, taxation, defence, foreign affairs and other matters of national importance. Revenue is raised mostly from taxes, the bulk of it being expended on administration and grants. The federal government budget, which comes down in August each year, makes note of all the federal government's transactions. Pension funds and government savings are held by the Trust Fund and the Loan Fund lends money to the states. Companies and individuals have to pay income tax to the commonwealth government.

STATE

State government is responsible for law, order, education, child welfare, transport, provision of water supply and sewerage services, harbour facilities, electricity and gas, housing, banking and similar matters directly affecting the state. Some states are funded by taxes and borrowing, and others charge for their services.

LOCAL

Local government responsibilities may include road maintenance, building and land development, administrating regulations on weights and measures, registering dogs etc. as well as hospitals, charitable institutions, recreation grounds, parks, swimming pools, libraries, museums etc. They are only responsible to the ratepayer, but are overseen by the state government.

National Accounts

The production and use of goods and services, and transfers of income or capital are transactions in the economy and summarised in national accounting. Product income and expenditure consist of the following:

GROSS DOMESTIC PRODUCT

Gross domestic product (GDP) is the total market value of goods and services produced in Australia after deduction of the cost of goods and services used up during production but before deducting allowances for the consumption of fixed capital. GDP is therefore measured at market prices. It is the same as gross national expenditure plus exports of goods and services less imports of goods and services. Gross farm product comes from production in agriculture and services to agriculture. Gross non-farm product comes from production in all the other industries.

GROSS NATIONAL EXPENDITURE

Gross national expenditure is the total expenditure on final goods and services (i.e. excluding goods and services used up during the period in the process of production) bought by Australian residents. It is the same as the gross domestic product plus imports of goods and services less exports of goods and services.

HOUSEHOLD INCOME

Household income is the total income, whether in cash or kind, received by Australian residents in return for productive activity (such as wages, salaries, and supplements, incomes of unincorporated enterprises etc.) and transfer incomes (such as cash, social security benefits, interest etc.). It includes the imputed interest of life offices and superannuation funds, which is the benefit adding up to policies taken out by members from the investment income of the funds. It also includes third party motor vehicle and public risk insurance claims paid to persons in respect of policies taken out by enterprises, any property income received by non-profit organisations such as private schools, churches, charitable organisations etc. It excludes any income which might be said to add up to persons in the form of undistributed company income.

DOMESTIC PRODUCTION ACCOUNT ($ MILLION)

	1994–1995	1995–1996
Wages, salaries and supplements	223 960	239 954
Gross operating surplus — Trading enterprises —		
Private corporate	68 728	73 204
Other	103 233	109 281
Government		
Financial enterprises	7 762	7 938
Less imputed bank service charge	4 462	4 659
Total	175 261	185 764
Gross domestic product at factor cost	399 221	425 718
Indirect taxes less subsidies	56 395	60 366
Gross domestic product	455 616	486 045
Gross farm product	10 959	14 474
Gross non-farm product	444 657	471 580

The comparison chart below shows Australia's financial position in September 1996 in relation to the leading 20 nations with populations of more than 1 million. The ranking is by GDP with all amounts in US dollars. Current account figures are surplus or (deficit) on 12 months trading. Exact figures fluctuate according to currency exchange rates.

	GDP (US$)	Pop'n (millions)	Pop'n Growth	CPI	Exports (US$)	Current Account	Life Expect.
United States	25 950	267	1.0	2.9	554 bn	($153 bn)	77
Switzerland	24 480	7	0.6	0.7	84 bn	$20 bn	78
Hong Kong	23 100	6	2.1	6.4	174 bn	$1bn	78
Singapore	21 500	3	2.0	1.1	124 bn	$15 bn	76
Japan	21 350	126	0.3	0.3	445 bn	$92 bn	80
Canada	21 270	30	1.3	1.4	185 bn	($7 bn)	78
Germany	20 170	83	0.7	1.7	496 bn	($17 bn)	76
France	19 770	59	0.6	2.4	262 bn	17.5 bn	77
AUSTRALIA	**19 700**	**18.4**	**1.2**	**2.7**	**78 bn**	**($16 bn)**	**78**
Italy	18 600	57.5	0.2	4.3	211 bn	$23 bn	78

	GDP (US$)	Pop'n (millions)	Pop'n Growth	CPI	Exports (US$)	Current Account	Life Expect.
Britain	18 140	58.5	0.3	2.2	230 bn	($10.6 bn)	76
New Zealand	17 050	3.6	1.0	3.5	13.6 bn	($2.5 bn)	76
Taiwan	13 250	22	1.0	2.8	114 bn	($5.2 bn)	75
Saudi Arabia	11 180	19.5	4.3	4.5	39.0 bn	($9 bn)	70
South Korea	10 540	45	0.9	5.5	131 bn	($11.7 bn)	72
Malaysia	8 770	21	2.4	3.6	74.8 bn	($7.2 bn)	72
Mexico	7 490	93	1.9	34.0	84.6 bn	($0.1 bn)	71
Thailand	6 890	62	1.5	5.5	54.2 bn	($13.5 bn)	69
Brazil	5 670	165	1.9	18.2	48.0 bn	($17 bn)	67
Turkey	5 560	63	2.1	82.0	17.4 bn	($2.3 bn)	67

Sources: Available sources, World Bank, OECD, Reserve Bank of Australia.

Banking

For the first 30 years of Australian colonisation, there was no banking system because the British thought of Australia as solely a penal settlement with no need for currency. The settlers used imported coins and a bartering system. The Bank of New South Wales opened in 1817 and is still one of Australia's largest trading banks, changing its name to Westpac in 1982.

BANKS

Australia's currency is in decimal dollars and cents. The Reserve Bank of Australia helps to ensure that Australian currency remains stable, employment remains stable and that the population is more economically prosperous. The board of the Reserve Bank informs the government on monetary and banking policies and also controls the issue of bank notes.

The major banks in Australia are the Commonwealth Bank of Australia (CBA), the Australia and New Zealand Banking Group (ANZ), Westpac Banking Corporation, National Australia Bank (NAB) and St George Bank. At December 1996, the banks operated about 6500 branches with 3880 of these in metropolitan areas. The total number of bank agencies in Australia is about 11 960, with approximately half of these in metropolitan areas. Whilst the number of branches of banks is declining, particularly in country areas, the number of automatic telling machines (ATM) has increased enormously so that now they are in excess of 7000, easily outnumbering bank branches.

MAJOR TRADING AND SAVINGS BANKS
ASSETS AND LIABILITIES, 1995–1996

Bank	Assets (millions)	Liabilities (millions)
National Australia Bank	93 615	82 347
Commonwealth Bank	86 953	82 762
Westpac Banking Corporation	76 800	69 937
ANZ Banking Group	70 459	64 308
St George Bank	18 059	16 552
Colonial State Bank	16 572	15 501
Advance Bank Australia	15 640	14 704
Total all banks in Australia	**509 370**	**467 327**

BANKING STATISTICS, OCTOBER 1996

Type	Amount
Total deposits	295 940
Lending to government	30 795
Lending to persons	195 550
Housing finance	162 935
Fixed loans	19 130
Overdrafts	3 670
Credit cards	7 035
Commercial lending	268 245
Agriculture, forestry, fishing	115
Mining	90
Manufacturing	210
Construction	95
Transport, storage	25
Finance, investment, insurance	135
Property, business services	200
Wholesale trade	75
Retail trade	160
Other	272
Foreign currency liabilities	72 095
Foreign currency assets	34 890
Coin and cash with Reserve Bank	8 285

OTHER FINANCIAL INSTITUTIONS

A permanent building society can take money deposits, borrows predominantly from its members and mainly offers its members housing loans. Co-operative housing societies cannot take money deposits, can only raise money through loans and can only offer its members housing loans. Credit co-operatives mainly borrow from and provide loans to their members. Money market corporations can borrow funds from the Reserve Bank at a high rate for at least seven days as long as they keep the bank informed of their operations, invest minimum loans in approved securities, buy and sell approved securities and stay within their limits. There are also money market corporations who cannot borrow from the Reserve Bank, but provide loans to authorised dealers and businesses.

At October 1996, permanent building societies had a total of $13 700 million in assets; credit co-operatives had a total of $16 295 million; money market corporations had a total of $61 300 million. Finance companies had a total $35 805 million in assets.

CASH MANAGEMENT TRUSTS

This is a public unit trust which mainly invests in financial securities and the units can be returned to the unit holder on demand.

PUBLIC UNIT TRUSTS

A public unit trust is a fund which is controlled by a trust deed between a management company and a trustee company; it is open to the public in Australia and the unit holders receive income or capital gains from their investment; they can also dispose of their units quickly.

GENERAL INSURANCE AND SUPERANNUATION

The main purpose of these schemes and funds is to provide retirement benefits. The Insurance and Superannuation Commission was established in 1987 and was a reflection of the growing national economic and social importance of the insurance and superannuation industries. The Commission has responsibility for the Commonwealth's insurance and superannuation supervisory and policy advising functions. The level of assets of the insurance and superannuation companies which the Commission controls is about $260 billion.

In 1996, there were 183 general insurance companies and 51 life insurance companies in Australia. In 1995, the federal government introduced compulsory superannuation for all employees. There are currently approximately 6.5 million members of superannuation funds, and in the four quarters of 1995–1996, the income from these funds was $4.8 billion, $5.5 billion, $2.8 billion and $3.6 billion

Foreign Trade

Investment from overseas supports many Australian economic enterprises. Since the early 19th century, the government sought British capital to develop industry and public works and from the 1950s onwards other nations invested in Australia. Investment from overseas in real estate (particularly from Asia) has increased dramatically in the past ten years. The Australian economy is particularly reliant on foreign trade because the country is a major producer of commodities and primary produce. Its major exports are coal, iron ore, copper, bauxite, manganese, nickel, mineral sands, diamonds, gold, uranium, natural gas, wool, meat, wheat, coarse grains, rice, cotton and sugar. In return it imports large quantities of manufactured goods.

ASIA PACIFIC ECONOMIC CO-OPERATION (APEC)

APEC has membership of 18 countries in the Asia–Pacific area and was established as a major economic trading group alliance in 1989. In an APEC leaders summit in Bogor, Indonesia in 1994, a motion was passed to remove all trade barriers between participating nations by 2020, with the so-called advanced nations achieving this by the year 2010. At that time Australia unilaterally made a pledge to reduce its tariff barriers to an average of 5% by the year 2000. Whilst current progress indicates that it will achieve this aim, in late 1996 the Commonwealth government announced that it would review its commitment to continue to lower its tariff rate after the year 2000, taking into account the progress of other APEC members.

APEC accounts for more than 50% of world production and 40% of its population. Australia's merchandise trade with APEC has been steadily growing by more than 10% a year since 1985 and now accounts for 75% of Australia's total merchandise trade figures.

IMPORTS

The Commonwealth government controls customs and excise. Following the 1970s recession, import controls were placed on the textile, clothing, footwear, motor vehicle and cheese industries to protect employment and investment. Whilst in general tariffs have been reduced or dispensed with entirely, some quotas still remain.

In 1995–1996, the total imports came to $77 094 million: the total consumption goods came to $19,863 million; the total capital goods came to $19 171 million, and the total intermediate and other goods came to $38 000 million.

EXPORTS

The Australian Trade Commission (Austrade) provides assistance to exporters by way of grants and rebates which help companies with overseas marketing, market research, fares, representation, advertising and helping with the cost of participating in trade fairs. It also encourages industry to become more export orientated. Through its worldwide network, Austrade can channel information on commercial opportunities to Australian companies.

In 1995–1996, total exports came to $75 305 million: total rural exports $21 290 million; total non-rural $54 015 million; meat and meat preparations $3290 million; cereal grains and cereal preparations $4926 million; total manufacturing $18 361 million, and total minerals and metals $33 612 million.

MERCHANDISE TRADE WITH AUSTRALIA
BY COUNTRY, 1995–1996

Country	Imports ($ million)	Exports ($ million)
USA	17 550	4 615
Japan	10 820	16 415
Hong Kong	970	3 070
Republic of Korea	2 295	6 615
China	4 010	3 780
Germany	4 860	1 150
United Kingdom	4 885	2 825
New Zealand	3 595	5 600
ASEAN	7 335	11 750
Other	20 774	19 485
Total	**77 094**	**75 305**

EXPORTS AND IMPORTS, 1995–96

Export Goods	Amount ($ million)	Import Goods	Amount ($ million)
Minerals and metals	33 612	Consumption goods	19 863
Rural	21 290	Capital goods	19 171
Total non-rural	54 015	Intermediate and	
Meat & meat preparations	3 290	other goods	38 060
Cereals & cereal preparations	4 926		
Sugar & honey	1 711		
Wool and sheepskins	3 606		
Total manufacturing	18 361		
Total exports	**75 305**	**Total imports**	**77 094**

AUSTRALIA'S FOREIGN TRADE

Financial Year	Exports (A$ million)	Imports (A$ million)
1990–1991	52 400	48 900
1993–1994	64 550	64 465
1995–1996	75 305	77 094

BALANCE OF PAYMENTS

Australia's balance of payments show the amount of its foreign assets and liabilities, its debt and its transactions with the rest of the world. It helps to determine which external influences affect the domestic economy. At the end of September 1996, the Australian balance of payments trade deficit (current account) for the previous 12 months stood at $20.1 billion.

Prices

The Consumer Price Index (CPI) regularly checks the price of a selection of goods and services used by metropolitan wage earners. It only measures price changes and does not take note of changing quality or quantity in the goods and services. The selection includes food, clothing, housing, household goods, transportation, tobacco, alcohol, health, personal care, recreation and education and these groups are then subdivided. Each selection has a fixed weight or measure of its importance.
The CPI for 1995–1996 was 112.7.

Employment, Social Security & Welfare

EMPLOYMENT

The labour force in Australia consists of everyone over 15 years of age who is employed or unemployed. Employed means doing any work regardless of the hours involved. Comparing employment levels to population levels shows the country's job growth. Industries are judged by the size of their workforce and the hours worked. Labour supplied to industry can be estimated by comparing employment and hours worked.

Unemployment

If someone is not employed, but is free to work and looking for work, then they are considered unemployed. The economic and social features of unemployment are judged by the length of time that someone is unemployed and their qualifications. Job vacancy statistics also help the government work out the demand for labour. There is a section of the community who are not in the labour force because they are unable to get work due to their age, lack of training or education, language problems or lack of local work.

Wages

After the economic depression in the 1890s, the trade union movement tried to ensure its members had a realistic standard of living, so guaranteed basic wages were developed. In 1907, the owner of the Sunshine Harvester works asked the Commonwealth Arbitration and Conciliation Court to declare that his company's wages were fair, so that his company would not have to pay excise duties. After an investigation, the court decided that the minimum wage for a family of five was two pounds and two shillings a week. As a result the company lost the case and wages for unskilled labour were increased by nearly 20%.

These guidelines were used until 1913 when the cost of living was adjusted and it was automatically adjusted every month from 1921. Employers were allowed to reduce their wages by 10% during the Depression in the 1930s. From 1934, full wages were restored and divided into the basic wage and different categories for skill, experience and the state of the economy.

From the 1920s to the 1950s, the female basic wage was 54% of the male rate. It was then made up to 75% and in 1969 the female rate of pay was made equal to the male. The wages for many traditional female occupations are, however, lower than those for many traditional male occupations. In 1967, the Australian Conciliation and Arbitration Commission introduced a 'total' wage which varied basic and marginal components and a minimum wage was introduced.

The federal and state government industrial tribunals decide on the awards for minimum wages. Superannuation is the highest non-wage benefit that all wage earners now receive and following that are leave benefits.

(See chapter 5, 'Population'.)

Trade Unions

A trade union is an association of workers in any trade or several similar trades who have joined together to protect and better their wages, hours of work, conditions of employment etc. Anyone working in a job that is covered by a union can become a member of that union; however, it is not compulsory to join.

Unionism developed in the Australian colonies as large numbers of free immigrants arrived from England in the 1820s. A great percentage of these settlers were skilled tradesmen who brought with them a unionist tradition already well established overseas. Between 1831 and 1850, a number of trade associations were set up in all colonies. Unionism was particularly prominent in the printing, building, transport and engineering industries. One of the first industrial unions was the Operative Stonemasons' Society. The objective of these unions was to reduce the working week to 48 hours. This was achieved in certain industries in New South Wales and Victoria during the 1850s but only after prolonged strike action, and it took several further decades to become the norm throughout the country.

As individual unions increased in numbers and strength there were moves towards centralised and cooperative organisations. The first permanent Trades Council was formed in New South Wales in 1871, followed by Queensland, Tasmania, South Australia and Victoria in the 1880s, and Western Australia in 1891.

Trade unions were given legal status in the different states from the late 1880s to the early 1890s. By the mid-1880s, there were about 100 unions with an estimated total membership of 50 000 people. Rural workers did not have full union representation until the 1890s. One of the first rural unions was the Amalgamated Shearers' Union, formed in 1887; with groups such as the Queensland Shearers' Union, it formed the Australian Workers' Union in 1904.

In the 1890s, the unions realised that they needed direct representation in parliament when strikes as a means of protest failed to work. The federation of the colonies as the Australian Commonwealth in 1901 was accompanied by the interstate political alliance of unions in the first Australian Labor Party. The Commonwealth Court of Conciliation and Arbitration was established in 1904 under the Commonwealth Conciliation and Arbitration Act. It had the authority to conciliate and arbitrate in industrial matters. In a historic decision in 1907, it introduced the concept of the basic wage, a 'fair and reasonable wage' which employers were required to pay. In 1921, a labour congress proposed uniting labour organisations into one big union but the arbitration court refused to license the organisation.

The Australian Council of Trades Unions (ACTU) was founded in 1927 although the Australian Workers' Union (AWU), the nation's largest union, refused to join. The post-war period saw increased union agitation for better wages and reduced hours. There were 869 strikes in 1946 and the figure increased by 50% within a decade.

The union and Labor movements both suffered increased internal division, particularly over the issue of communist influence. In 1960, the Menzies

Liberal government attempted to introduce the *Communist Party Dissolution Act* to outlaw the Communist Party and prevent its members holding office in the trades unions. This move was successfully challenged in the High Court by the Waterside Workers Federation and the Ironworkers Association. Industrial candidates were elected who successfully opposed communist influence within the unions. The continuing issue of communist infiltration eventually caused a rift in the Labor Party and the emergence of the Democratic Labor Party (DLP) in 1956.

The structure and interests of trades unions have changed since the 1950s. Through amalgamation the number of unions fell, while the number of unionists more than doubled in the same period. Also reflecting general trends in the union movement is the increase in white-collar unionism. The largest central organising body is the ACTU with which many unions are affiliated. The ACTU represents about 2.7 million workers or approximately one third of the total workforce. Union membership is obligatory under certain awards but the coalition government which came to power in 1996 announced its intention of changing industrial relations legislation to give employees greater freedom of choice.

(*See* chapter 5, 'Population'.)

ENTERPRISE BARGAINING

Enterprise bargaining allows businesses and their employees to negotiate workplace agreements that suit their particular needs. While many claim that it allows for greater equality and representation in all levels of business, others argue that it disempowers workers. The first enterprise agreements in Australia were registered in October 1991 and now cover around 30% of workers.

TRAINING PROGRAMS

The commonwealth government has a number of labour force incentives which promote work experience and training. These include training for industry and apprenticeships for adults, youths, long-term unemployed and aboriginals. They also offer monetary and child care support. (*See* chapter 13, 'Education, Employment & Training'.)

SOCIAL SECURITY & WELFARE

Government and charitable organisations ensure that people in difficulty can maintain an acceptable standard of living.

Towards the end of the 19th century, colonial governments recognised the need for legislation on matters of health and education. In 1901, the old-age pension was introduced in New South Wales and Victoria. In 1908, a limited means-tested invalid and old-age pension was introduced throughout Australia by the federal government. The Harvester Judgement in 1907 introduced the payment of a basic wage (see 'Economy', p. 312), which became a yardstick for the assessment of welfare payments. The depression in the 1930s caused the government to introduce emergency measures to provide for the huge numbers of unemployed, and unemployment and sickness benefits were eventually introduced in 1944. Child benefits were introduced in 1941 and widows' benefits in 1942.

The Commonwealth and state governments and welfare organisations provide social security and welfare services. The Commonwealth Department of Social Security provides old-age pensions, invalid pensions, widows' pensions, supporting parents' pensions, family allowances, orphans' pensions, handicapped children's' pensions, unemployment benefit and sickness benefit. All households pay taxes to the government through income tax or taxes on goods and services and all households receive benefits from the government, whether directly in benefits, or through services provided.

(*See* chapter 12, 'Health'.)

REGISTERED CHARITIES

There are more than 12 000 registered charities in Australia today. The largest three are, the Salvation Army, the St Vincent de Paul Society and the Smith Family.

The Salvation Army started in Adelaide in 1880 and provided religious and charitable support to ex-prisoners, prostitutes and neglected children. The Salvation Army is most famous for aid in times of war and economic depression and it still provides food and shelter for the homeless throughout Australia. In 1996, its national budget for Social and Community Service operations was $144 million. The annual Red Shield Appeal in the same year collected $37.76 million.

The St Vincent de Paul Society began in Sydney in 1881. Originally it was a voluntary service which visited families in need. Now operating throughout Australia, its facilities include hostels for the homeless, homes for the aged, nursing homes and advisory assistance for migrants. In 1995–1996, the St Vincent de Paul Society in New South Wales alone collected about $86.6 million from donations and through its opportunity shops, with expenditure of approximately $85.5 million.

In 1922, a Christmas party at a Sydney children's home, sponsored by five anonymous businessmen, led to the founding of the Smith Family charity which operates in New South Wales and Victoria. The Smith Family distributes food, clothing, furniture and money to the needy, gives counselling, and provides welfare visitors and housing schemes for the aged. In 1996, the Smith Family collected about $25.3 million in donations and helped more than 253 300 people, about 132 000 of whom were children. The Smith Family is also the largest textile and clothing waste recycler in Australia.

Health Care

High standards of nutrition and medical care have raised the average life expectancy in Australia. (*See* chapter 5, 'Population'.) Private and public health education is directed towards healthier lifestyles.

There have been various approaches to financing personal health care in Australia. Generally, Labor governments favour a health care service to ensure free or heavily subsidised medical care for all Australian residents. Liberal and coalition governments believe that the individual should be responsible for medical treatment through private health insurance schemes.

Policy concerning health insurance and medical benefits fluctuated considerably in the 1970s. In 1975, the Whitlam Labor government tried to introduce a universal medical and hospital benefits system known as Medibank. This scheme was changed by the following Liberal-National Country Party government, who introduced voluntary private insurance and imposed an income levy on those wishing to use Medibank. Between 1981 and 1984, only those in genuine need (about 25% of the population) were allowed free medical and hospital care. During that period, the rest of the community had to pay their own medical and hospital expenses and were encouraged to insure themselves with a health insurance fund.

The Medicare scheme, established in February 1984, covers the entire resident population of Australia. (See chapter 12, 'Health'.)

Australian Stock Exchange

The first stock exchange in Australia is believed to have been the Melbourne Stock Exchange, which was formed in 1861. Until quite recently every Australian State had its own stock exchange but by far the majority of sales went through the Melbourne and Sydney exchanges. In 1987 the six existing stock exchanges in Adelaide, Brisbane, Hobart, Melbourne, Perth and Sydney were amalgamated into one and called the Australian Stock Exchange or its widely used abbreviation ASX.

Shares are listed in two main sections: Industrials, which includes banks and service industries, and mining and oil. There are also what are called 'second boards' for the smaller listed companies which do not trade so frequently. The total number of companies listed on the ASX at 30 June 1996 was about 1185, with $114 046 million turned over in Industrials and $45 284 million turned over in mining and oil. The total turnover in

1995–1996 amounted to $159 billion. All trading is now computerised and appears on screen. There is no trading on what used to be called the floor of the stock exchange.

At the beginning of 1997, the Australian Stock Exchange was still a non-profit organisation using its income to improve facilities and services to the public. Its income is mainly derived from selling information and in 1995–1996 it showed a surplus of $19.4 million from total revenue of $113 million respectively. Almost 60% of all share trading takes place in Sydney. The ASX expects that it will require $75 million to pay for expanded technology over the next few years and a proposal is currently being considered by members whereby the ASX will be floated as a public company with individual shareholders limited to holdings of 10% to prevent any take over.

The following list shows the top 100 public companies in Australia according to their sharemarket valuation.

100 LARGEST COMPANIES IN AUSTRALIA
STOCK MARKET VALUATION AT 3 JANUARY 1997

Company name	Capitalisation ($ million)	Industry
1. BHP	35807	Mining/diversified
2. News Ltd	22447	Media
3. National Australia Bank	22253	Banking
4. Westpac Banking Corp	13478	Banking Commonwealth
5. CRA	12565	Mining/diversified
6. ANZ Bank	11831	Banking
7. Commonwealth Bank	10911	Banking
8. Western Mining Corp	8724	Mining/diversified
9. Fletcher Challenge	8253	Paper/packaging
10. Coca-Cola Amatil	7205	Food/soft drinks
11. Woodside Petroleum	6093	Oil & gas
12. Lend Lease	6075	Developers/contractors
13. Coles Myer	5682	Retailing
14. Brambles	5592	Transport
15. Amcor	5354	Paper/packaging
16. Fosters Brewing	5044	Brewing/wine
17. CSR	4320	Sugar/building products
18. Boral	4090	Building products
19. ICI Australia	3837	Chemicals
20. Comalco	3633	Mining/smelting
21. Brierley Investments	3587	Diversified
22. Pioneer International	3429	Diversified building mats
23. Woolworths	3408	Retailing

Company name	Capitalisation ($ million)	Industry
24. Normandy	3394	Gold mining
25. Pacific Dunlop	3234	Diversified industrial
26. National Mutual	3111	Diversified property trust
27. Publishing and Broadcasting	3042	Media
28. General Property Trust	2877	Diversified property trust
29. MIM Holdings	2851	Mining
30. Westfield Trust	2803	Retail property trust
31. Mayne Nickless	2702	Transport
32. Santos	2698	Oil/gas
33. North Ltd	2591	Mining
34. Advance Bank	2575	Banking
35. Southcorp	2407	Diversified/wine
36. Qantas Airways	2249	Air transport
37. John Fairfax Holdings	2186	Media/newspapers
38. Lihir Gold	2141	Gold mining
39. Wesfarmers	2061	Diversified industrial
40. Australian Gas Light (AGL)	2060	Gas distribution
41. Westfield Holdings	2057	Retail developers
42. St George Bank	1990	Banking
43. Goodman Fielder	1965	Food manufacturing
44. GIO Australia	1937	Insurance
45. QBE	1918	Insurance
46. Howard Smith	1909	Shipping/diversified
47. Tabcorp Holdings	1791	Leisure/gambling
48. Lion Nathan	1665	Brewing
49. Pasminco	1552	Mining
50. James Hardie Industries	1503	Building materials
51. Crown	1466	Leisure/gambling
52. Leighton	1413	Construction
53. WH Soul Pattinson	1384	Retail/pharmacies
54. Seven Network	1305	Media/television
55. Aus Fond Investments	1304	Investments & financial Serv
56. Burns Philp	1280	Diversified/trading
57. Macquarie Bank	1272	Banking
58. Sydney Casino	1230	Leisure/gambling
59. Bank of Melbourne	1191	Banking
60. WA Newspapers	1175	Media/newspapers
61. Arnotts	1174	Food/distribution
62. QCT Resources	1172	Mining/coal
63. Stockland	1161	Diversified trust
64. Newcrest	1160	Mining/gold

Company name	Capitalisation ($ million)	Industry
65. Bank West	1154	Banking
66. Renison Goldfields (RGC)	1143	Mining/diversified
67. Placer Pacific	1134	Mining/gold
68. Southern Pacific	1129	Oil & gas
69. Oil Search	1123	Oil& gas
70. HIH Winterthur	1116	Insurance
71. Email	1106	Diverse/electrical manufacturing
72. Energy Resources Australia	1087	Mining/uranium
73. Village Roadshow	1078	Leisure/entertainment
74. Plutonic	1075	Mining/gold
75. Faulding	1063	Pharmaceuticals
76. QNI	1042	Mining/nickel
77. Central Pacific	1001	Mining
78. Rothmans	993	Food/tobacco
79. ANI	990	Engineering
80. Indochina	950	Gold mining
81. Schroder PF	946	Finance/investment
82. Orogen	935	Diversified resources
83. Great Central	889	Mining/gold
84. Metway Bank	885	Banking
85. Pacific Magazines and Printing	886	Media
86. Futuris Corp	858	Diversified manufacturing
87. George Weston	847	Food & household
88. Hudson Conway	819	Real estate/leisure
89. Reinsurance	815	Insurance
90. Caltex	801	Oil refining/distribution
91. Sons of Gwalia	797	Mining/gold
92. Centaur Mining	792	Mining
93. Transurban	783	Toll roads
94. Commonwealth Serum Labs	776	Pharmaceutical
95. Davids	774	Retailing
96. Amalgamated Holdings	763	Tourism & leisure
97. Coal & Allied	761	Mining/coal
98. Capral	723	Metals
99. Hoyts	706	Media/entertainment
100. Franked Inc.	705	Investment/financial services

Australian Securities Commission

The Australian Securities Commission (ASC), an independent government body, was established by the *Australian Securities Commission Act 1989* to protect the interests of investors and companies by providing information about companies, helping businesses to interpret the law and taking action against those found guilty of such misconduct as insolvent trading.

The responsibilities of the ASC are to ensure fair play in business, to prevent corporate crime, to protect investors and to help Australia's business reputation abroad.

Primary Industries

AGRICULTURE

The establishment of agriculture was a matter of urgency for the colonists of the First Fleet in 1788 who were dependent on supplies brought with them, or sent from England. The first successful farms were established near Parramatta to the west of Sydney, the earliest being James Ruse's Experiment Farm at Rose Hill (renamed Parramatta in 1791) and John and Elizabeth Macarthur's Elizabeth Farm at Camden in 1793.

Later on, large wheat crops were produced in South Australia, which became the leading wheat growing state from the 1840s. Cattle raising developed into a major industry in Queensland and the western region of New South Wales, and now Australia is one of the three leading red meat producers in the world. Dairying is concentrated in the wetter south-eastern corner of the country, while sugarcane is grown on the coastal belt which extends up the eastern coast from northern New South Wales to far north Queensland.

The most important agricultural and pastoral industries produce cereals (mostly wheat), sheep, beef cattle, dairy cattle, wool, sugar, honey, fruit and grapes for wine.

Historically, agricultural products comprised more than 80% of Australia's exports. Recently, however, Australia's exports from the agricultural sector have declined as a percentage. This is largely due to an increase in the quantity and values of the exports from our mining and manufacturing industries. There are about 146 260 establishments throughout the country involved in agricultural activity. The farm sector contributes about 3% of Australia's total GDP.

GROSS VALUE OF AGRICULTURAL COMMODITIES PRODUCED, 1994–1995

Commodity	Gross Value ($ million)
Livestock products	
Wool	3 264
Milk	2 574
Eggs	241
Livestock slaughtering	
Cattle	3 960
Sheep	738
Pigs	609
Poultry	927
Crops	
Wheat for grain	1 927
Barley for grain	564
Oats for grain	162
Other cereal grains	550
Sugar cane	1 103
Fruit and nuts	2 000
Grapes	570
Vegetables	1 517
All other crops	2 964
Total	**23 180**

CEREALS AND WHEAT

Australia's main cereal crops are wheat, barley, oats, sorghum, maize, rice, rye and millet. Barley is used for feeding cattle and for producing vinegar and malt extract; maize and wheat make breakfast foods; wheaten flour makes bread, cakes, biscuits and breakfast foods; and pasta is based on semolina (a wheat product). Adhesives and industrial alcohol are also made from flour. Cellulose, which can be extracted from wheat straw, can be used to make paper.

Wheat is grown throughout Australia and is its most important crop in terms of production and exports. In 1788, wheat was first grown at Farm Cove (now Sydney's Royal Botanic Gardens), however diseases prevented it from growing successfully until the 1820s. Victoria and South Australia started growing wheat in the 1830s, but Tasmania was the chief growing area because its climate suited the English wheat. In the early 1900s, wheat yields improved with the expansion of rail transport, the use of fertilisers, and the introduction of new farming technology and methods. William Farrer introduced a hardier wheat strain more appropriate to Australia's climate and throughout the 1950s the wheat industry continued to strengthen and expand.

In 1995–1996, farm incomes grew substantially, especially for growers of wheat and barley. Today Australia is the third largest wheat exporter in the world. Approximately 15 million tonnes are exported per annum and this is 85% of the Australian crop. In 1994, a total of 16 480 million tonnes was produced. About 80% of the wheat is made into bread and the market is becoming increasingly specialised. All customers have specific requirements which are met from using wheat grown in different soil and climatic areas of Australia.

LIVESTOCK AND DAIRY PRODUCTS

The major revenue from Australian beef cattle comes through export. The size of beef cattle herds can be affected by droughts or floods. There was a long drought in the 1970s which made cattle production drop by about 9 million head of cattle. The Shorthorn, Hereford, Aberdeen Angus and Devon breeds are the most popular, with more exotic breeds being introduced gradually. Australia is the fifth largest meat consumer in the world with about 77 kilograms eaten per capita.

DAIRYING

Dairying in Australia has been a major rural industry from the end of the 19th century. It is the fourth largest rural industry after wheat, wool and beef. Australia has a very efficient dairy industry due to large herd sizes and improved farming methods. Victoria accounts for 60% of Australia's total milk production. Milk production in 1995 was about 9000 million litres. Although Australia produces less than 2% of the world's milk, it accounts for around 7% of the world trade in dairy products. About 30% is consumed in liquid milk form and on average Australians drink 100 litres of milk a year per capita. With the recent consumer interest in health and nutrition; a greater percentage of the milk sold has been low fat or skim milk. The most popular dairy breeds are Friesian, Illawarra Shorthorn, Jersey, Guernsey, Ayrshire, Red Poll and Dairy Shorthorn.

SHEEP

The first sheep came to Australia in 1788 with the First Fleet. They were Cape Fat Tails and had hairy fleeces and fat tails and were suitable mainly for food, not for wool production. At the end of the 18th century, when Captain John Macarthur started breeding from pure Spanish Merinos brought from South Africa, Australia's wool industry was born.

In 1793, Macarthur had bought 60 Bengal and three Irish sheep. He discovered that when he crossed the two breeds, the offspring produced a mingled fleece of hair and wool. The idea came to him of producing fine wool and his purchase of Cape Merinos gave him this opportunity. In 1803, Macarthur went to England to sell his wool. He returned to Sydney two years later with authority from Lord Camden, the Colonial Minister, to select an area of land for himself, providing he devoted his grazing activities from then on to fine wool production. He shipped his first bale of wool to England in 1807. Up until 1822, German wool led the market, but due to overbreeding their exports declined and Australia soon took over as the market leader.

In the early 1840s, wool prices fell and there were three years of drought. Graziers then began boiling sheep for tallow until the discovery of gold in 1851 started a minor agricultural revolution. Shepherds and other employees on the sheep stations left their jobs to search for gold, and the flocks were left to look after themselves. To the delight of the graziers, the sheep did very well. No longer did the industry need such a big workforce and with their increased freedom both the sheep and the quality of their wool improved. Many more sheep could be run, expenses were reduced and the sheep grew more fleece. Another result of the gold rushes was that, with the large increase in population, there developed a profitable market for mutton and beef. Many settlers who had concentrated on Merino flocks now changed to cattle and others to long-woolled sheep.

The worst Depression in the history of the wool industry began in 1929 and lasted for almost ten years. Prices for commodities other than wool fell drastically also, but halving the price of wool, Australia's biggest export product, was a prime cause of the economic depression that affected almost the whole community in the early 1930s. Wool provided nearly half of Australia's income from exports before the crash in 1929 and about one third in the depressed years of the early 1930s.

Today, more than 75% of all Australian sheep are Merinos. Most of the others are crossbreds derived from carefully crossing the Merino with breeds of British origin to produce a heavier carcass for meat production.

Australia is the world's largest supplier of apparel wool, growing more than one quarter of all the world's wool and almost one-half of its Merino wool. Australia has about 140 million sheep and experts believe that this number is far too high. About 40% of Australia's sheep population is in New South Wales. Wool production in the 1990s has decreased by about half from the boom years of the 1980s.

The Australian Wool Corporation was established in 1973 to serve the interests of woolgrowers by increasing their returns. The Wool Corporation facilitates wool marketing, promotes wool use and funds and administers wool research and development. It is funded by a self-imposed tax on the woolgrowers. For several years, the Wool Corporation established a basic floor price and wool that did not reach this price at the regular wool auctions was bought in by the corporation and sold later when the price has risen again. This practice was discontinued in 1992.

SUGAR

There are different types of sugar which can be produced from sugar cane: sugarbeet, lactose (which comes from milk) and fructose (which is found in some fruit and honey).

In 1788, sugar cane was brought to Australia with the First Fleet and the first successful plantation was at Port Macquarie in 1821, although it was abandoned ten years later. The first successful Queensland crop was in Brisbane in 1862 and the Queensland industry was well established by the late 1860s. In the late 1830s, the first sugar refinery was built by the Australian Sugar Company and bought by the Colonial Sugar Refining Company (CSR) in 1855. Today, CSR is the main sugar producer in Australia.

About 95% of the country's sugarcane is grown in Queensland. The Commonwealth and Queensland governments control the sugar growing, refining, marketing and exporting. In 1994, there were 338 000 hectares under cultivation with sugar cane, producing about 31.3 million tonnes. One-quarter of Australia's sugar is produced for the domestic market, the rest is exported as raw bulk sugar. The main importers of Australian sugar are Asian and Southeast Asian countries.

FRUIT

Introduced fruit species are the basis of Australia's fruit industry. The First Fleet brought seeds and plants and fruit-growing soon developed in populated areas for the domestic market. Different states produce specialised fruits suited to their climate: Queensland produces tropical fruit, while Tasmania produces apples and berries. Fruit exports have grown noticeably in the past few years, the most important exports of these are; sultanas, fresh pears and quinces, canned pears, and fresh or dried apples. Australia is becoming highly successful in the production of exotic fruit, grown predominantly in Queensland.

GRAPES AND WINE

The most important of all fruit produced are grapes, both wine and table varieties. The main grape growing areas are the Hunter Valley and outer Sydney area of New South Wales, the Barossa Valley and riverland area of South Australia, the Yarra Valley and peninsula areas of Victoria and the Margaret River area of Western Australia. Grapes are grown in all states.

Governor Arthur Phillip planted the first vines at Farm Cove (now the Royal Botanic Gardens), however, the sea air and too rich a soil did not produce good wine grapes. James Busby subsequently planted vines in the Hunter Valley and by 1852 the area was producing 270 000 litres of wine and 4500 litres of brandy every year. These days, South Australia is by far the largest wine producing state. Up until the 1960s, most of Australia's wine was sweet fortified wine such as sherry, port and muscat, but consumer demand meant that more table wine came to be produced and many new types of grape were planted. In 1995, about 480 million litres of wine were produced, of which roughly 10% was exported and this percentage continues to increase. In a relatively short time, Australia has developed its winemaking techniques to equal the best in the world and Australian wines are renowned for their consistent superior quality.

COTTON

First planted in Queensland during the 1860s, cotton growing soon started up in other states. Up until the 1920s, output was very small, but then the government offered assistance and protection to the industry and significant development took place. In particular, mechanical harvesting and better pest control have stabilised the industry. Today most of Australia's cotton is grown in Queensland and 80% of our national requirement is now produced within the country so that only a small amount of long-fibred cotton has to be imported. In 1994, 788 000 tonnes of cotton were produced with a value of $652 million.

Forestry

The total area of native forest in Australia was estimated at more than 41 million hectares in 1995, in addition to which there were 1 105 080 ha of plantations, mainly softwood. Forests provide many important products and benefits to the nation and with proper management they will continue to do so for a long time. Forestry also provides much rural employment and in recent years the destruction of Australian rainforests has become a controversial issue. A federal government scheme is in place to plant one billion trees in ten years. (*See* chapter 4, 'Environment'.)

Within the Commonwealth Scientific Industrial Research Organisation (CSIRO) is a department called the Division of Forestry and Forest Products which researches wood production and the use of forest land (including the ecology and management of forests). Each State has control and management over its own forests but the Department of Primary Industries and Energy is responsible for forests at a national level.

The export of forest products amounted to $777 million in 1993, of which 54% were woodchips and about 25% were paper and related products.

Fishing

Australia's fishing industry is underdeveloped in terms of its resource potential of 14 million square kilometres, when compared with other parts of the world. Commercial fishing is currently valued at $1.3 billion with catches totalling 200 000 tonnes a year. It is estimated, however, that the industry could be worth between $5 and $10 billion by 2020. More than 60% of fish exports go to Japan and Taiwan.

The administration of the Australian fishing industry is handled by the state or territory of the coastal water concerned, fishing beyond the continental shelf is handled by the Commonwealth government. Many coastal ports have fishing fleets and some have fish processing factories which support the small seaside communities. The northern coast's most important commercial species is the barramundi; in the south-east and south-west mullet, bream, Australian salmon and herring are the most important. There is also a large tuna industry off the east coast.

The most valuable seafood in Australia's fishing industry are prawns which are caught in offshore waters, estuaries and along coasts in all states of Australia except Tasmania. The north coast between Cape York and Cape Londonderry is the largest fishery for prawns. Crabs, lobsters, squid and scampi are mainly taken from the west. The shell from the Australian rock oyster is used for buttons and knife handles; it is harvested in the tropical waters around northern Australia.

GROSS VALUE OF MAJOR FISHERIES CATEGORIES, 1994

Type of seafood	Gross Value ($ million)
Prawns	280
Rock lobster	420
Tuna	115
Other fin fish	325
Abalone	175
Scallops	70
Oysters	50
Other	175
Total	1 610

AQUACULTURE

Australia or fish farming is an increasingly profitable alternative to harvesting of ocean fish. It ensures sustainable yields and is currently having great success with pearl oysters, Atlantic salmon and freshwater trout. In 1994, the value of acquaculture production had risen to an all time high of $303

PEARLING

Commercial pearling started in Australia in 1861 on the north-western coast. This industry developed quickly and became the economic basis for many coastal towns. Pearling luggers were operating off northern Queensland and in the Torres Strait by 1868. Pearl oysters were firstly sought for their shells which were used to make mother-of-pearl buttons and other items. At one time Australia produced 80% of the world's output of mother-of-pearl. The industry continued until 1960 when plastics began to take over. Several Japanese companies set up cultured pearl farms in the 1960s and the centre of the industry is at Broome in Western Australia. In recent years, the Australian pearling industry has seen a renaissance backed by strong marketing. In 1994, the gross value of the industry was $124 million.

Mining

Most minerals of economic importance are found throughout Australia and generally speaking there are adequate deposits for domestic and export uses. The principal mining is for bauxite (aluminium), black coal, clays, copper, diamonds, gold, iron ore, lead, manganese, natural gas, nickel, salt, silver, tin, uranium and zinc. All mineral rights in Australia are held by the commonwealth, but each state or territory has its own mining regulations and collects mineral royalties. The commonwealth is responsible for offshore mining rights beyond three nautical miles from the shore. Mining income in Australia is not subject to company tax.

MINING PRODUCTION, 1994

Type of mineral	Amount mined
Bauxite	43 305 kilotonnes
Black coal	177 875 kilotonnes
Brown coal	49 685 kilotonnes
Copper concentrate	1 320 kilotonnes
Copper precipitate	16 190 tonnes
Gold bullion	274 685 kilograms
Iron ore	123 630 kilotonnes
Lead concentrate	875 kilotonnes
Manganese ore	815 kilotonnes
Mineral sands	2 250 kilotonnes
Uranium concentrate	1 455 tonnes
Zinc concentrate	1 890 kilotonnes

Australia is the world's leading exporter of alumina, diamonds, black coal, ilmenite, rutile and zircon. It is the sixth largest exporter of iron ore, aluminium, lead and zinc, and the third largest producer and exporter of gold; an industry valued at $5.5 billion. It is the second largest producer in the world of silver with silver exports valued at about $62 million in 1995–1996.

Energy

Australia has enough reserves of coal at current consumption rates to last 300 years, enough gas for 45 years and enough uranium for 145 years. These will meet both export and domestic demands. Coal is mined in New South Wales, Queensland and small areas of Western Australia, South Australia and Tasmania. Petroleum is extracted mainly from Bass Strait and the Timor Sea region. Natural gas comes from the Cooper basin or the North West Shelf off the coast of Western Australia. Uranium is mined in Queensland, the Northern Territory, Western Australian and South Australia.

There is a growing awareness of the polluting effects of burning fossil fuels (e.g. coal, oil) and considerable thought is being given to reduction of carbon monoxide by simple measures such as time control systems. These will turn down the power on lighting, air conditioning and office equipment during the night. Another measure is the double use of power so that less energy is used.

The oil and gas industries were valued at $8.2 billion in 1996.

COAL

Coal is the largest source of energy in Australia. Discovered near Newcastle in 1791, it was already being exported to India by 1799. Australia's coal-fields were slow to develop until steam trains, steamships and the use of gas were introduced at the end of the 19th century. The production of coal was very important in Australia's economic development for both domestic and export income. The late 1980s were difficult years for the coal industry. There was a record production level, but the export revenue declined due to reduced prices in the world markets. Australia was the largest exporter with 40% more tonnage than the United States, its nearest rival. It accounts for about one-third of the world's seaborne coal trade.

PETROLEUM

Petroleum is known as crude oil in its liquid form. Natural gas is the gaseous hydrocarbon which ignites easily and burns with little waste. In the 1860s, the first petroleum products made in Australia came from shale oil deposits and New South Wales made a large contribution to petrol needs during World War II.

Until the 1950s, Australia was thought to have very few oil and gas deposits. Serious exploration began after oil was discovered in Western Australia in 1953 and oil was later found in commercial quantities in Queensland in 1961. The first gas fields were found in 1963 in South Australia. Exploration for oil began in the Bass Strait in the early 1960s and by mid-1982 oil and natural gas were being produced from Queensland, the Bass Strait, South Australia and Western Australia. Australia now produces more than two-thirds of its petroleum needs and more than enough natural gas. Australia's crude oils are what are termed 'light' and so heavy crude oil for special applications is imported from the Middle East and refined locally.

Each state is responsible for petroleum exploration and development rights which are only granted when the government is satisfied that the company or individual has adequate funds to complete the research. Roughly $750 million was spent on private petroleum exploration in 1994. The commonwealth government owns offshore petroleum rights and there is a royalty arrangement with each state.

Because Australia is a large country with a relatively small population, the federal government has encouraged rationalisation between the companies in the oil refinery and petroleum distribution business. As a result there are oil refineries located in each State to take care of local needs.

The world's largest floating offshore oil rig will begin operating in 1999, situated 550 km north-west of Darwin. This joint venture will invest more than $1 billion to extract the 250 million barrels in known reserves from the floor of the Timor Sea, located in Australian waters. At 1997, it is expected that the project will boost Australia's self-sufficiency by up to 20%.

NUCLEAR

Australia is rich in uranium, but due to much public opposition to nuclear energy for negative purposes, the Hawke/Keating Labor governments followed a policy of limiting production to just a few mines. The Liberal/National coalition government is currently considering opening up the uranimum mining industry.

SOLAR

The inexhaustible supply of solar power is taken advantage of in some remote areas of the country, where more than 10 000 houses in 3000 communities generate their own electricity. About 5% of Australian dwellings use solar energy for water heating. The figure in the Northern Territory is far higher, however, with almost 60% of houses using solar heating.

WIND

The Bass Strait, Western Australia, South Australia and Tasmania all have coastal areas with high wind energy. Wind is mainly used for windmills to pump water and for small wind turbine generators. Some remote homesteads near hot artesian bores are beginning to use wind in preference to diesel generators.

OCEAN

The open ocean only has a rise and fall within a range of one metre, but on the north-west coast this can increase to 11 metres through the gravitational effect on tides. Waves are generated by wind over a large expanse of water and at present ocean energy is more expensive to harness than coal fired energy. The cost of electricity generated by wave power plants is, at present, uncertain.

HYDRO-ELECTRIC

Australia, with the exception of Tasmania, has few good hydro-electric resources due to its low average rainfall and few mountainous regions. Tasmania has considerable potential, but with a small, isolated population and almost no heavy industry, hydro-electric power is not likely to be developed much further in the foreseeable future. As well as this, the damming of rivers in the state has come in conflict with both the environment lobby and the rapidly expanding tourist industry.

BIOMASS

The energy from biomass which is agriculture, crops and forestry waste is currently only converted by burning wood and bagasse (the fibrous waste from sugar cane). It does have a possible use as a source of liquid fuel, but it is small and is not competitive with petroleum-based fuels.

Housing

The first European settlers used primitive building materials and techniques. The earliest homes were generally two-roomed cottages made from materials easily available, such as wattle and daub, mud bricks, bark, timber and stone. Most people had separate homes on large allotments because of the availability of land. Houses became more substantial with the growth in industry and the consequent prosperity. Terraced houses were first built in Australia in the 1860s to provide urban accommodation on a rental basis. At the end of the 19th century, English-style homes of brick and timber with tile or corrugated iron roofs were the most popular. By 1900, 70% of Australians lived in metropolitan areas, but after World War I there was a housing shortage and semi-detached cottages were constructed in the inner city and suburbs because they were cheaper to build and used less land.

Beginning in the 1930s, detached houses and flats became popular due to the new laws on minimum allotment sizes. In 1945, there was another housing shortage and under the Commonwealth–state housing loan agreements, low-cost housing was provided for sale or rental, with preference given to returned servicemen and their families. During the following 20 years, many flats were built as an alternative to houses, and in the 1960s there was a boom in private flat building and public high-rise flats. Since the 1970s, there has been a sharp reduction in the number of flats built and an increasing trend towards town houses, home units and row houses, but the construction of detached houses still accounts for most of the building in Australia.

Australia has one of the highest rates of private house ownership in the world. About 67% of Australians own or are buying their own house and most houses are free-standing with an average of five rooms on 0.05 hectares. The state of the housing industry in Australia is generally considered to reflect the economic state of the nation. About 44% of total construction activity in 1995 was in the area of residential building, with about $17 370 million being spent.

The government helps pay for public housing, support accommodation services, crisis accommodation, mortgage and rent relief.

AUSTRALIAN DWELLINGS, 1991 CENSUS

Type of Dwelling	Percentage of Total No. of Dwellings
Separate house	76.7
Semi-detached	7.9
Flat/Apartment	12.1
Caravan	1.4
Other	1.9

Tourism

Australia has become a popular destination for foreign tourists particularly since travel has become cheaper and easier. In the past three decades tourism has become one of the largest growth industries. The tourist industry involves travel, accommodation, catering, hospitality, retail sales, meetings and conventions as well as many other related activities. With the 2000 Olympics imminent, the tourism industry will greatly expand in the next few years. It is estimated that tourism now accounts for 6.6% of Australia's gross domestic product (GDP) and employs more than 6% of the workforce; about 500 000 jobs.

In 1995–1996, there were 3.97 million short-term visitors to Australia. The largest numbers come from New Zealand followed by Britain, Ireland and the United States. Visitors from Europe, Japan and Southeast Asia continue to increase. In the same period there was a total of 172 370 hotel/motel rooms with an occupancy rate of 58.7%; 197 250 caravan park sites with an occupancy rate of 41%, and 39 960 places in holiday flats and units with an occupancy rate of 53.6%.

The Australian Tourist Commission (ATC) is a statutory body formed in 1967 and funded by the commonwealth and state governments as well as by the tourist industry itself. It has worldwide branches and its role is one of good will, to increase the number of visitors to Australia.

Manufacturing

In the early 19th century, the Australian manufacturing industry was still very small and concentrated on the production of salt, cloth and leather. In the 1850s, the industry developed rapidly but then people were lured away by the gold rush and many of the industries collapsed. In the 1890s, there was another surge and tariffs were introduced which sheltered locally made goods from overseas competition. World War I saw the development of the iron, steel, clothing, electrical goods and timber industries because imported goods were unavailable. When World War II began, Australia experienced an enormous expansion of the machine tools, aircraft, shipbuilding and munitions industries.

Since 1980 the growth of trade in manufactured goods has averaged 7.6% per annum, whereas the growth in clothing manufacturing had been 10.2% and telecommunications and computer equipment 12.5%.

The Australian Manufacturing Council believes that more agricultural products should be exported, and that the computer, telecommunications, motor car, chemical and pharmaceutical industries could be improved. The high cost of financing in Australia compared to overseas further hinders the local industry, while high interest rates have kept the value of the Australian dollar too high; this has encouraged imports and hindered exports. Without exports the Australian market is too small to make the manufacturing of many products viable. About 70% of the balance of payments deficit is due to imported manufactured goods and these are mainly consumer goods. Imports from the Far East can be very cheap despite transportation costs because of countries such as Japan or Germany investing in cheap labour, modern equipment and very high quality, low-cost shipping. Another problem for local industry is that some Australians perceive Australian products as being inferior, a legacy of early manufacturing processes.

To counteract this, the Australian Chamber of Manufactures has been running a marketing campaign to promote Australian manufactured goods. The use of an 'Australian-made' label on goods was hoped to make the consumers buy more Australian products. Unfortunately surveys by magazines and major newspapers found that 77% of Australian made brands were more expensive than the imported ones. They surveyed 64 product categories and in more than one third of the categories there were no Australian-made brands at all.

In 1995–1996, the manufacturing sector employed about 1 111 300 people, with 186 industrial disputes in progress during this period.

MANUFACTURING INDUSTRIES' TURNOVER, 1993

Industry	Turnover ($ million)
Food, beverages and tobacco	37 000
Textiles, clothing, footwear, leather	8 850
Wood and paper product	9 910
Printing, publishing, recorded media	11 540
Petroleum, coal, chemical and assoc. product	27 550
Non-metallic mineral product	8 360
Metal product	31 310
Machinery and equipment	30 780
Other	4 800
Total	**170 100**

Retail

In the early days of colonisation, there was a general store which sold everything for the householder and also gave personal service. As the population increased and industry prospered there were more goods available and speciality shops appeared. In the early 1900s, the population grew and moved to the suburbs. Small retail shops and department stores started to grow. In the 1950s, the changing economic conditions and technological progress had an enormous impact on the retail trade. The widespread use of the motor car together with refrigeration meant that larger quantities of products could be bought less frequently thereby heralding the arrival of supermarkets. The 1960s saw shopping centres appear in suburbs with a proportionate decline and change of emphasis in retailing in the centre of cities. These expanded to giant mall complexes in the 1970s, 80s and 90s, meaning the decline of suburban strip shopping centres. Recently there has been a push to return the retail heart to the cities and encourage shoppers back into city centres.

TURNOVER OF RETAIL SALES, 1995–1996

Type of Goods	Amount Sold ($ million)
Food	48 518
Department stores	11 607
Clothing/soft goods	8 222
Household goods	13 104
Recreational goods	6 970
Other	11 178
Hospitality and services	21 171
Total	**120 770**

Note: This is not a complete table and is only shown as an indication of turnover.

10

Transport & Communications

Telecommunications

*U*ntil *the second half of the 19th century, Australia could only communicate with the rest of the world by ship. The telegraph first came to Australia in 1854, and, in 1872, the Overland Telegraph Line was completed. This line connected major cities to Darwin, and was then linked by submarine telegraph cable to Java which, in turn, was linked to the British telegraph network.*

HISTORY

Telephone exchanges were being established in the capital cities as early as the 1870, the first opening in Melbourne in 1880 with 44 users. Exchanges gradually changed over from manual call connection to automatic from 1912 onwards. The Postmaster-General's Department managed all postal and telephone services after Federation in 1901. It was also responsible for radio broadcasting after the first services began in the 1920s.

In the wake of World War II, the vital nature of international communications was recognised and, in 1946, the Overseas Telecommunications Commission was established to develop and administer these essential links. Further changes came in 1975, when the Postal and Telecommunications Department was opened and two commissions were formed: Australian Telecommunications Commission (Telecom) and the Australian Postal Commission (Australia Post).

The *Telecommunications Act 1989* opened the industry to competition, and the Australian Telecommunications Authority (AUSTEL) was established to regulate the industry. Telecom and OTC merged in 1992 to become the Australian and Overseas Telecommunications Corporation and then, in 1995, Telstra. Optus Communications, Australia's first private phone company, was also established in 1992. Both organisations were issued with general and mobile carrier licences, while Vodafone received a mobile licence only. From July 1997, the limit on the number of telecommunications carriers will be lifted.

AUSTRALIAN TELECOMMUNICATIONS AUTHORITY

The *Telecommunications Act 1991* sets out the functions of the Australia Telecommunications Authority (AUSTEL). Its objectives include the protection of consumers and the promotion of competition and fair market conduct. It manages the national numbering plan, issues equipment permits, sets and maintains technical standards, provides advice and assistance to industry and consumers, provides reports and advice to the

Minister for Communications and the Arts, and implements the Federal government's telecommunications policies.

AUSTEL also examines issues such as possible anti-competitive practices of the carriers, privacy, cabling, installation of mobile phone towers and access to services.

From July 1997, AUSTEL's responsibility for eliminating anti-competitive conduct in the telecommunications industry will be transferred to the Australian Competition and Consumer Commission (*see* chapter 8, 'Law'). In the same month, AUSTEL will merge with the Spectrum Management Agency to become the Australian Telecommunications and Spectrum Management Authority.

SPECTRUM MANAGEMENT AUTHORITY (SMA)

Established in 1993 by the Federal government, SMA manages access to and use of the radio spectrum, providing a means for communicating information such as voice, pictures, music and data via electromagnetic waves. The SMA is responsible for the planning of the overall use of the spectrum, setting prices for its use, the management of licensing schemes, the setting of equipment standards and managing electromagnetic interference.

Currently the SMA has approximately 100 000 clients who hold licences giving them access to the spectrum, allowing them to watch television, listen to the radio, make mobile phone calls and use equipment such as remote controls.

TELSTRA

Telstra provides a number of services involved with telephones. These include: installing and maintaining private, corporate and public telephones, customer billing, telephone products (including answering machines, mobile and cordless phones), operator-assisted services, disability and rural area services and directories. As well as telephone services, Telstra also handles a vast amount of communications through computers, the Internet and television.

At the end of June 1996, Telstra's revenue was up 8.2% to $15.2 billion, and it showed a record profit of 2304.7 million, up 31.5%. Approximately one in four Australians has a mobile phone. More than 60% of these were with Telstra, with its analogue and digital networks reaching more than 91% of the population.

In 1996, after the first year of Internet management, the international Internet links went from 6 Mbps to 32 Mbps to deal with a 250% increase in traffic volume.

FOXTEL, a cable television joint venture between Telstra and News Corporation Ltd, began in 1995 offering more than 20 channels, reaching an estimated 1.2 million homes in 1996. In December 1996, the Federal government's plan to sell one-third of Telstra was given the go-ahead. The government's ambition is to raise between $8 billion and $10 billion from this partial privatisation.

OPTUS COMMUNICATIONS

Optus was selected as the second Australian carrier to compete with Telecom (as it was then known) in 1991, and was fully established the next year. That same year it purchased AUSSAT, the company that owned, operated and managed Australia's National Satellite System. Optus now comprises four communications satellites, a national network of satellite earth stations including two command and control centres based in Sydney and Perth, and a number of international satellite earth stations. The company has a monopoly of domestic satellite communications services until July 1997.

Specialising in long distance, mobile communications and business network, the company has achieved an annual revenue in excess of $1.5 billion, and invested almost $2 billion in capital expenditure. It achieved a profit of $60 million in less than five years. The principal shareholders include the Australian companies Mayne Nickless (25% and AMP Society (10%), with 49% of equity held equally by BellSouth of the USA and Cable and Wireless of the UK.

Optus is also a major shareholder (46%) in Optus Vision, which offered 20 pay TV channels in 1995, on the road to reaching three million Australian homes by the end of 1998. In 1996, it had secured more than 100 000 pay TV subscribers.

TELEPHONE CHARGES

Local calls from public telephones cost 40 or 50 cents, and 25 cents from residential phones. STD is charged at different rates, depending on the distance covered and the time the call begins. All STD rates are expressed as charges for time used.

FACSIMILE

Developed around the turn of the century, facsimile transmission or picture-grams were first introduced by the Australian Post Office in 1929. On 9 September, the first photographs were transmitted between Sydney and Melbourne. The first picture sent to Melbourne was of the Sydney Harbour Bridge, under construction at the time.

By 1975, all facsimile business was being transmitted along Telecom lines. Recent years have seen an enormous increase in the use of facsimile machines and the trend for future developments in this field is to increase the transmission speed of documents, thus making the service even cheaper.

SATELLITES

Satellites are machines which orbit the earth and transmit radio signals to earth stations using a beam which is kept as small as possible to maximise its strength and minimise the power required. They have two main uses; communications and observation. The speed at which they revolve around the earth is determined by their altitude, so the higher the orbit the lower the speed.

Some satellites, usually those used for communication, are positioned 36 000 km from earth above the equator, and revolve around the earth once every 24 hours. This is called a geostationary orbit. Observation satellites, on the other hand, are kept as low as possible for clarity of picture and usually operate in a near polar orbit. Their speed is such that, at an elevation of 350 km, they would orbit the earth 14 times in every 24 hours.

The National Satellite System was commissioned in 1979, and AUSSAT was formed in 1981 to own and operate three A-series spacecraft. AUSSAT developed satellite control facilities in Sydney and Perth along with satellite earth stations in other capital cities. In 1985, the first two satellites — A1 and A2 — were launched from the NASA space shuttles, while A3 was launched in 1987. Optus Communications took over these systems in 1992 when it acquired AUSSAT, and the original spacecraft have been gradually replaced by the new B-series of satellites. In total, six satellites have been launched, with A1 retired in 1993 and B2 destroyed at launch.

The International Telecommunications Satellite Organisation (Intelsat), set up in 1964, provides tracking, telemetry, command and monitoring services to its eight spacecraft over the Indian and Pacific oceans region. In total, it has about 20 spacecraft, and Telstra is its sixth largest user and shareholder.

The International Maritime Satellite Organisation (Inmarsat) provides a similar service for aviation, maritime and land based mobile markets.

The primary application of satellite technology is to provide the remote parts of Australia with better television, radio and data transmissions. Other uses include a better air traffic control network, remote and long distance education, private network voice, video and data services, mobile communications, entertainment distribution, and aid in health and medical services.

RADIOCOMMUNICATION STATIONS

By 1994, there were about 928 230 authorised radiocommunication stations in Australia, divisible as follows: 328 010 land mobile services, 397 180 citizens band (CB) stations, 77 370 marine services and 57 650 fixed services.

Postal Services

HISTORY

In the early days of the colony, reasonable communication between Australia and Britain and also between settlers was extremely important and very difficult. Letters, which were mostly official, had to be sent by ship between Australia and Britain.

The Australian postal system began officially in Sydney in 1809 in response to a number of cases of mail pilfering on board incoming ships. Isaac Nichols was asked to distribute overseas mail in addition to his work as Principal Superintendent of Convicts.

The first post office in Sydney was authorised in 1810 in Mr Nichols' home in George Street in the centre of the city; in his first year, Nichols handled a few hundred items. In 1828, the first seven post offices outside the General Post Office in New South Wales were opened and postmasters appointed in Bathurst, Campbelltown, Liverpool, Newcastle, Parramatta, Penrith and Windsor. The first postman, an assigned convict, was appointed in Sydney in 1828. He was the private servant of Sydney's first Postmaster-General.

Over the next 15 years, other States followed suit. In 1831, recipients paid the cost of postage (two pence) to the GPO, and in the same year the first post boxes were installed. In 1852, Australia was one of the first countries in the world to introduce prepaid adhesive stamps.

Early methods of transporting the mail were by convicts on foot and lone horse-riders. From the 1850s, domestic mail was carried by coach or rail, and a regular steamship service to the UK was introduced. Telegraphy was being used extensively by the 1860s, and by the 1870s the Overland Telegraph line was ready for operation.

POSTMASTER-GENERAL'S DEPARTMENT

Upon Federation, responsibility for the country's postal service was passed from the individual States to the Commonwealth, effective from 1 March 1901. This was controlled by the newly established Postmaster-General's Department (PMG).

The first airmail from London to Sydney began to arrive in 1919, but a regular service between the two countries was not established until 1934. Within Australia, the first regular airmail began in 1922 in Western Australia, and, in the same year, a service between Cloncurry and Charleville was started by the Queensland and Northern Territory Aerial Services Ltd, a company that later became Australia's international and domestic airline, Qantas.

Australia Post

The first major overhaul of the organisation of Australia's postal services since Federation was undertaken in 1975. The Australian Postal Commission (later Corporation) assumed responsibility for the operation and management of Australia's postal services. To reduce congestion and handling time at the large exchanges, a system of regional sorting and distribution centres was established and new suburban parcel centres were set up to further reduce congestion.

In October 1988, the International Express Post service was launched. The Australian Postal Corporation was renamed in December 1988 and has since been known as Australia Post. Its function is to provide efficient postal services to the whole nation, especially to the people who live in the country, and to operate at a profit. At present it is the only national postal system within Australia, but following deregulation in the communications industry Australia Post may be open to competition in the near future.

Australia has roughly 4000 post offices and post office agencies. The main services and products of Australia Post are surface and express post, parcel post; electronic post; fax services, money orders; private boxes and bags; express courier; the sale of padded envelopes, stationery and postage stamps; the collection of departure tax and passport applications. It also processes applications for tax file numbers for the Australian Taxation Office, and acts as agent for other Commonwealth, State and local government departments and authorities.

Australia Post delivers to almost 7.7 million addresses and this number increases by about 160 000 every year. In 1996, it processed about 3920 million items. During this period approximately 93.6% of enveloped mail was delivered by the next day, and 98.8% was delivered within two days.

Over 1994–1995, Australia Post had an operating profit of $331.6 million, and employed 31 600 full-time and 4000 part-time staff. In 1996, the basic postage rate was 45¢ following a five year price freeze enforced in 1993.

Document Exchange

The AUSDOC Document Exchange (DX) was created in 1971 and caters for the business and government communities by transporting general business documents, letters, inter-office mail and legal documents within the state, interstate and overseas. It currently has 20 000 members, of whom 35% are legal firms, 17% government departments and the remainder businesses. Members receive a DX box number in their chosen exchange (of which there are 580 throughout Australia). At that exchange they clear their own box and place documents in other members' boxes. Documents are exchanged overnight by a network of couriers. Some remote country locations may require second-day delivery. There are also overnight interstate and international delivery services. The DX also links with city, metropolitan area and country courier services between branch offices, and bulk mail distribution to members and non-members.

Transport

Each Census asks about the method used to travel to work that day. In 1991, the responses were as follows:

Method	Number
Car as driver	3 827 410
Car as passenger	573 580
Train	372 115
Bus	310 535
Ferry/tram	50 325
Taxi	28 945
Motorcycle	62 960
Bicycle	92 505
Walked only	336 055
Other	86 624

People in the Australian Capital Territory make an average of 84 public transport journeys each year; the greatest number for all the States and Territories. New South Wales follows at 73 and Victoria at 71, while people in the Northern Territory make the least number of journeys at 18, followed by Tasmania at 26 and Queensland at 29 journeys.

ROAD BUILDING

In New South Wales, the first road was a 2-km track from the Governor's house to the Battery at Dawes Point. Between 1789 and 1791, a road was built between the settlement in Parramatta and Sydney. As Lachlan Macquarie arrived to run the colony in 1810, work began to plan, build and maintain all existing roads; 444 km in total. One of the most important of these was the one linking Sydney to Bathurst across the Blue Mountains.

When the colony began extending along the coasts and to Van Diemen's Land (now Tasmania), roads began to improve. In 1807, a 4-km road was built between Hobart and New Town in Tasmania, and in 1835 the road between Sydney and Melbourne was started, followed by a road-mail service four years later.

The first roads were dirt tracks on which it was hazardous to travel. In the 1850s, however, the gold rush made a proper road system a priority. In order to cope with the greatly increased usage, Road Boards were created in South Australia and Victoria to plan and administer the roads and collect tolls. Until the railways were developed in the 1850s and 1860s, a great deal was spent on building and maintaining roads.

The arrival of the car had a major effect on road building, especially after World War I. In the 1920s, the Main Road Boards of State governments organised road building and maintenance. During World War II, 6000 km of new roads were built and 8000 km were improved, including the highway from Darwin in the Northern Territory to Port Augusta in Adelaide. In 1934, the National Association of Australian State Road Authorities (NAASRA) was established, and, in 1947, the government passed the Commonwealth Aid Roads Rural Works Act to improve the standard of all roads.

The 1950s saw a national road policy developed due to increased road traffic, and in 1960 NAASRA founded the Australian Road Research Board to undertake and sponsor road and road transport research. The Board disseminates this information through conferences and publications, maintaining close contact with similar organisations in other countries.

In July 1989, AUSTROADS was established to replace NAASRA with a brief 'to pursue the effective management and use of the nation's roads as part of the Australian transport system, by the development and promotion of national policies and practices'.

There are many difficulties in building and maintaining roads in Australia due to the long distances involved between major cities and the often harsh climate. By June 1995, there were 801 402 km of roads in Australia, with just 300 460 km of these being bitumen or concrete. In the June 1996 Federal Budget, national funding for roads was cut by $622 million.

ROAD DISTANCES

Road Route	Distance (km)
Sydney–Brisbane	
via Pacific Highway	980
via New England Highway	1014
via Putty Road and New England Highway	1005
Sydney–Melbourne	
via Hume Highway	805
via Princes Highway	1043
via Olympic Way	893
Canberra–Cooma–Cann River	1030

Road Route	Distance (km)
Sydney–Adelaide	
via Mid-Western Highway	1414
via Sturt Highway	1418
via Barrier Highway	1666
Melbourne–Adelaide	
via Western and Dukes Highways	731
via Princes Highway West	929
Sydney–Darwin	
via Dubbo, Bourke, Charleville and Mt Isa	4006
via New England Highway, Toowoomba,	
Blackall and Mt Isa	4253
via Pacific Highway, Brisbane and Townsville	4751
Brisbane–Cairns	
via Bruce Highway	1711
Perth–Darwin	
via North West Coastal Highway	4189
via Great Northern Highway	4006
Adelaide–Darwin	
via Stuart Highway	3026
Adelaide–Perth	
via Eyre Highway	2691
Alice Springs–Uluru	
via Erldunda, Curtin Springs Homestead and	
Yulara Tourist Resort	455

Road Transport

CARS

From the 1880s onwards, Australia started building motor cars. One of the earliest successful petrol-powered cars was made by the Tarrant Motor and Engineering Company in Melbourne in 1897. From the 1920s, motor manufacturing and car sales gradually increased, but the Depression of the

1930s caused sales and production to decrease sharply and all but the biggest car manufacturers went bankrupt. There were about 600 000 motor vehicles in the country by this time.

After World War II, the car industry picked up considerably and in 1948 the first completely Australian made car, the 48/215 Holden, was manufactured by General Motors-Holden. It was so successful that by 1951 the Holden became Australia's top selling car.

By 1968, over 80% of the car industry was controlled by Ford, Chrysler, General Motors-Holden and two smaller companies, BMC and Australian Motor Industries (AMI). The rest of the market was filled by about 50 companies, and there were about 900 different types of car from which to choose. In 1973–1974, there was a boom in local car manufacturing. Many cars were still imported, but expensive petrol prices made small models increasingly popular.

The top motor vehicle producers in Australia today are overseas-based international companies such as General Motors-Holden, Ford, Toyota and Mitsubishi. Regulations demand, however, that Australian-produced cars must have more than 80% locally made parts. Up to 30% of all passenger vehicles are imported.

Australia is one of the largest motor vehicle consumers in the world. About 590 motor vehicles are registered for every 1000 people, with 638 910 new vehicles registered in 1994–1995. In a survey conducted by the Australian Bureau of Statistics on Australian household expenditure in 1994, out of a total average weekly expenditure of $602, the third greatest cost after income tax and food was transport at $94.

Road transport accounts for about 25% of the energy consumed in Australia; this is a 20% higher fuel use per head than the OECD urban average.

BUSES

Buses are used extensively around Australia, operated both by State and local government bodies and private operators. These different services cater for a wide range of routes: local services, intercity and interstate. Buses are also often run in connection with government rail services.

Government and/or municipal bus services are located in every capital city and also in Newcastle (New South Wales), Rockhampton (Queensland) and Burnie and Launceston (Tasmania). Private services cover many other cities and towns, with the largest operators located in Melbourne. Private long-distance bus services are the cheapest form of interstate transport, undercutting most rail fares over long distances.

The Sydney and Newcastle government bus system is one of the largest in the world, with 1450 buses covering about 1250 route km over 300 routes. In all of New Souh Wales, government buses travel about

62 million km each year, with over 189 million passenger journeys. By the 1990s, government and private buses throughout the country carried more people than any other form of public transport (except in Melbourne).

Compressed natural gas has been used as an alternative bus fuel in recent years, beginning with trials in Sydney in 1992 and Canberra in 1993. Buses using this fuel produce approximately 25% less greenhouse emissions than diesel buses. (*See* chapter 4, 'Environment'.)

ROAD TRAFFIC ACCIDENTS

While the number of road deaths has steadily declined as advertising campaigns, public education, random breath testing, the popularity of light beer and Driver Reviver stops have all appeared to take effect, there was an increase in the number of deaths from 1994 to 1995.

NUMBER OF DEATHS DUE TO ROAD TRAFFIC ACCIDENTS

Year	*No. of deaths*
1989	2804
1990	2331
1991	2113
1992	1952
1993	1952
1994	1934
1995	2017

Rail Transport

TRAINS

Until the middle of the 1800s, Australians travelled around the country by horse-drawn transport and by coastal shipping services. From 1854, when the first steam railway between Melbourne and Port Melbourne started, the railway system of the eastern States developed rapidly. Initially all track and rolling stock was imported, although by the 1880s most of the equipment was being made locally. Although the railways were initially run by private companies, the various State governments were soon forced to assume control as the companies ran into financial problems.

By Federation, all States (except Western Australia) were linked by rail and more than 20 000 km of track had been laid. Three different gauges had been used, however: standard gauge in New South Wales, broad gauge in Victoria and the southern part of South Australia, and narrow gauge in Tasmania, Queensland, Western Australia and the north of South Australia. This meant that, in 1917, if you wanted to travel from Perth to Brisbane, you had to change trains six times. It was not until 1970 that the situation improved sufficiently so that a passenger could remain on the same train on a journey from Perth to Sydney. Three different gauges still exist in Australia, but the state capitals are now linked by one uniform gauge.

Steam locomotion was used until the 1950s when diesel-electric engines began to take over. Steam engines were completely withdrawn in the 1970s, but tourist trips are still available on scenic routes in New South Wales and Victoria.

Suburban electric trains operate in New South Wales, Victoria, Queensland and Western Australia.

GOVERNMENT-OWNED RAILWAY SYSTEMS, 1995

Railway	Amount of track (km)
State Rail Authority of NSW (SRA)	9 810
Public Transport Corporation Victoria	5 107
Queensland Railways	9 357
State Transport Authority, South Australia	120
Western Australian Government Railways (Westrail)	5 583
National Rail Corporation Ltd (NR)	n.a.
Australian National Railways Commission (Australian National)	6 235
Total	**36 212**

Australian National (AN) was set up as a statutory authority in 1978 to control Commonwealth, Tasmanian and South Australia country lines. In November 1996, the Federal government announced its intention to privatise AN by 30 June 1997. As well as selling its three famous passenger services the Indian Pacific, the Ghan and the Overlander, the government will put its 40% stake in National Rail, the interstate rail freight operator in South Australia and Tasmania, on the market.

The privatisation move is a response to reports that AN's debts may be as large as $1 billion, with additional losses in the 1995–1996 financial year estimated at anywhere between $148 and $250 million. In preparation for the sell off, the government will spend $2 billion bailing out AN. The government will keep 6118 km of AN track in public hands, to be managed by a new national track authority.

The National Rail Corporation was established in 1991 to manage all interstate rail freight on the mainland network. Its shareholders are the

New South Wales, Victoria and Western Australia State governments along with the Federal government.

During the period 1993–1994, government railways carried 212.3 million tonnes of freight earning $2642.4 million. The total number of passenger journeys in the same period was 407.2 million.

During the period 1994–1995, the non-government railways, not including trains run inside harbour precincts, mines, quarries and industrial estates, carried 173.4 million tonnes: 121.6 million of iron ore; 31.8 million of sugar; 7.9 million of coal, and 12.1 million tonnes of other raw materials or goods.

FREIGHT MOVEMENT

The majority of freight moved around Australia in 1994–1995 was carried by rail. The figures shown below exclude all freight movements within urban areas and journeys of less than 25 km in rural areas.

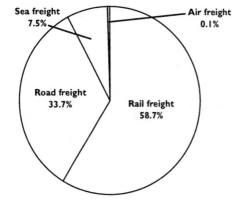

Sea freight 7.5%

Air freight 0.1%

Road freight 33.7%

Rail freight 58.7%

Freight Movement in Australia
In 1994–1995, a total of 656.6 million tonnes of freight was moved by either rail, road, sea or air.

SPEEDRAIL

By December 1996, the Federal Minister for Transport was expressing strong support for the proposed high-speed rail service between Sydney and Canberra, with a possible later extension to Melbourne. The 300 km/h service between Sydney and the national capital would take approximately 80 minutes, with the fare set at half the economy airfare. The target date for operation is currently the year 2001. Services would commence from Sydney's Central Station and/or Parramatta, stopping at Mascot Airport, Goulburn and the Southern Highlands.

It is estimated that the project would involve capital expenditure of $1.8 billion, including $160 million on new track to be shared with State Rail.

LONG-DISTANCE AND/OR TOURIST PASSENGER TRAINS, 1995

Train	Route	Distance (km)	Max. Speed (km/h)
Australind	Perth–Bunbury	184	120
Ghan	Adelaide–Alice Springs	1559	115
Gulflander	Normanton–Croydon	152	60
Kuranda	Cairns–Kuranda	33	60
Indian Pacific	Perth–Sydney	4355	115
Overland	Melbourne–Adelaide	774	115
Prospector	Perth–Kalgoorlie	659	140
Queenslander	Brisbane–Cairns	1681	100
Xplorer	ACT–NSW	various	140
XPT	Sydney–Melbourne	960	160
	Sydney–Brisbane	1074	130
	Sydney–NSW country	various	160
Spirit of Capricorn	Brisbane–Rockhampton	639	120
Spirit of the Outback	Brisbane–Longreach	1326	100

MONORAIL

On 21 July 1988, a monorail system operated by a private company was opened in Sydney which links the city's central business district with Darling Harbour. There are seven stations at present, with one more due to be completed in 1997. The rolling stock is of Australian/Swiss manufacture and the monorail can achieve a maximum speed of 33 km/h. No accidents have been recorded since the opening.

TRAMS/LIGHT RAIL

The first horse-drawn tram ran between 1861 and 1866, from Circular Quay to Central Station in Sydney. In 1879, steam-powered trams were introduced especially to coincide with an international exhibition held in Sydney. In 1886, a cable car was developed for the steep hills of North Sydney.

Melbourne and Brisbane introduced tram services in 1885, Adelaide from 1878, Hobart from 1893 and Perth from 1899. The first regular electric trams ran between Box Hill and Doncaster in Victoria in October 1889, and during the next 15 years most trams in Australia gradually converted to electricity.

Today, the only trams used for urban purposes are those in Melbourne (330 km of track) and one 11-km route between Adelaide and Glenelg in South Australia.

There are two 'light rail' services, one operating in Adelaide, South Australia, and another scheduled for Sydney in 1997.

Water Transport

SHIPPING

HISTORY

A government ship building yard was established in Sydney Cove in 1797, remaining in operation until 1833. In 1798, the *Rose Hill Packet* was the first ship to be built in Australia in 1798, and was used to transport goods and passengers up and down the Parramatta River. That same year, James Underwood opened the first private shipyard and others soon followed in Sydney and along the developing coasts. There were 20 ships being built by 1804.

In order to protect the East India Company, the building of oceangoing ships was restricted by the British Government until the beginning of the 1800s. From 1813, when the monopoly ended, ship building flourished and soon became established with most of the colonies building fishing and transport vessels. The first shipyard in Victoria was built on the Yarra River in Melbourne in 1939. Tasmania also became a leading builder of large ships, thanks largely to its wealth of timber.

During World War I, many naval vessels were built, but by the late 1920s and early 1930s there was little demand for new ships, either naval or commercial, and many of the shipyards closed. The possibility of another world war reopened the shipyards, and, in 1941, the Australian Shipbuilding Board was developed to initiate and coordinate construction.

From the 1960s, cargo and passenger ships, as well as some smaller vessels, were built, but in the late 1970s major yards closed and Australia stopped producing large ships. Up to the end of 1975, Australian shipyards had completed 329 vessels valued at approximately $734 million. The closing of Newcastle's Carrington Slipways in 1990, the only remaining yard capable of building large oceangoing ships, was the end of an era.

In the 1980s, the industry began building new technology catamarans, luxury motor yachts and specialised fishing vessels aimed at international markets, with an emphasis on high-quality, innovative designs. In the 1990s, the most successful shipyards also constructed ferries and offshore supply vessels. There was a resurgence in the naval shipbuilding industry in the 1990s, with a series of Anzac class frigates being built in Williamstown, Victoria, and Collins class submarines coming out of the Australian Submarine Corporation's base in Port Adelaide, South Australia.

SEA CARGO

Until the 1920s, when the commercial aircraft was developed, Australia's only trading link with the world was by sea. Today, the sea is still a cheap way of importing and exporting bulk goods.

By 1995, Australia's trading fleet consisted of 332 ships over 150 gross tonnes, including a coastal fleet of 96 ships and an overseas fleet of 56 ships. Between 1994 and 1995, 46.0 million tonnes of cargo were discharged, with 45.3 million tonnes loaded. The largest inward cargo grouping was machinery, equipment, apparatus and appliances. The largest outward cargo grouping was coal, coke and briquettes. The greatest amount of cargo was discharged in New South Wales (17.6 million tonnes), followed by Queensland (13.1 million tonnes); while the greatest amount was loaded in Queensland (11.7 million tonnes), Western Australia (9.8 million tonnes) and Victoria (8.2 million tonnes). In general, coal is transported from New South Wales to Victoria and South Australia; sugar from Queensland to New South Wales and Victoria, and iron ore from Western Australia to New South Wales.

On 1 July 1989, the successor to the Australian Coastal Shipping Commission, the Australian Shipping Commission which operates a fleet called the Australian National Line, became ANL Limited, a public company. The Federal government's attempts to sell the loss-making ANL Limited in 1995 were unsuccessful.

As at 30 June 1996, it had a fleet of 12 ships, eight of which are deployed in overseas trades and four in coastal trade. ANL is involved with many shipping-related activities, including freight forwarding, customs agency, ship management services, container management and others.

RIVERBOATS AND FERRIES

RIVERBOATS

In the 19th century, riverboats were widely used as transport on many of Australia's rivers. The rivers were shallow and so the steam-powered boats had to be flat-bottomed. The most important riverboats worked on the Murray, Darling and Murrumbidgee Rivers in the 1850s. They carried goods, passengers and produce to the townships along the banks. Goolwa and Echuca were the main riverports on the Murray–Darling system in the mid-1860s.

The development of the railways and roads led to the decline of the riverboats by the 1930s. In more recent times, some have been restored and river ports, such as Echuca and Swan Hill on the Murray River, are preserved as part of the Australian heritage.

FERRIES

Many of the colonial capitals relied on ferries for local transport and for crossing at convenient points before the development of roads and bridges. The first sailing ferry in Australia was the *Rose Hill Packet* which began to operate in 1789 on the route between Sydney Cove and Parramatta (earlier called Rose Hill). The first steam-powered ferry in Australia was the British-built *Sophia Jane*, used between Sydney and Newcastle from 1831. The Surprise was the first Australian-built steamship and plied the Parramatta-Sydney route for a year in 1831 before transferring to Hobart. The *Experiment*, built in 1832 and used on the Parramatta route, was the first paddlewheel ship built in Australia. Four horses powered the capstan which turned the paddlewheels.

For 20 years from the early 1840s, ferry services expanded and began to call at many of the new suburbs springing up around Sydney. By the 1930s, many of these steam-driven boats were being converted to diesel. When the Sydney Harbour Bridge opened in 1932, however, the need for vehicle-carrying and passenger ferries declined so dramatically that the New South Wales government took the ferries over in 1951.

The faster Rivercat ferries began operating between Parramatta and Circular Quay in 1992. All New South Wales ferry services are now run by the State Transit Authority.

In Brisbane, ferries run by private companies and the Brisbane City Council operate between the city and suburbs. Vehicular ferries operate between Moreton and Stradbroke Islands. In Perth, State government ferries travel between the city and South Perth, while private operators run between the city and Rottnest Island. Ferries along the Murray River in South Australia have always been important. They now operate to Berri, Mannum and Hindmarsh Islands. In Tasmania, ferries travel across the Mersey at Devonport, while vehicular ferries link mainland Tasmania with Bruny Island. The *Spirit of Tasmania* began operating between Melbourne and Devonport in 1993, and there are also privately operated ferries travelling along Hobart's Derwent River.

Aviation

HISTORY

Australian research into aviation began in the 1840s. In 1889 and 1893 respectively, Lawrence Hargrave, the Australian aviation pioneer later to be internationally acclaimed, invented his compressed air engine and the box kite. The former was the forerunner of the internal combustion engine used in many early aircraft, while the latter revealed principles that were applied in the development of powered flight.

Aircraft were built in Australia from 1910, after John Duigan's first powered flight, and mass production of de Havilland Gypsy Moths began in the 1920s. After World War II, the Commonwealth Aircraft Corporation (CAC) was formed and began to build the Wirraway aeroplane. The CAC and Government Aircraft Factory built a large number of military aircraft including the Mustang fighter, the Beaufighter and Beaufort fighter bombers, the Lincoln heavy bombers and later the Canberra jet bombers and Sabre jet fighters. Since World War II, Australia has tried, with little commercial success, to build light aircraft.

In the years between the two world wars, Australia became an important pioneer of trans-oceanic flights. Bert Hinkler made the first solo flight from Britain to Australia in 1928, and in the same year Charles Kingsford Smith became the first pilot to fly from the United States to Australia. This was also the year that the Australian Inland Mission's Flying Doctor Service (now the Royal Flying Doctor Service) began operating from Queensland.

In more recent times, the Federal government announced the deregulation of the airline industry with the two airline policy ending in 1990. After almost 40 years, new airlines were allowed access to interstate trunk routes and airlines were able to set their own fare rates and capacity. These were previously regulated by the government. Compass Airlines entered the field, but was unable to compete under deregulation conditions that allowed drastic fare discounting. In 1993, Compass ceased operations.

In 1994–1995, it is estimated that 23 423 million passenger km were flown in civil aviation aircraft on regular domestic services. This was a marked increase on the 1992–1993 estimate of 18 996 million passenger km.

AIRLINE FLEETS

QANTAS

Qantas is the world's second oldest airline, founded in 1920 as Queensland and Norther Territory Aerial Services Ltd. Today, it employs nearly 30 000 staff across its network, operating an average of 552 flights a day to 52 Australian destinations. It also operates 360 international flights a week to 44 destinations in 26 countries, as well as flying to nine ports throughout the Pacific. In 1992, Qantas was permitted to buy Australian Airlines. In 1995, 51% of Qantas shares were floated and made available to the public. The remaining 49% is owned by overseas shareholders, of which British Airways is the largest.

In the year ending June 1996, Qantas carried 9 386 000 passengers domestically (53% of the domestic market), and 6 165 000 on international flights (38.5% of the market). The regional subsidiaries carried 1 935 000 passengers. In the same period, Qantas increased its profit by about 37% to $246.7 million, while revenue increased by about 6% to $7.6 billion.

In 1996, Qantas had a fleet of 96 aircraft: the majority of which are Boeing 737s, 747s and 767s. Its subsidiaries include such regional airlines as Eastern Australian Airlines, Southern Australia Airlines, Sunstate and Airlink, and these operate a mixed fleet of 46 de Havilland Canada, British Aerospace, Shorts and Cessna aircraft. On average, the aircraft are used for 11.8 hours per day.

MAJOR OVERSEAS VISITORS

Source country	1993 ('000)	1995 ('000)
Japan	670.8	782.7
New Zealand	499.3	538.4
United Kingdom	310.3	347.9
United States of America	281.3	304.9
Total	**2 996.2**	**3 725.8**

MAJOR DESTINATIONS OF AUSTRALIAN TRAVELLERS

Country	1993 ('000)	1995 ('000)
New Zealand	347.2	371.4
United States of America	300.1	314.0
United Kingdom	241.1	265.4
Indonesia	198.8	222.2
Total	**2 267.1**	**2 518.6**

ANSETT AUSTRALIA

Ansett Australia began operating in 1936, and was solely a domestic carrier until the Federal government announced fundamental changes to aviation policy in its 1992 'One Nation' statement, including an end to the Single Designation Policy. Flights to Bali began in September 1993, and Ansett now flies to nine international destinations.

Ansett is jointly owned by News Corporation Ltd and Air New Zealand. Its fleet comprises seventeen Airbus A320s, four Boeing 727-LRs, twenty-two Boeing 737-300s, nine Boeing 767-200s, three Boeing 747-300s, one Boeing 767-300ER, seven BAe 146-200s, five Fokker 28-4000s and five BAe 146-300s. There are three aircraft operating solely as freighters.

REGIONAL SERVICES

There are also about 45 commuter operators which make regular public transport flights to about 230 Australian airports. As well as these, much business is done in charter work, aerial work, aerial agriculture, training and other operations. In 1995, it was estimated that regional operators carried 2.8 million passengers.

INTERNATIONAL AIRLINES

At June 1995, 46 international airlines were operating regular passenger services in and out of Australia. An estimated 27 500 flights arrived in the country carrying 5.34 million passengers, while 27 280 flights departed with 5.28 million passengers.

REGISTRATIONS AND LICENCES

At the end of 1995, about 9630 aircraft were registered in Australia. There are about 35 700 people holding current aeroplane pilot licences, including both private and commercial pilots.

AVIATION ACCIDENTS AND CASUALTIES

Year	Accidents	Fatalities
1985	205	41
1986	210	43
1987	224	31
1988	245	58
1989	250	46
1990	269	64
1991	259	45
1992	233	49
1993	256	46
1994	206	51
1995	221	37

INTERNATIONAL AGREEMENTS

At December 1995, Australia had 39 full treaty air service agreements with other countries, while six arrangements do not have full treaty status. These allow the renegotiation of passenger numbers and routes in the light of ever increasing public demand.

Australia is also a member of the International Civil Aviation Organisation (ICAO) and has been on the governing council since its establishment in 1947. Australia is also one of the 15 members of the Air Navigation Commission responsible for determining international safety standards and maximum navigational efficiency.

11
Defence

Australia's Defence Policy

*A*ustralia's defence policy is one of self-reliance, within the framework of overseas alliances and agreements. This policy is set out in a document called the 1994 White Paper on Defence, Defending Australia, which highlights the agenda for defence strategy and development into the next century. The White Paper recognises the public expectation that Australia will be able to defend itself against any likely threat. It also recognises changes in the strategic circumstances of our region and major developments in military technology.

With the end of the Cold War, the threat of global war has been significantly reduced, but at other levels, the use of military force has not diminished and Australia must re-assert its position against any possible armed force. Australia's future security, like its economy, is closely linked to Asia and the Pacific region and the importance of its relationship with these areas cannot be overstated.

Australia's area of direct military interest is identified as Australia, its territories and adjacent ocean areas, as well as Papua New Guinea, New Zealand and other neighbouring countries of the south-west Pacific Ocean. This area constitutes approximately 10% of the world's surface, stretching as it does for 7000 km east–west and 5000 km north–south.

Australia's location, population, size and infrastructure make it unique in terms of its defence capabilities and provides both advantages and challenges. As an island continent, priority is placed on the defence of sea and air approaches. Planning focuses on defence capabilities rather than imminent threats. Due to Australia's size and the likelihood of any attack coming from the north, it was decided to develop a new command in the north of the country known as NORCOM.

In response to changes in strategic and regional developments, the Royal Australian Navy (RAN) has established itself as a two ocean navy, with major installations on both the Pacific and Indian Ocean coasts. HMAS Stirling in Western Australia is being developed as a main naval base and home for half of our surface and submarine fleet. There will be six Collins Class submarines based there by the turn of the century. As part of the Stirling expansion program, the Royal Australian Navy will also put in place six destroyers/frigates and 12 offshore patrol vessels. Early detection systems are in place which can detect enemy planes and ships when they are still over the horizon. This will enable an early response to any attack.

Of Australia's present alliances, the ANZUS Treaty is seen as among the most significant. Although the treaty has broken down between the United States and New Zealand, due to the New Zealand ban on nuclear ships, Australia maintains its ties with both countries.

Under the Five Power Defence Arrangement (FPDA), Australia, New Zealand and the United Kingdom combine to support the security of Singapore and Malaysia. Australia also maintains a formal agreement with Papua New Guinea, both for historical associations and because of its strategic location.

Over the past few years, the military relationship between Indonesia and Australia has intensified and is now our most significant defence relationship in the region. Combined exercises with the Indonesian military are beneficial in providing closer strategic links and goodwill for both countries.

KEY DEFENCE PRIORITIES

The key defence priorities are identified as:
1. to continue to fulfil defence and national commitments of the day with a very high level of professionalism and integrity;
2. to sustain and strengthen Australia's capability for national defence, which will also provide options to contribute to multilateral security efforts;
3. to promote strategic stability and security in our region globally, and to maintain strong alliances;
4. to strengthen the partnership between the Australian Defence Force (ADF) and the Australian community, enhance the capability of Australian industry to support the ADF and, where practicable, establish a support base for the region; and
5. to attract and retain sufficient number of well-trained, highly motivated personnel to support a high technology ADF into the next century and ensure the use of best personnel practices.

The corner stone of Australia's defence policy is self-reliance. The ADF applies its defence strategy — one of 'defence in depth' — through the following means:
- by ensuring that its is able to defend Australia from armed attack;
- by sustaining its alliances; and
- by contributing to a global and regional environment of peace.

DEFENCE OBJECTIVES

- To establish Australia's place in emerging patterns of global strategic relationships and shape them to meet Australia's needs.
- To undertake peacetime operational tasks as directed by government.
- To deal effectively with raids, harassment, incursions and other situations that could arise in the short term.
- To provide a framework for expansion of forces capable of coping with higher levels of threat if Australia's strategic circumstances deteriorate in the longer term.

THE AUSTRALIAN DEFENCE FORCE

The Australian Defence Force (ADF) is made up of three services: the Australian Army, the Royal Australian Air Force and the Royal Australian Navy. It also includes the Australian Defence Force Executive.

Defence Structure

THE MINISTERS

As set out by the *Defence Act 1903*, responsibility for the administration and broad control of the Australian Defence Force rests with the Federal Minister of Defence. Since 1987, the Minister for Defence Science and Personnel has assumed responsibilities within the Defence portfolio for the Defence Science and Technology Organisation and the personnel concerns of the ADF. The Minister of Defence is a member of Cabinet and a junior minister is responsible for Defence Science and Personnel.

CHIEF OF THE DEFENCE FORCE

Headed by the Chief of the Defence Force (CDF), the Australian Defence Force Command provides planning, operational and logistical direction to the services. The CDF is also the principal military adviser to the Minister for Defence and has joint responsibility with the Secretary of the Department of Defence for the administration of the Australian Defence Force.

Together they advise the Minister on human resources policy requirements, including conditions of service for the ADF; the efficient use of its resources; and recommendations for promotions and postings. The CDF may be an admiral, general or air chief marshal.

The Vice Chief of the Defence Force is the CDF's principal staff officer and chief of the headquarters staff. Supervising the operation of Headquarters Australian Defence Force (HQADF), the vice chief directs development of ADF long-term planning, including military defence planning.

THE SECRETARY, DEPARTMENT OF DEFENCE

The Secretary of the Department of Defence is the principal civilian adviser to the Minister on matters of policy, resources, organisation and the use of public funds. As previously mentioned, the Secretary shares responsibility for the administration of the Australian Defence Force with the CDF.

CHIEFS OF STAFF

Each of Australia's three Defence Forces is run by a Chief of Staff; thus the Navy is commanded by the Chief of Naval Staff; the Army by the Chief of the General Staff; and the Air Force by the Chief of the Air Staff.

DEFENCE COMMITTEE SYSTEM

This system was established to formulate policy to achieve government defence objectives, and to make decisions on matters of defence administration, including resource management, and on joint service planning and doctrine. The most important committees are:

THE COUNCIL OF DEFENCE Matters relating to the control and administration of the Defence Force are referred to the Council of Defence by the Minister for Defence, who is a member of the Council along with the Minister for Defence Science and Personnel, the Secretary, the CDF, the service Chiefs of Staff and the Vice Chief of the Defence Force.

THE DEFENCE COMMITTEE The Defence Committee advises the Minister on defence policy, the co-ordination of military, strategic, economic, financial and external affairs, defence policy and joint service or interdepartmental matters. Chaired by the Secretary, the other members of the committee are the CDF, the Chiefs of Staff, and the Secretaries to the Departments of: the Prime Minister and Cabinet; Treasury; and Foreign Affairs and Trade.

DEFENCE FORCE DEVELOPMENT COMMITTEE This committee advises the Minister on force development and resource management, including major equipment and facilities acquisitions, and formulation of the Five-Year Defence Program and annual budgets. Chaired by the Secretary, the committee's members are the CDF and the Chiefs of Staff.

THE CHIEFS OF STAFF COMMITTEE Chaired by the CDF, this committee advises the Chief of the Defence Force in his role as commander.

THE MINISTER AND CHIEFS OF THE ADF AS OF 1 APRIL 1997

Position	*Currently held by*
Minister for Defence	Ian McLachlan
Junior Minister in Charge of Defence Science and Personnel	Bronwyn Bishop
Chief of Defence Force	Lt General John Baker
Secretary, Department of Defence	Mr A Ayers

Position	Currently held by
Vice Chief of the Defence Force	Rear Admiral Robert Walls
Chief of Naval Staff	Vice Admiral Rod Taylor
Chief of the General Staff	Lt General John Sanderson
Chief of the Air Staff	Air Marshal Les Fisher
Chief Defence Scientist	Dr Richard Brabin-Smith

ORGANISATION

The structure which has been established to enable the government to carry out its defence responsibilities is identified by the following programs:
1. Defence Force Executive
2. Navy
3. Army
4. Air Force
5. Strategy and Intelligence
6. Acquisition and Logistics
7. Budget and Management
8. Science and Technology

RANKS

COMMISSIONED OFFICERS

Navy	Army	Air Force
Admiral	General	Air Chief Marshal
Vice Admiral	Lieutenant General	Air Marshal
Rear Admiral	Major General	Air Vice Marshal
Commodore	Brigadier	Air Commodore
Captain	Colonel	Group Captain
Commander	Lieutenant Colonel	Wing Commander
Lieutenant Commander	Major	Squadron Leader
Lieutenant	Captain	Flight Lieutenant
Sub Lieutenant	Lieutenant	Flying Officer
	2nd Lieutenant	Pilot Officer

WARRANT AND NON-COMMISSIONED OFFICERS

Navy	Army	Air Force
Warrant Officer	Warrant Officer Class 1	Warrant Officer
Chief Petty Officer	Warrant Officer Class 2	
	Staff Sergeant	Flight Sergeant
Petty Officer	Sergeant	Sergeant
Leading Seaman	Corporal or Bombardier	Corporal

Personnel

The Australian Defence Force (ADF) is one of Australia's largest employers. The actual staffing level of the ADF at June 1996 (including Reserves) was 106 460 personnel. The relative sizes of each service are shown below.

DISTRIBUTION OF SERVICE PERSONNEL AND CIVILIAN STAFF AS AT JUNE 1996

Location	No. of personnel
Permanent Forces:	
Navy	14 404
Army	25 694
Air Force	17 212
Civilian:	
Forces Executive	623
Navy	3 820
Army	5 503
Air Force	2 133
Strategy & Intelligence	1 054
Aquisitions & Logistics	1 478
Budget & Management	3 220
Science & Technology	2 541
Sub Total	**77 952**
Reserves:	
Navy	1 227
Army	22 274
Air Force	1 348
Ready Reserves:	
Navy	278
Army	3 116
Air Force	265
Sub Total	**28 508**
TOTAL	**106 460**

WOMEN IN THE AUSTRALIAN DEFENCE FORCE

After the *Sex Discrimination Act* was passed and the new Australian Defence Force (ADF) employment policies were adopted in 1984, the percentage of women in all three areas increased dramatically. The percentage of women in the Army rose from 6.1% to 11.1%.

The number of women in the ADF has increased by more than 1000 since 1987. Women now occupy more than 13% of all regular service positions and more than 10% of total personnel. In 1988, the Chief of the Defence Force Army Prize for the most outstanding graduate of the Australian Defence Force Academy went, for the first time, to a woman.

Since December 1992, women have been eligible to compete for about 99% of Royal Australian Navy and Royal Australian Air Force positions and 67% of Army positions. Apart from some minor areas related to specific occupational health concerns, the only categories of employment not open to women are mine clearance diver in the Navy, combat arms in the Army and airfield defence guards in the Air Force.

PERMANENT SERVICE PERSONNEL BY SEX AS AT JUNE 1996

	Navy	Army	Air Force	Total
Men	12 232	23 225	14 425	49 882
	(84.9%)	(89.5%)	(83.8%)	(86.6%)
Women	2 172	2 739	2 754	7 698
	(15.1%)	(10.5%)	(16.2%)	(13.4%)
Total	14 404	25 964	17 012	57 580

Note: The figures reflect all members of the permanent ADF, whether paid or unpaid. Reserves on full-time duty are not included.

AUSTRALIAN DEFENCE FORCE — ENLISTMENTS AS AT 30 JUNE 1996

	Navy		Army		Air Force		ADF	
	Men	Women	Men	Women	Men	Women	Men	Women
Trained force								
Officers	6	0	48	16	0	0	54	16
Other ranks	6	0	554	74	0	0	560	74
Training force								
Officers	162	71	302	65	360	92	824	228
Other ranks	1 042	289	1923	450	575	186	3 540	925
Apprentices	0	0	0	0	0	0	0	0
Total	1 216	360	2 827	605	935	278	4 978	1 243

TOTAL RESERVE FORCE STRENGTH
AS AT 30 JUNE 1996

	Men	Women	Total
Navy	1 025	202	1 227
Army	18 068	4 206	22 274
Air Force	1 082	266	1 348
ADF Total	20 175	4 674	24 849

Note: The figures for reserves are for those with training obligations.

TOTAL READY RESERVE FORCE
STRENGTH AS AT 30 JUNE 1996

	Men	Women	Total
Navy	257	21	278
Army	2 968	148	3 116
Air Force	265	0	265
ADF Total	3 490	169	3 659

Expenditure

The 1995–1996 Defence budget was $10 009.9 million, with the actual outlay being $10 010.6 million.

RESOURCES AND FINANCIAL PROGRAMS

There are three principal categories of Defence spending: investment, which accounts for 26.9% of total budget, personnel 38.7% and operating costs of 34.3%. These proportions are expected to remain relatively unchanged until next century. Commencing in 1996–1997, the government will provide Defence with a five-year budget commitment to facilitate more efficient strategic planning and deployment of funds.

DEFENCE EXPENDITURE BY MAJOR ITEM (1995–1996)

Item	1995–1996 Actual (%)	1996–1997 Estimated (%)
Major and minor capital equipment	22.5	23.0
Facilities	8.1	7.2
Housing	2.5	1.7

Item	1995–1996 Actual (%)	1996–1997 Estimated (%)
Service salaries	29.1	30.3
Civilian salaries	8.6	8.5
Production costs	0.3	0.3
Defence co-operation	0.7	0.7
Maintenance stores	15.2	15.2
Administration expenses	12.9	12.7
Other	0.2	0.2

Training & Education

The Australian Defence Force (ADF) has adopted a through-career approach to military education which focuses on the profession of arms. Military education may be conducted in-house, for example, at the School of Army Education, the various staff colleges, the Australian Defence Force Academy and the Australian College of Defence and Strategic Studies. The ADF also uses a variety of secondary and tertiary educational institutions throughout Australia to provide education where this is more cost-effective, for example, in the training of medical and legal officers.

AUSTRALIAN DEFENCE FORCE ACADEMY

Following a federal government decision in 1977, the Australian Defence Force Academy (ADFA) opened in Canberra in January 1986 as a tri-service training centre. It has a student population of 1500, comprising 900 cadets, 100 undergraduates and 500 post-graduates. There are about 807 military and academic staff. Its main role is to provide a balanced and liberal university education to cadets for the Australian Defence Force's three services, within a military environment. By 1995, after nine graduating classes, the Academy had turned out 1660 young officers. The pass rate of cadets is approximately 60% and about 23% of the cadets are female.

Australian Defence Force Command

The Australian Defence Force (ADF) Command is headed by the Chief of the Defence Force (CDF) and serves to provide support for the dual role of this position; as the principal military adviser to the Minister for Defence and Commander of the Australian Defence Force. It is based at Headquarters Australian Defence Force (HQADF) in Canberra which, reflecting the value of an integrated command for the ADF, has developed and grown in recent years. The ADF Command provides planning, operational and logistical direction to the services.

The Vice Chief of the Defence Force is the CDF's principal staff officer and chief of the headquarters staff.

Other responsibilities of the ADF Command are to ensure that the ADF is in 'readiness' to deal with short-term contingencies and otherwise organise joint operations.

ACTIVITIES ORGANISED BY ADF COMMAND IN 1995–1996

PEACEKEEPING FORCES
The Australian Defence Force's contribution to United Nations (UN) and other multinational peace operations has included medical teams, engineers, movement control personnel, communicators, aviation and self-contained units including infantry battalions and naval task groups.

Australian troops have been deployed in Cambodia, Mozambique, Namibia, Somalia, Rwanda and the Middle East. In 1995–1996, HMAS Melbourne was deployed in the Middle East to provide support for the UN resolutions against Iraq.

NON UNITED NATIONS OPERATIONS
Australia currently provides a contingent of 27 Australian Defence Force personnel and a Force Commander in the Sinai region of Egypt, as part of a multinational force of observers. The South Pacific Peace Keeping Force in Bougainville is another non-UN peace operation.

INTERNATIONAL PROGRAMS In 1993, Australian military communications personnel helped to safeguard general elections in Cambodia and engineers continue to provide mine clearing advice and technical support to the Cambodian military. Army signallers provided communication support to the UN in the Western Sahara. Medical support and training was provided to the Solomon Islands Government and construction personnel assisted with accommodation construction in Vanuatu. In 1995–1996, Army personnel continued to oversee the destruction of Iraqi methods of mass destruction and continued work in Cambodia providing technical advice and training on the detection and clearance of mines. Mine clearance operations and education programs in Mozambique, under way since 1994, continued in 1995–1996.

COMBINED EXERCISES   During 1995–1996, Australian forces took part in combined military exercises with Canada, Japan, Chile, Republic of Korea, Papua New Guinea, Thailand, Indonesia, New Zealand, Malaysia, Singapore and the United States. The ADF plans to continue and expand upon the current program of international training and exercise activities into the next decade and beyond.

The Royal Australian Navy

HISTORY

At the time of federation in 1901, Australia's naval resources consisted of ships of the Royal (British) Navy stationed in Australian waters; an auxiliary squadron provided through an 1887 agreement with Britain which was paid for partly by the Australian government and could only be deployed in local waters; and some boats transferred to the Commonwealth government from state governments.

Captain R. Cresswell, formerly Queensland's naval commandant, was made director of Australia's naval forces in December 1904 and subsequently became the principal naval adviser to the newly formed Council of Defence, formed in 1905.

In 1910, the Labor Minister for Defence, Senator Pearce, organised for a recently retired Royal Navy admiral, Sir Reginald Henderson, to formulate a blueprint for the Australian navy's development. Henderson came up with a grandiose plan, projected over a period of 22 years, and although the Commonwealth government rejected the overall scheme they did undertake to implement some of its suggestions. A ship-building program was set in motion which would provide Australia with battlecruisers, cruisers, destroyers and submarines. Some of this fleet was commissioned from overseas shipwrights, while others were built at Cockatoo Island in Sydney.

In July 1911, the title Royal Australian Navy (RAN) was formally approved by King George V and, on 4 October 1913, Australia's new fleet sailed proudly into Sydney Harbour. The RAN's first commander was Rear Admiral Sir George Patey.

ROLE

The role of the Royal Australian Navy (RAN) is to provide maritime forces for Australia's defence and to protect Australian interests in its proximity. It must also be able to provide protection in any likely maritime contingency and have the capacity for future expansion when and if it is required.

The RAN maintains operational effectiveness through joint operations with the Army and Air Force and also with the New Zealand and United States navies.

The Chief of Naval Staff (CNS) is the senior Navy Officer. The RAN's headquarters are at the Department of Defence (Navy Office) in Canberra and its Maritime Headquarters are in Sydney.

THE RAN FLEET

Type of Vessel	Name	Location
3 guided missile destroyers	HMAS *Perth*	Sydney NSW
	HMAS *Hobart*	Sydney NSW
	HMAS *Brisbane*	Sydney NSW
6 guided missile frigates	HMAS *Adelaide*	Garden Is. WA
	HMAS *Canberra*	Sydney NSW
	HMAS *Sydney*	Garden Is. WA
	HMAS *Darwin*	Sydney NSW
	HMAS *Melbourne*	Sydney NSW
	HMAS *Newcastle*	Sydney NSW
3 River class	HMAS *Torrens*	Garden Is. WA
destroyer escorts	HMAS *Derwent*	Garden Is. WA
	HMAS *Swan*	Garden Is. WA
4 Oberon class submarines	HMAS *Ovens*	Sydney NSW
	HMAS *Onslow*	Sydney NSW
	HMAS *Orion*	Garden Is. WA
	HMAS *Otama*	Sydney NSW
2 Collins class submarines	HMAS *Collins*	Garden Is. WA
	HMAS *Farncomb*	Garden Is. WA
2 minehunter inshore	HMAS *Rushcutter*	Sydney NSW
	HMAS *Shoalwater*	Sydney NSW
1 amphibious heavy lift ship	HMAS *Tobruk*	Sydney NSW
6 landing craft heavy	LCH *Wewak*	Cairns Qld
	HMAS *Balikpapan*	Darwin NT
	HMAS *Tarakan*	Cairns Qld
	HMAS *Labuan*	Cairns Qld
	HMAS *Betano*	Sydney NSW
	HMAS *Brunei*	Sydney NSW
15 Fremantle class patrol boats	HMAS *Fremantle*	Sydney NSW
	HMAS *Wollongong*	Darwin NT

Type of Vessel	Name	Location
	HMAS Dubbo	Darwin NT
	HMAS Geraldton	Garden Is. WA
	HMAS Bunbury	Garden Is. WA
	HMAS Ipswich	Cairns Qld
	HMAS Townsville	Cairns Qld
	HMAS Bendigo	Cairns Qld
	HMAS Whyalla	Cairns Qld
	HMAS Gladstone	Cairns Qld
	HMAS Warrnambool	Sydney NSW
	HMAS Cessnock	Darwin NT
	HMAS Launceston	Darwin NT
	HMAS Gawler	Darwin NT
	HMAS Geelong	Darwin NT
1 fleet oiler	HMAS Success	Sydney NSW
1 auxiliary tanker	HMAS Westralia	Garden Is. WA
2 hydrographic survey ships	HMAS Moresby	Garden Is. WA
	HMAS Flinders	Cairns Qld
4 survey motor launches	HMAS Paluma	Cairns Qld
	HMAS Mermaid	Cairns Qld
	HMAS Shepparton	Cairns Qld
	HMAS Benalla	Cairns Qld
1 trials & safety vessel	HMAS Protector	Garden Is. WA
2 general purpose vessels	GPV Banks	Sydney NSW
	GPV Ardent	Sydney NSW
3 auxiliary minesweepers	AM Koraaga	Sydney NSW
	AM Brolga	Sydney NSW
	AM Bermagui	Sydney NSW
2 auxiliary minesweepers	AM Bandicoot	Sydney NSW
— tugs	AM Wallaroo	Sydney NSW
1 youth sail training ship	STS Young Endeavour	Cairns Qld

FLEET AIR ARM

The Fleet Air Arm operates 7 Westland Sea King Mk50, Mk 50A, 3 Bell Kiowa 206B1, 16 Seahawk S-70B-2, 6 Squirrel AS 350B helicopters and 2 Hawker Siddeley HS748 electronic warfare training aircraft from HMAS Albatross, the Naval Air Station at Nowra in New South Wales. The RAN also operates Jindivik pilotless target aircraft from Jervis Bay airfield, as realistic target aircraft for defence force missile practices.

COMMISSIONED ESTABLISHMENTS

Establishment	Name	Location
Headquarters–Area Administration	HMAS *Kuttabul*	Sydney NSW
Naval air station	HMAS *Albatross*	Nowra NSW
Submarine base	HMAS *Platypus*	Sydney NSW
Ship and submarine base	HMAS *Stirling*	Garden Is. WA
Patrol boat base	HMAS *Cairns*	Cairns Qld
Patrol boat base and communications station	HMAS *Coonawarra*	Darwin NT
Mine warfare and patrol boat base	HMAS *Waterhen*	Sydney NSW
Training establishments	HMAS *Cerberus*	Crib Point Vic.
	HMAS *Creswell*	Jervis Bay ACT
	HMAS *Penguin*	Middle Head NSW
	HMAS *Watson*	Watsons Bay NSW
Communications station/ Area administration	HMAS *Harman*	Canberra ACT

NON-COMMISSIONED ESTABLISHMENTS

Establishments	Location
Jervis Bay Range Facility	Jervis Bay ACT
Naval Supply Centre	Sydney NSW
Naval Supply Depot	Randwick NSW
Naval Armament Depots	Newington NSW
	Kingswood NSW
	Somerton Vic.
Naval armament and equipment depots	Garden Is. WA
	Maribyrnong Vic.
RAN Missile Maintenance Establishment	Kingswood NSW
RAN Torpedo Maintenance Establishment	North Sydney NSW
RAN Training Establishment	Salisbury SA
Naval Communication Stations	Canberra ACT
	Exmouth WA
	Darwin NT
Naval Communications Area Master Station Australia (NAVCAMAUS)	Canberra ACT
Naval Communications Area Local Stations (NAVCALS)	Sydney NSW
	Nowra NSW
	Cairns Qld
	Fremantle WA

Establishments	Location
Naval Support Offices	Brisbane Qld
	Adelaide SA
	Hobart Tas.

NAVAL ASSISTANCE TO THE COMMUNITY

- assistance with coastal surveillance
- search and rescue
- assistance to the community following natural disasters such as bushfires
- recompression chambers at HMAS Stirling and HMAS Penguin used for treatment of diving related accidents

NAVAL ENTRY REQUIREMENTS AND EARLY TRAINING

Various entry schemes are available depending on age, educational standard, final employment and interests. New entry training is conducted at the following places:

- HMAS *Nirimba* at Quakers Hill. Centre for trade training, including courses for apprentices aged between 15 and 18 years, and direct entry tradesmen, and for training general duties sailors.
- HMAS *Cerberus* at Crib Point, Victoria, training centre for all general entry, non-apprentice recruits aged between 16 and 28. Common basic training is given followed by category training courses.
- Advanced category training is conducted at various establishments at HMAS *Penguin* and HMAS *Watson* in Sydney and the Naval Air Station at Nowra, New South Wales. Specialist courses are conducted in the United States and United Kingdom.

OFFICER ENTRY

AUSTRALIAN DEFENCE FORCE ACADEMY

Permanent commission applicants must be between 17 and 20 years of age and must meet service selection criteria and matriculation requirements of the University of NSW in their specialised subject. Successful applicants study for a degree at the Australian Defence Force Academy, with additional service, military and professional studies. Officer appointees specialise in Seaman, Supply and Secretariat, Engineering or Instruction Branches.

ROYAL AUSTRALIAN NAVAL COLLEGE

Short service commissions are for nine years (including two years training) and have an age requirement of 17–24 years. Matriculation to a degree course at an Australian university or institute of technical and further education, or four passes at Year 12 level are also required. Initial training is at the Royal Australian Naval College at Jervis Bay, then in RAN ships and establishments.

Direct Entry

Professionally qualified personnel including doctors, nurses, teachers, engineers and lawyers below the age of 31 years are eligible as Direct Entry Officers. Their initial training is at Jervis Bay.

RAN Staff College

The RAN Staff College at HMAS *Penguin*, New South Wales prepares RAN officers of Lieutenant Commander and Lieutenant rank for command and staff appointments. Each year there are two courses of 22 weeks duration. The student capacity of 28 usually comprises 20 naval officers, one officer from each of the Army, the Royal Australian Air Force, the United States Navy and the Royal New Zealand Navy, as well as two Public Service commission officers and two Defence Co-operation Program students.

ROYAL AUSTRALIAN NAVAL RESERVE

The Royal Australian Naval Reserve (RANR) involves a commitment of at least 28 days part-time training each year, made up of about 3 nights training a month and one annual period of 12 days continuous training either at sea or ashore. The pay for all reserve forces is tax free. Reserve personnel must be from 17–34 years of age; 20–42 years of age for officers.

The Australian Army

History

Upon federation in 1901, responsibility for defence passed from the states to the federal government. The combined military forces at that time consisted of 29 000 men, of whom 1500 were regular soldiers, and a naval force of less than 2000 men, of which 250 were on full-time service.

The states' forces were not formally transferred to the Commonwealth until 1 March 1901, and the first Federal Department of Defence was formed from the staff of the Victorian Department, who were transferred on 1 June 1901. The first commander of the Australian Forces was a senior British officer, Major General Sir Edward Hutton, who arrived in Australia to take up his position at the end of January 1902.

Hutton returned to England in late 1904 and was replaced by three military personnel and two civilians, one of them the Minister of Defence. Known as the Australian Military Board, they started work on 12 January

1905 and such was the success of this system that it remained in place for 70 years (with a brief break during World War II).

In September 1905, the Australian National Defence League, an independent organisation, was set up in Sydney. This small but vociferous body advocated universal military training for men as a necessary step in raising a national defence force. To promote their ideas they produced a magazine called *The Call*.

In 1907, the then Prime Minister Alfred Deakin announced to parliament that his government would introduce compulsory training and a Bill to this effect was introduced and passed in September 1908. The requirement was for compulsory drilling of boys aged 12–17 years and annual training for 18- to 20-year-olds with the citizen forces.

This scheme was implemented in July 1911 with an amendment suggested by Field Marshal Lord Kitchener on an Australian visit, that the age limit be raised to include 25-year-olds. Kitchener had also suggested that a military college be established to train the staff officers who would be needed to manage a compulsory training scheme.

In June 1911, the Royal Military College was opened in Canberra, the planned site for the new capital. That year, when compulsory training began, more than 90 000 youths were involved and this grew by 20 000 more each year for the next two years. There were 28 000 prosecutions for non-attendance in the first three months of the scheme and 5732 youths were jailed; others were fined.

ROLE

The role of the Army is to provide ground forces for Australia's defence, with the capacity for expansion to meet future requirements. The Chief of General Staff is the senior officer of the Australian Army.

The Army is divided into three commands: Land, Logistic and Training Commands.

LAND COMMAND   With headquarters in Sydney, the Land Command controls the training and readiness of all field army units of the Australian Army, Regular and Army Reserve.

LOGISTIC COMMAND   Based in Melbourne, the Logistic Command controls the principal logistic elements of the Australian Army, i.e. transport, repair and supply support (the largest of the three commands).

TRAINING COMMAND   Based in Sydney, the Training Command is responsible for all individual training and commands all Army training establishments and schools except the Royal Military College, Duntroon, which is under the command of the Chief of the General Staff.

MILITARY DISTRICTS

Administrative support for the Commands is provided by the seven Military Districts into which the country is divided. Military District Headquarters also handle matters which involve state and Commonwealth governments.

1st Military District —	the state of Queensland
2nd Military District —	the state of New South Wales, excluding southern and south-western New South Wales
3rd Military District —	the state of Victoria and part of southern New South Wales
4th Military District —	the state of South Australia, plus part of south-western New South Wales
5th Military District —	the state of Western Australia, less the Kimberley local government area
6th Military District —	the state of Tasmania
7th Military District —	the Northern Territory, plus the Kimberley local government area of Western Australia

CORPS

The Australian Army is composed of 23 functional groups, or Corps. Each member of the Army, whether he or she be a regular or reserve soldier, belongs to a Corps.

COMBAT

The Royal Australian Armoured Corps (RAAC)
The Royal Regiment of Australian Artillery (RAA)
The Royal Australian Infantry Corps (RA Inf)
The Australian Army Aviation Corps (AA Avn)

COMBAT SUPPORT

The Royal Australian Engineers (RAE)
The Royal Australian Corps of Signals (RA Sigs)
Australian Intelligence Corps (Aust Int Corps)
The Royal Australian Corps of Transport (RACT)
The Royal Australian Army Ordnance Corps (RAAOC)
The Royal Australian Electrical and Mechanical Engineers (RAEME)

COMBAT SERVICE SUPPORT

The Royal Australian Survey Corps (RA Svy)
The Royal Australian Army Medical (RAAMC)
The Royal Australian Dental Corps (RAADC)
The Royal Australian Nursing Corps (RAANC)

The Australian Army Psychology Corps (AAPSYCH)
Royal Australian Corps of Military Police (RACMP)
The Australian Army Catering Corps (AACC)
The Royal Australian Army Chaplains Department (RAAChD)
The Australian Army Legal Corps (AALC)
The Royal Australian Army Educational Corps (RAAEC)
Australian Army Band Corps (AABC)
The Royal Australian Army Pay Corps (RAAPC)
Australian Army Public Relations Service (AAPRS)

COMBAT FORCE

The structure of the Army combat force is based on provision of:
* a ready deployment force;
* a manoeuvre force;
* ready deployment force augmentation units;
* expansion base force for higher levels of conflict; and
* communication support forces.

These forces enable the Army to deploy highly mobile forces to any part of Australia, and to conduct operations in harsh terrain which lacks infrastructure and resources.

THE ARMY RESERVE

Applicants for the Army Reserve must be at least 17 years of age and under 35 years. If a reservist has a particular skill, this age limit may be raised to 42 years. Reservists must also have or be applying for Australian citizenship. Minimum height is 152 cm (5 ft). The commitment is a minimum of 26 days per year, 14 of which are full-time.

ARMY ENTRY REQUIREMENTS AND EARLY TRAINING

There are a number of different forms of entry to the Army. However, the basic requirements for enlistment follow.

AGE   There are different age limits depending on the type of entry into the Army sought.

HEIGHT   Applicants must be at least 152 cm (men *and* women) in height.

MEDICAL   Applicants must meet Army fitness standards (a history of epilepsy or asthma, for example, bars an applicant from being accepted into the Army).

CITIZENSHIP   The applicant must be an Australian citizen or eligible for grant of citizenship, or must undertake to apply for citizenship when eligible to do so.

SOLDIERS/GENERAL ENTRY

There are approximately 3500 vacancies for general entry to the Army each year. Applicants must be over the age of 17 and under 35 (or up to 42 if the applicant has specialist skills). They are selected through interview, aptitude and medical tests conducted at the Defence Force Recruiting Centre.

Various trade, apprentice, musician and adult trade enlistment schemes also exist under general entry, with varying entry requirements.

All soldiers enlist initially for a period of four years under the Open Ended Enlistment Scheme. Early discharge will only be given if:

(i)   a minimum period of 4 years has been served;
(ii)   any Return of Service Obligation incurred by long-term schooling or overseas postings has been paid back; and
(iii)   a minimum notice period of six months is given.

Only in exceptional circumstances will discharge be granted prior to the completion of four years service.

SOLDIER TRAINING

All non-commissioned enlistees to the Army, except those who come in under the apprentice scheme, receive 12 weeks basic training at the 1st Recruiting Training Battalion in Kapooka, Wagga Wagga, New South Wales.

This basic training includes field craft, shooting, drill, physical training, Army customs and procedures, first aid and small arms training. Emphasis is on teamwork, self-organisation and self-discipline. Graduation from the course is with the rank of private or equivalent (depending on the Corps allocated). This initial training is followed by advanced training for a specialist role, conducted at a Corps school.

Apprenticeship enlistees can learn one of a number of trades. Their first two years are spent at the Army Apprentices School at Bonegilla (near Wodonga) in Victoria, where they receive military and trade training.

OFFICER ENTRY

Officers and cadets are given a Queen's Commission on appointment. Resignation is by agreement of the Governor-General only, and is not accepted when an Officer has a Return of Service Obligation (one year of service is owed for each year of training, plus one year, so 3 years training = 4 years Return of Service Obligation).

AUSTRALIAN DEFENCE FORCE ACADEMY

The Australian Defence Force Academy (AFDA) has approximately 372 vacancies a year for Cadet Officers. There is an age limit of 17–19 years, although applicants who are younger than 17 may be accepted.

Successful applicants must meet University of NSW entry requirements and the subject requirements of the University College.

Cadet Officers take a three-year degree courses in science, engineering or the arts, followed by a year of military training at the Royal Military College Duntroon, then graduation as a lieutenant. Honours students in arts and science and all engineering students return to the AFDA to complete their degrees.

Students have a fully paid appointment as an officer cadet while studying for a degree, and dress in uniform. Cadets of all three services study together at the AFDA, which was opened in January 1986 as a college of the University of NSW.

ROYAL MILITARY COLLEGE DUNTROON

The Royal Military College Duntroon has approximately 240 vacancies a year. Applicants should be 18–22 years of age, or up to 25 years of age for tertiary qualified entrants and 27 years of age for in-service entrants. They must hold passes in English and three other subjects at Year 12 level.

Training takes the form of an 18-month leadership, management and military skills course which leads on conclusion to a commission as Lieutenant (General Service Officer).

AUSTRALIAN COLLEGE OF DEFENCE AND STRATEGIC STUDIES

The Australian College of Defence and Strategic Studies has approximately 40 vacancies a year. One-third of these positions are open to overseas participants. The course is one year in duration.

DIRECT ENTRY

To satisfy its continuing needs for professional medical and technical staff, the Army has a number of direct entry recruitment schemes which offer applicants with specific qualifications and skills a commission at varying levels of rank.

SPECIALIST SERVICE OFFICERS   Direct entry as a Specialist Service Officer (SSO) is offered to graduates in the following professions: Medical Officer, Pharmaceutical Officer, Medical Technical Officer, Dental Officer, Nursing Officer, Education Officer, Psychologist, Public Relations Officer, Legal Officer and Pilot.

Appointments are made for an initial period of two to five years. Newly commissioned SSOs attend a course at the Land Warfare Centre, Canungra, Queensland.

GENERAL SERVICE OFFICERS   Direct Entry as a General Service Officer (GSO) can currently be made in the following categories: Engineer, Computer Scientist, Food Technologist and Fuel Technologist.

Initially appointed for five years, of which the first 18 months is probationary, GSOs may apply for a permanent commission after four years.

THE UNDERGRADUATE SCHEME

Applicants for the Undergraduate Scheme must be at least 18 years old and be partly qualified in one of the following disciplines: medicine, a technical medical course, pharmacy, dentistry, psychology, nursing, engineering or computer science.

Applicants must continue to study in a course approved by the Army. Vacancies in the various professions vary each year.

THE ARMY RESERVE

Officer Cadet Training Units, located in each military district provide precommissioning training for the majority of officers for the Army Reserve.

The Royal Australian Air Force

HISTORY

In early 1909, the Aerial League of Australia was formed in Sydney, championing the idea that Australia should establish an aviation corps. Although there was some pressure on the government at this time to develop the idea, it held off until the end of 1911. In June that year, the Minister of Defence, Senator Pearce, attended an imperial conference in Britain and on his return the government decided to go ahead and advertised positions for two flight instructors in the *Commonwealth of Australia Gazette*.

In July 1912, the positions were filled and four aircraft ordered from Britain. The Flying School began in February 1914 on 295 hectares of land purchased at Point Cook in Victoria and the first intake began training on 17 August that year.

The Australian Flying Corps was created during World War I, in 1916. Four Australian squadrons were formed during the war using some of the pilots trained at Point Cook. The Corps saw active duty on the western front and in the Middle East. In 1921, the Royal Australian Air Force (RAAF) came into being.

ROLE

The role of the RAAF is to provide air forces suitable for the defence of Australia, working in conjunction with maritime and land forces, and designed for longer term expansion as necessary. The Chief of Air Staff is the senior Air Force officer.

There are two functional commands within the RAAF: Air Command and Support Command.

AIR COMMAND   The RAAF Air Command organises air operations and operational training. It has headquarters at Glenbrook in New South Wales and has a number of subdivisions.

SUBDIVISIONS OF THE RAAF AIR COMMAND

Group	Aircraft	Location
Strike/Reconnaissance Group	F-111/RF-111C	Amberley Qld
Tactical Fighter Group	F/A-18	Williamtown Vic.
	F/A-18	Tindal NT
Maritime Patrol Group	P3C Orion	Edinburgh SA
Tactical Transport Group	Caribou	Amberley Qld
	Caribou	Townsville Qld
Special Transport Squadron	DA 900 (Falcon)	Fairbairn ACT
	HS 748	East Sale Vic.
Aircraft Research & Development	F/A-18	Edinburgh SA
	Macchi MB.326H	
	Pilatus PC-9/A	
	UH-1H Iroquois	
	C-47 Dakota	
	Nomad	

SUPPORT COMMAND   Responsible for basic training logistics and maintenance of RAAF equipment, the Support Command has its headquarters in Melbourne.

SUPPORT COMMAND AIRCRAFT AND TRAINING LOCATIONS

Usage	Aircraft	Location
Basic Pilot Training	CT4, Macchi, PC9	Point Cook, Pearce
Instructor Pilot Training	CT4, Macchi, PC9	East Sale
Navigator Training	HS748	East Sale

TRAINING

AUSTRALIAN DEFENCE FORCE ACADEMY
The Australian Defence Force Academy (AFDA) is the primary source of tertiary-qualified entrants to the General Duties, Engineer and Supply branches of the Officer Corps.

OFFICER TRAINING RAAF COLLEGE
This college at Point Cook, Victoria, trains officers other than those entering through the Australian Defence Force Academy. It also conducts a Basic Staff Course.

BASIC AIRCREW TRAINING
See Support Command Aircraft & Location table on previous page.

Aircrew (Flight Engineers, Loadmasters and Air Electronics Analysts) are given basic training at Edinburgh and Laverton.

STAFF COLLEGE
The RAAF Staff College, Fairbairn, conducts staff courses running for 11 months for senior officers intended for staff and command appointments. It takes 46 new students per year.

GROUND TRAINING Initial basic training takes place at Edinburgh School of Radio, Laverton. The School of Technical Training Wagga includes Catering, Clerical and Man Management courses.

Acquisition & Logistics

Acquisition and Logistics plans and implements long-term investment in equipment and infrastructure, particularly through the use of Australian industry and resources.

There are three specific areas of activity: procurement of capital equipment and capital facilities; logistics and Australian industry involvement and contracting. In 1995–1996, the following program levels were achieved:

SUMMARY OF RESOURCES

Subprogram	Outlay ($'000)	No. of Personnel
Major capital equipment	2 145 601	1 584
Logistics	47 380	671
Industry involvement and contracting	39 643	241
Total	2 232 624	2 496

PROCUREMENT OF CAPITAL FACILITIES

This is the development of the infrastructure of bases, airfields, communications stations, training and other facilities in accordance with the government's policy, which reflects the emphasis on operations in the north and north-west of Australia.

In 1995–1996, expenditure on capital equipment and facilities in Australia (other than housing) totalled $1 994 987 000. Expenditure overseas was $906 771 000. Major work included: the acquisition of new Collins class submarines from the Australian Submarine Corporation; the construction of radar sites in Queensland and Western Australia for the Jindalee Operational Radar Network; the acquisition of new ANZAC class frigates; construction facilities for the Minehunter Coastal (MHC) project at Newcastle, New South Wales; and upgraded accommodation at various Navy, Army and Air Force establishments.

LOGISTICS

The role of the Defence Logistics Organisation is to plan and implement logistic support to the ADF in the most efficient and economic manner feasible, using civil resources where possible, and maintaining the capacity for expansion to meet longer term contingencies.

The Defence Logistics Organisation is composed as follows: Logistics Projects, Logistics Policy, Logistics Resources, Defence Quality Assurance and Joint Movements and Transport.

AUSTRALIAN INDUSTRY INVOLVEMENT

The Australian Industry Involvement policy is described in the 1994 Defence White Paper. The aim is to make use of Australian resources for existing needs (ranging from capital equipment through to rations), and to foster Australian technology and support facilities (from research through to manufacture).

In 1995–1996, some 80% of ADF expenditure on facilities, equipment, goods and services was spent in Australia. This percentage, which represents a major increase over the last decade, is largely the result of Australian industry involvement in major equipment projects. These projects increased the share of capital equipment expenditure in Australia from 25% in 1984–1985 to almost 69% in 1995–1996.

As well as this, there is a government owned and managed industrial base to research, develop and manufacture supplies and equipment as required by the ADF. Australian industry involvement ranges from major ship repair and heavy engineering (such as gun manufacture) through chemicals, explosives and clothing manufacture, to the maintenance of complex weapons systems. A government-owned company was formed in 1989 to manage the defence factories and Garden Island Dockyard called Australian Defence Industries Pty Ltd.

AUSTRALIAN DEFENCE INDUSTRIES

Australian Defence Industries (ADI) operates in four business divisions.
1. Naval Engineering Division — ADI Garden Island Facility
   ADI St Marys Electronics Facility
2. Ammunition and Missiles Division — ADI Footscray Facility
   ADI Mulwala Facility
   ADI St Marys Facility
   ADI Salisbury Facility
3. Weapons and Engineering Division — ADI Bendigo Facility
   ADI Maribyrnong Facility
   ADI Lithgow Facility
4. Military Clothing Division — ADI Coburg Facility

The Forces Executive

The Forces Executive provides the command structure for the Australian Defence Force. Its responsibilities are divisible into seven major areas:
1. Strategic Operations and Plans
2. Military Strategic and Force Development
3. Personnel
4. Emergency Management Australia
5. Executive Support
6. Australian Defence Force Superannuation
7. Defence Housing

DISTRIBUTION OF RESOURCES IN 1995–1996

Area	Outlay ($m)	Personnel
Strategic Operations and Plans	58 907	331
Military Strategic and Force Development	12 260	157
Personnel	167 300	1 904
Emergency Management Australia	11 262	59
Executive Support	36 442	1 305
Australian Defence Force Superannuation	14 604	-
Defence Housing	318 443	7 336

SUPERANNUATION

The Military Superannuation and Benefits Scheme (MSBS) was introduced in October 1991 and superseded the Defence Force Retirement and Death Benefits Scheme. The scheme aims to provide members of the ADF with an occupational superannuation scheme that meets the needs of serving and retiring service personnel and accords with community standards.

RETIREMENT BENEFITS There is compulsory retirement in the ADF at 55 years of age. From enlistment, a percentage of salary is paid into the MSBS. After a certain number of years service, retirement pay is calculated at a percentage of current salary; the rate rises for each additional year of service (e.g. 51.25% for 30 years of service and 76.5% after 40 years).

INVALIDITY BENEFIT A lump sum or pension is paid depending on the amount of incapacity. In the event of death, pensions are payable to eligible dependants.

EMERGENCY MANAGEMENT AUSTRALIA

Emergency Management Australia (EMA) co-ordinates practical assistance from Commonwealth sources including the Australian Defence Force. It also plans, advises and co-ordinates the Commonwealth disaster response in the south-west Pacific and Papua New Guinea, on behalf of the Australian International Development Assistance Bureau.

The organisation produces publications and holds seminars to promote public awareness and preparedness for natural disasters such as floods and cyclones, and other disasters such as oil spills and airport emergencies.

DEFENCE HOUSING

Defence Housing, as its name suggests, provides and maintains housing for eligible ADF personnel and, where applicable, for civilian personnel.

Budget & Management

This division oversees five areas of the Australian Defence Force: personnel and management; finance; program delivery assessment; regional support and facilities, including property assets.

The Budget and Management division consists of the central divisions and agencies which provide overall services to the Defence organisation.

RESOURCES EXPENDED ON
CORPORATE SERVICES IN 1993–94

Area	Outlay ($'000)	Personnel
Personnel and management	118 212	583
Finance	4 580	366
Program delivery assessment	8 875	126
Regional support	163 992	1 933
Facilities	533 447	164
Total	829 106	3 172

PERSONNEL AND MANAGEMENT

The objective in this area is to develop and oversee policies on personnel, management and support; organisational and administrative resources; legal and security services; and to manage associated information systems and services.

HUMAN RESOURCES Activities include principles of:
- generalist graduate recruitment to improve the quality of the administration of the Public Service and Defence. In 1995, the target for Graduate Administrative Assistants in Canberra was 50 people. Ninety offers were made to graduates and 39 were accepted. Recruitment is difficult in several professional and technical areas, e.g. Computer Systems Officers;
- internal mobility to provide staff with greater job variety;
- training and development of civilian personnel: supervisors have responsibility for the training and development of their staff;
- equal employment opportunity.

Strategy & Intelligence

The objective of this area of the Australian Defence Force is to develop strategic and international defence policy and guidance, and co-ordinate Defence programs and budgets. Its four divisions are: International and Strategic Policy; Force Development and Planning; Intelligence and Program Management.

INTERNATIONAL STRATEGIC POLICY AND DEFENCE CO-OPERATION

This division promotes Australia's security interests in the South Pacific and South East Asia (particularly Papua New Guinea and the ASEAN countries) and organises co-operative defence activities with countries in those regions, encouraging their defence self-reliance, and view of Australia as a primary defence partner. It is also involved in United Nations and other international endeavours which promote Australia's security.

STRATEGIC POLICY   Based on the Defence White Paper, this policy aims to:
- extend understanding of the strategic factors that could affect the security of the Australian region and the ADF's role in overcoming them;
- analyse the nature of conflict in Australia's strategic environment in the context of regional political and military developments;
- support the development of operational concepts and plans, including the definition of priorities.

International policy also falls within this area, with key activities being with the United States, New Zealand, Papua New Guinea and the South Pacific, Asia, Europe-NATO and the United Nations.

INTELLIGENCE

There are two defence intelligence organisations; the Defence Signals Directorate and the Defence Intelligence Organisation.

DEFENCE SIGNALS DIRECTORATE   Active in the areas of foreign signals intelligence and communications and computer security. The DSD operates in conjunction with joint and single Service staffs and other intelligence and security agencies, and with counterpart agencies overseas.

DEFENCE INTELLIGENCE ORGANISATION   Formed in March 1989 by the merger of the Joint Intelligence Organisation and the Headquarters of the Australian Defence Force (HQADF) intelligence staff, the Defence Intelligence

Organisation compiles and assesses information about international events relevant to Australia's strategic environment, defence policy formulation and military planning.

The Joint Intelligence Organisation provides support to Australia's contributions to UN Peacekeeping activities in areas such as the Middle East, Africa and Asia. It also provides assistance to Papua New Guinea and other South Pacific countries (including disaster relief) and assistance in relation to arms control matters.

Science & Technology

DEFENCE SCIENCE AND TECHNOLOGY ORGANISATION

The Defence Science and Technology Organisation (DSTO) has as its main objective the enhancement of Australia and its people through the application of science and technology. DSTO also contributes to the development of new or enhanced defence capabilities by assisting the defence organisation with evaluation of purchasing options, extending the life of existing equipment, and developing technologies to meet specific Australian defence requirements and conditions. DSTO research comprises three key areas: aeronautical and maritime research; electronics and surveillance research; and the executive, which provides corporate management, policy advice, management of DSTO's interaction with industry, and administrative support.

The Chief Defence Scientist is the chief adviser on science and technology to the Secretary and the Chief of the Defence Forces, and is head of the DSTO.

DEFENCE SATELLITE NETWORK   This network consists of 11 sites including Canberra and Adelaide. It provides high quality communications links for the defence integrated secure communications network.

KURU MUNA (EYE IN THE DARK)   Kuru Muna is an advanced system of thermal imaging, wide-area surveillance and infra-red target identification which is transportable.

SEARCH AND RESCUE DYE MARKER   This is used in the location of people or vessels in distress at sea. It is visible for up to 8 km from an altitude of 1500 m.

Defence Force Awards

COLLECTIVE AWARDS

WARLIKE OPERATIONS
- The Australian Active Service Medal

NON-WARLIKE OPERATIONS
- The Australian Service Medal

INDIVIDUAL AWARDS

OPERATIONAL
FOR GALLANTRY
- The Victoria Cross for Australia
- The Star of Gallantry
- The Medal for Gallantry
- The Commendation for Gallantry

FOR DISTINGUISHED SERVICE
- The Distinguished Service Cross
- The Distinguished Service Medal
- The Commendation for Distinguished Service

UNIT CITATIONS
- The Unit Citation for Gallantry
- The Meritorious Unit Citation

OPERATIONAL/NON-OPERATIONAL
- The Nursing Service Cross

NON-OPERATIONAL
- The Conspicuous Service Cross
- The Conspicuous Service Medal
- The Champion Shots Medal

LONG SERVICE AWARDS (ESTABLISHED 1982)
- Defence Force Service Medal
- Reserve Force Decoration
- Reserve Force Medal
- Australian Service Medal

To date, the areas of operations which have been declared as prescribed areas for the award of the Australian Service Medal are: Uganda, for members of the Commonwealth Military Training Team; Namibia, for members of the United Nations Transition Assistance Group; Iran/Iraq, for members of the United Nations Iran/Iraq Military Observer Group; and Sinai, for members of the Military Observer Group and Multinational Force.

Australian Security Intelligence Organisation

The Australian Security Intelligence Organisation (ASIO) was established in 1949. ASIO is controlled by the following Acts of Parliament: the *Australian Security Intelligence Organisation Act 1979*; the *Telecommunications (Interception) Act 1979*; and the *Inspector-General of Intelligence and Security Act 1986*.

ASIO is an advisory body intended to obtain, analyse and impart, where appropriate, intelligence relevant to security, including foreign intelligence obtained within Australia, and to advise Ministers and Commonwealth authorities on security matters.

ASIO's policies are not subject to any party political or sectional bias. Its role is to pre-empt acts which threaten Australia's security. ASIO gathers information on people whose actions might threaten security, advising authorities so that the necessary action can be taken. ASIO's task is to attain the highest standards in the relevance, accuracy and timeliness of its intelligence reporting.

ASIO has no powers to interrogate, detain or arrest people, but it may take steps to discourage or inhibit activities prejudicial to security. ASIO may inform other agencies (e.g. police or customs) of suspected activities.

THE ATTORNEY-GENERAL

The Attorney-General is the Minister responsible for the activities of ASIO. He has the authority to direct the Director-General, but cannot overrule the Director-General's opinion on the nature of advice given by the Organisation. The Attorney-General can, however, overrule the opinion of the Director-General on whether the investigation of an individual would be justified on security grounds. In such a case, the Inspector-General of Intelligence and Security and the Prime Minister must be informed.

The Attorney-General must grant prior approval of ASIO's intention to cooperate with any foreign authorities.

The Attorney-General's warrant is required to authorise ASIO's use of its special powers to:
- enter and search premises and inspect or extract records;
- use listening equipment without consent of the subject;
- intercept and inspect post and telecommunications.

The Minister may certify the withholding of information, e.g. from the subject of a security assessment or from the Parliamentary Joint Committee on ASIO. Similarly, when the Minister issues guidelines to the Director-General, the Minister decides whether the guidelines should be tabled in Parliament or made available to the Parliamentary Joint Committee on ASIO (in a complete or abridged form).

THE DIRECTOR-GENERAL OF SECURITY

The Director-General of Security is responsible for ASIO and to the Attorney-General. The Director-General is required to ensure that ASIO fulfils its statutory functions, and does not engage in activities beyond those functions. Only the Director-General or his delegate may impart intelligence on ASIO's behalf. It is an offence for an ASIO employee or agent to communicate ASIO information without authority.

The Director-General is required to keep the Leader of the Opposition informed on matters relating to security.

The Director-General alone has the authority to request the Attorney-General's authorisation for ASIO's use of its special powers under the ASIO Act. In an emergency, the Director-General can issue a 48-hour warrant. In all cases, the Director-General must inform the Minister at the expiry of the warrant, to the extent to which the action taken has assisted ASIO.

In ASIO's provision of security assessments to Commonwealth agencies, the Director-General's opinion is the basis for any adverse or qualified assessment, and if there is an application for review to the Security Appeals Tribunal, the Director-General must supply the Tribunal with the background information.

ASIO staff are employed under individual agreements with the Director-General and are not members of the Australian Public Service.

The Director-General is required to issue an annual report on ASIO's activities to the Attorney-General (to be tabled in Parliament) and the Leader of the Opposition.

THREATS TO SECURITY

ASIO is responsible for dealing with threats to national security. These fall into two broad categories: acts of foreign interference; and politically motivated violence.

Acts of Foreign Interference

Clandestine or threatening intelligence or political activities detrimental to Australia's interests which are conducted by or for a foreign power are considered acts of foreign interference. The most significant activity in this area is the gathering of intelligence on Australia by foreign agencies whose agents enter the country posing as legitimate diplomatic staff, students, business representatives, visitors or long-term residents.

Politically Motivated Violence

Acts or threats of violence intended or likely to achieve a political objective, whether in Australia or elsewhere, are considered politically motivated violence. Domestic politically motivated violence is primarily prompted by Australian issues and events, and is carried out by Australian residents in Australia. International politically motivated violence may involve threats to foreign interests in Australia or overseas, and may be carried out by Australian residents or by people visiting this country.

Responses to Threat

Exclusion or expulsion from Australia can be actioned on ASIO's recommendations by the Department of Foreign Affairs and Trade, or the Department of Immigration, Local Government and Ethnic Affairs. Expulsion from a country can be executed privately or publicly, depending on the attitude of the host government towards the intolerable activity of the individual or individuals involved, and the host government's attitude towards continuing relations with the foreign government involved.

Intelligence Gathering

Intelligence is gathered by a repetitive or cyclical process. The process involves four phases:
1. investigation planning;
2. collection;
3. analysis;
4. review.

Investigation Planning

SECURITY OPERATIONS PROGRAMS Security Operations Program (SOP) is the name given to the series of documents that begin the investigation planning phases. SOPs:
- provide a factual description of the subject;
- relate the subject's activity to the appropriate categories of security;
- specify ASIO's objectives and strategies;
- give details of information collection requirements.

COLLECTION SOURCES

The amount of information sought relates directly to the assessed threat to security.

- Overt sources: members of the public offering information, government agencies and publicly available material.
- Official records: Commonwealth and state databases and records, including foreign material.
- Intelligence co-operation: other Australian intelligence agencies, e.g. Australian Secret Intelligence Service (ASIS), Defence Signals (DSD), Joint Intelligence Organisation (JIO) and Office of National Assessment (ONA), Australian law enforcement authorities, foreign security, intelligence and law enforcement agencies, as authorised by the Attorney-General.
- Surveillance: mobile and static, using photographic, video and other equipment.
- Human sources: members of subject groups and others with relevant information.
- Audio-technical collection: telephone interception and listening devices (UNDER WARRANT).
- Interception of recorded communications: mail, facsimile and telex interception (UNDER WARRANT).
- Search: overt or covert entry and search of premises (UNDER WARRANT).

WARRANT DOCUMENTATION PROCEDURES   ASIO requires the Attorney-General's authorisation to collect information under warrant. All warrants are issued for a fixed period which may not exceed:

- 7 days for entry and search;
- 90 days for inspections of postal articles;
- 6 months for use of listening devices or interception of telegrams or telecommunications.

Before expiry, a warrant is reviewed to decide if it should be renewed or allowed to lapse. Warrants can be revoked before expiry if the objectives of the warrant have been achieved.

The Attorney-General may revoke a warrant at any time before expiry. Warrants can be renewed through a system similar to the initial authorisation procedure.

ANALYSIS

Information is collated, evaluated and assessed and further investigation undertaken where necessary. The resulting intelligence allows conclusions to be drawn regarding the threat to security and arguments for further action to be prepared.

ASIO's intelligence is used to advise Ministers and Commonwealth authorities through security assessments, threat assessments or recommendations for executive action. In some cases, ASIO's intelligence is communicated to foreign authorities.

REVIEW

ASIO assesses the quality and usefulness of the intelligence product against the methods and resources used in obtaining it. Investigation may then be dropped, decreased, adjusted, or increased, in which case the intelligence cycle is renewed.

12
Health

Commonwealth Department of Health and Community Services

*T*he Commonwealth Department of Health and Community Services provides services for aged people, children, people with disabilities and people who need housing assistance. It is also involved in the the fight against the misuse of illegal and legal drugs, the promotion of health and medical research, access to health care and maintaining the quality and safety of therapeutic goods.

The Health and Community Services portfolio is very large and is therefore divided on a federal level into two areas overseen by two Ministers. The Minister for Human Services and Health is the senior minister and co-ordinates the portfolio as a whole, having particular responsibility for major policy decisions and budget matters. The other Minister is primarily responsible for Family Services.

ADMINISTRATION

Developing and implementing national health care policy is the responsibility of the Commonwealth, which also provides grants and benefits to organisations and regulates health insurance. It is up to State and Territory governments, however, to provide health services, with each State and Territory having one Minister responsible for these services. Local government, semi-voluntary agencies, and non-government organisations also have a role in providing health care.

EXPENDITURE

The Federal government spent about $38 billion on health programs in 1994–1995. This was an increase on the $36.5 billion spent in 1993–94 and $35 billion in 1992–1993. Health expenditure per person increased at about 2.8% in real terms between 1983 and 1994. As a proportion of gross domestic product, health expenditure was estimated at 8.5% in June 1994.

Health Insurance

Over the years, there have been various approaches to health care in Australia. Labor governments have tended to opt for free or heavily subsidised health care for all Australians, while the Liberal and Coalition governments have, in the past, maintained that the individual should be responsible for medical costs through private health insurance schemes.

Government policy on health began to change considerably during the 1970s. In 1975, the Whitlam Labor government introduced a universal health care system known as Medibank.

Medibank was abolished by the Liberal–National Country Party government, who introduced voluntary private insurance and imposed an income levy on those using Medibank. Only people considered by the Fraser Government to be in genuine need (about 25% of the population) were allowed free medical and hospital care from 1981 to February 1984 (when Medicare was introduced). Others had to pay their own medical and hospital expenses and were encouraged to join a private health insurance fund.

MEDICARE

Medicare was introduced by the Hawke Labor government in February 1984 to help Australians pay for essential medical and hospital care. All permanent Australian residents are entitled to Medicare. Visitors from overseas countries such as the United Kingdom, New Zealand, Italy, Sweden, the Netherlands, Finland and Malta, which have signed special agreements with Australia, are also entitled to Medicare benefits. In return, Australians in these countries have restricted access to those country's public hospitals for immediate and essential medical services.

Medicare has 269 offices nationwide and is overseen by the Health Insurance Commission in Canberra.

COST

The cost of Medicare was estimated in 1995–1996 to be almost $6.1 billion (fee for service only) in that year. From this total, the government received $3.35 billion from the Medicare levy. This levy is an income tax raised by the Commonwealth government and administered by the Australian Taxation Office to help pay for the cost of medical care.

LEVIES

Most Australians pay 1.5% of their taxable income to Medicare, while those on higher incomes pay 2.5%. Single people earning less than about $13 000 a year or $14 000 a year for couples or sole parents, do not pay the Medicare levy. Payment is phased in over an income range.

EXTENT OF COVER

Medicare helps pay for doctors' consultations in hospital, at home or in the doctor's surgery with the general practitioner (GP) chosen by the patient. It also covers X-rays and blood tests, as well as eye tests and certain types of oral surgery. Glasses, contact lenses, general dental work and physiotherapy are not covered. Hospital accommodation and treatment is free under Medicare for public patients in public hospitals, although the hospital chooses the doctor. To have your own doctor in a public hospital, you must become a private patient and pay for your accommodation. Medicare does provide a benefit for private patients in private and public hospitals, but does not cover theatre fees or accommodation.

BENEFITS

For non in-patient services, Medicare pays 85% of the schedule fee (see schedule fees) and the patient pays the difference which cannot exceed $50 (indexed annually). If charged more than the schedule fee, then the patient has to pay that difference, known as the 'patient gap', which is usually about 15–20%. If doctors or optometrists direct bill (or bulk bill) then the patient pays nothing at all. When gap payments reach about $280 in one financial year, Medicare will repay up to 100% of the the schedule fee for any further claims. Gap payments for private patients in a hospital do not count towards this $280 total.

Medicare only pays 75% of the schedule fee for the doctor's services to private patients in either a public or private hospital. Private health insurance will cover up to 25% of the scheduled fee. Insurers are not permitted to provide payment above the schedule fee unless covered by a private health insurance contract.

SCHEDULE FEES

The Medicare Benefits Schedule lists medical services and the schedule (standard) fee for each of these. Up until 1985, schedule fees were set by independent bodies appointed by the government, including the Australian Medical Association (AMA). From 1986, schedule fees have been updated by the government in consultation with the medical profession.

MEDICARE BENEFITS — NATIONAL TOTALS, 1995-96

Type of Service	Amount ($m)
GP consultation	2314.4
Specialist consultation	887.9
Obstetrics	58.7
Anaesthetics	121.6
Pathology	812.8
Diagnostic imaging	875.9
Operations	560.7
Optometry	141.9
Other	264.6
Total	**6038.5**

Payments

New South Wales received the most in Medicare benefits in 1995–1996, with benefits reaching $2236.9 million. Victoria received $1517.6 million, Queensland $1042.8 million, Western Australia $514.4 million, South Australia $476.2 million, Tasmania $136.5 million, Australian Capital Territory $82.2 million and Northern Territory $31.5 million.

Pharmaceutical Benefits Scheme

The Pharmaceutical Benefits Scheme (PBS) is designed to give all Australians access to affordable prescription drugs. The government subsidises the cost of prescriptions provided by pharmacists. Prescriptions written under the Scheme are supplied by pharmacists to the patient who pays the first $16.80. People holding a concession card pay $3.20 a prescription. Pharmacists claim the balance from the government, who pay within 15–30 days of receiving the claim.

Cost of the PBS

In 1995–1996, the total cost of the scheme, including patient contribution, was $2207.4 million. In the past couple of years the cost of the scheme has doubled. It is increasing because of new and more complex drugs, increased numbers receiving social security and an ageing population.

Safety Net Provisions

Safety nets refer to a ceiling placed on the amount which can be paid by an individual or family who, because of chronic illness, need a lot of pharmaceutical drugs. The expenditure threshold varies according to a patient's circumstances, but for most families the amount is $600 each year. Once this amount of drugs has been used, concessional PBS drugs cost only $2.60 per prescription for the rest of the year.

Top Ten Drugs by Prescription Counts, 1994

Drug	Condition/Use	Total users
amoxicillin	antibiotic	5 865 380
salbutamol	asthma	4 398 580
paracetamol	analgesic	4 137 020
codeine	narcotic analgesic	3 655 410
amoxicillin with clavulanic acid	antibiotic	3 416 260
enalapril	high blood pressure	3 126 970
temazepam	insomnia	3 032 220
ranitidine	ulcers	2 968 680

Drug	Condition/Use	Total users
betamethasone	skin inflammation	2 791 320
doxycycline	antibiotic	2 756 180

Top Ten Drugs by Cost to the Government, 1994

Drug	Condition/Use	Cost ($m)
simvastatin	high cholesterol	95.00
ranitidine	ulcers	82.30
enalapril	high blood pressure	77.3
captopril	high blood pressure/ heart failure	58.70
omeprazole	ulcers	55.00
ipratropium bromide	asthma	45.1
salbutamol	asthma	43.30
fluoxetine	antidepressant	34.7
felodipine	high blood pressure	34.40
budenoside	asthma/hay fever	32.00

PRIVATE HEALTH INSURANCE

People who have private health insurance are also covered by Medicare, and have the choice of seeking treatment as a private or public hospital patient. In 1996, there were 48 registered health funds in Australia, with 14 to 15 of these covering about 80% of the market. The largest funds include MBF, HCF and Medibank Private.

It is recommended that health insurance contributors contact their health fund prior to receiving costly hospital treatment to find out what rebates they will be entitled to. Contributors should also ask their doctor what medical service charges will be raised.

After the Budget of August 1996, some health funds announced premium increases of up to 40%. By December 1996, the two largest funds, Medibank Private and MBF, had increased premiums by about 15%.

The levels of health insurance cover include: ancillary cover, basic hospital cover, intermediate hospital cover, top hospital cover, cut-price hospital cover and doctors' fees (out-of-pocket costs).

ANCILLARY COVER   This provides services for such services as physiotherapy, chiropractic, massage, dental, optical, psychology and podiatry. Tables can also include rebates for such things as gym shoes and/or gym membership depending on health fund policy. In 1994–1995, 33.2% of the Australian population had ancillary cover.

BASIC HOSPITAL COVER   This is generally sufficient to cover accommodation in a shared ward of a public hospital as a private patient able to choose their own doctor. It also covers any surgically implanted prostheses which are required. Rebates would also contribute to accommodation in a private hospital, but there would generally be a substantial patient co-payment. In 1994–1995, 35% of the Australian population had basic table health insurance.

INTERMEDIATE HOSPITAL COVER   This traditional intermediate table would offer rebates suitable for a private room in a public hospital, or shared ward accommodation in a private hospital with a patient co-payment.

TOP HOSPITAL COVER   Funds generally offer substantial rebates under these tables and may cover shared-ward and single-room private hospital accommodation and many other charges fully, although this '100%' cover may be restricted to hospitals which have a contract with the patient's health fund.

CUT-PRICE HOSPITAL COVER   The contribution rate for this cover can be reduced if a contributor chooses a front-end deductible table or a select and save table. Front-end deductible tables involve contributors agreeing to pay a specified amount at the time they make their first hospital claim in each year. This amount, which would otherwise have been payable by the health fund, varies between tables and health funds and ranges from $100–$1000 or more. Select and save tables have restrictions on the types of services for which benefits will be payable. Benefits for hip replacements or obstetrics, for example, may be excluded from the cover.

DOCTORS' FEES (OUT-OF-POCKET COSTS)   All hospital tables also rebate 25% of the Medicare Benefits Schedule (MBS) fee which, when added to the Medicare rebate of 75% of the MBS fee, means that private patients are fully covered up to 100% of the MBS fees for doctors' services while they are in hospital. Patients will face out-of-pocket costs, however, if their doctor charges more than the MBS fee. If the doctor has a contract with the patient's health fund, the fund will refund up to an agreed fee.

Legislative reforms introduced in May 1995, allow health funds to contract with hospitals and, for the first time, with doctors, to enable the health funds to pay rebates of up to 100% of both hospital and doctors' charges. These arrangements allow health funds to provide benefits for services where patients' out-of-pocket expenses would be reduced or at least confined to a known amount. The contracts may include funding mechanisms other than those included in the above tables.

INCENTIVES TO TAKE OUT AND MAINTAIN HEALTH INSURANCE
As announced in the 1996 Budget, the government will implement a strategy that will work on two fronts. From 1 July 1997, lower and middle income earners will be able to claim an incentive payment if they have private health insurance, and higher income earners (singles earning more than $50 000 or couples and families earning more than $100 000) will face an increased Medicare levy surcharge if they do not choose to take out private heatlth insurance.

Singles earning under $35 000 a year will be eligible for up to $125 each year towards the cost of their private health insurance premiums. Couples earning under $70 000 will receive up to $250, and families with one child earning under the same amount will receive up to $450. The income threshold for families will rise by $3000 for each additional child, in line with the government's Family Tax Initiative.

PRIVATE HEALTH INSURANCE COMPLAINTS COMMISSIONER
The Private Health Insurance Complaints Commissioner has been set up to deal with inquiries and complaints about any aspect of private health insurance. The Commissioner is totally independent of the private health funds, private and public hospitals and the government.

The Hospital System

In 1994–1995, hospital funding grants by the Federal Government totalling $3980 million to the States and Territories, provided $3878 million for hospitals and related services. Australia's public hospitals are, however, widely regarded as overcrowded and underfunded, with waiting lists growing and doctors having to do more with less money. One of the main problems is that as Australia's population ages more people are using the hospital system. Also, advanced medical technology is becoming more expensive, but hospital spending has remained the same instead of matching this increased cost. The August 1996 Budget announced a $320 million reduction in hospital funding over four years.

FUNDING

PUBLIC AND PRIVATE HOSPITALS
The basic difference between public and private hospitals is that public hospitals offer affordable medical treatment to all Australians, while private hospitals only cater to those who can pay independently for their services.

At June 1995, there were a total of 1149 hospitals in Australia: 688 recognised public hospitals, 334 private hospitals and 127 day hospital facilities. These provided 4.32 beds per 1000 population. At June 1994, hospital funding grants by the Commonwealth government came to a total of $5246 million. There was also $33 million spent on expanding post-acute and palliative care facilities.

HOSPITAL BEDS AVAILABLE

Hospital	June 1993	June 1994	June 1995
Public hospitals	55 410	54 050	53 910
Private hospitals	21 650	22 380	23 270
Day hospital facilities	615	290	315
All beds	**77 675**	**76 720**	**77 495**

REPATRIATION HOSPITALS

Repatriation general hospitals exist specifically for eligible veterans, treating the general community only after the needs of the entitled have been met. These hospitals offer a range of services, including out-patient facilities, and come under the responsibility of the Department of Veterans' Affairs. Veterans and their dependents can also seek treatment in public or private hospitals, nursing homes and psychiatric institutions, often at the expense of the Department of Veteran Affairs.

PSYCHIATRIC HOSPITALS

There are currently 50 public psychiatric hospitals operating in Australia. In recent years, Australia has followed the lead of other countries in treating the mentally ill. Treatment has shifted from policies of institutionalisation to a range of mental health services provided for in-patients and out-patients at psychiatric hospitals, psychiatric units in general hospitals and admission facilities and within residential care facilities 25 for psychogeriatric patients and those persons with intellectual disabilities.

See Mental Health for policy, funding and treatment.

The Medical Profession

GENERAL PRACTITIONERS

The ratio of doctors to patients is quite high in Australia (about 30 per 10 000 inhabitants in 1995) compared with similar countries (USA 21.4, Canada 19.6, New Zealand 17.4, UK 16.4 and Japan 15.1). At June 1995, there were approximately 255 400 people employed in the health services sector throughout Australia. About 152 900 of these were nurses, and 93% of these were women. There were an estimated 29 700 general practitioners (GPs) (71% men) and 13 500 specialists (75.5% men). In addition, there were 9600 dentists, 12 900 pharmacists, 6100 occupational therapists, 1800 optometrists, 7800 physiotherapists, 2500 speech pathologists, 2700 chiropractors/osteopaths, 1500 podiatrists and 6000 radiographers.

The August 1996 Budget announced plans to restrict newly qualified doctors' access to Medicare provider numbers. While the government claims that there is a Medicare cost blow-out with too many doctors competing for insufficient patients, medical professionals fear that this issue sets a precedent for government control of medical practice.

NUMBER OF PATIENTS PER DOCTOR, 1995

Country	Number
Italy	195
New Zealand	321
United States	387
Australia	438
Japan	545
Great Britain	581
Indonesia	6786
Afghanistan	7358
Papua New Guinea	12 500

CONSULTATIONS   Health care in Australia starts with a visit to the general practitioner. An average consultation will take 10 minutes, and at the end the GP will prescribe medication, or refer the patient to a specialist for further diagnosis and treatment. Many observers believe that it is at this level of general practice that our health care system has fallen down. They believe that health care costs are increasing because GPs are sending too many patients to specialists to complete the diagnosis, resulting in too many visits to specialists. Some GPs say the problem is that they are not being rewarded under the Medicare system.

Aboriginal and Torres Strait Islander Health

Responsibility for indigenous health was transferred from the Aboriginal and Torres Strait Islander Commission (ATSIC) to the Department of Health and Community Services in 1995. Here, the federal government can determine state health funding; a power ATSIC did not have. It was felt that indigenous people were in greater need of the major health programs implemented by the federal government as part of its $34 billion annual budget.

Despite the fact that Aboriginal and Torres Strait Islanders made up 1.6% of the Australian population in 1993–1994, ATSIC had only $55 million or 1.26% of the total health budget to spend on indigenous health.

Government Health Bodies

AUSTRALIAN INSTITUTE OF HEALTH AND WELFARE

The Australian Institute of Health and Welfare (AIHW) was set up in 1987 by the Commonwealth government, primarily as a health statistics and research agency. Its main aim is to keep an eye on resources given to health services and to help improve the overall health of Australians. In achieving these aims, it tends to focus on the recurring issues of cost, use, access, facilities, resources and efficiency of health services.

NATIONAL OCCUPATIONAL HEALTH AND SAFETY COMMISSION

Otherwise known as Worksafe Australia, the National Occupational Health and Safety Commission was set up to develop and introduce national occupational health and safety procedures. It is made up of government, employee and employer representatives.

The commission has pinpointed six major areas of concern: occupational back pain, noise-induced hearing loss, dealing with chemicals at work, occupational skin disorders, cancer and mechanical equipment injuries. The Science and Research Division has research projects ongoing: a continuing study of work-related deaths, the psychological factors in accidents and the effects of chemicals on the immune system.

See Occupational Health.

NATIONAL HEALTH AND MEDICAL RESEARCH COUNCIL

The National Health and Medical Research Council (NHMRC) is a statutory authority within the Commonwealth Department of Health and Community Services. It advises both governments and communities on issues relating to public health and ethics. It aims to promote debate on ethics and health policy, encouraging high quality research and the application of this research. The NHMRC draws on the expertise of people from a wide range of areas from scientific organisations, consumer groups, ATSIC and various health departments.

AUSTRALIAN QUARANTINE AND INSPECTION SERVICE

The Australian Quarantine and Inspection Service (AQIS) inspects all exported and imported food, including meat, fish, dairy products, dried food, grains, vegetables and fruit, and live animals. It must ensure that the animal and plant health requirements of Australia and importing countries are complied with fully. AQIS is involved at an international level in the development of food safety standards and hygiene, and manufacturing practice issues.

THERAPEUTIC GOODS ADMINISTATION

Therapeutic goods must be evaluated before they come on to the market. Therapeutic goods include intra-ocular lenses, intra-uterine contraceptive devices (IUDs), prosthetic heart valves, cardiac pacemakers, and drug infusion systems. The Therapeutic Goods Administation (TGA) tests these items for quality, safety and effectiveness, and manufacturers are also inspected to ensure that they maintain acceptable manufacturing standards.

Nutrition

There are many food and nutrition policies developed by the government and the National Health and Medical Research Council, and promoted through community education across Australia. Nutrition guidelines are also promoted in conjunction with the national 'Life Be In It' campaign, which has been a long-running and very successful fitness and exercise campaign run across all media.

AUSTRALIAN RECOMMENDED DAILY INTAKE (RDI) OF VITAMINS AND MINERALS

Vitamins/Minerals	Men	Women
Vitamin A	750 mcg	750 mcg
Vitamin C	40 mg	30 mg
Thiamin or vitamin B1	1.1 mg	0.8 mg
Riboflavin or vitamin B2	1.7 mg	1.2 mg
Niacin	18–20 mg	12–14 mg
Calcium	800 mg	800 mg

Health Organisations

As well as the government initiated health programs, there are numerous independent health organisations receiving limited government funding.

ROYAL FLYING DOCTOR SERVICE OF AUSTRALIA

The idea of using aircraft and radio to reach and then treat ill or injured people in the outback is a uniquely Australian one. It first began to take shape when Presbyterian minister Reverend John Flynn arrived in the outback in 1911. By 15 May 1928, the Australian Aerial Medical Service began operating from Cloncurry in outback Queensland. In 1942, it became the Flying Doctor Service and in 1955, after the Queen's visit, the Royal Flying Doctor Service.

Today, there are 16 bases nationwide. The Royal Flying Doctor Service operates about 39 aircraft, which cost a minimum of $3.5 million to replace. Outback homesteads make contact with the doctor by high frequency radio or telephone, and doctors are available 24 hours a day. Each homestead also has a medicine chest which helps people to deal with emergencies until the doctor gets there.

PATIENTS

The Royal Flying Doctor Service proudly boasts that it can reach any patient within two hours. In 1995–1996, 159 571 consultations were carried out, with 17 094 emergency evacuations and 4743 field clinics set up.

Each year, the aircraft cover over 11 316 368 kilometres, travelling over 80% of the continent. About 40% of the patients treated are Aboriginal, with the highest percentage being from the Kimberley, Cairns and Mt Isa.

The service provides its emergency, telephone consultation and routine healthcare services free. Some services to private organisations are fee based.

FUNDING

In recent years, the Commonwealth government has supported the Royal Flying Doctor Service by matching State and Territory operation funding. In addition, the Commonwealth has contributed towards the service's capital needs of new major items of expenditure, and by special grants towards funding the replacement of medical supplies to the patients' Royal Flying Doctor Service medical chests.

OTHER FLYING MEDICAL SERVICES

There are other aerial medical services apart from the Royal Flying Doctor Service. The Northern Territory Aerial Medical Service runs from bases in

Darwin, Gove and Alice Springs, and the Flying Surgeon Service based in Queensland runs between its Longreach and Roma bases.

AUSTRALIAN RED CROSS

The Australian Red Cross is a voluntary relief organisation, run on a non-profit basis which provides community services to the nation. Amongst the more well known programs is Meals on Wheels, which provides regular hot meals for elderly people in their homes. Other services for the aged include hospital visiting, entertainment and craft programs and day outings.

For young people, there is the Red Cross Youth and the Junior Red Cross, which provide educational activities for Australia's youth. Babysitting, childcare courses and migrant youth orientation schemes are also run by the Red Cross.

RED CROSS BLOOD TRANSFUSION SERVICE

This service is run throughout Australia. As well as permanent centres, mobile units make stops at companies and schools to collect blood from voluntary donors. It is possible to donate blood from the ages of 16 to 70, although doctor's approval is required for those over 65 and parental consent for those under 18 years of age. Since May 1985, the Red Cross has screened all blood for the AIDS antibody, as well as testing for syphilis and hepatitis.

The Red Cross Blood Transfusion Service is funded by the Commonwealth and state governments (98%) and the Red Cross (2%). In 1993–1994, the service cost $93.1 million.

THE NATIONAL HEART FOUNDATION OF AUSTRALIA

The National Heart Foundation is a national voluntary organisation established in 1960 to fight heart disease, the greatest killer of Australians. The foundation funds research into heart disease and how to reduce it. It also provides information and education programs for individuals, health professionals and special groups like schools. The foundation runs mostly on donations. In 1994, income totalled $24.3 million, of which $17.5 million came from donations and bequests. Most of this money ($15 million) went to research, education and community service.

WORLD HEALTH ORGANISATION

The World Health Organisation (WHO) was set up by the United Nations and aims to achieve the highest possible level of health for people world-wide. Australia contributes to this goal within its assigned region, the Western Pacific, whose headquarters are in Manila in The Philippines. In 1995, Australia contributed $7.8 million to WHO.

INTERNATIONAL AGENCY FOR RESEARCH ON CANCER

Established in 1965, the International Agency for Research on Cancer (IARC) aims to provide for the planning and encouragement of research that leads either to the treatment or prevention of cancer. The headquarters are in Lyon in France. In 1994, Australia contributed $1.1 million to the agency.

Drugs in Australia

NATIONAL CAMPAIGN AGAINST DRUG ABUSE

When drug abuse amongst the young began to show an alarming increase in the 1980s, the Hawke government launched a long-term program. The National Drug Strategy deals with the widespread social and health ramifications of drug abuse.

The National Campaign Against Drug Abuse (NCADA) aims to reduce demand for drugs through education, treatment, and rehabilitation programs and also to restrict the supply of drugs. Its greatest success appears to be in the declining number of deaths per 100 000 population that can be linked to tobacco and alcohol abuse.

COMMON DRUGS IN AUSTRALIA

CAFFEINE
Caffeine is probably the world's most popular drug, widely found in tea and coffee. Today, world consumption of caffeine is estimated at about 70 mg per person per day. Approximately 54% of world caffeine consumption is from coffee, 43% from tea, with 3% ingested in other forms.

Research into the effects of caffeine are not conclusive, but evidence points to it being a carcinogenic agent and indicates that an intake of 600 mg/day may aggravate heart problems. There is 6–100 mg in a cup of instant coffee, 80–350 mg in a cup of fresh coffee, 2–4 mg in a cup of decaffeinated coffee, and 8–90 mg in a cup of tea.

SMOKING
Next to caffeine, nicotine from tobacco is the most widely used stimulant in Australia. In the 1993–1994 period, 31.6 billion cigarettes were manufactured. About 32.1% of men and 24.7% of women in Australia are smokers. There has been an increase in the number of young people smoking, with young women taking up smoking at higher rates than young men. Among 17-year-olds, 26% of boys have never smoked compared to only 24% of girls.

THE EFFECTS OF SMOKING   The long-term effects of smoking include increased risk of heart attack, emphysema, coronary heart disease, cervical cancer, stomach ulcers and cancer of the lungs, mouth, larynx, oesophagus, bladder, kidney and pancreas. Smoking also causes premature ageing.

If a person gives up smoking, within ten years of kicking the habit the risk of getting smoking-related illnesses falls almost to the level of someone who has never smoked. The risk of suffering from many other diseases falls even sooner. In 1994, a national law was introduced which ensures that one-third of the area of every cigarette packet carries a health department warning.

ALCOHOL

Alcohol is a depressant and is also toxic. About 90% of Australian adults have had alcohol at one time or other; about 75% of men and 50% of women drink occasionally, and around 5% of adults are alcohol dependent. It is believed that at least 500 000 Australians drink alcohol in quantities large enough to risk their health, or to develop alcohol related injuries. Around 25% of high school children in Australia drink at least once a week.

DRINK DRIVING   In all States and Territories, the legal limit for drinking and driving is 0.05% blood alcohol level (Class A licence) and 0.02% or 0.00% for those holding provisional licences (depending on the State). Penalties for breaking this law include disqualification from driving (three months to three years), fines and imprisonment (3–12 months) for repeat offenders.

Random breath testing (RBT) was introduced to help enforce this law in 1982. Any driver or motorcyclist on the road is under legal obligation to take a breathalyser test if pulled over.

CANNABIS

Marijuana, cannabis and hashish all come from the hemp plant. Cannabis is the most widely used illegal drug. It is estimated that about 35% of 18- to 25-year-olds have used it at some time in their lives. A group called NORML (National Organisation to Reform Marijuana Laws) has been lobbying for a number years to have marijuana legalised on the basis that a significant number of Australians use it, but has so far been unsuccessful. In the Australian Capital Territory and South Australia, the possession of cannabis for personal use has been decriminalised, and other States are endeavouring to review their laws regarding the drug.

COCAINE

Cocaine is not a widely used drug in Australia in comparison to marijuana, heroin and amphetamines. It shows no signs of escalating into the epidemic proportions it has reached in the United States, where cocaine is presently used by between 5 million and 10 million Americans, with the cheaper substitute, crack, also widely used.

HEROIN
Heroin is a very powerful and addictive drug. Because it is illegal, it is difficult to estimate the number of people who use it regularly. Most authorities agree that in Australia the figure is between 10 000 and 20 000 people, an estimate based on arrests and admissions to hospitals.

HALLUCINOGENS
Hallucinogens like LSD, Ecstasy, Angel Dust and Magic Mushrooms are not usually taken on a regular basis, but are rather occasional or 'party' drugs. It is against the law to possess, use, manufacture or deal in any of these drugs in Australia.

Communicable Diseases

QUARANTINE
Australia's relative isolation and stringent quarantine laws have kept it comparatively free of some of the diseases which have caused considerable damage overseas. The *Quarantine Act 1908* and the *Biological Control Act 1984* are designed to prevent diseases affecting humans, animals and plants from entering Australia, while also enabling the safe importation of agricultural products. In 1994–1995, quarantine inspections were carried out on 6000 ships, 31 000 aircraft, 6.3 million crew and passengers, one million cargo containers and 1.8 million airfreight consignments.

HUMANS
Authorities overseeing all air and sea traffic arriving in Australia are obliged to tell Commonwealth officials of any illnesses on board. The contagious diseases causing most concern are cholera, yellow fever, typhus and viral haemorrhagic fevers. All these diseases require the afflicted person to go through a period of quarantine.

ANIMALS
Only nominated species from certain countries with the same quarantine regulations are permitted to enter Australia, while animal products must pass stringent inspections. Quarantine stations can be found in most capital cities, with a high-security station situated on the Cocos Islands.

PLANTS

Plant material is inspected upon arrival; the main aim is to keep out pests or disease that could cause serious harm and economic losses to Australia's agricultural, horticultural and forest industries, as well as to the native flora.

IMMUNISATION

Immunisation is recommended for all children, and there are immunisation centres located in every capital city in Australia. Immunisation protects against childhood diseases such as whooping cough, tetanus, measles, diphtheria and poliomyelitis. A new measles/mumps/rubella vaccine has also been introduced for all children aged 12–15 months. Babies are immunised against hepatitis B, if it is thought that their mother is part of a community where the carrier rate exceeds 5%. In schools throughout Australia, rubella immunisation programs have been implemented for girls aged between 10 and 15 years.

IMMUNISATION PROGRAM

Age	Injection
Birth	First injection of hepatitis B vaccine
1–2 months	First injection of triple antigen*
	First dose of Sabin vaccine given by mouth (protects against poliomyelitis)
	Second injection of hepatitis B vaccine
4 months	Second injection of triple antigen
	Second dose of Sabin vaccine by mouth
6 months	Third injection of triple antigen
	Third injection of hepatitis B vaccine
	Third dose of Sabin vaccine by mouth
5 months	One injection of combined measles/mumps vaccine
8 months	Booster injection of combined triple antigen
5 years	Booster injection of CDT combined
	Booster dose of Sabin vaccine given by mouth
Girls under 15	Injection of rubella vaccine (protects against German measles)
15 years	Booster injection of adult diphtheria and tetanus
	Booster dose of Sabin vaccine by mouth

* Triple antigen is a three-in-one vaccine for protection against diphtheria, whooping cough and tetanus.

Acquired Immune Deficiency Syndrome

Causes

Acquired immune deficiency syndrome (AIDS) is caused by a virus known as human immunodeficiency virus (HIV) which attacks the immune system, the body's natural defence against illness, infection and some forms of cancer. HIV breaks down the immune system and the infected person can die from infectious diseases that would not normally affect them.

AIDS is primarily a sexually transmitted disease, but it can also be spread through the sharing of needles and syringes, or through receipt of contaminated blood, blood components or tissue.

AIDS in Australia

The first case of AIDS was reported in Australia in November 1982. By 1994, 18 769 cases of HIV had been diagnosed: 15 780 men and 881 women. Of these cases, about 100 were reported in children under 13 years of age. AIDS was subsequently diagnosed in 5732 of these cases: 5510 men and 204 women. Almost 60% of these cases were diagnosed in New South Wales. Victoria had the second highest rate followed by Queensland, Western Australia, South Australia, Australian Capital Territory, Tasmania and the Northern Territory in that order. An estimated 75% of these deaths occurred in the 30–49 years of age category. By far the highest transmission category, contributing about 81% of all cases, is that of male-to-male sexual contact, but the mortality rate is higher for those people infected by blood, blood components or tissue. The Commonwealth government granted $52 million to the treatment of AIDS patients in public hospitals in 1994.

Prevention

To prevent infection with HIV, it is suggested that a person have a monogamous sexual relationship. Condoms should be used during sex, although they are not 100% safe. Intravenous drug users should always use a clean needle, and never share needles or syringes. Infection as a result of blood transfusions or tissue is no longer a risk in Australia due to stringent screening procedures.

NEEDLE EXCHANGE PROGRAM   The Needle Exchange Program, set up in 1988, aims to minimise the risk of AIDS for intravenous drug users. Free needles can be obtained wherever the exchange logo of two arrows forming a circle is displayed. Exchange outlets also operate at some hospitals, pharmacies, health and welfare agencies.

Treatment

There is no cure for AIDS. There are, however, some drugs available to treat the infections AIDS sufferers develop and there has been some success in delaying the onset of full-blown AIDS with drug therapy. Other drugs such as the antiviral drug zidovudine, known as Retrovir or AZT, are undergoing trials. Approval for use of AZT was previously restricted to people with advanced cases of AIDS, but, in 1990, restrictions were removed after lobbying followed reports of positive results from US trials.

WOMEN AND AIDS

AIDS is largely viewed as a disease affecting the male homosexual community. Although the number of infected women is low, women are at risk through unprotected intercourse and the sharing of needles and syringes. It is believed that women are more at risk of catching the AIDS virus from infected men than men are from infected women.

Infected pregnant women can pass the AIDS virus to their baby, who will be born with it. There is also the risk of infection through breastfeeding.

THE AIDS FUNDING PROGRAM

The AIDS Funding Program is a Commonwealth government initiative. It funds AIDS-prevention activities such as the National AIDS Program, which conducts research and education, and the Matched Funding Program, which provides funds to the States and Territories who match it dollar for dollar. This latter program funds services such as the screening of donated blood to ensure Australia's donated blood stocks remain uncontaminated.

Death

See chapter 5, 'Population'.

Occupational Health

The workplace is not always a safe environment. Every year over 500 Australians are killed in work-related accidents, with about 300 000 cases of work-related injuries or disease occurring in the same period, resulting in a total annual cost in compensation of about $4.8 billion.

COMMON WORKPLACE INJURIES

There are six main, serious injuries that occur in the workplace:
- Occupational back pain hits three out of four Australians once in their lives and accounts for a quarter of all compensated injuries.

- 250 000–500 000 Australians experience noise-induced hearing loss through being exposed to high noise levels at work.
- Australian workers are exposed to some 80 000 industrial chemicals which, when used improperly, can cause injury and disease.
- Skin disorders, such as dermatitis and skin cancer, account for half of all compensated diseases. One affected area is the food processing industry.
- Work-related cancers make up a significant proportion of all cancers. Exposure to blue asbestos is associated with the rare cancer mesothelioma which had already killed over 1500 people by the early 1990s.
- At least one in three of all compensated injuries are caused by machinery or equipment. High-risk industries are mining, agriculture, forestry and manufacturing.
- Women suffer fewer compensated injuries and diseases in the workplace than men, but lose more time off work. Only 1.4% of women were recorded as being injured in the workplace, whereas 3.4% of men suffered injuries during the same period.

WORKSAFE AUSTRALIA
See Government Health Bodies, pp. 404–5.

Mental Health

Over the years there have been a number of approaches to caring for the mentally ill in Australia. It was the advent of drug therapy and the growth of the human rights movement in the mid-1950s, however, which really influenced and changed the philosophy behind the treatment of mentally ill people.

During the 1960s and early 1970s, policies of non-institutional care were implemented and a process of discharging long-stay patients occurred in the belief that new drug therapies would allow many people to be managed as outpatients, thus eliminating the dehumanising effects of long-term institutional care. It is a scheme not without its own hazards, however, as many suffering from mental disorders suffer human rights abuses out in the community.

NATIONAL MENTAL HEALTH STRATEGY
Commonwealth funding of $269 million has been committed from 1992 through to 1998. It is being used to implement the National Mental Health Strategy designed to reform and overhaul the mental health sector. About

$189 million of this is directly for the States and Territories, placing the responsibility for the delivery of specialist public mental health services in their hands. National programs receive $68 million, while $5 million is dedicated to mental health research.

State and Territory projects include:
- the creation of community crisis services open for extended hours;
- more mental health workers placed in rural communities;
- establishment of community-based respite care services;
- more places made available in appropriate accommodation;
- specialist programs for children and adolescents.

National projects include:
- community awareness programs to educate the general population about mental health disorders and therefore dispel myths and eliminate the abuse, injustice, stigma and discrimination surrounding the issue;
- programs to educate the non-English speaking community about mental health issues, and fully inform them of services available for those in need;
- examining ways in which various government departments could integrate to ensure greater access to improved services and support;
- an inquiry into the educational and training necessities in the mental health workforce;
- the development of effective mental health legislation.

INCIDENCE

Approximately 20% of the adult population will be affected by mental health problems in their lifetime, while between 10% and 15% of young people will be afflicted in the space of a year.

Women have a poorer mental health status and use mental health services more than men. At 14–15 years of age, depression in adolescent girls stands at 29.4% of the total population; more than double that for boys at 12.9%. This pattern continues through adult life to old age, where women have a higher risk of developing dementia than men. Men, however, have higher rates of suicide and increased incidence of alcohol abuse, while homeless men exhibit a high rate of mental disorder.

SENILE DEMENTIA

The rate of mental disorders such as dementia increases with advancing years. It is estimated that up to 2% of the population aged 65–70 years, and up to 20% after the age of 80 years, will have some form of dementia. The incidence of dementia is expected to increase by over 70% in the next 20 years due to Australia's ageing population.

SCHIZOPHRENIA

Schizophrenia is estimated to affect 1% of the population. The term covers several disorders that vary symptomatically and in terms of treatment. There are generally considered to be two forms: acute, when the sufferer is not in touch with reality, experiences delusions, has hallucinations and disordered thoughts; and chronic, when the personality appears to break down. Emotions are dulled or inappropriate, and the sufferer withdraws from social contact, lacking energy, insight and volition.

Researchers believe that schizophrenia is a result of genetic and biochemical factors. Antipsychotic drugs have revolutionised the treatment of the disorder, working to correct the chemical imbalance in the brain. Used in conjuction with appropriate psychotherapy, most sufferers are able to live in the community. Between 50% and 90% of sufferers relapse if they stop taking the medication.

Care for the Elderly

Through its Aged Residential Care Program, the Commonwealth government is trying to promote quality of life for the rapidly increasing population of elderly people, by offering a range of home and community care and a network of hostels and nursing homes.

HOME NURSING ASSISTANCE

Hostels or nursing homes are not necessarily the only option for frail elderly people who have a relative or other carer willing to look after them in their own homes. These carers may receive the Carer Pension subject to a means test, however, the person being cared for must be frail, aged or severely disabled. The carer need not live in the same house, but must be able to show that constant, substantial care is given.

HOME AND COMMUNITY CARE

Under the Commonwealth government's Review of the Aged Care Reform Strategy, elderly people are able to stay in their homes for as long as possible instead of being forced to move to a nursing home or hostel. An assessment program works to ensure that the aged receive appropriate care based on their physical, psychological, emotional and social needs and the needs of those who care for them.

SERVICES

A wide range of services are available, including home help (cleaning, cooking, banking, washing, ironing), personal care, home maintenance, food services (shopping and Meals on Wheels), community respite care (giving carers a break from their role), transport, community nursing and paramedical aid (physiotherapy and podiatry at a community centre or in the home).

RESIDENTIAL CARE FOR OLDER PEOPLE

This section covers some of the alternatives to home or community care that exist for older people.

HOSTELS

Hostels do not provide full nursing care, but instead offer help with daily tasks. Accommodation is usually a single room, which can be furnished with the resident's own belongings, and a private bathroom. Staff help with personal care such as bathing, dressing and eating, and are on call 24 hours a day to help when needed. Living in a hostel is affordable even if the only income is the aged pension.

At July 1995, there were about 1450 hostels Australia-wide, offering 59 900 places. Commonwealth expenditure in the preceding year reached $363.1 million. (There was also additional capital expenditure on hostels and nursing homes of $107.1 million.)

SPECIAL SERVICES

Special services exist to help organise activities for hostel residents who suffer from conditions like Alzheimer's disease. There are also day therapy services to hostels and community residents.

NURSING HOMES

Nursing homes cater for people who need to have continuous nursing care and a lot of daily help with personal care. Accommodation is usually a mix of four-bed, two-bed and private rooms, with adjoining day lounge, activity and dining rooms. A registered nurse is available 24 hours a day. Some smaller nursing homes cater for specific groups such as Aboriginal and Torres Strait Islander people, ethnic groups and rural communities.

In 1987, the Commonwealth government introduced standard daily nursing home fees and standard government benefits. Operating costs for nursing homes were split into two areas: nursing, personal care and staff; and infrastructure costs such as food, cleaning and laundry. At July 1995, Commonwealth expenditure on nursing homes reached $1804.7 million. The 1996–1997 Coalition Budget announced the means testing of nursing homes, permitting them to charge upfront fees that could average $26 000.

Disabled People

People with intellectual, physical, sensory or psychiatric disabilities are able to apply for assistance from a number of government programs to assist them with employment, job placement, training, recreation, accommodation, independent living and care. The government also funds services and programs which provide rehabilitation, hearing aids and other audiological services. These services are provided under the *Disability Services Act 1986* working in conjunction with the 1993 Commonwealth/State Disability Agreement (CSDA). The agreement rationalises the provision of services, determining that the Commonwealth administers employment programs while the states and territories manage accommodation and other support services. It is roughly estimated that 18% of the population have one or more disabilities, with about 95% of these people living in households.

ACCOMMODATION

The Home and Community Care Program funds community groups and accommodation services that help disabled people stay at home. Respite care services are offered for short term relief for families or other unpaid carers, or for disabled people caring for themselves. Other services offer home help and maintenance, personal care, transport services and community nursing. Special needs programs are also funded for those from non-English speaking backgrounds, Aboriginal and Torres Strait Islanders and young people, amongst other groups.

EMPLOYMENT AND TRAINING

Services exist to help disabled people gain paid employment in the general workforce at, or above, award wages.

The Competitive Employment Training and Placement Services place people who have a disability, but do not require substantial support in award wage jobs. Training and support designed to meet the specific needs of the worker are provided for about two years, until it is felt that the person can work independently. The worker's progress is monitored with the aim of encouraging them towards financial independence.

The Commonwealth government has operated the Commonwealth Rehabilitation Service (CRS) since 1948. It provides working age disabled people with vocational and rehabilitation services, with the expectation that a job or independent living are achievable goals. The services provided include physiotherapy, occupational and speech therapy, aids and appliances, home, car and workplace modifications and appropriate housing and training allowances.

AUSTRALIAN HEARING SERVICES

This statutory authority offers hearing assessment, selection and fitting of hearing aids and other devices to eligible people. Services operate out of about 55 permanent and 75 visiting hearing centres in cities and towns throughout Australia, including some in remote areas.

To be eligible to use the services, a person must be younger than 21 years old, have a Commonwealth Seniors Health or Pensioner Concession Card, or be an eligible veteran.

Childcare

Childcare is an important facility in the growth of equal opportunity for women. With increasing numbers of women entering the workforce, the issue of adequate childcare increases in importance.

CHILDREN'S SERVICE PROGRAM

This program is concerned with the improvement of childcare: its supply, affordability and quality.

In June 1983, there were just 46 000 funded childcare places, while in the year ending June 1995 this number had increased to about 269 000. It is estimated that by the year 2001 there will be 354 000 funded places. These places include community and private long daycare places, family daycare places, occasional care places, Aboriginal Children's Service places and outside school hours care places.

At June 1995, it was estimated that approximately 396 720 children were attending childcare services. The majority (about 133 500) were going to private centres, followed by 88 700 attending family day care and 77 700 attending community long day care. About 63 900 children attended an outside school hours care service.

TYPES OF CHILDCARE AVAILABLE

CENTRE-BASED CHILD CARE   These centres take care of children under school age while their parents are working or training to enter the workforce, and are open a minimum of eight hours a day, five days a week for at least 48 weeks of the year.

FAMILY DAY CARE   This service takes children under school age and from 5–12 years and supervises them in private homes of childcare-trained staff.

OUTSIDE SCHOOL HOURS AND HOLIDAY CARE   These centres operate before and after school hours and during the school holidays, and are attended by children from 5–12 years.

MULTIFUNCTIONAL CENTRES   These centres are located in rural areas and take care of children whether their parents work or not.

OCCASIONAL CARE   These places are open for parents who want to take a break, especially those with children under school age. Parents can leave their children in care while they go shopping or while they have an appointment, but only for a short period of time.

SPECIAL SERVICES   Childcare centres exist which look after children from Aboriginal backgrounds, non-English speaking families and those children who are disabled, offering services which take into account their different cultural backgrounds or special needs.

CHILDCARE CASH REBATE

In 1994, a 30% Childcare Cash Rebate was introduced for work-related childcare. A limit is set on per week expenses: about $115 for one child and $225 for two or more. By June 1995, there were more than 252 000 families registered for the Rebate. If the service costs more, parents have to bridge the gap.

CHILDCARE ASSISTANCE

This service gives special consideration to low- and middle-income families wishing to place their children into care. The threshold for maximum assistance is connected to the Social Security's Additional Family Payment.

In the year ending June 1995, about 240 000 families using long day care received government financial assistance through the scheme. About 40% of these families received the maximum amount of assistance.

13

Education, Employment & Training

The Commonwealth's Role

*T*he Commonwealth government is committed to increasing employment opportunities, reducing unemployment, improving the skills base and promoting equity in higher education and training in the labour market.

The Commonwealth's main role is to act as a national coordinator for education, employment and training by developing and implementing policies in these areas. These policy responsibilities include external territories such as Christmas Island, Norfolk Island and the Cocos Islands, as well as the Aboriginal and Torres Strait Islander population and migrants to Australia.

The Commonwealth also provides limited funding to the States and total funding for higher education institutions and student assistance schemes. The States and the two Territories administer their own systems of primary, secondary and technical and further education and provide substantial funding of their own.

Department of Employment, Education, Training and Youth Affairs

The Commonwealth Department of Employment, Education, Training and Youth Affairs (DEETYA) advises on and implements government policies for achieving immediate and long-term economic goals through programs aimed at improving Australia's employment, education and training systems.

In 1996, greater emphasis was placed on assisting the nation's young people, with the inclusion of 'Youth Affairs' in the Department's name.

DEETYA PROGRAM OBJECTIVES

SCHOOLS   Supporting schools so as to enable all young people to share equally in the benefits of education.

HIGHER EDUCATION   Using higher education resources effectively so that Australia may meet its ever-increasing need for an educated and skilled work force. It also aims to encourage and maintain a system that takes a long-term and independent approach in pursuing teaching, scholarly work and research.

VOCATIONAL EDUCATION AND TRAINING Contributing to the improvement of the workforce's productivity and skills, and thereby increasing the nation's economic competitiveness.

EMPLOYMENT Enabling the labour market to function efficiently by ensuring equitable access to employment prospects and opportunities to improve skills.

STUDENT, YOUTH AND ABORIGINAL AND TORRES STRAIT ISLANDER EDUCATION SUPPORT Improving access to, participation and retention in, and completion of education, training and work experience. Special priority is given to encouraging indigenous people into education.

LEGISLATION

The Portfolio administers a total of 35 items of legislation. The key acts are:
- the *Employment, Education and Training Act 1988*;
- the *Employment Services Act 1994*;
- the *Higher Education Funding Act 1988*;
- the *Student and Youth Assistance Act 1973*; and
- the *Vocational Education and Training Funding Act 1992*.

STATUTORY BODIES

A number of statutory bodies have been established by legislation administered by the portfolio. These bodies complement the work of DEETYA:
- Anglo-Australian Telescope Board
- Australian Maritime College
- Australian National Training Authority
- Australian National University
- Employment Services Regulatory Authority
- National Board of Employment, Education and Training
- University of Canberra.

EXPENDITURE

In the year ending June 1996, DEETYA's total expenses reached $1 004 059 000; an increase on the previous year's figure of $978 692 000. The net cost of services was $983 773 000, with revenue from the government totalling $1 045 415 000. The total revenue less expenses came to $61 641 000.

The Education System

COMMONWEALTH FUNDING

The Commonwealth government hands down funding for education to the States and Territories, who distribute this accordingly between preschool, primary and secondary schooling, TAFE, tertiary education and other educational institutions eligible for government funding. Total government spending on education in 1993–1994 came to $22 125 million: 5.2% of gross domestic product (GDP). This marked a steady increase from 1988–1989 when the $15 761 million spent represented 4.6% of GDP.

Private final expenditure went from $5658 million in 1992–1993 to $5960 million in 1993–1994; a rise of 5.3%. This remained constant at 1.3% of GDP.

Schooling

AUSTRALIA'S SCHOOLS

Australia's first school was that now known as Parramatta Marist High School, founded in 1821 by Father John Terry. In 1832, two Anglican schools opened in Sydney and Parramatta (the King's school), providing a liberal English education. Despite the existence of these and other schools, education did not become compulsory in Australia until 1869.

In 1994, there were 9679 schools in Australia: 7159 government schools and 2520 non-government schools. Government schools receive about 90% of their funding from their State or Territory governments with the Commonwealth contribution representing about 10%. Non-government schools charge tuition fees, as well as receiving about 65% of their funding from the Commonwealth. The States and Territories provide about 35%. Approximately 2 214 940 students attended the government schools: 1 360 770 at primary level and 854 167 at secondary level. There were about 884 440 students attending non-government schools: 91 890 in primary school and 419 470 in secondary school.

The retention rate of secondary students staying on until Year 12 fell in all States and Territories from 76.6% in 1993 to 74.6% in 1994. The highest retention rates are amongst females at non-government schools, while the lowest rates are for males at government schools. The rate for indigenous students was 31% in 1995, and the rates for low socio-economic status and rural or remote students are also lower than for the general school population.

In the same period, there were approximately 143 380 teaching staff at government schools, and 56 960 at non-government schools.

LEVELS OF SCHOOLING IN AUSTRALIA

There are four levels of schooling in Australia: preschool, primary, junior secondary (Years 7–10) and senior secondary (Years 11 and 12). It is compulsory for children to begin school by the age of six and they can legally leave once they turn 15 (16 in Tasmania). Age requirements for starting school vary from State to State. In New South Wales, for example, children may begin preschool at 3 years 9 months, while in Western Australia children cannot enter preschool until they turn five years of age.

Examination methods also vary. Most States examine school students in both Year 10 and 12, although Victoria, Tasmania and the Northern Territory also hold exams in Year 11.

NATIONAL CURRICULUM

Since 1988, the Commonwealth, States and Territories have been working together to establish a national curriculum. Eight key learning areas have been identified: English, mathematics, science, technology, studies of society and the environment, the arts, health and physical education, and languages other than English.

SPECIAL PROGRAMS

The Commonwealth government funds a wide range of school programs which focus on groups of students with special needs and encourages them to take part in education at all levels. Such programs are aimed at students disadvantaged by lower income backgrounds or geographical isolation, disabled children and students not likely to finish secondary schooling.

There are also special programs which aim to improve the teaching of English as a second language (ESL). Aboriginal and Torres Strait Islander children are also served by special programs which, in some cases, offer bilingual classes in communities where the child's first language is not English. These programs are often backed up by the deployment of indigenous teachers' aides.

Other programs focus on children with learning difficulties, while there are also programs for students recognised as gifted.

GRANTS

There are two major programs that deal with the funding of schools in Australia. The general recurrent grants provide financial support for government and non-government schools. In 1995, $2513 million was allocated, covering 2 244 000 students in government schools and 897 000 students in non-government schools.

The Capital Grants Program assists schools in improving school facilities and educational outcomes in relation to the broader curriculum and new technologies. It also aims to ensure that indigenous and rural students have access to facilities. In 1995, $320 million was allocated for school building projects.

NATIONAL EQUITY PROGRAM FOR SCHOOLS

There are four major elements to this government-funded program: access, equity, national priorities and incentives. Each of these elements is further broken up into a number of parts:

Components	1995 funding (million)
Access	
English as a second language	$106.7
Special education	$74.4
Equity	
Disadvantaged schools	$66.6
Country areas	$15.4
National priorities	
Early literacy	$8.9
Literacy and learning	$1.7
Students at risk	$7.2
Transition support	$2.2
Gifted and talented	$1.1
Incentives	
Students with disabilities	$9.9
Gender equity	$1.4

LANGUAGES AND ASIAN STUDIES PROGRAM

Recognising Australia as a multicultural society, this program promotes the study of foreign languages and the quality teaching and learning of Asian Studies. In 1995, the community languages element of the program was allocated $11 million which was used to support over 230 000 students studying more than 60 languages.

SCHOOLS OF THE AIR/ DISTANCE EDUCATION CENTRES

Education of children in the vast and sparsely settled areas of outback Australia has always been a major problem. Children isolated from regular schools due to distance, health, or because they are travelling for extended periods of time with their families, can enrol in Schools of the Air which operate in New South Wales, South Australia, Queensland, Western Australia and the Northern Territory. Children are taught using a variety of media from print, audio, radio, video and graphics to fax, teleconferencing and networked personal computers. This is combined with home visits. Pupils must attend three compulsory air lessons each week, complete the correspondence course work and whenever possible take advantage of the field services provided by the school. Video and audio tapes, slides, pictures, library books and corrected work are posted free of charge between child and teacher. Students can use Schools of the Air from preschool through to Years 10–12, although most will leave home for their secondary education.

The first School of the Air was established at Alice Springs on 8 June 1951, although it was not until 1953 that a teacher was officially appointed to the school by the South Australian Department of Education. To make broadcasts to children in the area, the School borrowed the Royal Flying Doctor Service's radio network. Today it operates on its own frequencies using modern radio technology.

Higher Education

Higher education began when Australia's first higher education institution, Sydney University, was established on 1 October 1850. Although tertiary education was originally set up on a fee-paying basis, the Whitlam Labor government abolished fees in 1972 on the basic principle that education was a right and not a privilege. Since 1989, however, students have once again paid fees in the form of the Higher Education Contribution Scheme (HECS).

As of 1996, there were 36 public universities belonging to the Unified National System of Higher Education with over 600 000 students enrolled. Female students outnumbered male students, the proportion of female students being about 54%.

The areas of study with the greatest number of students were arts, humanities and social sciences (23%); economics and business administration (21%); and science (15%). About 59% of these students were enrolled in full-time study, 29% in part-time study and 12% in external studies. Approximately 60% of students are aged 24 years or under.

COMMONWEALTH FUNDING

The Commonwealth provides funds for higher education under the *Higher Education Funding Act 1988*. In 1994, funding totalled $4968 million, increasing to $5065 million in 1995.

OTHER FUNDING SOURCES

Contributions from students under the Higher Education Contribution Scheme (HECS) are also expected to make an increasing contribution to higher education funding. In 1995–1996, the HECS financial contribution from individuals came to $391 475 000. About $185 861 000 came from HECS receipts paid through the taxation system, while $175 546 000 came from up-front payments by students to institutions.

In this same period, it was estimated that the total HECS debt estimated to be outstanding was $3 304 803 000. An estimated 17.2% of this is unlikely to be repaid. This is because individuals do not make repayments on their debt through the Australian Taxation Office unless their taxable income reaches an indexed minimum ($27 675 for the 1995–1996 period).

In 1994, the proportion of funding from sources other than the Commonwealth government and HECS came to about 27%; a dramatic increase from the 11% of 1983.

Some of the other sources include: State and Territory governments (2%), investment income (2%), donations and bequests (1%) and fees and charges (11%). About 12% came from such sources as research products, loans and the proceeds of the sale of assets and products.

HIGHER EDUCATION CONTRIBUTION SCHEME (HECS)

With the higher education system costing the taxpayer around $3000 million a year, a committee headed by former NSW Premier, Neville Wran, was set up in 1987 to examine alternative ways of funding the education system. In April 1988, the Wran Committee recommended the Higher Education Contribution Scheme (HECS), which came into effect on 1 January 1989.

In December 1996, the Coalition government introduced a number of significant changes to HECS. All courses are now placed in one of three categories using a formula that takes into account the cost of the degree and the earning potential of graduates. While existing students continue to pay a flat fee of $2500, new students in the humanities, social sciences, visual and performing arts and nursing pay $3300 a year, and those in science, architecture, computing, engineering, business or economics pay $4700. New students enrolled in dentistry, law, medicine and veterinary science pay $5500 each year.

Students begin to repay their HECS debt when their income reaches $20 700; the previous income threshold was $28 000. Graduates pay their debt in instalments deducted from their pay. Students with a dependent spouse and children who are exempt from the Medicare levy will also be exempt from repaying HECS.

From 1998, universities will be able to 'sell' up to 25% of their places per course to Australian residents. These students must be able to pay for the full cost of a degree, which could be as high as $30 000. It is expected that these places will raise up to $1 billion a year for universities.

Between 1997 and 2000, the government will award 4000 merit scholarships which will be exempt from HECS. These are aimed at students who are economically disadvantaged, including indigenous students and those from rural and isolated areas. The average duration of these scholarships is four years.

AMALGAMATION — A UNIFIED NATIONAL SYSTEM

To be an eligible member of the unified national system, higher education institutions must have a minimum enrolment of at least 2000 full-time students. If not, they must merge with a larger institution which negotiates with the Commonwealth for funding on their behalf. Institutions on common or adjacent sites must combine under a single management structure and have a single educational profile — a further condition for membership of the unified national system. From 1990, only institutions in the national network are fully funded. Those not in the network are funded on a contract basis for teaching purposes only.

Before the amalgamation policy was implemented in 1989, there were 79 higher education institutions in Australia. The Federal government reduced this number by more than half.

ADMISSION TO HIGHER EDUCATION

For school leavers entering higher education, admission is based on a tertiary entrance score, calculated on academic achievement in the final one or two years of study and, in some cases, on aptitude as well. Many courses in high demand, such as medicine, dentistry and law, select candidates on the basis of their tertiary entrance score.

Institutions make special entry provisions for mature-age applicants who may lack normal entrance qualifications, and for those who have suffered disadvantage in their schooling.

TERTIARY ADMISSION CENTRES

Tertiary admission centres receive and process applications for admission to participating institutions and advise applicants of their selection and matriculation status. To matriculate, students must have completed their last year of senior secondary school and must have taken their final exams in Year 12.

AUSTRALIAN UNIVERSITIES, 1996

Institution	Location	Established
University of Sydney	Sydney	1850
University of Melbourne	Melbourne	1853
University of Adelaide	Adelaide	1874
Royal Melbourne Institute of Technology	Melbourne	1887
University of Tasmania	Hobart	1890
University of Queensland	Brisbane	1909
University of Western Australia	Perth	1911
Australian National University	Canberra	1946
University of New South Wales	Sydney	1949
University of New England	Armidale, NSW	1954
Monash University	Melbourne	1958
La Trobe University	Melbourne	1964
Macquarie University	Sydney	1964
University of Newcastle	Newcastle, NSW	1965
Flinders University	Adelaide	1966
James Cook University	Townsville, Qld	1970
Griffith University	Brisbane	1971
Murdoch University	Perth	1973
Deakin University	Geelong, Vic.	1974
University of Wollongong	Wollongong, NSW	1975
Bond University (private)	Gold Coast, Qld	1987
Curtin University of Technology	Perth	1987
Northern Territory University	Darwin	1988
University of Technology	Sydney	1988
Charles Sturt University	Bathurst, NSW	1989
University of Western Sydney	St Marys	1989
Queensland University of Technology	Brisbane	1989
Victoria University of Technology	Footscray	1990
Central Queensland University	Rockhampton	1990
University of Canberra	Canberra	1990
University of South Australia	Adelaide	1991
Edith Cowan University	Nedlands, WA	1991
Australian Catholic University	Sydney	1991
University of Southern Queensland	Toowoomba	1992
Swinburne University of Technology	Melbourne	1992
Notre Dame University (private)	Fremantle, WA	1992
University of Ballarat	Ballarat, Vic.	1994
Southern Cross University	Lismore, NSW	1994

PRIVATE EDUCATIONAL INSTITUTIONS

There are a number of educational institutions that, although they must be approved by the Department of Employment, Education, Training and Youth Affairs, receive no government support and are funded solely by the private sector.

BOND UNIVERSITY

Bond University was Australia's first privately funded tertiary institution, situated on Queensland's Gold Coast. The university opened in May 1989, and has five schools: the School of Information and Computing Sciences; the School of Business; the School of Humanities and Social Sciences; the School of Law; and the Graduate School of Science and Technology. The university's grounds include the University Park Hotel, and the Bond University Research Park, where business and industry representatives reside alongside students.

NON-GOVERNMENT COLLEGES

Most non-government colleges cater for overseas students paying full fees and offer professional and occupational training courses in areas such as business, economics and engineering.

A large percentage of overseas students study at the more than 120 English language colleges (ELICOS), where courses range from four weeks to 12 months. Costs vary according to the length and content of the course. Educational bodies such as the Workers Educational Association and a range of voluntary groups help meet adult education needs in the community through a variety of courses and programs.

UNIVERSITY OF SOUTHERN QUEENSLAND

Australia's first solely Internet-based university course — Open and Distance Learning Graduate Certificate Course — began in July 1996. Funded by the telecommunications giant AT&T, there are students from the US, Canada, Singapore, the Solomon Islands, Malaysia, the UK, Brazil and Mexico.

Aboriginal Education

The Commonwealth government is responsible for ensuring that indigenous Australians have equality of access to, participation and retention in and completion of education. The National Aboriginal and Torres Strait Islander Education Policy was introduced in 1990, receiving the support of indigenous communities throughout the country.

In 1995–1996, $292 million was provided for DEETYA's Aboriginal Education program; an increase from the $253 million spent in 1994–1995. The program has three main components: ABSTUDY, Aboriginal Education Direct Assistance (AEDA) and the Aboriginal Education Strategic Initiatives Program.

1. ABSTUDY

This financial assistance scheme encourages indigenous students to complete secondary school and move on to further education. In 1995–1996, about 48 000 students benefitted from the scheme; an increase of 4.7% from the previous year. Government expenditure was $129 million; an increase of 12.4% over the previous year.

2. ABORIGINAL EDUCATION DIRECT ASSISTANCE (AEDA)

ABORIGINAL TUTORIAL ASSISTANCE SCHEME   Assistance by more than 10 000 tutors was given to about 50 000 students. The expenditure of $32 million in 1995–1996 was spread evenly between primary, secondary and tertiary students.

VOCATIONAL AND EDUCATIONAL GUIDANCE FOR ABORIGINALS SCHEME   About 550 projects received a total of $2.3 million in funding in 1995–1996.

ABORIGINAL STUDENT SUPPORT AND PARENT AWARENESS PROGRAM School-based parent groups received $16.5 million in funding, to help them increase the participation and attendance of indigenous students. About 10 000 parents in 3000 groups were involved, representing about 84 000 students.

3. ABORIGINAL EDUCATION STRATEGIC INITIATIVES PROGRAM

The Aboriginal Education Strategic Initiatives Program (AESIP) is one of the main bodies responsible for ensuring the implementation of the National Aboriginal and Torres Strait Islander Education Policy. In 1995–1996, the program received $84 million to improve outcomes in all education sectors except higher education.

Student Assistance

As with tertiary education, all student assistance is fully funded by the Commonwealth government. In 1994, the government spent $1602 million in this area. The three main areas of student assistance are AUSTUDY, Assistance for Isolated Children (AIC) and the Loan Supplement Scheme.

STUDENT ASSISTANCE SPENDING, 1994

Program	No. assisted	Funding ($ million)
AUSTUDY (secondary)	225 690	566
AUSTUDY (tertiary)	252 570	898
ABSTUDY (school)	26 280	45
ABSTUDY (tertiary)	17 990	69
Assistance for isolated children	13 040	24

AUSTUDY

AUSTUDY provides an annual living allowance to full-time students aged 16 years or over, who are Australian citizens or have Australian residency and are enrolled in approved secondary or tertiary courses. In 1995–1996, 481 600 students received assistance.

Although AUSTUDY is granted on a non-competitive basis, it is subject to a parental and family income and assets test. About 275 000 beneficiaries come from families whose incomes are in the bottom 40% of Australian family incomes.

The main AUSTUDY benefit is paid in three ways:

* standard rate;
* away from home rate (for country and outer metropolitan students); and
* independent rate (for those over 22 years of age who have spent at least three of the past four years in the workforce, or who are married with a dependent child or without parental support. An income and assets test applies).

If a student qualifies for a living allowance, they may be entitled to one or more of the following: fares allowance; dependent spouse allowance and/or childcare assistance (for some single parents).

PAYMENTS

All AUSTUDY payments are made fortnightly. Approximately $552 million was paid to secondary students in 1995–1996, while tertiary students received $1021 million.

ASSISTANCE FOR ISOLATED CHILDREN SCHEME

The Assistance for Isolated Children Scheme (AIC) assists families of primary, secondary and, in some cases, tertiary students who do not have daily access to a government school offering classes at the student's level. Some students may be geographically isolated, while others have a condition, disability or special educational need, or live in a family that is forced to move regularly due to work demands. These benefits are not income or assets tested.

It is believed that Year 12 retention rates for rural areas have increased from 58% in 1989 to 64% in 1994 partly because of this scheme. Rates for remote students have also increased from 47% to 58% in the same period.

Expenditure in 1995–1996 came to $28.1 million, with approximately 11 700 students assisted.

LOAN SUPPLEMENT SCHEME

This is a voluntary loan scheme whereby tertiary students can obtain additional financial assistance to help meet their living expenses. Loan recipients fall into two categories:

- tertiary students eligible for AUSTUDY or ABSTUDY who are allowed to trade in up to $3500 of their grant for a loan of twice that amount (i.e. up to $7000); and
- tertiary students ineligible for AUSTUDY or ABSTUDY because of the parental income test, but whose parents' adjusted income is less than $53 138 (in 1996). Students in this category can obtain a loan for up to $2000.

The Commonwealth Bank of Australia provides these supplement loans under an agreement with the Commonwealth government.

RESEARCH GRANTS AND AWARDS

POSTGRADUATE AWARDS SCHEME

Each year the government offers a number of competitive awards, based on academic merit, to selected higher education students undertaking Masters and PhD programs at Australian higher education institutions.

LARGE GRANTS Research projects by individuals and/or teams are allocated funds, with 667 of 2832 applications successful in 1996.

SMALL GRANTS In 1996, a total of $26.2 million was given to institutions, mostly to fund academics at the beginning of their careers.

COLLABORATIVE GRANTS This scheme encourages research collaboration between industry and higher education institutions. About $18.6 million was allocated in 1996 with 108 new grants and 159 continuing grants.

INTERNATIONAL FELLOWSHIPS These fellowships offer Australian positions to about 15 postdoctoral researchers from overseas, with fellowship periods ranging from four to twelve months.

AUSTRALIAN POSTGRADUATE AWARDS This program offers awards to students pursuing postgraduate studies at Australian institutions. About $76.6 million was allocated in 1996 for awards with stipend, with 1550 new awards given. About 3000 awards in this category were continued from previous years.

Awards designed to promote industry-based research began in 1990 with 150 new awards in 1996 allocated about $7.9 million.

In 1996, about 22 000 awards specifically granting HECS exemptions to postgraduate students were offered.

RESEARCH FELLOWSHIPS About $26 million was allocated in 1996 to outstanding researchers carrying out research both in Australian higher education institutions and other organisations. One hundred fellowships were granted of the 715 applications received.

OVERSEAS POSTGRADUATE RESEARCH SCHOLARSHIPS Outstanding overseas research students are attracted to Australia under this scheme, and are granted tuition fees and health insurance costs. In 1996, there were 300 new scholarships granted, with the cost for both new and continuing awards totalling approximately $15 million.

Overseas Students

Overseas students have become a significant part of Australian education with the export of education services rapidly growing and becoming a potentially important part of the Australian economy. There are currently 80 000 overseas students enrolled in Australian universities and colleges and paying full fees.

RECOGNITION OF OVERSEAS SKILLS

In order to take advantage of the skills and qualifications of migrants, enabling them to participate fully in the workforce, the National Office of Skills Recognition (NOOSR) provides three forms of assessment: educational, occupational and occupational by examination. The latter are conducted in such fields as dentistry, pharmacy, physiotherapy and veterinary science. NOOSR also aims to improve labour mobility with a particular emphasis on the Asia–Pacific region.

In the period 1995–1996, about 2060 educational, 1260 occupational and 395 examination assessments were carried out.

Bridging courses and training programs are available in a number of areas to assist those with overseas qualifications. These labour market programs prepare professionals to meet local recognition requirements. In 1995–1996, a total of 407 participants took part in bridging courses, with the greatest number being doctors, nurses, dentists and accountants.

Educational Administration

Aside from DEETYA, there are a number of other national organisations responsible for the administration of educational matters.

NATIONAL BOARD OF EMPLOYMENT, EDUCATION AND TRAINING

The National Board of Employment, Education and Training advises the government on relevant matters of policy, coordinating the input of business, union and industry organisations. It is assisted by six councils: the Australian International Education Foundation Council, the Australian Language and Literacy Council, the Australian Research Council, the Employment and Skills Formation, the Higher Education Council and the Schools Council.

MINISTERIAL COUNCIL ON EDUCATION, EMPLOYMENT, TRAINING AND YOUTH AFFAIRS

The council's prime responsibility is to establish links between labour-market programs and education and training, from pre-primary through to higher education and vocational training. It coordinates national policies, negotiating and developing national agreements on shared interests and objectives.

AUSTRALIAN COUNCIL FOR EDUCATIONAL RESEARCH

The Australian Council for Educational Research receives annual grants from State, Territory and the Commonwealth grants, but operates as an independent research organisation. It conducts and contracts research into the evaluation and measurement of education, learning and teaching.

NATIONAL CENTRE FOR VOCATIONAL EDUCATION RESEARCH

Established in 1980, this government-funded centre conducts and funds research, as well as maintaining statistics on vocational education and training. It also publishes research reports and journals, as well as housing the International Labour Organisation.

STANDARDS AND CURRICULUM COUNCIL

The Standards and Curriculum Council was formed to ensure that national competency standards and curriculum assessments are developed efficiently and effectively. It is also responsible for the management of the Australian Qualifications Framework, introduced in January 1995, in relation to vocational education and training.

Training

TECHNICAL AND FURTHER EDUCATION (TAFE)

TAFE is a vital element of Australia's post-school education and training system and is funded largely by the States and Territories. Most courses are held at TAFE centres, although some courses are taught at higher education institutions, agricultural colleges and adult education authorities spread throughout metropolitan and country areas. Courses vary from entry-level training, specialised instruction and vocational training prior to employment, to adult education courses available for personal interest and leisure.

ENTRY INTO TAFE

TAFE's non-discriminatory access policy means that courses are open to all permanent residents of Australia who have left school, although TAFE also operates with high schools to provide courses for their students in selected areas. TAFE also caters for groups in the community with special needs, such as Aboriginal and Torres Strait Islanders, senior citizens, people in remote areas, unemployed people, people with disabilities, or those from non-English speaking backgrounds.

TAFE COURSES AND AWARDS

TAFE offers a range of courses: skills training in a trade; courses specially tailored to industry or government needs; vocational training; programs to help people get back into studying or work, and enrichment programs.

The training programs are broadly classified on the higher education model of 12 fields of study: land and marine resources, animal husbandry; architecture and building; arts, humanities and social sciences; business administration and economics; education; engineering and surveying; health and community services; law and legal studies; science; veterinary science and animal care; hospitality and transport services; and TAFE multi-field education.

The awards given for a pass in a TAFE course mirror the educational level and duration of the course.

TAFE FUNDING

In 1994, the TAFE system received about $2600 million in funding: about 70% of this came from the States and Territories, while the Commonwealth provided about 20%. The other 10% came from fees and various other sources. Capital funding for the same period came to $348 million, with the Commonwealth providing 65% and the States and Territories 35%.

Leisure and enrichment courses were once free at TAFE and training cost considerably less than it does now. In 1989, however, an annual TAFE administration charge was introduced. Overseas students must pay full fees to attend TAFE.

ENROLMENTS

In 1993, there were 1 121 340 TAFE students, with part-time students accounting for 974 920 of this total. The ratio of women to men is almost equal, with 597 280 men enrolled. TAFE courses are most popular with the 30–39 years age group, with this group accounting for 227 410 of the total number of students. The 20–24 years age group accounted for 209 710 of the student population.

The most popular faculties in 1993 were TAFE multi-field education (602 140); business administration and economics (327 750), and arts, humanities and social sciences (236 770).

SOME GOVERNMENT INITIATIVES

AUSTRALIAN NATIONAL TRAINING AUTHORITY

The Commonwealth government funds the Australian National Training Authority (ANTA) with money distributed amongst the States and Territories in support of a national vocational, education and training system. In the period 1995–1996, about $788 million was spent on national programs which included: equity programs designed to address gender imbalance; group training schemes for small companies; skills centres formed in conjunction with industry, business, TAFE colleges and governments; adult and community education funding.

MODERN AUSTRALIAN APPRENTICESHIP
AND TRAINEESHIP SYSTEM

The aim of the Modern Australian Apprenticeship and Traineeship System (MAATS) is to modernise the national training system, making it more responsive to the needs of industry. MAATS is an industry-led system that aims to provide a greater number of training opportunities by promoting access and equity, recognising it as essential that Australian businesses regard training programs as an attractive and beneficial proposition.

The Coalition government has allocated $207 million from 1996–2000 towards the implementation of MAATS.

NATIONAL EMPLOYMENT AND TRAINING TASKFORCE

The National Employment and Training Taskforce (NETTFORCE) was established to encourage more employers to create positions for the unemployed and to increase the number of training places offered at entry-level, especially for young people. In pursuit of this goal, NETTFORCE has set up 26 industry training companies (ITCs) to match up trainees and jobs across a broad range of industries.

In 1995–1996, there was a total of about 37 600 trainee commencements, with numbers dramatically increased in manufacturing and metals, small business, administration, recreation, automotive, tourism and hospitality and health and community services. Government funding for ITCs in this period was $4.4 million.

AUSTRALIAN STUDENT TRAINEESHIP FOUNDATION

Established in 1994, the Australian Traineeship Foundation promotes the gaining of workplace knowledge and experience by secondary school students. It encourages workplace partnerships between students and businesses/industry, so that skills relevant to the labour market can be developed.

Grants totalling more than $10 million fund structured workplace programs for a projected 25 000 students. Many of the programs lead directly into traineeships and apprenticeships.

AUSTRALIAN VOCATIONAL TRAINING SYSTEM

The Australian Vocational Training System (AVTS) provides opportunities for combining education, training and experience in workplaces, based on business and industry endorsed standards of competency. In the 1995–1996 period, about 145 projects were running throughout Australia: 110 were based in workplaces, while the others were based in institutions (usually schools). Expenditure on these projects reached $6.6 million.

A survey found that six months after completing projects, about 63% of the participants were employed. Approximately 88% of the participants based in workplaces were employed.

Employment

The Department of Employment, Education, Training and Youth Affairs (DEETYA) contributes to the efficient functioning of the Australian labour market through the Commonwealth Employment Service (CES). The CES offers a broad range of services to the workforce and to Australian business and industry.

COMMONWEALTH EMPLOYMENT SERVICE

Australia's only public employment service, the Commonwealth Employment Service (CES), helps employers find the workers they need and job seekers find employment. When matching up people and jobs, CES staff provide counselling and advice on opportunities, as well as arranging referrals and giving the latest information on the employment scene, with emphasis on the special requirements of job seekers who are disadvantaged.

By going into the CES regularly, job seekers are kept up-to-date with new employment opportunities. Regular contact is also a condition for receiving any of the categories of Unemployment Benefits ('the dole'). In 1995, approximately 74% of vacancies notified were filled.

FUNCTIONS OF THE COMMONWEALTH EMPLOYMENT SERVICE

While primarily registering job seekers and filling job vacancies, the CES also plays a number of other vital roles: job referral; identification of job seekers needing special assistance; referral of these job seekers to specialist units; case management of the long-term unemployed (those unemployed for 12 months and more) through Employment Assistance Australia (EAA); advice on and placement in labour market programs, and the promotion of these programs to employers.

SPECIALIST SERVICES

Specialist officers are trained to cater for those with specific needs that may not be met by the general CES service. They target specific groups such as the long term unemployed, migrants with English language difficulties, people with disabilities, Aboriginal and Torres Strait Islanders, women, sole parents, people with low literacy levels and young people.

Specialist services available include Youth Access, Career Reference and Student Assistance Centres, Aboriginal and Torres Strait Islander Education Units, the Remote Area Field Service for remote clients, particularly indigenous communities, Templine for those seeking temporary employment only, and Recruitment Services Australia acting on behalf of the Australian Public Service.

EMPLOYMENT ASSISTANCE AUSTRALIA

Working in close collaboration with the CES, Employment Assistance Australia (EAA) case-manages the long-term unemployed and other disadvantaged job seekers under the provisions of the *Employment Services Act 1994*. The particular skills and needs of the job seeker are identified and a scheme is developed to assist them find and retain a job.

EAA costs in 1995–1996 came to approximately $162 million. About 458 000 job seekers had their cases managed through this scheme, with 2000 case managers working in more than 300 locations. The highest proportion of participants (50%) were the very long term unemployed, while other specific groups identified included women (31%), indigenous people (7%), people from a non-English speaking background (17%) and people with disabilities (18%).

The EAA regards an 'outcome' as the gaining of full- or part-time work, returning to full-time education and/or gaining subsidised employment using specific labour market programs.

EAA PARTICIPANTS AND OUTCOMES, 1995–1996

Job seeker type	Total no.	No. of outcomes
Long-term unemployed	120 534	39 655
Very long term unemployed	230 876	128 553
Women	142 918	70 700
Indigenous	30 207	14 768
Non-English speaking backgrounds	79 327	35 175
People with disabilities	81 420	39 257

ABORIGINAL EMPLOYMENT AND TRAINING ASSISTANCE

The Commonwealth government aims to increase the numbers of indigenous Australians in the workforce using a number of strategies and programs. One of the main programs, the Training for Aboriginals and Torres Strait Islanders (TAP), uses Employment Strategies and Direct Assistance to further this aim.

The Employment Strategies element gives funding for agreements with employers to initiate recruitment and career development programs targeted at indigenous people. About $16 million was spent in this area in 1995–1996, with 1300 people recruited and 89 Employment Strategy agreements in place.

Delivered through the CES, Direct Assistance offers skills development, formal training and transition assistance. A participant in the scheme can move from training and work experience to subsided on-the-job training.

In 1995–1996, there were a total of 11 500 job commencements under TAP, with job placements in this scheme representing about 40% of all CES placements for indigenous clients. The total cost of TAP was about $37 million.

MIGRANT EMPLOYMENT

The Migrant Service Improvement Strategy (MSIS) aims to give migrants greater access to job opportunities. Migrant liaison officers are a bridge between the CES and the ethnic communities and employers, while Migrant Advisory Committees provide feedback to the CES on ethnic community needs. Interpreter services are also provided by the CES or case managers in the job-seeking client's preferred language. Expenditure for interpreter services in 1995–1996 was $2.4 million.

One of the employment support services specifically aimed at ethnic communites, is the Advanced English for Migrants Program. Advanced English as a Second Language training aims to assist job seekers over the language barrier so that they may participate fully in employment, vocational education and training. State and Territory governments receive grants to fund courses usually operating through TAFE of a registered ESL training centre. In 1996, $5.1 million was provided to assist about 4000 participants.

PRIVATE EMPLOYMENT AGENCIES

Private employment agencies receive no government support, but are financed through the private sector. While the 1980s were a growth period for the staffing industry, with the temporary personnel area experiencing a particularly sharp boom, many of these agencies have closed down in the 1990s. The industry has become more professional, with most agency staff holding a qualification from the Institute of Personnel Consultants.

Income Support

Several types of income support are provided by the Department of Social Security to those who are unemployed and willing and able to work.

YOUTH TRAINING ALLOWANCE

YTA is paid to people under the age of 18 who are taking part in education, training or work experience.

NEWSTART ALLOWANCE

The Newstart Allowance is paid to those people between the ages of 18 and 65 who are temporarily unemployed, but actively seeking work while registered with the CES.

SPECIAL BENEFIT

People in dire financial need, but unable to claim any other allowance or pension are eligible for this payment. The circumstances in which it is granted are determined by the Department of Social Security.

Employment Support Services

There are a range of labour market programs to assist eligible jobseekers into employment by providing services such as:
* training for the unemployed;
* assistance to employers who give jobs to the unemployed;
* assistance for individuals, enterprises and specific regions.

JOBSTART

This is a general wage subsidy program that emphasises equity of access to employment. Wage subsidies are paid for periods of up to 26 weeks to those who employ and improve the general employment prospects of disadvantaged job seekers. The scheme is aimed at those who have been unemployed for six months or more, or those who face other disadvantages such as a disability.

At June 1996, some 101 000 placements had been recorded at a cost of $236 million. In the previous year, 56.3% of those who had been in the scheme were taking part in unsubsidised employment, education or training three months after participation.

FORMAL TRAINING ASSISTANCE

This benefit is paid to job seekers receiving training to improve their employment prospects. Those eligible for this payment may receive income support as well as books, equipment, fares and tutorial assistance.

Formal Training Assistance (FTA) is available to those involved in any of the following schemes: JobTrain, Special Intervention Program, Accredited

Training for Youth, SkillShare, Training for Aboriginals and Torres Strait Islanders Program (TAP), New Enterprise Incentive Scheme Training Program, Special Assistance Program, National Skills Shortage, National Office of Overseas Skills Recognition Bridging Courses for the Overseas Trained, and Advanced English for Migrants.

JobTrain

This program, which began in 1988, provides opportunities for the long-term unemployed, people with disabilities, women returning to the workforce and other job seekers with special needs. Preference is given to those who have been unemployed for at least 12 months. The training assistance given is tailored to suit available opportunities in the local area, with courses provided by TAFE, private agencies, industry bodies and community-based organisations.

With a budget of $165 million in 1995–1996, 93 000 people were assisted. Three months after participating in the program, there was a success rate of almost 43%.

Employment Training

The three programs in this area combine on- and off-the-job training with practical work experience. The Landcare and Environment Action Program, JobSkills and New Work Opportunities were popular with case managers, but the results for the 1995–1996 period were disappointing with only 32% of participants in unsubsidised employment, education or training three months after completing the program. Expenditure came to $860 million, with around 89 000 people taking part.

Community-based Assistance

SkillShare

Skillshare is targeted at long-term unemployed people of all ages, and also at other disadvantaged groups such as young people 'at risk', indigenous Australians; migrants with English language difficulties, sole parents, offenders and ex-offenders, and homeless people.

Skillshare aims to provide employment-related training and assistance to those people most in need through community-based organisations, in response to local market conditions and the personal needs of participants. The local community provides about 15% of the total operating costs of SkillShare.

In 1995–1996, there were 405 projects across the country along with a range of specialist services such as Disability Access Support Units, Disadvantaged Young People Services and Mature Workers Centres.

About 165 000 participants were assisted in 1995–1996 at a total cost of $134 million. About 47% of clients were in unsubsidised employment, education or training three months after completing a SkillShare program.

PARTICIPATION IN AND POSITIVE OUTCOMES OF EMPLOYMENT PROGRAMS, 1995–1996

Program	No. commencing	Positive outcomes (%)
JobStart	100 520	56
National Training Wage	33 460	n.a.
JobSkills	27 410	38
Landcare and Environment Action Program	13 490	34
New Work Opportunities	49 400	25
JobTrain	92 800	43
Special Intervention	90 030	39
Accredited Training for Youth	1660	41
SkillShare	164 840	47
Job Clubs	45 790	44
Mobility Assistance	48 800	85
Other	4340	40

14
The Media

Changes in the Australian media

*B*ig changes have occurred in the Australian media in the past decade. The print media is dominated by just two main players: Kerry Packer and Rupert Murdoch. By 1995, the Murdoch share in the newspaper market stood at 66%, with Fairfax slipping to 22%. The country's magazine market, the biggest per population in the world, has possibly reached saturation point, with the launch of many new magazines over the past five years.

The electronic media has also been turned upside down by the rapid series of radio and television station sales that have occurred in the past decade and with the introduction of new cable and pay TV networks.

This section looks at the current state of the Australian print, radio and television media; who owns what and what regulations are applied to keep our media in check. For the purposes of this chapter, the Australian media is divided into two parts:
1. the publicly owned Australian Broadcasting Corporation (ABC) and the Special Broadcasting Service (SBS); and
2. the commercial broadcasting sector.

Both areas follow regulations set out by the *1942 Broadcasting Act* and its subsequent amendments. The Act is enforced by the Australian Broadcasting Authority (ABA).

Regulation of the Commercial Media

OWNERSHIP AND CONTROL PROVISIONS

COMMERCIAL TELEVISION
A person may not have a 'prescribed interest' (any direct or traceable interest above 15% in a licensee company) in:
- commercial television licences which have a combined audience reach of more than 60% of the nation;
- two or more commercial television licenses in the same state or the same metropolitan area.

At December 1996, the foreign ownership limit stands at 20%, with some networks calling for this to be raised to 35%; this is the amount currently permitted for pay television.

COMMERCIAL RADIO

From 1990, newspaper companies could not have more than a 15% holding in a radio station. From July 1992, commercial operators were permitted to own two stations in a single market. A person may not have a 'prescribed' interest (any direct or traceable interest above 15% in a licensee company) in:
- each of 17 or more commercial radio licences in Australia; or
- more than one licence within one area with allowance for up to 30% audience reach in the overlap between licences;
- each of a number of commercial radio licences which have a national audience reach of more than 50%.

PRINT

At December 1996, foreign ownership of major newspapers was limited to 25% for any one individual. Total foreign investment in local newspaper companies is limited to 30%.

CROSS-MEDIA LIMITS

Under cross-media limits, person may not have a 'prescribed interest' in more than one of the following in a Defined Service Area:
- a licence for a commercial television station;
- a licence for a commercial radio station;
- an associated newspaper.

At the end of 1996, almost all the nation's media companies were calling for an end to these restrictions, arguing that new technologies now make the cross-media rules out of date. They believe that integrated media companies are necessary as the Internet, global satellite and cable television compete with traditional media.

The current Howard Federal government appears to be strongly considering the scrapping of these limits, believing that they are too inflexible and too difficult to administer. The government favours the regulation of ownership by new general competition laws that will include a 'public interest' test for media ownership, with the Australian Competition and Consumer Commission (ACCC), operating under the *Trade Practices Act*, having the power to block deals which threaten to reduce ownership diversity seriously.

The Media Entertainment and Arts Alliance (MEAA) supports the retention of the cross-media limits.

FOREIGN LEVELS OF OWNERSHIP
At December 1996, the Federal government had set up a review to examine the issue of foreign ownership. It is strongly believed that the review will result in the abolishing of the current restriction on ownership of both a television network and newspaper in the same metropolitan market.

A Decade of Media Ownership

1986

- The Hawke/Keating government announces new laws to break up existing media empires.

1987

- Rupert Murdoch's News Ltd acquires the Herald and Weekly Times group for $2.5 billion and sells the group's television and radio assets.
- Cross-media ownership rules are introduced into the *Broadcasting Act*. The two television station rule is abolished and media companies are forced to specialise in either newspapers or television.
- Alan Bond buys Kerry Packer's Nine Network stations in Sydney and Melbourne for $1 billion.
- Ten Network stations in Sydney and Melbourne sold by News Ltd to Frank Lowy.
- Warwick Fairfax Jnr launches a successful privatisation bid for the Fairfax group.
- Fairfax group sells all its television interests to Christopher Skase in a deal worth $780 million.

1988

- Kerry Packer's Australian Consolidated Press (ACP) acquire the bulk of Fairfax's magazines.
- Cross-ownership laws extended to limit holdings by newspaper companies in radio stations to 5%.

1989

- Christopher Skase buys two more television networks from Robert Holmes à Court's Bell Group; seven months later, Skase's Quintex

Entertainment collapses and the market value of Skase's two public companies halves.

1990

- Packer buys back the Nine Network for $250 million when Alan Bond proves unable to pay the $800 million he owed after buying it three years earlier.
- Warwick Fairfax Jnr sacks the Fairfax board and becomes chairman and chief executive. With debts of $1.7 billion, the Fairfax group is put into receivership. This marks the collapse of a 149-year-old-empire just three years after Warwick Jnr took the helm.

1991

- Matt Handbury buys Murdoch Magazines from News Ltd.
- Cross-media laws reformed with changes to the definition of control and an increase in ownership limits in television and radio from 5% to 15%.
- Conrad Black's Tourang consortium buys Fairfax from its receivers at auction. The sale is opposed by former Prime Ministers Gough Whitlam and Malcolm Fraser and Packer is forced to withdraw from the consortium.;
- The bankers of the collapsed Quintex Entertainment set up Television Holdings Ltd to run the Seven network.

1992

- Australian Consolidated Press (ACP) is floated as a public company.
  Pacific Magazines and Printing is floated as a public company.
  News Corp takes a 14.6% stake in the Seven Network, while Telstra buys 10%.
  Broadcasting Services Act replaces the *Broadcasting Act*, bringing in cross-media rules for satellite subscriber television and incorporating cross-media rules for print and free-to-air television.
  The Australian Broadcasting Authority established.
  John Fairfax Holding Ltd is floated on the stock exchange.
  Packer increases his stake in Fairfax newspapers to the 15% maximum permitted under the cross-media laws.
  Ten network sold to a consortium including a 15% share to Canada's CanWest.
  Pay TV legislation allocates two channels to the ABC and offers two commercial satellite licences of four channels each.

1993

- Packer, Murdoch and Telstra form PMT consortium to enter pay TV market;
- News Ltd takes a 15% stake in the Seven Network;
- Conrad Black granted permission to lift Tourang's stake in Fairfax from 15% to 25%.
- Television Holdings Ltd float the Seven Network as a public company, with the share offer oversubscribed.

1994

- PMT consortium collapses and Murdoch and Telstra form Foxtel Pay TV venture.
- Kerry Packer forms rival Optus Vision with Optus Communications and Continental Cablevision.
- Australian Consolidated Press (ACP) absorbs Syme Magazines, establishing a new company to publish Southeast Asian editions of several of its magazines.

1995

- On 26 January, pay TV begins transmission.
- Kerry Packer and Rupert Murdoch go to war over Super League.
- Packer increases his stake in Fairfax to 16.4%.
- Federal government sets a new 20% limit in cross-media laws.

1996

- Australian Competition and Consumer Commission blocks the merger of Foxtel and satellite Pay TV company Australis Media. Six months later, the latter company signs a deal with Optus Vision.
- Kerry Packer reduces his stake in Fairfax to 14.99%.
- News Ltd sells its 5% stake in Fairfax.
- Conrad Black's Tourang consortium sells 80% of its stake in John Fairfax Holdings Ltd to New Zealand's Brierley Investments for approximately $553.8 million.

Program Standards — Australian Content and Quotas

Australian content standards aim to protect and foster local industry, both regional versus metropolitan and Australian versus foreign. If these requirements are not met, a licence may be revoked or not renewed.

TELEVISION

From January 1996, a new program standard for Australian content on commercial television came into effect:

- an increase in Australian programming, with the transmission quota increasing from 50 to 55 per cent in 1998;
- first-release Australian children's drama to be doubled from 16 hours a year in 1996 to 32 hours a year in 1998;
- eight hours of Australian children's drama to be repeated each year;
- the total 130 hours of annual preschool children's programs must be Australian;
- ten hours of first run Australian documentaries per year;
- minimum levels of new Australian drama guaranteed;
- sketch comedy supported by its inclusion within the first release Australian drama quota;
- 'Australian program' defined, in all categories, as that produced under the creative control of Australians;
- support for Australian feature films as a part of the drama quota, even those having had cinema, video and pay TV release;
- 80% of advertising time broadcast by licensees between 6 a.m. and midnight to be used for Australian produced advertisements.

Government Broadcasting

AUSTRALIAN BROADCASTING CORPORATION

The Australian Broadcasting Corporation (ABC), founded as the Australian Broadcasting Commission on 1 July 1932, became the Australian Broadcasting Corporation on 1 July 1983. The ABC provides Australia with informative and entertaining programs that aim to reflect the cultural diversity in Australian society. The organisation operates under the *Australian Broadcasting*

Corporation Act 1983, making it accountable to parliament, but able to make independent broadcasting decisions on behalf of the Australian people.

Government funding for the ABC has come to about $523 million a year, but, at January 1997, the Federal government was threatening the broadcaster with budget cuts of up to 20%.

ABC TELEVISION

ABC-TV provides a national television service to all capital cities and regional areas, as well as to remote areas through the ABC Satellite Service.

ABC RADIO

The ABC provides radio services in all capital cities, while people in rural areas are provided with at least two radio services, a national youth network and shortwave stations aimed at the Northern Territory's Aboriginal communities. They are ABC Classic FM, ABC Network Program Unit, Parliamentary and News Network, Radio Australia, Triple J-FM and Radio National. The latter is the national ideas and information network of the ABC, broadcasting to capital cities and more than 230 regional centres across the country.

NEW SOUTH WALES   2BL 702, RN 576 AM
VICTORIA   3LO, RN 621 AM
QUEENSLAND   4QR, RN 792 AM
SOUTH AUSTRALIA   5AN, RN 729 AM
WESTERN AUSTRALIA   720 6WF, RN 810 AM
TASMANIA   7NT, 7ZR, RN 585 AM
NORTHERN TERRITORY   8DDD FM, RN 657 AM, ABC Territory Radio
AUSTRALIAN CAPITAL TERRITORY   2CN, RN 846 2

RADIO AUSTRALIA

Radio Australia broadcasts news and information in nine languages to an estimated 5 million weekly listeners. The service has satellite and rebroadcast arrangements on local networks to provide better reception.
1. English Language service, with main target areas being Asia and the Pacific, North America and Europe: an estimated 1 million listeners.
2. Foreign Language service, broadcasting in eight languages to Asia, the Pacific, the Indian Ocean, the Gulf States and Africa. Vietnamese broadcasts have 500 000 listeners; Mandarin and Cantonese have 650 000; Thai up to 300 000; French have 250 000, Indonesian have 2.5 million; Tokpisan (Papua New Guinea) have 800 000, and Khmer broadcasts have an unknown number of listeners.

The Federal government budget cuts to the ABC may force the closure of this respected international service, even though its existence is laid down in the ABC's charter. In 1996, its running costs were $13 million, with an additional $14 million in transmission costs.

SYDNEY   Head Office, ABC Ultimo Centre, 700 Harris Street, Ultimo NSW 2007. Ph: (02) 9333 1500. Fax: (02) 9333 1400.

MELBOURNE   Southbank Centre, Southbank Boulevard, South Melbourne VIC 3205. Ph: (03) 9626 1600. Fax: (03) 9626 1621.

BRISBANE   Middenbury, Radio Building, 600 Coronation Drive, Toowong QLD 4066. Ph: (07) 3377 5222. Fax: (07) 3377 5307.

ADELAIDE   85 Main North East Road, Collinswood SA 5081. Ph: (08) 8343 4000. Fax: (08) 8343 4800.

PERTH   191 Adelaide Terrace, Perth WA 6000. Ph: (09) 220 2700. Fax: (09) 220 2919.

HOBART   Broadcasting Centre, Cnr Brooker & Tasman Highway, Hobart TAS 7000. Ph: (03) 6335 3333. Fax: (03) 6235 3661.

DARWIN   1 Cavenagh Street, Darwin NT 0800. Ph: (089) 43 3172. Fax: (089) 43 3175.

SPECIAL BROADCASTING SERVICE (SBS)

SBS was created on 1 January 1978 by the Commonwealth government to provide multilingual radio and, in August 1978, multilingual television services, using Australia's sole UHF-only television network (SBS-TV). Emphasis is on multicultural and multilingual programming, with subtitling undertaken by SBS. It also provides multilingual radio to various metropolitan and regional areas across Australia.

The Broadcasting Service Act 1991 states: 'The principle function of the SBS is to provide multilingual and multicultural radio and television services that inform, educate and entertain all Australians and, in doing so, reflect Australia's multicultural society.'

SYDNEY   Head Office, 14 Herbert Street, Artarmon NSW 2064. Ph: (02) 9430 2828. Fax: (02) 9430 3700.

MELBOURNE   SBS Melbourne Radio, 2 Kavanagh Street, South Melbourne VIC 3205. Ph: (03) 9685 2828. Fax: (03) 9686 7501.

Television

Television began in Australia on 16 September 1956, when the commercial station TCN-9 Sydney first broadcast in black and white. ABN-2 Sydney began broadcasting on 5 November the same year followed later that month by ABN-2 Melbourne. In 1974, the first colour test transmissions were made in Melbourne and, by March 1975, Australians were able to watch their favourite television shows in colour.

Currently there are almost 50 commercial television stations in Australia and three remote television stations. Public access stations operate on restricted licences on UHF bands and the first pay television stations were established in 1995.

LICENCES

Television licences are renewed by the Australian Broadcasting Authority for a period of 12 months to three years.

RATINGS

Ratings for television are put out 365 days a year, via people meters installed in a sample of homes by Nielsen AC Australia. One full ratings survey equals four weeks viewing. The unofficial off ratings period takes place over the summer, although ratings are still taken.

TELEVISION STATIONS

NATIONAL
ABN Channel 2
Television Studios, 221 Pacific Highway, Gore Hill NSW 2065.
Ph: (02) 9950 3000. Fax: (02) 9950 3102.

ABV Channel 2 Melbourne
8 Gordon Street, Elsternwick VIC 3185.
Ph: (03) 9528 4444. Fax: (03) 9528 2221.

SBS TV
Television Studios, 14 Herbert Street, Artarmon NSW 2064.
Ph: (02) 9430 2828. Fax: (02) 9430 3700.

METROPOLITAN

SYDNEY

ATN 7 Sydney
Licensee: Amalgamated Television Services Pty Ltd
Mobbs Lane, Epping NSW 2121. Ph: (02) 9877 7777. Fax: (02) 9877 7888.
Opened: 2 December 1956

TCN 9 Sydney
Licensee: TCN Channel Nine Pty Ltd
24 Artarmon Road, Willoughby NSW 2068.
Ph: (02) 9906 9999. Fax: (02) 9965 2119.
Opened: 16 September 1956

Network 10 Sydney
Licensee: Network Ten Limited
1 Saunders Street, Pyrmont NSW 2009.
Ph: (02) 9844 1010. Fax: (02) 9844 1364.
Opened: 5 April 1965

MELBOURNE

Channel 10 Melbourne
Licensee: Network Ten Limited
620 Chapel Street, South Yarra VIC 3141.
Ph: (03) 9275 1010. Fax: (03) 9275 1011.
Opened: 1 August 1964

GTV 9 Melbourne
Licensee: General Television Corporation Pty Ltd
22 Bendigo Street, Richmond VIC 3121.
Ph: (03) 9420 3111. Fax: (03) 9429 1977.
Opened: 19 January 1957

HSV Channel 7
Licensee: HSV Channel 7 Pty Ltd
119 Wells Street, South Melbourne VIC 3205.
Ph: (03) 9697 7777. Fax: (03) 9697 7888.
Opened: 4 November 1956

BRISBANE

BTQ 7 Brisbane
Licensee: Brisbane TV Limited
Sir Samuel Griffith Drive, Mount Coot-tha QLD 4066.
Ph: (07) 3369 7777. Fax: (07) 3368 2970.
Opened: 1 November 1959

QTQ 9 Brisbane
Licensee: Queensland Television Ltd
Sir Samuel Griffith Drive, Mt Coot-tha QLD 4066.
Ph: (07) 3214 9999. Fax: (07) 3369 3512.
Opened: 16th August 1959

TVQ 10 Brisbane
Licensee: Network Ten Ltd
Sir Samuel Griffith Drive, Mt Coot-tha QLD 4066.
Ph: (07) 3214 1010. Fax: (07) 3214 1040.
Opened: 1 July 1965

ADELAIDE
ADS 10 Adelaide
Licensee: Network Ten (Adelaide) Ltd
125 Strangways Terrace, North Adelaide SA 5006.
Ph: (08) 8239 1010. Fax: (08) 8239 0007.
Opened: 24 October 1959

NWS 9 Adelaide
Licensee: Southern Television Corporation Pty Ltd
202-208 Tynte Street, North Adelaide SA 5006.
Ph: (08) 8267 0111. Fax: (08) 8267 3996.
Opened: 31 August 1959

SAS 7 Adelaide
Licensee: South Australian Telecasters Limited
45-49 Park Terrace, Gilberton SA 5081.
Ph: (08) 8342 7777. Fax: (08) 8342 7717.
Opened: 26 July 1965

PERTH
STW 9 Perth
Licensee: Swan Television & Radio Broadcasters Limited
9 Gay Street, Dianella WA 6062.
Ph: (09) 449 9999. Fax: (09) 449 9902.
Opened: 12 June 1965

New Channel 10
Licensee: West Coast Telecasters Limited
Cottonwood Crescent, Dianella Heights WA 6062.
Ph: (09) 345 1010. Fax: (09) 344 8076.
Opened: 20 May 1988

TVW 7 Perth
Licensee: TVW Enterprises Limited
Osborne Road, Tuart Hill WA 6060.
Ph: (09) 344 0777. Fax: (09) 344 0606.
Opened: 16 October 1959

HOBART
WIN Television Tasmania
Licensee: WIN Television Tasmania
52 New Town Road, Hobart TAS 7008.
Ph: (03) 6228 8999. Fax: (03) 6228 8995.
Opened: 23rd May 1960

CANBERRA
Prime Television Canberra
Licensee: Prime Television (Southern) Pty Ltd
Lot 5, Antill Street, Watson ACT 2602.
Ph: (06) 242 3700. Fax: (06) 242 3888.
Opened: 31 March 1989

Ten Capital
Licensee: Southern Cross Broadcasting Australia Limited
Aspinall Street, Watson ACT 2602.
Ph: (06) 242 2400. Fax: (06) 241 7230.

WIN Television Canberra
84 Wentworth Avenue, Kingston ACT 2604
Ph: (06) 234 5699. Fax: (06) 239 6644.

DARWIN
NTD 8 Darwin
Licensee: Territory Television Pty Ltd
Blake Street, Gardens Hill Darwin NT 0800.
Ph: (08) 8981 8888. Fax: (08) 8981 6802.
Opened: 11 November 1971

REGIONAL
NEW SOUTH WALES   New South Wales has six regional television stations,
two community stations and five subscription stations. The main ones are:

NBN Television Newcastle
Licensee: NBN Limited
11-17 Mosbri Crescent, Newcastle NSW 2300.
Ph: (049) 29 2933. Fax: (049) 26 2936.

Prime Television Network
Licensee: Prime Television
1 Pacific Highway, North Sydney NSW 2060.
Ph: (02) 9965 7700. Fax: (02) 9965 7729.

WIN TV NSW Pty Ltd
Licensee: TWT Limited
Television Avenue, Mount St Thomas NSW 2500.
Ph: (042) 23 4199. Fax: (042) 27 3682.

VICTORIA   The state has three regional stations, one community station and one subscription station. The main ones are:

Prime Television Victoria
Licensee: Prime Television Limited
Sunraysia Highway, Mitchell Park, Ballarat VIC 3353.
Ph: (053) 37 1777. Fax: (053) 37 1700.

Ten Victoria
Licensee: Southern Cross Communications Limited
Lily Street, Bendigo VIC 3550. Ph: (054) 30 2888. Fax: (054) 30 2700.

WIN Television
Licensee: WIN Television Victoria Pty Ltd
Cnr Walker and Simpson Streets, Ballarat VIC 3350.
Ph: (053) 20 1366. Fax: (053) 33 1598.

QUEENSLAND   The state has seven regional stations, one community station and one subscription station. The main ones are:

Prime Television — Gold Coast
Licensee: Prime Television (Northern) Pty Ltd
60 High Street, Southport QLD 4215.
Ph: (07) 5573 8777. Fax: (07) 5531 4630.

WIN Television Queensland
Licensee: WIN Television Queensland Pty Ltd
Dean Street, Rockhampton QLD 4700.
Ph: (079) 30 4499. Fax: (079) 30 4495.

Seven Queensland
Licensee: Sunshine Television Network Limited
140-42 Horton Parade, Maroochydore QLD 4558.
Ph: (07) 5430 1777. Fax: (07) 5443 9373.

SOUTH AUSTRALIA   The state has three regional stations and one community station. The main ones are:

GTS Channel 4
Licensee: Spencer Gulf Telecasters Ltd
76 Wandearah Road, Port Pirie SA 5540.
Ph: (086) 32 2555. Fax: (086) 33 0984.

SES 8 Mt Gambier
Licensee: South East Telecasters Limited
51 John Watson Drive, Mt Gambier SA 5290.
Ph: (087) 25 6366. Fax: (087) 23 0114.

WESTERN AUSTRALIA   The state has two regional stations and one community station. The main one is:

Golden West Network (GWN)
Licensee: Golden West Network Pty Ltd
Roberts Crescent, Bunbury WA 6230. Ph: (097) 21 4466. Fax: (097) 91 2601.

TASMANIA   The state has three regional stations and one subscription station. The main one is:

TNT 9 Southern Cross TV
Licensee: Southern Cross Television (TNT 9) Pty Ltd
Watchorn Street, Launceston TAS 7250
Ph: (03) 6344 0202. Fax: (03) 6343 0340.

NORTHERN TERRITORY   The territory has three regional stations. The main one is:

Imparja Television
Licensee: Imparja Television Pty Ltd
Shop 6, Todd Mall, Alice Springs NT 0870.
Ph: (08) 9850 1411. Fax: (08) 8953 4441.

ABORIGINAL TELEVISION
The first Aboriginal controlled and operated television station in Australia, Imparja Television, opened in Alice Springs on 2 January 1988. Run by the multi-award winning Central Australian Aborigines Media Association (CAAMA), it also includes a radio and shortwave network operating throughout the outback. It is aimed specifically at the Northern Territory's Aboriginal population, although CAAMA often produces programs in conjunction with government departments and Alice Springs media.

CABLE/PAY TELEVISION

FOXTEL
Foxtel Management Pty Ltd
Wharf 8, Pyrmont NSW 2009.
Ph: (02) 9200 1000. Fax: (02) 9200 1111.
21 channels

GALAXY TV
Galaxy Media Pty Ltd
55 Pyrmont Bridge Road, Pyrmont NSW 2009.
Ph: (02) 9776 2000. Fax: (02) 9776 2111.
Eight channels

OPTUS VISION
Optus Vision Pty Ltd
821 Pacific Highway, Chatswood NSW 2067.
Ph: (02) 9775 9775. Fax: (02) 9775 9000.
17 channels

SATELLITE TELEVISION

QUEENSLAND SATELLITE TELEVISION: QSTV
12 The Strand, Townsville QLD 4810.
Ph: (077) 21 3377. Fax: (077) 21 1705.

SKY CHANNEL
2/81 Frenchs Forest Road, Frenchs Forest NSW 2086.
Ph: (02) 9451 0888 Fax: (02) 9452 4520.

Radio

Australia's first radio broadcasting was the 'sealed set' system introduced in 1923. Under this system, the set was tuned so it could only receive one radio station and each station would charge a listening fee. With only 2FC and 2BL in Sydney, 3AR in Melbourne and 6WF in Perth running these stations, the system changed, dividing stations into either A or B Class stations (B Class being commercial radio).

2SB was the first commercial radio station to broadcast when it began in 1923. By the end of 1926, 12 B Class stations had opened. Then, in 1928, A Class radio stations were nationalised, forming the beginning of the ABC's national network.

Today in Australia there are more than 273 radio licences: 142 commercial, 2 supplementary and 79 public licences. There are 123 AM licences in Australia and 96 FM licences. Stations on the AM band transmit within the frequency range 525-1605KHz and on the FM band within the range 88-108 MHz.

LICENCES

Radio licences are renewed by the Australian Broadcasting Authority for a duration of 12 months to three years. Community and limited broadcasting licences are renewed every three to six months.

RATINGS

AGB McNair carries out ratings surveys for all metropolitan and regional radio stations on behalf of the Federation of Australian Radio Broadcasters. In metropolitan areas surveys are carried out eight times over a 39-week period each year with a break each Christmas period. Survey times vary in the regional markets.

NATIONAL RADIO STATIONS

Australian Broadcasting Corporation (ABC)
See Government broadcasting.

METROPOLITAN RADIO STATIONS

SYDNEY
Radio 2CH
Radio Superhighway Pty Ltd
33 Berry Street, North Sydney NSW 2060. Ph: (02) 9900 1170.
Fax: (02) 9956 7000. Format: Easy listening

2DAY FM
Austereo Ltd
500 Oxford Street, Bondi Junction NSW 2022. Ph: (02) 9375 1041.
Fax: (02) 9386 9810. Format: Better music and more of it

Radio 2GB
Harbour Radio Limited
368 Sussex Street, Sydney NSW 2000. Ph: (02) 9269 0646.
Fax: (02) 9287 2701. Format: News, talk and sport

Radio 2KY
2KY Broadcasters Pty Ltd
20–22 Wentworth Street, Parramatta NSW 2150. Ph: (02) 9633 9333.
Fax: (02) 9633 9304. Format: Sport and talk

Triple M Sydney
The Triple M Broadcasting Company Pty Ltd
500 Oxford Street, Bondi Junction NSW 2022. Ph: (02) 9387 1000.
Fax: (02) 9387 5207. Format: Contemporary rock

Radio Kick AM 1269
Kick Media Pty Ltd
186 Blues Point Road, North Sydney NSW 2060. Ph: (02) 9922 1270.
Fax: (02) 9954 3117. Format: Cool country, rock 'n' blues

Radio 2UE
Radio 2UE 954
176 Pacific Highway, Greenwich NSW 2065. Ph: (02) 9930 9954.
Fax: (02) 9906 7757. Format: News, information and sport

Mix 106.5 FM
Commonwealth Broadcasting Corporation Pty Ltd
11 Rangers Road, Neutral Bay NSW 2089. Ph: (02) 9968 5000.
Fax: (02) 9908 2746. Format: Sydney's best mix of the '70s, '80s and '90s

2WS FM 101.7
Australian Radio Network
2 Leabons Lane, Seven Hills NSW 2147. Ph: (02) 9671 2411.
Fax: (02) 9621 3729. Format: Best songs of all time

MELBOURNE
Radio 3AK
Fusion Media Pty Ltd
432 St Kilda Road, Melbourne VIC 3004. Ph: (03) 9866 8666.
Fax: (03) 9867 3363. Format: Middle of the road music, 40+ years

Radio 3AW
Southern Cross Broadcasting
43 Bank Street, South Melbourne VIC 3205. Ph: (03) 9243 2000.
Fax: (03) 9690 0773. Format: Information, news, entertainment and sport

Radio 3 FOX FM
Austereo Limited

180 St Kilda Road, St Kilda VIC 3182. Ph: (03) 9205 1111.
Fax: (03) 9536 8899. Format: Better music and more of it for the '80s and '90s

Radio 104.3 Gold FM
Australian Radio Network
21–31 Goodwood Street, Richmond VIC 3121. Ph: (03) 9240 1043.
Fax: (03) 9420 1150. Format: The best songs of all time

Radio Magic 693
Southern Cross Broadcasting Pty Ltd
43 Bank Street, South Melbourne VIC 3205. Ph: (03) 9243 2000.
Fax: (03) 9682 9234. Format: All-time favourites

Radio 3MP
Goulburn Valley Broadcasters Pty Ltd
43B Davey Street, Frankston VIC 3199. Ph: (03) 9781 3311.
Fax: (03) 9770 2438. Format: Easy music

Triple M Melbourne
Melbourne FM Radio Pty Ltd
180 St Kilda Road, St Kilda VIC 3182. Ph: (03) 9230 1051.
Fax: (03) 9534 8011. Format: Modern rock with great classics, 18–39 years

3XY Radio Hellas
264–72 Rosslyn Street, West Melbourne VIC 3003. Ph: (03) 9328 2310.
Fax: (03) 9328 2310. Format: Current affairs, entertainment, news, sport
and music

Radio TTFM
Double T Radio Pty Ltd
21–31 Goodwood Street, Richmond VIC 3121 Ph: (03) 9420 1011.
Fax: (03) 9420 1055. Format: Contemporary hits and memories

BRISBANE
Radio 4BC
Radio 4BC Brisbane Pty Ltd
30 Macrossan Street, Brisbane QLD 4000. Ph: (07) 3831 1311.
Fax: (07) 3832 2949. Format: News, sport and talk

Today's B105 FM
B105 FM Pty Ltd (Austereo Ltd)
16 Campbell Street, Bowen Hills QLD 4006. Ph: (07) 3257 1053.
Fax: (07) 3252 3022. Format: Adult rock

Brisbane's Easy Listening 4BH 882
Queensland Radio 2000 Pty Ltd
Cnr Pine Mountain Road & Hill Street, Raymonds Hill QLD 4305.
Ph: (07) 3201 5882. Fax: (07) 3201 6369. Format: Easy listening

Radio 4KQ
Australian Radio Network
444 Logan Road, Stones Corner QLD 4120. Ph: (07) 3394 1777.
Fax: (07) 3849 0642. Format: Greatest memories and latest hits

FM 104 Triple M Brisbane
FM 104 Pty Ltd
Level 3, 549 Queen Street, Brisbane QLD 4000. Ph: (07) 3361 0104.
Fax: (07) 3832 3954. Format: Rock 40

QFM 106.9
Ipswich and West Morton Broadcasting Corporation Pty Ltd
Cnr Hill Street and Pine Mountain Road, Raymonds Hill QLD 4305.
Ph: (07) 3201 6000. Fax: (07) 3812 3060. Format: Contemporary

ADELAIDE
Radio 5AA (5-Double-A)
Festival City Broadcasters Limited
Pulteney Court, Adelaide SA 5000. Ph: (08) 8224 0224.
ax: (08) 8232 0981. Format: Interviews, talkback, sport

5AD FM 102.3 Today's Easy Listening 5AD
Australian Radio Network
201 Tynte Street, North Adelaide SA 5006. Ph: (08) 8300 1000.
Fax: (08) 8300 1030. Format: Easy listening

Radio 5DN
Australian Radio Network
201 Tynte Street, North Adelaide SA 5006. Ph: (08) 8305 1300.
Fax: (08) 8300 1030. Format: News, talk and information

Triple M Adelaide
Adelaide FM Radio Pty Ltd
128 Greenhill Road, Unley SA 5061. Ph: (08) 8290 1047.
Fax: (08) 8357 9575. Format: Contemporary

SA FM (5SSA)
Austereo Limited

128 Greenhill Road, Unley SA 5061. Ph: (08) 8301 1071.
Fax: (08) 8373 3733. Format: Better music and more of it from the '70s, '80s and '90s

PERTH
Radio PM-FM 92.9
Consolidated Broadcasting System (WA) Pty Ltd
283 Rokeby Road, Subiaco WA 6008. Ph: (09) 382 0111.

Fax: (09) 381 3183. Format: Contemporary music
6IX AM 1080
Southern Cross Radio Pty Ltd
169 Hay Street, East Perth WA 6004. Ph: (09) 325 3311.
Fax: (09) 325 2806. Format: Adult contemporary, gold

94.5 FM
JMB Pty Ltd
283 Rokeby Road, Subiaco WA 6008. Ph: (09) 381 3945.
Fax: (09) 381 2945. Format: Adult contemporary

Radio 6PR
Western Broadcasting Services Pty Ltd
169 Hay Street, East Perth WA 6004. Ph: (09) 325 3311.
Fax: (09) 325 2806. Format: Talkback, news and sport

Triple M Perth
New Broadcasting Limited
111 Wellington Street, East Perth WA 6004. Ph: (09) 325 9611.
Fax: (09) 325 6173. Format: Contemporary hit radio

HOBART
Radio HO-FM
Commercial Broadcasters Pty Ltd
254 Liverpool Street, Hobart TAS 7000. Ph: (03) 6231 0277.
Fax: (03) 6231 1141. Format: Adult contemporary

100.9 TTT FM
Southern Tasmanian FM Stereo Pty Ltd
75 Liverpool Street, Hobart TAS 7000. Ph: (03) 6224 1009.
Fax: (03) 6234 3030. Format: Contemporary rock

DARWIN
Radio Hot 100 FM
NT FM Limited

4 Peary Street, Darwin NT 0800. Ph: (08) 8941 9999.
Fax: (08) 8981 4299. Format: Contemporary hits

CANBERRA
Radio 2CA 1053
Austereo Ltd
65–67 Northbourne Avenue, Canberra City ACT 2600. Ph: (06) 257 1053.
Fax: (06) 247 3833. Format: Best songs of all time

Radio 2CC 1206 AM
Radio Canberra Pty Ltd
44 Hoskins St, Mitchell ACT 2911. Ph: (06) 241 1911.
Fax: (06) 242 0666. Format: Talk and easy favourites

Radio FM 104.7 Canberra
Austereo Ltd
65–67 Northbourne Avenue, Canberra City ACT 2601. Ph: (06) 257 1047.
Fax: (06) 247 3833. Format: Better music from the 70s, 80s and 90s

Radio 106.3 Canberra FM
Capital City Broadcasters Pty Ltd
Bellenden Street, Gungahlin ACT 2912. Ph: (06) 241 1566.
Fax: (06) 241 2704. Format: Soft adult contemporary

METROPOLITAN PUBLIC BROADCASTING

New South Wales has 16 of these stations, Victoria 18, and Queensland and
South Australia both have seven. Western Australia has eight metropolitan
and regional public broadcasting stations, Tasmania has nine and the
Northern Territory has seven.

REGIONAL STATIONS

NEW SOUTH WALES
New South Wales has 40 regional AM stations, 22 regional FM stations and
26 regional public broadcasting stations. The main ones are:

Radio 2HD
2HD Broadcasters Pty Ltd
173–175 Maitland Road Sandgate NSW 2304. Ph: (049) 67 6111.
Fax: (049) 67 2129. Format: News, talk, sport and lifestyle

NX FM 106.9
Radio Newcastle Pty Ltd

252 Pacific Highway, Charlestown NSW 2290. Ph: (049) 42 3333.
Fax: (049) 42 1426. Format: Hot adult contemporary

Radio i 198 FM
WIN Radio Pty Ltd
Television Avenue, Mount St Thomas, Wollongong NSW 2500.
Ph: (042) 23 4198. Fax: (042) 23 4192. Format: Adult contemporary

2WL Wave FM
Wollongong Broadcasters Pty Ltd
Cnr Church & Edward Streets, Wollongong NSW 2500. Ph: (042) 29 4233.
Fax: (042) 26 1925. Format: Adult with music from the '60s to the 90s

VICTORIA
Victoria has 14 regional AM stations, 13 regional FM stations and 12
regional public broadcasting stations. The main ones are:

Radio 3CV 1071 AM
Broadcast Media Group
401–405 High Street, Golden Square VIC 3555. Ph: (054) 41 1071.
Fax: (054) 41 3937. Format: Adult 35+

Radio Bay FM
Bay FM Pty Ltd
83 Moorabool Street, Geelong VIC 3220. Ph: (052) 29 2939.
Fax: (052) 23 1341. Format: Soft rock and talk

Radio 3GG
Votraint No 691 Pty Ltd
31 Warragul-Korumburra Road, Warragul VIC 3820. Ph: (056) 22 2531.
Fax: (056) 22 2534. Format: Adult contemporary

Radio 3TR
ACE Radio Broadcasters Limited
Cnr Princes Hwy and Coonac Road, Traralgon VIC 3844.
Ph: (051) 76 1242. Fax: (051) 76 1177. Format: Adult contemporary

QUEENSLAND
Queensland has 28 regional AM stations, 14 regional FM stations and seven
regional public broadcasting stations. The main ones are:

Radio 4AM
Regional Broadcasters (Australia) Pty Ltd
175A Byrnes Street, Mareeba QLD 4880. Ph: (070) 92 4558.
Fax: (070) 92 4676. Format: Contemporary

90.9 SEA FM
SEA FM Pty Ltd
12–14 Marine Parade, Southport QLD 4215. Ph: (07) 5591 5000.
Fax (07) 5591 6080. Format: Adult rock/contemporary, 10-39 years

4MK
Barrier Reef Broadcasting Pty Ltd/Rural Press
85 Sydney Street, Mackay QLD 4740. Ph: (079) 53 5353.
Fax: (079) 51 2358. Format: Hits and memories

Hot FM Mt Isa
North Queensland Broadcasting Corporation Pty Ltd
67 West Street, Mt Isa QLD 4825. Ph: (077) 43 3444. Fax: (077) 43 3633.
Format: Hot rock

92.7 MIX FM
Sunshine Coast Broadcasters Pty Ltd/Sea FM Ltd
161 Currie Street, Nambour QLD 4560. Ph: (074) 41 1522.
Fax: (074) 41 5277. Format: Adult contemporary

SOUTH AUSTRALIA
South Australia has ten regional AM stations and four regional public
broadcasting stations. The main ones are:

Radio 5AU
5AU Broadcasters Pty Ltd
6 Denton Court, Port Augusta SA 5700. Ph: (086) 42 2444.
Fax: (086) 42 4330. Format: A better music mix

5CC
Coast and Country Broadcasting Services Pty Ltd
22 Washington Street, Port Lincoln SA 5606. Ph: (086) 82 5000.
Fax: (086) 82 6223. Format: Contemporary

Radio 5RM (Riverland)
5AU Broadcasters Pty Ltd
19 Vaughan Terrace, Berri SA 5343. Ph: (085) 82 1800.
Fax: (085) 82 3140. Format: Contemporary

Western Australia

Western Australia has 19 regional AM stations and three regional FM stations. The main ones are:

Radio 6KA
Northwest Radio Pty Ltd
31 Bond Place, Karratha WA 6714. Ph: (091) 44 4333.
Fax: (091) 44 2944. Format: Contemporary hit radio
6TZ
Radio West Broadcasters Pty Ltd
Spencer Street, Bunbury WA 6230. Ph: (097) 91 2899
Fax: (097) 91 2661. Format: Adult contemporary

Warringarri Radio (6WR)
Kununurra Waringarri Aboriginal Corporation
2229 Speargrass Road, Kununurra WA 6743. Ph: (091) 68 2214.
Fax: (091) 69 1010. Format: Local news, music, indigenous languages, sport, current affairs

Northern Territory

There are a total of six AM and FM stations and seven public broadcasting stations in the Northern Territory. The main ones are:

8HA Alice Springs
Alice Springs Commercial Broadcasters Pty Ltd
South Stuart Highway, Alice Springs NT 0871. Ph: (08) 8952 2900.
Fax: (08) 8952 8276. Format: Adult contemporary

SUN FM
Alice Springs Commercial Broadcasters
South Sturt Hwy, Alice Springs NT 0870. Ph: (08) 8955 5969.
Fax: (08) 8952 8276. Format: Top 40 hits

CAAMA Radio 8KIN FM
Central Australian Aboriginal Media Association
101 Todd Street, Alice Springs NT 0870. Ph: (08) 8952 9204.
Fax: (08) 8952 9214. Format: Indigenous broadcasting

TEABBA Radio
Top End Aboriginal Bush Broadcasting Association
Rapid Creek Shopping Centre, Rapid Creek NT 0810. Ph: (08) 8948 3023.
Fax: (08) 8948 3027. This station has the capacity to broadcast in 15 languages to more than 25 Aboriginal communities.

TASMANIA
7LA Launceston
Bass Strait Media Pty Ltd
109 York Street, Launceston TAS 7250. Ph: (03) 6331 4844.
Fax: (03) 6331 2720. Format: Adult contemporary

Print

Australia's first newspaper, The *Sydney Gazette and NSW Advertiser* hit the streets on 5 March 1803. The editor was George Howe. Then, in October 1824, Australia's first privately owned newspaper, the weekly *Australian*, was published by William Charles Wentworth and Robert Wardell, continuing until 1848. The country's first national daily, *The Australian*, began publication on 15 July 1964.

Breakdown of Advertising Expenditure across the Media

Newspapers 37.7% at
 $2.3 billion
TV 30.7% at $1.87 billion
Radio 7.1% at $433 million
Magazines 5.6% at
 $354 million
Other 18.7%

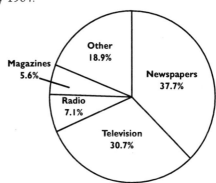

NATIONAL NEWSPAPERS

THE AUSTRALIAN   On 15 July 1964, *The Australian* became the first national daily newspaper. Its current circulation is 122 500 for the Monday to Friday edition, with the *Weekend Australian* selling about 311 000 copies per edition.

THE AUSTRALIAN FINANCIAL REVIEW   First published as a weekly newspaper in September 1951, the *Financial Review* became a Monday to Friday paper in 1963. Current circulation is 83 700 copies per day.

METROPOLITAN NEWSPAPERS

SYDNEY
Daily Telegraph Circulation: Monday to Friday 443 180; Saturday 351 650
The Sydney Morning Herald Circulation: 234 980
The Sunday Telegraph Circulation: 701 330

The Sunday Telegraph Circulation: 701 330
The Sun-Herald Circulation: 557 960

MELBOURNE
The Herald Sun Circulation: Monday to Friday 565 984; Saturday 522 835
The Age Circulation: 232 000
Sunday Age Circulation: 194 000
Sunday Herald Sun Circulation: 512 720

BRISBANE
The Courier-Mail Circulation: Monday to Friday 218 820; Saturday 338 995
The Sunday Mail Circulation: 590 000

ADELAIDE
Adelaide Advertiser Circulation: Monday to Friday 200 465; Saturday 264 352
The Sunday Mail Circulation: 339 120

PERTH
The West Australian Circulation: Monday to Friday 238 460; Saturday 384 760
Sunday Times Circulation: 350 090

DARWIN
The Northern Territory News Circulation: Monday to Friday 22 190; Saturday 29 260
Sunday Territorian Circulation: 24 460

HOBART
The Mercury Circulation: 51 774
The Sunday Tasmanian Circulation: 54 080

CANBERRA
The Canberra Times Circulation: Monday to Friday 42 600; Saturday 73 320; Sunday 40 300
The Canberra Chronicle Circulation: 120 175

SUBURBAN NEWSPAPERS

There are about 160 suburban newspapers in Australia: 40 in Sydney, 63 in Melbourne, 24 in Brisbane, 11 in Adelaide and 23 in Perth. Tasmania has 15 suburban/regional papers and the Northern Territory has eight in this same category.

REGIONAL NEWSPAPERS

There are more than 400 regional newspapers in Australia: 161 in New South Wales, 94 in Victoria, 30 in South Australia, 95 in Queensland and 27 in Western Australia.

OTHER

There are 108 publications for the ethnic community in Australia. Rural newspapers are also popular: *The Land* has the largest circulation at 59 310 copies.

MAGAZINES AND OTHER PUBLICATIONS

BROADCASTING AND TV GUIDES
TV Week Circulation: 442 850. Pacific Publications

BUSINESS AND FINANCIAL INTERESTS
Business Review Weekly Circulation: 72 923. BRW Media
The Bulletin with Newsweek Circulation: 99 342. Australian Consolidated Press
Asian Business Review Circulation: 30 203. Asian Business Review Pty Ltd
Personal Investment Monthly Circulation: 60 072. BRW Publications

CARS
Wheels Circulation: 59 760. ACP Syme

FASHION
Elle Australia Circulation: 66 710. Hachette/Australian Consolidated Press
Mode Circulation: 35 975. Australian Consolidated Press
Vogue Australia Circulation: 70 210. Conde Nast Publications Pty Ltd
Marie Claire Circulation: 92 795. Murdoch Magazines

GENERAL INTEREST
Australian Geographic Circulation: 208 000. John Fairfax Holdings
Australian Gourmet Traveller Circulation: 61 100. Australian Consolidated Press
Australasian Post Circulation: 81 640. Pacific Publications
Reader's Digest Circulation: 505 477. Readers Digest (Australia) Pty Ltd
Time Australia Circulation: 110 808. Time Australia Magazine Pty Ltd
Who Weekly Circulation: 230 470. Time Australia Magazine Pty Ltd
Cinema Papers Circulation: 13 000. MTV Publishing Ltd
Inside Sport Circulation: 80 025. Gemkilt Publishing Pty Ltd

HOME AND GARDEN
Australian Home Beautiful Circulation: 81 496. Pacific Publications
Belle Circulation: 47 820. Australian Consolidated Press

Vogue Entertaining Guide Circulation: 85 100. Conde Nast Publications Pty Ltd
Vogue Living Circulation: 90 130. Conde Nast Publications Pty Ltd
Better Homes and Gardens Circulation: 293 892. Murdoch Magazines
Australian House & Garden Circulation: 102 642. Australian
Consolidated Press

YOUTH

TV Hits Circulation: 126 040. Pacific Publications
Rolling Stone Circulation: 36 490. Next Media
Smash Hits Circulation: 52 080. Mason Stewart Publishing Pty Ltd
Dolly Circulation: 174 722. Australian Consolidated Press
Girlfriend Circulation: 132 020. Pacific Publications

MEN

Australian Penthouse Circulation: 124 030. Gemkilt Publishing Pty Ltd
Australian Playboy Circulation: 36 780. Mason Stewart Publishing Pty Ltd
The Picture Circulation: 104 970. Australian Consolidated Press
People Circulation: 104 970. Australian Consolidated Press
Australian Hustler Circulation: 50 000. JT Publishing Australia Pty Ltd

WOMEN

Australian Women's Forum Circulation: 33 270. Gemkilt Publications Pty Ltd
Australian Family Circle Circulation: 253 515. Murdoch Magazines
Cleo Circulation: 263 355. Australian Consolidated Press
Cosmopolitan Circulation: 237 580. Australian Consolidated Press
HQ Circulation: 34 865. Australian Consolidated Press
New Idea Circulation: 616 430. Pacific Publications
New Woman Circulation: 111 350. Murdoch Magazines
Woman's Day Circulation: 990 680. Australian Consolidated Press
New Weekly Circulation: 220 590. Australian Consolidated Press
That's Life Circulation: 496 310. Pacific Publications
Australian Women's Weekly Circulation: 994 750. Australian
Consolidated Press
She Circulation: 100 600. Australian Consolidated Press

Print Media Ownership

Advertiser Newspapers Limited
Incorporated in SA
Chairman: B. L. Sallis. Holding company: The News Corporation Ltd
Media interests: *The Advertiser* (Adelaide), *Sunday Mail* (Adelaide) (50%),
Messenger Newspapers Pty Ltd (Adelaide Suburban Press).

ACP Publishing Pty Ltd
Incorporated in NSW
Chairman: K Packer. Media shareholders: Publishing & Broadcasting Ltd,
Consolidated Press Holdings Ltd
Major media interests: *Australian Women's Weekly, The Bulletin with Newsweek,
Australian Business, Woman's Day, Cosmopolitan* (50%), *Elle* (49%), *Cleo, HQ,
Dolly, People, Picture, Mode Australia, Belle, New Weekly, Australian Gourmet
Traveller, Australian House & Garden, Modern Motor, Wheels* (50%), *Street
Machine* (50%), *Deals on Wheels, Auto Super Market, Unique Cars, Rugby
League Week, TV Week* (50%), *Australian Personal Computer, PC Week, IT
Review, Australian PC User, Handmade, Trade-a-Boat*.

Australian Provincial Newspapers Holdings Limited
Incorporated in the ACT
Chairman: L. Healy. Major owner: Kelsal Pty Ltd
Major media interests: *The Gladstone Observer, The Morning Bulletin,
Maryborough-Hervey Bay Chronicle, Hervey Bay Observer, Sunshine Coast
Sunday, Sunshine Coast Weekly, Queensland Times, Bribie Weekly, Warwick
Bush Telegraph, Gold Coast Mail, Gold Coaster, Stanhope Border Post, The
Chronicle* (50%), *Bundaberg Guardian, Capricorn Coast Mirror, Mackay Daily
Mercury, Capricorn Coast Mirror, The Gatton Star* (50%), *The Northern Star,
North Coast Advocate, Byron Shire News, Richmond River Express Examiner,
Tweed Extra, The Grafton Daily Examiner, Rivertown Times*.

Cumberland Newspaper Group
Incorporated in ACT
Chairman: P. J. Macourt. Major shareholder: Herald & Weekly Times Ltd
Ultimate owner: News Limited
Major media interests: *Bankstown Express, Blacktown Advocate, Canterbury
Express, Central Coast Express Advocate, Fairfield Advance, Glebe and Inner
City News, Hills Shire Times, Inner Western Weekly, Lake Macquarie News,
Liverpool Leader, Macarthur Chronicle, Manly Daily, Mosman Daily, Northern
District Times, Parramatta Advertiser, Penrith Press*.

Davies Brothers Limited
Incorporated in Tasmania
Chairman: K. M. Drake. Major shareholder: Herald & Weekly Times Ltd
Ultimate owner: News Limited
Major media interests: *The Hobart Mercury, The Sunday Tasmanian, The
Saturday Mercury, Tasmanian Country, Treasure Islander, Derwent Valley Gazette,
Community Express*.

John Fairfax Holdings Limited
Incorporated in ACT
Chairman: Sir Lawrence Street, D.W. Colson. Major owners: Daily Telegraph Holding BV, Nine Network Australia Pty Ltd. In December 1996, Conrad Black's Tourang consortium sold its 25% stake of Fairfax to New Zealand's Brierley Investments for approximately $553.8 million.
Major media interests: *Australian Financial Review, Sydney Morning Herald, Sun-Herald, Newcastle Herald, Illawarra Mercury, Blacktown Sun, Fairfield City Companion, Penrith Sun, District Times, The Hills Sun, The Newcastle Post, Wollongong Advertiser, Auburn Review Pictorial* (50%), *Cooks River Valley News* (50%), *Port Stephens Examiner* (40%), *Tuggerah Lakes News* (25%), *Terrigal Times* (25%), *Central Coast Bowler* (25%), *Shepparton News* (46.5%), *City of Casey Journal, Werribee Banner, Williamstown Advertiser*, The Advocate, *Benalla Ensign, South Gippsland Sentinel Times* (50%), *Business Review Weekly, Personal Investment Monthly, Australian Geographic, Good Weekend, Homes Pictorial, Australian Greyhound Weekly* (50%), *Caravan World* (50%), *Inside Football* (50%), *Jack High* (50%), *Trotting Weekly* (50%), *Wheels* (50%).

Federal Capital Press of Australia Pty Ltd
Incorporated in ACT
Chairman: K. Stokes. Owner: North Alston Pty Ltd
Media interests: *The Canberra Times, Canberra Chronicle, The Valley View.*

Herald and Weekly Times Limited
Incorporated in Victoria
Chairman: Ms Janet Calvert-Jones. Major owner: The News Corporation Ltd
Media interests: *The Herald Sun News-Pictorial, Sunday Herald Sun, The Weekly Times, The Midweek Globe, The Sporting Globe.*

Peter Isaacson Publications
Incorporated in Victoria
Major owner: APN Holdings Limited.
Major media interests: *Brighton Southern Cross, Caulfield Southern Cross, Emerald Hill Times, This Week in Brisbane/Melbourne/Sydney/Darwin/ Tasmania/ Canberra, The Miner, Ink* (51%), *Waste Management and Environment* (51%), *Family PC* (80%), *Computer Week*, plus a series of annual publications.

Leader Newspaper Group
Incorporated in Victoria
Major owner: The News Corporation Ltd
Major media interests: *Whittlesea Post, Brimbank Messenger, Moreland Courier, Preston Post Times, Moreland Sentinel, Northcote Leader, Melbourne Yarra Leader, Progress Press, Diamond Valley News, Heidelberger, Whitehorse Gazette, Ringwood Croydon Mail, Waverley Gazette, Knox News, Free Press,*

Malvern Prahran Leader, Moorabbin Glen Eira Standard, Mordialloc Chelsea News, Frankston Standard, Cranbourne, Berwick Leader.

Marinya Media Pty Ltd
Incorporated in ACT
Major owner: Marinya Holdings Pty Ltd
Major media interests: The company owns the majority of Rural Press Limited, JB Fairfax Press Pty Ltd, 75% of Gore and Osment Publications Pty Ltd and half of Eastern Suburbs Newspapers. The latter company, in turn, owns Federal Publishing Company Pty Ltd.

The News Corporation Limited
Incorporated in SA
Chairman: R. Murdoch
Major media interests: *The Australian, Daily Telegraph, Herald Sun, Courier-Mail, Adelaide Advertiser, Hobart Mercury, NT Times, Sunday Telegraph, Sunday Sun Herald, Sunday Times, Sunday Mail, Sunday Territorian, Sporting Globe, Weekly Times, Sportsman, Cairns Post, Townsville Bulletin, Centralian Advocate, Bowen Independent, Innisfail Advocate, Herbert River Express, New Idea, TV Week, Australasian Post, Home Beautiful, Your Garden.*
News Corp also owns a number of overseas publications.

Pacific Publications
Incorporated in Victoria
Ultimate owner: Pacific Magazines and Printing Ltd in which The News Corporation Ltd has a 45% share.
Media interests: *New Idea, TV Week, Girlfriend, TV Hits, Sports Weekly, Disney Adventures, Australian Home Beautiful, Australasian Post, Your Garden, Best Bets.*

Queensland Press Limited
Incorporated in Queensland
Chairman: K.H. McDonald. Major owners: Cruden Investments Pty Ltd and The News Corporation Ltd
Media interests: *The Courier-Mail, The Sunday Mail, Gold Coast Bulletin, The Cairns Post.*

Quest Community Newspapers
Incorporated in the ACT
Chairman: P.J. Macourt. Major owner: Quest is a division of Nationwide News Pty Ltd owned by News Ltd.
Major media interests: *Albert and Logan News, Caboolture Shire Herald, Northside Chronicle, Westside News, Wynnum Herald, Southern Star, Pine Rivers Press, Southern News, Northern News, City News, City and Shire Leader, Northern Times.*

Rural Press Limited
Incorporated in NSW
Chairman: J. B. Fairfax.
Major owner: Marinya Media Pty Ltd
Major media interests: National magazines: *Australian Farm Journal, Australian Horticulture, Australian Flowers, Hoofs and Horns, Turfcraft, Beef, Crops, Wool, Lot Feeding.* National newspapers: *Australian Cotton Outlook, Good Fruit and Vegetable.* State magazines: *The Grower.* State newspapers: *Queensland Country Life, North Queensland Register, The Land, Stock and Land, Stock Journal, Farm Weekly, Farmer and Stockowner, Queensland Farmer, Queensland Farmer and Grazier, The Cattleman, NSW Agriculture Today.* Regional: *Country Leader, Gippsland Farmer, Nornews Rural, Northern Daily Leader, Maitland Mercury, Daily Liberal, Central Western Daily, Western Advocate, Goulburn Post, Gympie Times, Ballarat Courier, The Examiner, Town and Country Magazine, Western Magazine, Sapphire Sun, Southern Weekly Magazine, South Coast and Southern Tablelands Magazine, Tasmanian Travelways, On the Coast, X-Press Magazine.* Community: *Tenterfield Star, Glen Innes Examiner, Inverell Times, Armidale Express, The New Englander, Tamworth City Times, Muswellbrook, Hunter Valley News, Singleton Argus, Hunter Valley Star News, Cessnock Advertiser, Newcastle Star, Newcastle Times, Hibiscus Happenings, Mid-Coast Observer, Port Macquarie News, Port Macquarie Express, Hastings Happenings, Hastings Gazette, Camden Haven Courier, Manning River Times, Manning-Great Lakes Extra, Great Lakes Happenings, Dungog Chronicle, Hawkesbury Courier, Blue Mountains Gazette, Western Sunday, Mailbox Shopper, Mid-State Observer, Central West Sunday, Western Times, Cowra Guardian, Champion Post, Highlands Post, Southern Highlands News, Property Press, Post Weekly, Queanbeyan Age, Cooma-Monaro Express, Snowy Times, Shoalhaven and Nowra News, South Coast Register, Moruya Examiner, Imlay Magnet, Capricorn Local News, Leisuretime Community News, Noosa Citizen, Sunshine Coast Citizen, Ipswich Advertiser, Great Southern Star, Barossa and Light Herald, Northern Argus, Flinders News, The Transcontinental, Whyalla News/Leisuretime, Port Lincoln Times, Fresh Eyre, Ballarat News, Gippsland Times and Maffra Spectator, Traralgon Journal, Latrobe Valley Express, Morwell Advertiser, Moe and Narracan News, Bunbury Mail, Mandurah Mail, Augusta-Margaret River Mail, Avon Valley Advocate, Central Midlands and Coastal Advocate, Sunday Examiner, Launceston Week, Sun Coast News.* Suburban: *Ipswich Advertiser, Redland Times, Bayside Bulletin.* Annual: *Australian Sugar Yearbook, Hortguide, Flower Register.* Overseas: *New Zealand Farmer, Farm Equipment News, Southerner, Dairyman, AgTrader, Rural Waikato, New England Farmer, New York Farmer, Kentucky Farmer, Maryland Farmer, North Carolina Farmer, Tennessee Farmer, Virginia Farmer, Alabama Farmer, Georgia Farmer, Arkansas Farmer, Louisiana Farmer, Mississippi Farmer, Southern Hogs, Southern Cattle, Southern Poultry, Farm Business.*

David Syme & Co Limited
Incorporated in Victoria
Managing Director: J. C. Reynolds. Owner: John Fairfax & Sons Ltd
Major media interests: *The Age, The Sunday Age, Australian Auto Action* (50%), *National Greyhound Weekly* (50%), *Australian Motorcycle News* (50%), *Caravan World* (50%), *4 Wheeler* (50%), *Inside Football* (50%), *Motor* (50%), *National Trotting Weekly* (50%), *Street Machine* (50%), *Which Car?* (50%), *Wheels* (50%), *Tourist Park Guide, View, Jack High* (50%), *Football Plus* (25%).

Time Inc. Magazines Co Pty Ltd
Incorporated in Victoria
Owner: Time Inc., subsidiary of Time Warner Inc
Major media interests: *Time Australia, Who Weekly.*

West Australian Newspapers Ltd
Incorporated in WA
Chairman: T. R. Eastwood. Owner: West Australian Newspaper Holdings Ltd
Major media interests: *The West Australian, Kalgoorlie Miner, South Western Times, Warren Blackwood Times, Coastal Times, Busselton-Margaret Times, Harvey Reporter, Mandurah Telegraph, Sound Telegraph, Bunbury Weekender, Albany Advertiser, Northern Guardian, Great Southern Herald, North-West Telegraph, Broome Advertiser, Narrogin Observer, Albany Extra, Canning-Melville Times* (49.9%), *News Chronicle* (49.9%), *Comment News* (49.9%), *Eastern Suburbs Reporter* (49.9%), *Fremantle Cockburn Gazette* (49.9%), *Midland-Kalamunda Reporter* (49.9%), *Melville Fremantle* (49.9%), *Southern Gazette* (49.9%), *Stirling Times* (49.9%), *Wanneroo Times* (49.9%), *Weekend Courier* (49.9%), *Countryman, Goldfields Magazine.*

Regulatory Bodies

AUSTRALIAN BROADCASTING AUTHORITY

The Australian Broadcasting Authority (ABA) is an independent federal statutory authority responsible for the regulation of the broadcasting industry. It replaced the former Australian Broadcasting Tribunal previously known as the Broadcasting Control Board.

Some of the authority's major functions include granting, renewing, suspending and revoking of licences; approving changes in ownership and control of the media; determining program standards; and assembling information about broadcasting. The ABA was created by the *Broadcasting Services Act 1992,* which sets out a number of policy objectives:

- provide appropriate access to the broadcasting services bands of the radio frequency spectrum and allocate and administer broadcasting licences for radio and television;
- ensure that control of commercial television broadcasting services rests with Australians and that diversity of control of the more influential broadcasting services is maintained;
- encourage service providers to be responsive to the diverse broadcasting needs, interests and values of the Australian community;
- promote the role of broadcasting services in developing and reflecting a sense of Australian identity, character and cultural diversity;
- establish the authority as a principal source of expert advice and information on broadcasting issues for the government, the broadcasting industry and the community;
- ensure the optimum operation of the authority by pursuing continual improvement in the management of its resources; and
- develop the commitment and professionalism of staff to enhance the effectiveness of the authority.

AUSTRALIAN PRESS COUNCIL

The Australian Press Council, a self-regulatory body of the print media, consists of representatives of the public and of the press with an independent chairperson. It was established in 1976 and is funded by the print media. It has two main functions:

- the receiving of, and dealing with, complaints from the public against newspapers and magazines published in Australia. Such complaints must be directed at the editorial and article section of the publication. (A separate body deals with complaints about advertising.);
- the resisting of threats to the freedom of the press in doing its job, and the promotion of reforms in the legal and statutory environment in which the press operates to facilitate that freedom.

About 20% of complaints are adjudicated by the Australian Press Council, with about 415 complaints received each year.

ADVERTISING STANDARDS COUNCIL

The Advertising Standards Council (ASC), established in 1974, acts on complaints received from the public involving advertising in the press and other media, and publishes statistical data on these complaints in an annual report. The Council also monitors the advertising industry through their five Advertising Codes, authorised by the Trades Practices Commission for the benefit of the consumer. It is funded by a 0.01% levy on media advertising.

FEDERATION OF AUSTRALIAN COMMERCIAL TELEVISION STATIONS

The Federation of Australian Commercial Television Stations (FACTS) administers the commercial television industry's Code of Practice. In accordance with the *Broadcasting Services Act 1992*, the code demonstrates the self-regulation of broadcasting operations in strict accordance with community standards.

FEDERATION OF AUSTRALIAN RADIO BROADCASTERS

The Federation of Australian Radio Broadcasters (FARB) acts as a clearance body for radio advertisements before they are heard on radio.

Unions

MEDIA, ENTERTAINMENT AND ARTS ALLIANCE

The Australian Journalists Association (AJA) was founded in 1910 at a meeting of 100 newspaper journalists in Melbourne. In 1944, it adopted a code of ethics, and in 1992 it amalgamated with other unions to form the Media, Entertainment and Arts Alliance (MEAA). In 1995, it had a membership of more than 13 000 journalists, artists and photographers. This number includes about 1000 radio and television technicians, 5500 in newspapers and other publications, 1500 in television and 1500 in radio.

Members of the union employed in the media are expected to observe and enforce the Jounalists' Code of Ethics:

1. They shall report and interpret the news with scrupulous honesty by striving to disclose all essential facts and by not suppressing relevant, available facts, or distorting by wrong or improper emphasis;
2. They shall not place unnecessary emphasis on gender, race, sexual preference, religious belief, marital status or physical or mental disability;
3. In all circumstances they shall respect all confidences received in the course of their calling;
4. They shall not allow personal interests to influence them in their professional duties;
5. They shall not allow their professional duties to be influenced by any consideration, gift or advantage offered and, where appropriate, shall disclose any such offer;
6. They shall not allow advertising or commercial considerations to influence them in their professional duties;

7. They shall use fair and honest means of obtaining news, films, tapes and documents;
8. They shall identify themselves and their employers before obtaining any interview for publication or broadcast;
9. They shall respect private grief and personal privacy and shall have the right to resist compulsion to intrude on them;
10. They shall do their utmost to correct any published or broadcast information found to be harmfully inaccurate.

AUSTRALIAN MANUFACTURING WORKERS' UNION

This union covers printers, with about 10 000 of the 43 000 members employed in newspapers and other publications.

News Agencies

News agencies began as information carriers during the era of world colonisation. News of the colonies or news from the home country would be transmitted from colonies to the imperial country or vice versa. These days, agencies have enormous power and resources as newspapers can no longer afford their own foreign correspondents. To supply international news, papers must subscribe to an agency, with subscription costs varying from medium to medium, according to information needs, publication size and circulation.

Established in 1935 as a cooperative of 13 newspapers, AAP gathers and distributes general news, sport, finance and politics. It supplies more than 80 daily newspapers both in Australia and overseas, 150 commercial radio and television stations and non-daily and provincial newspapers with news, graphics and photos. By the mid-1990s, it had nine Australian bureaus operating overseas.

AAP Information Services Pty Ltd
9 Lang Street, Sydney NSW 2000. Ph: (02) 9322 8000. Fax: (02) 9322 8888.

Reuters Australia Pty Ltd
60 Margaret Street, Sydney NSW 2000. Ph: (02) 9373 1800.
Fax: (02) 9262 4727.

Industry Awards

THE WALKLEY AWARDS

Recognised as the pinnacle of journalistic excellence in Australia, the prestigious Walkley Awards are held each year by the Australian Journalists' Association as a national competition for reporters sub-editors, photographers and artists in all facets of the media. Recent winners include Alan Tate and Paul Bailey of the *Sydney Morning Herald*, David Bentley of the *Brisbane Courier Mail*, Monica Attard of ABC Radio, Jenny Brockie of ABC TV, Philip Chubb and Sue Spencer of ABC TV and Peter McEvoy of ABC Radio National.

TV WEEK LOGIES

The Logies are the Australian television industry awards and are presented annually. Logie winners are voted for by TV Week readers. The most prestigious award on the night is the Gold Logie given to the entertainer voted most popular.

GOLD LOGIE WINNERS SINCE THE AWARD'S INCEPTION

Year	Winner
1959	Graham Kennedy and Panda (Victoria only)
1960	Graham Kennedy TV Week 'Star of the Year'
1961	Bob Dyer
1962	Tommy Hanlon and Lorrae Desmond
1963	Michael Charlton
1964	Bobby Limb
1965	Jimmy Hannan
1966	Gordon Chater
1967	Graham Kennedy
1968	Brian Henderson
1969	Graham Kennedy
1970	Barry Crocker and Maggie Tabberer
1971	Gerard Kennedy and Maggie Tabberer
1972	Gerard Kennedy
1973	Tony Barber
1974	Graham Kennedy and Pat McDonald
1975	Ernie Sigley and Denise Drysdale
1976	Garry McDonald ('Norman Gunston') and Denise Drysdale
1977	Don Lane and Jeannie Little

Year	Winner
1978	Graham Kennedy
1979	Bert Newton
1980	Mike Walsh
1981	Bert Newton
1982	Bert Newton
1983	Daryl Somers
1984	Bert Newton
1985	Rowena Wallace
1986	Daryl Somers
1987	Ray Martin
1988	Kylie Minogue
1989	Daryl Somers
1990	Craig McLachlan
1991	Steve Vizard
1992	Jana Wendt
1993	Ray Martin
1994	Ray Martin
1995	Ray Martin

SOME OTHER RADIO AWARDS

The Awgie Awards are presented by the Australian Writers' Guild for best scripts for stage, cinema, television and radio. Winners include David Williamson, Robert Caswell and Michael Gow.

Other radio industry awards include the Payter Awards, the Hi-Fi Awards and the Golden Stave Awards, which are based on votes from the advertising industry.

15
The Arts

Overview

*I*t is estimated that approximately 100 000 people were employed in the arts industry in 1996, which includes libraries, media and publishing as well as dance, theatre, film and music in their many forms. The arts industry has been growing at a rate of 4% a year since the 1980s, making it one of the fastest growing industries in the country.

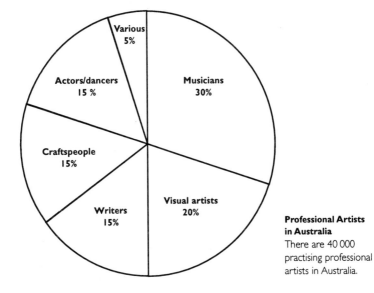

Professional Artists in Australia
There are 40 000 practising professional artists in Australia.

1990–1991 AUDIENCES FOR THE ARTS

Artform/Art space	Number of Visits per Year
Art galleries	9.7 million
Museums	8.3 million
Theatre	5.8 million
Music theatre (incl. opera)	5.3 million
Dance	3.5 million
Film	65 million
Popular music	13.6 million
Classical music	3.1 million

*A*ustralians are avid readers, spending more than $1000 million on books in 1994, an average of more than $50 per head. The Australian Book Publishers Association estimated retail book sales for the same year to be approximately $1 billion, with Australian books accounting for 50% of this market. About 5000 new Australian titles are published each year, 10% of which are works of literature.

In 1996, there were approximately 870 cinema screens in Australia and total box office revenue in the same year was in excess of $470 million. There are approximately 2800 video rental outlets in Australia. It is estimated that 99% of Australian households have one or more televisions and almost 60% of these have video recorders/players.

There is a large number of organisations administrating and funding the arts in Australia. Some of the major ones are: the Copyright Council of Australia, the Australasian Performing Rights Association, the Federal and State crafts councils, the State arts funding agencies, the Australian Society of Authors, the Australian Writers' Guild and the National Association of the Visual Arts.

Major Organisations

THE AUSTRALIA COUNCIL

The Australia Council is the Federal governments principal arts funding and advisory body. Its goals are to promote excellence in the arts; to support the creation of new work; to foster participation and appreciation of the arts by all Australians; to promote Aboriginal and Torres Strait Islander arts and recognise cultural diversity and to increase audiences for Australian arts.

In 1996–1997, a budget of $63.8 million was allocated to the Australia Council by the Federal government. Of this, $55.5 million (87%) was used for direct financial support for arts activities and the balance of $8.3 million (13%) was used for other support for arts activities, administration and general purposes.

Within the Australia Council, there are several divisions and artform funds. The Strategy and Policy Division provides support to the council and coordinates policy, planning, research, library, public affairs and arts infrastructure support. The Audience Development and Advocacy Division was established to strengthen and expand audiences for the arts, both within Australia and internationally. It aims to improve marketing and advocacy skills in the Australian arts community.

The various funds and the Aboriginal and Torres Strait Islander Arts Board are the Australia Council's main decision-making bodies for grants and provide advice on the development of arts policy. The funds are: Community Cultural Development, Dance, Literature, Major Organisations, Music, Theatre, Visual Arts/Craft and New Media Arts.

ABORIGINAL AND TORRES STRAIT ISLANDER BOARD

The Aboriginal and Torres Strait Islander Arts Board assists indigenous Australians in claiming, controlling and enhancing their cultural inheritance. The board supports these rights through its grant programs and through the development of a national indigenous arts policy.

The initial allocation for the board in 1996–1997 was $4.4 million.

COMMUNITY CULTURAL DEVELOPMENT FUND

The Community Cultural Development Fund assists the expression of Australian culture by supporting artists and communities working together. It supports community-based arts practice that affirms the principle of self-determination. Community cultural development enables communities to advance their artistic, social and economic aspirations.

The initial allocation for the fund in 1996–1997 was $5.8 million.

DANCE FUND

The Dance Fund fosters the development of Australian dance and movement arts through supporting companies, ensembles, freelance artists and independent initiatives. It encourages artists to create and present the highest quality work that contributes to the diversity and originality of Australia's performing arts.

The initial allocation for the fund in 1996–1997 was $3.3 million.

LITERATURE FUND

The Literature Fund encourages the creation, publication, translation, critical appraisal and awarenesss of high-quality contemporary Australian literature. It encourages new and established writers through individual grants and supports related activities such as community projects, festivals, residencies, literary magazines and journals and international promotion.

The initial allocation for the fund in 1996–1997 was $4.2 million.

MAJOR ORGANISATIONS FUND

The Major Organisations Fund aims to promote the effective delivery of artistic excellence by Australian arts organisations of national standing. The Fund selects organisations for inclusion on the basis of their significant cultural role, their size, the scope of their programs and their financial viability. These organisations must have demonstrated a high profile nationally or internationally, and shown a commitment to developing the professional skills of Australian artists.

The initial allocation for the fund in 1996–1997 was $12.5 million.

MUSIC FUND

The Music Fund fosters the highest quality work by encouraging artistic innovation in content, development and presentation across the broad range of Australian music practice. The fund's programs aim to achieve diversity and originality in Australia's performing arts.

The initial allocation for the fund in 1996–1997 was $4.3 million.

THEATRE

The Theatre Fund supports theatre that exhibits creative energy and a commitment to innovation and cultural diversity and a variety of practices in the development and presentation of Australian theatre. The fund fosters a wide range of approaches to the creation of theatre including text-based theatre, devised work, contemporary performance, puppetry, visual theatre, youth theatre, circus and physical theatre.

The initial allocation for the fund in 1996–1997 was $8.2 million.

VISUAL ARTS/CRAFT FUND

The Visual Arts/Craft Fund supports the creation, presentation and interpretation of contemporary Australian visual arts and craft, both nationally and internationally. The fund's programs are designed to expand opportunities to produce and present new Australian visual arts and craft to ensure that visual artists and craftspeople are valued and fairly rewarded for their work in Australia, and to promote understanding and enjoyment of contemporary art and craft.

The fund gives financial support to a number of established arts organisations, galleries and museums around Australia. The initial allocation for the fund in 1996–1997 was $6.2 million.

NEW MEDIA ARTS FUND

The New Media Arts Fund supports the collaboration between the arts, often with new technologies, but not based in any single arts discipline. The fund provides policy advice to the Australia Council and allocated funds to support the hybrid and the emerging digital arts. It maintains an overview of interdisciplinary arts practices and seeks to develop the potential of convergence of both artforms and media.

The initial allocation for the Fund in 1996–1997 was $2.6 million.

THE ARTS COUNCIL OF AUSTRALIA

There are arts councils in the Australian Capital Territory and each State of Australia which work within the country communities to bring arts to people in regional areas. They are independent organisations which receive support from Federal, State and local governments. The Arts Council of Australia was founded in 1946 to arrange tours of performing arts in schools and for adults and to arrange tours of exhibitions. The Arts Councils run workshops in all branches of the arts to stimulate and coordinate arts activities. Its role is primarily one of support, giving advice and information to help local arts and community bodies develop.

Arts Festivals

There are about 400 festivals in Australia devoted partly or solely to the arts. The Adelaide Arts Festival, a biennial event, and the annual Perth Festival are the largest of these, both attracting artists and performers from around Australia and overseas. Other major festivals and the month they are held appear below.

MAJOR ARTS FESTIVALS IN AUSTRALIA

Festivals	Month
Festival of Sydney	January
Sydney Gay and Lesbian Mardi Gras	February
Festival of Perth	February
Moomba (Melbourne)	March
Adelaide Arts Festival	March, biennial
Canberra Festival	March
Hobart Arts Festival	May
Hobart Film Festival	May
Sydney Film Festival	June
Melbourne Film Festival	July
Brisbane Film Festival	August
Queensland Festival of the Arts	August
Festival of Darwin	August
Carnivale, Sydney	September
Melbourne International Festival	October

Dance

THE AUSTRALIAN BALLET

The Australian Ballet was established in 1962 by the Australian Elizabethan Theatre Trust with Dame Peggy Van Praagh as the first Artistic Director. They gave their first performance, a full-length production of *Swan Lake*, on 2 November 1962 at Her Majesty's Theatre in Sydney.

The Ballet employs 143 staff: 62 dancers, 38 artistic, music, production and technical staff and 43 administrative staff. They perform an average of 14 ballets a year, giving around around 180 performances both in Australia and overseas.

The Australian Ballet Foundation is the corporate entity behind the Australian Ballet. It was registered as an incorporated company on 16 October 1970. It receives funding from a number of sources, including the Major Organisation Fund of the Australia Council ($3.5 million for 1996), the Victorian and New South Wales Ministries of the Arts, corporate sponsors, private foundations and patrons.

ARTISTIC DIRECTORS OF THE AUSTRALIAN BALLET

Year	Artistic Director
1962–1974	Dame Peggy Van Praagh
1965	Sir Robert Helpmann became co-Artistic Director with Dame Peggy Van Praagh
1974	Sir Robert Helpmann became sole Director
1976	Anne Woolliams
1978	Dame Peggy Van Praagh
1978–May 1982	Marilyn Jones
May–Dec 1982	Marilyn Rowe Maver (Ballet Director)
1983–1996	Maina Gielgud
1997–	Ross Stretton

ABORIGINAL ISLANDER DANCE THEATRE

Aboriginal Islander Dance Theatre (AIDT) is the professional performing arm of the National Aboriginal and Islander Skills and Development Association (NAISDA) Inc.

NAISDA also run a College that provides training in dance and related arts subjects. The College offers three programs of study: Certificate in Dance, Associate Diploma in Dance and a Diploma of Dance, for Aboriginal and Torres Strait Islander people. The courses place a strong emphasis on the preservation of the Aboriginal and Torres Strait Islander cultures, enabling tutors to travel from traditional communities to pass on their knowledge to students. In exchange, the students travel to these same communities to gain first hand experience of the culture and its people.

NAISDA receives funding from the Department of Communication and the Arts, the Aboriginal and Torres Strait Islander Unit of the Australia Council, the Aboriginal and Torres Strait Islander Commission (ATSIC), the Ministry for the Arts and the Department of Employment, Education, Training and Youth Affairs.

In 1997, NAISDA took up residence in The Rocks in one of the vaults under the Sydney Harbour Bridge.

SYDNEY DANCE COMPANY

Originally formed as an educational dance company in 1965, the Dance Company of NSW, as it was then known, became the State's first funded, full-time professional dance company in 1971. Today, it is one of the most respected Australian dance companies both here and overseas, due largely to the efforts of Artistic Director Graeme Murphy and Assistant Director Janet Vernon.

When first appointed as Director in 1976, Murphy announced the aim to nurture Australian choreographers, composers and designers. This goal has made the company a leader in the Australian arts industry.

The company is headed by a board of eight directors from the business community and is chaired by Rowan Ross. Office and rehearsal studios are located at The Wharf, Walsh Bay, but the company's performance home is the Sydney Opera House, where it gives two major seasons each year.

Film

HISTORY

The first films shown before a paying public in Australia, were screened at the Opera House in Melbourne on 22 August 1896. These were screened as part of a variety bill by the English illusionist Carl Hertz.

The first cinema, Salon Cinimatographie, was opened in Pitt Street, Sydney, in the same year. After France, USA and Germany, Australia was fourth in the world to exhibit films in an auditorium designed solely for that purpose.

The first films made in Australia were taken by Marius Sestier, who came to Sydney from Paris in September 1896. These were short scenes taken around Sydney. The first dramatic Australian films were produced by Major Joseph Perry of the Salvation Army, Melbourne, beginning in 1897. Among these was *Soldiers of the Cross*.

Made in 1906, *The Story of the Kelly Gang* is reputed to be one of the world's first feature-length films. It ran for more than an hour, whereas most other films being made at the time ran for ten minutes or less. The film was produced by the Melbourne company J. & N. Tait.

CLASSIFICATION OF FILMS, VIDEOTAPES, PUBLICATIONS AND COMPUTER GAMES

The *Classification (Publications, Films and Computer Games) Act 1995* establishes the Classification Board as a full-time statutory body within the Attorney-General's portfolio. The Office of Film and Literature Classification provides administrative support to the board.

The Classification Board is responsible for the classification of films, videos, publications and computer games in accordance with the requirements of the Act. When making classification decisions, the board applies criteria which are set out in the National Classification Code and the classification guidelines which are approved by Commonwealth, State and Territory Censorship Ministers. Enforcement of classification decisions is the responsibility of the States and Territories.

Classifications

G	General (suitable for all ages)
PG	Parental Guidance (parental guidance recommended for persons under 15 years)
M 15+	Mature (recommended for mature audiences aged 15 years and over)
MA 15+	Mature Accompanied (restrictions apply to persons under the age of 15 years)
R 18+	Restricted (restricted to adults aged 18 years and over)
NVE *	Contains non-violent sexually explicit material (restricted to adults aged 18 years and over)

* Videos have a classification that does not apply to cinema-release films, the 'NVE' classssification. Material rated NVE can only be sold or hired in the Australian Capital Territory and the Northern Territory, and must not show children or violent sex.

CONSUMER ADVICE

Since May 1989, films and videos classified PG, M, MA, R and X carry, in addition to the classification symbol, a consumer advice line. This advises of the principal elements which have contributed to the classification of a film or video, and indicates their intensity and/or frequency. Consumer advice now appears prominently on the cover of each videotape, and in advertisements for films and videotapes.

AUSTRALIAN FILM, TELEVISION AND RADIO SCHOOL

The Australian Film, Television and Radio School (AFTRS) was set up in 1973 and is funded by the Commonwealth government. It is the national training centre for these media.

The school offers a number of courses including a post-graduate program that has a duration of one, two or three years. This program leads to awards, the titles of which will be announced pending accreditation. It offers a short program including seminars, conferences and forums in a variety of specialist subjects and it also offers a 28-week full-time course in commercial radio.

The aim of the AFTRS in regard to training is to identify and develop new and emerging talent and to provide working professionals with opportunities to gain additional skills not available in their employment. Training is directed towards those people with demonstrated creative potential and clear ability and commitment.

Full-time study courses are conducted at the AFTRS Sydney base, with short courses available in Melbourne, Brisbane, Perth, Adelaide and Hobart.

AUSTRALIAN FILM COMMISSION

The Australian Film Commission (AFC) was established in 1975. It is a federal statutory authority whose objective is the development of Australian film-making through funding, or otherwise assisting, the making, promotion, distribution and broadcasting of Australian programs. Part of its brief is to give special attention to encouraging experimental and highly creative programs and also to the proper archival storage of Australian recordings.

The AFC gives a broad definition to the word film and uses it to include video and all gauges of film.

AUSTRALIAN FILM INSTITUTE

The Australian Film Institute (AFI) is an independent company established in October 1958. It receives some financial support from the Australian Film Commission, State government arts bodies, corporate sponsors and members. Its aim is 'to promote knowledge, appreciation and enjoyment of the art of film amongst Australian film-makers and audiences with particular emphasis on Australian film'.

The Australian Film Institute has cinemas in Sydney and Hobart, and had 7460 members nationally in 1996. It also controls AFI Distribution, which provides distribution for independent film and video Australia-wide.

AFI AWARDS

The first Australian Film Awards were held in 1958 as part of the Melbourne Film Festival. They were initiated by the Festival Director Erwin Rado. The aim of the awards was to 'direct public attention to Australian films and to encourage high standards in their production'. The Australian Film Institute was established after this time, with Erwin Rado as its Director and the awards as its major objective.

The 1958 awards had four categories: documentary, educational, open and advertising. Over the years, the categories and awards have evolved and grown in number in reaction to the growth in Australian film-making. In 1983, the awards were presented for the first time as the AFI awards, with television awards introduced for the first time in 1986.

WINNERS OF THE AFI AWARDS

Year/Award	Title
1958	
Silver awards	
Documentary	*Conquest of the Rivers*
Documentary	*Hard to Windward*
Open	*The Forerunner*
1959	
Silver awards	
Documentary	*The Edge of the Deep, The Power Makers*
Open	*Grampians Wonderland*
Teaching	*Think Twice*
Advertising	Shell television commercial
1960	
Silver awards	
Experimental	*The Black Man and His Wife*
Teaching	*Biological Control of Insects*
Advertising	*Visual Squeeze* — ICA, Tip Top Slide
Special award	*The Terrific Adventures of the Terrible Ten* Special certificate for Children's Film
1961	no awards presentation
1962	
First prize winners	
Open	*A Report on the Political Development in the Territory of Papua New Guinea*
Experimental	*Conference Room*
Public Relations	*Gateway to a City*
Advertising	Shell Car Family
Children's	*The Prize*

Year/Award	Title
1963	
Grand Prix	*Adam and Eve*
Gold awards	
Documentary	*The Land That Waited*
Nature	*Dancing Orpheus*
Experimental	*Adam and Eve*
1964	
Gold awards	
Documentary	*The Dancing Class*
	I, the Aboriginal
1965	
Gold awards	
Open	*Faces in the Sun*
Travel	*From the Tropics to the Snow*
1966	
Golden Reels	
Documentary	*Concerto for Orchestra*
Public Relations	*People Make Papers*
1967	
Golden Reel	
Documentary	*Cardin in Australia*
1968	
Golden Reels	
Documentary	*The Change at Groote*
	The Talgai Skull
Teaching	*Drama Lesson*
1969	
Golden Reels	
Documentary	*Bullocky*
	The Die-Hard 'The Legend of Lasseter's Lost Gold Reef'
1970	
Grand Prix	*Three To Go: Michael*
Golden Reels	
Documentary	*The Gallery*
Public Relations	*Symphony in Steel*

Year/Award	Title
1971	
Grand Prix	*Homesdale*
Golden Reels	
Fiction	*Paddington Lace*
Documentary	*A Big Hand for Everyone*
General	*This Man*
Best Direction	Peter Weir, *Homesdale*
Best Performance	Monica Maughan, *A City's Child*
1972	
Gold awards	
Fiction	*Stork*
Documentary	*Jackpot Town*
Advertising	*Adelaide — Darwin on Steel*
Best Direction	Tim Burstall, *Stork*
Best Performance	Bruce Spence and Jackie Weaver, *Stork*
1973	
Gold awards	
Fiction	*The Child Episode of Libido*
	27A
Documentary	*Tidiwaka and Friends*
Best Actor	Robert McDarra, *27A*
Best Actress	Judy Morris, *The Child Episode of Libido*
Best Direction	Eric Porter, *Marco Polo Junior Versus the Red Dragon*
1974–1975	
Golden Reels	
Feature	*Sunday Too Far Away*
Documentary	*Mr Symbol Man*
General	*Billy and Percy*
Best Actor	Jack Thompson, *Petersen, Sunday Too Far Away*
	Martin Vaughan, *Billy and Percy*
Best Actress	Julie Dawson, *Who Killed Jenny Langby?*
Best Direction	John Power, *Billy and Percy*
1976	
Best Film	*The Devil's Playground*
Best Actor	Simon Burke and Nick Tate, *The Devil's Playground*
Best Actress	Helen Morse, *Caddie*
Best Direction	Fred Schepisi, *The Devil's Playground*

Year/Award	Title

1977
Best Film   *Storm Boy*
Best Actor   John Meillion, *The Fourth Wish*
Best Actress   Pat Bishop, *Don's Party*
Best Direction   Bruce Beresford, *Don's Party*

1978
Best Film   *Newsfront*
Best Actor   Bill Hunter, *Newsfront*
Best Actress   Angela Punch, *The Chant of Jimmy Blacksmith*
Best Direction   Phillip Noyce, *Newsfront*

1979
Best Film   *My Brilliant Career*
Best Actor   Mel Gibson, *Tim*
Best Actress   Michele Fawdon, *Cathy's Child*
Best Direction   Gillian Armstrong, *My Brilliant Career*

1980
Best Film   *Breaker Morant*
Best Actor   Jack Thompson, *Breaker Morant*
Best Actress   Tracey Mann, *Hard Knocks*
Best Direction   Bruce Beresford, *Breaker Morant*

1981
Best Film   *Gallipoli*
Best Actor   Mel Gibson, *Gallipoli*
Best Actress   Judy Davis, *Winter of Our Dreams*
Best Direction   Peter Weir, *Gallipoli*

1982
Best Film   *Lonely Hearts*
Best Actor   Ray Barrett, *Goodbye Paradise*
Best Actress   Noni Hazlehurst, *Monkey Grip*
Best Direction   George Miller, *Mad Max 2*

1983
Best Film   *Careful. He Might Hear You*
Best Actor   Norman Kaye, *Man of Flowers*
Best Actress   Wendy Hughes, *Careful, He Might Hear You*
Best Direction   Carl Schultz, *Careful, He Might Hear You*

Year/Award	Title
1984	
Best Film	*Annie's Coming Out*
Best Actor	John Hargreaves, *My First Wife*
Best Actress	Angela Punch McGregor, *Annie's Coming Out*
Best Direction	Paul Cox, *My First Wife*
1985	
Best Film	*Bliss*
Best Actor	Chris Hayward, *A Street To Die*
Best Actress	Noni Hazlehurst, *Fran*
Best Direction	Ray Lawrence, *Bliss*
1986	
Best Film	*Malcolm*
Best Actor	Colin Friels, *Malcolm*
Best Actress	Judy Davis, *Kangaroo*
Best Direction	Nadia Tass, *Malcolm*
1987	
Best Film	*The Year My Voice Broke*
Best Actor	Leo McKern, *Travelling North*
Best Actress	Judy Davis, *High Tide*
Best Direction	John Duigan, *The Year My Voice Broke*
1988	
Best Film	*The Navigator*
Best Actor	John Waters, *Boulevard of Broken Dreams*
Best Actress	Nadine Garner, *Mullaway*
Best Direction	Vincent Ward, *The Navigator*
1989	
Best Film	*Evil Angels*
Best Actor	Sam Neill, *Evil Angels*
Best Actress	Meryl Streep, *Evil Angels*
Best Direction	Fred Schepisi, *Evil Angels*
1990	
Best Film	*Flirting*
Best Actor	Max von Sydow, *Father*
Best Actress	Catherine McClements, *Weekend with Kate*
Best Direction	Ray Argall, *Return Home*

Year/Award	Title
1991	
Best Film	*Proof*
Best Actor	Hugo Weaving, *Proof*
Best Actress	Sheila Florence, *A Woman's Tale*
Best Direction	Jocelyn Moorhouse, *Proof*
1992	
Best Film	*Strictly Ballroom*
Best Actor	Russell Crowe, *Romper Stomper*
Best Actress	Lisa Harrow, *The Last Days of Chez Nous*
Best Direction	Baz Luhrmann, *Strictly Ballroom*
1993	
Best Film	*The Piano*
Best Actor	Harvey Keitel, *The Piano*
Best Actress	Holly Hunter, *The Piano*
Best Direction	Jane Campion, *The Piano*
1994	
Best Film	*Muriel's Wedding*
Best Actor	Nicholas Hope, *Bad Boy Bubby*
Best Actress	Toni Colette, *Muriel's Wedding*
Best Direction	Rolf de Heer, *Bad Boy Bubby*
1995	
Best Film	*Angel Baby*
Best Actor	John Lynch, *Angel Baby*
Best Actress	Jacqueline McKenzie, *Angel Baby*
Best Direction	Michael Rymer, *Angel Baby*

FILM AUSTRALIA

Film Australia is Australia's national production house. Their role is to produce, promote and distribute films, videos and television programs.

They often undertake projects in conjunction with the ABC, SBS and Australia's commercial networks as well as with many international partners such as Channel Four, the BBC, United States Public Broadcasting and the National Film Board of Canada. Currently, Film Australia has a catalogue of more than 2000 titles, which have earned more than 500 awards from around the world.

Originally known as the Cinema Branch, Film Australia was formed to provide footage of Australia for the campaign to encourage migrants from

Britain. It began in 1911 with a staff of one, James Pinkerton Campbell, a photographer and movie-maker. Pinkerton was only provided with basic equipment and had to find his own studio, which he did, sharing with a friend.

In 1917, Frank Hurley and Herbert Wilkins were appointed as war correspondents and sent to the Middle East and France. After World War I, the emphasis again turned to immigration and Campbell's replacement, Bert Ives, and his two assistants, were moved to the Commonwealth Immigration Office.

Eminent Australian Director Raymond Longford and his star turned co-director Lottie Lyall were taken on as contractors in the 1920s to produce films for an exhibition in London in 1923. It was decided around this time to expand into producing shorts for cinema release. This idea was very successful and one short was made each week for MGM and Paramount.

Soon after the outbreak of World War II, the Cinema Branch was transferred to the newly formed Department of Information. A film unit of five was sent to the Middle East and the footage they recorded was shown by Cinesound and Movietone in their weekly newsreels. Australia won its first Academy Award in 1947 with the film *Kokoda Frontline*, which Cinesound made from Damien Parer's war footage.

In 1951, the Cinema Branch was known as the National Film Board and had become part of the Department of the Interior. That year they produced 180 films. In 1954, the board became the Commonwealth Film Unit and made the first feature-length colour film produced in Australia, *The Queen in Australia*. Upon the establishment of the Australian Film Commission in 1975, the Film Unit finally became Film Australia, the production arm of the Film Commission.

In 1988, Film Australia became a statutory company and entered into a production contract with the government. Their role now is the production of material which reflects the Australian people and their lifestyle and deals with matters of national interest.

Fine Arts

NATIONAL GALLERY OF AUSTRALIA

The National Gallery of Australia is situated on the shores of Lake Burley Griffin in Canberra on a 5.6-hectare site which includes a sculpture garden set over 2 hectares. Home of the National Collection of art, the National Gallery is very young in comparison with its international counterparts. Although the Commonwealth government has been acquiring art since 1911, serious collecting of Australian art did not begin until 1967, followed by international art in 1972.

The National Gallery was officially opened on 12 October 1982. Since this time the Gallery has become an integral part of Australian cultural life and the international art world. It has initiated and hosted major exhibitions, and lent works to similar exhibitions in Australia and overseas. It is a recognised source of art scholarship and also increases public access through a range of services including in-house and travelling exhibitions, education services and guided tours. It also has a research library and conservation department to preserve and maintain the collection.

NATIONAL GALLERY OF AUSTRALIA COLLECTIONS

AUSTRALIAN ART   The Australian collection tells the story of European settlement over the past two hundred years. Displays combine paintings, sculptures, drawings and watercolours, prints and photographs, folk and popular arts, as well as decorative arts in all media.

ABORIGINAL AND TORRES STRAIT ISLANDER ART   The oldest art tradition in Australia is that of the country's original inhabitants and their descendants. Aboriginal art is not a static relic of a bygone era, but a vital expression of current human concerns. Aboriginal artists may work in either traditional media or adopt new techniques, but the values permeating their art are consistently and distinctively Aboriginal.

AFRICAN, OCEANIC AND PRE-COLOMBIAN ART   This collection affirms Australia's location in the Pacific region by its small, but excellent representation of the art produced by its Oceanic neighbours. It also includes a range of material from further afield — works originating in Africa and Pre-Colombian America.

ASIAN ART   The Asian collection introduces Australian audiences to brilliant achievements in the visual arts of the many Asian and Islamic cultures. Although small, these collections embody some of the great social and national themes of Asian history.

INTERNATIONAL ART   This collection parallels the gallery's holdings of Australian art over the past two hundred years. It contains paintings, sculptures, photographs, prints, drawings, illustrated books and decorative arts, including theatre arts and fashion. The collection concentrates on the achievements of European and American artists, and finds its strengths in the twentieth century. It represents the major schools and movements in art from 1850 to the present and includes a small but historically significant collection of European art before 1850.

SCULPTURE   Sculptures from the collections are on show in the sculpture garden, which is designed to display up to 50 works in 'outdoor rooms' created by native Australian trees and shrubs, a slate-paved court and a marsh pond.

THE ARCHIBALD PRIZE

When he died in 1991, J. F. Archibald, the founder of the *Bulletin* magazine, left provision in his will for a prize to be awarded for the best portrait 'preferentially of some man or woman distinguished in Art, Letters, Science or Politics, painted by any artist resident in Australasia during the six months preceding the date fixed by the Trustees for sending in the pictures'. The current value of the prize is $20 000. It was first awarded in 1921.

Probably the most prestigious award in Australian art, it has been the subject of controversy more than once. In 1944, Mary Edwards and Joseph Wolinski took legal action to stop the award of the prize money to William Dobell, whose portrait of Joshua Smith had won the 1943 prize. They considered the painting to be a caricature rather than a portrait. After a legal battle of two years the court found that the prize judges' decision was binding. In 1953, students demonstrated when, for the seventh time, the award went to William Dargie. In 1975, John Bloomfield's winning portrait of Tim Burstall was disqualified when it was found that it had been painted from a photograph rather than from life as the conditions of the prize require.

ARCHIBALD PRIZE WINNERS

Year	Title	Artist
1921	*Desbrowe Annear*	W. B. McInnes
1922	*Professor Harrison Moore*	W. B. McInnes
1923	*Portrait of a Lady*	W. B. McInnes
1924	*Miss Collins*	W. B. McInnes
1925	*Maurice Moscovitch*	John Longstaff
1926	*Silk and Lace*	W. B. McInnes
1927	*Mrs Murdoch*	George W. Lambert
1928	*Dr Alexander Leeper*	John Longstaff
1929	*W. A. Holman, K.C.*	John Longstaff
1930	*Drum-Major Harry McClelland*	W. B. McInnes
1931	*Sir John Sulman*	John Longstaff
1932	*Sir William Irvine*	Ernest Buckmaster
1933	*Ambrose Pratt*	Charles Wheeler
1934	*Self Portrait*	Henry Hanke
1935	*A. B. (Banjo) Paterson*	John Longstaff
1936	*Dr Julian Smith*	W. B. McInnes
1937	*Self Portrait*	Normand Baker
1938	*Mme Elink Schuurman*	Nora Heysen

Year	Title	Artist
1939	The Hon. G. J. Bell, Speaker of the House of Representatives	Max Meldrum
1940	Dr J. Forbes McKenzie	Max Meldrum
1941	Sir James Elder, K.B.E.	William Dargie
1942	Corporal Jim Gordon, V.C.	William Dargie
1943	Joshua Smith	William Dobell
1944	S. Rosevear, M.H.R., Speaker	Joshua Smith
1945	Lt. General The Hon. Edmund Herring, K.B.E., D.S.O., M.C., E.D.	William Dargie
1946	L. C. Robson, M.C., M.A.	William Dargie
1947	Sir Marcus Clarke, K.B.E.	William Dargie
1948	Margaret Olley	William Dobell
1949	Bonar Dunlop	Arthur Murch
1950	Sir Leslie McConnan	William Dargie
1951	Laurie Thomas	Ivor Hele
1952	Mr Essington Lewis, C.H.	William Dargie
1953	Sir Henry Simpson Newland, C.B.E., D.S.O., M.S., F.R.C.S.	Ivor Hele
1954	Rt Hon. R.G. Menzies, P.C., C.H., Q.C., M.P.	Ivor Hele
1955	Robert Campbell	Ivor Hele
1956	Mr Albert Namatjira	William Dargie
1957	Self Portrait	Ivor Hele
1958	Mr Ray Walker	William Pidgeon
1959	Dr Edward MacMahon	William Dobell
1960	Stanislaus Rapotec	Judy Cassab
1961	Rabbi Dr I. Porush	William Pidgeon
1962	Patrick White	Louis Kahan
1963	Professor James McAuley	J. Carrington Smith
1964	no award	—
1965	R. A. Henderson	Clifton Pugh
1966	Charles Blackman	Jon Molvig
1967	Margo Lewers	Judy Cassab
1968	Lloyd Rees	William Pidgeon
1969	George Johnston	Ray Crooke
1970	Gruzman — Architect	Eric Smith
1971	Sir John McEwan	Clifton Pugh
1972	The Hon. E. G. Whitlam	Clifton Pugh
1973	Michael Boddy	Janet Dawson

Year	Title	Artist
1974	*Jockey Norman Stephens*	Sam Fulbrook
1975	*The Hon. Sir Frank Kitto, K.B.E.*	Kevin Connor
1976	*Self Portrait in the Studio*	Brett Whiteley
1977	*Robert Klippel*	Kevin Connor
1978	*Life, Art and the Other Thing*	Brett Whiteley
1979	*Portrait of Phillip Adams*	Wes Walters
1980	no award	—
1981	*Rudy Komon*	Eric Smith
1982	*Peter Sculthorpe*	Eric Smith
1983	*Chandler Coventry*	Nigel Thomson
1984	*Max Gillies*	Keith Looby
1985	*Flugelman with Wingman*	Guy Warren
1986	*Dr John Arthur McKelvey*	Shera Davida Allen
1987	*Equestrian Self Portrait*	William Robinson
1988	*John Beard*	Fred Cress
1989	*Portrait of Elwyn Lynn*	Brian Westwood
1990	*Dorothy Hewett*	Geoffrey Proud
1991–92	*Portrait of the Prime Minister, Paul Keating*	Bryan Westwood
1993	*Tom Thompson*	Garry Shead
1994	*Homage to John Reichardt*	Francis Giacco
1995	*Self Portrait with Stunned Mullet*	William Robinson
1996	*Self Portrait — As Diana of Erskineville*	Wendy Sharpe

SIR JOHN SULMAN PRIZE

Sir John Sulman was a trustee of the Art Gallery of NSW from 1899 until his death in 1934. Under the terms of a gift from his family, an award is given annually for paintings or mural designs judged to be the best subject painting, genre painting or design for an intended mural design done by an artist resident in Australia for two years preceding the date fixed by the trustees for sending in the pictures. The painting must have been executed in the preceding two years. The value of this prize is $5000. It was first awarded in 1936.

SIR JOHN SULMAN PRIZE WINNERS

Year	Title	Artist
1936	*La Gitana*	Henry Hanke
1937	no award	—
1938	*Atlanta's Eclipse*	Charles Meere
1939	Mural decoration Hotel Australia building	Gert Selheim
1940	*Vaucluse Interior*	Harold Abbott
1941	Historical mural Bathurst Public School	Douglas Annand
1942	*For Whom the Bell Tolls*	Jean Bellette
1943	Mural Le Coq d'Or restaurant	Elaine Haxton
1944	*Iphigenia in Tauris*	Jean Bellette
1945	Mural at Sydney University *Tribute to Shakespeare*	Virgil Lo Schiavo
1946	*Natives carrying wounded soldiers*	Sali Herman
1947	Mural Messrs Jantzen Pty Ltd	Douglas Annand
1948	*The Drovers*	Sali Herman
1949	Mural design New State building, Hobart	J. Carrington Smith
1950	*Summer Holiday*	Harold Greenhill
1951	Mural R.M.S. Oronsay restaurant	Douglas Annand
1952	*Darlinghurst Road*	Charles Doutney
1953	Mural *Convicts Berrima 1839* Old Court House, Berrima	Eric Smith
1954	*Sculptor and Model*	Wallace Thornton
1955	Mural design *Oriental Mural*	Wesley Penberthy
1956	*Prawning at Night*	Harold Greenhill
1957	*The Voice of Silence*	Michael Kmit
1958	no award	—
1959	*The Circus*	Susan Wright
1960	*The Burial*	Leonard French
1961	*Sea Movement and Rocks*	Robin Norling
1962	*Children Dancing*	John Rigby
1963	*Spring Walk*	Roy Fluke
1964	*The Private Public Preview*	Ken Reinhard
1965	*Grapepickers and Vineyards*	Gareth Jones Robert
1966	*It's Hot in Town*	Louis James

Year	Title	Artist
1967	Exercise in Variegation	Cec Burns
1968	Suzy 350	Tim Storrier
1969	Spyhole	Louis James
1970	Philopena	Michael Kmit
1971	Pyramid Shelf	James Meldrum
1972	Sun-torso 128 (Bunch)	Peter Powditch
1973	The Painter Transmogrified and Mrs Smith	Eric Smith
1974	Still Life and Comfy II	Keith Looby
1975	Transvestite (for Diane Arbus)	Alan Oldfield
	Untitled Jane	Geoffrey Proud
1976	Interior with Time Past	Brett Whiteley
1977	Woman's Life, Woman's Love 3	Salvatore Zofrea
1978	Yellow Nude	Brett Whiteley
1979	The Water Trap	Salvatore Zofrea
1980	The Old Physics Building	Brian Dunlop
1981	A French Family	William Delafield Cook
1982	Psalm 24	Salvatore Zofrea
1983	Marat, the Unsophisticated will be shocked at the Depiction of Your Death; or, the Artist Answers His Critics	Nigel Thompson
1984	The Burn	Tim Storrier
1985	Western Suburbs Magi	Victor Morrison
	Mural, Redfern	Public Art Squad
	Think Globally, Act Locally	(D. Humphries and R. Monk)
1986	Black Sun — Morning to Night	Wendy Sharpe
	The State Institution	Nigel Thompson
1987	Crutching the Ewes	Marcus Beilby
	The Grand Parade, Sydney Show	Bob Marchant
1988	Catching rabbits and yabbies at 5 Mile Dam	Bob Marchant
1989	Don Quixote Enters the Inn	John Olsen
1990	Going Away — Looking Back	Robert Hollingworth
1991-92	Najaf (Iraq) June 1991	Kevin Connor
1993	Life Series	John Montefiore
1994	Boy Dressed as Batman 2	Noel McKenna
1995	By the Banks of Her Own Lagoon	Juli Haas
1996	Grey-to-Grey	Aida Tomescu

WYNNE PRIZE

From the bequest of Richard Wynne, who died in 1895, an award is given annually for the best landscape or sculpture. This is the longest running art prize in Australia. The value of the prize is $10 000.

In addition to this prize, the award's trustees have, since 1961, awarded the Trustees Watercolour Prize. This $2000 prize is presented to the best watercolour if the Wynne prize is awarded to an oil painting or sculpture.

WYNNE PRIZE WINNERS

Year	Title	Artist
1897	*The Storm*	Walter Withers
1898	*The Last Gleam*	W. Lister Lister
1899	*Across the Blacksoil Plains*	G. W. Lambert
1900	*Still Autumn*	Walter Withers
1901	*Thunderstorm on the Darling*	W. C. Piguenit
1902	Bronze group *In Defence of the Flat*	James S. White
1903	*Glenora*	Edward Officer
1904	*Mystic Morn*	Hans Heysen
1905	*The Blue Noon*	Albert J. Hanson
1906	*The Golden Splendour of the Bush*	W. Lister Lister
1907	Plaster *Study of a Head*	G. W. L. Hirst
1908	*Noon, Burnside, S.A.*	Will Ashton
1909	Watercolour *Summer*	Hans Heysen
1910	*Mid Song of Birds and Insects Murmuring*	W. Lister Lister
1911	*Hauling Timber*	Hans Heysen
1912	*Sydney Harbour*	W. Lister Lister
1913	*Federal Capital Site*	W. Lister Lister
1914	*Landscape*	Penleigh Boyd
1915	Bronze group *Knowledge, Fine Art and Commerce*	J. C. Wright
1916	*Morning Light*	Elioth Gruner
1917	*Windswept Marshes*	W. Lister Lister
1918	*The Grey Road*	W. B. McInnes
1919	*Spring Frost*	Elioth Gruner
1920	*Toilers*	Hans Heysen
1921	*Valley of the Tweed*	Elioth Gruner
1922	*The Quarry*	Hans Heysen

Year	Title	Artist
1923	Sculpture	
	Study of a Head	G. W. L. Hirst
1924	Afternoon in Autumn	Hans Heysen
1925	Track through the Bush	W. Lister Lister
1926	Farmyard, Frosty Morning	Hans Heysen
1927	Plaster Head	Raynor Hoff
1928	Afternoon Light Goulburn Valley	Arthur Streeton
1929	On the Murrumbidgee	Elioth Gruner
1930	Kosciusko	Will Ashton
1931	Red Gums of the Far North	Hans Heysen
1932	Brachina Gorge	Hans Heysen
1933	Bronze	Lyndon Dadswell
	Youth	
1934	Murrumbidgee Ranges, Canberra	Elioth Gruner
1935	Winter Morning	J. Muir Auld
1936	An Australian Landscape	Elioth Gruner
1937	Weetangera, Canberra	Elioth Gruner
1938	The Approaching Storm	Sydney Long
1939	Morning Light, Middle Harbour	Will Ashton
1940	The Lake, Narrabeen	Sydney Long
1941	Valley Farms	Lorna Nimmo
1942	Backyards	Douglas Watson
1943	The Hilltop	Douglas Dundas
1944	McElhone Steps	Sali Herman
1945	Old Grain Stores, Greenough, W.A.	Douglas Watson
1946	January Weather	Lance Solomon
1947	Sofala	Russell Drysdale
1948	Storm Approaching, Wangi	William Dobell
1949	Two Rivers	George Lawrence
1950	The Harbour from	Lloyd Rees
	McMahons Point	
1951	Never Never Creek, Gleniffer	Charles Meere
1952	Summer at Kanmantoo	Charles Bush
1953	The River Bend	Lance Solomon
1954	Cooktown	Arthur Even Read
1955	Townsville Waterfront	Charles Bush
1956	The Chicory Kiln, Phillip Island	L. Scott Pendlebury
1957	Constitution Dock	L. Scott Pendlebury
1958	The Cliff	Ronald Pendlebury
1959	Harbour Cruise	Reinis Zusters
1960	Dairy Farm, Victoria	John Percival
	Old Farmhouse	L. Scott Pendlebury

Year	Title	Artist
1961	Landscape, Hill End	David Strachan
1962	The Devil's Bridge, Rottnest	Sali Herman
1963	Sandhills on the Darling	Sam Fullbrook
1964	Trees in a Landscape	Sam Fullbrook
1965	The Red House	Sali Herman
1966	Upway Landscape	Fred Williams
1967	Ravenswood 1	Sali Herman
1968	Road to Whistlewood	L. Scott Pendlebury
1969	The Chasing Bird Landscape	John Olsen
1970	Redfern — Southern Portal	Frederick Bates
1971	Karri Country	Margaret Woodward
1972	Falling Bark	Eric Smith
1973	Dry Landscape	Clem Millward
1974	Redfern Landscape	Eric Smith
1975	Murchison Sand Plain	Robert Juniper
1976	Mt Kosciusko	Fred Williams
1977	The Jacaranda Tree	Brett Whiteley
1978	Summer at Carcoar	Brett Whiteley
1979	Flood Creek	Robert Juniper
1980	A Waterfall	William Delafield Cook
1981	Hills of Ravendale	David Voight
1982	Morning on the Derwent	Lloyd Rees
1983	Life along the Coast	David Rankin
1984	South Coast after Rain	Brett Whiteley
1985	A Road to Clarendon, Autumn	John Olsen
1986	Sculpture Torso	Rosemary Madigan
1987	Landscape Painting II	Ian Bettinson
1988	Fire and Drought near Old Junee	Elwyn Lynn
	The Purple Noon's Transparent Might — An Asbestos Mine Wittenoom 1984–88	John Wolseley
1989	Landscape Painting IV, 1989	Ian Bettinson
1990	The Rainforest	William Robinson
1991–92	Maschera/Maschio/ Maschera Femina	Peter Schipperheyn
1993	Open Cut	George Gittoes
1994	Waratahs, Wedderburn Series	Suzanne Archer
1995	Seasons of Drought	David Aspden
1996	Creation Landscape, Earth and Sea	William Robinson

Theatre

AUSTRALIAN ELIZABETHAN THEATRE TRUST

The Australian Elizabethan Theatre trust was founded in 1954 to foster the development of the performing arts of theatre, opera, ballet and puppetry in Australia. Their aim was to fill the gap left when World War II halted British touring companies who had previously provided the majority of dramatic productions for Australian audiences.

Over the years, the Trust has helped to found and develop the Australian Opera, the Australian Ballet and NIDA. It currently administers Theatre of the Deaf, the only professional theatre company in Australia performing to both deaf and hearing audiences. The Trust also runs a number of programs through specific divisions such as the Australian Content Department, Australian Orchestral Enterprises, International Liaison, Business Liaison, Industry Support, Administrative Services, Commercial Hire and Audience Development Divisions.

Another division of the Australian Elizabethan Theatre Trust, launched in 1989, is the Australian Business Support of the Arts (ABSA) program which aims to increase support for the arts from the private sector. The Australian Orchestral Enterprises Division provides administration and art direction to the Elizabethan Sinfonietta (known internationally as the Australian Philharmonic Orchestra). The Australian Opera and Ballet Orchestra, formerly administered by the Trust and called the Elizabethan Philharmonic Orchestra, is now run by a board nominated by the Australian Ballet, Opera Australia and the players themselves.

NATIONAL INSTITUTE OF DRAMATIC ARTS

The National Institute of Dramatic Arts (NIDA) is Australia's national theatre school. It was established in 1958 under the patronage of the University of NSW and the Australian Elizabethan Theatre Trust, in association with the ABC. An independent company, NIDA is funded by the Commonwealth government through the Department of the Arts.

Originally housed in the old Randwick racecourse buildings on the campus of the University of NSW, the school has now moved into purpose-built premises completed in 1988.

The school offers courses in acting, design and technical production, which run for three years full-time. They also offer a postgraduate Director's course which runs for one year, and several workshops and classes for professionals. Admission is by an audition and interview held in all State capitals each year. The acting course in particular is very popular. From 1700 applications for the 1996 course, approximately 60 were successful.

THE ABC

The national public broadcaster, the ABC, was founded on 1 July 1932 as the Australian Broadcasting Commission. On 1 July 1983, it became the Australian Broadcasting Corporation.

The ABC continues to provide Australia's only non-commercial and free-to-air national and local radio and television services. ABC Radio and ABC Television remain the only broadcasting services heard and seen in all parts of Australia.

An important part of the ABC's program Charter is the support of Australian music. The ABC does this through many radio and television broadcasts as well as through the six State symphony orchestras. These orchestras have traditionally been operated and funded by the ABC. In 1995, however, the Sydney Symphony Orchestra became a subsidiary of the ABC and the other five orchestras (Melbourne, West Australian, Queensland, Adelaide and Tasmanian Symphonies) are expected to follow this model. This will mean that while the ABC will continue to broadcast and televise their performances, it will no longer directly fund the orchestras.

In 1990, the ABC launched its own highly successful record label. The emphasis is on Australian composition and performance: from classical music to country, jazz and children's.

Music

AUSTRALIAN RECORDING INDUSTRY ASSOCIATION

A non-profit organisation, the Australian Recording Industry Association (ARIA) was formed out of the Association of Australian Record Manufacturers, which dates back to 1956.

Its activities cover three main functions: to advocate on behalf of the music industry in Australia and overseas; to act as a focus for industry information and opinions; and to license and enforce copyright.

ARIA's combined membership, currently at 90 members, includes Australia's six major labels which produce approximately 90% of all recordings made in Australia.

THE ARIA AWARDS

The annual ARIA Awards were introduced in 1986. They recognise a range of different styles of music and media involved in the Australian recording industry; from classical to comedy, from Best Australian Album to Best Cover Artwork.

ARIA WINNERS

Year/Award	Artist	Single/Album
Best Australian Album		
1986	John Farnham	*Whispering Jack*
1987	Icehouse	*Man of Colours*
1988	Crowded House	*Temple of Low Men*
1989	Ian Moss	*Matchbook*
1990	Midnight Oil	*Blue Sky Mining*
1991	Baby Animals	*Baby Animals*
1992	Diesel	*Hepfidelity*
1993	The Cruel Sea	*The Honeymoon is Over*
1994	Tina Arena	*Don't Ask*
1995	You Am I	*Hourly Daily*
Best Australian Single		
1986	John Farnham	'You're the Voice'
1987	Midnight Oil	'Beds Are Burning'
1988	The Church	'Under the Milky Way'
1989	Peter Blakeley	'Crying in the Chapel'
1990	Absent Friends	'Nobody But You'
1991	Yothu Yindi	'Treaty'
1992	Wendy Matthews	'The Day You Went Away'
1993	The Cruel Sea	'The Honeymoon is Over'
1994	silverchair	'Tomorrow'
1995	Nick Cave and Kylie Minogue	'Where the Wild Roses Grow'
Best Australian Group		
1986	INXS	
1987	Crowded House	
1988	INXS	
1989	The Black Sorrows	
1990	Midnight Oil	
1991	INXS	
1992	Crowded House	
1993	The Cruel Sea	
1994	The Cruel Sea	
1995	You Am I	
Best Australian Female Artist		
1986	Jenny Morris	
1987	Jenny Morris	
1988	Kate Ceberano	

Year/Award	Artist	Single/Album
Best Australian Female Artist (continued)		
1989	Kate Ceberano	
1990	Wendy Matthews	
1991	Deborah Conway	
1992	Wendy Matthews	
1993	Wendy Matthews	
1994	Tina Arena	
1995	Christine Anu	
Best Australian Male Artist		
1986	John Farnham	
1987	John Farnham	
1988	Jimmy Barnes	
1989	Ian Moss	
1990	John Farnham	
1991	Jimmy Barnes	
1992	Diesel	
1993	Diesel	
1994	Diesel	
1995	Dave Graney	
Highest Selling Australian Single		
1986	John Farnham	'You're the Voice'
1987	Kylie Minogue	'Locomotion'
1988	Kylie Minogue	'I Should Be So Lucky'
1989	Kate Ceberano	'Bedroom Eyes'
1990	Craig McLachlan and Check 1-2	'Mona'
1991	Melissa	'Read My Lips'
1992	Wendy Matthews	'The Day You Went Away'
1993	Peter Andre	'Give Me a Little Sign'
1994	silverchair	'Tomorrow'
1995	CBD	'Let's Groove'
Highest Selling Australian Album		
1986	John Farnham	Whispering Jack
1987	Icehouse	Man of Colours
1988	John Farnham	Age of Reason
1989	Johnny Diesel and The Injectors	Johnny Diesel and The Injectors
1990	John Farnham	Chain Reaction
1991	Jimmy Barnes	Soul Deep

1992	Australian Cast	*Jesus Christ Superstar*
1993	John Farnham	*... then again*
1994	The 12th Man	*Wired World of Sports*
1995	Tina Arena	*Don't Ask*

OPERA AUSTRALIA

In 1956, Opera Australia, formed as a division of the Elizabethan Theatre Trust, performed their first season. It has toured Australia every year since then with the exceptions of 1959 and 1961. In 1970, the company became an independent body. The Sydney Opera House has been its permanent Sydney performance home since its opening in 1973, while the State Theatre in the Victorian Arts Centre became its permanent Melbourne home with its opening in 1984.

In 1996, the 40th anniversary of its foundation, Opera Australia announced its merger with the Victorian State Opera company and changed its name from The Australian Opera. The resulting company, headquartered in Sydney with an active Melbourne opera division, is the third busiest opera company in the world. In 1996, over an 11-month period, it gave 224 performances of 18 operas in Sydney, Melbourne, Adelaide and Brisbane.

Opera Australia's board is elected by members of the company and subscribers. The company is financed through a number of sources, the most important of which is box office which accounts for around 65% of revenue in a given year. Government funding received from the Federal government and the New South Wales and Victorian State governments accounts for about 24% of revenue. The remainder comes from private fundraising from both individuals and corporations.

Opera Australia is the largest performing arts organisation in Australia, employing more than 280 permanent staff (including principal singers, chorus and orchestra members) and up to 900 casual and temporary staff including more than 100 Australasian-born guest principal singers. Opera Australia and Ballet Orchestra, the orchestra which is the performance partner in Sydney of both the Australian Opera and the Australian Ballet, is part of the Australian Opera group company.

The Artistic Director is Moffatt Oxenbould and Adrian Collette is the General Manager.

ORCHESTRAS

Australia has a number of orchestras, one in each capital city, and two established by the Australian Elizabethan Theatre Trust. In 1990, the Elizabethan Philharmonic Orchestra changed its name to the Australian Opera and Ballet Orchestra and established an independent board.

STATE ORCHESTRAS

On the recommendation of Professor Bernard Heinze, who was appointed part time musical adviser to the ABC in 1934, the ABC started to establish studio broadcasting orchestras in each State.

The Sydney Symphony Orchestra (SSO) was formed in 1946 with the enlargement of the ABC's existing Sydney Orchestra from 45 to 72 members. Within the next four years Symphony Orchestras had been set up in each State; the Queensland Symphony Orchestra in March 1947; the Tasmanian Symphony Orchestra in 1948; the Melbourne Symphony Orchestra and the Adelaide Symphony Orchestra in July 1949; and the West Australian Symphony Orchestra in November 1950.

In 1995, the SSO became a subsidiary of the ABC and, at December 1996, the other orchestras looked set to follow this model.

MUSICA VIVA AUSTRALIA

Originally established as an ensemble called Sydney Musica Viva to give high-quality chamber music performances in Australia, the organisation gave its first public performance in December 1945 at the Sydney Conservatorium.

Since that time, Musica Viva Australia has evolved into an entrepreneur of fine music, and is believed to be the largest presenter of chamber music in the world, presenting more than 2000 concerts annually to an audience of more than 400 000 people through its national touring networks.

Musica Viva Australia presents subscription series, featuring major chamber music ensembles from Australia and overseas, in all capital cities and Newcastle (around 70 concerts per annum attracting around 7000 subscribers and around 60 000 single ticket buyers). It manages Musica Viva CountryWide, a regional touring program for Australian and visiting artists and ensembles (around 70 concerts per annum); Musica Viva Export, an international touring program for Australian artists run in association with the Department of Foreign Affairs and Trade (around 150 performances at international festivals and venues); and Musica Viva in Schools, an award-winning live music education program which operates in all States and territories, reaching some half a million school children.

Musica Viva Australia regularly collaborates with other major arts organisations, including the Sydney Symphony Orchestra and Opera Australia, to present chamber music concerts and recitals. It also presents the annual Yarra Valley Festival at Domaine Chandon.

TAMWORTH COUNTRY MUSIC FESTIVAL

The Tamworth Country Music Festival, which draws up to 40 000 visitors, is held in January every year. Running over ten days, the festival consists of more than 650 programmed events, including the Australasian Country

Music Awards and the Starmaker Quest. It is held in the New South Wales northern tablelands regional town of Tamworth, which is considered the country music capital of Australia.

THE AUSTRALASIAN COUNTRY MUSIC AWARDS

The Australasian Country Music Awards were first presented in January 1973. Eleven invited judges choose winners from records that have been released, in Australia and New Zealand, during the previous year. Each year, at least three new judges are chosen.

The award presented to winners is a solid bronze 'golden guitar' 23 cm high and mounted on a plinth of blackwood.

AUSTRALASIAN COUNTRY MUSIC AWARD WINNERS

Year	Artist	Album of the Year
1973	Slim Dusty	*Me and My Guitar*
1974	Slim Dusty	*Live at Tamworth*
1975	Slim Dusty	*Australiana*
1976	Slim Dusty	*Lights on the Hill*
1977	Slim Dusty	*Angel of Goulburn Hill*
1978	Hawking Brothers	*Country Travellin'*
1979	Hawking Brothers	*One Day at a Time*
1980	Slim Dusty	*Walk a Country Mile*
1981	Slim Dusty	*The Man Who Steadies the Lead*
1982	Jewel and Arthur Blanch	*The Lady and the Cowboy*
1983	Arthur Blanch	*Too Late For Regrets*
1984	Slim Dusty	*On the Wallaby*
1985	Slim Dusty	*Trucks on the Track*
1986	John Williamson	*Road Thru the Heart*
1987	John Williamson	*Mallee Boy*
1988	Slim Dusty	*Neon City*
1989	John Williamson	*Boomerang Cafe*
1990	John Williamson	*Warragul*
1991	Slim Dusty	*Coming Home*
1992	Anne Kirkpatrick	*Out of the Blue*
1993	Lee Kernaghan	*The Outback Club*
1994	Lee Kernaghan	*Three Chain Road*
1995	Graeme Connors	*Songs from the Homeland*

ROLL OF RENOWN

Year	Artist
1976	Tex Morton
1977	Buddy Williams

Year	Artist
1978	Smokey Dawson
1979	Slim Dusty
1980	Shirley Thoms
1981	Tim McNamara
1982	Gordon Parsons
1983	The McKean Sisters (Joy and Heather)
1984	Reg Lindsay
1985	Rick and Thel Carey
1986	Johnny Ashcroft
1987	Chad Morgan
1988	John Minson
1989	Hawking Brothers
1990	Stan Coster
1991	Barry Thornton
1992	Nev Nicholls
1993	Shorty Ranger
1994	Jimmy Little
1995	Ted Egan

Libraries

HISTORY

The first library open to the public in Australia was the Australian Subscription Library and Reading Room, which opened in Sydney on 7 March 1826. Members were elected by ballot and were subject to an entrance fee and annual subscription.

The first public library was opened in Victoria on 11 February 1856 and was followed by New South Wales in 1869 when the State government took over the Australian Subscription Library and renamed it the Sydney Free Library. There are now more than 13 000 libraries in Australia. This figure includes 10 000 school libraries and nearly 1400 public libraries. With these facilities, almost every Australian has access to a public library.

Every level of government contributes to library funding: university libraries are funded by the Commonwealth, while public libraries receive joint funding from state and local governments. Australian libraries employ more than 20 000 people. There are an estimated 130 000 000 items in Australian libraries. This figure includes books, magazines, tapes, CDs, pictures and other material. More than 27 000 000 of these are in public libraries, which, in 1995, lent more than 120 500 000 items to an estimated 6 500 000 users.

The National Library of Australia, situated in Canberra, was originally part of the Commonwealth Parliamentary Library established in 1901. In 1960, an Act of Parliament formally separated the two and the National Library came into existence in March 1961. Under the *Copyright Act 1968*, a copy of every book published in Australia must be deposited in the Library.

National Library of Australia
Parkes Place, Canberra ACT 2600
Ph: (06) 262 1111

New South Wales
State Library of New South Wales
Macquarie Street, Sydney NSW 2000
Ph: (02) 9230 1414

Victoria
State Library of Victoria
304-328 Swanston Street, Melbourne VIC 3000
Ph: (03) 9669 9888

Queensland
State Library of Queensland
Cnr Stanley and Peel Streets, Southbank, South Brisbane QLD 4101
Ph: (07) 3840 7666

South Australia
State Library of South Australia
North Terrace, Adelaide, SA 5001
Ph: (08) 8207 7200

Western Australia
Library and Information Services of Western Australia
Alexander Library Building, Perth Cultural Centre, Perth WA 6000
Ph: (09) 427 3111

Tasmania
State Library of Tasmania
91 Murray Street, Hobart TAS 7000
Ph: (03) 6233 8011
Northern Territory
Reference Library of the Northern Territory
25 Cavanagh Street, Darwin NT 0800
Ph: (08) 8999 7177

Literary Awards

MILES FRANKLIN LITERARY AWARD

Year	Author	Title
1957	Patrick White	*Voss*
1958	Randolph Stow	*To the Islands*
1959	Vance Palmer	*The Big Fellow*
1960	Elizabeth O'Connor	*The Irishman*
1961	Patrick White	*Riders in the Chariot*
1962	Thea Astley	*The Well Dressed Explorer*
	George Turner	*The Cupboard under the Stairs*
1963	Sumner Locke Elliott	*Careful, He Might Hear You*
1964	George Johnston	*My Brother Jack*
1965	Thea Astley	*The Slow Natives*
1966	Peter Mathers	*Trap*
1967	Thomas Keneally	*Bring Larks and Heroes*
1968	Thomas Keneally	*Three Cheers for the Paraclete*
1969	George Johnston	*Clean Straw for Nothing*
1970	Dal Stivens	*A Horse of Air*
1971	David Ireland	*The Unknown Industrial Prisoner*
1972	Thea Astley	*The Acolyte*
1973	no award	—
1974	Ronald McKie	*The Mango Tree*
1975	Xavier Herbert	*Poor Fellow My Country*
1976	David Ireland	*The Glass Canoe*
1977	Ruth Park	*Swords and Crowns and Rings*
1978	Jessica Anderson	*Tirra Lirra by the River*
1979	David Ireland	*A Woman of the Future*
1980	Jessica Anderson	*The Impersonators*
1981	Peter Carey	*Bliss*
1982	Rodney Hall	*Just Relations*
1983	no award	—
1984	Tim Winton	*Shallows*
1985	Christopher Koch	*The Doubleman*
1986	Elizabeth Jolley	*The Well*
1987	Glenda Adams	*Dancing on Coral*
1988	no award	—
1989	Peter Carey	*Oscar and Lucinda*
1990	Tom Flood	*Oceana Fine*
1991	David Malouf	*The Great World*
1992	Tim Winton	*Cloudstreet*
1993	Alex Miller	*The Ancestor Game*

Year	Author	Title
1994	Rodney Hall	The Grisly Wife
1995	Helen Darville	The Hand That Signed the Paper
1996	Christopher Koch	Journey to a War

THE AUSTRALIAN/VOGEL LITERARY AWARD

Year	Author	Title
1980	Paul Radley	Jack Rivers and Me (later withdrawn)
1981	Chris Matthews	Al Jazzar
	Tim Winton	An Open Swimmer
1982	Brian Castro	Birds of Passage
	Nigel Krauth	Matilda My Darling
1983	Jenny Summerville	Shields of Trell
1984	Kate Grenville	Lilian's Story
1985	no award	—
1986	Robin Walton	Glacé Fruits
1987	Jim Sakkas	Ilias
1988	Tom Flood	Oceana Fine
1989	Mandy Sayer	Mood Indigo
1990	Gillian Mears	The Mint Lawn
1991	Andrew McGahan	Praise
1992	Fotini Epanomitis	The Mule's Foal
1993	Helen Darville	The Hand That Signed the Paper
1994	Darren Williams	Swimming in Silk
1995	Richard King	Kindling Does for Firewood

CHILDREN'S BOOK COUNCIL AWARDS

Year	Author	Title
1985	James Aldridge	The True Story of Lili Stubeck
1986	Thurley Fowler	The Green Wind
1987	Simon French	All We Know
1988	John Marsden	So Much to Tell You
1989	Gillian Rubinstein	Beyond the Labyrinth
1990	Robin Klein	Came Back to Show You I Could Fly
1991	Gary Crew	Strange Objects
1992	Eleanor Nilsson	The House Guest
1993	Melina Marchetta	Looking for Alibrandi
1994	Isobelle Carmody	The Gathering
	Gary Crew	Angel's Gate

Year	Author	Title
1995	Gillian Rubinstein	*Foxspell*
1996	Catherine Jinks	*Pagan's Vows*

NATIONAL BOOK COUNCIL AWARDS/BANJO AWARDS

Year	Author	Title
1974	Roland Robinson	*The Drift of Things*
	Geoffrey Searle	*From Deserts the Prophets Come: The Creative Spirit in Australia, 1788–1972*
1975	Les Murray	*Lunch and Counter Lunch*
	Laurie Clancy	*A Collapsible Man*
	William Nagle	*The Odd Angry Shot*
	Frank Moorhouse	*The Electrical Experience*
	F. B. Vickers	*Without Map or Compass*
1976	Ray Ericksen	*Cape Solitary*
	John Blight	*Selected Poems, 1939–75*
1977	Harry Gordon	*An Eyewitness History of Australia*
	Joseph Johnson	*A Low Breed*
	Barry Hill	*The Schools*
1978	Helen Garner	*Monkey Grip*
	Kevin Gilbert	*Living Black*
1979	Christopher Koch	*The Year of Living Dangerously*
	Ray Ericksen	*Ernest Giles, Explorer and Traveller, 1835–1897*
1980	Murray Bail	*Homesickness*
	Elsie Webster	*Whirlwinds in the Plain: Ludwig Leichhardt — Friends, Foes and History*
1981	David Foster	*Moonlite*
	A. B. Facey	*A Fortunate Life*
1982	Geoffrey Searle	*John Monash: A Biography*
	Peter Carey	*Bliss*
1983	Dimitris Tsaloumas	*The Observatory*
	Olga Masters	*The Home Girls*
1984	Bernard Smith	*The Boy Adeodatus*
	Les A. Murray	*The People's Otherworld*
1985	Peter Carey	*Illywhacker*
	Morris Lurie	*The Night We Ate the Sparrow*
	Phillip Pepper and Tess de Araugo	*The Kurnai of Gippsland*
1986	no sponsorship and no awards	

Year	Author	Title
1987	Alan Wearne	*The Nightmarkets*
	Robert Drewe	*Fortune*
1988	C.M.H. Clark	*History of Australia*, Vol. 6
	Morris Lurie	*Whole Life*
1989	Peter Carey	*Oscar and Lucinda*
	Brenda Niall	*Martin Boyd: A Life*
1990	Thea Welsh	*The Story of the Year 1912 in the Village of Elsa Darzins*
	Michael Gallagher and Stephen Hawke	*Noonkanbah: Whose Land, Whose Law?*
1991	Tim Winton	*Cloudstreet*
	Glenda Adams	*Longleg*
	Drusilla Modjeska	*Poppy*
1992	Alan Gould	*To the Burning City*
	David Marr	*Patrick White: A Life*
	Roger Milliss	*Waterloo Creek*
1993	Roger MacDonald	*Shearers' Motel*
	Liam Davidson	*Soundings*
1994	Elizabeth Jolley	*The George's Wife*
	Dorothy Hewett	*Peninsula*
	Hazel Rowley	*Christina Stead*
1995	Sally Morrison	*Mad Meg*
	Peter Singer	*Rethinking Life and Death*
1996	Henry Reynolds	*Fate of a Free People*
	Abraham Biderman	*The World of My Past*
	Rod Jones	*Billy Sunday*

Publishing

AUSTRALIAN PUBLISHERS' ASSOCIATION

Originally called the Australian Book Publishers' Association (ABPA), it was formed in 1948. Membership is open to any organisation, of any size, engaged in publishing books in Australia. In 1948, membership was 20 organisations, about six of which were important Australian publishers. In 1996, the membership had climbed to about 140 members, producing approximately 80% of the turnover in Australian publishing, and it changed its name to the Australian Publishers' Association (APA). The aims of the APA are to assist in the development of original publishing in Australia, to encourage high standards and to establish Australia as a major force in international publishing.

16

Sport

*F*or a nation with a relatively small population, Australia has an outstanding record in international sporting competition. During the 1960s, Australia gained its reputation as one of the great sporting nations in the world, dominating the worlds of tennis, cricket, swimming and boxing. In the 1990s, Australian athletes continue their position at the top of their sporting fields with the moral support of a sports-loving nation and a renewed sense of national sporting pride.

This chapter looks at some of the most popular sports in Australia, and a selection of their greatest ever sportspeople.

STATISTICS   29% of Australians over the age of 15 participate in an organised sport. This figure includes 23% of women and 35% of men.

AUSTRALIAN INSTITUTE OF SPORT

Australia's performance in world sports began to decline in the late 1960s and 1970s, reaching an all-time low at the 1976 Montreal Olympics, where Australia did not win any gold medals. Public concern and criticism was so high that it prompted the government to set up what is now known as the Australian Institute of Sport. Situated in Canberra on a 65-hectare site, the institute provides first-class training and coaching opportunities for Australian athletes to help raise their performance at the Olympic Games, world championships and other international events. When the institute opened in 1981, it supported eight sports. It now provides instruction and training facilities for 17 established and internationally competitive sports.

DRUGS IN SPORT

DRUGS IN SPORT INQUIRY

Following a 'Four Corners' program aired on ABC television on 30 November 1987, which alleged widespread drug use by athletes, especially at the Australian Institute of Sport, a Senate Committee Inquiry was set up (headed by Senator John Black) on 19 May 1988 to investigate the use of performance-enhancing drugs by Australian sportspeople and the role played by Commonwealth agencies. The first interim report in June/July 1989, following some controversial public hearings and submissions, recommended the establishment of an independent drug testing agency and a tribunal to deal with disputed drug tests.

AUSTRALIAN SPORTS DRUG AGENCY

The Australian Sport Drugs Agency (ASDA), established in 1989, is funded by the Australian Sports Commission. Its role is not only to conduct independent drug testing, at all levels, but also to educate sportspeople and others about the dangers of drug taking in competitive sport.

THE NATIONAL PROGRAM ON DRUGS IN SPORT

Following the release of the Senate report, the Australian Sports Commission set up the Australian Sport Drugs Agency to develop sport drug testing procedures and to implement drug education programs. The existing program was set up in 1985. The National Program on Drugs in Sport received increased funding and random drug testing began at the Australian Institute of Sport.

Disabled Sport

Sport for disabled people is provided under the Australian Sports Commission's Disabled Sport Program (DSP), established in 1988. Many specific groups exist to organise sporting programs for particular disabilities, e.g the Australian Deaf Sports Federation, which has about 1500 members. The Australian government also contributes to the cost of sending athletes to compete in sporting events held overseas. The major international events which Australia enters are the Summer and Winter Paralympics, and the world championships.

AUSTRALIAN RECORD AT RECENT SUMMER PARALYMPIC GAMES

Year	Venue	Gold	Silver	Bronze	Total
1988	Seoul, South Korea	23	35	37	95
1992	Barcelona/Madrid, Spain	37	37	33	107
1996	Atlanta, USA	42	37	27	106

AUSTRALIAN RECORD AT RECENT WINTER PARALYMPIC GAMES

Year	Venue	Gold	Silver	Bronze	Total
1988	Innsbruck, Australia	–	–	–	–
1992	Albertville, France	1	1	2	4
1994	Lillehammer, Norway	3	2	3	8

PARALYMPIAN OF THE YEAR

This honour has been awarded by the Australian Paralympic Federation since 1994. It goes to the most outstanding performer in the Paralympic Games or world championships of that year.

Year	Winner	Sport
1994	Louise Sauvage, Western Australia	Athletics
1995	Priya Cooper, Western Australia	Swimming

The Olympic Games

Australia's Record at the Summer Olympic Games

Year	Venue	Gold	Silver	Bronze	Total
1896	Athens, Greece	2	–	–	2
1900	Paris, France	3	–	4	7
1904	St Louis, USA	–	–	–	–
1908	London, England	1	2	1	4
1912	Stockholm, Sweden	2	2	2	6
1916	Berlin, Germany	cancelled			
1920	Antwerp, Belgium	–	2	1	3
1924	Paris, France	3	1	2	6
1928	Amsterdam, Holland	1	2	1	4
1932	Los Angeles, USA	3	1	1	5
1936	Berlin, Germany	–	–	1	1
1940	Tokyo, Japan; Helsinki, Finland	cancelled			
1944	London, England	cancelled			
1948	London, England	2	6	5	13
1952	Helsinki, Finland	6	2	3	11
1956	Melbourne, Australia	13	8	14	35
1960	Rome, Italy	8	8	6	22
1964	Tokyo, Japan	6	2	10	18
1968	Mexico City, Mexico	5	7	5	17
1972	Munich, West Germany	8	7	2	17
1976	Montreal, Canada	-	1	4	5
1980	Moscow, USSR	2	2	5	9
1984	Los Angeles, USA	4	8	12	24
1988	Seoul, South Korea	3	6	5	14
1992	Barcelona, Spain	7	9	11	27
1996	Atlanta, USA	9	9	23	41
	TOTAL	**88**	**85**	**118**	**291**

2000 Olympics

Following an unsuccessful bid for the 1996 Olympics by Melbourne, Sydney was triumphant in its bid for the 2000 Olympics. This will be only the second time the Olympic Games have been held in the southern hemisphere. The suburb of Homebush in Sydney's west is the site of the Olympic village, stadiums and facilities. It will be the first time the triathlon will be an official Olympic event. The Australian federal government has allocated $135 million for the development and training of Australian athletes for the 2000 Olympics.

AUSTRALIAN SUMMER OLYMPIC RECORDS

- Three people share the record for the most gold medals won (4) by an Australian at the Olympics: swimmer Dawn Fraser (100 m freestyle, 4 x 100 freestyle relay 1956; 100 m freestyle 1960; 100 m freestyle 1964); athlete Betty Cuthbert (100 m, 200 m, 4 x 100 m relay 1956; 400 m 1964) and swimmer Murray Rose (400 m freestyle, 1500 m freestyle, 4 x 200 freestyle relay 1956; 400 m freestyle 1960).
- Swimmer Dawn Fraser holds the record for the most medals won by an Australian at the Olympics — 8 in total (4 gold and 4 silver).
- The record for the highest number of medals at a single Olympic Games by an Australian is held by swimmer Shane Gould. She won 5 medals (3 gold, 1 silver and 1 bronze) at the 1972 Munich Olypmic Games.
- Australia's youngest ever gold medallist is swimmer Sandra Morgan, who was a member of the victorious 4 x 100 m freestyle relay team at the age of 14 years 6 months in 1956 at the Melbourne Olympics.
- Australia's oldest ever gold medallist is yachtsman Bill Northam, who won gold in the 5.5 m class at the age of 50 years 26 days in the 1964 Tokyo Olympics.

THE WINTER OLYMPIC GAMES

Not surprisingly, given the country's hot climate and limited winter Olympic sport facilities, Australia has won only one medal at the Winter Olympics. This went to the men's speed skating 5000 m relay team in Lillehammer, Norway, in 1994. The team comprised: Kieran Hansen, Steven Bradbury, Andrew Murtha and Richard Nizielzki.

Australia does, however, have a world champion in winter sport. Freestyle skier Kirstie Marshall became world champion in competition at Nagano, Japan, site of the 1998 Winter Olympics. She has won nine World Cup events and is the first skier from the southern hemisphere to win an overall World Cup title. She was also ABC Sportswoman of the Year from 1990 to 1992. This spectacular discipline requires a high degree of nerve and control to complete the acrobatic movements necessary to become world-class.

The Commonwealth Games

The Commonwealth Games were first held in 1930 in Hamilton, Canada, when they were known as the British Empire Games. The Commonwealth Games are held at four-yearly intervals, however after the 1938 Games in Sydney, World War II put a stop to them until 1950. Australia has attended since the games began and has hosted the Commonwealth Games three times; first in Sydney in 1938, then Perth in 1962 and more recently in Brisbane in 1982.

In terms of medal tallies, Australia's best performance was at the 1994 Commonwealth Games in Victoria, where the team picked up 182 medals, including 87 gold. Its second best performance was the the 1990 Commonwealth Games in Auckland, New Zealand, where the team won 162 medals, including 52 gold.

AUSTRALIA'S RECORD AT THE COMMONWEALTH GAMES

Year	Venue	Gold	Silver	Bronze	Total
1930	Hamilton, Canada	3	4	1	8
1934	London, England	8	4	2	14
1938	Sydney, Australia	24	19	22	65
1950	Auckland, New Zealand	34	27	19	80
1954	Vancouver, Canada	20	11	17	48
1958	Cardiff, Wales	27	22	17	66
1962	Perth, Australia	38	36	31	105
1966	Kingston, Jamaica	23	28	22	73
1970	Edinburgh, Scotland	36	24	22	82
1974	Christchurch, New Zealand	29	28	25	82
1978	Edmonton, Canada	24	33	27	84
1982	Brisbane, Australia	39	39	29	107
1986	Edinburgh, Scotland	40	46	33	119
1990	Auckland, New Zealand	52	54	56	162
1994	Victoria, Canada	87	52	43	182
	TOTAL	**484**	**427**	**367**	**1278**

AUSTRALIA'S COMMONWEALTH GAMES RECORDS

- Swimmer Michael Wenden holds the record for the most Commonwealth Games gold medals won by an Australian man. He won 9 gold medals from 1966–1974.
- Four sportswomen hold the record for the most Commonwealth Games gold medals won by an Australian woman. Athlete Marjorie Jackson won 7 gold medals from 1950–1954; athlete Raelene Boyle won 7 gold medals from 1970–1982; swimmer Lisa Curry-Kenny won a total of 7 gold medals in 1982 and 1990; and swimmer Hayley Lewis won 7 gold medals from 1990–1994.
- The record for the most gold medals at a single games is held by athlete Decima Norman, swimmer Hayley Lewis and gymnast Kasumi Takahashi. Norman won 5 gold medals (100 yds, 220 yds, 4 x 110 yds, 660 yds medley relay, long jump) in 1938 at Sydney; Lewis won 5 gold medals (200 m freestyle, 400 m freestyle, 200 m butterfly, 200 m individual medley, 4 x 200 m freestyle relay) in 1990 at Auckland; and

Takahashi won 5 gold medals (gymnastics — hoop, ball, clubs, ribbons, all round) in 1994 at Victoria.

- The record for the highest number of Commonwealth Games medals won by an Australian man is held by shooter Phillip Adams, who won 17 gold medals from 1982 to 1994.
- The record for the highest number of Commonwealth Games medals won by an Australian woman is held by swimmer Hayley Lewis, who won 11 gold medals from 1990–1994.

Athletics

Olympic Games

Next to swimming, track and field events are Australia's strongest areas at the Olympics. Our first gold medal came at the inaugural Modern Olympics in 1896 in Athens, when Edwin Flack won the men's 800 m and 1500 m track events.

Australia's first woman gold medallist was runner Marjorie Jackson (*see* 'Outstanding Athletes'), who won the 100 m sprint at the 1952 Helsinki Olympics, equalling the world record of 11.5 seconds, and also the 200 m event at the same games.

Australia's Olympic Gold Medal Athletes

Year	Winner	Event
Men		
1896	Edwin Flack	800 m
1896	Edwin Flack	1500 m
1924	Nick Winter	Hop, step and jump
1948	John Winter	High jump
1960	Herb Elliot	1500 m
1968	Ralph Doubell	800 m
Women		
1952	Marjorie Jackson	100 m
1952	Marjorie Jackson	200 m
1952	Shirley Strickland	80 m hurdles
1956	Shirley Strickland	80 m hurdles
1956	Betty Cuthbert	100 m
1956	Betty Cuthbert	100 m
1956	Norma Croker, Fleur Mellor, Shirley Strickland, Betty Cuthbert	4 x 100 m relay

Year	Winner	Event
1964	Betty Cuthbert	400 m
1968	Maureen Caird	80 m hurdles
1984	Glynis Nunn	Heptathlon
1988	Debbie Flintoff-King	400 m hurdles

COMMONWEALTH GAMES

Australia's first Commonwealth Games medallist was Decima Norman, who took gold in the women's 100 yds at the 1938 Sydney Games, also winning the 220 yds, 440 yds relay, 660 yds relay and the long jump.

MARATHON

Some of Australia's outstanding marathon runners include George Perdon, who ran from Fremantle (Western Australia) to Sydney (New South Wales), a distance of 4662.3 km, in 47 days 1 hour 45 minutes in 1973. Tony Rafferty set a record for a run from Adelaide to Melbourne, finishing in nine days exactly.

In 1983, Victorian potato farmer Cliff Young created a sensation when he won the Westfield Sydney to Melbourne road race at 61 years of age. Yiannos Kouros won the same race in 1985, 1987, 1988, 1989 and 1990.

Bill Ermerton, an Australian, is remembered for being the first person to run the 201-km length of Death Valley in the USA in 1968. It took him 3 days 23 minutes in temperatures above 100°F (37.8°C).

CITY TO SURF

At least 35 000 people enter Sydney's City To Surf fun run (known as the Sun-Herald City To Surf) every August, making it the biggest race in the southern hemisphere. The 14-km course starts at the intersection of William and College Streets in the city centre and ends on the sand at Bondi Beach. The race was 25 years old in August 1995, and past winners include Australia's 'marathon man', Robert 'Deek' de Castella, who set a race record of 40 mins 8 secs.

OUTSTANDING ATHLETES

RON CLARKE

Ron Clarke is considered to have been one of Australia's most talented athletes and possibly its greatest middle distance runner. Although he never won an Olympic or Commonwealth gold medal, he did set 17 world records over a five-year period, 1963–1968, for distances ranging from 2 to 12 miles. Clarke lit the Olympic flame at the Melbourne Olympics in 1956.

His 5000 m and 10 000 m Australian track records amazingly still stand after 30 years.

BETTY CUTHBERT
Australia's 'Golden Girl', Betty Cuthbert won four Olympic gold medals (an Australian record) during her career. Three of these were in front of the home crowd at the 1956 Games in Melbourne for the 100 m, 200 m and 4 x 100 m relay, and the fourth was for the 400 m in the 1964 Tokyo Games. Tragically, she now suffers from multiple sclerosis.

ROBERT DE CASTELLA
Widely considered to be Australia's greatest marathon runner, Robert de Castella has taken gold medals for the marathon at the 1982 Brisbane Games and 1986 Edinburgh Commonwealth Games. In 1983, he also won gold at the inaugural World Athletics Championships held in Helsinki. He won the prestigious Boston Marathon in 1984, in the third-fastest time ever recorded in the world.

HERB ELLIOT
Herb Elliot was a brilliant runner who lost only one race over 1500 m or the mile during his career. His fame came largely through a number of records he set. During his career, he broke the four-minute mile barrier 17 times and, on 6 August 1968, ran the mile in a world record time of 3 mins 54.5 secs.

He won gold in the 1500 m at the 1960 Rome Olympic Games, setting a world record of 3 mins 35.6 secs. At the 1958 Commonwealth Games in Cardiff, he won gold medals for the 880 yds and the mile.

DEBBIE FLINTOFF-KING
One of Australia's greatest hurdlers, Debbie Flintoff-King rose to fame when she won gold at the 1982 Brisbane Commonwealth Games in the 400 m hurdles. At the 1986 Edinburgh Commonwealth Games, she took gold again in the 400 m hurdles and in the 400 m. An Olympic gold medal followed soon after at the 1988 Seoul Olympics, when she won the 400 m hurdles.

CATHY FREEMAN
In 1994, Cathy Freeman became the first Aboriginal woman to win a gold medal in an individual track event when she won both the 200 m and 400 m events at the Victoria Commonwealth Games. In 1990, she was part of the relay team that took gold at the Auckland Commonwealth Games. She was also a member of the Australian women's relay team that won gold at the 1995 world championships in Gothenburg, Sweden. In 1996, she won silver at the Atlanta Olympics in the 400 m, recording an Australian record time in the process. She was named Young Australian of the Year in 1990.

MARJORIE JACKSON
Nicknamed the 'Lithgow Flash', Jackson won six individual gold medals at Olympic and Commonwealth Games. She was the first Australian woman to win an Olympic Games gold medal, when she won the 100 m sprint at the 1952 Helsinki Olympics, equalling the world record of 11.5 secs in the semifinals and winning the final by 3 metres. In the 200 m heat, she equalled the world's longest standing world record (unbeaten since 1935) and won the final by 4 metres.

At the 1950 Auckland Games, she won gold in the 100 yds and 220 yds, and repeated this performance at the 1954 Vancouver Games, where she won another two gold medals.

Australian Rules

Devised in Melbourne from the roots of Gaelic football, Australian Rules was originally known as Victorian Rules and was designed to keep cricketers fit during the off-season. It was renamed in 1905, after officials found it hard to interest other states in a game called Victorian Rules!

The first game was held in Melbourne in 1856 and, in 1877, the Victorian Football Association (VFA) was set up, followed in 1897 by the breakaway Victorian Football League (VFL). The first official team was the Melbourne Football Club, set up in 1858 and still in competition today.

The three major Australian Rules competitions in Australia currently are the Australian Football League (AFL), formerly the VFL; the South Australian National Football League (SANFL); and the Western Australian National Football League (WNFL). In 1996, the AFL celebrated 100 years of competition.

The 1996 season was one of some turmoil for the AFL, with Fitzroy, one of the foundation clubs of the league, being forced to merge with the Brisbane Bears. From 1997, the Bears became known as the Brisbane Lions, taking the colours and nickname of the former Fitzroy club. Two new teams joined the AFL in 1997 — the Fremantle Dockers and Port Adelaide.

AFL MEDALS

THE BROWNLOW MEDAL
This medal was first awarded in 1924 to Geelong player Edward 'Cargie' Greeves. It is awarded annually by the Australian Football League to the best and fairest player in the home and away series, in memory of Charles Brownlow, a cricket and football star from Geelong. Haydn Bunton Snr (Fitzroy), Bob Skilton (South Melbourne), Ian Stewart (St Kilda) and Dick Reynolds have each won three medals.

John Coleman Medal

The John Coleman Medal is awarded to the highest goal kicker in the Australian Football League in the home and away series. John Coleman was a former Essendon full-forward who kick 537 goals for his club. The medal has been awarded since 1981 and winners include Tony Lockett (twice while playing for St Kilda and once while with the Sydney Swans), Gary Ablett (Geelong, three times) and Jason Dunstall (Hawthorn, three times).

VFL/AFL Records

- The record for the most goals in a match is held by Fred Fanning (Melbourne), who scored 18 goals against St Kilda in 1947.
- Peter Hudson (Hawthorn, 1971) and Bob Pratt (South Melbourne, 1934) share the record for the most goals in a VFL season (150).
- Collingwood's Gordon Coventry holds the record for the most goals in a career, having scored 1299 goals in a career that lasted from 1920-1937.
- Michael Tuck has made the most appearances in senior football in the VFL/AFL, having played 426 games for Hawthorn.
- The highest attendance for a VFL/AFL match was for the 1970 Grand Final between Carlton and Collingwood, when 121 696 people turned out to watch Carlton take the title.
- When Hawthorn defeated Essendon 20.20 (140) to 8.9 (57) in 1983 by a margin of 83 points, they set a new record for an VFL/AFL Grand Final winning margin; the previous record was 81 points.
- Geelong has had the most consecutive VFL senior wins, winning 26 matches in a row from July 1952 to August 1953.

AFL Premierships

Year	Winner	Runner-up	Year	Winner	Runner-up
1897	Essendon	Geelong	1910	Collingwood	Carlton
1898	Fitzroy	Essendon	1911	Essendon	Collingwood
1899	Fitzroy	Sth Melbourne	1912	Essendon	Sth Melbourne
1900	Melbourne	Fitzroy	1913	Fitzroy	St Kilda
1901	Essendon	Collingwood	1914	Carlton	Sth Melbourne
1902	Collingwood	Essendon	1915	Carlton	Collingwood
1903	Collingwood	Fitzroy	1916	Fitzroy	Carlton
1904	Fitzroy	Carlton	1917	Collingwood	Fitzroy
1905	Fitzroy	Collingwood	1918	Sth Melbourne	Collingwood
1906	Carlton	Fitzroy	1919	Collingwood	Richmond
1907	Carlton	Sth Melbourne	1920	Richmond	Collingwood
1908	Carlton	Essendon	1921	Richmond	Carlton
1909	Sth Melbourne	Carlton	1922	Fitzroy	Collingwood

Year	Winner	Runner-up	Year	Winner	Runner-up
1923	Essendon	Fitzroy	1960	Melbourne	Collingwood
1924	Essendon	Richmond	1961	Hawthorn	Footscray
1925	Geelong	Collingwood	1962	Essendon	Carlton
1926	Melbourne	Collingwood	1963	Geelong	Hawthorn
1927	Collingwood	Richmond	1964	Melbourne	Collingwood
1928	Collingwood	Richmond	1965	Essendon	St Kilda
1929	Collingwood	Richmond	1966	St Kilda	Collingwood
1930	Collingwood	Geelong	1967	Richmond	Geelong
1931	Geelong	Richmond	1968	Carlton	Essendon
1932	Richmond	Carlton	1969	Richmond	Carlton
1933	Sth Melbourne	Richmond	1970	Carlton	Collingwood
1934	Richmond	Sth Melbourne	1971	Hawthorn	St Kilda
1935	Collingwood	Sth Melbourne	1972	Carlton	Richmond
1936	Collingwood	Sth Melbourne	1973	Richmond	Carlton
1937	Geelong	Collingwood	1974	Richmond	Nth Melbourne
1938	Carlton	Collingwood	1975	Nth Melbourne	Hawthorn
1939	Melbourne	Collingwood	1976	Hawthorn	Nth Melbourne
1940	Melbourne	Richmond	1977	Nth Melbourne	Collingwood
1941	Melbourne	Essendon	1978	Hawthorn	Nth Melbourne
1942	Essendon	Richmond	1979	Carlton	Collingwood
1943	Richmond	Essendon	1980	Richmond	Collingwood
1944	Fitzroy	Richmond	1981	Carlton	Collingwood
1945	Carlton	Sth Melbourne	1982	Carlton	Richmond
1946	Essendon	Melbourne	1983	Hawthorn	Essendon
1947	Carlton	Essendon	1984	Essendon	Hawthorn
1948	Melbourne	Essendon	1985	Essendon	Hawthorn
1949	Essendon	Carlton	1986	Hawthorn	Carlton
1950	Essendon	Nth Melbourne	1987	Carlton	Hawthorn
1951	Geelong	Essendon	1988	Hawthorn	Melbourne
1952	Geelong	Collingwood	1989	Hawthorn	Geelong
1953	Collingwood	Geelong	1990	Collingwood	Essendon
1954	Footscray	Melbourne	1991	Hawthorn	West Coast
1955	Melbourne	Collingwood	1992	West Coast	Geelong
1956	Melbourne	Collingwood	1993	Essendon	Carlton
1957	Melbourne	Essendon	1994	West Coast	Geelong
1958	Collingwood	Melbourne	1995	Carlton	Geelong
1959	Melbourne	Essendon	1996	Nth Melbourne	Sydney

OUTSTANDING PLAYERS

GARY ABLETT   Gary Ablett started his VFL/AFL career with Hawthorn in 1982, but will forever be identified with Geelong, the team he has played for since 1984. He won the John Coleman Medal three times — in 1993,

1994 and 1995 — kicking more than 100 goals in each season. In 1995, he became the fifth player to score more than 1000 goals in the league.

RON BARASSI   Ron Barassi played 12 seasons for Melbourne, and a total of 203 senior games in the VFL. After helping Melbourne win six premierships, he switched to Carlton in 1964 as captain–coach and went on to lead them to their greatest ever winning performance in 1970's VFL Grand Final. He moved to North Melbourne as coach in 1973, coaching them to four consecutive Grand Finals and two premierships in 1975 and 1977, before switching to become coach of Melbourne from 1981–1985. In 1995, he celebrated 500 matches as a coach while with the Sydney Swans, a position he had taken up in 1993, and then retired at the end of that season.

HAYDN BUNTON   Haydn Bunton Snr was possibly the Australian Rules equivalent of cricket's Don Bradman. He played most of his career for Fitzroy and won six best and fairest medals in his senior career: three Brownlow medals (in VFL football) and three Sandover medals in the Western Australian National Football League competition.

ROY CAZALY   Even those who know nothing about football are familiar with the famous cry 'Up there Cazaly', which was the basis of a 1979 pop hit, and was also heard at football matches and used by Australians fighting in World War II. The cry refers to one of Australia's greatest footballers, Roy Cazaly, who began his career playing for St Kilda at the age of 16 in 1910. His career spanned five decades, during which he played 410 matches, 100 of these representing St Kilda, 99 with South Melbourne and 81 with New Town. He also coached numerous sides including Hawthorn, St Kilda and South Melbourne.

JACK DYER   Nicknamed 'Captain Blood' because of his aggression, Jack Dyer played 312 games for Richmond between 1929 and 1949, scoring 440 goals. One of the best ruckmen ever seen in Australian Rules, he was also player–coach of Richmond from 1941–1949, and then non-playing coach in 1950 and 1951.

GRAHAM 'POLLY' FARMER   'Polly' Farmer was an Aboriginal ruckman who helped develop the handpass from a defensive move into an attacking weapon, relieving pressure on a player unable to kick. He played 31 games for Western Australia and 5 for Victoria, and was awarded the Sandover Medal in 1956 and 1960, as well as the Simpson Medal in 1956, 1958, 1959 and 1969, and the Tassie Medal in 1956.

TONY LOCKETT   Tony Lockett started his VFL/AFL career with St Kilda in 1983, where he scored 898 goals before joining the Sydney Swans. He then became the fourth player to score more than 1000 goals in his career and is currently third on the all-time goal scoring list. He has also scored more than 100 goals in a season five time. Lockett became the only full forward to win the Brownlow Medal in 1987.

Rugby League

Rugby league began as a breakaway movement from rugby union in 1907, when union clubs refused to compensate their players for injuries. The first international match series, between New Zealand and Australia, was held that year, although organisers had difficulties putting together a team, as many Australian players were reluctant to leave the amateur code (rugby union) for the new professional league. When champion player Herbert Henry 'Dally' Messenger was lured away, however, for a reputed £80, the other stars soon followed and rugby league was born.

STATE OF ORIGIN

The first matches between New South Wales and Queensland were held in 1908, with New South Wales winning three out of three matches. In 1980, the old Queensland vs New South Wales matches were replaced by State of Origin clashes between the 'Maroons' (Queensland) and the 'Blues' (New South Wales). The decision to change the game's format was made after 15 successive wins by New South Wales between 1975 and 1980. Selection is now based on the player's birthplace or state of origin, a bonus for the Queensland team; in 1981, seven top players in the New South Wales team returned to play for Queensland. From 1990–1996, Queensland won two of the State of Origin series played, and New South Wales won five series. Dual international Michael O'Connor holds the record for the most points in a State of Origin match, 18 points (2 tries, 5 goals), scored for New South Wales against Queensland in 1985. He also holds the record for the most points for New South Wales — 129 (11 tries, 42 goals, 1 field goal).

AUSTRALIAN RUGBY LEAGUE

The New South Wales Rugby League (NSWRL) competition began as first-grade club premierships in 1908. In 1930, the first Grand Final was played, with compulsory Grand Finals beginning in 1954. By the time the Winfield Cup was introduced in 1982, South Sydney led the table, playing in 30 finals, and winning 20 of these. Since the introduction of interstate teams in the Sydney first-grade competition, the NSWRL has been known as the Australian Rugby League (ARL).

NSWRL/ARL PREMIERSHIPS

Year	Winner	Runner-up	Year	Winner	Runner-up
1908	South Sydney	Eastern Suburbs	1948	Western Suburbs	Balmain
1909	South Sydney	Balmain	1949	St George	South Sydney
1910	Newtown	South Sydney	1950	South Sydney	Western Suburbs
1911	Eastern Suburbs	Glebe	1951	South Sydney	Manly–Warringah
1912	Eastern Suburbs	Glebe	1952	Western Suburbs	South Sydney
1913	Eastern Suburbs	Newtown	1953	South Sydney	St George
1914	South Sydney	Newtown	1954	South Sydney	Newtown
1915	Balmain	Glebe	1955	South Sydney	Newtown
1916	Balmain	South Sydney	1956	St George	Balmain
1917	Balmain	South Sydney	1957	St George	Manly–Warringah
1918	South Sydney	Western Suburbs	1958	St George	Western Suburbs
1919	Balmain	Eastern Suburbs	1959	St George	Manly–Warringah
1920	Balmain	South Sydney	1960	St George	Eastern Suburbs
1921	North Sydney	Eastern Suburbs	1961	St George	Western Suburbs
1922	North Sydney	Glebe	1962	St George	Western Suburbs
1923	Eastern Suburbs	South Sydney	1963	St George	Western Suburbs
1924	Balmain	South Sydney	1964	St George	Balmain
1925	South Sydney	Western Suburbs	1965	St George	South Sydney
1926	South Sydney	University	1966	St George	Balmain
1927	South Sydney	St George	1967	South Sydney	Canterbury
1928	South Sydney	Eastern Suburbs	1968	South Sydney	Manly–Warringah
1929	South Sydney	Newtown	1969	Balmain	South Sydney
1930	Western Suburbs	St George	1970	South Sydney	Manly–Warringah
1931	South Sydney	Eastern Suburbs	1971	South Sydney	St George
1932	South Sydney	Western Suburbs	1972	Manly–Warringah	Eastern Suburbs
1933	Newtown	St George	1973	Manly–Warringah	Cronulla
1934	Western Suburbs	Eastern Suburbs	1974	Eastern Suburbs	Canterbury
1935	Eastern Suburbs	South Sydney	1975	Eastern Suburbs	St George
1936	Eastern Suburbs	Balmain	1976	Manly–Warringah	Parramatta
1937	Eastern Suburbs	South Sydney	1977	St George	Parramatta
		St George	1978	Manly-Warringah	Cronulla
1938	Canterbury	Eastern Suburbs	1979	St George	Canterbury
1939	Balmain	South Sydney	1980	Canterbury	Eastern Suburbs
1940	Eastern Suburbs	Canterbury	1981	Parramatta	Newtown
1941	St George	Eastern Suburbs	1982	Parramatta	Manly–Warringah
1942	Canterbury	St George	1983	Parramatta	Manly–Warringah
1943	Newtown	North Sydney	1984	Canterbury	Parramatta
1944	Balmain	Newtown	1985	Canterbury	St George
1945	Eastern Suburbs	Balmain	1986	Parramatta	Canterbury
1946	Balmain	St George	1987	Manly–Warringah	Canberra
1947	Balmain	Canterbury	1988	Canterbury	Balmain

Year	Winner	Runner-up	Year	Winner	Runner-up
1989	Canberra	Balmain	1993	Brisbane	St George
1990	Canberra	Penrith	1994	Canberra	Canterbury
1991	Penrith	Canberra	1995	Bulldogs	Manly–Warringah
1992	Brisbane	St George	1996	Manly–Warringah	St George

Rugby League Awards

Several awards are handed out annually to outstanding or exemplary rugby league players in the ARL competition. They are: the Rothmans Medal, awarded to the best and fairest first-grade player as voted by the referees; the Clive Churchill Medal, awarded to the best and fairest player in the Grand Final; the Rising Star Award, given to the most outstanding player in his debut season; and the Dally M Awards, which are given in several categories and are selected by the rugby league media.

Super League

In 1997, after a legal battle with the Australian Rugby League and Super League's subsequent win on appeal, a rival national rugby league competition has been held in Australia. Outstanding players and several clubs switched over from the ARL competition to play in the new league. Fielding teams from as far afield as Perth, Western Australia, and Auckland, New Zealand, Super League is trying to stage a truly national competition, with plans to extend its international base. The Super League competition is held concurrently with the ARL premiership.

There are currently ten teams in the Super League competition: Adelaide Rams, Auckland Warriors, Brisbane Broncos, Canberra Raiders, Canterbury Bulldogs, Cronulla Sharks, Hunter Mariners, North Queensland Cowboys, Penrith Panthers and the Western Reds (Perth).

Test Matches

Australia's rugby league football team, the Kangaroos, played their first match in England in 1908–1909 and drew 22-all. Their greatest triumph was in 1982, when they toured Great Britain and France undefeated.

Australia's Test Record*

Opponent	Won	Drawn	Lost	Total
Great Britain	54	4	53	111
France	32	2	12	46
New Zealand	53	1	21	75

Opponent	Won	Drawn	Lost	Total
Papua New Guinea	6	0	0	6
South Africa	2	0	0	2
Total	**147**	**7**	**86**	**240**

* As at 1996.

WORLD CUP

Australia has won the Rugby League World Cup eight times: in 1957, 1968, 1970, 1975 (international series), 1975, 1977 and 1988 (the 1988 final was from a series held over four years) and 1995.

RUGBY LEAGUE RECORDS

- The record crowd for a rugby league match in Australia is 87 161 people for a State of Origin match at the Melbourne Cricket Ground in 1994.
- The Kangaroos scored a record winning total against England in the 1963 Test series (on the 9 November) defeating them 50–12.
- Kerry Boustead began his Test career at the age of 18, making him the youngest ever Australian Test player.
- St George's Reg Gasnier played in 36 Tests, an Australian record.
- Graeme Langlands, or 'Changa', holds the record for the most international games, with 45 games in total (34 Tests and 11 World Cups).
- Michael O'Connor has been an outstanding player for both Australia and the New South Wales side in State of Origin clashes. In State of Origin matches, he holds the record for the most points for New South Wales (129), the most tries (11) and the most goals (42, plus 1 field goal). In Test matches, he holds the record for the most points in a match — 30 points (4 tries, 7 goals) — made in a match against Papua New Guinea in 1988. This latter achievement is a world record.

OUTSTANDING PLAYERS

'DALLY' MESSENGER   Herbert Henry 'Dally' Messenger was one of the great early Rugby League players. He was captain of the first Kangaroos team to play overseas in 1908–1909 and was also the first Australian to play professionally overseas. He toured with the New Zealand All Golds in 1907–1908 scoring 146 points (101 more points than anyone else on the team) and arrived home £200 richer. Some of Rugby League's most important awards are now named after him.

CLIVE CHURCHILL   Otherwise known as 'The Little Master', Clive Churchill was one of Australia's best footballers. He was the first World Cup captain in 1954, and coached the Kangaroos in 1959. He captained Australia 54 times in 24 Tests and 4 Internationals. In 1985 he received the Order of Australia but died that same year.

MICK CRONIN   Mick Cronin played for Parramatta, as well as playing 22 matches for Australia. He has won over 12 awards and retired in 1986. He holds the record for the most points scored in international games for Australia: 199 in 22 Tests and 11 World Cups. In 1986, he was awarded the Dally Messenger Award for service to rugby league.

WALLY LEWIS   Wally Lewis played 33 Tests for Australia, 14 of these against New Zealand and 23 as captain He played 31 State of Origin matches for Queensland. He has won numerous awards and in 1987 was elected into the Sport Australia Hall of Fame.

MAL MENINGA   Mal Meninga played for both the Kangaroos and for Queensland in State of Origin matches. His contribution to Australian rugby league was recognised in 1989, when he won the Dally Messenger Representative Player of the Year award. In 1990, when he was voted 'Best Player in the World' in the Adidas Golden Boot Awards. He retired in 1994.

ST GEORGE   St George is one of the more well known club sides, having won 11 successive first-grade Grand Finals from 1956-1966. In 1963, the club won all three grades, the first time this has happened at a senior level anywhere in Australia, and also became the first club side to defeat a visiting international team, New Zealand, by 22–7. Some of the greatest stars to play the game came from St George. Five captained Australia (Ken Kearney, Ian Walsh, Reg Gasnier, Graeme Langlands and Johny Raper) and between 1956 and 1964 the club provided 16 members to three Kangaroo sides.

Rugby Union

Australia is regarded as one of the world's top four rugby union nations, despite the game's lesser standing in this country. The first union matches were played in 1823. By 1864, Sydney University had formed the first club and four years later the first controlling body, the Southern Rugby Football Union was set up in New South Wales. Other states soon followed; by the time Queensland played in 1880, there were already more than 100 clubs in Sydney. From 1990–1995, there was an increase of more than 50% in participation in rugby union.

QUEENSLAND VS NEW SOUTH WALES

The games between Queensland and New South Wales in rugby union are on a par with rugby league's State of Origin matches. The first match was held in 1882, when New South Wales defeated Queensland 28–4 at the Association Ground now known as the Sydney Cricket Ground. The two teams have met 255 times, including this first match. New South Wales have won 170 of these clashes and Queensland have won 74. The other 11 matches have been drawn.

TEST MATCHES

The Bledisloe Cup is a Test series competition that dates back to 24 June 1899, when Australia played their first Test at the Sydney Cricket Ground, defeating the British Isles 13–3. It is now played between Australia and New Zealand, and, following the tradition of inter-Tasman rivalry, is commonly seen as the most important international series played by the Australians. The representative team for Australia is known as the Wallabies and some of the most famous and widely watched Test matches have been between the Wallabies and the All Blacks (New Zealand, widely regarded as the greatest rugby union team in recent times).

The Rugby Union World Cup began in 1987, and is played every four years between 16 qualifying nations. The Australian Wallabies won the World Cup in Britain in 1991 with a score of 12-6 against England.

WORLD CUP RESULTS

Year	Venue(s)	Final Result	Score
1987	Australia/New Zealand	New Zealand def. France	29–9
1991	England/France/Wales/ Scotland/Ireland	Australia def. England	12–6
1995	South Africa	South Africa def. New Zealand	15–12

RUGBY UNION RECORDS

- The record for the most points in a match is held by Matthew Burke. He scored 39 points (3 tries, 2 penalty goals, 9 conversions) in a match against Canada in 1996.
- The record for the most points in a career is held by Michael Lynagh. He scored 911 points (17 tries, 140 conversions, 170 penalty goals, 9 field goals) in 72 games from 1985–1985.
- Greg Cornelsen (NSW) and David Campese (ACT) share the record for the most tries in a Test. Cornelson scored 4 tries against New Zealand in 1978, and Campese scored 4 tries in a match against the United

States in 1993. Campese also hold the record for the most tries in a career (64) and the most Test matches (100).

OUTSTANDING PLAYERS

KEN CATCHPOLE   Catchpole is widely regarded as one of the best ever rugby union halfbacks. He represented Australia in 27 Tests, but was forced to retire from first-grade rugby after an injury in 1968.

THE ELLA BROTHERS   Nicknamed 'The Invincibles', these three brothers, Mark, Glen and Gary, are unforgettable rugby union players. The three Aboriginal kids, sick of racist taunts, started playing rugby union at school, and all three ended up representing Australia. Mark was the first to reach Test standard, playing 26 Tests before retiring in 1984. Glen and Gary have played only four Tests each.

Soccer

Soccer was firmly established in Australia when dissatisfied amateur clubs began a breakaway movement in 1957. Australian soccer suffered from this greatly over the next couple of decades. First the clubs lost their Olympic affiliation and then Australia was suspended in 1959 by FIFA (the international controlling body) for poaching European players. The Australian Soccer Federation had to pay $50 000 and wait until 1963 to be readmitted by FIFA, while the Australian Olympic Federation remained immovable until 1977.

NATIONAL SOCCER LEAGUE CHAMPIONSHIPS

The National Soccer League (NSL) was established in April 1977, with 14 clubs in its inaugural season. Although many predicted disaster, the first season was a great success and soccer continues to grow in popularity in Australia, with a strong supporter base throughout the country.

NSL CHAMPIONS

Year	Champions	Year	Champions
1977	Hakoah-Eastern Suburbs	1983	St George
1978	West Adelaide	1984	South Melbourne
1979	Marconi Fairfield	1985	Brunswick Juventus
1980	Sydney City	1986	Adelaide City
1981	Sydney City	1987	Apia Leichhard
1982	Sydney City	1988	Marconi Fairfield

Year	Champions	Year	Champions
1989	Marconi Fairfield	1992–93	Marconi Fairfield
1989–90	Sydney Olympic	1993–94	Adelaide City
1990–91	South Melbourne	1994–95	Melbourne Knights
1991–92	Adelaide City	1995–96	Melbourne Knights

INTERNATIONAL RESULTS

Australia has only once qualified for the finals of the world's most prestigious soccer competition, the World Cup. In the 1973 finals in West Germany, Australia came 14th, after losing twice to West Germany and drawing once with Chile.

SOCCER RECORDS

- Paul Wade has played 82 international matches (1986–1996), representing Australia more times than any other player.
- The record of Australia's top goal scorer in international matches is shared by Atti Abonyi and John Kosmina. Abonyi scored 25 goals in 60 full internationals from 1967–1977, and 36 for Australia in all matches. Kosmina also scored 25 goals for Australia, in 60 games from 1976–1988.
- In 1953, Joe Marsden became the first Australian to play in an English FA Cup Final, with the losing team Preston North End.

OUTSTANDING PLAYERS

REG DATE   Reg Date was one of Australia's best soccer players and played for 24 years, from the 1930s to the mid-1950s, scoring 664 goals in his career (an Australian record), and gaining national selection nine times. Date is also one of only two soccer players, along with Trevor Rumley, to kick 9 goals in one match.

CRAIG JOHNSTONE   Craig Johnstone, South African-born but educated in Newcastle, New South Wales, was only 17 when he was selected for the Middlesborough first division team in England. He became Australia's first million-dollar soccer player when he transferred from Middlesborough to Liverpool for $1.23 million in 1981, at 20 years of age. In 270 games for Liverpool, he netted 40 goals and was the first Australian to be a member of a winning team in both the FA Cup and European Cup in 1986.

Boxing

Boxing began in Australia when the first official bare knuckle fight was held on 7 January 1814, the fight lasted 56 rounds and was won by John Berringer who defeated Charles Lifton.

The infamous bushranger Ned Kelly was a bare knuckle boxer and used to attend matches while he was on the run. Gloves were not used in fights until 1834. On the 26 July 1884, the first championship fight with gloves was held.

WORLD CHAMPIONSHIPS

There are two main world boxing competitions, the World Boxing Council (WBC) titles, dating from the 1960s, and the International Boxing Federation (IBF) titles, founded in the early 1980s. Both groups were formed after there was a split in the original World Boxing Association (WBA). Of the two, the WBC titles are the most prestigious, although IBF titles attract boxers of the same calibre.

AUSTRALIAN WORLD CHAMPIONS
- Alfred Griffiths, known as 'Young Griffo', became Australia's first world champion on 2 September 1890, when he beat New Zealand's 'Torpedo' Billy Murphy in 15 rounds at the White Horse Hotel in Sydney, to win the world featherweight championship.
- Rocky Mattioli won the WBC junior welterweight title on 6 August 1977 in Berlin. He successfully defended the title twice in 1978, but lost to Maurice Hope (Antigua) on 4 March 1979 at San Remo, Italy.
- Lester Ellis won the IBF junior lightweight world title on 15 February 1985, but subsequently lost it — after one successful defence — to Australia's Barry Michael on 12 July 1985 in Melbourne.
- Barry Michael won the IBF junior lightweight world title on 12 July 1985. He successfully defended his title three times before losing to Rocky Lockridge of the USA on 9 August 1987.
- Jeff Harding won the WBC light heavyweight world championship on 24 June 1989, successfully defending his title twice before losing on 28 July 1990 to Great Britain's Dennis Andries. He regained his title the following year — from Andries on 11 September 1991 — and success-fully defended it twice before losing to Mike McCallum of Jamaica on 24 July 1994.

See 'Outstanding Boxers' for other world champions: Lionel Rose, Johny Famechon, Jimmy Carruthers and Jeff Fenech.

OLYMPIC MEDALLISTS

- Reginald 'Snowy' Baker won the silver medal for the middleweight section at the 1908 London Olympics.
- Kevin Hogarth won the bronze medal in the welterweight section at the 1956 Melbourne Olympics.
- Ollie Taylor brought home the bronze for the bantamweight section at the 1960 Rome Olympics.
- Tony Madigan won the bronze for the light heavyweight section at the 1960 Rome Olympics.
- Grahame Cheney won the silver for the light welterweight section at the 1988 Los Angeles Olympics.

COMMONWEALTH GAMES GOLD MEDALLISTS

- Leonard Cook took gold in the lightweight division at the London Games in 1934.
- William Smith won gold at the 1938 Sydney Games in the welterweight division.
- Wally Taylor took the gold medal in the featherweight division at the 1958 Cardiff Games.
- Tony Madigan won gold twice in Commonwealth Games, in 1958 and 1962 in the light heavyweight divisions.
- Geoff Dynevor took the gold medal in the bantamweight division at the 1962 Perth Games.
- Philip McElwaine won gold in the middleweight division at the 1978 Edmonton Games.
* Robert Peden won gold in the bantamweight division at the 1994 Victoria Games.

OUTSTANDING BOXERS

JIMMY CARRUTHERS   Carruthers won the world bantamweight title from Vic Toweel (South Africa), knocking him out in the first round on 15 November 1952 in Johannesburg. He successfully defended the title twice in 1953 and once in 1954, before retiring as undefeated champion on 16 May 1954.

JOHNNY FAMECHON   Famechon won the world featherweight title from Jose Legra (Cuba) on 21 January 1969 in London. He successfully defended the title twice in 1969 and 1970, but lost to Vicente Saldivar (Mexico) on 9 May 1970, in Rome, and retired the same year. He is considered by many of Australia's modern boxing heroes to have been the best defensive boxer in the world — elusive and almost impossible to hit.

JEFF FENECH   Jeff Fenech's three world titles speak for themselves. He is regarded as one of Australia's greatest modern boxers and is the only Australian to have won four world titles (Lester Ellis has won two). On 26 April 1985, he won the IBF world bantamweight title from Satoshi Shingaki of Japan. He successfully defended his title three times before switching to WBC and winning the super bantamweight title on 8 May 1987. He successfully defended this title twice. On 7 March 1988, he won his third title, the WBC featherweight title, defeating Victor Callejas of Mexico. After successfully defending this title three times, he moved to the super featherweight division, beating Azumah Nelson for the title on 28 June 1991. He lost to Nelson in his first defence on 28 June 1991 and unsuccessfully fought just one more title, the IBF lightweight, before retiring in 1996.

TONY MADIGAN   Tony Madigan was Australia's most successful amateur boxer. His biggest claim to fame is probably that he was the only Australian boxer ever to face Mohammed Ali. He also built up an impressive medal and title tally, including gold medals at the 1958 and 1962 Commonwealth Games, silver at the 1954 Vancouver Commonwealth Games and numerous Australian titles and championships.

TONY MUNDINE   Tony Mundine is one of Australia's greatest boxers. In his 15-year career (1969–1984), he never lost to another Australian boxer. He scored more knockout victories, 65 out of 96 wins, than any other Australian boxer and is the only Australian to earn a world ranking in three divisions, and win a Commonwealth title in two divisions. He held the Australian heavyweight title for 6 years 10 months and the light heavy-weight title for 8 years 5 months.

LIONEL ROSE   Rose was one of the first Aboriginal Australians, next to Evonne Goolagong, to win worldwide acclaim in sport, when he won the world bantamweight title from Fighting Harada (Japan) on 27 February 1968 in Tokyo. He was only 19 years old when he won, making him Australia's youngest bantamweight world champion and successfully defended the title twice in 1968, and once 1969. He was renowned for his speed, balance and combination of punches.

KOSTYA TSZYU   Born in Russia but now a naturalised Australian, Kostya Tszyu is currently Australia's most successful boxer. He won the IBF junior welterweight from Jake Rodriguez of the USA on 28 January 1995, and has successfully defended his title four times. Tszyu's professional record is exemplary, with 18 wins (14 KOs) from 18 bouts. His last fight to date was against Jan Bergman of South Africa on 14 September 1996, which he won by a knockout after 6 rounds.

Cricket

TEST MATCHES

The first Test match between Australia and England was held at the Melbourne Cricket Ground on 15 March 1877. Australia won, with batsman A. C. Bannerman scoring 165 runs (retired hurt), the first century in Test cricket. Australia has a long history of rivalry with England, its traditional cricket foes. Regular Test series are now played against England, the West Indies, Pakistan, India, Sri Lanka, New Zealand and South Africa.

THE BODYLINE SERIES — 1932–1933

In 1932, the English team, captained by Douglas Jardine, came to Australia for a five-Test series, which became infamously known as the 'Bodyline Series'. It was called bodyline because of England's orchestrated short-pitched bowling attacks on the leg stump, which often injured the Australian batsmen. The worst incident occurred at the Adelaide Test, when this tactic curbed the brilliant Australian batsman at whom it was aimed, Don Bradman, and injured most of the Australian team, sending Bert Oldfield to hospital with a fractured skull. England won by 338 runs. Crowds were furious and 400 policemen were sent to Adelaide Oval to line the fence, with another 400 mounted policemen standing by at a nearby oval in case the crowd got out of control.

Relations between the Australian and England cricket management deteriorated to such a point that diplomatic relations were almost broken off between the two countries. Today, short-pitched bowling is considered part of the game, although bowling bouncers at tailenders is still felt by most people to be against the spirit of cricket and there are rules covering intimidatory bowling.

THE TIED TESTS

The first of only two tied Tests ever was played during the West Indies 1960 summer tour. On the final day's play, Australia needed one run to win with two balls remaining, but as the two batsmen were running for what should have been the winning single, Ian Meckiff was run out by a brilliant shy at the stumps by West Indian fielder Joe Solomon. Both Australia and West Indies tied on a score of 737. The second tie was in a Test between Australia and India in Madras in 1986.

THE CENTENARY TEST — 12–17 MARCH 1977

Australia won the Centenary Test against England by 45 runs — remarkably this was the same margin that it had won by in the first ever Test on the same ground on 15–17 March 1877. Although it was a close finish, the

Centenary Test is mainly remembered for the number of records that were set that day.

On the fourth day, Rod Marsh ('Iron Gloves') became the first Australian wicket-keeper to score a Test century (110 not out), while on the second day Marsh passed Wally Grout's record of 187 Test dismissals by an Australian wicket-keeper.

English bowler Derek Underwood bagged his 250th Test wicket when he bowled Greg Chappell for 42 in the first innings.

AUSTRALIA'S TEST RESULTS*

Versus	No. of Tests	Won	Lost	Drawn	Tied
England	286	111	90	85	–
South Africa	59	31	13	15	–
West Indies	81	32	27	21	1
New Zealand	32	13	7	12	–
India	50	24	8	17	1
Pakistan	40	14	11	15	–
Sri Lanka	10	7	–	3	–

* As at September 1996.

WORLD SERIES CRICKET

The World Series Cup was set up in May 1977, by Australian media baron Kerry Packer, upsetting the Test cricket world by contracting Test players for one-day games, where each side receives 50 overs. Players wore national colours and a white ball was used instead of red. Openers were chosen for their hitting power and fast bowlers bowled to no slips, with fieldsmen spread out on the boundary.

'Packerball' was played from 1977 to 1979, before the first recognised game was held between Australia and the West Indies on 27 November 1979. World Series Cricket is now a regular part of Australia's cricket program, with matches being played between Australia and the touring Test team of that year, plus one other nation. The one-day game has grown in popularity around the cricket-playing nations, with a one-day international World Cup being held every four years between the Test-playing nations.

WORLD SERIES RESULTS

Year	Winner	Runner-up	Third Team
1979–1980	West Indies	England	Australia
1980–1981	Australia	New Zealand	India
1981–1982	West Indies	Australia	Pakistan

Year	Winner	Runner-up	Third Team
1982–1983	Australia	New Zealand	England
1983–1984	West Indies	Australia	Pakistan
1984–1985	West Indies	Australia	Sri Lanka
1985–1986	Australia	India	New Zealand
1986–1987	England	Australia	West Indies
1987–1988	Australia	New Zealand	Sri Lanka
1988–1989	West Indies	Australia	Pakistan
1989–1990	Australia	Pakistan	Sri Lanka
1990–1991	Australia	New Zealand	England
1991–1992	Australia	India	West Indies
1992–1993	West Indies	Australia	Pakistan
1993–1994	Australia	South Africa	New Zealand
1994–1995	Australia	Australia A	England
1995–1996	Australia	Sri Lanka	West Indies

WORLD CUP

Year	Host Nation(s)	Winner	Runner-up	Venue
1975	England	West Indies	Australia	Lord's
1979	England	West Indies	England	Lord's
1983	England	India	West Indies	Lord's
1987	India/Pakistan	Australia	England	Calcutta
1991–92	Australia/ New Zealand	Pakistan	England	Melbourne
1995–96	India/Pakistan/ Sri Lanka	Sri Lanka	Australia	Lahore

SHEFFIELD SHIELD

In 1892–1993, New South Wales, Victoria and South Australia played for the first time in this competition, named after Lord Sheffield of England, who brought the 1891-1892 English team to Australia and donated funds to help develop Australian cricket. The Sheffield Shield is now widely considered as the best domestic cricket competition in the world. Queensland joined in 1926–1927, Western Australia in 1947–1948 and Tasmania in 1977–1978.

New South Wales is the most successful state; Queensland has won only once; Tasmania has never won; and Victoria achieved the highest score, against New South Wales at the Melbourne Cricket Ground in 1926–1927, with a total of 1107 runs.

CRICKET FACTS

- More 200 000 people in Australia play cricket regularly, 194 000 men and 15 800 women.
- Australia's highest ever Test innings total was against the West Indies in 1954–1955 when it finished on 8 for 758. The lowest ever Australian innings total was 36 against England in 1902.
- Australia's biggest ever winning total (one-day) was against Sri Lanka on the 28 January 1985 winning by 232 runs, a world record, with only 2 wickets down.
- Thomas Matthews bowled two hat-tricks in the same Test against South Africa in 1912 (3 for 16) and (3 for 38). He is the only bowler in the history of Test cricket to take a hat-trick in each innings in a Test. He clean bowled two batsmen, caught and bowled two others and captured his other two leg before wicket.
- Fast bowler Craig McDermott holds the dubious honour of the most ducks (7) in Test cricket.
- Geoff Lawson holds the Australian record for the most maiden overs in one-day cricket, with 59 from 2488 balls bowled.
- The highest attendance for a one-day international was on 22 January 1984, when Australia played the West Indies (86 133 spectators).

WOMEN'S CRICKET

Women's cricket was first played in Australia at Bendigo, Victoria, in 1874. The first Test matches were played when England toured Australia and New Zealand, defeating Australia 2-0 (one Test drawn). Betty Archdale captained the first Australian Test team.

Australia's greatest all-rounder was Betty Rebecca Wilson, who began her Test career in a 1948 match against New Zealand. In 16 Test innings, she scored 862 runs including three centuries and took 66 wickets at 11.56, including the remarkable Test figures of 7 for 7 (which included a hat-trick) in 1957–1958. Bowler Zoe Goss is one woman cricketer to gain fame in recent years, and not just for her performance in women's cricket. In the 1995–1996 season, while playing in a testimonial match, she took the wicket of the outstanding West Indian batsman Brian Lara. Lara is holder of the record for the most runs scored in a Test innings.

OUTSTANDING PLAYERS

DAVID BOON David Boon is a batsman renowned for his gritty determination and prolific run-scoring. He was also an excellent close-in fieldsman for Australia, taking many catches close to the bat in both Tests and one-day internationals. He made his debut for Australia in the 1984–1985 Test series against the West Indies. He played on three Ashes tours

(1985, 1989, 1993) and in two World Cups. When he retired from international cricket in 1996, he had played 107 Tests and scored 7422 runs in Test cricket, at an average of 43.66.

ALLAN BORDER   Allan Border is one of Australia's best modern cricketers. He appeared in 156 Test matches (an Australian record) and was Australia's longest serving captain, with 93 Tests to his credit from 1984–1994. Border also holds several Australian records, including the most runs in a Test career; 11 174 (including 63 half-centuries and 27 centuries). His highest score is 205 runs and his batting average 50.56. He also holds the record for the most catches (156) in a career.

SIR DONALD BRADMAN   Widely regarded as Australia's greatest batsman, Don Bradman (The 'Don') had a batting average of 99.94 from 52 Tests and a total of 6996 runs, 13 half-centuries and 29 centuries in his career. He is the only batsman to score six triple centuries and scored his 100th first-class century on 15 November 1947. His highest score in first-class cricket was 452 not out for New South Wales against Queensland. His highest Test cricket score (334) has since been surpassed, although he still holds the world record for wicket partnerships — Bradman and Bill Ponsford made 415 against England in 1934; this was equalled in 1982–1983 by N. Mudassar and Javed Miandad (Pakistan) against India.

THE CHAPPELL BROTHERS   The two Chappell brothers, Ian and Greg, have made an outstanding contribution to Australian Test cricket. Greg, who played from 1970–1984, appeared in 88 Tests, making a total of 7110 runs, with a highest score of 247. His batting average was 40.70. Greg still holds the world record for the most runs in a season (686). He also shares the world record for the most catches by a fieldsman in a Test match (7), taken in a match against England in 1974-1975. He captained Australia for 48 Tests. Ian Chappell, who played from 1964–1980, made 76 Test appearances, scored 4345 runs and had a batting average of 65.80. He captained Australia in 29 Tests between 1970 and 1975. He holds the Australian record for the best one-day strike rate with 100.00.

CLARRIE GRIMMETT   Clarrie Grimmett is regarded by many as Australia's best ever spin bowler. He played in 37 Tests for Australia and was 32 years old when he played his first Test in 1924. He captured 216 Test wickets in his career and had a bowling average of 24.21. He holds the record for the most Sheffield Shield wickets with 513.

DENNIS LILLEE   Dennis Lillee is one of Australia's most famous bowlers. He played from 1970–1984, making 70 Test appearances, during which he set a world record of 355 wickets (since broken by Imran Khan, Kapil Dev,

Ian Botham and Richard Hadlee, who currently holds the record of 415). Lillee's best bowling figures are 7 for 83 and his bowling average is 23.92.

Renowned for his blistering pace and aggression, Lillee bowled 652 maiden overs from 18 647 balls in Test cricket — the highest for an Australian bowler. In one-day internationals, Lillee also holds the Australian record for the most number of wickets with 68 taken and the lowest ever bowling average of 18.35.

ROD MARSH   Rod Marsh remains Australia's most outstanding wicket-keeper. He appeared in 97 Tests from 1970–1984 and holds the world record for the most dismissals, 355, in a Test career. The Marsh/Lillee combination is the most famous in Test cricket history. Marsh took 95 (almost 40%) of the 239 Test catches taken off Lillee's bowling. This combination will probably never be equalled. In one-day cricket, he has taken a world record total of 78 wickets, and set a world record of four dismissals in one innings on 8 January 1981.

SHANE WARNE   Shane Warne is widely credited with the resurgence of the art of spin bowling in cricket. A right-arm bowler, he made his Test debut against India in 1992-1993. Warne has already taken more than 200 wickets in Test cricket, in a period of less than four years, the quickest any bowler has achieved this feat. He is renowned for the variety in his bowling arsenal, including his 'flipper', and is credited with several match-winning performances. His success has turned the role of the spin bowler from that of a stock bowler designed to keep up the over rate to one of being the spearhead in the strike attack.

Golf

Golf was first played in Australia during the 1820s and today it is the most popular sport in the country. More than 300 000 Australians are regular golf players. There are about 1400 golf clubs with 500 000 registered players and 500 000 non-registered players.

THE AUSTRALIAN OPEN

The Open is held annually and many of the world's greatest golfers have attempted to win the event. Those who have succeeded include Gene Sarazen, Jack Nicklaus, Arnold Palmer, Jerry Snead, Bill Rogers and Tom Watson (USA), and South Africans Bobby Locke and Gary Player. Player holds the record for the most Open wins (1958, 1963, 1964, 1965, 1969, 1970, 1974). He was runner-up in 1957 and 1968. Greg Norman has won four

Australian Open titles (1980, 1985, 1987, 1995). Fellow Australian Ossie Pickworth won the title three times in a row in 1946, 1947, 1948, a record for an Australian.

GOLFING FACTS

The world's most prestigious golf tournaments, similar to the tennis world's Grand Slam, include the British Open, the US Open, the US Masters and the US PGA. Australia has been well represented at these events, as well as producing golfers who have won a host of other important international golf tournaments.

- Jim Ferrier won the US PGA championship in 1947 and the Canadian Open in 1950 and 1951.
- Peter Thompson won the British Open five times in 1954, 1955, 1956, 1958 and 1965, and the US PGA Seniors championship in 1984.
- Kel Nagle won the British Open in 1960, as well as the Canadian Open in 1964 and the French Open in 1961.
- Bruce Crampton became the first Australian to win $1 million (US) in prize money on 1 July 1973 when he took his career earnings to $1 002 885 by finishing fourth in the Western Open in Chicago, USA.
- Greg Norman has twice won the British Open, for the first time in 1986 and again in 1983, while Ian Baker-Finch won in 1991.
- Wayne Grady won the US PGA tournament on 12 August 1990, winning $200 000 prize money. It was his first grand slam tournament win after turning professional in 1978. Steve Elkington won this same tournament in 1995.

WOMEN'S GOLF

The first Australian championship for women was held in 1894 in Geelong and was won by C. B. McKenzie. The first Australian Women's Open championship was held in 1974 at the Victoria Golf Club, with Australia's Penny Pulz finishing runner-up to Japan's Chako Higuichi. The Open ended after the 1978 event won by Debbie Austin (USA), due to lack of interest from sponsors, but was reintroduced in 1994.

The Australian Ladies' Masters is the second professional tournament in Australia. It was first staged in 1990.

GOLF RECORDS

- The youngest winner of a major Australian championship was Harry Llewelyn Williams (1915–1961), who was 16 when he won the Australian Amateur Championship at The Australian in 1931.
- Peter Thompson became the only Australian to play five tournament

rounds under 70 when he played the 1959 Pelaco Tournament in Melbourne, shooting 68, 68, 67, 67 and 69 on a 73-par course.

OUTSTANDING PLAYERS

DAVID GRAHAM   David Graham won the Australian Open in 1977, the US Open in 1981 (the only Australian to do so), the US PGA Championship in 1979, the World Match Play Championship in 1976 and the Japan Open in 1972.

GREG NORMAN   Greg Norman, or the 'Great White Shark', is undoubtedly one of the most well known Australian golfers and among the richest. He is currently ranked number one in the world. He was the leading earnings winner on the US golfing circuit as of July 1990, with $800 000. His total income, including sponsorship and other business deals, is rumoured to be about $10 million a year. Greg Norman won the British Open in 1986, the World Match Play Championship in 1980 and 1983, the Canadian Open in 1984, the French Open in 1980 and the US PGA Tournament in 1990.

MARGARET MASTERS   Australia's most successful professional woman player was Margaret Masters, who turned pro in 1965 after a brilliant amateur career, which included taking the national championships of South Africa in 1957, New Zealand in 1956 and Canada in 1964. In her first professional season she was named Rookie of the Year in the US and set a course record of 76 in her first US Open. By 1967, she had her first US title and had topped $100 000 in her career earnings by 1974.

JAN STEPHENSON   Jan Stephenson turned professional in 1972. In 1973, she won the Australian Ladies PGA title, and two other pro events in three weeks. She was named Rookie of the Year in 1974, won the 1975 King Hassan Trophy in Morocco in 1975, the Birmingham and Sarah Coventry Naples Classics in the USA in 1976, the Australian Open in 1977 and the US Open in 1983, taking her career earnings at the time to $850 960.

Horse Racing

THE MELBOURNE CUP

'The race that stops the nation' was first held on 7 November 1861. It received very little publicity, even though today it is the biggest all-age handicap in the world. It is now an annual event that has even non-punters stopping to watch the race on the first Tuesday of November every year. In 1933, Sir Charles Kingsford Smith flew the first film of the race to Sydney, where it was shown at Sydney's Regent Theatre some six hours after the event was run.

MELBOURNE CUP WINNERS

Year	Winner	Jockey	Trainer
1861	Archer*	J. Cutts	E. De Mestre
1862	Archer	J. Cutts	E. De Mestre
1863	Banker	H. Chifney	S. Waldock
1864	Lantern	S. Davis	S. Mahon
1865	Tory Boy	E. Cavanagh	P. Miley
1866	The Barb	W. Davis	J. Tait
1867	Tim Whiffler	J. Driscoll	E. De Mestre
1868	Glencoe	C. Stanley	J. Tait
1869	Warrior	J. Morrison	R. Sevior
1870	Nimblefoot	J. Day	W. Laing
1871	The Pearl	J. Cavanagh	J. Tait
1872	The Quack	W. Enderson	J. Tait
1873	Don Juan	W. Wilson	J. Wilson
1874	Haricot	R. Piggott	S. Harding
1875	Wollomai	R. Batty	S. Moon
1876	Briseis	P. St Albans	J. Wilson
1877	Chester	P. Piggott	E. De Mestre
1878	Calamia	T. Brown	E. De Mestre
1879	Darriwell	S. Cracknell	W. E. Dakin
1880	Grand Flaneur	T. Hales	T. Brown
1881	Zulu	J. Gough	T. Lamond
1882	The Assyrian	C. Hutchins	J. Saville
1883	Martini-Henri	J. Williamson	M. Fennelly
1884	Malua	A. Robertson	I. Foulsham
1885	Sheet Anchor	M. O'Brien	T. Wilson
1886	Arsenal	W. English	H. Raynor
1887	Dunlop	T. Sanders	J. Nicholson
1888	Mentor	M. O'Brien	W. Hickenbottom
1889	Bravo	J. Anwin	T. Wilson
1890	Carbine**	R. Ramage	W. Hickenbottom
1891	Malvolio	G. Redfern	J. Redfern
1892	Glenloth	G. Robson	M. Carmody
1893	Tarcoola	H. Cripps	J. Cripps
1894	Patron	H. G. Dawes	R. Bradfield
1895	Auraria	J. Stevenson	J. Hill
1896	Newhaven	H. Gardiner	W. Hickenbottom
1897	Gaulus	S. Callinan	W. Forrester
1898	The Grafter	J. Gough	W. Forrester

Year	Winner	Jockey	Trainer
1899	Merriwee	V. Turner	J. Wilson Jnr
1900	Clean Sweep	A. Richardson	J. Scobie
1901	Revenue	F. Dunn	H. Munro
1902	The Victory	R. Lewis	R. Bradfield
1903	Lord Cardigan	N. Godby	A. E. Cornwall
1904	Acrasia	T. Clayton	A. Wills
1905	Blue Spec	F. Bullock	W. Hickenbottom
1906	Poseidon	T. Clayton	I. Earnshaw
1907	Apologue	W. Evans	I. Earnshaw
1908	Lord Nolan	J. R. Flynn	E. A. Mayo
1909	Prince Foote	W. H. McLachlan	F. McGrath
1910	Comedy King	W. H. McLachlan	J. Lynch
1911	The Parisian	R. Cameron	C. Wheeler
1912	Piastre	A. Shanahan	R. O'Connor
1913	Posinatus	A. Shanahan	J. Chambers
1914	Kingsburgh	K. G. Meddick	I. Foulsham
1915	Patrobus	R. Lewis	C. Wheeler
1916	Sasanof	F. Foley	M. Hobbs
1917	Westcourt	W. H. McLachlan	J. Burton
1918	Nightwatch	W. Duncan	R. Bradfield
1919	Artilleryman	R. Lewis	P. Heywood
1920	Poitrel	K. Bracken	H. Robinson
1921	Sister Olive	E. O'Sullivan	J. Williams
1922	King Ingoda	A. Wilson	J. Scobie
1923	Bittali	A. Wilson	J. Scobie
1924	Backwood	P. Brown	R. Bradfield
1925	Windbag	J. Munro	G. Price
1926	Spearfelt	H. Cairns	V. O'Neill
1927	Trivalve	R. Lewis	J. Scobie
1928	Statesman	J. Munro	W. Kelso
1929	Nightmarch	R. Reed	A. McAuley
1930	Phar Lap	J. E. Pike	H. Telford
1931	White Nose	N. Percival	E. Hatwell
1932	Peter Pan	W. Duncan	F. McGrath
1933	Hall Mark	J. O'Sullivan	J. Holt
1934	Peter Pan	D. Munro	F. McGrath
1935	Marabou	K. Voitre	L. Robertson
1936	Wotan	0. Philips	J. Fryer
1937	The Trump	A. Reed	S. Reid
1938	Catalogue	F. Shean	A. McDonald
1939	Rivette	E. Preston	H. Bamber
1940	Old Rowley	A. Knox	J. Scully

Year	Winner	Jockey	Trainer
1941	Skipton	W. Cook	J. Fryer
1942	Colonus	H. McCloud	F. Manning
1943	Dark Felt	V. Hartney	R. Webster
1944	Sirius	D. Munro	E. Fisher
1945	Rainbird	W. Cook	S. Evans
1946	Russia	D. Munro	E. Hush
1947	Hiraji	J. Purtell	J. McCurley
1948	Rimfire***	R. Neville	S. Boyden
1949	Foxzami	W. Fellows	D. Lewis
1950	Comic Court	P. Glennon	J. M. Cummings
1951	Delta	N. Sellwood	M. McCarten
1952	Dalray	W. Williamson	C. McCarthy
1953	Wodalla	J. Purtell	R. Sinclair
1954	Rising Fast	J. Purtell	I. Tucker
1955	Toparoa	N. Sellwood	T. J. Smith
1956	Evening Pearl	G. Podmore	E. D. Lawson
1957	Straight Draw	N. McGrowdie	J. Mitchell
1958	Baystone	M. Schumacher	J. Green
1959	Macdougal	P. Glennon	R. W. Roden
1960	Hi Jinx	W. A. Smith	T. H. Knowles
1961	Lord Fury	R. Selkrig	F. B. Lewis
1962	Even Stevens	L. Coles	A. McGregor
1963	Gatum Gatum	J. Johnson	H. Heagney
1964	Polo Prince	R. Taylor	J. Carter
1965	Light Fingers	R. Higgins	J. B. Cummings
1966	Galilee	J. Miller	J. B. Cummings
1967	Red Handed	R. Higgins	J. B. Cummings
1968	Rain Lover	J. Johnson	M. L. Robbins
1969	Rain Lover	J. Johnson	M. L. Robbins
1970	Baghdad Note	E. Didham	R. Heasley
1971	Silver Knight	R. Marsh	E. Temperton
1972	Piping Lane	J. Letts	G. M. Hanlon
1973	Gala Supreme	F. Reys	R. J. Hutchins
1974	Think Big	H. White	J. B. Cummings
1975	Think Big	H. White	J. B. Cummings
1976	Van Der Hum	R. Skelton	L. Robinson
1977	Gold and Black	J. Duggan	J. B. Cummings
1978	Arwon	H. White	G. M. Hanlon
1979	Hyperno	H. White	J. B. Cummings
1980	Beldale Ball	J. Letts	C. S. Hayes
1981	Just a Dash	P. Cook	T. J. Smith
1982	Gurner's Lane	L. Dittman	G. T. Murphy

Year	Winner	Jockey	Trainer
1983	Kiwi	J. Cassidy	E. S. Lupton
1984	Black Knight	P. Cook	G. M. Hanlon
1985	What a Nuisance	P. Hyland	J. F. Meagher
1986	At Talaq	M. Clarke	C. S. Hayes
1987	Kensei	L. Olsen	L. J. Bridge
1988	Empire Rose	T. Allan	L. K. Laxon
1989	Tawriffic	R. S. Dye	D. L. Freedman
1990	Kingston Rule	D. Beadman	J. B. Cummings
1991	Let's Elope	S. King	J. B. Cummings
1992	Subzero	G. Hall	D. L. Freedman
1993	Vintage Crop	M. Kinane	D. Weld
1994	Jeune	W. Harris	D. Hayes
1995	Doriemus	D. Oliver	D. L. Freedman
1996	Saintly	D. Beadman	J. B. Cummings

* Archer was later immortalised on a postage stamp.
** Carbine is the heaviest weighted horse — at 10 st 5 lbs (66.5 kg) — to win the Melbourne Cup.
*** Rimfire won the Melbourne Cup at odds of 80–1.
**** Kingston Rule set a record time of 3 mins 16.3 secs in 1990.

THE CAULFIELD CUP

The Caulfield Cup is probably the most important handicap race on the racing calendar after the Melbourne Cup and is considered one of the most gruelling tests of stamina. Organised by the Victoria Amateur Racing Club (VARC), it was first held in 1879 and won by Newminster. After the first three races, it was switched from autumn to spring, to cash in on the huge crowds and horses the Melbourne Cup was attracting and became a springboard for the VARC's carnival. Rising Fast has won the race twice in a row, in 1954 and 1955, while Ming Dynasty has also won twice, in 1977 and 1980.

CAULFIELD CUP–MELBOURNE CUP

Winners of both the Caulfield Cup and the Melbourne Cup, a revered feat in the racing world, include The Trump in 1937, Rivette in 1939, Rising Fast in 1954, Even Stevens in 1962, Galilee in 1966 and Gurner's Lane in 1982.

POSEIDON

In 1906, Poseidon won the AJC Derby, the Caulfield Cup, the Victoria Derby and the Melbourne Cup, a record that has never been equalled, nor is it likely to be.

PHAR LAP

An Australian legend, Phar Lap's fame sparked a movie about him and his strapper, Tommy Woodcock, as well as numerous publications. Phar Lap had three starts in the Melbourne Cup. In the first in 1929 as a champion three-year-old, he started favourite and finished third. Just before the race started the following year, a failed attempt was made to shoot him. He went on to win the race by three lengths, starting favourite at 11–8 and carrying 9 st 12 lbs. At his last start in 1931 he carried a huge 10 st 10 lbs and finished eighth, after being sent in favourite at 3–1. In 1940, another attempt was made to shoot him.

Phar Lap eventually died in mysterious circumstances at Menlo Park, near San Francisco on 5 April 1932. The results from the autopsy were inconclusive and it was rumoured he had been poisoned. His body was brought back to Melbourne, where it has been on museum display ever since.

AUSTRALIAN JOCKEY CLUB (AJC)

Australia's oldest operating racing club, the AJC, was formed from the Australian Race Committee, set up in 1840 with the intention of regulating the industry. The most famous race organised by the AJC, the AJC Ledger, was first run at the old Homebush track in 1841 and is now staged at Randwick Racecourse.

Motor Racing

THE AUSTRALIAN GRAND PRIX

The first Australian Formula One Grand Prix was held on 31 March 1928 at Phillip Island, just out of Melbourne. It is the most important event on the international motor racing calendar and was held in Adelaide from 1989 to 1995. Despite some opposition and political controversy, the Australian Grand Prix has been held at the Albert Park Circuit in Melbourne since 1996.

AUSTRALIAN GRAND PRIX WINNERS

Date	Driver	Car
1928	A. C. R. Waite (Great Britain)	Austin 7
1929	A. J. Terdich	Bugatti
1930	W. B. Thompson	Bugatti
1931	C. Junker	Bugatti
1932	W. B. Thompson	Bugatti

Date	Driver	Car
1933	W. B. Thompson	Riley
1934	R. A. Lea-Wright	Singer
1935	L. Murphy	MG 'P-type'
1937	L. Murphy	MG 'P-type'
1938	P. N. Whitehead	ERA
1939	A. Tomlinson	MG
1947	W. B. Murray	MG
1948	L. F. Pratt	BMW
1949	J. Crouch	Delahaye
1950	D. Whiteford	Ford Special
1951	F. W. Pratley	Ford Special
1952	D. Whiteford	Lago-Talbot
1953	D. Whiteford	Lago-Talbot
1954	A. N. Davidson	(HWM Jaguar)
1955	Jack Brabham (Australia)	Cooper-Bristol
1956	Stirling Moss (Great Britain)	Maserati
1957	A. N. Davidson	Ferrari
1958	A. N. Davidson	Ferrari
1959	S. J. Jones	Maserati
1960	A. Mildren	Cooper-Maserati
1961	A. N. Davidson	Cooper-Climax
1962	B. McLaren (New Zealand)	Cooper-Climax
1963	Jack Brabham (Australia)	Repco-Brabham
1964	Jack Brabham (Australia)	Repco-Brabham
1965	B. McLaren (New Zealand)	Cooper-Climax
1966	Graham Hill (Britain)	BRM
1967	Jackie Stewart (Britain)	BRM
1968	J. Clarke (Britain)	Lotus-Ford
1969	C. Amon (New Zealand)	Ferrari
1970	F. Matich	McLaren-Repco
1971	F. Matich	Repco-Matich A50
1972	G. McRae (New Zealand)	Leda-Chevrolet
1973	G. McRae (New Zealand)	McRae GM2
1974	M. Stewart	Lola T330
1975	M. Stewart	Lola T400
1976	J. Goss	Matich-Repco A53
1977	W. Brown	Lola T430
1978	G. McRae (New Zealand)	McRae GM3
1979	J. Walker	Lola T332
1980	Alan Jones	Williams FW07
1981	R. Moreno (Brazil)	Ralt RT4
1982	Alain Prost (France)	Ralt RT4

Date	Driver	Car
1983	R. Moreno (Brazil)	Ralt RT4
1984	R. Moreno (Brazil)	Ralt RT4
1985	Keke Rosberg (Finland)	Williams FW10
1986	Alain Prost (France)	McLaren MP4/2C
1987	Gerhard Berger (Austria)	Ferrari F187
1988	Alain Prost (France)	McLaren-Honda MP4/4
1989	Thierry Boutsen (Belgium)	Williams FW13
1990	Nelson Piquet (Brazil)	Benetton-Ford B190
1991	Ayrton Senna (Brazil)	McLaren-Honda MP4/6
1992	Gerhard Berger (Austria)	McLaren-Honda MP4/7A
1993	Ayrton Senna (Brazil)	McLaren-Ford MP4/8
1994	Nigel Mansell (Great Britain)	Williams-Renault FW16
1995	Damon Hill (Great Britain)	Williams-Renault FW17
1996	Damon Hill (Great Britain)	Williams-Renault FW18

INDYCAR RACING

This is the most popular form of motor racing in the USA and races on the Grand Prix circuit are held in the USA, Canada and Australia. The cars resemble Formula 1 vehicles, but have narrower wheels, are heavier and run on methane rather than petrol. The first IndyCar Grand Prix was held in Australia in 1991 on a street circuit around Surfers Paradise on Queensland's Gold Coast. It is now held annually, attracting drivers and crowds from throughout Australia and the world.

AUSTRALIAN INDYCAR GRAND PRIX WINNERS

Year	Driver	Car
1991	John Andretti (USA)	Lola-Chevrolet
1992	Emerson Fittipaldi (Brazil)	Penske-Chevrolet
1993	Nigel Mansell (Great Britain)	Lola-Ford
1994	Michael Andretti (USA)	Reynard-Ford
1995	Paul Tracy (Canada)	Lola-Ford
1996	Jimmy Vasser (USA)	Reynard-Honda

BATHURST 1000

Perhaps Australia's most well known motor race for standard touring cars, the Bathurst 1000 is broadcast to millions of people around the world. International drivers and manufacturers enter the race every year.

It was first held in 1960 at Phillip Island, outside Melbourne, but was transferred to Mount Panorama near Bathurst, New South Wales, in 1963.

Originally known as the Armstrong 500, there have been numerous sponsorship and name changes since. In 1966 and 1967, it was referred to as the Gallaher 500, then from 1968 to 1973 as the Hardie Ferodo 500. In 1973, the race distance was increased from 500 miles to 1000 kilometres and in 1981 the race was re-named the James Hardie 1000, before becoming the Tooheys 1000 in 1988. It is now known as the Bathurst 1000.

BATHURST 1000 WINNERS

Date	Winners	Cars
1960	Frank Coad, John Roxburgh	Vauxhall Cresta
1961	Bob Jane, Harry Firth	Mercedes-Benz 220SE
1962	Bob Jane, Harry Firth	Ford Falcon
1963	Bob Jane, Harry Firth	Ford Cortina GT
1964	Bob Jane, George Reynolds	Ford Cortina GT
1965	Barry Seton, Midge Bosworth	Ford Cortina GT 500
1966	Rauno Aaltonen, Bob Holden	Morris Cooper S
1967	Harry Firth, Fred Gibson	Ford Falcon GT
1968	Bruce McPhee, Barry Mulholland	Holden Monaro GTS327
1969	Colin Bond, Tony Roberts	Holden Monaro GTS350
1970	Alan Moffatt	Ford-Falcon GTHO
1971	Alan Moffatt	Ford Falcon GTHO
1972	Peter Brock	Holden Torana XU-1
1973	Alan Moffatt, Ian Geoghegan	Ford Falcon GT
1974	John Goss, Kevin Bartlett	Ford Falcon GT
1975	Peter Brock, Brian Sampson	Holden Torana L34
1976	Bob Morris, John Fitzpatrick	Holden Torana L34
1977	Alan Moffatt, Jacky Ickx	Ford Falcon XC
1978	Peter Brock, Jim Richards	Holden Torana A9X
1979	Peter Brock, Jim Richards	Holden Torana A9X
1980	Peter Brock, Jim Richards	Holden Commodore VC
1981	Dick Johnson, John French	Ford Falcon XD
1982	Peter Brock, Larry Perkins	Holden Commodore VH
1983	Peter Brock, Larry Perkins, John Harvey	Holden Commodore VH
1984	Peter Brock, Larry Perkins	Holden Commodore VH
1985	John Goss, Armin Hahne	Jaguar XJS
1986	Allan Grice, Graeme Bailey	Holden Commodore VK
1987	Peter Brock, Peter McLeod, David Parsons	Holden Commodore VL
1988	Tony Longhurst, Tomas Mezera	Ford Sierra RS500
1989	Dick Johnson, John Bowe	Ford Sierra RS500
1990	Win Percy, Allan Grice	Holden Commodore VL
1991	Jim Richards, Mark Skaife	Nissan Skyline GT-R
1992	Jim Richards, Mark Skaife	Nissan Skyline GT-R
1993	Larry Perkins, Gregg Hansford	Holden Commodore VP

Date	Winners	Cars
1994	Dick Johnson, John Bowe	Ford Falcon EB
1995	Larry Perkins, Russell Ingall	Holden Commodore VR
1996	Craig Lowndes, Greg Murphy	Holden Commodore VR

AUSTRALIAN TOURING CAR CHAMPIONSHIP

Organisers of the inaugural championship were unsure about how this racing class would be received when it began in 1960. Today, however, touring car racing is one of the most popular branches of Australian motor sport and the initial single-race championship is now a national series. Ian Geoghegan and Dick Johnson have taken the most line honours in this event: Geoghegan five times in 1964, 1966, 1967, 1968, and 1969; and Johnson in 1981, 1982, 1984, 1988 and 1989.

AUSTRALIAN DRIVERS' CHAMPIONSHIP

This race was first held in 1957 when the Confederation of Australian Motor Sport offered a Gold Star Award to Australia's champion racing driver. After running under several different formats, it is now a series of races for Formula Holden cars, i.e. open-wheeled, single-seat vehicles powered by modified Holden Commodore V6 engines. Consecutive winners include Alfredo Costanzo (1980, 1981, 1982, 1983) and Bill Stillwell (1962, 1963, 1964, 1965).

OVERSEAS SUCCESS

The most famous victory by Australians in an international driving rally was when the Australians Ken Tubman, Andre Welinski and Jim Reddex (NSW) drove a Citroen to win the 1974 World Cup Rally over 17 700 km through England, the Sahara Desert and Europe.

Vern Schuppan, who is the only Australian to be successful in the classic Le Mans 24-hour race, shared the drive in the winning car in 1983. He is also the only Australian to get a place in the Indianapolis 500 and has been a champion endurance sports car driver for many years.

OUTSTANDING DRIVERS

JACK BRABHAM   Now Sir Jack Brabham, he was the first of two Australians to win the world drivers' championship three times, in 1959, 1960 and 1966. He was also the first driver to win the world championship in a car he had designed and built himself, in 1966. In 1961, he became the first Australian to drive in the Indianapolis 500, finishing ninth. Brabham also won the Australian Grand Prix in 1955, 1963, and 1964.

PETER BROCK   Brock holds the record for winning the most Bathurst 1000 races, in 1972, 1975, 1978, 1979, 1980, 1982, 1983, 1984 and 1987 (nine times). From 1980, he began driving Holden Commodores in the big race, and has since marketed his own Brock Commodore through Holden. He has also won the Australian Touring Car Championships three times — in 1974, 1978 and 1980.

BOB JANE   Bob Jane began his motor racing career in 1957 with a Maserati 300S. In 1961, he built the famous 3.8 racing Jaguar and won more than 300 races in Australia with it, including the 1962 and 1967 Australian Championships. He is the only Australian driver to win four consecutive times, from 1961-1964. He also won the Australian GT Championships in the famous Light Weight E Type and the 1971 and 1972 Australian Touring Car Championships in a 1969 Chevrolet Camaro.

ALAN JONES   Along with Sir Jack Brabham, Alan Jones is the only other Australian racing car driver to win the World Drivers' Championship. Jones began his racing career in Go-Karts, went to England and worked his way into Grand Prix racing via Formula Three and Formula Two cars and was runner-up in the 1979 World Championship before winning his first title in 1980. He also won the rich USA Can Am Championship in 1978 and 1979, and the Australian Grand Prix in 1980. He retired from Grand Prix racing in 1981, but had a short-lived comeback in January 1985.

ALLAN MOFFATT   Another Australian who has proven himself in Australia's toughest races is Allan Moffatt. He won the Australian Touring Car Championships three times, in 1973, 1976 and 1977. He has also won the great Bathurst 1000 race four times in 1970, 1971, 1973 (driving with Ian Geoghegan) and 1977 (with Jackie Ickx).

JOAN RICHMOND   Richmond was the first great woman driver in Australia. She was also the first Australian to compete in the Le Mans 24-hour race. She competed in the Monte Carlo Rally and in 1932 shared the winning drive with the Englishwoman Elsie Wisdom in a 1610-km race at Brooklands, becoming the first Australian woman to win a major overseas race.

Motorcycling

Motorcycling caught on more quickly in Australia than motorcar racing because bikes were cheaper and it was easier to organise races. Sydney to Melbourne record attempts were often made in the early days, with James Bolder becoming the first rider to cover the distance in less than 24 hours on 16 February 1913, with a time of 23 hrs 41 mins. The first rider to break 100 m.p.h. is a contentious issue, but it is thought to have been Harry Jenkins in 1916 when he rode at an average of 102 m.p.h.

Motorcycle racing is also the second biggest killer after speedway racing in Australian sport.

CASTROL SIX HOUR RACE

This is the most popular long-distance motorcycling race in Australia. Set up for production machines, it was first held at Amaroo Park near Sydney in 1970 and was won by Len Atlee. Today, it is staged every year, and attracts a large overseas entry and average crowds of 20 000 spectators, as well being beamed into the living rooms of an estimated 2.2 million people around Australia.

FIM WORLD MOTORCYCLE GRAND PRIX CHAMPIONSHIP (500CC)

The FIM World Motorcycle Grand Prix is an annual event. Rounds are held in different places around the world, 15 events in four classes, and each winner of a round receives a certain number of points. The outright winner of the whole competition is decided by the final points score. From 1997, the Australian round of the event has been held at Victoria's Phillip Island.

See Wayne Gardner, Michael Doohan under 'Outstanding Riders'.

500CC MOTORCYCLE WORLD CHAMPIONS SINCE 1985

Year	Rider	Machine
1985	Freddie Spencer, USA	Honda
1986	Eddie Lawson, USA	Yamaha
1987	Wayne Gardner, Australia	Honda
1988	Eddie Lawson, USA	Yamaha
1989	Eddie Lawson, USA	Honda
1990	Wayne Rainey, USA	Yamaha
1991	Wayne Rainey, USA	Yamaha
1992	Wayne Rainey, USA	Yamaha

Year	Rider	Machine
1993	Kevin Schwantz, USA	Suzuki
1994	Michael Doohan	Honda
1995	Michael Doohan	Honda
1996	Michael Doohan	Honda

SUPERBIKE WORLD CHAMPIONSHIP

This championship, which commenced in 1988, is based on road-going machines rather than purpose-built motorcyles. It is held over 12 rounds consisting of two races each.

SUPERBIKE WORLD CHAMPIONS

Year	Rider	Machine
1988	Fred Merkel, USA	Yamaha
1989	Fred Merkel, USA	Yamaha
1990	Raymond Roche, France	Ducati
1991	Doug Polen, USA	Ducati
1992	Doug Polen, USA	Ducati
1993	Scott Russell, USA	Kawasaki
1994	Carl Fogarty, Great Britain	Ducati
1995	Carl Fogarty, Great Britain	Ducati
1996	Troy Corser, Australia	Ducati

OUTSTANDING RIDERS

KEITH CAMPBELL
Keith Campbell was Australia's first world champion, winning the 1957 World 350cc Championship riding a works Moto-Guzzi. He died in 1958 in a racing accident in France.

KEL CARRUTHERS   In 1969, Kel Carruthers won the world 250cc championship; in 1970, he was runner-up in the 250cc and 350cc championships.

MICK DOOHAN   Currently at the top of the field in world 500cc motorcycle racing, Michael Doohan made his 500cc Grand Prix debut in 1989. Doohan was runner-up in the world championship in 1991, and again in 1992, when he would almost certainly have won the title but for a broken leg which forced him out of competition for five races. He has now won the FIM World Motorcycle Championship in the 500cc class three times, and is expected to take the title again in 1997. His first win was in 1994, followed by wins in 1995 and 1996.

STEPHEN GALL   Stephen Gall is a famous moto-cross rider, an event where participants race on a loosely surfaced course with sharp bends and artificial hills. On 2 June 1984, Gall won the first World Masters Supercross Championship in London on a Yamaha. He has also won championships in road racing, dirt track speedway racing and sprint and touring cars.

WAYNE GARDNER   Gardner is one of Australia's most successful motorcycle riders, although he was plagued by injury during his career. His outstanding international record includes the most important championship of them all, the FIM World Motorycle Championship, which Gardner won in 1987. He has also won the 1986 Spanish, Dutch and British Grands Prix; the 1987 Spanish, Austrian, Nations, Yugoslavian, Swedish, Czechoslovakian and Brazilian Grands Prix; the 1988 Dutch, Belgian, Yugoslavian and Czechoslovakian Grands Prix; and the 1989 Australian Grand Prix. In 1993, Gardner retired from motorcycle racing at the height of his career and on top of the rider's championship table.

Speedway Racing

Australia is the only country in the world to stage as many as 12 different types of speedway racing, many at the same meeting. These include solo, and sidecar motorcycle racing, moto-cross (racing on artificial hills and dirt tracks), speedcars, sprint cars, sedan cars, junior speedcars (TQs), micro midgets, hot rods, stock cars and stock motorcycles. Jack Brabham was one of the most famous drivers in speedway, starting his career on dirt tracks before switching to road racing. Speedway was particularly popular during the 1960s.

Speedway racing is the most dangerous Australian sport, almost 140 deaths have been recorded since 1906 when it began on a professional basis.

SPRINT CAR RACING

During the 1980s, sprint car racing (which developed from hot rods) has experienced a boom in popularity, due mainly to the small number of restrictions placed on entries. Cars can have extremely powerful engines and sophisticated engineering features and the faster ones often exceed 110 m.p.h. on short straights. Gary Rush is the most successful sprint car racer, winning six Australian championships.

Sailing

The first serious sailing competition was held in Tasmania on the Derwent River in 1827. Competition did not begin in Sydney until 1837, when the Anniversary Regatta was held. The main race was won by James Milson, after whom Milsons Point in Sydney is named. The first yacht clubs began in Sydney in the 1830s with the Royal Yacht Club of Victoria being established in Melbourne in 1853, followed by the Royal Sydney Yacht Squadron in 1862.

18-FOOTERS

The nippy 18-footers first appeared on Sydney Harbour in the summer of 1894. The class quickly developed, with designers devising hulls and masts capable of carrying enormous areas of sail. Although the boats were very fast, they also tended to capsize in high winds. Crews eventually shrank from 12 to 3 as more emphasis was placed on reducing weight.

RACING CLASSES

Australia has pioneered a range of internationally recognised classes and designs. They include 18-footers, 16-footers, Sabots, Vee Jays (a design created for junior members of the Vaucluse club in Sydney), Vee Ess's, Contenders, Moths and Gwen 12s, as well as a range of catamarans, one of which was selected by the International Yacht Racing Union as the international design for A Class catamaran racing.

SYDNEY TO HOBART YACHT RACE

Originally held as a pleasure cruise in 1945, the Sydney to Hobart Yacht Race is now an ocean classic. The field for the first race was a record low of nine yachts and the race line and handicap honours were won by Commander Illingworth's *Rani* in 6 days 2 hours 22 minutes. Only four other boats have won both line and handicap honours: R. Turner's *American Eagle* in 1972, J. B. Kilroy's *Kialoa* in 1977, the syndicate-owned *New Zealand* skippered by Peter Blake in 1980, and *Sovereign* in 1987. The first boat to win the race three years in succession was *Freya* (1963, 1964, 1965).

THE AMERICA'S CUP

1983 AUSTRALIAN VICTORY

One of Australia's greatest sporting victories in modern times was when Australia won the America's Cup on 26 September 1983. The Australian victory ended 112 years of American domination of the race. *Australia II* defeated the American entry, *Liberty*. *Australia II*, designed by Ben Lexcen, had a revolutionary winged keel, which caused a lot of controversy in the USA. The challenge was financed by Alan Bond, who had sponsored two previous challenges — in 1974 with *Southern Cross* and 1980 with *Australia*. The designer Lexcen, the skipper John Bertrand and Bond became household names. Australia defended the Cup in 1987 and competed in 1995 against an international fleet, but was defeated.

OTHER CHALLENGES

Other Australian entries in the America's Cup were *Gretel* in 1962, *Dame Pattie* in 1967 and *Gretel II* in 1970, along with the three Bond challenges of 1977, 1978 and 1980. During this period, Australian yachts won only three races. In 1987, *Kookaburra III*, skippered by Ian Murray, lost the challenge to the US boat *Stars and Stripes*, skippered by Dennis Conner.

THE ADMIRAL'S CUP

This ocean racing trophy is held every two years on the south coast of England, in the Solent off the Isle of Wight. Nine races are held, the longest and most dangerous being the 605 nautical mile (874 km) Fastnet race. Australia entered this race for the first time in 1965 with four yachts: *Camille*, *Caprice of Huon*, *Freya* and *Lorita Marie*. *Caprice of Huon* won the 225-mile (362 km) Channel Race and the 30-mile (48.3 km) Britannia Cup race around the Solent, came third in the New York Challenge Cup and finished fourth in the Fastnet with *Camille* third and *Freya* sixth. Great Britain won overall.

AUSTRALIAN VICTORY

Australia's first success in the Admiral's Cup came in 1967 when Australian yachts *Balandra* (Sir Robert Crichton-Brown), *Mercedes III* (Ted Kaufman) and *Caprice of Huon* (Gordon Huon) gained sufficient points to win from Great Britain and the USA.

In 1979, the Australian yachts *Impetuous* (Graeme Lambert), *Police Car* (Peter Cantwell) and *Ragamuffin* (Syd Fischer) won the Admiral's Cup for Australia again.

THE OLYMPICS

Yachting was first held at the 1900 Olympics in Paris, but Australia did not enter until 1948. At the 1956 Melbourne Games, Rolly Tasker and John Scott won a silver medal in the 12-metre class and Jock Sturrock, Devereaux Mytton and Douglas Buxton won bronze in the 5.5-metre class. However, it was not until the 1964 Tokyo Games that Australia won its first gold medal, with veteran Bill Northam skippering his boat *Barrenjoey* to victory, with crewmen Peter O'Donnell and Dick Sargeant, in the 5.5-metre class. At the 1972 Munich Olympics, Australia won gold in the Dragon class with a boat skippered by John Cunie and crewed by Tom Anderson and John Shaw, and gold in the Star class with David Forbes as skipper and John Anderson crew. The last Australian medal in sailing was won at the 1996 Atlanta Olympic Games, when Colin Beaschel and David Giles took bronze in the Star class.

OUTSTANDING YACHTSPEOPLE

JOHN BERTRAND   Most remembered for being the skipper of *Australia II*, the boat which took the 1983 America's Cup from Dennis Conner's *Liberty*, John Bertrand became a member of the Order of Australia in 1983. However, Bertrand had a remarkable sailing background even before the America's Cup made him a household name. At the 1976 Montreal Olympics, he took bronze in the Finn class yachting and was subsequently named Australian Yachtsman of the Year that same year and again in 1983, when he was also named World Sportsman of the Year.

IAIN MURRAY   Iain Murray is famous for his record-breaking feats in 18-footers as well as being a great boat designer and skipper. In 1977, at the age of 18, he became the youngest ever winner of the World 18-Footer Championships. He went on to win the event five more times in 1978, 1979, 1980, 1981 and 1982. He has also won the Australian 18-Footer Championships in 1978, 1979, 1980, 1981, and 1982 and was named Australian Yachtsman of the Year in 1984. In 1987, he was skipper of *Kookaburra III*, which unsuccessfully challenged Dennis Conner's *Stars & Stripes* for the America's Cup,

KAY COTTEE   Kay Cottee was the first woman to complete a solo, non-stop, unassisted circumnavigation of the globe. When she came into Sydney Harbour on 5 June 1988, 120 000 people lined the foreshores and 500 pleasure craft followed her in. She completed the trip (25 000 nautical miles) in 189 days in her 12-metre Cavalier 37 Sloop. In 1989, she was honoured with an Order of Australia and was named Australian of the Year.

Surfing

SURF LIFESAVING

Australia's famous bronzed lifeguards first appeared at the turn of the century when experienced surfers, alarmed at the growing rate of injury and drowning, formed clubs that organised beach patrols as well as competitions. Bondi, Manly and Bronte Clubs were amongst the first set up in Sydney. The first rescue took place at Bondi in 1906 when two boys, one the young Sir Charles Kingsford Smith, were rescued using a reel and rope. (The reel and rope method meant that the lifesaver was attached by a line to the beach; they could rescue the swimmer and then be hauled back into shore).

SURF LIFESAVING CLUBS

There are more than 260 surf lifesaving clubs in Australia, with a total membership of 73 000 people. These clubs all belong to the Royal Lifesaving Society, which has performed about 400 000 rescues since it began in 1906. Clubs receive some funding from the Federal government, which goes towards buying equipment; the balance is received from public fund-raising.

IRONMAN CHAMPIONSHIPS

The first ironman contest was held in Queensland during the 1965-1966 surf lifesaving season, and was won by Haydn Kenny (Grant Kenny's father). The ironman competition consists of four races; swimming, surfboard racing, running and a surf ski section. The standard of competition has improved immensely since the early days when ironman championships were often a swimmer's race. Today, only a good all-rounder can win, with former ironmen Ken Vidler, Grant Kenny and Trevor Hendy going on to Olympic performances. The Australian national ironman championship is the Uncle Toby's Super Series.

GREAT IRONMEN

The first ironman superchampions were Barry Rodgers ('Mr Surf'), who won the Australian title in 1966–1967 and 1967–1968, and Ken Vidler who won in 1972–1973, 1973–1974 and 1974–1975.

Grant Kenny holds the record for the greatest performance at an Australian championship carnival. At his debut in March 1980, Kenny won the Australian Senior Ironman title in Hobart. Ten minutes later, he entered and won the National Junior Ironman Championship. On the same day, he also won the Junior Single Ski title and finished second with John Atras in the Junior Double Ski title. Then, in December 1980, he repeated the Senior–Junior Ironman double on the same day at North Cronulla, Sydney.

In March 1981, Kenny added another double title when he won the New Zealand Ironman Championships at Oakura Beach. He retained his Australian Senior Ironman title in 1981–1982.

Other outstanding ironman competitors include New South Welshmen Guy Leech and the Mercer brothers, Dean and Darren.

Uncle Toby's Super Series Results

Year	Winner
1989–1990	Trevor Hendy, Queensland
1990–1991	Trevor Hendy, Queensland
1991–1992	Trevor Hendy, Queensland
1992–1993	Guy Andrews, Queensland
1993–1994	Guy Andrews, Queensland
1994–1995	Michael King, Queensland
1995–1996	Guy Andrews, Queensland

Ironwomen Championships

The national ironwomen championships began in 1994-1995 and have been dominated by two competitors, Reen Corbett and Karla Gilbert. The women's event features run, swim and board legs.

Devondale Ironwoman Series

Year	Winner
1994–1995	Reen Corbett, Queensland
1995–1996	Reen Corbett, Queensland

Surfing

Surfing was first introduced to Australia in 1915 when Hawaiian Duke Kahanamoku brought a board to Sydney and gave a demonstration at Freshwater Beach in Sydney. The original solid boards became hollow in the 1930s and in 1956 malibu boards were introduced. They were incredibly light and had a fin, making the board easy to manoeuvre.

Australian Titles

The first official Australian titles were staged by the Australian Surfriders' Association in 1964. Bernard 'Midget' Farrelly won the Men's Open Championship, Robert Coneeley won the Junior Men's title and Phyllis O'Donnell won the Women's Open.

WORLD SURFING CHAMPIONSHIPS

Australia is one of the world's leading surfing nations, with a long line of Australian surfers taking out the world surfing championships in amateur and professional competitions. Mark Richards took four consecutive world titles from 1979-1982.

The current world championship, the ASP World Championship, is run by the Association of Surfing Professionals (ASP). Both men's and women's events are held. The International Surfing Association (ISA) held an amateur world surfing championship from 1964–1994. This competition was superseded by the World Surfing Games in 1996, a championship which now includes professionals surfers and has seven different categories including kneeboarding and bodyboarding, as well as traditional shortboard and longboard events.

ASP WORLD CHAMPIONS

Year	Men's World Champion	Women's World Champion
1976	Peter Townsend, Australia	—
1977	Shaun Tomson, South Africa	Margo Oberg, USA
1978	Wayne Bartholomew, Australia	Lynne Boyer, USA
1979	Mark Richards, Australia	Lynne Boyer, USA
1980	Mark Richards, Australia	Margo Oberg, USA
1981	Mark Richards, Australia	Margo Oberg, USA
1982	Mark Richards, Australia	Debbie Beacham, USA
1983	Tom Carroll, Australia	Kim Mearig, USA
1984	Tom Carroll, Australia	Frieda Zamba, USA
1985	Tom Curren, USA	Frieda Zamba, USA
1986	Tom Curren, USA	Frieda Zamba, USA
1987	Damien Hardman, Australia	Wendy Botha, South Africa
1988	Barton Lynch, Australia	Frieda Zamba, USA
1989	Martin Potter, Great Britain	Wendy Botha, Australia*
1990	Tom Curren, USA	Pam Burridge, Australia
1991	Damien Hardman, Australia	Wendy Botha, Australia
1992	Kelly Slater, USA	Wendy Botha, Australia
1993	Derek Ho, Hawaii	Pauline Menczer, Australia
1994	Kelly Slater, USA	Lisa Andersen, USA
1995	Kelly Slater, USA	Lisa Andersen, USA
1996	Kelly Slater, USA	

* Wendy Botha changed her citizenship to Australian in 1989.

ISA WORLD CHAMPIONSHIP

Year	Men's World Champion	Women's World Champion
1964	Bernard 'Midget' Farrelly, Australia	Phyllis O'Donnell, Australia
1965	Felipe Pomer, Peru	Joyce Hoffman, USA
1966	Robert 'Nat' Young, Australia	Joyce Hoffman, USA
1968	Fred Hemmings, Hawaii	Margo Godfrey, USA
1970	Rolf Arness, USA	Sharon Webber, Hawaii
1972	Jim Blears, Hawaii	Sharon Webber, Hawaii
1978	Anthony Brodowicz, South Africa	not held
1980	Mark Scott, Australia	Alisa Schwarzstein, USA
1982	Tom Curren, USA	Jenny Gill, Australia
1984	Scott Farnsworth, USA	Janice Aragon, USA
1986	Mark Sainsbury, Australia	Connie Nixon, Australia
1988	Fabio Gouveia	Pauline Menczer, Australia
1990	Henry Tahutini, Tahiti	Kathy Newman, Australia
1992	Grant Frost, Australia	Lynette McKenzie, Australia
1994	Sasha Stocker, Australia	Alessandra Viera, Brazil
1996	Taylor Knox, USA	Neridah Falconer, Australia

Triathlon

The gruelling discipline of triathlon has experienced a phenomenal boom in popularity in both Australia and overseas in recent years. There is now a Triathlon tour, a series of seven national events for men and women with an emphasis on Olympic distance events; the Triathlon Grand Prix, which started in 1994 and has five rounds in a variety of formats; and the Australian Triathlon Championships, held annually over the four international standard distances. Internationally, there are the World Triathlon Championship, an annual event held over the Olympic distance at a different venue each year, and the ITU Triathlon World Cup, which combines a number of high-standard international triathlons, including the world championship.

Triathlon is to be included as an official Olympic sport for the first time in 2000, at the Sydney Olympic Games.

Australia has several outstanding triathletes in both the men's and women's competitions. Greg Welch has performed extremely well at international level and is considered a world-class triathlete, with success in the 1990 Men's Open World Triathlon Championships and the event considered the most gruelling of all, the Hawaii Triathlon. Brad Beven has won the men's section of Australia's Triathlon Grand Prix three times since its introduction in 1994 (1994, 1995, 1996). He has also won the international ITU Triathlon World Cup four times, from 1992–1995. Michellie Jones and Jackie Gallagher are both premier performers in the women's events.

Swimming

The first recorded swimming competition was staged in 1846 at baths located at Woolloomooloo Bay. In 1894, the first national championship was held, although it was restricted to men. The first national championships for women was not staged until 1930.

THE AUSTRALIAN CRAWL

Now known as modern freestyle, the Australian crawl was developed by Richard Cavill, after he won the 100 yds New South Wales championship in 1899 using the stroke and became the first man to swim 100 yds in less than a minute. The Cavill family are often called the royal family of Australian swimming. The father, Fred, was a marathon swimmer. His son Percy won the 440 yds and five mile world championships in 1897, his fourth son Arthur gained awards for lifesaving and his daughter Madeleine was also a notable swimmer. The fifth son, Sydney, was a swimming teacher in the USA, where he developed the butterfly stroke.

OLYMPIC GAMES

Australia has an outstanding record in swimming at the Olympic Games. Fred Lane was the first of many gold medallists, winning the 200 m freestyle and 200 m obstacle race (only ever held once) at the 1900 Paris Games. Sarah 'Fanny' Durack was the first Australian woman to win at the Olympic Games, taking gold in the 100 m freestyle, the first swimming event staged and the only one for women at the 1912 Stockholm Games. The silver went to another Australian, Wilhelmina Wylie. In the 1990s, the Australians are widely regarded as one of the teams to beat in international swimming competition, although at the 1996 Atlanta Olympic Games they were not as competitive as in the past. Kieren Perkins, however, won Australia's only gold medal in the pool with a courageous swim in the 1500 m freestyle, following on from his success in this event in 1992 at Barcelona.

COMMONWEALTH GAMES

Noel Ryan was the first gold medallist for Australia at the first Empire (Commonwealth) Games in Canada in 1930. Ryan won both the 440 yds and the 1500 yds freestyle. Clare Dennis was the first woman gold medallist, at the 1934 Commonwealth Games at London, winning the 200 yds breast stroke title.

OUTSTANDING SWIMMERS

KIEREN PERKINS   Dual Olympic gold medallist Kieren Perkins is possibly Australia's best ever male swimmer and certainly its best distance swimmer. He won silver medals in the 1500 m at the 1990 Auckland Commonwealth Games and the 1991 world championships. At the 1992 Olympics, he took out silver in the 400 m freestyle and gold in the 1500 m event in a world record time of 14 mins 43.48 secs. At the 1994 Commonwealth Games in Victoria, Canada, he won gold in the 200 m freestyle, 400 m freestyle, 4 x 200 m freestyle relay and 1500 m freestyle. In this latter event, he broke his own world record. Just two weeks later, he won two gold medals at the world swimming championships in the 400 m and 1500 m events. Perkins has set 11 world records, of which he currently holds five. He repeated his gold medal-winning effort in the 1992 Olympics at Atlanta in 1996, winning the 1500 m freestyle event after only just qualifying for the final.

DUNCAN ARMSTRONG   Armstrong won his first gold medal for swimming at the 1986 Edinburgh Commonwealth Games in the 400 m freestyle. Then, at the 1988 Seoul Olympics, he won the gold medal for the 200 m freestyle, and silver in the 400 m freestyle. That same year he received the best male athlete award at the Sport Australia Awards and in 1989 was named Young Australian of the Year.

LORRAINE CRAPP   Crapp set 16 individual and seven relay world records. On 25 August 1956, she became the first woman to break 5 minutes for the 400 m freestyle; in the same swim she set records for the 200 m and the 200 yds.

DAWN FRASER   At the 1964 Olympics, Dawn Fraser created a record that still stands today — being the only woman in Olympic history to win three successive 100 m freestyle gold medals. She established 27 individual world records and won a record 29 Australian Championships. She was also the first woman to beat one minute for the 110 yds freestyle with a world record time of 59.9 secs during Commonwealth Games preselection trials in Melbourne on 27 October 1962. During the Commonwealth Games in Perth, she broke that time with a world record 59.5 secs.

SHANE GOULD   In 1972, at the age of just 15, Shane Gould set five freestyle world records (in each recognised freestyle distance), won every Australian freestyle championship and won three gold medals at the 1972 Munich Olympics.

STEVE HOLLAND   Holland broke 11 individual world freestyle records between 1973 and 1976, and at the 1976 Australian championships set new world records for the 800 m and the 1500 m, in the same swim.

THE KONRADS   John Konrads set 26 individual world records and six world relay records in freestyle events. Both he and his sister Ilsa were born in Latvia, but emigrated to Australia in 1949, settling in Sydney. Both were trained by Don Talbot. Ilsa Konrads went on to set 12 individual world freestyle records and three world freestyle relay records.

HAYLEY LEWIS   Hayley Lewis won silver in the 800 m freestyle and bronze in the 400 m freestyle at the 1992 Olympics Games in Barcelona, Spain. She also won 5 gold medals (200 m freestyle, 400 m freestyle, 200 m butterfly, 200 m individual medley, 4 x 200 m freestyle relay) in 1990 at the Auckland Commonwealth Games. In 1991, she won a gold medal (in the 200 m freestyle), two silver (400 m freestyle and 400 m individual medley) and one bronze (200 m butterfly) in the world championships.

JOHN MARSHALL   Marshall broke 29 world records in a career which saw him set a total of 171 world, American national and Australian national records. At one stage of his career, he held 19 world records at the same time.

MURRAY ROSE   Rose set 15 world records over distances ranging from 400 m to 1500 m, and in relay events. He won three gold medals at the 1956 Melbourne Olympics and another in the 1960 Rome Games.

TRACEY WICKHAM   One of Australia's greatest swimmers, Tracey Wickham first hit the headlines when she set five world records in distances ranging from the 400m to the 1500 m freestyle at the 1978 Edmonton Games. Two of Wickham's records stood for almost a decade, until 1987: the 400 m which she had bettered three weeks after the world championships in Berlin and the 800 m. At the 1982 Brisbane Commonwealth Games, Wickham took gold in the 800 m freestyle and silver in the 200 m freestyle.

MARATHON SWIMMING

The first Australian to attempt the English Channel crossing was Frederick Cavill, but he failed twice. The first successful attempt was made by Linda McGill on 7 August 1965. McGill also holds the record for the fastest time by an Australian, making the crossing in 9 hrs 59 mins. John Koorey became the first Australian man to cross the Channel in September 1969, after failing twice the previous year. Des Renford has made 19 crossings, the most by any Australian. In July 1990, Suzie Maroney, from Sydney, became the youngest Australian woman to swim the English Channel, at just 16 years of age. In May 1997, she successfully swam from Cuba to Florida in the USA at her second attempt, the first time any person has done so.

Shelley Taylor-Smith is a world champion marathon swimmer. Having broken several world records and achieved unparalleled success in the water, Taylor-Smith contines to compete at the highest international level.

Tennis

WIMBLEDON

Wimbledon is surely the world's most prestigious tennis tournament. It is also the only Grand Slam tournament now played on grass. There have been many Australian Wimbledon champions; the first was Norman E. Brookes who won the men's singles title in 1907. During the 1950s, 1960s and early 1970s, Australian players more or less dominated Wimbledon, with the Australian men winning every singles and doubles final in the 1960s, with the exception of 1963.

AUSTRALIAN WIMBLEDON WINNERS

Year	Player
Men's Singles	
1907	Norman E. Brookes
1914	Norman E. Brookes
1919	Gerald L. Patterson
1922	Gerald L. Patterson
1933	Jack Crawford
1952	Frank Sedgman
1956	Lew Hoad
1957	Lew Hoad
1958	Ashley Cooper
1960	Neale Fraser
1961	Rod Laver
1962	Rod Laver
1964	Roy Emerson
1965	Roy Emerson
1967	John Newcombe
1968	Rod Laver
1969	Rod Laver
1970	John Newcombe
1971	John Newcombe
1987	Pat Cash

Year	Player
Women's singles	
1963	Margaret Court
1965	Margaret Court
1970	Margaret Court
1971	Evonne Goolagong
1980	Evonne Cawley née Goolagong
Men's doubles	
1907	Norman Brookes and Anthony Wilding
1914	Norman Brookes and Anthony Wilding
1919	R. V. Thomas and Pat O'Hara Wood
1922	James O. Anderson and Randolph Lycett
1935	Jack Crawford and Adrian Quist
1948	John Bromwich and Frank Sedgman
1950	John Bromwich and Adrian Quist
1951	Frank Sedgman and Ken McGregor
1952	Frank Sedgman and Ken McGregor
1953	Lew Hoad and Ken Rosewall
1954	Rex Hartwig and Mervyn Rose
1955	Rex Hartwig and Lew Hoad
1956	Lew Hoad and Ken Rosewall
1959	Roy Emerson and Neale Fraser
1961	Roy Emerson and Neale Fraser
1962	Bob Hewitt and Fred Stolle
1964	Bob Hewitt and Fred Stolle
1965	John Newcombe and Tony Roche
1966	John Newcombe and Ken Fletcher
1968	John Newcombe and Tony Roche
1969	John Newcombe and Tony Roche
1970	John Newcombe and Tony Roche
1971	Roy Emerson and Rod Laver
1974	John Newcombe and Tony Roche
1978	Ross Case and Geoff Masters
1980	Peter McNamara and Paul McNamee
1982	Peter McNamara and Paul McNamee
1989	John Fitzgerald and Anders Jarryd (Sweden)
1993	Mark Woodforde and Todd Woodbridge
1994	Mark Woodforde and Todd Woodbridge
1995	Mark Woodforde and Todd Woodbridge
1996	Mark Woodforde and Todd Woodbridge

Year	Player

Women's doubles

1964	Margaret Court and Leslie Turner
1969	Margaret Court and Jan Tegart
1974	Evonne Goolagong
1977	Mrs Helen Cawley and Joanne Russell
1978	Wendy Turnbull and Kerry Reid
1985	Liz Smiley and Cathy Jordan

Mixed doubles

1920	Gerald Patterson and Suzanne Lenglen
1922	Pat O'Hara Wood and Suzanne Lenglen
1930	Jack Crawford and Elizabeth Ryan
1947	John Bromwich and Louise Brough
1948	John Bromwich and Louise Brough
1951	Frank Sedgman and Doris Hart
1957	Mervyn Rose and Darlene Hard
1958	Bob Howe and Loraine Coghlan
1959	Rod Laver and Darlene Hard
1960	Rod Laver and Darlene Hard
1961	Fred Stolle and Lesley Turner
1962	Neale Fraser and Margaret du Pont
1963	Ken Fletcher and Margaret Court
1964	Fred Stolle and Lesley Turner
1965	Ken Fletcher and Margaret Court
1966	Ken Fletcher and Margaret Court
1967	Owen Davidson and Billie Jean King
1968	Ken Fletcher and Margaret Court
1969	Fred Stolle and P. F. Jones
1971	Owen Davidson and Billie Jean King
1973	Owen Davidson and Billie Jean King
1975	Marty Reissen and Margaret Court
1976	Tony Roche and Francoise Durr
1985	Paul McNamee and Martina Navratilova

THE GRAND SLAM

The Grand Slam refers to winning the Wimbledon, French Open, US Open and Australian Open titles in a single year. The first Australian man to win a Grand Slam was Rod Laver achieving this goal in 1962 and again in 1969. Margaret Court was the first Australian woman to achieve this feat, winning the Grand Slam in 1970. The first Australian men's doubles team to win a Grand Slam was Frank Sedgman and Ken McGregor in 1951. The pair was also the first doubles team to ever achieve this. The first mixed doubles pair to win the Grand Slam was Margaret Smith (Court) and Ken Fletcher in 1963, also a world first.

THE AUSTRALIAN OPEN

Previously known as the Australian Singles Championship, the first tournament was held in Melbourne in 1905. Rod Laver has won the most men's singles titles; six, between 1961 and 1967. Margaret Court holds the women's record with 11 women's singles titles between 1960 and 1973. John Bromwich and Adrian Quist won eight men's doubles titles between 1938 and 1950, while Thelma Coyne and Nancy Wynne won ten women's doubles titles between 1936 and 1952. The Australian Open is currently the first Grand Slam title on the international tennis calendar, being played in January each year at Flinders Park, Melbourne.

THE DAVIS CUP

Named after Dwight Filley Davis, a Harvard student who devised the event, the Davis Cup has grown from a single match between the USA and Great Britain to one of the largest and most prestigious team events in world tennis. Originally, Australia competed with New Zealand as Australasia. The two countries entered as separate teams from 1923.

Since 1981, the Cup has been sponsored and now carries prize money; more than 16 countries have been brought into the competition. Currently 85 countries compete.

DAVIS CUP FINALS SINCE 1983

Year	Venue	Result	Score
1983	Melbourne, Australia	Australia def. Sweden	3–2
1984	Gothenburg, Sweden	Sweden def. USA	4–1
1985	Munich, West Germany	Sweden def. West Germany	3–2
1986	Melbourne, Australia	Australia def. Sweden	3–2
1987	Gothenburg, Sweden	Sweden def. India	5–0
1988	Gothenburg, Sweden	West Germany def. Sweden	4–1
1989	Stuttgart, West Germany	West Germany def. Sweden	3–2
1990	St Petersburg, USA	USA def. Australia	3–2
1991	Lyon, France	France def. USA	3–1
1992	Forth Worth, USA	USA def. Switzerland	3–1
1993	Dusseldorf, Germany	Germany def. Australia	4–1
1994	Moscow, Russia	Sweden def. Russia	4–1
1995	Moscow, Russia	USA def. Russia	3–2

OUTSTANDING PLAYERS

EVONNE CAWLEY   Evonne Cawley (nee Goolagong) was one of the first Australian aboriginals to achieve worldwide sporting acclaim. She won the women's singles title at Wimbledon twice, once under her maiden name in 1971 (defeating Margaret Court) and then again in 1980, when she staged a remarkable comeback after years away from the international tennis circuit.

MARGARET COURT   Margaret Court (nee Smith) is widely regarded as Australia's greatest woman tennis player. In 1956, at age 18, she became the youngest Australian to win the Australian Open women's singles, going on to win the title a record 11 times between 1960 and 1973. Court also holds the Australian record for the most Wimbledon wins, taking the women's singles three times in 1963, 65 and 70. In 1970, she became the first Australian woman to win the grand slam.

With four wins, Court and Ken Fletcher also share the record for the most Wimbledon mixed doubles titles (including the grand slam) with Owen Davidson and Billie Jean King. Court has also won the Wimbledon women's doubles twice; with Leslie Turner in 1964 and with Jan Tegart in 1965.

ROD LAVER   Rod Laver, nicknamed the 'Rockhampton Rocket' holds the Australian record for winning the most men's singles titles at Wimbledon, in 1961, 1962, 1968 and 1969. He has also won five Wimbledon doubles titles, in 1961, 1962, 1968, 1969 and 1971. He was also the first Australian to win a singles grand slam in 1962.

JOHN NEWCOMBE   John Newcombe, has won the men's singles at Wimbledon three times, in 1967, 1970 and 1971, as well as forming the most successful Australian doubles partnership ever with Tony Roche. Together they won the Wimbledon doubles five times, in 1965, 1968, 1969, 1970 and 1974.

KEN ROSEWALL   In 1953, at age 18, Ken Rosewall became the youngest player to win the Australian men's singles title. In the same year, he won the French Open and, with Lew Hoad, the doubles titles for both the French and Australian tournaments. In 1972, he became the oldest player to win the Australian men's singles title at the age of 37, only retiring from major tournament tennis in 1979.

Netball

Netball is the most popular women's sport in Australia. It is estimated that more than one million women play the sport. In 1980, women's netball was incorporated into the Australian Institute of Sport in Canberra.

England failed to win in an official Test match against the Australian team until 1981. In the prestigious World Netball Championships, the Australian team is yet to finish without a place.

AUSTRALIA'S WORLD NETBALL CHAMPIONSHIPS RECORD

Year	Venue	Winner	Runner-up
1963	Eastbourne, England	Australia	New Zealand
1967	Perth, Australia	New Zealand	Australia
1971	Kingston, Jamaica	Australia	New Zealand
1975	Auckland, New Zealand	Australia	England
1979	Port of Spain, Trinidad	Australia/New Zealand/Trinidad (tie)*	
1983	Singapore	Australia	New Zealand
1987	Glasgow, Scotland	New Zealand	Australia/Trinidad*
1994	Sydney, Australia	Australia	New Zealand
1995	Birmingham, England	Australia	South Africa

* No final was played in 1979 and 1987.

OUTSTANDING PLAYERS

Joyce Brown was captain of the first world championship team in 1963 and now coaches Australian teams for international competition. Wilma Shakespeare was also a member of the first world championship team and became head coach at the Australian Institute of Sport in 1981.

Anne Sargeant has become a household name in Australia since netball began receiving more media coverage. One of Australia's leading senior players since 1978, she captained Australia between 1983 and 1987.

Hockey

Men's Hockey

The men's national hockey league was formed in 1991. Eight teams from Sydney, Melbourne, Brisbane, Adelaide, Perth, Canberra, Tasmania and North Queensland compete. Internationally, Australia competes in the Four Nations Tournament, the Manning Cup (against New Zealand), the Champions Trophy, the Hockey World Cup and the Olympic Games. Australia has won three silver medals (in 1968, 1976 and 1992) and two bronze medals (1964 and 1996) at the Olympics.

Men's Hockey World Cup Results

Year	Venue	Winner	Runner-up
1971	Barcelona, Spain	Pakistan	Spain
1973	Amsterdam, Netherlands	India	Netherlands
1975	Kuala Lumpur, Malaysia	India	Pakistan
1978	Buenos Aires, Argentina	Pakistan	Netherlands
1972	Bombay, India	Pakistan	West Germany
1986	London, England	Australia	England
1990	Lahore, Pakistan	Netherlands	Pakistan
1994	Sydney, Australia	Pakistan	Netherlands

Outstanding Players

Ric Charlesworth is one of Australia's best ever men's hockey players. He played 227 internationals for Australia and was captain of the victorious 1986 World Cup team. He took over as coach of the Australian women's hockey team in 1993. Mark Hagar has been another key figure in Australian men's hockey in recent years.

Women's Hockey

Women's hockey began in Australia in 1901, around the same time as men's hockey. However, while the men's first hockey team was sent to the Olympics in 1956, women's hockey was not played at the Olympics until the 1980 Moscow Games, which Australia boycotted.

It was not until 1984 that the Australian women's hockey team finally competed in the Olympic Games, coming a tied third with the United States, but subsequently losing the penalty shootout for the bronze medal. In 1988, at the Los Angeles Games, the Australian team won the gold medal. They repeated their success at the 1996 Atlanta Games.

THE WORLD CUP

Australia has entered the World Cup five out of the seven times it has been held. Apart from the Olympics, it is the most prestigious hockey competition in the world and is held between Olympiads.

WOMEN'S HOCKEY WORLD CUP RESULTS

Date	Venue	Winner	Runner-up
1974	Mandelieu, France	Netherlands	Argentina
1976	West Berlin, Germany	West Germany	Argentina
1978	Madrid, Spain	Netherlands	West Germany
1981	Buenos Aires, Argentina	West Germany	Netherlands
1983	Kuala Lumpur, Malaysia	Netherlands	Canada
1987	Amsterdam, Netherlands	Netherlands	West Germany
1990	Sydney, Australia	Netherlands	Australia
1994	Dublin, Republic of Ireland	Australia	Argentina

OUTSTANDING PLAYERS

Diane Gorman (nee Dowd) is probably Australia's most famous hockey player. She played for Australia between 1972 and 1980, four times as captain and twice as vice-captain. In 1980, she was the only Australian selected in the World Eleven which competed in the International Associations Jubilee Tournament in Scotland.

Other long-serving women hockey players include Miss E. Tazewell (1925–1936) and May Campbell (1933–1948). Sharon Buchanan (1980–1993), formerly captain of the Australian women's hockey team, holds the record for the most appearances with 187 games. Jackie Pereira (1986–1996) holds the record for the most number of goals scored by an Australian women's player, with 109 goals.

Some of the most well known players of recent times include Jackie Pereira, Rochelle Hawkes, Alyson Annan and Nova Peris-Kneebone, winner of the 1997 Young Australian of the Year.

Index

A

Ablett, Gary, 538, 539–40
Aboriginal and Torres Strait Islander
  arts, 491, 494–5, 505
  Central Australian Aborigines Media Association (CAAMA), 462
  seasons, 19–20
  television, 462
Aboriginal and Torres Strait Islander Arts Board, 494; see Australia Council
Aboriginal and Torres Strait Islander Commission (ATSIC), 283, 287, 403, 404, 494
Aboriginal Islander Dance Theatre, 494–5
Aboriginal peoples and Torres Strait Islanders, 43, 84, 85, 86, 87, 88, 131, 150, 158, 165, 172, 197–8, 201–3, 206, 208, 212–13, 215, 231, 283–5, 287, 536, 547
  European contact, 201–3, 212–13
  Deaths in Custody Royal Commission, 229, 230
  education, 423, 424, 432–3
  employment and training, 442–3
  health, 403–4
  Indigenous Land Fund, 284
  land rights, 224, 225, 227, 232–3
  Myall Creek Massacre, 212–13
  population, 167–8, 201
  resistance, 202
  right to vote, 215
  rock art, 59, 149, 150, 152, 157, 158, 197, 232
  Tasmanian, 202
Abrakurrie Cave, 59

acacias, 82, 85
acorn-worms, 119
acquired immune deficiency syndrome (AIDS), 407, 412–13
ACTU see Australian Council of Trade Unions
Adams, Phillip, 534
Adelaide, 8, 24–5
adelie penguin, 102
Administrative Appeals Tribunal, 285–6, 286
Admiral's Cup, 574
'Advance Australia Fair', 228
Advance Bank, 305, 316
advertising, 482
AFI see Australian Film Institute
age pension, 189–90
agriculture, 31, 49, 56, 62, 64, 68, 72, 92, 93, 143, 203–4, 212–13, 302, 318–23, 414
AIDS see acquired immune deficiency syndrome
AIF see Australian Imperial Force
air transport, 230, 351–4
Air Force see Royal Australian Air Force
airports, 274, 353
Albert Edward Range, 68
Albert's lyrebird, 110
alcohol, 300, 309, 409, 415
  drink driving, 409
  random breath testing (RBT), 409
Alice Springs, 6, 9, 16, 68, 207
allowances see pensions
America's Cup, 227, 573–4, 575
amphibians, 115, 143, 144
Anglican Church see Church of England
angophoras, 81–2
Annan, Alison, 590
Anne-A-Kananda Cave, 59, 60
annual ryegrass, 93
Ansett Airlines, 353
Antarctic prion, 103
Antarctica, 19, 31, 32, 37, 43, 44, 101, 104, 147, 158, 195, 200

anthozoa, 123–4
anti-Chinese riots, 209–10
ants, 131
ANZACs, 217, 219
ANZUS Treaty, 222, 228, 357
apple gums see angophoras
aquaculture, 324
arachnids, 125–7
Arafura Sea, 39, 47
Archibald Prize, 506–8
area of Australia, 37–8
Arkaroola, 56
Armistice, 218
Armstrong, Duncan, 581
Army see Australian Army
Arnhem Land, 42, 66, 161
artesian water, 49, 71–2
arthropods, 125–33
artificial lakes, 70
arts, 487–526
  festivals, 493
  funding, 490, 492, 494, 495, 496, 504, 514, 521
  major organisations, 490–3
Arts Council of Australia, 492–3
ash trees, 80–1
Ash Wednesday, 12, 227
Ashmore Reef, 46, 160
Asia–Pacific Economic Co-operation (APEC), 227, 307
ASIO see Australian Security Intelligence Organisation
Atherton Tableland, 55–6, 69
athletics, 534–7
Attorney-General, 231, 269, 281, 289, 388–9, 389, 391, 496
AUSSAT, 228, 337, 388
AUSTEL see Australian Telecommunications Authority
Austrade see Australian Trade Commission
Australasian Country Music Awards, 520–1
Australia and New Zealand Banking Group (ANZ), 304, 305, 315

Australia Council, 490–2, 494
Australia Day, 201
Australia Post, 335, 337, 340
Australian Airlines, 230, 352
Australian Alps, 6, 7, 8, 53, 55, 115
Australian and New Zealand Army Corps see ANZACs
Australian Antarctic Territory, 44
Australian Army, 359, 360, 361, 362, 363, 364, 372–8, 381
Australian Ballet, 491–3, 514
Australian Broadcasting Authority, 449, 457, 481–2
Australian Broadcasting Corporation (ABC), 449, 454–6, 503, 515
Australian brush-turkey, 105
Australian Bureau of Statistics, 165, 344
Australian bustard, 106
Australian Chamber of Manufactures, 331
Australian citizenship, 182
Australian Competition and Consumer Commission, 291
Australian Conciliation and Arbitration Commission (ACAC), 185, 278, 310
Australian conger eel, 118
Australian Conservation Foundation, 147
Australian Council of Trades Unions (ACTU), 226, 311, 312
Australian Defence Force Academy see Defence Force
Australian Defence Force Command see Defence Force
Australian Democrats, 259, 263
Australian Drivers' Championship, 568

Australian Elizabethan Theatre Trust, 493, 514, 518
Australian Farmers' Federal Organisation, 262
Australian Federal Police (AFP), 273–5
Australian Film Institute (AFI), 497
awards, 497–503
Australian Film Commission (AFC), 497, 504
Australian Film, Television and Radio School (AFTRS), 496–7
Australian Fishing Zone (AFZ), 40
Australian Football League (AFL), 537–41
Australian Hearing Service, 419
Australian hobby falcon, 105
Australian Imperial Force (AIF), 217
Australian Industrial Registry, 279
Australian Industrial Relations Commission, 185
Australian Institute of Health and Welfare, 404
Australian Institute of Sport (AIS), 529, 588, 530
Australian International Development Assistance Bureau, 383
Australian Jockey Club (AJC), 564
Australian kestrel, 105
Australian magpie, 111
Australian Manufacturing Council, 330
Australian Manufacturing Workers' Union, 484
Australian National Line (ANL), 350
Australian Nature Conservation Agency (ANCA), 145–6, 160
Australian Golf Open, 557
Australian Tennis Open, 586
Australian pelican, 103
Australian Press Council, 482

Australian Publishers' Association (APA), 490, 526
Australian Quarantine and Inspection Service, 405
Australian raven, 111
Australian Recording Industry Association (ARIA), 515
awards, 515–18
Australian republic, 227, 231, 233–4
Australian Rugby League (ARL), 541–3
Australian Rules (football), 536–41
Australian salmon, 118
Australian Secret Intelligence Service (ASIS), 227, 286, 391
Australian Securities Commission, 318
Australian Security Intelligence Organisation (ASIO), 223, 226, 286, 292, 388–92
Australian Sports Drug Agency, 529, 530
Australian Sports Commission, 529, 530
Australian Telecommunications Authority (AUSTEL), 335–6
Australian Touring Car Championship, 568
Australian Tourism Commission, 330
Australian Trade Commission (Austrade), 308
Australian/Vogel Literary Award, 524
Australian Wool Corporation, 230
AUSTROADS, 342
AUSTUDY, 434
aviation, 31, 32, 33, 221, 230, 330, 351–4
Awgie Awards, 486
Ayers Rock see Uluru

B
balance of payments, 309
Ballarat, 208, 209
Ballarat Reform League, 209
Balmain bug, 124

banded anteater, 97
banded hare-wallaby, 96, 135
bandicoots, 96
Bank of New South Wales see Westpac
banking, 221, 226, 228, 299, 230, 301, 304–6, 315, 316, 317
Banks, Joseph, 82, 200
banksias, 82–3, 85, 196
Barassi, Ron, 540
Barkly Tableland, 56
barn owls, 108
Barossa Valley, 16, 322
barrier beach coasts, 38, 39, 42
Bass Strait, 39, 47, 326, 327
Barton, Sir Edmund, 214, 216, 238, 248
Bathurst, 6, 16, 206, 207, 208, 341
Bathurst 1000, 566–8, 569
bats, 98–9
beaches, 39, 42, 140
beautiful firetail, 111
Beazley, Kim, 250
bêche-de-mer, 46
beef, 299, 318, 320, 321; see also livestock
bees, 131
beetles, 132
Bendigo, 209
benefits see pensions
Bennelong, 202–3
Bennelong Point, 202
Bernier Island, 96, 97
Bertrand, John, 575
bettongs, 96
Beven, Brad, 579
Bicentennial, 229
bilby, 98, 135
Bimberi Peak, 52, 53, 54
Bimberi-Franklin Brindabella Ranges, 47
biodiversity, 140, 143–4, 148
biomass, 328
bird-eating spiders, 125
birds of paradise, 109
birds, 45, 46, 82, 83, 100–11, 135, 143, 144, 196, 197
birds of prey, 104–5
births, 169–71
birth rate, 165, 169–70
fertility, 170
bitou bush, 93

bivalves, 121
Bjelke Petersen, Sir Joh, 229, 262
black bean tree, 83
black cockatoo, 84
black falcon, 105
black swan, 104, 134, 157
black-backed butcherbird, 111
blackberry, 92–3
black-lip oyster, 121
black-necked stork see jabiru
Blaxland, Gregory, 205
Bligh, William, 204
bloodwood gums, 80
Blue Lake, 52, 69
Blue Mountains, 6, 55, 87, 149, 205–6
blue petrel, 103
blue pointer shark, 116, 134
bluebottle see Portuguese man-of-war
blue-faced finch, 111
blue-ringed octopus, 122, 134
blue-tongue lizard, 114
blue-winged kookaburra, 109
bony fishes, 117–18
boobies, 103
Boon, David, 555–6
Border, Allan, 556
boronias, 85
Botany Bay, 200, 201
bottlebrushes, 83, 85
boundaries, state and territory, 46–8
Bourke, 4, 14
bowerbirds, 109–10
box jellyfish, 123, 133
box trees, 80
boxing, 529, 549–51
Boyle, Raelene, 533
Brabham, Jack, 568
brachiopods, 196
Brahe, William, 81, 207
Brisbane, 4, 7, 15, 16, 23–4, 32
brittle stars, 120
broad-faced potoroo, 96, 135
broad-shelled river turtle, 112
Brock, Peter, 569
brolga crane, 106
Broome, 4, 9, 10, 99
Brown, Joyce, 588

Brownlow Medal, 537
Bruce, Stanley
 Melbourne, 248, 262
brush-tailed bettong,
 96–7, 135
Buchan Caves, 58
Buddhists, 183
budgerigar, 107
budget, federal, 187, 399
buffalo, 100
bugs, 129
building societies, 305,
 306
building industry, 301
bull shark, 116
Bungle Bungle Range, 56
Bunton, Haydn, 540
Burdekin River, 67
Bureau of Meteorology,
 8, 12, 31–3
Burke and Wills, 81,
 207–8
Burke, Matthew, 546
burrowing bettong, 96,
 135
buses, 229, 344–5
bushfires, 12–13, 31, 32,
 80, 227, 231, 371
bushrangers, 58, 210
butcherbirds, 111
butterflies, 130–1
button-quails, 105

C
cable television see pay
 television
caffeine, 408
Cainozoic Era, 197
Cairns, 8, 12, 13, 56
Cairns, Dr Jim, 225
Calwell, Arthur, 223, 260
Cambridge Gulf, 68
Campbell, Keith, 571
Campese, David, 546–7
Canberra, 7, 18, 29–30,
 52, 216, 240–1
cancer, 173, 174, 404,
 408, 409, 414
cane toad, 115
cannabis, 409
Canning Basin, 57, 72
Cape Barren goose, 104
Cape Barren Island, 40
Cape Byron, 38, 52
Cape Howe, 46
Cape Parsley, 41
Cape York birdwing, 42,
 131
Cape York Peninsula, 38,
 40, 42, 49, 50, 55, 66,

86, 95, 105, 109, 148,
 161, 199, 200
carer pension, 190
Carruthers, Jimmy, 550
Carruthers, Kel, 571
cars, 343–4
Cartier Island, 46
cartilaginous fishes,
 115–17, 136
cash management trusts,
 306
Cash, Pat, 229
cassowaries, 100–1
Castrol Six Hour Race,
 570
casuarinas, 83
catbirds, 109–10
Catchpole, Ken, 547
catfish, 118
Catholic Church, 183
cattle see livestock
cattle ticks, 126
Caulfield Cup, 563
caves, 41, 56, 58–61,
 149, 150, 155, 157,
 158
Cawley, Evonne, 587
cays, 40, 41, 46, 160
Cazaly, Roy, 540
Census, 165, 175, 176,
 182, 214
centipedes, 127
Central Australian
 Standard Time, 48
Central Basin, 49
central hare-wallaby, 96,
 135
cephalopods, 122
cereals, 318, 319–20
CES see Commonwealth
 Employment Service
chamber magistrates, 287
Chamberlain, Lindy, 229,
 230
Channel Country, 50,
 153, 154
Chappell, Greg, 553,
 556
Chappell, Ian, 556
charities, 301, 302,
 313–14
Charlesworth, Ric, 589
Chifley, Joseph Benedict
 (Ben), 220, 221, 248,
 260
child support, 272
 Child Support Agency,
 272
childcare, 264, 312,
 419–20

Children's Book Council
 Awards, 524–5
children's python, 112
Chillagoe-Mugana-
 Rockwood-Redcap
 caves, 58
Chillagoe-Mungana
 National Park, 58
Chipp, Don, 263
chitons, 120
chlorofluorocarbons
 (CFCs), 143
Christmas Island, 45,
 146, 166, 273, 423
Church of England, 183
Churchill, Clive, 544–5
cicadas, 129
City to Surf, 535
Clarke, Ron, 535–6
Classification Board, 496
classification, film,
 videos, publications
 and computer games,
 496
Clean Up Australia Day,
 142
climate, 1–33, 44, 79,
 142–3
climatic data for capital
 cities, 21–30
climatic discomfort, 12,
 17
Clive Churchill Medal,
 543
Cloncurry, 17
cloud, 6
club mosses, 91
Clunies-Ross, John, 44–5
coal, 142, 196, 221, 307,
 325, 326, 347
coastal lakes, 69
coastline, 38–42
cocaine, 409–10
Cockatoo Island, 367
cockatoos, 107
cockroaches, 128
Cocos (Keeling) Islands,
 44–5, 166, 216, 410,
 423
coelenterates, 122–4, 196
colonisation, 201–3
common brushtail
 possum, 98
common death adder,
 112, 134
common diving-petrel,
 103
common koel, 108
common scaly-foot
 lizard, 114

common wombat, 98
Commonwealth Bank of
 Australia, 216, 299,
 304, 305, 315
Commonwealth
 Employment Service
 (CES), 188, 441, 442,
 443
Commonwealth
 Environment
 Protection Agency, 146
Commonwealth Games,
 532–4, 535, 550, 551,
 581–2
Commonwealth
 Meteorology Research
 Centre, 32
Commonwealth
 Scientific and
 Industrial Research
 Organisation (CSIRO),
 32, 33, 79, 323
communicable diseases,
 410–13
communications, 211,
 333–41
communism, 221–2,
 222, 223, 260, 311–12
Communist Party of
 Australia, 222, 312
Community Cultural
 Development Fund see
 Australia Council
community governments
 see local government
community legal centres,
 287
companies, largest 100,
 315–17
Compass Airlines, 230,
 352
Conciliation and
 Arbitration,
 Commonwealth Court
 of, 215, 310, 311
cone shells, 121, 133
conscription, 217–18,
 223, 259–60
conservation, 80,
 139–41, 143–4,
 145–8, 161
conservation areas, 146
Constitution, Australian,
 228, 233, 237–8, 241,
 242, 246, 269
Constitutions, State, 254
consumer affairs, 291
Consumer Price Index
 (CPI), 177, 309
continental islands, 40–1

continental shelf, 40
convict settlement, 201, 203–5
Cook, Captain James, 43, 98, 200, 201
Cook, Sir Joseph, 248
coolibah, 81, 153
Cooper Creek, 81, 207, 208
co-operative housing societies, 305
coral, 40, 44, 46, 123–4, 196
coral reefs, 40–1, 50, 117, 148, 153, 157, 160
Coral Sea, 39, 146
Coral Sea Islands Territory, 19, 45
cormorants, 103
Cornelsen, Greg, 546
Corra-Lynne Cave, 59, 60
corroboree frog, 115
corruption, 275–7
cost of living, 177–8
Cottee, Kay, 575
cotton, 68, 307, 323
cotton pygmy-goose, 104
coucals, 107–8
councils see local government
Country Party see National Party of Australia
County Courts, 272
Court, Margaret, 587
Cowen, Sir Zelman, 226, 249
Cox, William, 206
Cradle Mountain, 54
Cradle Mountain/Lake St Clair National Park, 69, 158
cranes, 106
Crapp, Lorraine, 581
crater lakes, 52, 56, 69
crayfish, 124
credit co-operatives, 305–6
Cresswell, Captain R., 367
crested tern, 106
cricket, 529, 552–7
crickets, 128
crime, 290, 292–6
crimson finch, 111
crimson rosella, 107
crocodiles, 114–15, 133, 157
Croesus Cave, 59

Cronin, Mick, 545
crops, 5, 11, 14, 15, 64, 68, 93, 319
cross-media limits, 450–1
crown of thorns, 119
crows, 111
crustaceans, 124, 324
CSIRO see Commonwealth Scientific and Industrial Research Organisation
cuckoos, 107–8
cunjevoi, 119
currawongs, 111
Curry-Kenny, Lisa, 533
Curtin, John, 220, 248, 260
Cuthbert, Betty, 532, 534, 535, 536
Cutta Cutta Cave, 59
cuttlefish, 122
cycads, 87, 196
cyclones, 3, 4, 5, 10, 13, 19, 31, 32, 45, 383

D
dairy industry, 56, 307, 318, 320
Dally M Awards, 543
Dampier, William, 200
dams, 70, 72–3
damselflies, 128
dance, 489, 493–5
Dance Fund see Australia Council
dangerous animals, 133–4
Darling Downs, 6, 57
Darling, Governor Ralph, 206, 207
Darwin, 4, 5, 7, 8, 13, 18, 28–9, 32
Darwin, Charles, 44
Date, Reg, 548
Davis Cup, 586
daylight saving, 48
de Castella, Robert, 535, 536
de facto relationships, 174, 190, 191
Deakin, Alfred, 215, 248, 373
deaths, 171–4
  infant mortality, 169–70, 172
deer, 100
defence, 31, 226, 301, 355–92

Defence Force Academy, 363, 365, 371, 377, 380
Command, 366–7
Defence Forces Executive, 382–3
Defence Intelligence Organisation, 385–6
Defence Satellite Network, 386
Defence Science and Technology Organisation (DSTO), 386
Defence Signals Directorate (DSD) 385, 391
dementia, senile, 415, 417
Democratic Labor Party (DLP) 260, 312
Democrats see Australian Democrats
demographics, 165–9
Depression (1890–1893), 210, 213–14, 310
Depression, Great, 218–19, 226, 321
deregulation, 228, 230, 299, 352
desert, 42, 51, 57, 64–5, 58, 66, 150, 154, 155, 157
desert rat-kangaroo, 96, 135
Derwent River, 51, 68, 70, 351
diamonds, 307, 325
dicotyledons, 89
Dig Tree, 81
dingos, 99
dinosaurs, 196
Director-General of Security, 389
Dirk Hartog Island, 38, 199
disabled people, 188, 395, 418–19, 445
disabled sport, 530
discovery of Australia, 198–200
discrimination, 281–3
distance education centres, 427–8
distances, road, 342–3
District Courts, 231, 272
diving-petrels, 103
divorce, 174, 175, 224, 271–2

Document Exchange (DX), 340–1
dole see pensions and benefits
dollarbird, 109
domestic production account, 303
Doohan, Mick, 571
Dorre Island, 96, 97
double dissolution, 216, 225, 226, 246
doves, 106–7
dragonflies, 128
dragons, 113
drink driving, 409
droughts, 11, 231, 320, 321
drugs, 274, 290, 293, 395, 398–9, 408–10
  in sport, 529–30
dry land salinity, 62
ducks, 105
dugongs, 99, 144, 157
Dukes-Fairy-Royal-Federal caves, 58
Dumaresq River, 46, 74
Durack Range, 56
dusky moorhen, 106
dust storms, 14
Dutch East India Company, 199
Dyer, Jack, 540

E
eagles, 105, 134
earthquakes, 53, 229
earwigs, 128
East India Company, 44, 200
Eastern Australian Standard Time, 48
eastern brown snake, 112
eastern hare-wallaby, 96, 135
eastern highlands, 49, 197
eastern pygmy possum, 98
eastern rosella, 107
eastern tiger snake, 112–13
Eastern Uplands, 49
echidnas, 95–6
echinoderms, 119
ecologically sustainable development, 139
economy, 221, 297–332
ecotourism, 141
education, 185, 224, 225, 301, 309, 312, 423–38

eels, 118
Eighty Mile Beach, 42
El Nino, 11
elderly care, 395, 416–17
elections, 43, 209, 214, 215, 218, 221, 223, 226, 227, 231, 253, 254, 255–8, 260, 261, 262, 263
electoral systems, 257–8
electrical storms, 13–14
electricity, 301
ELICOS (English Language Intensive Courses for Overseas Students), 432
eligibility to vote, 256
Ella, Mark, Gary and Glen, 547
Elliot, Herb, 534, 536
emancipation, 204
Emergency Management Australia, 383
employment, 183–4, 186, 309, 423, 424, 441–6
overtime, 184
women in the workforce, 185–6
Employment Assistance Australia, 442
Employment, Education, Training and Youth Affairs, Department of (DEETYA), 423–4, 441, 494
emus, 100–1
Endangered Species and Feral Pests Programs, 145
Endangered Species Protection Act, 144
endangered vertebrate fauna, 135–6
Endeavour, 200
Endeavour Strait, 38
energy, environment 326–8
enterprise bargaining, 312
environment, 92, 93, 137–62
Environment, Sport and Territories, Department of, 146
environmental crime, 293
environmental issues, 139–44
environmental organisations, 139, 145–8

ephiphytes, 79, 86, 87, 90
Ermerton, Bill, 535
estuaries, 39, 68
estuarine crocodiles *see* saltwater crocodiles
ethnic mix, 165, 180
eucalypts, 79, 80–81, 97
Eucumbene River, 67, 74
Eucla Basin, 72
Eureka Stockade, 209
evaporation, 10, 64, 79
Evans, George, 205–6
Evatt, Dr Herbert Vere, 222, 260
Exit Cave, 59, 60
Experiment Farm, 204, 318
exploration, 198–200, 205–8
exports, 302, 307, 308–9, 318, 319, 321, 322, 323
External Territories, Australian, 43–6, 273
extremities of Australia, 38
Eye in the Dark *see* Kuru Muna
Eyre, John Edward, 206

F
facsimiles, 337–8
Fadden, Arthur William, 220, 248, 262
fairy penguin, 101
fairy-wrens, 110
falcons, 105
false vampire bat *see* ghost bat
Famechon, Johnny
families, 171, 175–6
family law, 174–5, 269, 271–2
Family Court of Australia, 271–2, 288
Farmer, Graham 'Polly', 540
Farrer, William, 319
fauna, 95–136, 139, 141, 143–4, 146, 195, 196, 197, 198
faunal emblems, 134
fauna extinction rates, 143–4
feather stars, 120
Federal Court of Australia, 234, 269, 270–1, 272, 277, 279, 285

federal ministry, 249–50
federal shadow ministry, 250–1
Federal Supreme Court *see* High Court
federation, 165, 212, 214–16, 233, 237, 238–40, 244, 292, 311, 345, 367, 372
Fenech, Jeff, 551
feral cats, 144
feral mammals, 100, 144
ferns, 79, 91
ferries, 350–1
fierce snake, 113
Film Australia, 503–4
film, 489, 490, 495–504
finance, government, 300–1
fine arts, 489, 504–13
First Fleet, 165, 178, 201, 208, 211, 229, 318, 322
Fischer, Timothy, 249, 263
Fisher, Andrew, 216, 217, 248, 259
fishes, 115–20, 133, 136, 143, 144, 196
fishing, 324–5
Fitzgerald Inquiry, 229
Fitzroy River, 67
flag, Australian, 215
flannel flowers, 89
flatworms, 133
fleas, 130
flies, 130
Flinders Island, 39–40
Flinders Ranges, 50, 56
Flinders River, 68
Flintoff-King, 535, 536
floods, 11–12, 13, 14, 18, 31, 32
flora, 79–94, 139, 141, 143, 144, 146, 196, 198, 411
floral emblems, 94
Flying Surgeon Service, 407
fog, 6–7
Forde, Francis Michael, 248
foreign affairs, 301, 390
Foreign Affairs and Trade, Department of, 390
foreign debt, 299–300
foreign trade, 307–9
forest industries, 143, 323, 411, 414
fork-tailed swift, 108

fowl-like birds, 105–6
foxes, 100, 144
Franklin River, 147, 148, 158
Fraser, Dawn, 532, 581
Fraser, Eliza, 41
Fraser Island, 41, 63–4, 153, 162
Fraser, (John) Malcolm, 225, 226, 249, 261–2, 263
fraud, 274, 290, 292, 293
freckled duck, 104
Free Traders, 214, 216
Freedom of Information, 286
Freeman, Cathy, 536
freestyle skiing, 532
freight movement, 347
freshwater crocodiles, 115
frilled lizard, 113
frogmouths, 108
frost, 6, 18
fruit industry, 15, 318, 322
fulmars, 102
fungi, 90
funnel-web spiders, 125
Fusion Party, 216

G
galah, 107
gales, 15, 31
Gall, Stephen, 572
Gallagher, Jackie, 580
Gallipoli, 217
gang gang cockatoo, 107, 134
Garden Island Dockyard, 381, 382
Gardiner, Frank, 210
Gardner, Wayne, 572
gas, natural, 142, 301, 307, 315, 316, 317, 325, 326–7, 345
Gascoyne River, 68
Gasnier, Reg, 544, 545
gastropods, 121
geckoes, 113–14
geese, 104
General Motors-Holden (GMH), 344
general practitioners, 396, 402–3
geography, 35–76
Georgina-Daly Basin, 72
ghost bat, 99
giant kangaroos, 198
giant sensitive plant, 93

Gibson Desert, 51, 65, 66, 69, 156, 161
Gippsland, 50, 55
Gippsland Lakes, 70, 152
glacial lakes, 69
Glasshouse Mountains, 52, 55
global radiation, 9, 10
glossy ibis, 104
Gloucester Tree, 81
goannas, 113, 114
goats, 100, 144
gold, 178, 208–10, 211, 307, 316, 317, 321, 325, 342
gold rushes, 208–10
gold-lip oyster, 121
golf, 557–9
Gondwanaland, 195, 196
Goolie Cave, 58
Gorton, John Grey, 224, 248, 249, 261
goshawks, 105
Gould, John, 107
Gould, Shane, 532, 581
Gouldian finch, 111, 135
Gould's petrel, 103
government, 235–66; see also parliament, federal and state
government broadcasting, 449, 454–6
government expenditure, 301
government revenue, 300
Governors-General, 45, 214, 225, 226, 233, 237, 240, 242, 246, 251–3, 256, 260, 269, 278, 283, 288, 290, 376
Graham, David, 559
Grampians, The, 50, 55, 152
Grand Prix, Australian FIM Motorcycle (500 cc), 570, 572
Grand Prix, Australian Formula One, 564–6, 569
grapes, 318
graptolites, 196
grass trees, 88
grass-finches, 110–11
grasshoppers, 128
Great Artesian Basin, 49, 71, 72, 75
Great Australian Bight, 41, 47, 49, 51, 57, 207

Great Barrier Reef, 40–1, 45, 50, 99, 119, 139, 147, 161
  Marine Park, 40–1, 147
Great Dividing Range, 42, 46, 49, 50, 51, 55–6, 66, 67, 196, 211
Great Lake, 70
Great Sandy Desert, 42, 51, 57, 65, 66, 69, 161
Great Victoria Desert, 50, 57, 65, 66, 69, 155, 156, 161
great white shark, 116, 134, 136, 144
great-crested grebe, 101
greater glider, 98
grebes, 101
Green Island, 41
green pygmy-goose, 104
greenhouse effect, 30–1, 142–3, 146, 147, 345
Greening Australia, 146–7
Greenpeace, 147–8
Greens, Tasmanian, 259
Greenway, Francis, 205
grevilleas, 85
grey butcherbird, 111
grey nurse shark, 116, 136
grey teal duck, 104
grey-backed storm-petrel, 103
grey-headed flying fox, 98
Griffin, Walter Burley, 216, 241
Grimmett, Clarrie, 556
Grose, Major Francis, 204
Gross Domestic Product, 300, 302, 303–4, 318
gross farm product, 302, 303
gross national expenditure, 302
gross non-farm product, 302, 303
ground water, 70, 71–2
Gulf Country, 42
Gulf of Carpentaria, 42, 47, 49, 68, 71, 75, 207
gulls, 106
gum trees see eucalypts

H
Haddon Corner, 47
hagfish, 119
hail, 5, 14–15
Haines, Janine, 263

hairy-nosed wombat, 98, 134
hakeas, 85
Hall, Ben, 210
hallucinogens, 410
hammerhead shark, 116, 134
Hare, Alexander, 44–5
Hargrave, Lawrence, 351
Hargraves, Edward, 208
harriers, 105
Hartog, Dirk, 199
Hasluck, Sir Paul Meernaa Cadwalla, 225, 253
hawk owls, 108
Hawke, Robert (Bob) James Lee, 226–7, 228, 230, 249, 261, 396
Hawkes, Rochelle, 590
Hawkesbury River, 63, 67, 150, 203
Hayden, William (Bill) George, 226, 253, 261
health, 169, 172, 178, 185, 224, 225, 264, 312, 314, 393–420
Health and Community Services, Department of, 395
health insurance, 224, 228, 314, 395–401
Heard Island, 43–4, 53, 160
heart disease, 173, 174, 409
heatwaves, 8, 17
helmeted honeyeater, 134, 135
Henley-on-Todd Regatta, 68
Hercules moth, 131
hermit crabs, 124
heroin, 410
Heron Island, 41
herons, 104
High Court of Australia, 216, 222, 227, 228, 230, 232, 234, 237, 269–70, 272, 279, 312
higher education, 423, 428–32, 435–6
  private educational institutions, 432
Higher Education Contribution Scheme (HECS), 428, 429–30
Hinkler, Bert, 352
Hiroshima, 220

history, 193–234
hoary-headed grebe, 101
Hobart, 16, 17, 27–8
hockey, 589–90
Holland, Stephen, 582
Holt, Harold Edward, 223, 224, 248, 261, 262
home and community care, 416–17
home nursing assistance, 416
homicide, 293, 294, 295, 296
honey, 318
honeyeaters, 110
Hopetoun, the Earl of, 214, 240, 252
horse racing, 559–64
horsetails, 91
hospitals, 301, 396, 397, 401–2
hostels for the aged, 417
hours, average weekly working, 183, 184
houseflies, 130
Houses of Assembly, 254
House of Representatives, 224, 225, 240, 241, 242–4, 259, 260, 262, 263
households, 176–8, 302, 344
housing, 178, 185, 301, 309, 328–9
Hovell, William, 67, 206
Howard, John Winston, 227, 231, 232, 249, 261, 262
Hughes, William (Billy) Morris, 217–18, 248, 259–60, 262
human rights, 281–3
Human Rights and Equal Opportunity Commission, 281–3
Hume, Hamilton, 67, 206
humidity, 8–9, 10, 12, 18, 32
humpback whale, 99, 135
Hunter River, 67
Hunter Valley, 6, 322
Huon River, 51
Hutton, Major General Sir Edward, 372
hydro-electric power, 67, 142, 328
hydrozoa, 122–3

I

ibises, 104
Ice Tube-Growling
Swallet Cave, 59, 60
immigration, 167, 168,
169, 178–81, 221,
423
Immigration, Local
Government and
Ethnic Affairs,
Department of, 390
immunisation, 264, 411
imports, 299, 302, 307
income, 176–7, 185, 299
income support, 443–4
income tax, 177, 300,
301
Independent
Commission Against
Corruption (ICAC),
275–7, 293
Indian Ocean, 16, 39,
42, 44, 45, 146
industrial disputes, 186,
187, 213–14, 221, 311
industrial relations, 185,
270, 278–9
Industrial Relations
Commission, 278–9,
281
Industrial Relations
Court of Australia, 279
IndyCar Racing, 566
insects, 127–32, 196
Insurance and
Superannuation
Commission, 306
insurance, 15, 302, 306
intelligence *see also* ASIO
gathering of, 274, 275,
292, 388, 390–2
military, 385–6, 391
internal migration, 182
International Agency for
Research on Cancer
(IARC), 408
International Antarctic
Meteorological
Research Centre, 32
introduced animals, 100,
144
introduced plants, 92–3
invertebrates, 143, 195
ironbarks, 80, 153
ironman championships,
576–7
ironwoman
championships, 577
irrigation, 10, 49, 62,
72, 73–6

irrigation salinity, 63, 74
Israelite Bay, 58

J

jabiru, 104
Jackson, Marjorie, 533,
534
Jane, Bob, 569
Janz, Willem, 199
jawless fishes, 119
jellyfish, 123, 133, 195
Jenolan Caves, 58, 60
Jervis Bay National Park,
146, 147
Jervis Bay Territory, 43,
46, 47, 273, 370, 372
Jews, 183
Jinmium, 197
jockeys, 560–3
John Coleman Medal, 538
Johnstone, Craig, 548
Joint Intelligence
Organisation (JIO), 391
Jones, Alan, 569
Jones, Michellie, 580

K

Kakadu National Park,
19, 93, 146, 148, 157,
159, 162
Kalgoorlie, 210
Kanakas, 211–12
Kangaroo Island, 50, 97,
148
kangaroo paw, 86, 94
kangaroos, 96–7, 134,
198
karri, 81, 157
Keating, Paul, 226, 227,
230, 231, 233, 249,
261
Keeling, Captain
William, 44
Kelly, Ned, 210
Kenny, Grant, 576
Kerr, Sir John Robert,
225, 253, 260, 261
Khemlani, Tirath, 225
Kiandra, 18, 55
Kiernan, Ian, 142
killer whale, 99
Kilmore Gap, 50
Kimberley Plateau, 56,
65
Kimberley region, 7, 12,
13, 51, 57, 65, 66, 68,
197, 210, 232
King George Sound, 206
King, Governor Philip
Gidley, 204

King Island, 39
King, John, 81, 207–8
King Leopold Range, 56
king penguin, 101–2
King Sound, 51
king parrot, 107
kingfishers, 108
Kingsford Smith, Sir
Charles, 352, 559, 576
kites, 105
koalas, 97, 134
Konrads, Ilsa, 582
Konrads, John, 582
kookaburras, 108–9, 134
Koonalda Cave, 59
Korean War, 222
Kosciuszko National
Park, 55, 58, 150
Kow Swamp, 198
Kubla Khan Cave, 59, 60
Kuru Muna, 386

L

Labor Party, the
Australian, 214, 215,
216, 217–18, 219,
220, 221, 222, 223,
224, 225, 226–7, 228,
229, 231, 244, 250–1,
255, 259–61, 311,
312, 314, 327, 367,
395, 396
labour force, 183–7, 309
laburnum, 91
lacewings, 129–30
Lachlan River, 67, 74
lagoons, 39, 93, 149,
151, 158
Lake Alexandrina, 51, 66
Lake Argyle, 70, 73
Lake Barrine, 56, 69
Lake Boemingen, 41
Lake Corangamite, 69
Lake Eacham, 56, 69
Lake Eucumbene, 70,
72, 118
Lake Eyre, 3, 51, 53, 66,
69, 70, 71, 75, 155,
161, 206
Lake Gairdner, 70, 155
Lake George, 69
Lake Illawarra, 70
Lake Jindabyne, 70
Lake Macquarie, 69
Lake Mungo, 150, 198
Lake St Clair, 69, 70, 73
Lake Tantangara, 70
Lake Talbingo, 70
Lake Torrens, 70, 155,
206

Lake Wellington, 70
lakes, 69–70, 93
Lakes Entrance, 42, 70
Lalor, Peter, 209
Lambing Flat Riot,
209–10
lamprey, 119
lancelets, 119
land degradation, 62–4
land reform, 213
landform structures,
49–52
Langlands, Graeme, 544,
545
lantana, 91, 93
laughing kookaburra,
108–9
Launceston, 16
Laver, Rod, 587
Law Reform
Commission, 289–90
law, 267–96, 301
Lawson, William, 205
Leadbetter's possum,
134, 135, 152
leaf-tailed gecko, 114
leathery turtle *see* luth
turtle
legal aid, 287–8
Legislative Assemblies,
43, 254
Legislative Councils,
253, 254
legless lizards, 113, 114
Lewis, Hayley, 533, 534,
582
Lewis, Wally, 545
Liberal Party of Australia,
216, 221, 224, 225,
226, 227, 231, 234,
244, 249–50, 255,
259, 261–2, 263, 312,
314, 327, 396
libraries, 264, 301, 489,
521–2
lichens, 90
life expectancy, 171,
172–3, 314
light rail, 348
lightning, 14, 15
Lihou Reef Nature
Reserve, 45, 160
lilies, 86
Lillee, Dennis, 556–7
lilly pilly, 84
literary awards, 523–6
Literature Fund *see*
Australia Council
little brown bat, 99
little crow, 111

little eagle, 105
little grebe, 101
little raven, 111
liverworts, 90
livestock, 11, 14, 17, 319, 320–1
lizards, 111, 113–14
Loans Affair, 225
lobsters, 124
local government, 141, 263–6, 301
Lockett, Tony, 538, 540–1
locusts, 129
long-billed corella, 107
long-nosed bandicoot, 96
long-tailed moray eel, 118
long-tailed ray, 117
Lord Howe Island, 103, 161
lorikeets, 107
luth turtle, 45, 112, 136
Lynagh, Michael, 546
Lyons, Joseph Aloysius, 219, 248, 260, 262
lyrebirds, 110, 152

M
Macarthur, John, 204, 318, 320–1
McDonald Islands, 43–4, 160
Macdonnell Ranges, 56, 68
McEwen, John, 248, 261, 262
McGill, Linda, 582
McMahon, Sir William, 249, 261
McPherson Range, 46, 110
Macquarie, Governor Lachlan, 205, 206, 341
Macquarie Harbour, 203
Macquarie Island, 19, 31, 33, 158
McWilliams, W. J., 262
Mabo, 227, 230, 232–3, 234
Mabo, Eddie, 232
macadamia, 84
mackerel shark see blue pointer shark
Madigan, Tony, 551
magazines, 449, 475–6
magellanic penguin, 102
magnificent riflebird, 109

magpie goose, 104
mainland beach coasts, 38, 39, 42
Major Organisations Fund see Australia Council
mako shark see blue pointer shark
malacostraca, 124
mallee, 16, 50, 51, 63, 80, 150, 151, 152, 155
mallee fowl, 105
mammals, 95–100, 135, 143, 144, 196, 197
maned duck, 104
mangroves, 39, 51, 153, 157, 158
manta ray, 117
manufacturing, 299, 307, 318, 330–1, 343, 344, 414
Manx shearwater, 103
marathon, 535
marathon swimming, 583
marine and estuarine protected areas see national parks
maritime strike, the great, 213–14
Maroney, Suzie, 582–3
marriages, 174–5
duration of, 175
marital status, 175
Marsh, Rod, 553, 557
Marshall, John, 582
Marshall, Kirstie, 632
marsupial lion, 198
marsupial mole, 97
marsupials, 82, 95, 96–8, 144, 197, 198
Mason, Colin, 263
Masters, Margaret, 559
Mawson, Douglas, 19, 31
Mawson Peak, 53
Mawson Station, 19, 31, 44
mayflies, 127–8
meals on wheels, 264, 407
meat, 299, 307, 320; see also beef
media, 315, 316, 317, 447–86, 489
regulatory bodies, 481–3
Media, Entertainment and Arts Alliance, 483–4

media ownership, 451–3, 476–81
Medibank, 224, 226, 314, 396
medical profession, 402–3
Medicare, 227, 228, 314, 396–8, 399, 400, 401, 403
Meekatharra, 9
melaleucas, 83–4
Melbourne, 4, 8, 14, 15, 22–3
Melbourne Cup, 559–63, 564
Meninga, Mal, 545
mental health, 414–16
Menzies, Sir Robert Gordon, 219, 221–3, 248, 261, 262, 311
merinos, 320, 321
Mesozoic Era, 196
Messenger, 'Dally', 544
meteorology, 12, 19, 31–3, 45
Miles Franklin Literary Award, 523–4
military training, compulsory, 219, 373
milk see dairy industry
Millhouse, Robin, 263
millipedes, 127
mining, 72, 225, 299, 307, 308, 314, 315, 316, 317, 318, 325–6, 414
Mitchell, Sir Thomas, 207
mites, 125, 126
molluscs, 120–2, 196, 324, 325
money market corporations, 306
monocotyledons, 86–8
monoliths, 57
monorail, 348
monotremes, 95–6
Moreton Bay, 99
Moreton Bay bug, 124
Moreton Bay fig, 84
Morgan, 'Mad Dog', 210
Morgan, Sandra, 532
Mornington Peninsula, 50
moss animals, 132
mosses, 90–1
moths, 130–1
motor racing, 564–9

motorcycling, 570–2
mound builders, 105
Mount Augustus, 57
Mount Bartle Frere, 53, 54
Mount Bogong, 53, 54
Mount Buffalo, 54, 55, 152
Mount Elephant, 50
Mount Field, 17, 158
Mount Gambier, 51, 52, 69
Mount Hopeless, 81, 208
Mount Hotham, 53, 55
Mount Kosciuszko, 6, 53, 54, 55, 67
Mount Lofty Ranges, 16, 50, 56
Mount Meharry, 53
Mount Olga, 57
Mount Ossa, 53, 54
Mount Warning, 52
Mount Woodroffe, 53
Mount Zeil, 53, 54, 56
mountain ash, 80, 151, 152
mountains, 53, 54–7, 196
Movement, The, 260
Mullamullang Cave, 59, 60
Mundine, Tony, 551
Murphy, Lionel, 228
Murray cod, 118
Murray, Ian, 575
Murray Islands, 232
Murray River, 11, 46, 51, 55, 62, 66, 67, 73, 74, 118, 155, 206, 207, 211, 350
Murray–Darling Basin, 63, 72, 73, 74
Murray–Darling River system, 63, 66, 71, 73, 75, 118
Murrumbidgee River, 11, 52, 55, 67, 73, 74, 211, 350
Musgrave Ranges, 51
music, 489, 492, 515–21
Music Fund see Australia Council
Musica Viva, 519
Muslims, 183
musk duck, 104
Myall Creek Massacre, 212–13
Myall Lakes, 69
Mystery Creek Cave, 59, 60

N
nankeen see Australian kestrel
Narracoorte Range, 58–9
national accounts, 302–4
National Australia Bank, 304, 305, 315
National Book Council/ Banjo Awards, 525–6
National Campaign against Drug Abuse, 408
National Country Party see National Party of Australia
National Crime Authority (NCA), 231, 273, 275, 290–1, 293
National Gallery, Australian, 504–6
National Health and Medical Research Council, 404
National Heart Foundation of Australia, 407
National Institute of Dramatic Art (NIDA), 514
National Landcare Program, 140
National Library of Australia, 522
National Mental Health Strategy, 414–15
National Occupational Health and Safety Commission, 404
National Parks and Wildlife Service, 136, 148
national parks, 66, 141, 147, 148–60, 161
National Party of Australia, 229, 231, 234, 244, 227, 259, 261, 262–3, 327, 396
National Program on Drugs in Sport, 530
National Soccer League championships, 547–8
Nationalist Party, 218, 260
native title, 227, 231, 232–3, 234
nature conservation reserves see national parks
neoplasms, 173
net throwers, 126

netball, 588
New Media Arts Fund see Australia Council
news agencies, 484
Newcombe, John, 587
newspapers, 449, 450, 473–5
Niemeyer Plan, 218–19
nightjars, 108
Ninety Mile Beach, 42, 51, 70
Ningaloo Reef, 117, 148, 157
noisy scrub-bird, 110, 135
non-wage benefits, 185
Norfolk Island, 43, 146, 166, 178, 203, 273, 423
Norman, Decima, 533
Norman, Greg, 559
Northam, Bill, 532, 574
northern giant-petrel, 102
northern hairy-nosed wombat, 98, 135, 144
northern spotted barramundi, 118
Northern Territory Aerial Medical Service, 406–7
Northwest Cape, 4, 39, 199
NT Country Liberal Party, 244
nuclear energy, 142, 148, 327
Nuclear Disarmament Party, 228, 259
Nullarbor Plain, 41, 51, 57–8, 59, 65
numbats, 97, 134, 135
nursing homes, 417
nutrition, 405

O
occupational health, 413–14
O'Connor, Michael, 541, 544
octopuses, 122, 134
Office of Film and Literature Classification, 496
Olgas, The, 57
Olympic Games, 231, 330, 529, 531, 534, 535, 536, 537, 550, 574–5, 579, 580, 581, 582, 589

Summer Olympics, 501–2
Winter Olympics, 502
Olympic Federation, Australian, 547
Ombudsman, 280–1, 286
One Billion Trees scheme, 140, 146–7
Opera Australia, 230, 514, 518, 519
Optus Communications, 337, 338
orange-bellied parrot, 135, 144
orange-footed scrub fowl, 105
orchestras, 514, 518–19
orchids, 79, 86–7
Ord River, 68, 70, 157
Ord River Irrigation Scheme, 68, 75
organised crime, 274–5, 275, 290–1, 293
Orthodox Church, 183
ospreys, 105
Otway Ranges, 50
Overland Telegraph Line, 211, 335, 339
overseas students, 436–7
Overseas Telecommu- nications Commission (OTC), 335
owls, 108
Oxley, John, 206, 207
oysters, 121, 324, 325

P
Pacific black duck, 104
Pacific gull, 106
Page, Sir Earle, 248, 262
Palaeozoic Era, 195–6
palms, 86, 87–8
paperbarks, 83–4
Papuan frogmouth, 108
paradise riflebird, 109
Paralympic Games, 530
paralysis ticks see scrub ticks
Parkes, Henry, 238
Parliament, Federal, 214, 216, 237–51, 280, 281, 289, 301
Parliament House, Canberra, 229, 241
Parliament, State, 238, 253–5, 280, 281
parliamentary committees, 246–8
Parramatta, 204, 206, 318, 341

Parramatta River, 203
parrots, 107
Paterson's curse, 93
pay television, 336, 337, 449, 463
peacekeeping forces, 273, 366, 386
pearling, 121, 324, 325
pelicans, 103
penguins, 101–2
pensions, benefits and allowances, 187–91, 312–13, 382–3, 398–9, 443–6
perched lakes, 41
perching birds, 109–10
peregrine falcon, 105
Pereira, Jackie, 590
perentie goanna, 114
peripatus, 132
Peris-Kneebone, Nova, 590
Perkins, Kieren, 581
Perth, 9, 14, 18, 26–7, 32
petrels, 102–3
petroleum, 300, 315, 316, 317, 326–7, 344
Petrov Affair, 222–3, 260
Phar Lap, 561, 564
Pharmaceutical Benefits Scheme (PBS), 398–9
safety net provisions, 398
pheasant coucal, 107
pheasants, 105
Phillip, Governor Arthur, 201, 202, 203, 204, 205, 253, 322
pied butcherbird, 111
pied currawong, 111
pigeons, 106
pigs, 100, 144
pilot whale, 99
pilots, 229, 352
pink-eared duck, 104
placental mammals, 98–9
plains, 57–8
plains-wanderer, 105–6, 135
plateaus, 54–6
platypuses, 95, 134
plovers, 106
Poeppels Corner, 47, 48
Point Danger, 46
poisonous plants, 91–2
police, 273–5, 281
political parties, histories, 259–63

pollution, 140, 146, 148, 293, 326
population, 163–91, 221
  Aboriginal and Torres Strait Islander, 167–8
  ageing of, 165, 176, 398, 415
Port Arthur, 203, 231, 232, 294
Port Hedland, 4, 7, 9, 13, 17, 39, 42
Port Jackson shark, 116–17
Portuguese man-of-war, 122–3
Poseidon, 564
Possession Island, 200
possums, 98
postal services, 299, 339–41
potoroos, 96
praying mantises, 128
Pre-Cambrian Era, 195
prehistory, 195–8
  timeline, 195
Presbyterian Church, 183
print media, 449, 473–6
  ownership, 476–81
prices, 309
Prices and Incomes Accord, 226
primary industries, 318–26
primary products, 11, 212, 213, 218, 221, 299, 307
Prince Regent River, 66, 157, 161
prions, 102–3
private health insurance, 399–401
property crime, 293
Proserpine rock wallaby, 97, 135
Protectionist Party, 214, 216
protozoans, 133
providence petrel, 102–3, 135
psychiatric hospitals, 402
public unit trusts, 306
publishing, 489, 490, 491, 526
purple swamphen, 106

Q
Qantas, 230, 299, 316, 339, 352
quandong, 85
quarantine, 405, 410–11
Queen Elizabeth II, 229, 269, 406
Queen Victoria, 45, 214, 240
Queensland lungfish, 118
Quiros, Pedro Fernandez de, 198–9

R
RAAF see Royal Australian Air Force
rabbits, 100, 144
radio, 19, 338, 449, 450, 455, 456, 463–73
radiocommunications stations, 338
Rafferty, Tony, 535
rail transport, 210–11, 345–8
rails, 106
rainbow bee-eater, 108–9
rainbow lorikeet, 107
rainfall, 3–5, 11–12, 13, 14–15, 17, 18, 19–20, 21, 22, 23, 24, 25, 26, 27, 28, 29, 30, 32, 72, 79, 227
RAN see Royal Australian Navy
rat-kangaroos, 96
ravens, 111
rays, 117
recycling, 140–1, 147
Red Cross Society, Australian, 407
red fruit bat, 98–9
redback spiders, 125, 126, 134
red kangaroo, 96, 134
red-backed kingfisher, 108
red-bellied black snake, 113, 134
red-collared lorikeet, 107
red-eared firetail, 111
red-footed booby, 103
red-tailed black cockatoo, 107
referenda, 45, 215, 217, 218, 221, 222, 228, 237–8, 239, 240, 242, 258, 259, 270
refugees, 178, 179–80
Reid, George Houstoun, 214, 248
relative strain index (RSI), 12, 17
religious beliefs, 182–3
Renford, Des, 582
repatriation hospitals, 402
representative government, 253–4
reptiles, 111–15, 133, 136, 143, 144, 196
Republic Advisory Committee, 233
research grants, 435–6
Reserve Bank, 304, 306
retail, 331–2
ribbon worms, 132
Richmond, Joan, 569
ringtail possum, 98
river red gum, 81, 150, 154, 155
riverboats, 211, 350
rivers, 66–8
road building, 341–2
road transport, 341–5
  accidents, 229, 345
rock coasts, 38
rock shelter, 58, 59
rodents, 135
rollers, 108
Rose, Lionel, 551
Rose, Murray, 532, 582
Rosewall, Ken, 587
Rothmans Medal, 543
round worms, 132
royal albatross, 102
Royal Australian Air Force (RAAF), 359, 360, 361, 362, 363, 364, 372, 378–80
Royal Australian Navy (RAN), 43, 216, 357, 359, 360, 361, 362, 363, 364, 367–72
Royal Commissions, 222–3, 227, 228, 230, 231, 240, 260, 288–9, 290
Royal Flying Doctor Service, 352, 406
royal spoonbill, 104
rufous hare-wallaby, 97, 135
rufous scrub-bird, 110
rugby league, 541–5
rugby union, 541, 545–7
Rum Corps, 204–5
Rum Rebellion, 204–5
Ruse, James, 204, 318

S
sailing, 573–5
St George Bank, 305, 316
St Vincent de Paul Society, 313
St Vincent Gulf, 50
salt lakes, 69, 155, 157, 158
saltwater crocodiles, 114, 133
Salvation Army, 313
sand mining, 63–4
sandalwood, 85
Santamaria, B. A., 260
saprophytic orchids, 87
Sargeant, Anne, 588
sarus crane, 106
satellite television, 463
satellites, 19, 31, 32, 228, 337, 338
satin bowerbird, 109
Save the Bush scheme, 140
scallops, 121
scarlet honeyeater, 110
scarlet-chested parrot, 107
schizophrenia, 416
schooling, 423, 425–8
schools, 302, 425–6, 426–8, 382
  of the air, 427–8
Schuppan, Vern, 568
scorpion-flies, 130
scorpions, 125, 126–7
scrub ticks, 126
scrub-birds, 110
Scullin, James Henry, 218, 248, 260
sea anemones, 123
sea cucumbers, 120
sea squirts, 119
sea stars, 119–20
sea urchins, 120
sea wasp, 123, 133
seals, 144
segmented worms, 132
self-government, 254
Senate, 216, 224, 225, 240, 241, 244–6, 247, 259, 260, 263, 529, 530
serpent eel, 118
sex offences, 294
Shakespeare, Wilma, 588
Shark Bay, 4, 41, 96, 148, 156, 157, 162, 199
sharks, 116–17, 134, 144
shearwaters, 102–3
sheep, 11, 212, 213, 318, 320–1
sheep blowflies, 130

Sheffield Shield, 554
she-oaks see casuarinas
Shepparton, 14
shipping, 31, 32, 33, 211, 221, 330, 338, 345, 349–50
short-nosed bandicoot, 96
short-tailed goanna, 114
shrubs, 79, 85
silver gull, 106
silverfish, 127
Simpson Desert, 48, 50, 65, 66, 154, 155, 161, 207
skeleton weed, 93
skinks, 113, 114
Smith Family, 313–14
smoking, 408–9
snails, 121
snake stars see brittle stars
snakes, 111, 112–13, 134
Snedden, Billy, 225, 261
snow, 6, 16–17
Snowy Mountains, 4, 67; see also Australian Alps Hydro-Electric Scheme, 67, 70, 74, 221
Snowy River, 67, 74
soccer, 547–8
Social Security, Department of, 313
social security, 43, 187–8, 189–91, 302, 312–13; see also pensions, welfare
soil structure degradation, 64
soils, 61–4
conservation, 140
types of soil, 61–2
solar energy, 327
sole parents, 176, 187, 190
sooty albatross, 102
sooty owl, 108
sooty tern, 106
South Cape (Tas.), 38
South-East Asia Treaty Organisation (SEATO), 222
southern boobook, 108
southern cassowary, 101
southern emu-wren, 110
southern giant-petrel, 102
Southern Ocean, 3, 39, 47

Southern Oscillation Index (SOI), 4
southern right whale, 99, 135
Special Broadcasting Service (SBS), 449, 456, 503
Spectrum Management Authority (SMA), 336
speed skating, 532
Speedrail, 347
speedway racing, 572
Spencer Gulf, 50, 206
sperm whale, 99
spiders, 125–6, 134
spiny leaf insect, 129
splendid fairy-wren
sponges, 133
spoonbills, 104
sport, 527–90
spotted nightjar, 108
sprint car racing, 572
squatters, 212–13
Standley Chasm, 56
State and Territory courts, 269, 272
State and Territory Supreme Courts, 269, 271, 273, 277
State Premiers and Opposition Leaders, 255
State of Origin, 541
Steep Point (WA), 38
Stephenson, Jan
stick insects, 129
Stock Exchange, Australian, 314–17
Stony Desert, 206
storks, 104
storm-petrels, 103
straw-necked ibis, 104
strikes see industrial disputes
stringybarks, 80
stromatolites, 41, 156
Strzelecki, Paul de, 53
Stuart, John Macdougall, 207
student assistance, 433–6
Sturt, Charles, 65, 206–7
Sturt's desert pea, 89, 94
Sudden Infant Death Syndrome (SIDS), 172
suffrage, 209, 255–6
sugar, 211, 307, 318, 322, 347, 350
sugar glider, 98
Sulman Prize, Sir John, 508–10

sulphur-crested cockatoo, 107
sunshine, 9–10, 18
Sunshine Harvester Company, 215, 310
Super League, 543
superannuation, 306, 310
Superbike World Championship, 571
superb fairy-wren, 110
superb fruit-dove, 106–7
superb lyrebird, 110
superb parrot, 107
surf lifesaving, 576
surfing, 576–9
Sutherland, Dame Joan, 230
swans, 104
swifts, 108
swimming, 529, 580–3
Sydney, 4, 8, 21–2, 31, 231
Sydney Cove, 201, 203
Sydney Dance Company, 495
Sydney funnel-web spider, 125, 134
Sydney Harbour Bridge, 337, 351
Sydney Opera House, 495, 518
Sydney to Hobart Yacht Race, 573
Sydney trapdoor spider, 126

T
TAFE see Technical and Further Education
taipan, 113, 134
Takahashi, Kasumi, 533, 534
tallowwood, 81
Tamar-Esk River, 51
Tamworth Country Music Festival, 519–21
Tanami Desert, 66, 161
Tasman, Abel, 199, 208
Tasman Sea, 39, 47, 49
Tasmanian blue gum, 81, 94
Tasmanian mutton-bird, 102
Tasmanian tiger see thylacine
tawny frogmouth, 108
taxation, 300–1, 340
Taylor-Smith, Shelley, 583
tea trees, 83, 84–5

Technical and Further Education (TAFE), 423, 438–9
Telecom see Telstra
telecommunications, 291, 299, 335–8
telephones see Telstra, Optus Communications
television, 19, 336, 337, 338, 449, 454, 455, 456, 457–63
Telstra, 336–7, 338
temperature, 3, 7–8, 10, 12, 16, 17, 21, 22, 23, 24, 25, 26, 27, 28, 29, 30, 32
tennis, 529, 583–7
termites, 129, 159
terns, 106
Territory Chief Ministers and Opposition Leaders, 255
Tertiary Era, 197
theatre, 489, 492, 514–15
Theatre Fund see Australia Council
Therapeutic Goods Administration, 405
thunderstorms, 5, 15, 31
Thursday Island, 8, 18, 38
thylacine, 97, 134, 135
ticks, 125, 126, 133
tidal plains, 38, 39
tiger shark, 117, 134
time zones, 48
Timor Sea, 39, 46, 47, 326
Tobruk, 220
Todd River, 68
Torres Strait, 40, 199, 232
Torres Strait Islanders see Aboriginal peoples and Torres Strait Islander
Torresian crow, 111
tourism, 141, 330, 353
tornados, 15–16
trade, 307–9
trade unions, 185, 186, 213–14, 310–12, 483–4
training, 310, 312, 418, 423, 424, 438–40, 442, 443, 444–6
trains, 345–8
trams, 348
transport, 177, 178, 185, 210–11, 219, 301, 309, 341–54

transportation of convicts, 201, 203, 208
tree-climbing kangaroos, 96
trees, 79, 80–5
triathlon, 579–80
trilobites, 196
true crabs, 124
true quails, 105
trumpet manucode, 109
Tszyu, Kostya, 551
tube-nosed seabirds, 102–3
Turkish Bath Cave, 59
turtles, 45, 46, 112, 136, 160
TV Week Logies, 485–6
Tweed Volcano, 52
Twelve Apostles, 41–2

U
Uluru (Ayers Rock), 52, 57, 59, 229
Uluru-Kata Tjuta National Park, 146, 159, 162
Ulysses butterfly, 131
unemployment benefits *see* pensions
unemployment, 183, 187, 188, 218, 226, 310, 423
underground orchids, 87
United Australia Party, 221, 260
Uniting Church, 183
univalves *see* gastropods
universities, 224, 371, 428, 430, 431, 432
uranium, 228, 230, 317, 325, 326, 327

V
Van Diemen's Land, 47, 199, 200, 208, 341
variegated fairy-wren, 110
vegetation degradation, 64, 74
vegetation loss, 64, 74, 147
vegetative regions, 79
Victoria Fossil Cave, 59

Victoria's riflebird, 109
Vietnam War, 223–4
violent crime, 293
Visual Arts/Crafts Fund *see* Australia Council
vitamins and minerals, 405
Vlamingh, Willem de, 199
volcanic activity, 44, 50, 51, 52, 53, 55, 149, 150, 153, 154, 160, 196, 197
voting systems, 257–8

W
waders, 106
wages, 185, 219, 221, 302, 310, 312
  average weekly earnings, 185
  basic, 185, 213, 215, 218, 310, 311, 313
Walkley Awards, 485
wallabies, 96–7
wallaroos, 96
wandering albatross, 102
waratah, 85, 94
warblers, 110
Warburton Range, 65
Warne, Shane, 557
Warrumbungle National Park, 55, 150
Warrumbungles, 52, 55
wasps, 131–2
water erosion, 63
water hyacinth, 93
water transport, 211, 349–51
water resources, 70–3, 301
waterlogging *see* irrigation salinity
Watson, John Christian, 215, 248, 259
wattle, 82
wave energy, 328
weather, 3–30, 31, 44
  forecasts, 31, 32
  phenomena, 12–17
  seasonal, 3
  warnings, 31–2

wedge-tailed eagle, 105, 134
Welch, Greg, 579
welfare, 187–91, 221, 301, 312–13; *see also* pensions
Wenden, Michael, 533
Wentworth, William, 205
West Point, Dirk Hartog Island, 38
Western Australian Standard Time, 48
western barred bandicoot, 96, 135, 144
Western Front, 217
Western Shield, 49, 51
western swamp turtle, 136, 144
Westpac Banking Corporation, 304, 305, 315
whale sharks, 116, 117, 148
whales, 99, 135, 144, 147, 148
wheat, 15, 211, 218, 299, 307, 318, 319–20
White Australia Policy, 178, 212, 215
white collar crime, 292
white ibis, 104
white-bellied sea eagle, 105
white-faced heron, 104
white-rumped swiftlet, 108
white-throated needletail, 108
white-winged fairy-wren, 110
Whitlam, Edward Gough, 224–5, 226, 249, 260
Whitsunday Islands, 13
Wickham, Tracey, 582
Wik Decision, 234
wild dogs, 144
wild oats, 93
wilderness, 65–6, 158, 161
Wilderness Society, 147, 148

Willandra Lakes, 150, 161, 198
Willis Island, 19, 31
Wills, William *see* Burke and Wills
Wilsons Promontory, 38, 47, 152
Wilson's storm-petrel, 103
Wimbledon, 229, 583–5, 587
wind, 10–11, 12, 13, 15, 16, 18, 32, 328
wind erosion, 63–4
wine, 315, 318, 322–3
wireweed, 93
wombats, 98, 134, 135
wool industry, 211, 218, 221, 299, 307, 318, 319, 320–1
working week, 40-hour, 221
workplace injuries, 413–14
Worksafe Australia *see* National Occupational Health and Safety Commission
World Health Organisation, 407
World Heritage listing, 40, 65, 69, 139, 147, 161–2, 198
World Meteorological Organisation, 19, 32–3
World War I, 48, 216–18, 259, 329, 330, 342, 349, 378
World War II, 48, 178, 179, 219–21, 330, 342, 351, 352, 514
worms, 119, 132, 133
Wynne Prize, 511–13

Y
yabbies *see* crayfish
Yallingup Cave, 59
Yarrangobilly Caves, 58
yellow wattlebird, 110
yellow-bellied sea snake, 113
yellow-billed spoonbill, 104